Management Science

EDITION 14

Anderson/Cochran/Fry/Ohlmann/Sweeney/Williams/Camm

Australia • Brazil • Japan • Korea • Mexico • Singapore • Spain • United Kingdom • United States

Management Science
14 E

For product information and technology assistance, contact us at
Cengage Learning Customer & Sales Support, 1-800-354-9706

For permission to use material from this text or product, submit all requests online at **cengage.com/permissions**
Further permissions questions can be emailed to
permissionrequest@cengage.com

This book contains select works from existing Cengage Learning resources and was produced by Cengage Learning Custom Solutions for collegiate use. As such, those adopting and/or contributing to this work are responsible for editorial content accuracy, continuity and completeness.

Compilation © 2016 Cengage Learning

ISBN: 978-1-337-03485-2

Cengage Learning
20 Channel Center Street
Boston, MA 02210
USA

Cengage Learning is a leading provider of customized learning solutions with office locations around the globe, including Singapore, the United Kingdom, Australia, Mexico, Brazil, and Japan. Locate your local office at:
www.international.cengage.com/region.

Cengage Learning products are represented in Canada by Nelson Education, Ltd.

For your lifelong learning solutions, visit **www.cengage.com/custom.**

Visit our corporate website at **www.cengage.com.**

Acknowledgements

I would like to acknowledgement the following individuals, Dr. Gangaram Singh, Provost, Dr. Lena Rodriguez, Interim Dean School of Business and Management, Dr. Brian Simpson , Chair of Department of Economics and Finance, National University for their guidance and assistance in the development of this custom textbook. I would also like to thank my colleagues and my adjuncts faculties for their contributions

Dr. Reza Fadaei

Brief Contents

CHAPTER 1

Introduction

CONTENTS

Management science, an approach to decision making based on the scientific method, makes extensive use of quantitative analysis. A variety of names exists for the body of knowledge involving quantitative approaches to decision making; in addition to management science, two other widely known and accepted names are operations research and decision science. Today, many use the terms *management science, operations research,* and *decision science* interchangeably.

The scientific management revolution of the early 1900s, initiated by Frederic W. Taylor, provided the foundation for the use of quantitative methods in management. But modern management science research is generally considered to have originated during the World War II period, when teams were formed to deal with strategic and tactical problems faced by the military. These teams, which often consisted of people with diverse specialties (e.g., mathematicians, engineers, and behavioral scientists), were joined together to solve a common problem by utilizing the scientific method. After the war, many of these team members continued their research in the field of management science.

Two developments that occurred during the post–World War II period led to the growth and use of management science in nonmilitary applications. First, continued research resulted in numerous methodological developments. Probably the most significant development was the discovery by George Dantzig, in 1947, of the simplex method for solving linear programming problems. At the same time these methodological developments were taking place, digital computers prompted a virtual explosion in computing power. Computers enabled practitioners to use the methodological advances to solve a large variety of problems. The computer technology explosion continues; smart phones, tablets and other mobile-computing devices can now be used to solve problems larger than those solved on mainframe computers in the 1990s.

More recently, the explosive growth of data from sources such as smart phones and other personal-electronic devices provide access to much more data today than ever before. Additionally, the internet allows for easy sharing and storage of data, providing extensive access to a variety of users to the necessary inputs to management-science models.

As stated in the Preface, the purpose of the text is to provide students with a sound conceptual understanding of the role that management science plays in the decision-making process. We also said that the text is applications oriented. To reinforce the applications nature of the text and provide a better understanding of the variety of applications in which management science has been used successfully, Management Science in Action articles are presented throughout the text. Each Management Science in Action article summarizes an application of management science in practice. The first Management Science in Action in this chapter, Revenue Management at AT&T Park, describes one of the most important applications of management science in the sports and entertainment industry.

MANAGEMENT SCIENCE IN ACTION

REVENUE MANAGEMENT AT AT&T PARK*

Imagine the difficult position Russ Stanley, Vice President of Ticket Services for the San Francisco Giants, found himself facing late in the 2010 baseball season. Prior to the season, his organization had adopted a dynamic approach to pricing its tickets similar to the model successfully pioneered by Thomas M. Cook and his operations research group at American Airlines. Stanley desparately wanted the Giants to clinch a playoff birth, but he didn't want the team to do so *too quickly*.

When dynamically pricing a good or service, an organization regularly reviews supply and demand of the product and uses operations research to determine if the price should be changed to reflect these conditions. As the scheduled takeoff date for a flight nears, the cost of a ticket increases if seats for the flight are relatively scarce. On the other hand, the airline discounts tickets for an approaching flight with relatively few ticketed passengers. Through the use of optimization to dynamically set ticket prices, American Airlines generates nearly $1 billion annually in incremental revenue.

The management team of the San Francisco Giants recognized similarities between their primary product (tickets to home games) and the primary product sold by airlines (tickets for flights) and adopted a similar revenue management system. If a particular Giants' game is appealing to fans, tickets sell quickly and demand far exceeds supply as the date of the game approaches; under these conditions fans will be willing to pay more and the Giants charge a premium for the ticket. Similarly, tickets for less attractive games are discounted to reflect relatively low demand by fans. This is why Stanley found himself in a quandary at the end of the 2010 baseball season. The Giants were in the middle of a tight pennant race with the San Diego Padres that effectively increased demand for tickets to Giants' games, and the team was actually scheduled to play the Padres in San Francisco for the last three games of the season. While Stanley certainly wanted his club to win its division and reach the Major League Baseball playoffs, he also recognized that his team's revenues would be greatly enhanced if it didn't qualify for the playoffs until the last day

of the season. "I guess financially it is better to go all the way down to the last game," Stanley said in a late season interview. "Our hearts are in our stomachs; we're pacing watching these games."

Does revenue management and operations research work? Today, virtually every airline uses some sort of revenue-management system, and the cruise, hotel, and car rental industries also now apply revenue-management methods. As for the Giants, Stanley said dynamic pricing provided a 7% to 8% increase in revenue per seat for Giants' home games during the 2010 season. Coincidentally, the Giants did win the National League West division on the last day of the season and ultimately won the World Series. Several professional sports franchises are now looking to the Giants' example and considering implementation of similar dynamic ticket-pricing systems.

*Based on Peter Horner, "The Sabre Story," *OR/MS Today* (June 2000); Ken Belson, "Baseball Tickets Too Much? Check Back Tomorrow," *NewYork Times.com* (May 18, 2009); and Rob Gloster, "Giants Quadruple Price of Cheap Seats as Playoffs Drive Demand," *Bloomberg Business-week* (September 30, 2010).

1.1   PROBLEM SOLVING AND DECISION MAKING

Problem solving can be defined as the process of identifying a difference between the actual and the desired state of affairs and then taking action to resolve the difference. For problems important enough to justify the time and effort of careful analysis, the problem-solving process involves the following seven steps:

1. Identify and define the problem.
2. Determine the set of alternative solutions.
3. Determine the criterion or criteria that will be used to evaluate the alternatives.
4. Evaluate the alternatives.
5. Choose an alternative.
6. Implement the selected alternative.
7. Evaluate the results to determine whether a satisfactory solution has been obtained.

Decision making is the term generally associated with the first five steps of the problem-solving process. Thus, the first step of decision making is to identify and define the problem. Decision making ends with the choosing of an alternative, which is the act of making the decision.

Let us consider the following example of the decision-making process. For the moment assume that you are currently unemployed and that you would like a position that will lead to a satisfying career. Suppose that your job search has resulted in offers from companies in Rochester, New York; Dallas, Texas; Greensboro, North Carolina; and Pittsburgh, Pennsylvania. Thus, the alternatives for your decision problem can be stated as follows:

1. Accept the position in Rochester.
2. Accept the position in Dallas.

3. Accept the position in Greensboro.
4. Accept the position in Pittsburgh.

The next step of the problem-solving process involves determining the criteria that will be used to evaluate the four alternatives. Obviously, the starting salary is a factor of some importance. If salary were the only criterion of importance to you, the alternative selected as "best" would be the one with the highest starting salary. Problems in which the objective is to find the best solution with respect to one criterion are referred to as **single-criterion decision problems.**

Suppose that you also conclude that the potential for advancement and the location of the job are two other criteria of major importance. Thus, the three criteria in your decision problem are starting salary, potential for advancement, and location. Problems that involve more than one criterion are referred to as **multicriteria decision problems.**

The next step of the decision-making process is to evaluate each of the alternatives with respect to each criterion. For example, evaluating each alternative relative to the starting salary criterion is done simply by recording the starting salary for each job alternative. Evaluating each alternative with respect to the potential for advancement and the location of the job is more difficult to do, however, because these evaluations are based primarily on subjective factors that are often difficult to quantify. Suppose for now that you decide to measure potential for advancement and job location by rating each of these criteria as poor, fair, average, good, or excellent. The data that you compile are shown in Table 1.1.

You are now ready to make a choice from the available alternatives. What makes this choice phase so difficult is that the criteria are probably not all equally important, and no one alternative is "best" with regard to all criteria. Although we will present a method for dealing with situations like this one later in the text, for now let us suppose that after a careful evaluation of the data in Table 1.1, you decide to select alternative 3; alternative 3 is thus referred to as the **decision.**

At this point in time, the decision-making process is complete. In summary, we see that this process involves five steps:

1. Define the problem.
2. Identify the alternatives.
3. Determine the criteria.
4. Evaluate the alternatives.
5. Choose an alternative.

Note that missing from this list are the last two steps in the problem-solving process: implementing the selected alternative and evaluating the results to determine whether a satisfactory solution has been obtained. This omission is not meant to diminish the importance of each of these activities, but to emphasize the more limited scope of the term *decision making* as compared to the term *problem solving*. Figure 1.1 summarizes the relationship between these two concepts.

TABLE 1.1   DATA FOR THE JOB EVALUATION DECISION-MAKING PROBLEM

Alternative	Starting Salary	Potential for Advancement	Job Location
1. Rochester	$48,500	Average	Average
2. Dallas	$46,000	Excellent	Good
3. Greensboro	$46,000	Good	Excellent
4. Pittsburgh	$47,000	Average	Good

FIGURE 1.1   THE RELATIONSHIP BETWEEN PROBLEM SOLVING
AND DECISION MAKING

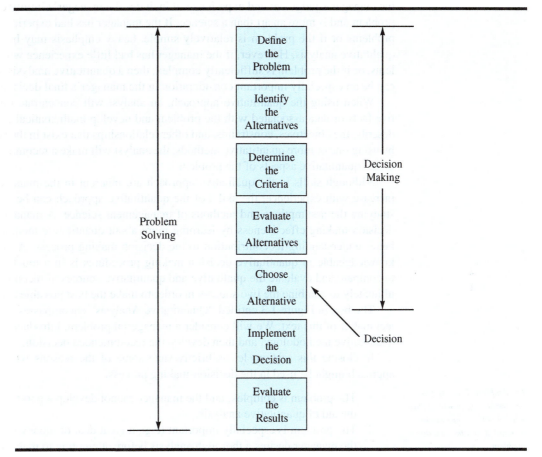

1.2   QUANTITATIVE ANALYSIS AND DECISION MAKING

Consider the flowchart presented in Figure 1.2. Note that it combines the first three steps of the decision-making process under the heading of "Structuring the Problem" and the latter two steps under the heading "Analyzing the Problem." Let us now consider in greater detail how to carry out the set of activities that make up the decision-making process.

FIGURE 1.2   AN ALTERNATE CLASSIFICATION OF THE DECISION-MAKING PROCESS

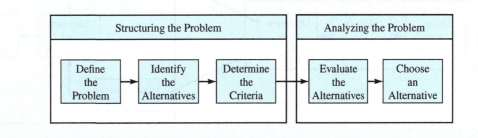

Figure 1.3 shows that the analysis phase of the decision-making process may take two basic forms: qualitative and quantitative. Qualitative analysis is based primarily on the manager's judgment and experience; it includes the manager's intuitive "feel" for the problem and is more an art than a science. If the manager has had experience with similar problems or if the problem is relatively simple, heavy emphasis may be placed upon a qualitative analysis. However, if the manager has had little experience with similar problems, or if the problem is sufficiently complex, then a quantitative analysis of the problem can be an especially important consideration in the manager's final decision.

When using the quantitative approach, an analyst will concentrate on the quantitative facts or data associated with the problem and develop mathematical expressions that describe the objectives, constraints, and other relationships that exist in the problem. Then, by using one or more quantitative methods, the analyst will make a recommendation based on the quantitative aspects of the problem.

Although skills in the qualitative approach are inherent in the manager and usually increase with experience, the skills of the quantitative approach can be learned only by studying the assumptions and methods of management science. A manager can increase decision-making effectiveness by learning more about quantitative methodology and by better understanding its contribution to the decision-making process. A manager who is knowledgeable in quantitative decision-making procedures is in a much better position to compare and evaluate the qualitative and quantitative sources of recommendations and ultimately to combine the two sources in order to make the best possible decision.

The box in Figure 1.3 entitled "Quantitative Analysis" encompasses most of the subject matter of this text. We will consider a managerial problem, introduce the appropriate quantitative methodology, and then develop the recommended decision.

In closing this section, let us briefly state some of the reasons why a quantitative approach might be used in the decision-making process:

Try Problem 4 to test your understanding of why quantitative approaches might be needed in a particular problem.

1. The problem is complex, and the manager cannot develop a good solution without the aid of quantitative analysis.
2. The problem is especially important (e.g., a great deal of money is involved), and the manager desires a thorough analysis before attempting to make a decision.

FIGURE 1.3   THE ROLE OF QUALITATIVE AND QUANTITATIVE ANALYSIS

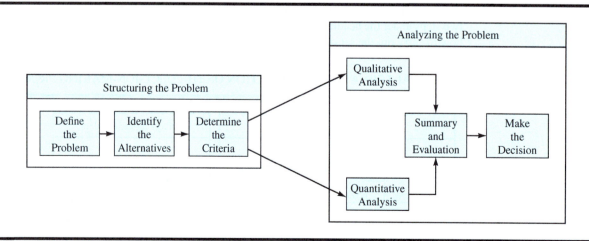

3. The problem is new, and the manager has no previous experience from which to draw.
4. The problem is repetitive, and the manager saves time and effort by relying on quantitative procedures to make routine decision recommendations.

1.3 QUANTITATIVE ANALYSIS

From Figure 1.3, we see that quantitative analysis begins once the problem has been structured. It usually takes imagination, teamwork, and considerable effort to transform a rather general problem description into a well-defined problem that can be approached via quantitative analysis. The more the analyst is involved in the process of structuring the problem, the more likely the ensuing quantitative analysis will make an important contribution to the decision-making process.

To successfully apply quantitative analysis to decision making, the management scientist must work closely with the manager or user of the results. When both the management scientist and the manager agree that the problem has been adequately structured, work can begin on developing a model to represent the problem mathematically. Solution procedures can then be employed to find the best solution for the model. This best solution for the model then becomes a recommendation to the decision maker. The process of developing and solving models is the essence of the quantitative analysis process.

Model Development

Models are representations of real objects or situations and can be presented in various forms. For example, a scale model of an airplane is a representation of a real airplane. Similarly, a child's toy truck is a model of a real truck. The model airplane and toy truck are examples of models that are physical replicas of real objects. In modeling terminology, physical replicas are referred to as **iconic models.**

A second classification includes models that are physical in form but do not have the same physical appearance as the object being modeled. Such models are referred to as **analog models.** The speedometer of an automobile is an analog model; the position of the needle on the dial represents the speed of the automobile. A thermometer is another analog model representing temperature.

A third classification of models—the type we will primarily be studying—includes representations of a problem by a system of symbols and mathematical relationships or expressions. Such models are referred to as **mathematical models** and are a critical part of any quantitative approach to decision making. For example, the total profit from the sale of a product can be determined by multiplying the profit per unit by the quantity sold. If we let x represent the number of units sold and P the total profit, then, with a profit of \$10 per unit, the following mathematical model defines the total profit earned by selling x units:

$$P = 10x \qquad\qquad (1.1)$$

The purpose, or value, of any model is that it enables us to make inferences about the real situation by studying and analyzing the model. For example, an airplane designer might test an iconic model of a new airplane in a wind tunnel to learn about the potential flying characteristics of the full-size airplane. Similarly, a mathematical model may be used to make inferences about how much profit will be earned if a specified quantity of a particular product is sold. According to the mathematical model of equation (1.1), we would expect selling three units of the product ($x = 3$) would provide a profit of $P = 10(3) = \$30$.

In general, experimenting with models requires less time and is less expensive than experimenting with the real object or situation. A model airplane is certainly quicker and less expensive to build and study than the full-size airplane. Similarly, the mathematical model in equation (1.1) allows a quick identification of profit expectations without actually requiring the manager to produce and sell x units. Models also have the advantage of reducing the risk associated with experimenting with the real situation. In particular, bad designs or bad decisions that cause the model airplane to crash or a mathematical model to project a $10,000 loss can be avoided in the real situation.

Herbert A. Simon, a Nobel Prize winner in economics and an expert in decision making, said that a mathematical model does not have to be exact; it just has to be close enough to provide better results than can be obtained by common sense.

The value of model-based conclusions and decisions is dependent on how well the model represents the real situation. The more closely the model airplane represents the real airplane, the more accurate the conclusions and predictions will be. Similarly, the more closely the mathematical model represents the company's true profit-volume relationship, the more accurate the profit projections will be.

Because this text deals with quantitative analysis based on mathematical models, let us look more closely at the mathematical modeling process. When initially considering a managerial problem, we usually find that the problem definition phase leads to a specific objective, such as maximization of profit or minimization of cost, and possibly a set of restrictions or **constraints,** such as production capacities. The success of the mathematical model and quantitative approach will depend heavily on how accurately the objective and constraints can be expressed in terms of mathematical equations or relationships.

A mathematical expression that describes the problem's objective is referred to as the **objective function.** For example, the profit equation $P = 10x$ would be an objective function for a firm attempting to maximize profit. A production capacity constraint would be necessary if, for instance, 5 hours are required to produce each unit and only 40 hours of production time are available per week. Let x indicate the number of units produced each week. The production time constraint is given by

$$5x \leq 40 \tag{1.2}$$

The value of $5x$ is the total time required to produce x units; the symbol $\leq$ indicates that the production time required must be less than or equal to the 40 hours available.

The decision problem or question is the following: How many units of the product should be scheduled each week to maximize profit? A complete mathematical model for this simple production problem is

$$\text{Maximize} \qquad P = 10x \quad \text{objective function}$$
$$\text{subject to (s.t.)}$$
$$\left. \begin{array}{r} 5x \leq 40 \\ x \geq 0 \end{array} \right\} \text{constraints}$$

The $x \geq 0$ constraint requires the production quantity x to be greater than or equal to zero, which simply recognizes the fact that it is not possible to manufacture a negative number of units. The optimal solution to this model can be easily calculated and is given by $x = 8$, with an associated profit of $80. This model is an example of a linear programming

FIGURE 1.4   FLOWCHART OF THE PROCESS OF TRANSFORMING MODEL INPUTS INTO OUTPUT

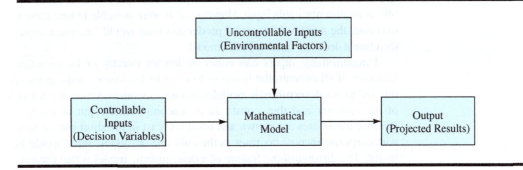

model. In subsequent chapters we will discuss more complicated mathematical models and learn how to solve them in situations where the answers are not nearly so obvious.

In the preceding mathematical model, the profit per unit ($10), the production time per unit (5 hours), and the production capacity (40 hours) are environmental factors that are not under the control of the manager or decision maker. Such environmental factors, which can affect both the objective function and the constraints, are referred to as **uncontrollable inputs** to the model. Inputs that are completely controlled or determined by the decision maker are referred to as **controllable inputs** to the model. In the example given, the production quantity x is the controllable input to the model. Controllable inputs are the decision alternatives specified by the manager and thus are also referred to as the **decision variables** of the model.

Once all controllable and uncontrollable inputs are specified, the objective function and constraints can be evaluated and the output of the model determined. In this sense, the output of the model is simply the projection of what would happen if those particular environmental factors and decisions occurred in the real situation. A flowchart of how controllable and uncontrollable inputs are transformed by the mathematical model into output is shown in Figure 1.4. A similar flowchart showing the specific details of the production model is shown in Figure 1.5.

FIGURE 1.5   FLOWCHART FOR THE PRODUCTION MODEL

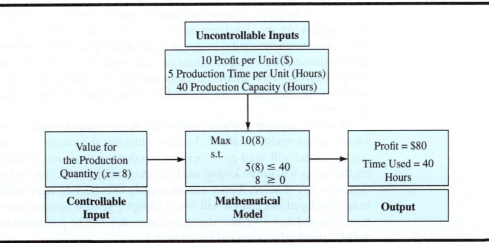

As stated earlier, the uncontrollable inputs are those the decision maker cannot influence. The specific controllable and uncontrollable inputs of a model depend on the particular problem or decision-making situation. In the production problem, the production time available (40) is an uncontrollable input. However, if it were possible to hire more employees or use overtime, the number of hours of production time would become a controllable input and therefore a decision variable in the model.

Uncontrollable inputs can either be known exactly or be uncertain and subject to variation. If all uncontrollable inputs to a model are known and cannot vary, the model is referred to as a **deterministic model.** Corporate income tax rates are not under the influence of the manager and thus constitute an uncontrollable input in many decision models. Because these rates are known and fixed (at least in the short run), a mathematical model with corporate income tax rates as the only uncontrollable input would be a deterministic model. The distinguishing feature of a deterministic model is that the uncontrollable input values are known in advance.

If any of the uncontrollable inputs are uncertain to the decision maker, the model is referred to as a **stochastic** or **probabilistic model.** An uncontrollable input to many production planning models is demand for the product. A mathematical model that treats future demand—which may be any of a range of values—with uncertainty would be called a stochastic model. In the production model, the number of hours of production time required per unit, the total hours available, and the unit profit were all uncontrollable inputs. Because the uncontrollable inputs were all known to take on fixed values, the model was deterministic. If, however, the number of hours of production time per unit could vary from 3 to 6 hours depending on the quality of the raw material, the model would be stochastic. The distinguishing feature of a stochastic model is that the value of the output cannot be determined even if the value of the controllable input is known because the specific values of the uncontrollable inputs are unknown. In this respect, stochastic models are often more difficult to analyze.

Data Preparation

Another step in the quantitative analysis of a problem is the preparation of the data required by the model. Data in this sense refer to the values of the uncontrollable inputs to the model. All uncontrollable inputs or data must be specified before we can analyze the model and recommend a decision or solution for the problem.

In the production model, the values of the uncontrollable inputs or data were $10 per unit for profit, 5 hours per unit for production time, and 40 hours for production capacity. In the development of the model, these data values were known and incorporated into the model as it was being developed. If the model is relatively small and the uncontrollable input values or data required are few, the quantitative analyst will probably combine model development and data preparation into one step. In these situations the data values are inserted as the equations of the mathematical model are developed.

However, in many mathematical modeling situations, the data or uncontrollable input values are not readily available. In these situations the management scientist may know that the model will need profit per unit, production time, and production capacity data, but the values will not be known until the accounting, production, and engineering departments can be consulted. Rather than attempting to collect the required data as the model is being developed, the analyst will usually adopt a general notation for the model development step, and then a separate data preparation step will be performed to obtain the uncontrollable input values required by the model.

Using the general notation

c = profit per unit

a = production time in hours per unit

b = production capacity in hours

the model development step of the production problem would result in the following general model:

$$\text{Max} \quad cx$$
$$\text{s.t.}$$
$$ax \leq b$$
$$x \geq 0$$

A separate data preparation step to identify the values for c, a, and b would then be necessary to complete the model.

Many inexperienced quantitative analysts assume that once the problem has been defined and a general model developed, the problem is essentially solved. These individuals tend to believe that data preparation is a trivial step in the process and can be easily handled by clerical staff. Actually, this assumption could not be further from the truth, especially with large-scale models that have numerous data input values. For example, a small linear programming model with 50 decision variables and 25 constraints could have more than 1300 data elements that must be identified in the data preparation step. The time required to prepare these data and the possibility of data collection errors will make the data preparation step a critical part of the quantitative analysis process. Often, a fairly large database is needed to support a mathematical model, and information systems specialists may become involved in the data preparation step.

Model Solution

Once the model development and data preparation steps are completed, we can proceed to the model solution step. In this step, the analyst will attempt to identify the values of the decision variables that provide the "best" output for the model. The specific decision-variable value or values providing the "best" output will be referred to as the **optimal solution** for the model. For the production problem, the model solution step involves finding the value of the production quantity decision variable x that maximizes profit while not causing a violation of the production capacity constraint.

One procedure that might be used in the model solution step involves a trial-and-error approach in which the model is used to test and evaluate various decision alternatives. In the production model, this procedure would mean testing and evaluating the model under various production quantities or values of x. Note, in Figure 1.5, that we could input trial values for x and check the corresponding output for projected profit and satisfaction of the production capacity constraint. If a particular decision alternative does not satisfy one or more of the model constraints, the decision alternative is rejected as being **infeasible,** regardless of the objective function value. If all constraints are satisfied, the decision alternative is **feasible** and a candidate for the "best" solution or recommended decision. Through this trial-and-error process of evaluating selected decision alternatives, a decision maker can identify a good—and possibly the best—feasible solution to the problem. This solution would then be the recommended decision for the problem.

Table 1.2 shows the results of a trial-and-error approach to solving the production model of Figure 1.5. The recommended decision is a production quantity of 8 because the feasible solution with the highest projected profit occurs at $x = 8$.

TABLE 1.2   TRIAL-AND-ERROR SOLUTION FOR THE PRODUCTION MODEL
OF FIGURE 1.5

Decision Alternative (Production Quantity) x	Projected Profit	Total Hours of Production	Feasible Solution? (Hours Used ≤ 40)
0	0	0	Yes
2	20	10	Yes
4	40	20	Yes
6	60	30	Yes
8	80	40	Yes
10	100	50	No
12	120	60	No

Although the trial-and-error solution process is often acceptable and can provide valuable information for the manager, it has the drawbacks of not necessarily providing the best solution and of being inefficient in terms of requiring numerous calculations if many decision alternatives are tried. Thus, quantitative analysts have developed special solution procedures for many models that are much more efficient than the trial-and-error approach. Throughout this text, you will be introduced to solution procedures that are applicable to the specific mathematical models that will be formulated. Some relatively small models or problems can be solved by hand computations, but most practical applications require the use of a computer.

Model development and model solution steps are not completely separable. An analyst will want both to develop an accurate model or representation of the actual problem situation and to be able to find a solution to the model. If we approach the model development step by attempting to find the most accurate and realistic mathematical model, we may find the model so large and complex that it is impossible to obtain a solution. In this case, a simpler and perhaps more easily understood model with a readily available solution procedure is preferred even if the recommended solution is only a rough approximation of the best decision. As you learn more about quantitative solution procedures, you will have a better idea of the types of mathematical models that can be developed and solved.

Try Problem 8 to test your understanding of the concept of a mathematical model and what is referred to as the optimal solution to the model.

After a model solution is obtained, both the management scientist and the manager will be interested in determining how good the solution really is. Even though the analyst has undoubtedly taken many precautions to develop a realistic model, often the goodness or accuracy of the model cannot be assessed until model solutions are generated. Model testing and validation are frequently conducted with relatively small "test" problems that have known or at least expected solutions. If the model generates the expected solutions, and if other output information appears correct, the go-ahead may be given to use the model on the full-scale problem. However, if the model test and validation identify potential problems or inaccuracies inherent in the model, corrective action, such as model modification and/or collection of more accurate input data, may be taken. Whatever the corrective action, the model solution will not be used in practice until the model has satisfactorily passed testing and validation.

Report Generation

An important part of the quantitative analysis process is the preparation of managerial reports based on the model's solution. In Figure 1.3, we see that the solution based on the quantitative analysis of a problem is one of the inputs the manager considers before making a final decision. Thus, the results of the model must appear in a managerial report that can be easily understood by the decision maker. The report includes the recommended decision and other pertinent information about the results that may be helpful to the decision maker.

A Note Regarding Implementation

As discussed in Section 1.2, the manager is responsible for integrating the quantitative solution with qualitative considerations in order to make the best possible decision. After completing the decision-making process, the manager must oversee the implementation and follow-up evaluation of the decision. The manager should continue to monitor the contribution of the model during the implementation and follow-up. At times this process may lead to requests for model expansion or refinement that will cause the management scientist to return to an earlier step of the quantitative analysis process.

Successful implementation of results is of critical importance to the management scientist as well as the manager. If the results of the quantitative analysis process are not correctly implemented, the entire effort may be of no value. It doesn't take too many unsuccessful implementations before the management scientist is out of work. Because implementation often requires people to do things differently, it often meets with resistance. People want to know, "What's wrong with the way we've been doing it?" and so on. One of the most effective ways to ensure successful implementation is to include users throughout the modeling process. A user who feels a part of identifying the problem and developing the solution is much more likely to enthusiastically implement the results. The success rate for implementing the results of a management science project is much greater for those projects characterized by extensive user involvement. The Management Science in Action, Quantitative Analysis and Supply Chain Management at the Heracles General Cement Company discusses the use of management science techniques to optimize the operations of a supply chain.

MANAGEMENT SCIENCE IN ACTION

QUANTITATIVE ANALYSIS AND SUPPLY CHAIN MANAGEMENT AT THE HERACLES GENERAL CEMENT COMPANY*

Founded in 1911, the Heracles General Cement Company is the largest producer of cement in Greece. The company operates three cement plants in the prefecture of Evoia; one each in Volos, Halkis, and Milaki. Heracles' annual cement production capacity is 9.6 million tons, and the company manages 10 quarries that supply limestone, clay, and schist. Seven of these quarries are in the vicinity of the cement plants, and three are managed by Heracles affiliate LAVA. The company also operates and maintains six distribution centers that are located across Greece; these distribution centers handle 2.5 million tons of domestic cement sales annually, which is over 40% of domestic sales in Greece.

Heracles faces a wide range of logistical challenges in transporting its products to customers. As a result, in 2005 the corporation decided to improve the efficiency of its supply chain by developing a platform for supply chain optimization and planning (SCOP) using mathematical programming.

Heracles' objectives in creating SCOP were to (1) improve the efficiency of decision-making processes throughout its supply chain operations by synchronizing production plans, inventory control, and transportation policies; (2) integrate the core business processes of planning and budgeting with supply chain operations; and (3) achieve system-wide cost reductions through global optimization.

SCOP has been extremely successful. In addition to achieving its three initial goals through the development and implementation of SCOP, the platform provides Heracles with guidance for optimal revision of policies and responses to demand and cost fluctuations. The impact and success of SCOP translates into improved internal coordination, lower costs, greater operational efficiency, and increased customer satisfaction.

*Based on G. Dikos and S. Spyropoulou, "SCOP in Heracles General Cement Company," *Interfaces* 43, no. 4 (July/August 2013): 297–312.

NOTES AND COMMENTS

1. Developments in computer technology have increased the availability of management science techniques to decision makers. Many software packages are now available for personal computers. Microsoft Excel and LINGO are widely used in management science courses and in industry.

2. Various chapter appendices provide step-by-step instructions for using Excel and LINGO to solve problems in the text. Microsoft Excel has become the most used analytical modeling software in business and industry. We recommend that you read Appendix A, Building Spreadsheet Models, located in the back of this text.

1.4   MODELS OF COST, REVENUE, AND PROFIT

Some of the most basic quantitative models arising in business and economic applications are those involving the relationship between a volume variable—such as production volume or sales volume—and cost, revenue, and profit. Through the use of these models, a manager can determine the projected cost, revenue, and/or profit associated with an established production quantity or a forecasted sales volume. Financial planning, production planning, sales quotas, and other areas of decision making can benefit from such cost, revenue, and profit models.

Cost and Volume Models

The cost of manufacturing or producing a product is a function of the volume produced. This cost can usually be defined as a sum of two costs: fixed cost and variable cost. **Fixed cost** is the portion of the total cost that does not depend on the production volume; this cost remains the same no matter how much is produced. **Variable cost,** on the other hand, is the portion of the total cost that is dependent on and varies with the production volume. To illustrate how cost and volume models can be developed, we will consider a manufacturing problem faced by Nowlin Plastics.

Nowlin Plastics produces a line of cell phone covers. Nowlin's best-selling cover is its Viper model, a slim but very durable black and gray plastic cover. Several products are produced on the same manufacturing line, and a setup cost is incurred each time a change-over is made for a new product. Suppose that the setup cost for the Viper is $3000. This setup cost is a fixed cost that is incurred regardless of the number of units eventually produced. In addition, suppose that variable labor and material costs are $2 for each unit produced. The cost-volume model for producing x units of the Viper can be written as

$$C(x) = 3000 + 2x \qquad (1.3)$$

where

$$x = \text{production volume in units}$$
$$C(x) = \text{total cost of producing } x \text{ units}$$

Once a production volume is established, the model in equation (1.3) can be used to compute the total production cost. For example, the decision to produce $x = 1200$ units would result in a total cost of $C(1200) = 3000 + 2(1200) = \$5400$.

Marginal cost is defined as the rate of change of the total cost with respect to production volume. That is, it is the cost increase associated with a one-unit increase in the production volume. In the cost model of equation (1.3), we see that the total cost $C(x)$ will increase by $2 for each unit increase in the production volume. Thus, the marginal cost is $2. With more complex total cost models, marginal cost may depend on the production volume. In such cases, we could have marginal cost increasing or decreasing with the production volume x.

Revenue and Volume Models

Management of Nowlin Plastics will also want information on the projected revenue associated with selling a specified number of units. Thus, a model of the relationship between revenue and volume is also needed. Suppose that each Viper cover sells for $5. The model for total revenue can be written as

$$R(x) = 5x \tag{1.4}$$

where

$$x = \text{sales volume in units}$$
$$R(x) = \text{total revenue associated with selling } x \text{ units}$$

Marginal revenue is defined as the rate of change of total revenue with respect to sales volume. That is, it is the increase in total revenue resulting from a one-unit increase in sales volume. In the model of equation (1.4), we see that the marginal revenue is $5. In this case, marginal revenue is constant and does not vary with the sales volume. With more complex models, we may find that marginal revenue increases or decreases as the sales volume x increases.

Profit and Volume Models

One of the most important criteria for management decision making is profit. Managers need to be able to know the profit implications of their decisions. If we assume that we will only produce what can be sold, the production volume and sales volume will be equal. We can combine equations (1.3) and (1.4) to develop a profit-volume model that will determine the total profit associated with a specified production-sales volume. Total profit, denoted $P(x)$, is total revenue minus total cost; therefore, the following model provides the total profit associated with producing and selling x units:

$$\begin{aligned} P(x) &= R(x) - C(x) \\ &= 5x - (3000 + 2x) = -3000 + 3x \end{aligned} \tag{1.5}$$

Thus, the profit-volume model can be derived from the revenue-volume and cost-volume models.

Breakeven Analysis

Using equation (1.5), we can now determine the total profit associated with any production volume x. For example, suppose that a demand forecast indicates that 500 units of the product can be sold. The decision to produce and sell the 500 units results in a projected profit of

$$P(500) = -3000 + 3(500) = -1500$$

In other words, a loss of $1500 is predicted. If sales are expected to be 500 units, the manager may decide against producing the product. However, a demand forecast of 1800 units would show a projected profit of

$$P(1800) = -3000 + 3(1800) = 2400$$

This profit may be enough to justify proceeding with the production and sale of the product.

We see that a volume of 500 units will yield a loss, whereas a volume of 1800 provides a profit. The volume that results in total revenue equaling total cost (providing $0 profit) is called the **breakeven point.** If the breakeven point is known, a manager can quickly infer that a volume above the breakeven point will result in a profit, whereas a volume below the breakeven point will result in a loss. Thus, the breakeven point for a product provides valuable information for a manager who must make a yes/no decision concerning production of the product.

Let us now return to the Nowlin Plastics example and show how the total profit model in equation (1.5) can be used to compute the breakeven point. The breakeven point can be found by setting the total profit expression equal to zero and solving for the production volume. Using equation (1.5), we have

$$P(x) = -3000 + 3x = 0$$
$$3x = 3000$$
$$x = 1000$$

Try Problem 12 to test your ability to determine the breakeven point for a quantitative model.

With this information, we know that production and sales of the product must be greater than 1000 units before a profit can be expected. The graphs of the total cost model, the total revenue model, and the location of the breakeven point are shown in Figure 1.6. In Appendix 1.1 we also show how Excel can be used to perform a breakeven analysis for the Nowlin Plastics production example.

FIGURE 1.6   GRAPH OF THE BREAKEVEN ANALYSIS FOR NOWLIN PLASTICS

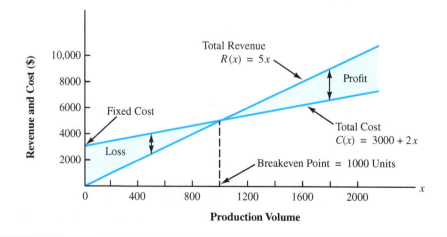

1.5 MANAGEMENT SCIENCE TECHNIQUES

In this section we present a brief overview of the management science techniques covered in this text. Over the years, practitioners have found numerous applications for the following techniques:

Linear Programming Linear programming is a problem-solving approach developed for situations involving maximizing or minimizing a linear function subject to linear constraints that limit the degree to which the objective can be pursued. The production model developed in Section 1.3 (see Figure 1.5) is an example of a simple linear programming model.

Integer Linear Programming Integer linear programming is an approach used for problems that can be set up as linear programs, with the additional requirement that some or all of the decision variables be integer values.

Distribution and Network Models A network is a graphical description of a problem consisting of circles called nodes that are interconnected by lines called arcs. Specialized solution procedures exist for these types of problems, enabling us to quickly solve problems in such areas as supply chain design, information system design, and project scheduling.

Nonlinear Programming Many business processes behave in a nonlinear manner. For example, the price of a bond is a nonlinear function of interest rates; the quantity demanded for a product is usually a nonlinear function of the price. Nonlinear programming is a technique that allows for maximizing or minimizing a nonlinear function subject to nonlinear constraints.

Project Scheduling: PERT/CPM In many situations, managers are responsible for planning, scheduling, and controlling projects that consist of numerous separate jobs or tasks performed by a variety of departments, individuals, and so forth. The PERT (Program Evaluation and Review Technique) and CPM (Critical Path Method) techniques help managers carry out their project scheduling responsibilities.

Inventory Models Inventory models are used by managers faced with the dual problems of maintaining sufficient inventories to meet demand for goods and, at the same time, incurring the lowest possible inventory holding costs.

Waiting-Line or Queueing Models Waiting-line or queueing models have been developed to help managers understand and make better decisions concerning the operation of systems involving waiting lines.

Simulation Simulation is a technique used to model the operation of a system. This technique employs a computer program to model the operation and perform simulation computations.

Decision Analysis Decision analysis can be used to determine optimal strategies in situations involving several decision alternatives and an uncertain or risk-filled pattern of events.

Goal Programming Goal programming is a technique for solving multicriteria decision problems, usually within the framework of linear programming.

Analytic Hierarchy Process This multicriteria decision-making technique permits the inclusion of subjective factors in arriving at a recommended decision.

Forecasting Forecasting methods are techniques that can be used to predict future aspects of a business operation.

Markov Process Models Markov process models are useful in studying the evolution of certain systems over repeated trials. For example, Markov processes have been used to describe the probability that a machine, functioning in one period, will function or break down in another period.

Methods Used Most Frequently

Our experience as both practitioners and educators has been that the most frequently used management science techniques are linear programming, integer programming, network models (including supply chain models), and simulation. Depending upon the industry, the other methods in the preceding list are used more or less frequently.

Helping to bridge the gap between the manager and the management scientist is a major focus of the text. We believe that the barriers to the use of management science can best be removed by increasing the manager's understanding of how management science can be applied. The text will help you develop an understanding of which management science techniques are most useful, how they are used, and, most importantly, how they can assist managers in making better decisions.

The Management Science in Action, Impact of Operations Research on Everyday Living, describes some of the many ways quantitative analysis affects our everyday lives.

MANAGEMENT SCIENCE IN ACTION

IMPACT OF OPERATIONS RESEARCH ON EVERYDAY LIVING*

In an interview with Virginia Postrel of the *Boston Globe*, Mark Eisner, associate director of the School of Operations Research and Industrial Engineering at Cornell University, once said that operations research "...is probably the most important field nobody's ever heard of." He further defines Operations Research as "...the effective use of scarce resources under dynamic and uncertain conditions." As Professor Eisner's definition implies, the impact of operations research on everyday living is substantial.

Suppose you schedule a vacation to Florida and use Orbitz to book your flights. An algorithm developed by operations researchers will search among millions of options to find the cheapest fare. Another algorithm will schedule the flight crews and aircraft used by the airline, and yet another algorithm will determine the price you are charged for your ticket. If you rent a car in Florida, the price you pay for the car is determined by a mathematical model that seeks to maximize revenue for the car rental firm. If you do some shopping on your trip and decide to ship your purchases home using UPS, another algorithm tells UPS which truck to put the packages on, the route the truck should follow to avoid congested roads, and where the packages should be placed on the truck to minimize loading and unloading time. Do you subscribe to NetFlix? The organization uses

operations research, ratings you provide for movies, and your history of movie selections to recommend other movies that will likely appeal to you. Political campaigns even use operations research to decide where to campaign, where to advertise, and how to spend campaign funds in a manner that will maximize the candidate's chance of getting elected.

Operations Research is commonly used in the healthcare industry. Researchers from the Johns Hopkins Bloomberg School of Public Health, Pittsburgh Supercomputing Center (PSC), University of Pittsburgh, and University of California, Irvine use operations research algorithms in the Regional Healthcare Ecosystem Analyst (RHEA). RHEA is used to assess how increases or decreases in vancomycin-resistant enterococci (VRE) at one hospital ultimately change the incidence of VRE in neighboring hospitals. Because VRE is one of the most common bacteria that cause infections in healthcare facilities, RHEA could dramatically reduce the length of hospital stays and the cost of treatment by reducing the incidence of VRE.

"Our study demonstrates how extensive patient sharing among different hospitals in a single region substantially influences VRE burden in those hospitals," states Bruce Y. Lee, MD, MBA, lead author and associate professor of International Health and Director of Operations Research,

International Vaccine Access Center, at the Johns Hopkins Bloomberg School of Public Health. "Lowering barriers to cooperation and collaboration among hospitals, for example, developing regional control programs, coordinating VRE control campaigns, and performing regional research studies could favorably influence regional VRE prevalence."

*Based on Virginia Postrel, "Operations Everything," *The Boston Globe*, June 27, 2004; "How Superbug Spreads Among Regional Hospitals: A Domino Effect,", *Science News*, July 30, 2013; and Bruce Y. Lee, S. Levent Yilmaz, Kim F. Wong, Sarah M. Bartsch, Stephen Eubank, Yeohan Song, et al., "Modeling the Regional Spread and Control of Vancomycin-Resistant Enterococci," *American Journal of Infection Control*, 41, no. 8 (2013):668–673.

NOTES AND COMMENTS

The Institute for Operations Research and the Management Sciences (INFORMS) and the Decision Sciences Institute (DSI) are two professional societies that publish journals and newsletters dealing with current research and applications of operations research and management science techniques.

SUMMARY

This text is about how management science may be used to help managers make better decisions. The focus of this text is on the decision-making process and on the role of management science in that process. We discussed the problem orientation of this process and in an overview showed how mathematical models can be used in this type of analysis.

The difference between the model and the situation or managerial problem it represents is an important point. Mathematical models are abstractions of real-world situations and, as such, cannot capture all the aspects of the real situation. However, if a model can capture the major relevant aspects of the problem and can then provide a solution recommendation, it can be a valuable aid to decision making.

One of the characteristics of management science that will become increasingly apparent as we proceed through the text is the search for a best solution to the problem. In carrying out the quantitative analysis, we shall be attempting to develop procedures for finding the "best" or optimal solution.

GLOSSARY

Analog model Although physical in form, an analog model does not have a physical appearance similar to the real object or situation it represents.

Breakeven point The volume at which total revenue equals total cost.

Constraints Restrictions or limitations imposed on a problem.

Controllable inputs The inputs that are controlled or determined by the decision maker.

Decision The alternative selected.

Decision making The process of defining the problem, identifying the alternatives, determining the criteria, evaluating the alternatives, and choosing an alternative.

Decision variable Another term for controllable input.

Deterministic model A model in which all uncontrollable inputs are known and cannot vary.

Feasible solution A decision alternative or solution that satisfies all constraints.

Fixed cost The portion of the total cost that does not depend on the volume; this cost remains the same no matter how much is produced.

Iconic model A physical replica, or representation, of a real object.

Infeasible solution A decision alternative or solution that does not satisfy one or more constraints.

Marginal cost The rate of change of the total cost with respect to volume.

Marginal revenue The rate of change of total revenue with respect to volume.

Mathematical model Mathematical symbols and expressions used to represent a real situation.

Model A representation of a real object or situation.

Multicriteria decision problem A problem that involves more than one criterion; the objective is to find the "best" solution, taking into account all the criteria.

Objective function A mathematical expression that describes the problem's objective.

Optimal solution The specific decision-variable value or values that provide the "best" output for the model.

Problem solving The process of identifying a difference between the actual and the desired state of affairs and then taking action to resolve the difference.

Single-criterion decision problem A problem in which the objective is to find the "best" solution with respect to just one criterion.

Stochastic (probabilistic) model A model in which at least one uncontrollable input is uncertain and subject to variation; stochastic models are also referred to as probabilistic models.

Uncontrollable inputs The environmental factors or inputs that cannot be controlled by the decision maker.

Variable cost The portion of the total cost that is dependent on and varies with the volume.

PROBLEMS

1. Define the terms *management science* and *operations research*.

2. List and discuss the steps of the decision-making process.

3. Discuss the different roles played by the qualitative and quantitative approaches to managerial decision making. Why is it important for a manager or decision maker to have a good understanding of both of these approaches to decision making?

4. A firm just completed a new plant that will produce more than 500 different products, using more than 50 different production lines and machines. The production scheduling decisions are critical in that sales will be lost if customer demands are not met on time. If no individual in the firm has experience with this production operation and if new production schedules must be generated each week, why should the firm consider a quantitative approach to the production scheduling problem?

5. What are the advantages of analyzing and experimenting with a model as opposed to a real object or situation?

6. Suppose that a manager has a choice between the following two mathematical models of a given situation: (a) a relatively simple model that is a reasonable approximation of the real situation, and (b) a thorough and complex model that is the most accurate mathematical representation of the real situation possible. Why might the model described in part (a) be preferred by the manager?

7. Suppose you are going on a weekend trip to a city that is d miles away. Develop a model that determines your round-trip gasoline costs. What assumptions or approximations are necessary to treat this model as a deterministic model? Are these assumptions or approximations acceptable to you?

8. Recall the production model from Section 1.3:

$$\text{Max} \quad 10x$$
$$\text{s.t.}$$
$$5x \leq 40$$
$$x \geq 0$$

Suppose the firm in this example considers a second product that has a unit profit of $5 and requires 2 hours of production time for each unit produced. Use y as the number of units of product 2 produced.
  a. Show the mathematical model when both products are considered simultaneously.
  b. Identify the controllable and uncontrollable inputs for this model.
  c. Draw the flowchart of the input-output process for this model (see Figure 1.5).
  d. What are the optimal solution values of x and y?
  e. Is the model developed in part (a) a deterministic or a stochastic model? Explain.

9. Suppose we modify the production model in Section 1.3 to obtain the following mathematical model:

$$\text{Max} \quad 10x$$
$$\text{s.t.}$$
$$ax \leq 40$$
$$x \geq 0$$

where a is the number of hours of production time required for each unit produced. With $a = 5$, the optimal solution is $x = 8$. If we have a stochastic model with $a = 3$, $a = 4$, $a = 5$, or $a = 6$ as the possible values for the number of hours required per unit, what is the optimal value for x? What problems does this stochastic model cause?

10. A retail store in Des Moines, Iowa, receives shipments of a particular product from Kansas City and Minneapolis. Let

x = number of units of the product received from Kansas City
y = number of units of the product received from Minneapolis

  a. Write an expression for the total number of units of the product received by the retail store in Des Moines.
  b. Shipments from Kansas City cost $0.20 per unit, and shipments from Minneapolis cost $0.25 per unit. Develop an objective function representing the total cost of shipments to Des Moines.
  c. Assuming the monthly demand at the retail store is 5000 units, develop a constraint that requires 5000 units to be shipped to Des Moines.

    d. No more than 4000 units can be shipped from Kansas City, and no more than 3000 units can be shipped from Minneapolis in a month. Develop constraints to model this situation.

    e. Of course, negative amounts cannot be shipped. Combine the objective function and constraints developed to state a mathematical model for satisfying the demand at the Des Moines retail store at minimum cost.

11. For most products, higher prices result in a decreased demand, whereas lower prices result in an increased demand. Let

$$d = \text{annual demand for a product in units}$$
$$p = \text{price per unit}$$

Assume that a firm accepts the following price-demand relationship as being realistic:

$$d = 800 - 10p$$

where p must be between \$20 and \$70.

    a. How many units can the firm sell at the \$20 per-unit price? At the \$70 per-unit price?

    b. What happens to annual units demanded for the product if the firm increases the per unit price from \$26 to \$27? From \$42 to \$43? From \$68 to \$69? What is the suggested relationship between the per-unit price and annual demand for the product in units?

    c. Show the mathematical model for the total revenue (TR), which is the annual demand multiplied by the unit price.

    d. Based on other considerations, the firm's management will only consider price alternatives of \$30, \$40, and \$50. Use your model from part (b) to determine the price alternative that will maximize the total revenue.

    e. What are the expected annual demand and the total revenue corresponding to your recommended price?

12. The O'Neill Shoe Manufacturing Company will produce a special-style shoe if the order size is large enough to provide a reasonable profit. For each special-style order, the company incurs a fixed cost of \$2000 for the production setup. The variable cost is \$60 per pair, and each pair sells for \$80.

    a. Let x indicate the number of pairs of shoes produced. Develop a mathematical model for the total cost of producing x pairs of shoes.

    b. Let P indicate the total profit. Develop a mathematical model for the total profit realized from an order for x pairs of shoes.

    c. How large must the shoe order be before O'Neill will break even?

13. Micromedia offers computer training seminars on a variety of topics. In the seminars each student works at a personal computer, practicing the particular activity that the instructor is presenting. Micromedia is currently planning a two-day seminar on the use of Microsoft Excel in statistical analysis. The projected fee for the seminar is \$600 per student. The cost for the conference room, instructor compensation, lab assistants, and promotion is \$9600. Micromedia rents computers for its seminars at a cost of \$120 per computer per day.

    a. Develop a model for the total cost to put on the seminar. Let x represent the number of students who enroll in the seminar.

    b. Develop a model for the total profit if x students enroll in the seminar.

    c. Micromedia has forecasted an enrollment of 30 students for the seminar. How much profit will be earned if their forecast is accurate?

    d. Compute the breakeven point.

14. Eastman Publishing Company is considering publishing a paperback textbook on spreadsheet applications for business. The fixed cost of manuscript preparation, textbook design, and production setup is estimated to be \$160,000. Variable production and material costs are estimated to be $6 per book. The publisher plans to sell the text to college and university bookstores for $46 each.

  a. What is the breakeven point?

  b. What profit or loss can be anticipated with a demand of 3800 copies?

  c. With a demand of 3800 copies, what is the minimum price per copy that the publisher must charge to break even?

  d. If the publisher believes that the price per copy could be increased to $50.95 and not affect the anticipated demand of 3800 copies, what action would you recommend? What profit or loss can be anticipated?

15. Preliminary plans are under way for the construction of a new stadium for a major league baseball team. City officials have questioned the number and profitability of the luxury corporate boxes planned for the upper deck of the stadium. Corporations and selected individuals may buy the boxes for $300,000 each. The fixed construction cost for the upper-deck area is estimated to be $4,500,000, with a variable cost of $150,000 for each box constructed.

  a. What is the breakeven point for the number of luxury boxes in the new stadium?

  b. Preliminary drawings for the stadium show that space is available for the construction of up to 50 luxury boxes. Promoters indicate that buyers are available and that all 50 could be sold if constructed. What is your recommendation concerning the construction of luxury boxes? What profit is anticipated?

16. Financial Analysts, Inc., is an investment firm that manages stock portfolios for a number of clients. A new client is requesting that the firm handle an $800,000 portfolio. As an initial investment strategy, the client would like to restrict the portfolio to a mix of the following two stocks:

Stock	Price/ Share	Maximum Estimated Annual Return/Share	Possible Investment
Oil Alaska	$50	$6	$500,000
Southwest Petroleum	$30	$4	$450,000

Let

$$x = \text{number of shares of Oil Alaska}$$
$$y = \text{number of shares of Southwest Petroleum}$$

  a. Develop the objective function, assuming that the client desires to maximize the total annual return.

  b. Show the mathematical expression for each of the following three constraints:

    (1) Total investment funds available are $800,000.

    (2) Maximum Oil Alaska investment is $500,000.

    (3) Maximum Southwest Petroleum investment is $450,000.

Note: Adding the $x \geq 0$ and $y \geq 0$ constraints provides a linear programming model for the investment problem. A solution procedure for this model will be discussed in Chapter 2.

17. Models of inventory systems frequently consider the relationships among a beginning inventory, a production quantity, a demand or sales, and an ending inventory. For a given production period j, let

$$s_{j-1} = \text{ending inventory from the previous period (beginning inventory for period } j)$$
$$x_j = \text{production quantity in period } j$$
$$d_j = \text{demand in period } j$$
$$s_j = \text{ending inventory for period } j$$

   a. Write the mathematical relationship or model that describes how these four variables are related.
   b. What constraint should be added if production capacity for period j is given by C_j?
   c. What constraint should be added if inventory requirements for period j mandate an ending inventory of at least I_j?

18. Esiason Oil makes two blends of fuel by mixing oil from three wells, one each in Texas, Oklahoma, and California. The costs and daily availability of the oils are provided in the following table.

Source of Oil	Cost per Gallon	Daily Gallons Available
Texas well	0.30	12,000
Oklahoma well	0.40	20,000
California well	0.48	24,000

Because these three wells yield oils with different chemical compositions, Esiason's two blends of fuel are composed of different proportions of oil from its three wells. Blend A must be composed of at least 35% of oil from the Texas well, no more than 50% of oil from the Oklahoma well, and at least 15% of oil from the California well. Blend B must be composed of at least 20% of oil from the Texas well, at least 30% of oil from the Oklahoma well, and no more than 40% of oil from the California well.

Each gallon of Blend A can be sold for $3.10 and each gallon of Blend B can be sold for $3.20. Long-term contracts require at least 20,000 gallons of each blend to be produced.

   Let

   x_i = number of gallons of oil from well i used in production of Blend A

   y_i = number of gallons of oil from well i used in production of Blend B

   i = 1 for the Texas well, 2 for the Oklahoma well, 3 for the California well

   a. Develop the objective function, assuming that the client desires to maximize the total daily profit.
   b. Show the mathematical expression for each of the following three constraints:
   (1) Total daily gallons of oil available from the Texas well is 12,000.
   (2) Total daily gallons of oil available from the Oklahoma well is 20,000.
   (3) Total daily gallons of oil available from the California well is 24,000.
   c. Should this problem include any other constraints? If so, express them mathematically in terms of the decision variables.

19. Brooklyn Cabinets is a manufacturer of kitchen cabinets. The two cabinetry styles manufactured by Brooklyn are contemporary and farmhouse. Contemporary style cabinets sell for $90 and farmhouse style cabinets sell for $85. Each cabinet produced must go through carpentry, painting, and finishing processes. The following table summarizes how much time in each process must be devoted to each style of cabinet.

	Hours per Process		
Style	Carpentry	Painting	Finishing
Contemporary	2.0	1.5	1.3
Farmhouse	2.5	1.0	1.2

Carpentry costs $15 per hour, painting costs $12 per hour, and finishing costs $18 per hour, and the weekly number of hours available in the processes is 3000 in carpentry, 1500 in painting, and 1500 in finishing. Brooklyn also has a contract that requires the company to supply one of its customers with 500 contemporary cabinets and 650 farmhouse style cabinets each week.

Let

x = the number of contemporary style cabinets produced each week

y = the number of farmhouse style cabinets produced each week

a. Develop the objective function, assuming that Brooklyn Cabinets wants to maximize the total weekly profit.

b. Show the mathematical expression for each of the constraints on the three processes.

c. Show the mathematical expression for each of Brooklyn Cabinets' contractual agreements.

20. PromoTime, a local advertising agency, has been hired to promote the new adventure film *Tomb Raiders* starring Angie Harrison and Joe Lee Ford. The agency has been given a $100,000 budget to spend on advertising for the movie in the week prior to its release, and the movie's producers have dictated that only local television ads and locally targeted Internet ads will be used. Each television ad costs $500 and reaches an estimated 7000 people, and each Internet ad costs $250 and reaches an estimated 4000 people. The movie's producers have also dictated that, in order to avoid saturation, no more than 20 television ads will be placed. The producers have also stipulated that, in order to reach a critical mass, at least 50 Internet ads will be placed. Finally, the producers want at least one-third of all ads to be placed on television.

Let

x = the number of television ads purchased

y = the number of Internet ads purchased

a. Develop the objective function, assuming that the movie's producers want to reach the maximum number of people possible.

b. Show the mathematical expression for the budget constraint.

c. Show the mathematical expression for the maximum number of 20 television ads to be used.

d. Show the mathematical expression for the minimum number of Internet ads to be used.

e. Show the mathematical expression for the stipulated ratio of television ads to Internet ads.

f. Carefully review the constraints you created in part (b), part (c), and part (d). Does any aspect of these constraints concern you? If so, why?

Case Problem SCHEDULING A GOLF LEAGUE

Chris Lane, the head professional at Royal Oak Country Club, must develop a schedule of matches for the couples' golf league that begins its season at 4:00 P.M. tomorrow. Eighteen couples signed up for the league, and each couple must play every other couple over the course of the 17-week season. Chris thought it would be fairly easy to develop a schedule, but after working on it for a couple of hours, he has been unable to come up with a schedule. Because Chris must have a schedule ready by tomorrow afternoon, he asked you to help him. A possible complication is that one of the couples told Chris that they may have to cancel for the season. They told Chris they will let him know by 1:00 P.M. tomorrow whether they will be able to play this season.

Managerial Report

Prepare a report for Chris Lane. Your report should include, at a minimum, the following items:

1. A schedule that will enable each of the 18 couples to play every other couple over the 17-week season.
2. A contingency schedule that can be used if the couple that contacted Chris decides to cancel for the season.

Appendix 1.1   USING EXCEL FOR BREAKEVEN ANALYSIS

In Section 1.4 we introduced the Nowlin Plastics production example to illustrate how quantitative models can be used to help a manager determine the projected cost, revenue, and/or profit associated with an established production quantity or a forecasted sales volume. In this appendix we introduce spreadsheet applications by showing how to use Microsoft Excel to perform a quantitative analysis of the Nowlin Plastics example.

Refer to the worksheet shown in Figure 1.7. We begin by entering the problem data into the top portion of the worksheet. The value of 3000 in cell B3 is the fixed cost, the value of 2 in cell B5 is the variable labor and material costs per unit, and the value of 5 in cell B7 is the selling price per unit. As discussed in Appendix A, whenever we perform a quantitative analysis using Excel, we will enter the problem data in the top portion of the worksheet and reserve the bottom portion for model development. The label "Model" in cell A10 helps to provide a visual reminder of this convention.

FIGURE 1.7   FORMULA WORKSHEET FOR THE NOWLIN PLASTICS PRODUCTION EXAMPLE

	A	B
1	**Nowlin Plastics**	
2		
3	**Fixed Cost**	3000
4		
5	**Variable Cost Per Unit**	2
6		
7	**Selling Price Per Unit**	5
8		
9		
10	**Model**	
11		
12	**Production Volume**	800
13		
14	**Total Cost**	=B3+B5*B12
15		
16	**Total Revenue**	=B7*B12
17		
18	**Total Profit (Loss)**	=B16-B14

Cell B12 in the Model portion of the worksheet contains the proposed production volume in units. Because the values for total cost, total revenue, and total profit depend upon the value of this decision variable, we have placed a border around cell B12 and screened the cell for emphasis. Based upon the value in cell B12, the cell formulas in cells B14, B16, and B18 are used to compute values for total cost, total revenue, and total profit (loss), respectively. First, recall that the value of total cost is the sum of the fixed cost (cell B3) and the total variable cost. The total variable cost—the product of the variable cost per unit (cell B5) and the production volume (cell B12)—is given by B5*B12. Thus, to compute the value of total cost we entered the formula =B3+B5*B12 in cell B14. Next, total revenue is the product of the selling price per unit (cell B7) and the number of units produced (cell B12), which is entered in cell B16 as the formula =B7*B12. Finally, the total profit (or loss) is the difference between the total revenue (cell B16) and the total cost (cell B14). Thus, in cell B18 we have entered the formula =B16-B14. The worksheet shown in Figure 1.7 shows the formulas used to make these computations; we refer to it as a formula worksheet.

To examine the effect of selecting a particular value for the production volume, we entered a value of 800 in cell B12. The worksheet shown in Figure 1.8 shows the values obtained by the formulas; a production volume of 800 units results in a total cost of $4600, a total revenue of $4000, and a loss of $600. To examine the effect of other production volumes, we only need to enter a different value into cell B12. To examine the effect of different costs and selling prices, we simply enter the appropriate values in the data portion of the worksheet; the results will be displayed in the model section of the worksheet.

FIGURE 1.8   SOLUTION USING A PRODUCTION VOLUME OF 800 UNITS FOR THE NOWLIN PLASTICS PRODUCTION EXAMPLE

Nowlin

	A	B
1	**Nowlin Plastics**	
2		
3	**Fixed Cost**	$3,000
4		
5	**Variable Cost Per Unit**	$2
6		
7	**Selling Price Per Unit**	$5
8		
9		
10	**Model**	
11		
12	**Production Volume**	800
13		
14	**Total Cost**	$4,600
15		
16	**Total Revenue**	$4,000
17		
18	**Total Profit (Loss)**	−$600

In Section 1.4 we illustrated breakeven analysis. Let us now see how Excel's Goal Seek tool can be used to compute the breakeven point for the Nowlin Plastics production example.

Determining the Breakeven Point Using Excel's Goal Seek Tool

The breakeven point is the production volume that results in total revenue equal to total cost and hence a profit of $0. One way to determine the breakeven point is to use a trial-and-error approach. For example, in Figure 1.8 we saw that a trial production volume of 800 units resulted in a loss of $600. Because this trial solution resulted in a loss, a production volume of 800 units cannot be the breakeven point. We could continue to experiment with other production volumes by simply entering different values into cell B12 and observing the resulting profit or loss in cell B18. A better approach is to use Excel's Goal Seek tool to determine the breakeven point.

Excel's Goal Seek tool allows the user to determine the value for an input cell that will cause the value of a related output cell to equal some specified value (called the *goal*). In the case of breakeven analysis, the "goal" is to set Total Profit to zero by "seeking" an appropriate value for Production Volume. Goal Seek will allow us to find the value of production volume that will set Nowlin Plastics' total profit to zero. The following steps describe how to use Goal Seek to find the breakeven point for Nowlin Plastics:

Step 1. Select the **Data** tab at the top of the Ribbon
Step 2. Select **What-If Analysis** in the **Data Tools** group
Step 3. Select **Goal Seek** in What-If Analysis
Step 4. When the **Goal Seek** dialog box appears:
        Enter *B18* in the **Set cell** box
        Enter *0* in the **To value** box
        Enter *B12* in the **By changing cell** box
        Click **OK**

The completed Goal Seek dialog box is shown in Figure 1.9, and the worksheet obtained after selecting **OK** is shown in Figure 1.10. The Total Profit in cell B18 is zero, and the Production Volume in cell B12 has been set to the breakeven point of 1000.

FIGURE 1.9   GOAL SEEK DIALOG BOX FOR THE NOWLIN PLASTICS
                  PRODUCTION EXAMPLE

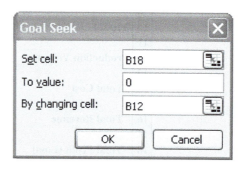

FIGURE 1.10 BREAKEVEN POINT FOUND USING EXCEL'S GOAL SEEK TOOL FOR THE NOWLIN PLASTICS PRODUCTION EXAMPLE

	A	B
1	**Nowlin Plastics**	
2		
3	**Fixed Cost**	$3,000
4		
5	**Variable Cost Per Unit**	$2
6		
7	**Selling Price Per Unit**	$5
8		
9		
10	**Model**	
11		
12	**Production Volume**	1000
13		
14	**Total Cost**	$5,000
15		
16	**Total Revenue**	$5,000
17		
18	**Total Profit (Loss)**	$0

CHAPTER 2

An Introduction to Linear Programming

CONTENTS

Linear programming is a problem-solving approach developed to help managers make decisions. Numerous applications of linear programming can be found in today's competitive business environment. For instance, IBM uses linear programming to perform capacity planning and to make capacity investment decisions for its semiconductor manufacturing operations. GE Capital uses linear programming to help determine optimal lease structuring. Marathon Oil Company uses linear programming for gasoline blending and to evaluate the economics of a new terminal or pipeline. The Management Science in Action, Timber Harvesting Model at MeadWestvaco Corporation, provides another example of the use of linear programming. Later in the chapter another Management Science in Action illustrates how IBM uses linear programming and other management science tools to plan and operate its semiconductor supply chain.

To illustrate some of the properties that all linear programming problems have in common, consider the following typical applications:

1. A manufacturer wants to develop a production schedule and an inventory policy that will satisfy sales demand in future periods. Ideally, the schedule and policy will enable the company to satisfy demand and at the same time *minimize* the total production and inventory costs.
2. A financial analyst must select an investment portfolio from a variety of stock and bond investment alternatives. The analyst would like to establish the portfolio that *maximizes* the return on investment.
3. A marketing manager wants to determine how best to allocate a fixed advertising budget among alternative advertising media such as radio, television, newspaper, and magazine. The manager would like to determine the media mix that *maximizes* advertising effectiveness.
4. A company has warehouses in a number of locations throughout the United States. For a set of customer demands, the company would like to determine how much each warehouse should ship to each customer so that total transportation costs are *minimized.*

MANAGEMENT SCIENCE IN ACTION

TIMBER HARVESTING MODEL AT MEADWESTVACO CORPORATION*

MeadWestvaco Corporation is a major producer of premium papers for periodicals, books, commercial printing, and business forms. The company also produces pulp and lumber, designs and manufactures packaging systems for beverage and other consumables markets, and is a world leader in the production of coated board and shipping containers. Quantitative analyses at MeadWestvaco are developed and implemented by the company's Decision Analysis Department. The department assists decision makers by providing them with analytical tools of quantitative methods as well as personal analysis and recommendations.

MeadWestvaco uses quantitative models to assist with the long-range management of the company's timberland. Through the use of large-scale linear programs, timber harvesting plans are developed to cover a substantial time horizon. These models consider wood market conditions, mill pulpwood requirements, harvesting capacities, and general forest management principles. Within these constraints, the model arrives at an optimal harvesting and purchasing schedule based on discounted cash flow. Alternative schedules reflect changes in the various assumptions concerning forest growth, wood availability, and general economic conditions.

Quantitative methods are also used in the development of the inputs for the linear programming models. Timber prices and supplies as well as mill requirements must be forecast over the time horizon, and advanced sampling techniques are used to evaluate land holdings and to project forest growth. The harvest schedule is then developed using quantitative methods.

*Based on information provided by Dr. Edward P. Winkofsky.

These examples are only a few of the situations in which linear programming has been used successfully, but they illustrate the diversity of linear programming applications. A close scrutiny reveals one basic property they all have in common. In each example, we were concerned with *maximizing* or *minimizing* some quantity. In example 1, the manufacturer wanted to minimize costs; in example 2, the financial analyst wanted to maximize return on investment; in example 3, the marketing manager wanted to maximize advertising effectiveness; and in example 4, the company wanted to minimize total transportation costs. *In all linear programming problems, the maximization or minimization of some quantity is the objective.*

All linear programming problems also have a second property: restrictions, or **constraints,** that limit the degree to which the objective can be pursued. In example 1, the manufacturer is restricted by constraints requiring product demand to be satisfied and by the constraints limiting production capacity. The financial analyst's portfolio problem is constrained by the total amount of investment funds available and the maximum amounts that can be invested in each stock or bond. The marketing manager's media selection decision is constrained by a fixed advertising budget and the availability of the various media. In the transportation problem, the minimum-cost shipping schedule is constrained by the supply of product available at each warehouse. *Thus, constraints are another general feature of every linear programming problem.*

2.1 A SIMPLE MAXIMIZATION PROBLEM

Par, Inc., is a small manufacturer of golf equipment and supplies whose management has decided to move into the market for medium- and high-priced golf bags. Par Inc.'s distributor is enthusiastic about the new product line and has agreed to buy all the golf bags Par, Inc., produces over the next three months.

After a thorough investigation of the steps involved in manufacturing a golf bag, management determined that each golf bag produced will require the following operations:

1. Cutting and dyeing the material
2. Sewing
3. Finishing (inserting umbrella holder, club separators, etc.)
4. Inspection and packaging

The director of manufacturing analyzed each of the operations and concluded that if the company produces a medium-priced standard model, each bag will require $7/10$ hour in the cutting and dyeing department, $1/2$ hour in the sewing department, 1 hour in the finishing department, and $1/10$ hour in the inspection and packaging department. The more expensive deluxe model will require 1 hour for cutting and dyeing, $5/6$ hour for sewing, $2/3$ hour for finishing, and $1/4$ hour for inspection and packaging. This production information is summarized in Table 2.1.

Par Inc.'s production is constrained by a limited number of hours available in each department. After studying departmental workload projections, the director of manufacturing estimates that 630 hours for cutting and dyeing, 600 hours for sewing, 708 hours for finishing, and 135 hours for inspection and packaging will be available for the production of golf bags during the next three months.

The accounting department analyzed the production data, assigned all relevant variable costs, and arrived at prices for both bags that will result in a profit contribution[1] of $10 for

---

[1]From an accounting perspective, profit contribution is more correctly described as the contribution margin per bag; for example, overhead and other shared costs have not been allocated.

TABLE 2.1 PRODUCTION REQUIREMENTS PER GOLF BAG

Department	Production Time (hours)	
	Standard Bag	**Deluxe Bag**
Cutting and Dyeing	$7/10$	1
Sewing	$1/2$	$5/6$
Finishing	1	$2/3$
Inspection and Packaging	$1/10$	$1/4$

It is important to understand that we are maximizing profit contribution, not profit. Overhead and other shared costs must be deducted before arriving at a profit figure.

every standard bag and $9 for every deluxe bag produced. Let us now develop a mathematical model of the Par, Inc., problem that can be used to determine the number of standard bags and the number of deluxe bags to produce in order to maximize total profit contribution.

Problem Formulation

Problem formulation, or **modeling,** is the process of translating the verbal statement of a problem into a mathematical statement. Formulating models is an art that can only be mastered with practice and experience. Even though every problem has some unique features, most problems also have common features. As a result, *some* general guidelines for model formulation can be helpful, especially for beginners. We will illustrate these general guidelines by developing a mathematical model for the Par, Inc., problem.

Understand the Problem Thoroughly   We selected the Par, Inc., problem to introduce linear programming because it is easy to understand. However, more complex problems will require much more thinking in order to identify the items that need to be included in the model. In such cases, read the problem description quickly to get a feel for what is involved. Taking notes will help you focus on the key issues and facts.

Describe the Objective   The objective is to maximize the total contribution to profit.

Describe Each Constraint   Four constraints relate to the number of hours of manufacturing time available; they restrict the number of standard bags and the number of deluxe bags that can be produced.

Constraint 1:   Number of hours of cutting and dyeing time used must be less than or equal to the number of hours of cutting and dyeing time available.

Constraint 2:   Number of hours of sewing time used must be less than or equal to the number of hours of sewing time available.

Constraint 3:   Number of hours of finishing time used must be less than or equal to the number of hours of finishing time available.

Constraint 4:   Number of hours of inspection and packaging time used must be less than or equal to the number of hours of inspection and packaging time available.

Define the Decision Variables   The controllable inputs for Par, Inc., are (1) the number of standard bags produced and (2) the number of deluxe bags produced. Let

$$S = \text{number of standard bags}$$
$$D = \text{number of deluxe bags}$$

In linear programming terminology, S and D are referred to as the **decision variables.**

Write the Objective in Terms of the Decision Variables   Par Inc.'s profit contribution comes from two sources: (1) the profit contribution made by producing S standard bags and (2) the profit contribution made by producing D deluxe bags. If Par, Inc., makes \$10 for every standard bag, the company will make \$10S if S standard bags are produced. Also, if Par, Inc., makes \$9 for every deluxe bag, the company will make \$9D if D deluxe bags are produced. Thus, we have

$$\text{Total Profit Contribution} = 10S + 9D$$

Because the objective—maximize total profit contribution—is a function of the decision variables S and D, we refer to $10S + 9D$ as the *objective function*. Using "Max" as an abbreviation for maximize, we write Par Inc.'s objective as follows:

$$\text{Max } 10S + 9D$$

Write the Constraints in Terms of the Decision Variables

Constraint 1:

$$\begin{pmatrix} \text{Hours of cutting and} \\ \text{dyeing time used} \end{pmatrix} \le \begin{pmatrix} \text{Hours of cutting and} \\ \text{dyeing time available} \end{pmatrix}$$

Every standard bag Par, Inc., produces will use $7/10$ hour cutting and dyeing time; therefore, the total number of hours of cutting and dyeing time used in the manufacture of S standard bags is $7/10 S$. In addition, because every deluxe bag produced uses 1 hour of cutting and dyeing time, the production of D deluxe bags will use $1D$ hours of cutting and dyeing time. Thus, the total cutting and dyeing time required for the production of S standard bags and D deluxe bags is given by

$$\text{Total hours of cutting and dyeing time used} = 7/10 S + 1D$$

The units of measurement on the left-hand side of the constraint must match the units of measurement on the right-hand side.

The director of manufacturing stated that Par, Inc., has at most 630 hours of cutting and dyeing time available. Therefore, the production combination we select must satisfy the requirement

$$7/10 S + 1D \le 630 \tag{2.1}$$

Constraint 2:

$$\begin{pmatrix} \text{Hours of sewing} \\ \text{time used} \end{pmatrix} \le \begin{pmatrix} \text{Hours of sewing} \\ \text{time available} \end{pmatrix}$$

From Table 2.1, we see that every standard bag manufactured will require $\frac{1}{2}$ hour for sewing, and every deluxe bag will require $5/6$ hour for sewing. Because 600 hours of sewing time are available, it follows that

$$\frac{1}{2} S + 5/6 D \le 600 \tag{2.2}$$

Constraint 3:

$$\left(\begin{array}{c}\text{Hours of finishing} \\ \text{time used}\end{array}\right) \leq \left(\begin{array}{c}\text{Hours of finishing} \\ \text{time available}\end{array}\right)$$

Every standard bag manufactured will require 1 hour for finishing, and every deluxe bag will require ⅔ hour for finishing. With 708 hours of finishing time available, it follows that

$$1S + \tfrac{2}{3}D \leq 708 \tag{2.3}$$

Constraint 4:

$$\left(\begin{array}{c}\text{Hours of inspection and} \\ \text{packaging time used}\end{array}\right) \leq \left(\begin{array}{c}\text{Hours of inspection and} \\ \text{packaging time available}\end{array}\right)$$

Every standard bag manufactured will require ⅒ hour for inspection and packaging, and every deluxe bag will require ¼ hour for inspection and packaging. Because 135 hours of inspection and packaging time are available, it follows that

$$\tfrac{1}{10}S + \tfrac{1}{4}D \leq 135 \tag{2.4}$$

We have now specified the mathematical relationships for the constraints associated with the four departments. Have we forgotten any other constraints? Can Par, Inc., produce a negative number of standard or deluxe bags? Clearly, the answer is no. Thus, to prevent the decision variables S and D from having negative values, two constraints

$$S \geq 0 \quad \text{and} \quad D \geq 0 \tag{2.5}$$

must be added. These constraints ensure that the solution to the problem will contain nonnegative values for the decision variables and are thus referred to as the **nonnegativity constraints.** Nonnegativity constraints are a general feature of all linear programming problems and may be written in the abbreviated form:

$$S, D \geq 0$$

Try Problem 24(a) to test your ability to formulate a mathematical model for a maximization linear programming problem with less-than-or-equal-to constraints.

Mathematical Statement of the Par, Inc., Problem

The mathematical statement or mathematical formulation of the Par, Inc., problem is now complete. We succeeded in translating the objective and constraints of the problem into a set of mathematical relationships referred to as a **mathematical model.** The complete mathematical model for the Par, Inc., problem is as follows:

$$
\begin{aligned}
\text{Max} \quad & 10S + 9D \\
\text{subject to (s.t.)} \quad & \\
& \tfrac{7}{10}S + 1D \le 630 \quad \text{Cutting and dyeing} \\
& \tfrac{1}{2}S + \tfrac{5}{6}D \le 600 \quad \text{Sewing} \\
& 1S + \tfrac{2}{3}D \le 708 \quad \text{Finishing} \\
& \tfrac{1}{10}S + \tfrac{1}{4}D \le 135 \quad \text{Inspection and packaging} \\
& S, D \ge 0
\end{aligned}
\tag{2.6}
$$

Our job now is to find the product mix (i.e., the combination of S and D) that satisfies all the constraints and, at the same time, yields a value for the objective function that is greater than or equal to the value given by any other feasible solution. Once these values are calculated, we will have found the optimal solution to the problem.

This mathematical model of the Par, Inc., problem is **a linear programming model,** or **linear program.** The problem has the objective and constraints that, as we said earlier, are common properties of all *linear* programs. But what is the special feature of this mathematical model that makes it a linear program? The special feature that makes it a linear program is that the objective function and all constraint functions are linear functions of the decision variables.

Mathematical functions in which each variable appears in a separate term and is raised to the first power are called **linear functions.** The objective function $(10S + 9D)$ is linear because each decision variable appears in a separate term and has an exponent of 1. The amount of production time required in the cutting and dyeing department $(\tfrac{7}{10}S + 1D)$ is also a linear function of the decision variables for the same reason. Similarly, the functions on the left-hand side of all the constraint inequalities (the constraint functions) are linear functions. Thus, the mathematical formulation of this problem is referred to as a linear program.

Try Problem 1 to test your ability to recognize the types of mathematical relationships that can be found in a linear program.

Linear *programming* has nothing to do with computer programming. The use of the word *programming* here means "choosing a course of action." Linear programming involves choosing a course of action when the mathematical model of the problem contains only linear functions.

NOTES AND COMMENTS

1. The three assumptions necessary for a linear programming model to be appropriate are proportionality, additivity, and divisibility. *Proportionality* means that the contribution to the objective function and the amount of resources used in each constraint are proportional to the value of each decision variable. *Additivity* means that the value of the objective function and the total resources used can be found by summing the objective function contribution and the resources used for all decision variables. *Divisibility* means that the decision variables are continuous. The divisibility assumption plus the nonnegativity constraints mean that decision variables can take on any value greater than or equal to zero.

2. Management scientists formulate and solve a variety of mathematical models that contain an objective function and a set of constraints. Models of this type are referred to as *mathematical programming models*. Linear programming models are a special type of mathematical programming model in that the objective function and all constraint functions are linear.

2.2 GRAPHICAL SOLUTION PROCEDURE

A linear programming problem involving only two decision variables can be solved using a graphical solution procedure. Let us begin the graphical solution procedure by developing a graph that displays the possible solutions (S and D values) for the Par, Inc., problem. The graph (Figure 2.1) will have values of S on the horizontal axis and values of D on the vertical axis. Any point on the graph can be identified by the S and D values, which indicate the position of the point along the horizontal and vertical axes, respectively. Because every point (S, D) corresponds to a possible solution, every point on the graph is called a *solution point*. The solution point where $S = 0$ and $D = 0$ is referred to as the origin. Because S and D must be nonnegative, the graph in Figure 2.1 only displays solutions where $S \geq 0$ and $D \geq 0$.

Earlier, we saw that the inequality representing the cutting and dyeing constraint is

$$\tfrac{7}{10}S + 1D \leq 630$$

To show all solution points that satisfy this relationship, we start by graphing the solution points satisfying the constraint as an equality. That is, the points where $\tfrac{7}{10}S + 1D = 630$. Because the graph of this equation is a line, it can be obtained by identifying two points that satisfy the equation and then drawing a line through the points. Setting $S = 0$ and solving for D, we see that the point ($S = 0, D = 630$) satisfies the equation. To find a second point satisfying this equation, we set $D = 0$ and solve for S. By doing so, we obtain

FIGURE 2.1 SOLUTION POINTS FOR THE TWO-VARIABLE PAR, INC., PROBLEM

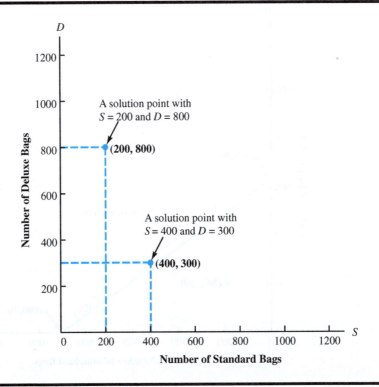

$\frac{7}{10}S + 1(0) = 630$, or $S = 900$. Thus, a second point satisfying the equation is ($S = 900$, $D = 0$). Given these two points, we can now graph the line corresponding to the equation

$$\frac{7}{10}S + 1D = 630$$

This line, which will be called the cutting and dyeing *constraint line,* is shown in Figure 2.2. We label this line "C & D" to indicate that it represents the cutting and dyeing constraint line.

Recall that the inequality representing the cutting and dyeing constraint is

$$\frac{7}{10}S + 1D \le 630$$

Can you identify all of the solution points that satisfy this constraint? Because all points on the line satisfy $\frac{7}{10}S + 1D = 630$, we know any point on this line must satisfy the constraint. But where are the solution points satisfying $\frac{7}{10}S + 1D < 630$? Consider two solution points: ($S = 200$, $D = 200$) and ($S = 600$, $D = 500$). You can see from Figure 2.2 that the first solution point is below the constraint line and the second is above the constraint line. Which of these solutions will satisfy the cutting and dyeing constraint? For the point ($S = 200$, $D = 200$), we see that

$$\frac{7}{10}S + 1D = \frac{7}{10}(200) + 1(200) = 340$$

FIGURE 2.2   THE CUTTING AND DYEING CONSTRAINT LINE

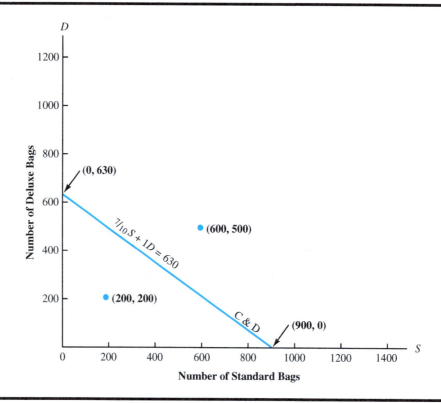

Because the 340 hours is less than the 630 hours available, the ($S = 200$, $D = 200$) production combination, or solution point, satisfies the constraint. For the point ($S = 600$, $D = 500$), we have

$$\tfrac{7}{10}S + 1D = \tfrac{7}{10}(600) + 1(500) = 920$$

The 920 hours is greater than the 630 hours available, so the ($S = 600$, $D = 500$) solution point does not satisfy the constraint and is thus not feasible.

Can you graph a constraint line and find the solution points that are feasible? Try Problem 2.

If a solution point is not feasible for a particular constraint, then all other solution points on the same side of that constraint line are not feasible. If a solution point is feasible for a particular constraint, then all other solution points on the same side of the constraint line are feasible for that constraint. Thus, one has to evaluate the constraint function for only one solution point to determine which side of a constraint line is feasible. In Figure 2.3 we indicate all points satisfying the cutting and dyeing constraint by the shaded region.

We continue by identifying the solution points satisfying each of the other three constraints. The solutions that are feasible for each of these constraints are shown in Figure 2.4.

Four separate graphs now show the feasible solution points for each of the four constraints. In a linear programming problem, we need to identify the solution points that satisfy *all* the constraints *simultaneously.* To find these solution points, we can draw all four constraints on one graph and observe the region containing the points that do in fact satisfy all the constraints simultaneously.

FIGURE 2.3   FEASIBLE SOLUTIONS FOR THE CUTTING AND DYEING CONSTRAINT, REPRESENTED BY THE SHADED REGION

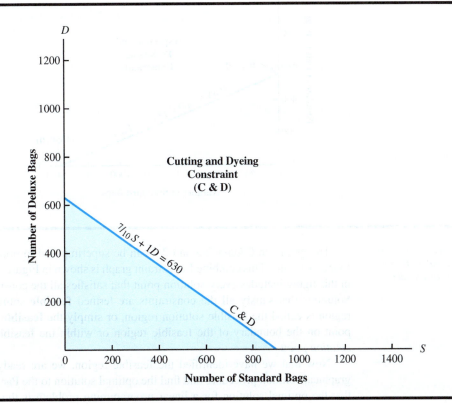

FIGURE 2.4   FEASIBLE SOLUTIONS FOR THE SEWING, FINISHING, AND INSPECTION
AND PACKAGING CONSTRAINTS, REPRESENTED BY THE SHADED REGIONS

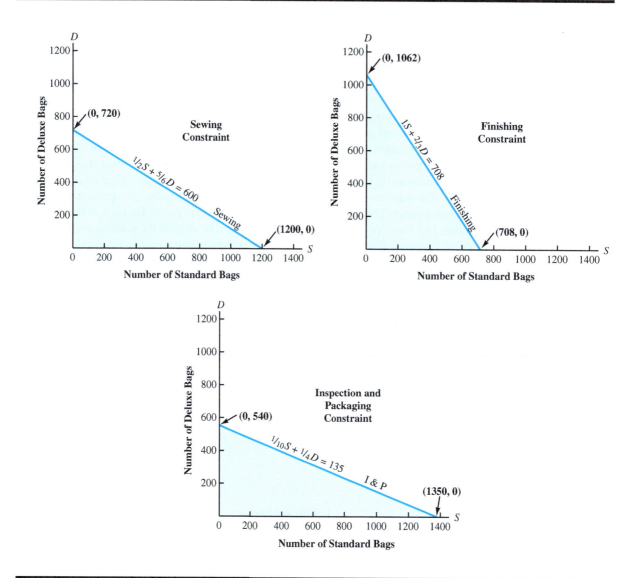

Try Problem 7 to test your ability to find the feasible region given several constraints.

The graphs in Figures 2.3 and 2.4 can be superimposed to obtain one graph with all four constraints. This combined-constraint graph is shown in Figure 2.5. The shaded region in this figure includes every solution point that satisfies all the constraints simultaneously. Solutions that satisfy all the constraints are termed **feasible solutions,** and the shaded region is called the feasible solution region, or simply the **feasible region.** Any solution point on the boundary of the feasible region or within the feasible region is a *feasible solution point.*

Now that we have identified the feasible region, we are ready to proceed with the graphical solution procedure and find the optimal solution to the Par, Inc., problem. Recall that the optimal solution for a linear programming problem is the feasible solution that

FIGURE 2.5 COMBINED-CONSTRAINT GRAPH SHOWING THE FEASIBLE REGION FOR THE PAR, INC., PROBLEM

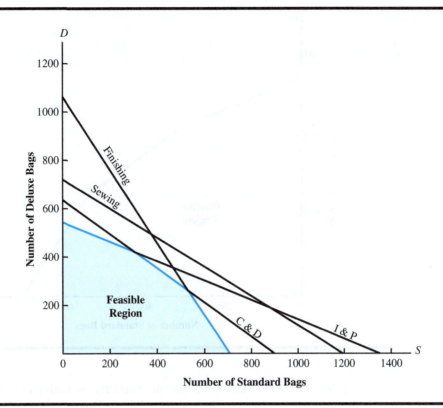

provides the best possible value of the objective function. Let us start the optimizing step of the graphical solution procedure by redrawing the feasible region on a separate graph. The graph is shown in Figure 2.6.

One approach to finding the optimal solution would be to evaluate the objective function for each feasible solution; the optimal solution would then be the one yielding the largest value. The difficulty with this approach is the infinite number of feasible solutions; thus, because one cannot possibly evaluate an infinite number of feasible solutions, this trial-and-error procedure cannot be used to identify the optimal solution.

Rather than trying to compute the profit contribution for each feasible solution, we select an arbitrary value for profit contribution and identify all the feasible solutions (S, D) that yield the selected value. For example, which feasible solutions provide a profit contribution of $1800? These solutions are given by the values of S and D in the feasible region that will make the objective function

$$10S + 9D = 1800$$

This expression is simply the equation of a line. Thus, all feasible solution points (S, D) yielding a profit contribution of $1800 must be on the line. We learned earlier in this section how to graph a constraint line. The procedure for graphing the profit or objective function line is the same. Letting $S = 0$, we see that D must be 200; thus, the solution

FIGURE 2.6   FEASIBLE REGION FOR THE PAR, INC., PROBLEM

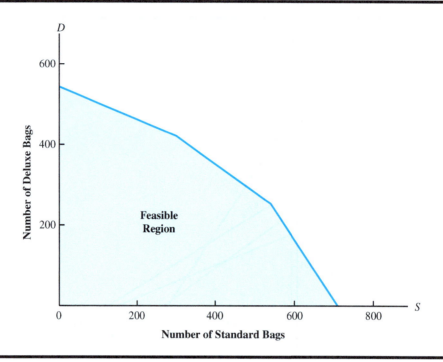

point ($S = 0$, $D = 200$) is on the line. Similarly, by letting $D = 0$, we see that the solution point ($S = 180$, $D = 0$) is also on the line. Drawing the line through these two points identifies all the solutions that have a profit contribution of $1800. A graph of this profit line is presented in Figure 2.7.

Because the objective is to find the feasible solution yielding the largest profit contribution, let us proceed by selecting higher profit contributions and finding the solutions yielding the selected values. For instance, let us find all solutions yielding profit contributions of $3600 and $5400. To do so, we must find the S and D values that are on the following lines:

$$10S + 9D = 3600$$

and

$$10S + 9D = 5400$$

Using the previous procedure for graphing profit and constraint lines, we draw the $3600 and $5400 profit lines as shown on the graph in Figure 2.8. Although not all solution points on the $5400 profit line are in the feasible region, at least some points on the line are, and it is therefore possible to obtain a feasible solution that provides a $5400 profit contribution.

Can we find a feasible solution yielding an even higher profit contribution? Look at Figure 2.8, and see what general observations you can make about the profit lines already drawn. Note the following: (1) the profit lines are *parallel* to each other, and (2) higher

FIGURE 2.7 $1800 PROFIT LINE FOR THE PAR, INC., PROBLEM

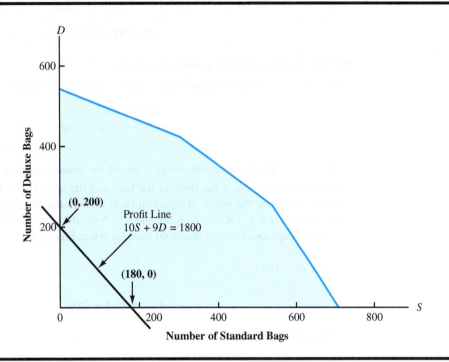

FIGURE 2.8   SELECTED PROFIT LINES FOR THE PAR, INC., PROBLEM

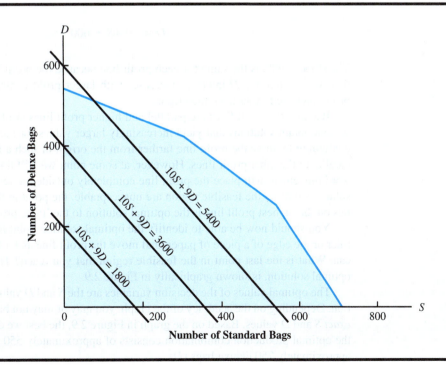

profit lines are obtained as we move farther from the origin. These observations can also be expressed algebraically. Let P represent total profit contribution. The objective function is

$$P = 10S + 9D$$

Solving for D in terms of S and P, we obtain

$$9D = -10S + P$$
$$D = -\tfrac{10}{9}S + \tfrac{1}{9}P \qquad\qquad (2.7)$$

Equation (2.7) is the *slope-intercept form* of the linear equation relating S and D. The coefficient of S, $-\tfrac{10}{9}$, is the slope of the line, and the term $\tfrac{1}{9}P$ is the D intercept (i.e., the value of D where the graph of equation (2.7) crosses the D axis). Substituting the profit contributions of $P = 1800$, $P = 3600$, and $P = 5400$ into equation (2.7) yields the following slope-intercept equations for the profit lines shown in Figure 2.8:

For $P = 1800$,

$$D = -\tfrac{10}{9}S + 200$$

For $P = 3600$,

$$D = -\tfrac{10}{9}S + 400$$

For $P = 5400$,

$$D = -\tfrac{10}{9}S + 600$$

Can you graph the profit line for a linear program? Try Problem 6.

The slope $(-\tfrac{10}{9})$ is the same for each profit line because the profit lines are parallel. Further, we see that the D intercept increases with larger profit contributions. Thus, higher profit lines are farther from the origin.

Because the profit lines are parallel and higher profit lines are farther from the origin, we can obtain solutions that yield increasingly larger values for the objective function by continuing to move the profit line farther from the origin in such a fashion that it remains parallel to the other profit lines. However, at some point we will find that any further outward movement will place the profit line completely outside the feasible region. Because solutions outside the feasible region are unacceptable, the point in the feasible region that lies on the highest profit line is the optimal solution to the linear program.

You should now be able to identify the optimal solution point for this problem. Use a ruler or the edge of a piece of paper, and move the profit line as far from the origin as you can. What is the last point in the feasible region that you reach? This point, which is the optimal solution, is shown graphically in Figure 2.9.

The optimal values of the decision variables are the S and D values at the optimal solution. Depending on the accuracy of the graph, you may or may not be able to determine the *exact* S and D values. Based on the graph in Figure 2.9, the best we can do is conclude that the optimal production combination consists of approximately 550 standard bags (S) and approximately 250 deluxe bags (D).

FIGURE 2.9   OPTIMAL SOLUTION FOR THE PAR, INC., PROBLEM

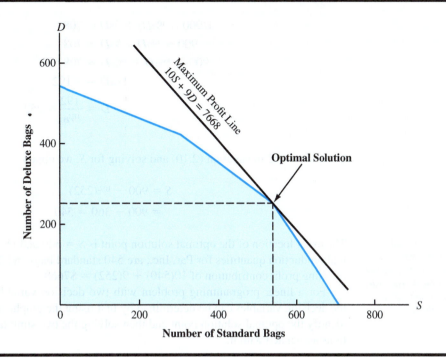

A closer inspection of Figures 2.5 and 2.9 shows that the optimal solution point is at the intersection of the cutting and dyeing and the finishing constraint lines. That is, the optimal solution point is on both the cutting and dyeing constraint line

$$\tfrac{7}{10}S + 1D = 630 \tag{2.8}$$

and the finishing constraint line

$$1S + \tfrac{2}{3}D = 708 \tag{2.9}$$

Thus, the optimal values of the decision variables S and D must satisfy both equations (2.8) and (2.9) simultaneously. Using equation (2.8) and solving for S gives

$$\tfrac{7}{10}S = 630 - 1D$$

or

$$S = 900 - \tfrac{10}{7}D \tag{2.10}$$

Substituting this expression for S into equation (2.9) and solving for D provides the following:

$$1(900 - {}^{10}\!/_7 D) + {}^2\!/_3 D = 708$$

$$900 - {}^{10}\!/_7 D + {}^2\!/_3 D = 708$$

$$900 - {}^{30}\!/_{21} D + {}^{14}\!/_{21} D = 708$$

$$-{}^{16}\!/_{21} D = -192$$

$$D = \frac{192}{{}^{16}\!/_{21}} = 252$$

Using $D = 252$ in equation (2.10) and solving for S, we obtain

$$S = 900 - {}^{10}\!/_7 (252)$$

$$= 900 - 360 = 540$$

Although the optimal solution to the Par, Inc., problem consists of integer values for the decision variables, this result will not always be the case.

The exact location of the optimal solution point is $S = 540$ and $D = 252$. Hence, the optimal production quantities for Par, Inc., are 540 standard bags and 252 deluxe bags, with a resulting profit contribution of $10(540) + 9(252) = \$7668$.

For a linear programming problem with two decision variables, the exact values of the decision variables can be determined by first using the graphical solution procedure to identify the optimal solution point and then solving the two simultaneous constraint equations associated with it.

A Note on Graphing Lines

Try Problem 10 to test your ability to use the graphical solution procedure to identify the optimal solution and find the exact values of the decision variables at the optimal solution.

An important aspect of the graphical method is the ability to graph lines showing the constraints and the objective function of the linear program. The procedure we used for graphing the equation of a line is to find any two points satisfying the equation and then draw the line through the two points. For the Par, Inc., constraints, the two points were easily found by first setting $S = 0$ and solving the constraint equation for D. Then we set $D = 0$ and solved for S. For the cutting and dyeing constraint line

$$^7\!/_{10} S + 1D = 630$$

this procedure identified the two points $(S = 0, D = 630)$ and $(S = 900, D = 0)$. The cutting and dyeing constraint line was then graphed by drawing a line through these two points.

All constraints and objective function lines in two-variable linear programs can be graphed if two points on the line can be identified. However, finding the two points on the line is not always as easy as shown in the Par, Inc., problem. For example, suppose a company manufactures two models of a small tablet computer: the Assistant (A) and the Professional (P). Management needs 50 units of the Professional model for its own salesforce, and expects sales of the Professional to be at most one-half of the sales of the Assistant. A constraint enforcing this requirement is

$$P - 50 \le {}^1\!/_2 A$$

or

$$2P - 100 \le A$$

or

$$2P - A \le 100$$

Using the equality form and setting $P = 0$, we find the point ($P = 0, A = -100$) is on the constraint line. Setting $A = 0$, we find a second point ($P = 50, A = 0$) on the constraint line. If we have drawn only the nonnegative ($P \ge 0, A \ge 0$) portion of the graph, the first point ($P = 0, A = -100$) cannot be plotted because $A = -100$ is not on the graph. Whenever we have two points on the line but one or both of the points cannot be plotted in the nonnegative portion of the graph, the simplest approach is to enlarge the graph. In this example, the point ($P = 0, A = -100$) can be plotted by extending the graph to include the negative A axis. Once both points satisfying the constraint equation have been located, the line can be drawn. The constraint line and the feasible solutions for the constraint $2P - A \le 100$ are shown in Figure 2.10.

As another example, consider a problem involving two decision variables, R and T. Suppose that the number of units of R produced had to be at least equal to the number of units of T produced. A constraint enforcing this requirement is

$$R \ge T$$

or

$$R - T \ge 0$$

FIGURE 2.10 FEASIBLE SOLUTIONS FOR THE CONSTRAINT $2P - A \le 100$

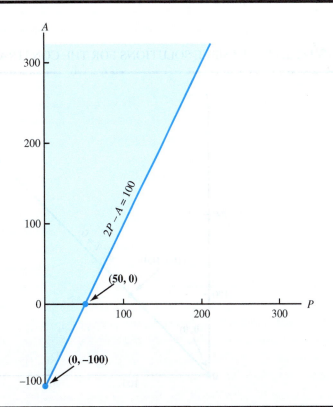

Can you graph a constraint line when the origin is on the constraint line? Try Problem 5.

To find all solutions satisfying the constraint as an equality, we first set $R = 0$ and solve for T. This result shows that the origin ($T = 0$, $R = 0$) is on the constraint line. Setting $T = 0$ and solving for R provides the same point. However, we can obtain a second point on the line by setting T equal to any value other than zero and then solving for R. For instance, setting $T = 100$ and solving for R, we find that the point ($T = 100$, $R = 100$) is on the line. With the two points ($R = 0$, $T = 0$) and ($R = 100$, $T = 100$), the constraint line $R - T = 0$ and the feasible solutions for $R - T \geq 0$ can be plotted as shown in Figure 2.11.

Summary of the Graphical Solution Procedure for Maximization Problems

For additional practice in using the graphical solution procedure, try Problems 24(b), 24(c), and 24(d).

As we have seen, the graphical solution procedure is a method for solving two-variable linear programming problems such as the Par, Inc., problem. The steps of the graphical solution procedure for a maximization problem are summarized here:

1. Prepare a graph of the feasible solutions for each of the constraints.
2. Determine the feasible region by identifying the solutions that satisfy all the constraints simultaneously.
3. Draw an objective function line showing the values of the decision variables that yield a specified value of the objective function.
4. Move parallel objective function lines toward larger objective function values until further movement would take the line completely outside the feasible region.
5. Any feasible solution on the objective function line with the largest value is an optimal solution.

FIGURE 2.11   FEASIBLE SOLUTIONS FOR THE CONSTRAINT $R - T \geq 0$

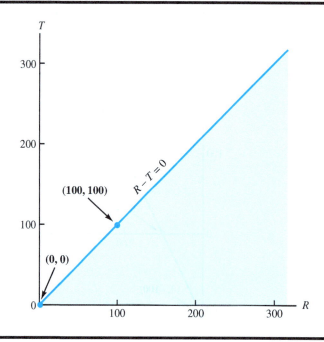

Slack Variables

In addition to the optimal solution and its associated profit contribution, Par Inc.'s management will probably want information about the production time requirements for each production operation. We can determine this information by substituting the optimal solution values ($S = 540, D = 252$) into the constraints of the linear program.

Constraint	Hours Required for $S = 540$ and $D = 252$	Hours Available	Unused Hours
Cutting and dyeing	$7/10(540) + 1(252) = 630$	630	0
Sewing	$1/2(540) + 5/6(252) = 480$	600	120
Finishing	$1(540) + 2/3(252) = 708$	708	0
Inspection and packaging	$1/10(540) + 1/4(252) = 117$	135	18

Thus, the complete solution tells management that the production of 540 standard bags and 252 deluxe bags will require all available cutting and dyeing time (630 hours) and all available finishing time (708 hours), while $600 - 480 = 120$ hours of sewing time and $135 - 117 = 18$ hours of inspection and packaging time will remain unused. The 120 hours of unused sewing time and 18 hours of unused inspection and packaging time are referred to as *slack* for the two departments. In linear programming terminology, any unused capacity for a $\leq$ constraint is referred to as the *slack* associated with the constraint.

Can you identify the slack associated with a constraint? Try Problem 24(e).

Often variables, called **slack variables,** are added to the formulation of a linear programming problem to represent the slack, or idle capacity. Unused capacity makes no contribution to profit; thus, slack variables have coefficients of zero in the objective function. After the addition of four slack variables, denoted S_1, S_2, S_3, and S_4, the mathematical model of the Par, Inc., problem becomes

$$\text{Max}\quad 10S + 9D + 0S_1 + 0S_2 + 0S_3 + 0S_4$$
$$\text{s.t.}$$
$$7/10 S + 1D + 1S_1 \qquad\qquad\qquad = 630$$
$$1/2 S + 5/6 D \qquad + 1S_2 \qquad\qquad = 600$$
$$1S + 2/3 D \qquad\qquad + 1S_3 \qquad = 708$$
$$1/10 S + 1/4 D \qquad\qquad\qquad + 1S_4 = 135$$
$$S, D, S_1, S_2, S_3, S_4 \geq 0$$

Can you write a linear program in standard form? Try Problem 18.

Whenever a linear program is written in a form with all constraints expressed as equalities, it is said to be written in **standard form.**

Referring to the standard form of the Par, Inc., problem, we see that at the optimal solution ($S = 540$ and $D = 252$), the values for the slack variables are

Constraint	Value of Slack Variable
Cutting and dyeing	$S_1 = \ \ 0$
Sewing	$S_2 = 120$
Finishing	$S_3 = \ \ 0$
Inspection and packaging	$S_4 = \ \ 18$

Could we have used the graphical solution to provide some of this information? The answer is yes. By finding the optimal solution point in Figure 2.5, we can see that the cutting and dyeing and the finishing constraints restrict, or *bind,* the feasible region at this point. Thus, this solution requires the use of all available time for these two operations. In other words, the graph shows us that the cutting and dyeing and the finishing departments will have zero slack. On the other hand, the sewing and the inspection and packaging constraints are not binding the feasible region at the optimal solution, which means we can expect some unused time or slack for these two operations.

As a final comment on the graphical analysis of this problem, we call your attention to the sewing capacity constraint as shown in Figure 2.5. Note, in particular, that this constraint did not affect the feasible region. That is, the feasible region would be the same whether the sewing capacity constraint were included or not, which tells us that enough sewing time is available to accommodate any production level that can be achieved by the other three departments. The sewing constraint does not affect the feasible region and thus cannot affect the optimal solution; it is called a **redundant constraint.**

NOTES AND COMMENTS

1. In the standard-form representation of a linear programming model, the objective function coefficients for slack variables are zero. This zero coefficient implies that slack variables, which represent unused resources, do not affect the value of the objective function. However, in some applications, unused resources can be sold and contribute to profit. In such cases, the corresponding slack variables become decision variables representing the amount of unused resources to be sold. For each of these variables, a nonzero coefficient in the objective function would reflect the profit associated with selling a unit of the corresponding resource.

2. Redundant constraints do not affect the feasible region; as a result, they can be removed from a linear programming model without affecting the optimal solution. However, if the linear programming model is to be re-solved later, changes in some of the data might make a previously redundant constraint a binding constraint. Thus, we recommend keeping all constraints in the linear programming model even though at some point in time one or more of the constraints may be redundant.

2.3   EXTREME POINTS AND THE OPTIMAL SOLUTION

Suppose that the profit contribution for Par Inc.'s standard golf bag is reduced from $10 to $5 per bag, while the profit contribution for the deluxe golf bag and all the constraints remain unchanged. The complete linear programming model of this new problem is identical to the mathematical model in Section 2.1, except for the revised objective function:

$$\text{Max } 5S + 9D$$

How does this change in the objective function affect the optimal solution to the Par, Inc., problem? Figure 2.12 shows the graphical solution of this new problem with the revised objective function. Note that without any change in the constraints, the feasible region does not change. However, the profit lines have been altered to reflect the new objective function.

By moving the profit line in a parallel manner toward higher profit values, we find the optimal solution as shown in Figure 2.12. The values of the decision variables at this point

FIGURE 2.12   OPTIMAL SOLUTION FOR THE PAR, INC., PROBLEM WITH AN
OBJECTIVE FUNCTION OF $5S + 9D$

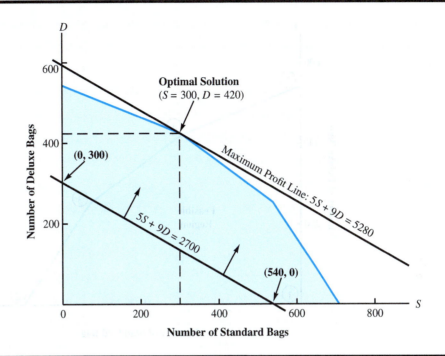

are $S = 300$ and $D = 420$. The reduced profit contribution for the standard bag caused a
change in the optimal solution. In fact, as you may have suspected, we are cutting back the
production of the lower-profit standard bags and increasing the production of the higher-
profit deluxe bags.

    What observations can you make about the location of the optimal solutions in the
two linear programming problems solved thus far? Look closely at the graphical solutions
in Figures 2.9 and 2.12. Notice that the optimal solutions occur at one of the vertices, or
"corners," of the feasible region. In linear programming terminology, these vertices are
referred to as the **extreme points** of the feasible region. The Par, Inc., feasible region
has five vertices, or five extreme points (see Figure 2.13). We can now formally state our
observation about the location of optimal solutions as follows:

*For additional practice
in identifying the extreme
points of the feasible
region and determining
the optimal solution by
computing and comparing
the objective function value
at each extreme point, try
Problem 13.*

    The optimal solution to a linear program can be found at an extreme point of the
feasible region.[2]

    This property means that if you are looking for the optimal solution to a linear pro-
gram, you do not have to evaluate all feasible solution points. In fact, you have to consider

_____

[2]We will discuss in Section 2.6 the two special cases (infeasibility and unboundedness) in linear programming that have
no optimal solution, and for which this statement does not apply.

FIGURE 2.13   THE FIVE EXTREME POINTS OF THE FEASIBLE REGION
FOR THE PAR, INC., PROBLEM

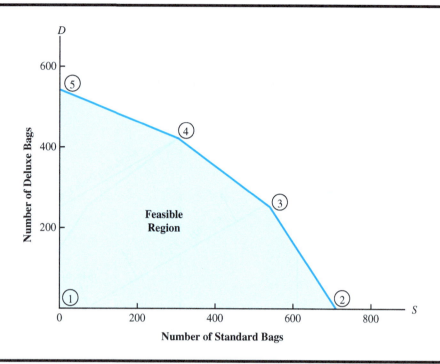

only the feasible solutions that occur at the extreme points of the feasible region. Thus, for the Par, Inc., problem, instead of computing and comparing the profit contributions for all feasible solutions, we can find the optimal solution by evaluating the five extreme-point solutions and selecting the one that provides the largest profit contribution. Actually, the graphical solution procedure is nothing more than a convenient way of identifying an optimal extreme point for two-variable problems.

2.4   COMPUTER SOLUTION OF THE PAR, INC., PROBLEM

Computer programs designed to solve linear programming problems are now widely available. After a short period of familiarization with the specific features of the package, users are able to solve linear programming problems with few difficulties. Problems involving thousands of variables and thousands of constraints are now routinely solved with computer packages. Some of the leading commercial packages include CPLEX, Gurobi, LINGO, MOSEK, Excel Solver, and Analytic Solver Platform for Excel. Packages are also available for free download. A good example is Clp (COIN-OR linear programming).

The solution to Par, Inc. is shown in Figure 2.14. The authors have chosen to make this book flexible and not rely on a specific linear programming package. Hence, the output in Figure 2.14 is generic and is not an actual printout from a particular software package. The output provided in Figure 2.14 is typical of most linear programming packages. We use this output format throughout the text. Two common software packages for solving linear programs are LINGO and Excel Solver; descriptions of these two packages are provided in the appendices. In Appendix 2.1 we show how to solve the Par, Inc., problem using LINGO.

FIGURE 2.14   THE SOLUTION FOR THE PAR, INC., PROBLEM

Optimal Objective Value =   7668.00000

Variable	Value	Reduced Cost
S	540.00000	0.00000
D	252.00000	0.00000

Constraint	Slack/Surplus	Dual Value
1	0.00000	4.37500
2	120.00000	0.00000
3	0.00000	6.93750
4	18.00000	0.00000

Variable	Objective Coefficient	Allowable Increase	Allowable Decrease
S	10.00000	3.50000	3.70000
D	9.00000	5.28571	2.33333

Constraint	RHS Value	Allowable Increase	Allowable Decrease
1	630.00000	52.36364	134.40000
2	600.00000	Infinite	120.00000
3	708.00000	192.00000	128.00000
4	135.00000	Infinite	18.00000

Par

In Appendix 2.2 we show how to formulate a spreadsheet model for the Par, Inc., problem and use Excel Solver to solve the problem.

Interpretation of Computer Output

Let us look more closely at the output in Figure 2.14 and interpret the computer solution provided for the Par, Inc., problem. The optimal solution to this problem will provide a profit of $7668. Directly below the objective function value, we find the values of the decision variables at the optimal solution. We have $S = 540$ standard bags and $D = 252$ deluxe bags as the optimal production quantities.

Recall that the Par, Inc., problem had four less-than-or-equal-to constraints corresponding to the hours available in each of four production departments. The information shown in the Slack/Surplus column provides the value of the slack variable for each of the departments. This information is summarized here:

Constraint Number	Constraint Name	Slack
1	Cutting and dyeing	0
2	Sewing	120
3	Finishing	0
4	Inspection and packaging	18

From this information, we see that the binding constraints (the cutting and dyeing and the finishing constraints) have zero slack at the optimal solution. The sewing department has 120 hours of slack or unused capacity, and the inspection and packaging department has 18 hours of slack or unused capacity.

The rest of the output in Figure 2.14 can be used to determine how changes in the input data impact the optimal solution. We shall defer discussion of reduced costs, dual values, allowable increases and decreases of objective function coefficients and right-hand-side values until Chapter 3, where we study the topic of sensitivity analysis.

NOTES AND COMMENTS

Linear programming solvers are now a standard feature of most spreadsheet packages. In Appendix 2.2 we show how Excel can be used to solve linear programs by using Excel Solver to solve the Par, Inc., problem.

2.5   A SIMPLE MINIMIZATION PROBLEM

M&D Chemicals produces two products that are sold as raw materials to companies manufacturing bath soaps and laundry detergents. Based on an analysis of current inventory levels and potential demand for the coming month, M&D's management specified that the combined production for products A and B must total at least 350 gallons. Separately, a major customer's order for 125 gallons of product A must also be satisfied. Product A requires 2 hours of processing time per gallon and product B requires 1 hour of processing time per gallon. For the coming month, 600 hours of processing time are available. M&D's objective is to satisfy these requirements at a minimum total production cost. Production costs are $2 per gallon for product A and $3 per gallon for product B.

To find the minimum-cost production schedule, we will formulate the M&D Chemicals problem as a linear program. Following a procedure similar to the one used for the Par, Inc., problem, we first define the decision variables and the objective function for the problem. Let

$$A = \text{number of gallons of product A}$$
$$B = \text{number of gallons of product B}$$

With production costs at $2 per gallon for product A and $3 per gallon for product B, the objective function that corresponds to the minimization of the total production cost can be written as

$$\text{Min } 2A + 3B$$

Next, consider the constraints placed on the M&D Chemicals problem. To satisfy the major customer's demand for 125 gallons of product A, we know A must be at least 125. Thus, we write the constraint

$$1A \geq 125$$

For the combined production for both products, which must total at least 350 gallons, we can write the constraint

$$1A + 1B \geq 350$$

Finally, for the limitation of 600 hours on available processing time, we add the constraint

$$2A + 1B \leq 600$$

After adding the nonnegativity constraints ($A, B \geq 0$), we arrive at the following linear program for the M&D Chemicals problem:

$$\text{Min} \quad 2A + 3B$$

s.t.

$$
\begin{array}{lll}
1A & \geq 125 & \text{Demand for product A} \\
1A + 1B & \geq 350 & \text{Total production} \\
2A + 1B & \geq 600 & \text{Processing time} \\
A, B & \geq 0 &
\end{array}
$$

Because the linear programming model has only two decision variables, the graphical solution procedure can be used to find the optimal production quantities. The graphical solution procedure for this problem, just as in the Par, Inc., problem, requires us to first graph the constraint lines to find the feasible region. By graphing each constraint line separately and then checking points on either side of the constraint line, the feasible solutions for each constraint can be identified. By combining the feasible solutions for each constraint on the same graph, we obtain the feasible region shown in Figure 2.15.

FIGURE 2.15   THE FEASIBLE REGION FOR THE M&D CHEMICALS PROBLEM

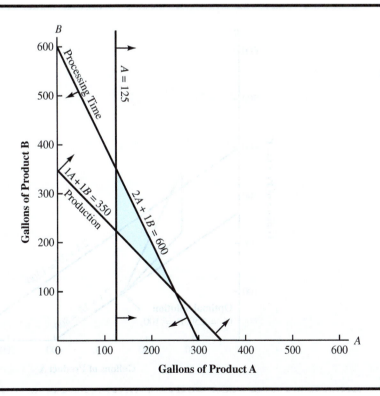

To find the minimum-cost solution, we now draw the objective function line corresponding to a particular total cost value. For example, we might start by drawing the line $2A + 3B = 1200$. This line is shown in Figure 2.16. Clearly, some points in the feasible region would provide a total cost of $1200. To find the values of A and B that provide smaller total cost values, we move the objective function line in a lower left direction until, if we moved it any farther, it would be entirely outside the feasible region. Note that the objective function line $2A + 3B = 800$ intersects the feasible region at the extreme point $A = 250$ and $B = 100$. This extreme point provides the minimum-cost solution with an objective function value of 800. From Figures 2.15 and 2.16, we can see that the total production constraint and the processing time constraint are binding. Just as in every linear programming problem, the optimal solution occurs at an extreme point of the feasible region.

Summary of the Graphical Solution Procedure for Minimization Problems

Can you use the graphical solution procedure to determine the optimal solution for a minimization problem? Try Problem 31.

The steps of the graphical solution procedure for a minimization problem are summarized here:

1. Prepare a graph of the feasible solutions for each of the constraints.
2. Determine the feasible region by identifying the solutions that satisfy all the constraints simultaneously.

FIGURE 2.16   GRAPHICAL SOLUTION FOR THE M&D CHEMICALS PROBLEM

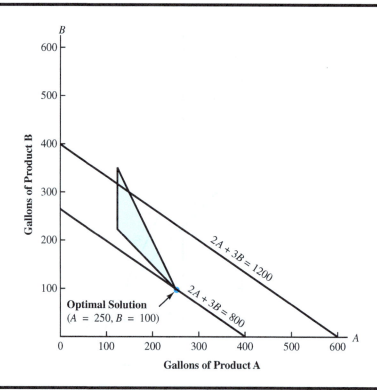

3. Draw an objective function line showing the values of the decision variables that yield a specified value of the objective function.
4. Move parallel objective function lines toward smaller objective function values until further movement would take the line completely outside the feasible region.
5. Any feasible solution on the objective function line with the smallest value is an optimal solution.

Surplus Variables

The optimal solution to the M&D Chemicals problem shows that the desired total production of $A + B = 350$ gallons has been achieved by using all available processing time of $2A + 1B = 2(250) + 1(100) = 600$ hours. In addition, note that the constraint requiring that product A demand be met has been satisfied with $A = 250$ gallons. In fact, the production of product A exceeds its minimum level by $250 - 125 = 125$ gallons. This excess production for product A is referred to as *surplus*. In linear programming terminology, any excess quantity corresponding to a $\geq$ constraint is referred to as surplus.

Recall that with a $\leq$ constraint, a slack variable can be added to the left-hand side of the inequality to convert the constraint to equality form. With a $\geq$ constraint, a **surplus variable** can be subtracted from the left-hand side of the inequality to convert the constraint to equality form. Just as with slack variables, surplus variables are given a coefficient of zero in the objective function because they have no effect on its value. After including two surplus variables, S_1 and S_2, for the $\geq$ constraints and one slack variable, S_3, for the $\leq$ constraint, the linear programming model of the M&D Chemicals problem becomes

$$\text{Min} \quad 2A + 3B + 0S_1 + 0S_2 + 0S_3$$

$$\text{s.t.}$$

$$1A \qquad - 1S_1 \qquad\qquad = 125$$
$$1A + 1B \qquad - 1S_2 \qquad = 350$$
$$2A + 1B \qquad\qquad + 1S_3 = 600$$
$$A, B, S_1, S_2, S_3 \geq 0$$

Try Problem 35 to test your ability to use slack and surplus variables to write a linear program in standard form.

All the constraints are now equalities. Hence, the preceding formulation is the standard-form representation of the M&D Chemicals problem. At the optimal solution of $A = 250$ and $B = 100$, the values of the surplus and slack variables are as follows:

Constraint	Value of Surplus or Slack Variables
Demand for product A	$S_1 = 125$
Total production	$S_2 = 0$
Processing time	$S_3 = 0$

Refer to Figures 2.15 and 2.16. Note that the zero surplus and slack variables are associated with the constraints that are binding at the optimal solution—that is, the total production and processing time constraints. The surplus of 125 units is associated with the nonbinding constraint on the demand for product A.

In the Par, Inc., problem all the constraints were of the $\leq$ type, and in the M&D Chemicals problem the constraints were a mixture of $\geq$ and $\leq$ types. The number and types of constraints encountered in a particular linear programming problem depend on the specific conditions existing in the problem. Linear programming problems may have some ≤ constraints, some = constraints, and some ≥ constraints. For an equality constraint, feasible solutions must lie directly on the constraint line.

Try Problem 34 to practice solving a linear program with all three constraint forms.

An example of a linear program with two decision variables, G and H, and all three constraint forms is given here:

$$\text{Min} \quad 2G + 2H$$
$$\text{s.t.}$$
$$1G + 3H \leq 12$$
$$3G + 1H \geq 13$$
$$1G - 1H = 3$$
$$G, H \geq 0$$

The standard-form representation of this problem is

$$\text{Min} \quad 2G + 2H + 0S_1 + 0S_2$$
$$\text{s.t}$$
$$1G + 3H + 1S_1 \qquad = 12$$
$$3G + 1H \qquad -1S_2 = 13$$
$$1G - 1H \qquad = 3$$
$$G, H, S_1, S_2 \geq 0$$

The standard form requires a slack variable for the ≤ constraint and a surplus variable for the ≥ constraint. However, neither a slack nor a surplus variable is required for the third constraint because it is already in equality form.

When solving linear programs graphically, it is not necessary to write the problem in its standard form. Nevertheless, you should be able to compute the values of the slack and surplus variables and understand what they mean, because the values of slack and surplus variables are included in the computer solution of linear programs.

A final point: The standard form of the linear programming problem is equivalent to the original formulation of the problem. That is, the optimal solution to any linear programming problem is the same as the optimal solution to the standard form of the problem. The standard form has not changed the basic problem; it has only changed how we write the constraints for the problem.

Computer Solution of the M&D Chemicals Problem

The optimal solution to M&D is given in Figure 2.17. The computer output shows that the minimum-cost solution yields an objective function value of $800. The values of the decision variables show that 250 gallons of product A and 100 gallons of product B provide the minimum-cost solution.

The Slack/Surplus column shows that the ≥ constraint corresponding to the demand for product A (see constraint 1) has a surplus of 125 units. This column tells us that production of product A in the optimal solution exceeds demand by 125 gallons. The Slack/Surplus values are zero for the total production requirement (constraint 2) and the processing time limitation (constraint 3), which indicates that these constraints are binding at the optimal solution. We will discuss the rest of the computer output that appears in Figure 2.17 in Chapter 3 when we study the topic of sensitivity analysis.

FIGURE 2.17   THE SOLUTION FOR THE M&D CHEMICALS PROBLEM

Optimal Objective Value =   800.00000

Variable	Value	Reduced Cost
A	250.00000	0.00000
B	100.00000	0.00000

Constraint	Slack/Surplus	Dual Value
1	125.00000	0.00000
2	0.00000	4.00000
3	0.00000	-1.00000

WEB file

M&D

Variable	Objective Coefficient	Allowable Increase	Allowable Decrease
A	2.00000	1.00000	Infinite
B	3.00000	Infinite	1.00000

Constraint	RHS Value	Allowable Increase	Allowable Decrease
1	125.00000	125.00000	Infinite
2	350.00000	125.00000	50.00000
3	600.00000	100.00000	125.00000

2.6   SPECIAL CASES

In this section we discuss three special situations that can arise when we attempt to solve linear programming problems.

Alternative Optimal Solutions

From the discussion of the graphical solution procedure, we know that optimal solutions can be found at the extreme points of the feasible region. Now let us consider the special case in which the optimal objective function line coincides with one of the binding constraint lines on the boundary of the feasible region. We will see that this situation can lead to the case of **alternative optimal solutions;** in such cases, more than one solution provides the optimal value for the objective function.

To illustrate the case of alternative optimal solutions, we return to the Par, Inc., problem. However, let us assume that the profit for the standard golf bag (S) has been decreased to $6.30. The revised objective function becomes $6.3S + 9D$. The graphical solution of this problem is shown in Figure 2.18. Note that the optimal solution still occurs at an extreme point. In fact, it occurs at two extreme points: extreme point ④ ($S = 300$, $D = 420$) and extreme point ③ ($S = 540$, $D = 252$).

The objective function values at these two extreme points are identical; that is

$$6.3S + 9D = 6.3(300) + 9(420) = 5670$$

FIGURE 2.18   PAR, INC., PROBLEM WITH AN OBJECTIVE FUNCTION OF $6.3S + 9D$ (ALTERNATIVE OPTIMAL SOLUTIONS)

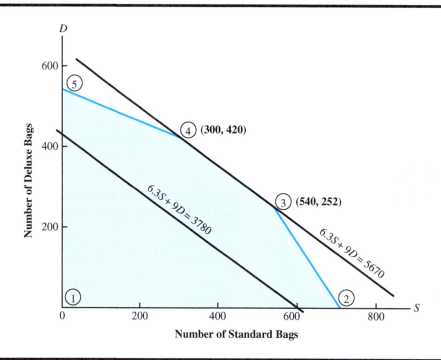

and

$$6.3S + 9D = 6.3(540) + 9(252) = 5670$$

Furthermore, any point on the line connecting the two optimal extreme points also provides an optimal solution. For example, the solution point ($S = 420$, $D = 336$), which is halfway between the two extreme points, also provides the optimal objective function value of

$$6.3S + 9D = 6.3(420) + 9(336) = 5670$$

A linear programming problem with alternative optimal solutions is generally a good situation for the manager or decision maker. It means that several combinations of the decision variables are optimal and that the manager can select the most desirable optimal solution. Unfortunately, determining whether a problem has alternative optimal solutions is not a simple matter.

Infeasibility

Problems with no feasible solution do arise in practice, most often because management's expectations are too high or because too many restrictions have been placed on the problem.

Infeasibility means that no solution to the linear programming problem satisfies all the constraints, including the nonnegativity conditions. Graphically, infeasibility means that a feasible region does not exist; that is, no points satisfy all the constraints and the nonnegativity conditions simultaneously. To illustrate this situation, let us look again at the problem faced by Par, Inc.

Suppose that management specified that at least 500 of the standard bags and at least 360 of the deluxe bags must be manufactured. The graph of the solution region may now be constructed to reflect these new requirements (see Figure 2.19). The shaded area in the

FIGURE 2.19 NO FEASIBLE REGION FOR THE PAR, INC., PROBLEM WITH MINIMUM PRODUCTION REQUIREMENTS OF 500 STANDARD AND 360 DELUXE BAGS

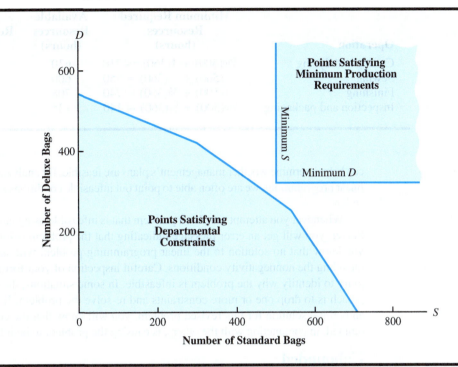

lower left-hand portion of the graph depicts those points satisfying the departmental constraints on the availability of time. The shaded area in the upper right-hand portion depicts those points satisfying the minimum production requirements of 500 standard and 360 deluxe bags. But no points satisfy both sets of constraints. Thus, we see that if management imposes these minimum production requirements, no feasible region exists for the problem.

How should we interpret infeasibility in terms of this current problem? First, we should tell management that given the resources available (i.e., production time for cutting and dyeing, sewing, finishing, and inspection and packaging), it is not possible to make 500 standard bags and 360 deluxe bags. Moreover, we can tell management exactly how much of each resource must be expended to make it possible to manufacture 500 standard and 360 deluxe bags. Table 2.2 shows the minimum amounts of resources that must be available, the amounts currently available, and additional amounts that would be required to accomplish this level of production. Thus, we need 80 more hours for cutting and dyeing, 32 more hours for finishing, and 5 more hours for inspection and packaging to meet management's minimum production requirements.

If, after reviewing this information, management still wants to manufacture 500 standard and 360 deluxe bags, additional resources must be provided. Perhaps by hiring another person to work in the cutting and dyeing department, transferring a person from elsewhere in the plant to work part-time in the finishing department, or having the sewing people help out periodically with the inspection and packaging, the resource requirements can be met. As you can see, many possibilities are available for corrective management action, once we discover the lack of a feasible solution. The important thing to realize is that linear programming analysis

TABLE 2.2   RESOURCES NEEDED TO MANUFACTURE 500 STANDARD BAGS
AND 360 DELUXE BAGS

Operation	Minimum Required Resources (hours)	Available Resources (hours)	Additional Resources Needed (hours)
Cutting and dyeing	$\frac{7}{10}(500) + 1(360) = 710$	630	80
Sewing	$\frac{1}{2}(500) + \frac{5}{6}(360) = 550$	600	None
Finishing	$1(500) + \frac{2}{3}(360) = 740$	708	32
Inspection and packaging	$\frac{1}{10}(500) + \frac{1}{4}(360) = 140$	135	5

can help determine whether management's plans are feasible. By analyzing the problem using linear programming, we are often able to point out infeasible conditions and initiate corrective action.

Whenever you attempt to solve a problem that is infeasible using either LINGO or Excel Solver, you will get an error message indicating that the problem is infeasible. In this case you know that no solution to the linear programming problem will satisfy all constraints, including the nonnegativity conditions. Careful inspection of your formulation is necessary to try to identify why the problem is infeasible. In some situations, the only reasonable approach is to drop one or more constraints and re-solve the problem. If you are able to find an optimal solution for this revised problem, you will know that the constraint(s) that was omitted, in conjunction with the others, is causing the problem to be infeasible.

Unbounded

The solution to a maximization linear programming problem is **unbounded** if the value of the solution may be made infinitely large without violating any of the constraints; for a minimization problem, the solution is unbounded if the value may be made infinitely small. This condition might be termed *managerial utopia;* for example, if this condition were to occur in a profit maximization problem, the manager could achieve an unlimited profit.

However, in linear programming models of real problems, the occurrence of an unbounded solution means that the problem has been improperly formulated. We know it is not possible to increase profits indefinitely. Therefore, we must conclude that if a profit maximization problem results in an unbounded solution, the mathematical model doesn't represent the real-world problem sufficiently. Usually, what has happened is that a constraint has been inadvertently omitted during problem formulation.

As an illustration, consider the following linear program with two decision variables, X and Y:

$$\text{Max} \quad 20X + 10Y$$
$$\text{s.t.}$$
$$1X \qquad \geq 2$$
$$1Y \leq 5$$
$$X, Y \geq 0$$

In Figure 2.20 we graphed the feasible region associated with this problem. Note that we can only indicate part of the feasible region because the feasible region extends indefinitely in the direction of the X axis. Looking at the objective function lines in Figure 2.20, we see that the solution to this problem may be made as large as we desire. That is, no matter what solution we pick, we will always be able to reach some feasible solution with a larger value. Thus, we say that the solution to this linear program is *unbounded.*

FIGURE 2.20   EXAMPLE OF AN UNBOUNDED PROBLEM

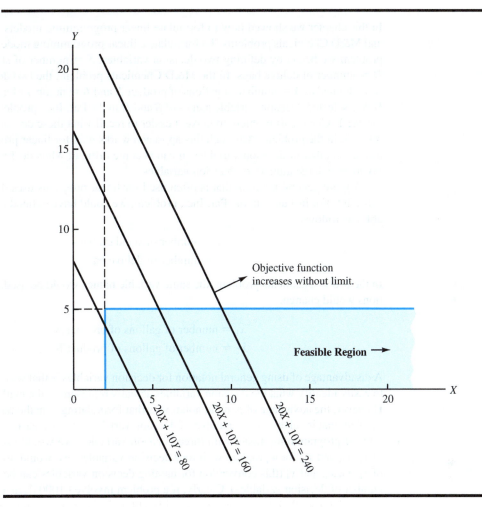

Can you recognize whether a linear program involves alternative optimal solutions or infeasibility, or is unbounded? Try Problems 42 and 43.

Whenever you attempt to solve a problem that is unbounded using either LINGO or Excel Solver you will get a message telling you that the problem is unbounded. Because unbounded solutions cannot occur in real problems, the first thing you should do is to review your model to determine whether you incorrectly formulated the problem. In many cases, this error is the result of inadvertently omitting a constraint during problem formulation.

NOTES AND COMMENTS

1. Infeasibility is independent of the objective function. It exists because the constraints are so restrictive that no feasible region for the linear programming model is possible. Thus, when you encounter infeasibility, making changes in the coefficients of the objective function will not help; the problem will remain infeasible.

2. The occurrence of an unbounded solution is often the result of a missing constraint. However, a change in the objective function may cause a previously unbounded problem to become bounded with an optimal solution. For example, the graph in Figure 2.20 shows an unbounded solution for the objective function Max $20X + 10Y$. However, changing the objective function to Max $-20X - 10Y$ will provide the optimal solution $X = 2$ and $Y = 0$ even though no changes have been made in the constraints.

2.7   GENERAL LINEAR PROGRAMMING NOTATION

In this chapter we showed how to formulate linear programming models for the Par, Inc., and M&D Chemicals problems. To formulate a linear programming model of the Par, Inc., problem we began by defining two decision variables: S = number of standard bags and D = number of deluxe bags. In the M&D Chemicals problem, the two decision variables were defined as A = number of gallons of product A and B = number of gallons of product B. We selected decision-variable names of S and D in the Par, Inc., problem and A and B in the M&D Chemicals problem to make it easier to recall what these decision variables represented in the problem. Although this approach works well for linear programs involving a small number of decision variables, it can become difficult when dealing with problems involving a large number of decision variables.

A more general notation that is often used for linear programs uses the letter x with a subscript. For instance, in the Par, Inc., problem, we could have defined the decision variables as follows:

$$x_1 = \text{number of standard bags}$$
$$x_2 = \text{number of deluxe bags}$$

In the M&D Chemicals problem, the same variable names would be used, but their definitions would change:

$$x_1 = \text{number of gallons of product A}$$
$$x_2 = \text{number of gallons of product B}$$

A disadvantage of using general notation for decision variables is that we are no longer able to easily identify what the decision variables actually represent in the mathematical model. However, the advantage of general notation is that formulating a mathematical model for a problem that involves a large number of decision variables is much easier. For instance, for a linear programming model with three decision variables, we would use variable names of x_1, x_2, and x_3; for a problem with four decision variables, we would use variable names of x_1, x_2, x_3, and x_4 (this convention for naming decision variables can be extended to any number of decision variables). Clearly, if a problem involved 1000 decision variables, trying to identify 1000 unique names would be difficult. However, using the general linear programming notation, the decision variables would be defined as $x_1, x_2, x_3, \ldots, x_{1000}$.

To illustrate the graphical solution procedure for a linear program written using general linear programming notation, consider the following mathematical model for a maximization problem involving two decision variables:

$$\text{Max} \quad 3x_1 + 2x_2$$
$$\text{s.t.}$$
$$2x_1 + 2x_2 \leq 8$$
$$1x_1 + 0.5x_2 \leq 3$$
$$x_1, x_2 \geq 0$$

We must first develop a graph that displays the possible solutions (x_1 and x_2 values) for the problem. The usual convention is to plot values of x_1 along the horizontal axis and values of x_2 along the vertical axis. Figure 2.21 shows the graphical solution for this two-variable problem. Note that for this problem the optimal solution is $x_1 = 2$ and $x_2 = 2$, with an objective function value of 10.

FIGURE 2.21   GRAPHICAL SOLUTION OF A TWO-VARIABLE LINEAR PROGRAM
WITH GENERAL NOTATION

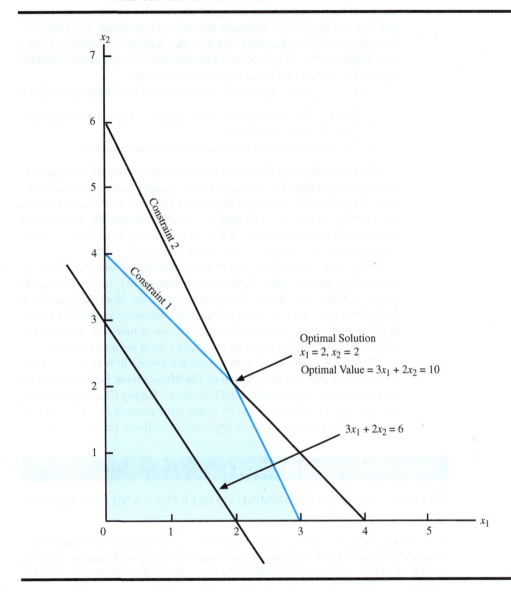

Using general linear programming notation, we can write the standard form of the
preceding linear program as follows:

$$\text{Max} \quad 3x_1 + 2x_2 + 0s_1 + 0s_2$$

s.t.

$$2x_1 + 2x_2 + 1s_1 \qquad\quad = 8$$
$$1x_1 + 0.5x_2 + \qquad\quad 1s_2 = 3$$
$$x_1, x_2, s_1, s_2 \geq 0$$

Thus, at the optimal solution $x_1 = 2$ and $x_2 = 2$; the values of the slack variables are $s_1 = s_2 = 0$.

SUMMARY

We formulated linear programming models for two problems: the Par, Inc., maximization problem and the M&D Chemicals minimization problem. For both problems we showed a graphical solution procedure and provided a computer solution to the problem in a generic solution table. In formulating a mathematical model of these problems, we developed a general definition of a linear programming model.

A linear programming model is a mathematical model with the following characteristics:

1. A linear objective function that is to be maximized or minimized
2. A set of linear constraints
3. Variables that are all restricted to nonnegative values

Slack variables may be used to write less-than-or-equal-to constraints in equality form and surplus variables may be used to write greater-than-or-equal-to constraints in equality form. The value of a slack variable can usually be interpreted as the amount of unused resource, whereas the value of a surplus variable indicates the amount over and above some stated minimum requirement. When all constraints have been written as equalities, the linear program has been written in its standard form.

If the solution to a linear program is infeasible or unbounded, no optimal solution to the problem can be found. In the case of infeasibility, no feasible solutions are possible, whereas, in the case of an unbounded solution, the objective function can be made infinitely large for a maximization problem and infinitely small for a minimization problem. In the case of alternative optimal solutions, two or more optimal extreme points exist, and all the points on the line segment connecting them are also optimal.

This chapter concludes with a section showing how to write a linear program using general linear programming notation. The Management Science in Action, IBM Uses Linear Programming to Help Plan and Execute its Supply Chain Operations, provides another example of the widespread use of linear programming by organizations. In the next two chapters we will see many more applications of linear programming.

MANAGEMENT SCIENCE IN ACTION

IBM USES LINEAR PROGRAMMING TO HELP PLAN AND EXECUTE ITS SUPPLY CHAIN OPERATIONS*

A semiconductor technically refers to the material, usually silicon, used to build integrated circuits that become the main building components for electronic devices. But in casual usage, semiconductor manufacturing refers to the design and production of the actual integrated circuit that performs the calculations necessary to power your computers, smart phones, tablets, and virtually every other electronic device with which you are familiar.

Semiconductor supply chains are very complex because they typically stretch across the globe and include many different suppliers, manufacturers, distributors, and customers. Hundreds of operations are required to produce semiconductors and lead times are often very long. To produce a finished semiconductor, the three-dimensional circuits must be deposited onto the base layer of semiconductive material through a process of deposition, photolithography, etching, and ion implantation. The circuits must then be thoroughly tested and packaged for shipment to customers. Small deviations in the manufacturing process result in different quality (speed) of devices. These different devices can sometimes be used as a substitute in times of shortages. For instance, if there are no medium-speed devices available for a certain manufacturing step, a high-speed device can be used instead, but a medium-speed device cannot be substituted for a high-speed device. This creates a multitude of different possible flows through the supply chain that must be constantly managed.

IBM has been producing semiconductors for more than 50 years. IBM manufactures semiconductors in Asia and in North America, and they distribute them around the world. IBM has been using management science techniques for many years to plan and execute its supply chain strategies. IBM's Central Planning Engine (CPE) is the set of tools the company uses to manage its supply chain activities for semiconductors. The CPE uses a combination of management science tools including linear programming. The model constraints include limitations on production capacities, raw material availabilities, lead time delays, and demand requirements. There are also constraints to enforce the substitution possibilities for certain devices. While many different problem-solving methods are used in the CPE, linear programming is used in several different steps including the allocation of production capacity to devices based on available capacities and materials.

IBM uses the CPE to perform both long-term strategic planning and short-term operational execution for its semiconductor supply chain. Due to the clever use of specific management science tools, these complex calculations can be completed in just a few hours. These fast solution times allow IBM to run several different possible scenarios in a single day and implement sensitivity analysis to understand possible risks in its supply chain. IBM credits the use of the CPE to increasing on-time deliveries by 15% and reducing inventory by 25% to 30%.

*Based on Alfred Degbotse, Brian T. Denton, Kenneth Fordyce, R. John Milne, Robert Orzell, Chi-Tai Wang, "IBM Blends Heuristics and Optimization to Plan Its Semiconductor Supply Chain," *Interfaces* (2012): 1–12.

GLOSSARY

Alternative optimal solutions   The case in which more than one solution provides the optimal value for the objective function.

Constraint   An equation or inequality that rules out certain combinations of decision variables as feasible solutions.

Decision variable   A controllable input for a linear programming model.

Extreme point   Graphically speaking, extreme points are the feasible solution points occurring at the vertices or "corners" of the feasible region. With two-variable problems, extreme points are determined by the intersection of the constraint lines.

Feasible region   The set of all feasible solutions.

Feasible solution   A solution that satisfies all the constraints.

Infeasibility   The situation in which no solution to the linear programming problem satisfies all the constraints.

Linear functions   Mathematical expressions in which the variables appear in separate terms and are raised to the first power.

Linear program   Another term for linear programming model.

Linear programming model   A mathematical model with a linear objective function, a set of linear constraints, and nonnegative variables.

Mathematical model   A representation of a problem where the objective and all constraint conditions are described by mathematical expressions.

Nonnegativity constraints   A set of constraints that requires all variables to be nonnegative.

Problem formulation   The process of translating the verbal statement of a problem into a mathematical statement called the *mathematical model*.

Redundant constraint   A constraint that does not affect the feasible region. If a constraint is redundant, it can be removed from the problem without affecting the feasible region.

Slack variable   A variable added to the left-hand side of a less-than-or-equal-to constraint to convert the constraint into an equality. The value of this variable can usually be interpreted as the amount of unused resource.

Standard form   A linear program in which all the constraints are written as equalities. The optimal solution of the standard form of a linear program is the same as the optimal solution of the original formulation of the linear program.

Surplus variable   A variable subtracted from the left-hand side of a greater-than-or-equal-to constraint to convert the constraint into an equality. The value of this variable can usually be interpreted as the amount over and above some required minimum level.

Unbounded   If the value of the solution may be made infinitely large in a maximization linear programming problem or infinitely small in a minimization problem without violating any of the constraints, the problem is said to be unbounded.

PROBLEMS

1. Which of the following mathematical relationships could be found in a linear programming model, and which could not? For the relationships that are unacceptable for linear programs, state why.
    a. $-1A + 2B \leq 70$
    b. $2A - 2B = 50$
    c. $1A - 2B^2 \leq 10$
    d. $3\sqrt{A} + 2B \geq 15$
    e. $1A + 1B = 6$
    f. $2A + 5B + 1AB \leq 25$

2. Find the solutions that satisfy the following constraints:
    a. $4A + 2B \leq 16$
    b. $4A + 2B \geq 16$
    c. $4A + 2B = 16$

3. Show a separate graph of the constraint lines and the solutions that satisfy each of the following constraints:
    a. $3A + 2B \leq 18$
    b. $12A + 8B \geq 480$
    c. $5A + 10B = 200$

4. Show a separate graph of the constraint lines and the solutions that satisfy each of the following constraints:
    a. $3A - 4B \geq 60$
    b. $-6A + 5B \leq 60$
    c. $5A - 2B \leq 0$

5. Show a separate graph of the constraint lines and the solutions that satisfy each of the following constraints:
    a. $A \geq 0.25 (A + B)$
    b. $B \leq 0.10 (A + B)$
    c. $A \leq 0.50 (A + B)$

6. Three objective functions for linear programming problems are $7A + 10B$, $6A + 4B$, and $-4A + 7B$. Show the graph of each for objective function values equal to 420.

7. Identify the feasible region for the following set of constraints:

$$0.5A + 0.25B \geq 30$$
$$1A + 5B \geq 250$$
$$0.25A + 0.5B \leq 50$$
$$A, B \geq 0$$

8. Identify the feasible region for the following set of constraints:

$$2A - 1B \le 0$$
$$-1A + 1.5B \le 200$$
$$A, B \ge 0$$

9. Identify the feasible region for the following set of constraints:

$$3A - 2B \ge 0$$
$$2A - 1B \le 200$$
$$1A \le 150$$
$$A, B \ge 0$$

10. For the linear program

$$\text{Max} \quad 2A + 3B$$
$$\text{s.t.}$$
$$1A + 2B \le 6$$
$$5A + 3B \le 15$$
$$A, B \ge 0$$

find the optimal solution using the graphical solution procedure. What is the value of the objective function at the optimal solution?

11. Solve the following linear program using the graphical solution procedure:

$$\text{Max} \quad 5A + 5B$$
$$\text{s.t.}$$
$$1A \le 100$$
$$1B \le 80$$
$$2A + 4B \le 400$$
$$A, B \ge 0$$

12. Consider the following linear programming problem:

$$\text{Max} \quad 3A + 3B$$
$$\text{s.t.}$$
$$2A + 4B \le 12$$
$$6A + 4B \le 24$$
$$A, B \ge 0$$

a. Find the optimal solution using the graphical solution procedure.
b. If the objective function is changed to $2A + 6B$, what will the optimal solution be?
c. How many extreme points are there? What are the values of A and B at each extreme point?

13. Consider the following linear program:

$$\text{Max} \quad 1A + 2B$$
$$\text{s.t.}$$
$$1A \le 5$$
$$1B \le 4$$
$$2A + 2B = 12$$
$$A, B \ge 0$$

    a. Show the feasible region.
    b. What are the extreme points of the feasible region?
    c. Find the optimal solution using the graphical procedure.

14. RMC, Inc., is a small firm that produces a variety of chemical products. In a particular production process, three raw materials are blended (mixed together) to produce two products: a fuel additive and a solvent base. Each ton of fuel additive is a mixture of ⅖ ton of material 1 and ⅗ of material 3. A ton of solvent base is a mixture of ½ ton of material 1, ⅕ ton of material 2, and ³⁄₁₀ ton of material 3. After deducting relevant costs, the profit contribution is $40 for every ton of fuel additive produced and $30 for every ton of solvent base produced.

    RMC's production is constrained by a limited availability of the three raw materials. For the current production period, RMC has available the following quantities of each raw material:

Raw Material	Amount Available for Production
Material 1	20 tons
Material 2	5 tons
Material 3	21 tons

Assuming that RMC is interested in maximizing the total profit contribution, answer the following:
    a. What is the linear programming model for this problem?
    b. Find the optimal solution using the graphical solution procedure. How many tons of each product should be produced, and what is the projected total profit contribution?
    c. Is there any unused material? If so, how much?
    d. Are any of the constraints redundant? If so, which ones?

15. Refer to the Par, Inc., problem described in Section 2.1. Suppose that Par, Inc., management encounters the following situations:
    a. The accounting department revises its estimate of the profit contribution for the deluxe bag to $18 per bag.
    b. A new low-cost material is available for the standard bag, and the profit contribution per standard bag can be increased to $20 per bag. (Assume that the profit contribution of the deluxe bag is the original $9 value.)
    c. New sewing equipment is available that would increase the sewing operation capacity to 750 hours. (Assume that $10A + 9B$ is the appropriate objective function.)
If each of these situations is encountered separately, what is the optimal solution and the total profit contribution?

16. Refer to the feasible region for Par, Inc., problem in Figure 2.13.
    a. Develop an objective function that will make extreme point ⑤ the optimal extreme point.
    b. What is the optimal solution for the objective function you selected in part (a)?
    c. What are the values of the slack variables associated with this solution?

17. Write the following linear program in standard form:

$$\text{Max} \quad 5A + 2B$$

s.t.

$$1A - 2B \leq 420$$
$$2A + 3B \leq 610$$
$$6A - 1B \leq 125$$
$$A, B \geq 0$$

18. For the linear program

$$\text{Max} \quad 4A + 1B$$

s.t.

$$10A + 2B \le 30$$
$$3A + 2B \le 12$$
$$2A + 2B \le 10$$
$$A, B \ge 0$$

   a. Write this problem in standard form.
   b. Solve the problem using the graphical solution procedure.
   c. What are the values of the three slack variables at the optimal solution?

19. Given the linear program

$$\text{Max} \quad 3A + 4B$$

s.t.

$$-1A + 2B \le 8$$
$$1A + 2B \le 12$$
$$2A + 1B \le 16$$
$$A, B \ge 0$$

   a. Write the problem in standard form.
   b. Solve the problem using the graphical solution procedure.
   c. What are the values of the three slack variables at the optimal solution?

20. For the linear program

$$\text{Max} \quad 3A + 2B$$

s.t.

$$A + B \ge 4$$
$$3A + 4B \le 24$$
$$A \qquad \ge 2$$
$$A - B \le 0$$
$$A, B \ge 0$$

   a. Write the problem in standard form.
   b. Solve the problem.
   c. What are the values of the slack and surplus variables at the optimal solution?

21. Consider the following linear program:

$$\text{Max} \quad 2A + 3B$$

s.t.

$$5A + 5B \le 400 \quad \text{Constraint 1}$$
$$-1A + 1B \le 10 \quad \text{Constraint 2}$$
$$1A + 3B \ge 90 \quad \text{Constraint 3}$$
$$A, B \ge 0$$

Figure 2.22 shows a graph of the constraint lines.

FIGURE 2.22   GRAPH OF THE CONSTRAINT LINES FOR EXERCISE 21

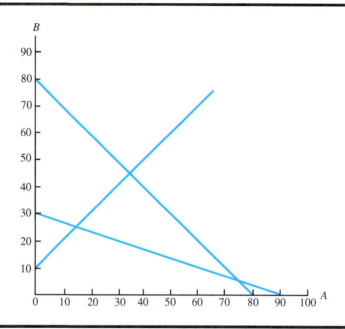

a. Place a number (1, 2, or 3) next to each constraint line to identify which constraint it represents.
b. Shade in the feasible region on the graph.
c. Identify the optimal extreme point. What is the optimal solution?
d. Which constraints are binding? Explain.
e. How much slack or surplus is associated with the nonbinding constraint?

22. Reiser Sports Products wants to determine the number of All-Pro (A) and College (C) footballs to produce in order to maximize profit over the next four-week planning horizon. Constraints affecting the production quantities are the production capacities in three departments: cutting and dyeing; sewing; and inspection and packaging. For the four-week planning period, 340 hours of cutting and dyeing time, 420 hours of sewing time, and 200 hours of inspection and packaging time are available. All-Pro footballs provide a profit of $5 per unit and College footballs provide a profit of $4 per unit. The linear programming model with production times expressed in minutes is as follows:

$$\text{Max} \quad 5A + 4C$$
s.t.
$$12A + 6C \leq 20{,}400 \quad \text{Cutting and dyeing}$$
$$9A + 15C \leq 25{,}200 \quad \text{Sewing}$$
$$6A + 6C \leq 12{,}000 \quad \text{Inspection and packaging}$$
$$A, C \geq 0$$

A portion of the graphical solution to the Reiser problem is shown in Figure 2.23.
a. Shade the feasible region for this problem.
b. Determine the coordinates of each extreme point and the corresponding profit. Which extreme point generates the highest profit?

FIGURE 2.23 PORTION OF THE GRAPHICAL SOLUTION FOR EXERCISE 22

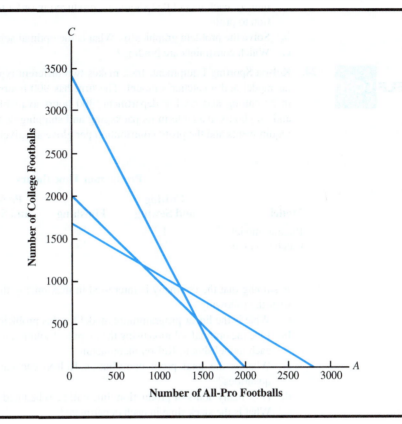

c. Draw the profit line corresponding to a profit of $4000. Move the profit line as far from the origin as you can in order to determine which extreme point will provide the optimal solution. Compare your answer with the approach you used in part (b).

d. Which constraints are binding? Explain.

e. Suppose that the values of the objective function coefficients are $4 for each All-Pro model produced and $5 for each College model. Use the graphical solution procedure to determine the new optimal solution and the corresponding value of profit.

23. Embassy Motorcycles (EM) manufactures two lightweight motorcycles designed for easy handling and safety. The EZ-Rider model has a new engine and a low profile that make it easy to balance. The Lady-Sport model is slightly larger, uses a more traditional engine, and is specifically designed to appeal to women riders. Embassy produces the engines for both models at its Des Moines, Iowa, plant. Each EZ-Rider engine requires 6 hours of manufacturing time and each Lady-Sport engine requires 3 hours of manufacturing time. The Des Moines plant has 2100 hours of engine manufacturing time available for the next production period. Embassy's motorcycle frame supplier can supply as many EZ-Rider frames as needed. However, the Lady-Sport frame is more complex and the supplier can only provide up to 280 Lady-Sport frames for the next production period. Final assembly and testing requires 2 hours for each EZ-Rider model and 2.5 hours for each Lady-Sport model. A maximum of 1000 hours of assembly and testing time are available for the next production period. The company's accounting department projects a profit contribution of $2400 for each EZ-Rider produced and $1800 for each Lady-Sport produced.

a. Formulate a linear programming model that can be used to determine the number of units of each model that should be produced in order to maximize the total contribution to profit.

b. Solve the problem graphically. What is the optimal solution?

c. Which constraints are binding?

24. Kelson Sporting Equipment, Inc., makes two different types of baseball gloves: a regular model and a catcher's model. The firm has 900 hours of production time available in its cutting and sewing department, 300 hours available in its finishing department, and 100 hours available in its packaging and shipping department. The production time requirements and the profit contribution per glove are given in the following table:

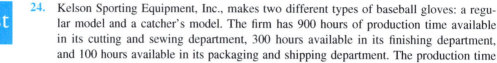

Production Time (hours)

Model	Cutting and Sewing	Finishing	Packaging and Shipping	Profit/Glove
Regular model	1	$\frac{1}{2}$	$\frac{1}{8}$	$5
Catcher's model	$\frac{3}{2}$	$\frac{1}{3}$	$\frac{1}{4}$	$8

Assuming that the company is interested in maximizing the total profit contribution, answer the following:

a. What is the linear programming model for this problem?

b. Find the optimal solution using the graphical solution procedure. How many gloves of each model should Kelson manufacture?

c. What is the total profit contribution Kelson can earn with the given production quantities?

d. How many hours of production time will be scheduled in each department?

e. What is the slack time in each department?

25. George Johnson recently inherited a large sum of money; he wants to use a portion of this money to set up a trust fund for his two children. The trust fund has two investment options: (1) a bond fund and (2) a stock fund. The projected returns over the life of the investments are 6% for the bond fund and 10% for the stock fund. Whatever portion of the inheritance he finally decides to commit to the trust fund, he wants to invest at least 30% of that amount in the bond fund. In addition, he wants to select a mix that will enable him to obtain a total return of at least 7.5%.

a. Formulate a linear programming model that can be used to determine the percentage that should be allocated to each of the possible investment alternatives.

b. Solve the problem using the graphical solution procedure.

26. The Sea Wharf Restaurant would like to determine the best way to allocate a monthly advertising budget of $1000 between newspaper advertising and radio advertising. Management decided that at least 25% of the budget must be spent on each type of media, and that the amount of money spent on local newspaper advertising must be at least twice the amount spent on radio advertising. A marketing consultant developed an index that measures audience exposure per dollar of advertising on a scale from 0 to 100, with higher values implying greater audience exposure. If the value of the index for local newspaper advertising is 50 and the value of the index for spot radio advertising is 80, how should the restaurant allocate its advertising budget in order to maximize the value of total audience exposure?

a. Formulate a linear programming model that can be used to determine how the restaurant should allocate its advertising budget in order to maximize the value of total audience exposure.

b. Solve the problem using the graphical solution procedure.

27. Blair & Rosen, Inc. (B&R), is a brokerage firm that specializes in investment portfolios designed to meet the specific risk tolerances of its clients. A client who contacted B&R this past week has a maximum of $50,000 to invest. B&R's investment advisor decides to recommend a portfolio consisting of two investment funds: an Internet fund and a Blue Chip fund. The Internet fund has a projected annual return of 12%, whereas the Blue Chip fund has a projected annual return of 9%. The investment advisor requires that at most $35,000 of the client's funds should be invested in the Internet fund. B&R services include a risk rating for each investment alternative. The Internet fund, which is the more risky of the two investment alternatives, has a risk rating of 6 per thousand dollars invested. The Blue Chip fund has a risk rating of 4 per thousand dollars invested. For example, if $10,000 is invested in each of the two investment funds, B&R's risk rating for the portfolio would be $6(10) + 4(10) = 100$. Finally, B&R developed a questionnaire to measure each client's risk tolerance. Based on the responses, each client is classified as a conservative, moderate, or aggressive investor. Suppose that the questionnaire results classified the current client as a moderate investor. B&R recommends that a client who is a moderate investor limit his or her portfolio to a maximum risk rating of 240.

  a. What is the recommended investment portfolio for this client? What is the annual return for the portfolio?

  b. Suppose that a second client with $50,000 to invest has been classified as an aggressive investor. B&R recommends that the maximum portfolio risk rating for an aggressive investor is 320. What is the recommended investment portfolio for this aggressive investor? Discuss what happens to the portfolio under the aggressive investor strategy.

  c. Suppose that a third client with $50,000 to invest has been classified as a conservative investor. B&R recommends that the maximum portfolio risk rating for a conservative investor is 160. Develop the recommended investment portfolio for the conservative investor. Discuss the interpretation of the slack variable for the total investment fund constraint.

28. Tom's, Inc., produces various Mexican food products and sells them to Western Foods, a chain of grocery stores located in Texas and New Mexico. Tom's, Inc., makes two salsa products: Western Foods Salsa and Mexico City Salsa. Essentially, the two products have different blends of whole tomatoes, tomato sauce, and tomato paste. The Western Foods Salsa is a blend of 50% whole tomatoes, 30% tomato sauce, and 20% tomato paste. The Mexico City Salsa, which has a thicker and chunkier consistency, consists of 70% whole tomatoes, 10% tomato sauce, and 20% tomato paste. Each jar of salsa produced weighs 10 ounces. For the current production period, Tom's, Inc., can purchase up to 280 pounds of whole tomatoes, 130 pounds of tomato sauce, and 100 pounds of tomato paste; the price per pound for these ingredients is $0.96, $0.64, and $0.56, respectively. The cost of the spices and the other ingredients is approximately $0.10 per jar. Tom's, Inc., buys empty glass jars for $0.02 each, and labeling and filling costs are estimated to be $0.03 for each jar of salsa produced. Tom's contract with Western Foods results in sales revenue of $1.64 for each jar of Western Foods Salsa and $1.93 for each jar of Mexico City Salsa.

  a. Develop a linear programming model that will enable Tom's to determine the mix of salsa products that will maximize the total profit contribution.

  b. Find the optimal solution.

29. AutoIgnite produces electronic ignition systems for automobiles at a plant in Cleveland, Ohio. Each ignition system is assembled from two components produced at AutoIgnite's plants in Buffalo, New York, and Dayton, Ohio. The Buffalo plant can produce 2000 units of component 1, 1000 units of component 2, or any combination of the two components each day. For instance, 60% of Buffalo's production time could be used to produce component 1 and 40% of Buffalo's production time could be used to produce component 2; in this case, the Buffalo plant would be able to produce $0.6(2000) = 1200$ units of component

1 each day and 0.4(1000) = 400 units of component 2 each day. The Dayton plant can produce 600 units of component 1, 1400 units of component 2, or any combination of the two components each day. At the end of each day, the component production at Buffalo and Dayton is sent to Cleveland for assembly of the ignition systems on the following workday.

a. Formulate a linear programming model that can be used to develop a daily production schedule for the Buffalo and Dayton plants that will maximize daily production of ignition systems at Cleveland.

b. Find the optimal solution.

30. A financial advisor at Diehl Investments identified two companies that are likely candidates for a takeover in the near future. Eastern Cable is a leading manufacturer of flexible cable systems used in the construction industry, and ComSwitch is a new firm specializing in digital switching systems. Eastern Cable is currently trading for $40 per share, and ComSwitch is currently trading for $25 per share. If the takeovers occur, the financial advisor estimates that the price of Eastern Cable will go to $55 per share and ComSwitch will go to $43 per share. At this point in time, the financial advisor has identified ComSwitch as the higher risk alternative. Assume that a client indicated a willingness to invest a maximum of $50,000 in the two companies. The client wants to invest at least $15,000 in Eastern Cable and at least $10,000 in ComSwitch. Because of the higher risk associated with ComSwitch, the financial advisor has recommended that at most $25,000 should be invested in ComSwitch.

a. Formulate a linear programming model that can be used to determine the number of shares of Eastern Cable and the number of shares of ComSwitch that will meet the investment constraints and maximize the total return for the investment.

b. Graph the feasible region.

c. Determine the coordinates of each extreme point.

d. Find the optimal solution.

31. Consider the following linear program:

$$\text{Min} \quad 3A + 4B$$
$$\text{s.t.}$$
$$1A + 3B \geq 6$$
$$1A + 1B \geq 4$$
$$A, B \geq 0$$

Identify the feasible region and find the optimal solution using the graphical solution procedure. What is the value of the objective function?

32. Identify the three extreme-point solutions for the M&D Chemicals problem (see Section 2.5). Identify the value of the objective function and the values of the slack and surplus variables at each extreme point.

33. Consider the following linear programming problem:

$$\text{Min} \quad A + 2B$$
$$\text{s.t.}$$
$$A + 4B \leq 21$$
$$2A + B \geq 7$$
$$3A + 1.5B \leq 21$$
$$-2A + 6B \geq 0$$
$$A, B \geq 0$$

a. Find the optimal solution using the graphical solution procedure and the value of the objective function.

    b. Determine the amount of slack or surplus for each constraint.

    c. Suppose the objective function is changed to max $5A + 2B$. Find the optimal solution and the value of the objective function.

34. Consider the following linear program:

$$\text{Min} \quad 2A + 2B$$
$$\text{s.t.}$$
$$1A + 3B \leq 12$$
$$3A + 1B \geq 13$$
$$1A - 1B = 3$$
$$A, B \geq 0$$

    a. Show the feasible region.

    b. What are the extreme points of the feasible region?

    c. Find the optimal solution using the graphical solution procedure.

35. For the linear program

$$\text{Min} \quad 6A + 4B$$
$$\text{s.t.}$$
$$2A + 1B \geq 12$$
$$1A + 1B \geq 10$$
$$1B \leq 4$$
$$A, B \geq 0$$

    a. Write the problem in standard form.

    b. Solve the problem using the graphical solution procedure.

    c. What are the values of the slack and surplus variables?

36. As part of a quality improvement initiative, Consolidated Electronics employees complete a three-day training program on teaming and a two-day training program on problem solving. The manager of quality improvement has requested that at least 8 training programs on teaming and at least 10 training programs on problem solving be offered during the next six months. In addition, senior-level management has specified that at least 25 training programs must be offered during this period. Consolidated Electronics uses a consultant to teach the training programs. During the next quarter, the consultant has 84 days of training time available. Each training program on teaming costs $10,000 and each training program on problem solving costs $8000.

    a. Formulate a linear programming model that can be used to determine the number of training programs on teaming and the number of training programs on problem solving that should be offered in order to minimize total cost.

    b. Graph the feasible region.

    c. Determine the coordinates of each extreme point.

    d. Solve for the minimum cost solution.

37. The New England Cheese Company produces two cheese spreads by blending mild cheddar cheese with extra sharp cheddar cheese. The cheese spreads are packaged in 12-ounce containers, which are then sold to distributors throughout the Northeast. The Regular blend contains 80% mild cheddar and 20% extra sharp, and the Zesty blend contains 60% mild cheddar and 40% extra sharp. This year, a local dairy cooperative offered to provide up to 8100 pounds of mild cheddar cheese for $1.20 per pound and up to 3000 pounds of extra sharp cheddar cheese for $1.40 per pound. The cost to blend and package the cheese spreads, excluding the cost of the cheese, is $0.20 per container. If each container of

Regular is sold for $1.95 and each container of Zesty is sold for $2.20, how many containers of Regular and Zesty should New England Cheese produce?

38. Applied Technology, Inc. (ATI), produces bicycle frames using two fiberglass materials that improve the strength-to-weight ratio of the frames. The cost of the standard grade material is $7.50 per yard and the cost of the professional grade material is $9.00 per yard. The standard and professional grade materials contain different amounts of fiberglass, carbon fiber, and Kevlar as shown in the following table:

	Standard Grade	Professional Grade
Fiberglass	84%	58%
Carbon fiber	10%	30%
Kevlar	6%	12%

ATI signed a contract with a bicycle manufacturer to produce a new frame with a carbon fiber content of at least 20% and a Kevlar content of not greater than 10%. To meet the required weight specification, a total of 30 yards of material must be used for each frame.
   a. Formulate a linear program to determine the number of yards of each grade of fiberglass material that ATI should use in each frame in order to minimize total cost. Define the decision variables and indicate the purpose of each constraint.
   b. Use the graphical solution procedure to determine the feasible region. What are the coordinates of the extreme points?
   c. Compute the total cost at each extreme point. What is the optimal solution?
   d. The distributor of the fiberglass material is currently overstocked with the professional grade material. To reduce inventory, the distributor offered ATI the opportunity to purchase the professional grade for $8 per yard. Will the optimal solution change?
   e. Suppose that the distributor further lowers the price of the professional grade material to $7.40 per yard. Will the optimal solution change? What effect would an even lower price for the professional grade material have on the optimal solution? Explain.

39. Innis Investments manages funds for a number of companies and wealthy clients. The investment strategy is tailored to each client's needs. For a new client, Innis has been authorized to invest up to $1.2 million in two investment funds: a stock fund and a money market fund. Each unit of the stock fund costs $50 and provides an annual rate of return of 10%; each unit of the money market fund costs $100 and provides an annual rate of return of 4%.

   The client wants to minimize risk subject to the requirement that the annual income from the investment be at least $60,000. According to Innis's risk measurement system, each unit invested in the stock fund has a risk index of 8, and each unit invested in the money market fund has a risk index of 3; the higher risk index associated with the stock fund simply indicates that it is the riskier investment. Innis's client also specified that at least $300,000 be invested in the money market fund.
   a. Determine how many units of each fund Innis should purchase for the client to minimize the total risk index for the portfolio.
   b. How much annual income will this investment strategy generate?
   c. Suppose the client desires to maximize annual return. How should the funds be invested?

40. Eastern Chemicals produces two types of lubricating fluids used in industrial manufacturing. Both products cost Eastern Chemicals $1 per gallon to produce. Based on an analysis of current inventory levels and outstanding orders for the next month, Eastern Chemicals' management specified that at least 30 gallons of product 1 and at least 20 gallons of product 2

must be produced during the next two weeks. Management also stated that an existing inventory of highly perishable raw material required in the production of both fluids must be used within the next two weeks. The current inventory of the perishable raw material is 80 pounds. Although more of this raw material can be ordered if necessary, any of the current inventory that is not used within the next two weeks will spoil—hence, the management requirement that at least 80 pounds be used in the next two weeks. Furthermore, it is known that product 1 requires 1 pound of this perishable raw material per gallon and product 2 requires 2 pounds of the raw material per gallon. Because Eastern Chemicals' objective is to keep its production costs at the minimum possible level, the firm's management is looking for a minimum cost production plan that uses all the 80 pounds of perishable raw material and provides at least 30 gallons of product 1 and at least 20 gallons of product 2. What is the minimum cost solution?

41. Southern Oil Company produces two grades of gasoline: regular and premium. The profit contributions are $0.30 per gallon for regular gasoline and $0.50 per gallon for premium gasoline. Each gallon of regular gasoline contains 0.3 gallons of grade A crude oil and each gallon of premium gasoline contains 0.6 gallons of grade A crude oil. For the next production period, Southern has 18,000 gallons of grade A crude oil available. The refinery used to produce the gasolines has a production capacity of 50,000 gallons for the next production period. Southern Oil's distributors have indicated that demand for the premium gasoline for the next production period will be at most 20,000 gallons.

   a. Formulate a linear programming model that can be used to determine the number of gallons of regular gasoline and the number of gallons of premium gasoline that should be produced in order to maximize total profit contribution.

   b. What is the optimal solution?

   c. What are the values and interpretations of the slack variables?

   d. What are the binding constraints?

42. Does the following linear program involve infeasibility, unbounded, and/or alternative optimal solutions? Explain.

$$\begin{aligned} \text{Max} \quad & 4A + 8B \\ \text{s.t.} \quad & \\ & 2A + 2B \le 10 \\ & -1A + 1B \ge 8 \\ & A, B \ge 0 \end{aligned}$$

43. Does the following linear program involve infeasibility, unbounded, and/or alternative optimal solutions? Explain.

$$\begin{aligned} \text{Max} \quad & 1A + 1B \\ \text{s.t.} \quad & \\ & 8A + 6B \ge 24 \\ & 2B \ge 4 \\ & A, B \ge 0 \end{aligned}$$

44. Consider the following linear program:

$$\begin{aligned} \text{Max} \quad & 1A + 1B \\ \text{s.t.} \quad & \\ & 5A + 3B \le 15 \\ & 3A + 5B \le 15 \\ & A, B \ge 0 \end{aligned}$$

a. What is the optimal solution for this problem?
b. Suppose that the objective function is changed to $1A + 2B$. Find the new optimal solution.

45. Consider the following linear program:

$$\text{Max} \quad 1A - 2B$$
$$\text{s.t.}$$
$$-4A + 3B \leq 3$$
$$1A - 1B \leq 3$$
$$A, B \geq 0$$

a. Graph the feasible region for the problem.
b. Is the feasible region unbounded? Explain.
c. Find the optimal solution.
d. Does an unbounded feasible region imply that the optimal solution to the linear program will be unbounded?

46. The manager of a small independent grocery store is trying to determine the best use of her shelf space for soft drinks. The store carries national and generic brands and currently has 200 square feet of shelf space available. The manager wants to allocate at least 60% of the space to the national brands and, regardless of the profitability, allocate at least 10% of the space to the generic brands. How many square feet of space should the manager allocate to the national brands and the generic brands under the following circumstances?
a. The national brands are more profitable than the generic brands.
b. Both brands are equally profitable.
c. The generic brand is more profitable than the national brand.

47. Discuss what happens to the M&D Chemicals problem (see Section 2.5) if the cost per gallon for product A is increased to $3.00 per gallon. What would you recommend? Explain.

48. For the M&D Chemicals problem in Section 2.5, discuss the effect of management's requiring total production of 500 gallons for the two products. List two or three actions M&D should consider to correct the situation you encounter.

49. PharmaPlus operates a chain of 30 pharmacies. The pharmacies are staffed by licensed pharmacists and pharmacy technicians. The company currently employs 85 full-time equivalent pharmacists (combination of full time and part time) and 175 full-time equivalent technicians. Each spring management reviews current staffing levels and makes hiring plans for the year. A recent forecast of the prescription load for the next year shows that at least 250 full-time equivalent employees (pharmacists and technicians) will be required to staff the pharmacies. The personnel department expects 10 pharmacists and 30 technicians to leave over the next year. To accommodate the expected attrition and prepare for future growth, management stated that at least 15 new pharmacists must be hired. In addition, PharmaPlus's new service quality guidelines specify no more than two technicians per licensed pharmacist. The average salary for licensed pharmacists is $40 per hour and the average salary for technicians is $10 per hour.
a. Determine a minimum-cost staffing plan for PharmaPlus. How many pharmacists and technicians are needed?
b. Given current staffing levels and expected attrition, how many new hires (if any) must be made to reach the level recommended in part (a)? What will be the impact on the payroll?

50. Expedition Outfitters manufactures a variety of specialty clothing for hiking, skiing, and mountain climbing. Its management decided to begin production on two new parkas designed

for use in extremely cold weather: the Mount Everest Parka and the Rocky Mountain Parka. The manufacturing plant has 120 hours of cutting time and 120 hours of sewing time available for producing these two parkas. Each Mount Everest Parka requires 30 minutes of cutting time and 45 minutes of sewing time, and each Rocky Mountain Parka requires 20 minutes of cutting time and 15 minutes of sewing time. The labor and material cost is $150 for each Mount Everest Parka and $50 for each Rocky Mountain Parka, and the retail prices through the firm's mail order catalog are $250 for the Mount Everest Parka and $200 for the Rocky Mountain Parka. Because management believes that the Mount Everest Parka is a unique coat that will enhance the image of the firm, they specified that at least 20% of the total production must consist of this model. Assuming that Expedition Outfitters can sell as many coats of each type as it can produce, how many units of each model should it manufacture to maximize the total profit contribution?

51. English Motors, Ltd. (EML) developed a new all-wheel-drive sports utility vehicle. As part of the marketing campaign, EML produced a video tape sales presentation to send to both owners of current EML four-wheel-drive vehicles as well as to owners of four-wheel-drive sports utility vehicles offered by competitors; EML refers to these two target markets as the current customer market and the new customer market. Individuals who receive the new promotion video will also receive a coupon for a test drive of the new EML model for one weekend. A key factor in the success of the new promotion is the response rate, the percentage of individuals who receive the new promotion and test drive the new model. EML estimates that the response rate for the current customer market is 25% and the response rate for the new customer market is 20%. For the customers who test drive the new model, the sales rate is the percentage of individuals that make a purchase. Marketing research studies indicate that the sales rate is 12% for the current customer market and 20% for the new customer market. The cost for each promotion, excluding the test drive costs, is $4 for each promotion sent to the current customer market and $6 for each promotion sent to the new customer market. Management also specified that a minimum of 30,000 current customers should test drive the new model and a minimum of 10,000 new customers should test drive the new model. In addition, the number of current customers who test drive the new vehicle must be at least twice the number of new customers who test drive the new vehicle. If the marketing budget, excluding test drive costs, is $1.2 million, how many promotions should be sent to each group of customers in order to maximize total sales?

52. Creative Sports Design (CSD) manufactures a standard-size tennis racquet and an oversize tennis racquet. The firm's racquets are extremely light due to the use of a magnesium-graphite alloy that was invented by the firm's founder. Each standard-size racquet uses 0.125 kilograms of the alloy and each oversize racquet uses 0.4 kilograms; over the next two-week production period only 80 kilograms of the alloy are available. Each standard-size racquet uses 10 minutes of manufacturing time and each oversize racquet uses 12 minutes. The profit contributions are $10 for each standard-size racquet and $15 for each oversize racquet, and 40 hours of manufacturing time are available each week. Management specified that at least 20% of the total production must be the standard-size racquet. How many racquets of each type should CSD manufacture over the next two weeks to maximize the total profit contribution? Assume that because of the unique nature of their products, CSD can sell as many racquets as they can produce.

53. Management of High Tech Services (HTS) would like to develop a model that will help allocate their technicians' time between service calls to regular contract customers and new customers. A maximum of 80 hours of technician time is available over the two-week planning period. To satisfy cash flow requirements, at least $800 in revenue (per technician) must be generated during the two-week period. Technician time for regular customers generates $25 per hour. However, technician time for new customers only generates

an average of $8 per hour because in many cases a new customer contact does not provide billable services. To ensure that new customer contacts are being maintained, the technician time spent on new customer contacts must be at least 60% of the time spent on regular customer contacts. Given these revenue and policy requirements, HTS would like to determine how to allocate technician time between regular customers and new customers so that the total number of customers contacted during the two-week period will be maximized. Technicians require an average of 50 minutes for each regular customer contact and 1 hour for each new customer contact.

a.   Develop a linear programming model that will enable HTS to allocate technician time between regular customers and new customers.

b.   Find the optimal solution.

54.   Jackson Hole Manufacturing is a small manufacturer of plastic products used in the automotive and computer industries. One of its major contracts is with a large computer company and involves the production of plastic printer cases for the computer company's portable printers. The printer cases are produced on two injection molding machines. The M-100 machine has a production capacity of 25 printer cases per hour, and the M-200 machine has a production capacity of 40 cases per hour. Both machines use the same chemical material to produce the printer cases; the M-100 uses 40 pounds of the raw material per hour and the M-200 uses 50 pounds per hour. The computer company asked Jackson Hole to produce as many of the cases during the upcoming week as possible; it will pay $18 for each case Jackson Hole can deliver. However, next week is a regularly scheduled vacation period for most of Jackson Hole's production employees; during this time, annual maintenance is performed for all equipment in the plant. Because of the downtime for maintenance, the M-100 will be available for no more than 15 hours, and the M-200 will be available for no more than 10 hours. However, because of the high setup cost involved with both machines, management requires that each machine must be operated for at least 5 hours. The supplier of the chemical material used in the production process informed Jackson Hole that a maximum of 1000 pounds of the chemical material will be available for next week's production; the cost for this raw material is $6 per pound. In addition to the raw material cost, Jackson Hole estimates that the hourly cost of operating the M-100 and the M-200 are $50 and $75, respectively.

a.   Formulate a linear programming model that can be used to maximize the contribution to profit.

b.   Find the optimal solution.

55.   The Kartick Company is trying to determine how much of each of two products to produce over the coming planning period. There are three departments, A, B and C, with limited labor hours available in each department. Each product must be processed by each department and the per-unit requirements for each product, labor hours available, and per-unit profit are as shown below.

Labor required in each department

Department	Product 1	Product 2	Labor Hours Available
	Product (hours/unit)		
A	1.00	0.30	100
B	0.30	0.12	36
C	0.15	0.56	50
Profit Contribution	$33.00	$24.00	

A linear program for this situation is as follows:

Let

x_1 = the amount of product 1 to produce

x_2 = the amount of product 2 to produce

Maximize $33\, x_1 + 24\, x_2$

s.t.

$$1.0\, x_1 + .30\, x_2 \leq 100 \quad \text{Department A}$$
$$.30\, x_1 + .12\, x_2 \leq 36 \quad \text{Department B}$$
$$.15\, x_1 + .56\, x_2 \leq 50 \quad \text{Department C}$$
$$x_1, x_2 \geq 0$$

Mr. Kartick (the owner) used trial and error with a spreadsheet model to arrive at a solution. His proposed solution is $x_1 = 75$ and $x_2 = 60$, as shown in Figure 2.24. He said he felt his proposed solution is optimal.

Is his solution optimal? Without solving the problem, explain why you believe this solution is optimal or not optimal.

FIGURE 2.24   MR. KARTICK'S TRIAL-AND-ERROR MODEL

	A	B	C	D	E
1	**Kartick**				
2	**Data**				
3				Hours	
4	Department	Prod 1	Prod 2	Available	
5	A	1.00	0.30	100	
6	B	0.30	0.12	36	
7	C	0.15	0.56	50	
8	Per unit				
9	Contribution	$33.00	$24.00		
10					
11	**Decisions**				
12					
13		Prod 1	Prod 2		
14	Quantity	75	60		
15					
16					
17	**Model**				
18		Hours	Unused		
19	Department	Used	Hours		
20	A	93	7		
21	B	29.7	6.3		
22	C	44.85	5.15		
23					
24	Contribution	$3,915.00			

56. Assume you are given a minimization linear program that has an optimal solution. The problem is then modified by changing an equality constraint in the problem to a less-than-or-equal-to constraint. Is it possible that the modified problem is infeasible? Answer yes or no and justify.

57. Assume you are given a minimization linear program that has an optimal solution. The problem is then modified by changing a greater-than-or-equal-to constraint in the problem to a less-than-or-equal-to constraint. Is it possible that the modified problem is infeasible? Answer yes or no and justify.

58. A consultant was hired to build an optimization model for a large marketing research company. The model is based on a consumer survey that was taken in which each person was asked to rank 30 new products in descending order based on their likelihood of purchasing the product. The consultant was assigned the task of building a model that selects the minimum number of products (which would then be introduced into the marketplace) such that the first, second, and third choice of every subject in the survey is included in the list of selected products. While building a model to figure out which products to introduce, the consultant's boss walked up to her and said: "Look, if the model tells us we need to introduce more than 15 products, then add a constraint which limits the number of new products to 15 or less. It's too expensive to introduce more than 15 new products." Evaluate this statement in terms of what you have learned so far about constrained optimization models.

Case Problem 1   WORKLOAD BALANCING

Digital Imaging (DI) produces color printers for both the professional and consumer markets. The DI consumer division recently introduced two new color printers. The DI-910 model can produce a 4" × 6" borderless color print in approximately 37 seconds. The more sophisticated and faster DI-950 can even produce a 13" × 19" borderless color print. Financial projections show profit contributions of $42 for each DI-910 and $87 for each DI-950.

The printers are assembled, tested, and packaged at DI's plant located in New Bern, North Carolina. This plant is highly automated and uses two manufacturing lines to produce the printers. Line 1 performs the assembly operation with times of 3 minutes per DI-910 printer and 6 minutes per DI-950 printer. Line 2 performs both the testing and packaging operations. Times are 4 minutes per DI-910 printer and 2 minutes per DI-950 printer. The shorter time for the DI-950 printer is a result of its faster print speed. Both manufacturing lines are in operation one 8-hour shift per day.

Managerial Report

Perform an analysis for Digital Imaging in order to determine how many units of each printer to produce. Prepare a report to DI's president presenting your findings and recommendations. Include (but do not limit your discussion to) a consideration of the following:

1. The recommended number of units of each printer to produce to maximize the total contribution to profit for an 8-hour shift. What reasons might management have for not implementing your recommendation?

2. Suppose that management also states that the number of DI-910 printers produced must be at least as great as the number of DI-950 units produced. Assuming that the objective is to maximize the total contribution to profit for an 8-hour shift, how many units of each printer should be produced?

3. Does the solution you developed in part (2) balance the total time spent on line 1 and the total time spent on line 2? Why might this balance or lack of it be a concern to management?

4. Management requested an expansion of the model in part (2) that would provide a better balance between the total time on line 1 and the total time on line 2. Management wants to limit the difference between the total time on line 1 and the total time on line 2 to 30 minutes or less. If the objective is still to maximize the total contribution to profit, how many units of each printer should be produced? What effect does this workload balancing have on total profit in part (2)?

5. Suppose that in part (1) management specified the objective of maximizing the total number of printers produced each shift rather than total profit contribution. With this objective, how many units of each printer should be produced per shift? What effect does this objective have on total profit and workload balancing?

For each solution that you develop, include a copy of your linear programming model and graphical solution in the appendix to your report.

Case Problem 2   PRODUCTION STRATEGY

Better Fitness, Inc. (BFI), manufactures exercise equipment at its plant in Freeport, Long Island. It recently designed two universal weight machines for the home exercise market. Both machines use BFI-patented technology that provides the user with an extremely wide range of motion capability for each type of exercise performed. Until now, such capabilities have been available only on expensive weight machines used primarily by physical therapists.

At a recent trade show, demonstrations of the machines resulted in significant dealer interest. In fact, the number of orders that BFI received at the trade show far exceeded its manufacturing capabilities for the current production period. As a result, management decided to begin production of the two machines. The two machines, which BFI named the BodyPlus 100 and the BodyPlus 200, require different amounts of resources to produce.

The BodyPlus 100 consists of a frame unit, a press station, and a pec-dec station. Each frame produced uses 4 hours of machining and welding time and 2 hours of painting and finishing time. Each press station requires 2 hours of machining and welding time and 1 hour of painting and finishing time, and each pec-dec station uses 2 hours of machining and welding time and 2 hours of painting and finishing time. In addition, 2 hours are spent assembling, testing, and packaging each BodyPlus 100. The raw material costs are $450 for each frame, $300 for each press station, and $250 for each pec-dec station; packaging costs are estimated to be $50 per unit.

The BodyPlus 200 consists of a frame unit, a press station, a pec-dec station, and a leg-press station. Each frame produced uses 5 hours of machining and welding time and 4 hours of painting and finishing time. Each press station requires 3 hours machining and welding time and 2 hours of painting and finishing time, each pec-dec station uses 2 hours of machining and welding time and 2 hours of painting and finishing time, and each leg-press station requires 2 hours of machining and welding time and 2 hours of painting and finishing time. In addition, 2 hours are spent assembling, testing, and packaging each Body Plus 200. The raw material costs are $650 for each frame, $400 for each press station, $250 for each pec-dec station, and $200 for each leg-press station; packaging costs are estimated to be $75 per unit.

For the next production period, management estimates that 600 hours of machining and welding time, 450 hours of painting and finishing time, and 140 hours of assembly, testing, and packaging time will be available. Current labor costs are $20 per hour for machining and welding time, $15 per hour for painting and finishing time, and $12 per hour for assembly, testing, and packaging time. The market in which the two machines must compete suggests a retail price of $2400 for the BodyPlus 100 and $3500 for the BodyPlus 200, although some flexibility may be available to BFI because of the unique capabilities of the new machines. Authorized BFI dealers can purchase machines for 70% of the suggested retail price.

BFI's president believes that the unique capabilities of the BodyPlus 200 can help position BFI as one of the leaders in high-end exercise equipment. Consequently, he has stated that the number of units of the BodyPlus 200 produced must be at least 25% of the total production.

Managerial Report

Analyze the production problem at Better Fitness, Inc., and prepare a report for BFI's president presenting your findings and recommendations. Include (but do not limit your discussion to) a consideration of the following items:

1. What is the recommended number of BodyPlus 100 and BodyPlus 200 machines to produce?
2. How does the requirement that the number of units of the BodyPlus 200 produced be at least 25% of the total production affect profits?
3. Where should efforts be expended in order to increase profits?

Include a copy of your linear programming model and graphical solution in an appendix to your report.

Case Problem 3   HART VENTURE CAPITAL

Hart Venture Capital (HVC) specializes in providing venture capital for software development and Internet applications. Currently HVC has two investment opportunities: (1) Security Systems, a firm that needs additional capital to develop an Internet security software package, and (2) Market Analysis, a market research company that needs additional capital to develop a software package for conducting customer satisfaction surveys. In exchange for Security Systems stock, the firm has asked HVC to provide $600,000 in year 1, $600,000 in year 2, and $250,000 in year 3 over the coming three-year period. In exchange for their stock, Market Analysis has asked HVC to provide $500,000 in year 1, $350,000 in year 2, and $400,000 in year 3 over the same three-year period. HVC believes that both investment opportunities are worth pursuing. However, because of other investments, they are willing to commit at most $800,000 for both projects in the first year, at most $700,000 in the second year, and $500,000 in the third year.

HVC's financial analysis team reviewed both projects and recommended that the company's objective should be to maximize the net present value of the total investment in Security Systems and Market Analysis. The net present value takes into account the estimated value of the stock at the end of the three-year period as well as the capital outflows that are necessary during each of the three years. Using an 8% rate of return, HVC's financial analysis team estimates that 100% funding of the Security Systems project has a net present value of $1,800,000, and 100% funding of the Market Analysis project has a net present value of $1,600,000.

HVC has the option to fund any percentage of the Security Systems and Market Analysis projects. For example, if HVC decides to fund 40% of the Security

Systems project, investments of 0.40($600,000) = $240,000 would be required in year 1, 0.40($600,000) = $240,000 would be required in year 2, and 0.40($250,000) = $100,000 would be required in year 3. In this case, the net present value of the Security Systems project would be 0.40($1,800,000) = $720,000. The investment amounts and the net present value for partial funding of the Market Analysis project would be computed in the same manner.

Managerial Report

Perform an analysis of HVC's investment problem and prepare a report that presents your findings and recommendations. Include (but do not limit your discussion to) a consideration of the following items:

1. What is the recommended percentage of each project that HVC should fund and the net present value of the total investment?
2. What capital allocation plan for Security Systems and Market Analysis for the coming three-year period and the total HVC investment each year would you recommend?
3. What effect, if any, would HVC's willingness to commit an additional $100,000 during the first year have on the recommended percentage of each project that HVC should fund?
4. What would the capital allocation plan look like if an additional $100,000 is made available?
5. What is your recommendation as to whether HVC should commit the additional $100,000 in the first year?

Provide model details and relevant computer output in a report appendix.

Appendix 2.1   SOLVING LINEAR PROGRAMS WITH LINGO

LINGO is a product of LINDO Systems. It was developed by Linus E. Schrage and Kevin Cunningham at the University of Chicago.

In this appendix we describe how to use LINGO to solve the Par, Inc., problem. When you start LINGO, two windows are immediately displayed. The outer or main frame window contains all the command menus and the command toolbar. The smaller window is the model window; this window is used to enter and edit the linear programming model you want to solve. The first item we enter into the model window is the objective function. Recall that the objective function for the Par, Inc., problem is Max $10S + 9D$. Thus, in the first line of the LINGO model window, we enter the following expression:

$$\text{MAX} = 10*S + 9*D;$$

Note that in LINGO the symbol * is used to denote multiplication and that the objective function line ends with a semicolon. In general, each mathematical expression (objective function and constraints) in LINGO is terminated with a semicolon.

Next, we press the Enter key to move to a new line. The first constraint in the Par, Inc., problem is $0.7S + 1D \leq 630$. Thus, in the second line of the LINGO model window we enter the following expression:

$$0.7*S + 1*D <= 630;$$

Note that LINGO interprets the $<=$ symbol as $\leq$. Alternatively, we could enter $<$ instead of $<=$. As was the case when entering the objective function, a semicolon is required at

WEB file

Par

the end of the first constraint. Pressing the Enter key moves us to a new line as we continue the process by entering the remaining constraints as shown here:

$$0.5*S + \tfrac{5}{8}*D <= 600;$$
$$1*S + \tfrac{2}{3}*D <= 708;$$
$$0.1*S + 0.25*D <= 135;$$

The model window will now appear as follows:

$$MAX = 10*S + 9*D;$$
$$0.7*S + 1*D <= 630;$$
$$0.5*S + \tfrac{5}{8}*D <= 600;$$
$$1*S + \tfrac{2}{3}*D <= 708;$$
$$0.1*S + 0.25*D <= 135;$$

When entering a fraction into LINGO it is not necessary to convert the fraction into an equivalent or rounded decimal number. For example, simply enter the fraction $\tfrac{2}{3}$ into LINGO as $\tfrac{2}{3}$ and do not worry about converting to a decimal or how many decimal places to use. Enter $\tfrac{7}{10}$ either as $\tfrac{7}{10}$ or 0.7. Let LINGO act as a calculator for you.

LINGO is very flexible about the format of an equation and it is not necessary to have the variables on the left-hand side of an equation and the constant term on the right. For example

$$0.7*S + 1*D <= 630;$$

could also be entered as

$$0.7*S <= 630 - 1*D;$$

This feature will be very useful later when writing models in a clear and understandable form. Finally, note that although we have expressly included a coefficient of 1 on the variable D above, this is not necessary. In LINGO, $1*D$ and D are equivalent.

If you make an error in entering the model, you can correct it at any time by simply positioning the cursor where you made the error and entering the necessary correction.

To solve the model, select the **Solve** command from the **LINGO** menu or press the **Solve** button on the toolbar at the top of the main frame window. LINGO will begin the solution process by determining whether the model conforms to all syntax requirements. If the LINGO model doesn't pass these tests, you will be informed by an error message. If LINGO does not find any errors in the model input, it will begin to solve the model. As part of the solution process, LINGO displays a Solver Status window that allows you to monitor the progress of the solver. LINGO displays the solution in a new window titled "Solution Report." The output that appears in the Solution Report window for the Par, Inc., problem is shown in Figure 2.25.

The first part of the output shown in Figure 2.25 indicates that an optimal solution has been found and that the value of the objective function is 7668. We see that the optimal solution is $S = 540$ and $D = 252$, and that the slack variables for the four constraints (rows 2–5) are 0, 120, 0, and 18. We will discuss the use of the information in the Reduced Cost column and the Dual Price column in Chapter 3 when we study the topic of sensitivity analysis.

FIGURE 2.25   PAR INC., SOLUTION REPORT USING LINGO

```
Global optimal solution found.
Objective value:                              7668.000
Infeasibilities:                              0.000000
Total solver iterations:                             2
Elapsed runtime seconds:                          0.17

Model Class:                                        LP

Total variables:                 2
Nonlinear variables:             0
Integer variables:               0

Total constraints:               5
Nonlinear constraints:           0

Total nonzeros:                 10
Nonlinear nonzeros:              0


              Variable              Value           Reduced Cost
        --------------       --------------       ----------------
                     S           540.0000               0.000000
                     D           252.0000               0.000000


                   Row     Slack or Surplus           Dual Price
        --------------       --------------       ----------------
                     1           7668.000               1.000000
                     2           0.000000               4.375000
                     3           120.0000               0.000000
                     4           0.000000               6.937500
                     5           18.00000               0.000000
```

Appendix 2.2   SOLVING LINEAR PROGRAMS WITH EXCEL SOLVER

The Excel add-in Analytic Solver Platform (ASP), which is used in Chapter 12 of this textbook for simulation problems, can also be used to solve linear programs. ASP uses more sophisticated algorithms for solving optimization problems and can solve larger problems than Excel Solver. However, since all optimization problems in this textbook can be solved using Excel Solver, we do not specifically discuss the use of ASP for optimization problems.

In this appendix we will use Excel Solver to solve the Par, Inc., linear programming problem. We will enter the problem data for the Par, Inc., problem in the top part of the worksheet and develop the linear programming model in the bottom part of the worksheet.

Formulation

Whenever we formulate a worksheet model of a linear program, we perform the following steps:

Step 1.   Enter the problem data in the top part of the worksheet.
Step 2.   Specify cell locations for the decision variables.
Step 3.   Select a cell and enter a formula for computing the value of the objective function.
Step 4.   Select a cell and enter a formula for computing the left-hand side of each constraint.
Step 5.   Select a cell and enter a formula for computing the right-hand side of each constraint.

FIGURE 2.26   FORMULA WORKSHEET FOR THE PAR, INC., PROBLEM

	A	B	C	D
1	Par, Inc.			
2				
3		**Production Time**		
4	**Operation**	**Standard**	**Deluxe**	**Time Available**
5	Cutting and Dyeing	0.7	1	630
6	Sewing	0.5	0.83333	600
7	Finishing	1	0.66667	708
8	Inspection and Packaging	0.1	0.25	135
9	**Profit Per Bag**	10	9	
10				
11				
12	**Model**			
13				
14		**Decision Variables**		
15		**Standard**	**Deluxe**	
16	**Bags Produced**			
17				
18	**Maximize Total Profit**	=B9*B16+C9*C16		
19				
20	**Constraints**	**Hours Used (LHS)**		**Hours Available (RHS)**
21	Cutting and Dyeing	=B5*B16+C5*C16	<=	=D5
22	Sewing	=B6*B16+C6*C16	<=	=D6
23	Finishing	=B7*B16+C7*C16	<=	=D7
24	Inspection and Packaging	=B8*B16+C8*C16	<=	=D8

The formula worksheet that we developed for the Par, Inc., problem using these five steps is shown in Figure 2.26. Note that the worksheet consists of two sections: a data section and a model section. The four components of the model are highlighted, and the cells reserved for the decision variables are B16 and C16. Figure 2.26 is called a formula worksheet because it displays the formulas that we have entered and not the values computed from those formulas. In a moment we will see how Excel Solver is used to find the optimal solution to the Par, Inc., problem. But first, let's review each of the preceding steps as they apply to the Par, Inc., problem.

Step 1.   Enter the problem data in the top part of the worksheet.
Cells B5:C8 show the production requirements per unit for each product. Note that in cells C6 and C7, we have entered the exact fractions. That is, in cell C6 we have entered $=5/6$ and in cell C7 we have entered $=2/3$.
Cells B9:C9 show the profit contribution per unit for the two products.
Cells D5:D8 show the number of hours available in each department.

Step 2.   Specify cell locations for the decision variables.
Cell B16 will contain the number of standard bags produced, and cell C16 will contain the number of deluxe bags produced.

Step 3.   Select a cell and enter a formula for computing the value of the objective function.
Cell B18: =B9*B16+C9*C16

Step 4.   Select a cell and enter a formula for computing the left-hand side of each constraint.
With four constraints, we have
Cell B21: =B5*B16+C5*C16
Cell B22: =B6*B16+C6*C16
Cell B23: =B7*B16+C7*C16
Cell B24: =B8*B16+C8*C16

Step 5.   Select a cell and enter a formula for computing the right-hand side of each constraint.
With four constraints, we have
Cell D21: =D5
Cell D22: =D6
Cell D23: =D7
Cell D24: =D8

Note that descriptive labels make the model section of the worksheet easier to read and understand. For example, we added "Standard," "Deluxe," and "Bags Produced" in rows 15 and 16 so that the values of the decision variables appearing in cells B16 and C16 can be easily interpreted. In addition, we entered "Maximize Total Profit" in cell A18 to indicate that the value of the objective function appearing in cell B18 is the maximum profit contribution. In the constraint section of the worksheet we added the constraint names as well as the "<=" symbols to show the relationship that exists between the left-hand side and the right-hand side of each constraint. Although these descriptive labels are not necessary to use Excel Solver to find a solution to the Par, Inc., problem, the labels make it easier for the user to understand and interpret the optimal solution.

Appendix A provides a discussion of how to properly build and structure a good spreadsheet model.

Excel Solution

The standard Excel Solver developed by Frontline Systems can be used to solve all of the linear programming problems presented in this text.

The following steps describe how Excel Solver can be used to obtain the optimal solution to the Par, Inc., problem:

Step 1.   Select the **Data** tab on the **Ribbon**
Step 2.   Select **Solver** from the **Analysis** Group
Step 3.   When the **Solver Parameters** dialog box appears (see Figure 2.27):
Enter *B18* into the **Set Objective** box
Select the **To: Max** option
Enter *B16:C16* into the **By Changing Variable Cells** box
Step 4.   Select **Add**
When the **Add Constraint** dialog box appears:
Enter *B21:B24* in the left-hand box of the **Cell Reference** area
Select **<=** from the middle drop-down button
Enter *D21:D24* in the **Constraint** area
Click **OK**
Step 5.   When the **Solver Parameters** dialog box reappears:
Select the checkbox for **Make Unconstrained Variables Non-Negative**
Step 6.   In the **Select a Solving Method** dropdown menu
Select **Simplex LP**
Step 7.   Click **Solve**
Step 8.   When the **Solver Results** dialog box appears:
Select **Keep Solver Solution**
Click **OK**

FIGURE 2.27   SOLVER PARAMETERS DIALOG BOX FOR THE PAR, INC., PROBLEM

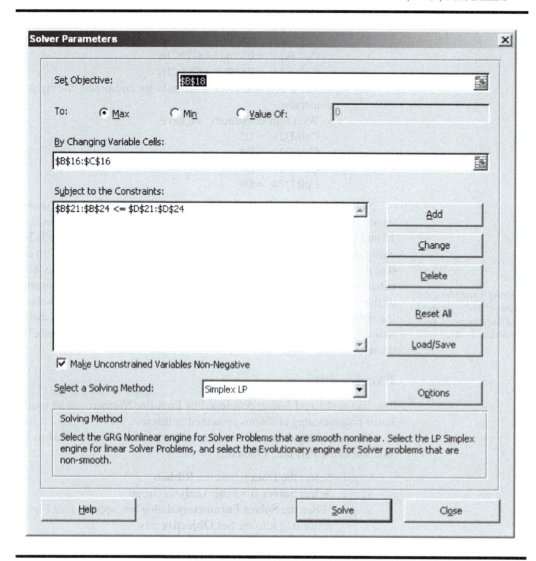

Figure 2.27 shows the completed **Solver Parameters** dialog box, and Figure 2.28 shows the optimal solution in the worksheet. The optimal solution of 540 standard bags and 252 deluxe bags is the same as we obtained using the graphical solution procedure. In addition to the output information shown in Figure 2.28, Solver has an option to provide sensitivity analysis information. We discuss sensitivity analysis in Chapter 3.

In Step 5 we selected the **Make Unconstrained Variables Non-Negative** checkbox to avoid having to enter nonnegativity constraints for the decision variables. In general, whenever we want to solve a linear programming model in which the decision variables are all restricted to be nonnegative, we will select this option. In addition, in Step 4 we entered all four less-than-or-equal-to constraints simultaneously by entering *B21:B24* in

FIGURE 2.28   EXCEL SOLUTION FOR THE PAR, INC., PROBLEM

	A	B	C	D
4	**Operation**	**Standard**	**Deluxe**	**Time Available**
5	Cutting and Dyeing	0.7	1	630
6	Sewing	0.5	0.833333333	600
7	Finishing	1	0.666666667	708
8	Inspection and Packaging	0.1	0.25	135
9	**Profit Per Bag**	10	9	
10				
11				
12	**Model**			
13				
14		**Decision Variables**		
15		**Standard**	**Deluxe**	
16	**Bags Produced**	540.00000	252.00000	
17				
18	**Maximize Total Profit**	7668		
19				
20	**Constraints**	**Hours Used (LHS)**		**Hours Available (RHS)**
21	Cutting and Dyeing	630	<=	630
22	Sewing	480.00000	<=	600
23	Finishing	708	<=	708
24	Inspection and Packaging	117.00000	<=	135

the left-hand box of the **Cell Reference** area, selecting **<=**, and entering *D21:D24* in the right-hand box. Alternatively, we could have entered the four constraints one at a time.

As a reminder, when entering a fraction into Excel, it is not necessary to convert the fraction into an equivalent or rounded decimal number. For example, simply enter the fraction ⅔ into Excel as =⅔ and do not worry about converting to a decimal or how many decimal places to use. Enter ⁷⁄₁₀ either as =⁷⁄₁₀ or =0.7. When entering a fraction, the "=" sign is necessary; otherwise, Excel will treat the fraction as text rather than a number.

CHAPTER 3

Descriptive Statistics: Numerical Measures

CONTENTS

STATISTICS (in) PRACTICE

SMALL FRY DESIGN*
SANTA ANA, CALIFORNIA

Founded in 1997, Small Fry Design is a toy and accessory company that designs and imports products for infants. The company's product line includes teddy bears, mobiles, musical toys, rattles, and security blankets and features high-quality soft toy designs with an emphasis on color, texture, and sound. The products are designed in the United States and manufactured in China.

Small Fry Design uses independent representatives to sell the products to infant furnishing retailers, children's accessory and apparel stores, gift shops, upscale department stores, and major catalog companies. Currently, Small Fry Design products are distributed in more than 1000 retail outlets throughout the United States.

Cash flow management is one of the most critical activities in the day-to-day operation of this company. Ensuring sufficient incoming cash to meet both current and ongoing debt obligations can mean the difference between business success and failure. A critical factor in cash flow management is the analysis and control of accounts receivable. By measuring the average age and dollar value of outstanding invoices, management can predict cash availability and monitor changes in the status of accounts receivable. The company set the following goals: The average age for outstanding invoices should not exceed 45 days, and the dollar value of invoices more than 60 days old should not exceed 5% of the dollar value of all accounts receivable.

In a recent summary of accounts receivable status, the following descriptive statistics were provided for the age of outstanding invoices:

Mean	40 days
Median	35 days
Mode	31 days

*The authors are indebted to John A. McCarthy, President of Small Fry Design, for providing this Statistics in Practice.

Small Fry Design uses descriptive statistics to monitor its accounts receivable and incoming cash flow.

Interpretation of these statistics shows that the mean or average age of an invoice is 40 days. The median shows that half of the invoices remain outstanding 35 days or more. The mode of 31 days, the most frequent invoice age, indicates that the most common length of time an invoice is outstanding is 31 days. The statistical summary also showed that only 3% of the dollar value of all accounts receivable was more than 60 days old. Based on the statistical information, management was satisfied that accounts receivable and incoming cash flow were under control.

In this chapter, you will learn how to compute and interpret some of the statistical measures used by Small Fry Design. In addition to the mean, median, and mode, you will learn about other descriptive statistics such as the range, variance, standard deviation, percentiles, and correlation. These numerical measures will assist in the understanding and interpretation of data.

In Chapter 2 we discussed tabular and graphical presentations used to summarize data. In this chapter, we present several numerical measures that provide additional alternatives for summarizing data.

We start by developing numerical summary measures for data sets consisting of a single variable. When a data set contains more than one variable, the same numerical measures can be computed separately for each variable. However, in the two-variable case, we will also develop measures of the relationship between the variables.

Numerical measures of location, dispersion, shape, and association are introduced. If the measures are computed for data from a sample, they are called **sample statistics**. If the measures are computed for data from a population, they are called **population parameters**. In statistical inference, a sample statistic is referred to as the **point estimator** of the corresponding population parameter. In Chapter 7 we will discuss in more detail the process of point estimation.

In the chapter appendixes we show how Minitab and Excel can be used to compute the numerical measures described in the chapter.

3.1   Measures of Location

Mean

The mean is sometimes referred to as the arithmetic mean.

Perhaps the most important measure of location is the **mean**, or average value, for a variable. The mean provides a measure of central location for the data. If the data are for a sample, the mean is denoted by $\bar{x}$; if the data are for a population, the mean is denoted by the Greek letter μ.

In statistical formulas, it is customary to denote the value of variable x for the first observation by x_1, the value of variable x for the second observation by x_2, and so on. In general, the value of variable x for the ith observation is denoted by x_i. For a sample with n observations, the formula for the sample mean is as follows.

The sample mean $\bar{x}$ is a sample statistic.

SAMPLE MEAN

$$\bar{x} = \frac{\Sigma x_i}{n} \tag{3.1}$$

In the preceding formula, the numerator is the sum of the values of the n observations. That is,

$$\Sigma x_i = x_1 + x_2 + \cdots + x_n$$

The Greek letter Σ is the summation sign.

To illustrate the computation of a sample mean, let us consider the following class size data for a sample of five college classes.

$$46 \quad 54 \quad 42 \quad 46 \quad 32$$

We use the notation x_1, x_2, x_3, x_4, x_5 to represent the number of students in each of the five classes.

$$x_1 = 46 \qquad x_2 = 54 \qquad x_3 = 42 \qquad x_4 = 46 \qquad x_5 = 32$$

Hence, to compute the sample mean, we can write

$$\bar{x} = \frac{\Sigma x_i}{n} = \frac{x_1 + x_2 + x_3 + x_4 + x_5}{5} = \frac{46 + 54 + 42 + 46 + 32}{5} = 44$$

The sample mean class size is 44 students.

To provide a visual perspective of the mean and to show how it can be influenced by extreme values, consider the dot plot for the class size data shown in Figure 3.1. Treating the horizontal axis used to create the dot plot as a long narrow board in which each of the

FIGURE 3.1   THE MEAN AS THE CENTER OF BALANCE FOR THE DOT PLOT OF THE
CLASSROOM SIZE DATA

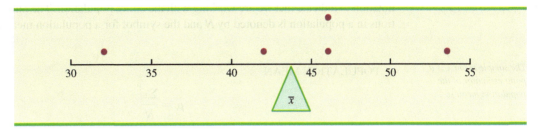

dots has the same fixed weight, the mean is the point at which we would place a fulcrum
or pivot point under the board in order to balance the dot plot. This is the same principle
by which a see-saw on a playground works, the only difference being that the see-saw is
pivoted in the middle so that as one end goes up, the other end goes down. In the dot plot
we are locating the pivot point based upon the location of the dots. Now consider what happens to the balance if we increase the largest value from 54 to 114. We will have to move
the fulcrum under the new dot plot in a positive direction in order to reestablish balance.
To determine how far we would have to shift the fulcrum, we simply compute the sample
mean for the revised class size data.

$$\bar{x} = \frac{\Sigma x_i}{n} = \frac{x_1 + x_2 + x_3 + x_4 + x_5}{5} = \frac{46 + 114 + 42 + 46 + 32}{5} = \frac{280}{5} = 56$$

Thus, the mean for the revised class size data is 56, an increase of 12 students. In other
words, we have to shift the balance point 12 units to the right to establish balance under
the new dot plot.

Another illustration of the computation of a sample mean is given in the following situation. Suppose that a college placement office sent a questionnaire to a sample of business
school graduates requesting information on monthly starting salaries. Table 3.1 shows the
collected data. The mean monthly starting salary for the sample of 12 business college
graduates is computed as

$$\bar{x} = \frac{\Sigma x_i}{n} = \frac{x_1 + x_2 + \cdots + x_{12}}{12}$$

$$= \frac{3850 + 3950 + \cdots + 3880}{12}$$

$$= \frac{47,280}{12} = 3940$$

TABLE 3.1   MONTHLY STARTING SALARIES FOR A SAMPLE OF 12 BUSINESS SCHOOL
GRADUATES

DATA *file*

2012StartSalary

Graduate	Monthly Starting Salary ($)	Graduate	Monthly Starting Salary ($)
1	3850	7	3890
2	3950	8	4130
3	4050	9	3940
4	3880	10	4325
5	3755	11	3920
6	3710	12	3880

Equation (3.1) shows how the mean is computed for a sample with n observations. The formula for computing the mean of a population remains the same, but we use different notation to indicate that we are working with the entire population. The number of observations in a population is denoted by N and the symbol for a population mean is μ.

The sample mean $\bar{x}$ is a point estimator of the population mean μ.

POPULATION MEAN

$$\mu = \frac{\Sigma x_i}{N} \qquad\qquad (3.2)$$

Weighted Mean

In the formulas for the sample mean and population mean, each x_i is given equal importance or weight. For instance, the formula for the sample mean can be written as follows:

$$\bar{x} = \frac{\Sigma x_i}{n} = \frac{1}{n}\left(\sum x_i\right) = \frac{1}{n}(x_1 + x_2 + \cdots + x_n) = \frac{1}{n}(x_1) + \frac{1}{n}(x_2) + \cdots + \frac{1}{n}(x_n)$$

This shows that each observation in the sample is given a weight of $1/n$. Although this practice is most common, in some instances the mean is computed by giving each observation a weight that reflects its relative importance. A mean computed in this manner is referred to as a **weighted mean**. The weighted mean is computed as follows:

WEIGHTED MEAN

$$\bar{x} = \frac{\Sigma w_i x_i}{\Sigma w_i} \qquad\qquad (3.3)$$

where

$$w_i = \text{weight for observation } i$$

When the data are from a sample, equation (3.3) provides the weighted sample mean. If the data are from a population, μ replaces $\bar{x}$ and equation (3.3) provides the weighted population mean.

As an example of the need for a weighted mean, consider the following sample of five purchases of a raw material over the past three months.

Purchase	Cost per Pound ($)	Number of Pounds
1	3.00	1200
2	3.40	500
3	2.80	2750
4	2.90	1000
5	3.25	800

Note that the cost per pound varies from $2.80 to $3.40, and the quantity purchased varies from 500 to 2750 pounds. Suppose that a manager wanted to know the mean cost per pound of the raw material. Because the quantities ordered vary, we must use the formula for a weighted mean. The five cost-per-pound data values are $x_1 = 3.00$, $x_2 = 3.40$, $x_3 = 2.80$, $x_4 = 2.90$, and $x_5 = 3.25$. The weighted mean cost per pound is found by weighting each cost by its corresponding quantity. For this example, the weights are $w_1 = 1200$, $w_2 = 500$, $w_3 = 2750$, $w_4 = 1000$, and $w_5 = 800$. Based on equation (3.3), the weighted mean is calculated as follows:

$$\bar{x} = \frac{1200(3.00) + 500(3.40) + 2750(2.80) + 1000(2.90) + 800(3.25)}{1200 + 500 + 2750 + 1000 + 800}$$

$$= \frac{18,500}{6250} = 2.96$$

Thus, the weighted mean computation shows that the mean cost per pound for the raw material is $2.96. Note that using equation (3.1) rather than the weighted mean formula in equation (3.3) would provide misleading results. In this case, the sample mean of the five cost-per-pound values is $(3.00 + 3.40 + 2.80 + 2.90 + 3.25)/5 = 15.35/5 = \$3.07$, which overstates the actual mean cost per pound purchased.

The choice of weights for a particular weighted mean computation depends upon the application. An example that is well known to college students is the computation of a grade point average (GPA). In this computation, the data values generally used are 4 for an A grade, 3 for a B grade, 2 for a C grade, 1 for a D grade, and 0 for an F grade. The weights are the number of credit hours earned for each grade. Exercise 16 at the end of this section provides an example of this weighted mean computation. In other weighted mean computations, quantities such as pounds, dollars, or volume are frequently used as weights. In any case, when observations vary in importance, the analyst must choose the weight that best reflects the importance of each observation in the determination of the mean.

Median

The **median** is another measure of central location. The median is the value in the middle when the data are arranged in ascending order (smallest value to largest value). With an odd number of observations, the median is the middle value. An even number of observations has no single middle value. In this case, we follow convention and define the median as the average of the values for the middle two observations. For convenience the definition of the median is restated as follows.

MEDIAN

Arrange the data in ascending order (smallest value to largest value).

(a) For an odd number of observations, the median is the middle value.
(b) For an even number of observations, the median is the average of the two middle values.

Let us apply this definition to compute the median class size for the sample of five college classes. Arranging the data in ascending order provides the following list.

32   42   46   46   54

Because $n = 5$ is odd, the median is the middle value. Thus the median class size is 46 students. Even though this data set contains two observations with values of 46, each observation is treated separately when we arrange the data in ascending order.

Suppose we also compute the median starting salary for the 12 business college graduates in Table 3.1. We first arrange the data in ascending order.

3710   3755   3850   3880   3880   3890   3920   3940   3950   4050   4130   4325

Middle Two Values

Because $n = 12$ is even, we identify the middle two values: 3890 and 3920. The median is the average of these values.

$$\text{Median} = \frac{3890 + 3920}{2} = 3905$$

The procedure we used to compute the median depends upon whether there is an odd number of observations or an even number of observations. Let us now describe a more conceptual and visual approach using the monthly starting salary for the 12 business college graduates. As before, we begin by arranging the data in ascending order.

3710   3755   3850   3880   3880   3890   3920   3940   3950   4050   4130   4325

Once the data are in ascending order, we trim pairs of extreme high and low values until no further pairs of values can be trimmed without completely eliminating all the data. For instance, after trimming the lowest observation (3710) and the highest observation (4325) we obtain a new data set with 10 observations.

~~3710~~   3755   3850   3880   3880   3890   3920   3940   3950   4050   4130   ~~4325~~

We then trim the next lowest remaining value (3755) and the next highest remaining value (4130) to produce a new data set with eight observations.

~~3710~~   ~~3755~~   3850   3880   3880   3890   3920   3940   3950   4050   ~~4130~~   ~~4325~~

Continuing this process, we obtain the following results.

~~3710~~   ~~3755~~   ~~3850~~   3880   3880   3890   3920   3940   3950   ~~4050~~   ~~4130~~   ~~4325~~

~~3710~~   ~~3755~~   ~~3850~~   ~~3880~~   3880   3890   3920   3940   ~~3950~~   ~~4050~~   ~~4130~~   ~~4325~~

~~3710~~   ~~3755~~   ~~3850~~   ~~3880~~   ~~3880~~   3890   3920   ~~3940~~   ~~3950~~   ~~4050~~   ~~4130~~   ~~4325~~

At this point no further trimming is possible without eliminating all the data. So, the median is just the average of the remaining two values. When there is an even number of observations, the trimming process will always result in two remaining values, and the average of these values will be the median. When there is an odd number of observations, the trimming process will always result in one final value, and this value will be the median. Thus, this method works whether the number of observations is odd or even.

The median is the measure of location most often reported for annual income and property value data because a few extremely large incomes or property values can inflate the mean. In such cases, the median is the preferred measure of central location.

Although the mean is the more commonly used measure of central location, in some situations the median is preferred. The mean is influenced by extremely small and large data values. For instance, suppose that the highest paid graduate (see Table 3.1) had a starting salary of $10,000 per month (maybe the individual's family owns the company). If we change the highest monthly starting salary in Table 3.1 from $4325 to $10,000 and recompute the mean, the sample mean changes from $3940 to $4413. The median of $3905, however, is unchanged, because $3890 and $3920 are still the middle two values. With the extremely high starting salary included, the median provides a better measure of central location than the mean. We can generalize to say that whenever a data set contains extreme values, the median is often the preferred measure of central location.

Geometric Mean

The **geometric mean** is a measure of location that is calculated by finding the nth root of the product of n values. The general formula for the geometric mean, denoted $\bar{x}_g$, follows.

GEOMETRIC MEAN

$$\bar{x}_g = \sqrt[n]{(x_1)(x_2) \cdots (x_n)} = [(x_1)(x_2) \cdots (x_n)]^{1/n} \qquad \textbf{(3.4)}$$

The geometric mean is often used in analyzing growth rates in financial data. In these types of situations the arithmetic mean or average value will provide misleading results.

To illustrate the use of the geometric mean, consider Table 3.2, which shows the percentage annual returns, or growth rates, for a mutual fund over the past 10 years. Suppose we want to compute how much $100 invested in the fund at the beginning of year 1 would be worth at the end of year 10. Let's start by computing the balance in the fund at the end of year 1. Because the percentage annual return for year 1 was -22.1%, the balance in the fund at the end of year 1 would be

$$\$100 - .221(\$100) = \$100(1 - .221) = \$100(.779) = \$77.90$$

The growth factor for each year is 1 plus .01 times the percentage return. A growth factor less than 1 indicates negative growth, while a growth factor greater than 1 indicates positive growth. The growth factor cannot be less than zero.

Note that .779 is identified as the growth factor for year 1 in Table 3.2. This result shows that we can compute the balance at the end of year 1 by multiplying the value invested in the fund at the beginning of year 1 times the growth factor for year 1.

The balance in the fund at the end of year 1, $77.90, now becomes the beginning balance in year 2. So, with a percentage annual return for year 2 of 28.7%, the balance at the end of year 2 would be

$$\$77.90 + .287(\$77.90) = \$77.90(1 + .287) = \$77.90(1.287) = \$100.2573$$

Note that 1.287 is the growth factor for year 2. And, by substituting $100(.779) for $77.90 we see that the balance in the fund at the end of year 2 is

$$\$100(.779)(1.287) = \$100.2573$$

In other words, the balance at the end of year 2 is just the initial investment at the beginning of year 1 times the product of the first two growth factors. This result can be generalized to

TABLE 3.2   PERCENTAGE ANNUAL RETURNS AND GROWTH FACTORS FOR THE MUTUAL FUND DATA

Year	Return (%)	Growth Factor
1	−22.1	0.779
2	28.7	1.287
3	10.9	1.109
4	4.9	1.049
5	15.8	1.158
6	5.5	1.055
7	−37.0	0.630
8	26.5	1.265
9	15.1	1.151
10	2.1	1.021

show that the balance at the end of year 10 is the initial investment times the product of all 10 growth factors.

$$\$100[(.779)(1.287)(1.109)(1.049)(1.158)(1.055)(.630)(1.265)(1.151)(1.021)] =$$

$$\$100(1.334493) = \$133.4493$$

The nth root can be computed using most calculators or by using the POWER function in Excel. For instance, using Excel, the 10th root of 1.334493 = POWER (1.334493,1/10) or 1.029275.

So, a \$100 investment in the fund at the beginning of year 1 would be worth \$133.4493 at the end of year 10. Note that the product of the 10 growth factors is 1.334493. Thus, we can compute the balance at the end of year 10 for any amount of money invested at the beginning of year 1 by multiplying the value of the initial investment times 1.334493. For instance, an initial investment of \$2500 at the beginning of year 1 would be worth \$2500(1.334493) or approximately \$3336 at the end of year 10.

But, what was the mean percentage annual return or mean rate of growth for this investment over the 10-year period? Let us see how the geometric mean of the 10 growth factors can be used to answer to this question. Because the product of the 10 growth factors is 1.334493, the geometric mean is the 10th root of 1.334493 or

$$\bar{x}_g = \sqrt[10]{1.334493} = 1.029275$$

The geometric mean tells us that annual returns grew at an average annual rate of $(1.029275 - 1)100\%$ or 2.9275%. In other words, with an average annual growth rate of 2.9275%, a \$100 investment in the fund at the beginning of year 1 would grow to $\$100(1.029275)^{10} = \$133.4493$ at the end of 10 years.

It is important to understand that the arithmetic mean of the percentage annual returns does not provide the mean annual growth rate for this investment. The sum of the 10 annual percentage returns in Table 3.2 is 50.4. Thus, the arithmetic mean of the 10 percentage annual returns is 50.4/10 = 5.04%. A broker might try to convince you to invest in this fund by stating that the mean annual percentage return was 5.04%. Such a statement is not only misleading, it is inaccurate. A mean annual percentage return of 5.04% corresponds to an average growth factor of 1.0504. So, if the average growth factor were really 1.0504, \$100 invested in the fund at the beginning of year 1 would have grown to $\$100(1.0504)^{10} = \$163.51$ at the end of 10 years. But, using the 10 annual percentage returns in Table 3.2, we showed that an initial \$100 investment is worth \$133.45 at the end of 10 years. The broker's claim that the mean annual percentage return is 5.04% grossly overstates the true growth for this mutual fund. The problem is that the sample mean is only appropriate for an additive process. For a multiplicative process, such as applications involving growth rates, the geometric mean is the appropriate measure of location.

While the applications of the geometric mean to problems in finance, investments, and banking are particularly common, the geometric mean should be applied any time you want to determine the mean rate of change over several successive periods. Other common applications include changes in populations of species, crop yields, pollution levels, and birth and death rates. Also note that the geometric mean can be applied to changes that occur over any number of successive periods of any length. In addition to annual changes, the geometric mean is often applied to find the mean rate of change over quarters, months, weeks, and even days.

Mode

Another measure of location is the **mode**. The mode is defined as follows.

MODE

The mode is the value that occurs with greatest frequency.

To illustrate the identification of the mode, consider the sample of five class sizes. The only value that occurs more than once is 46. Because this value, occurring with a frequency of 2, has the greatest frequency, it is the mode. As another illustration, consider the sample of starting salaries for the business school graduates. The only monthly starting salary that occurs more than once is $3880. Because this value has the greatest frequency, it is the mode.

Situations can arise for which the greatest frequency occurs at two or more different values. In these instances more than one mode exists. If the data contain exactly two modes, we say that the data are *bimodal*. If data contain more than two modes, we say that the data are *multimodal*. In multimodal cases the mode is almost never reported because listing three or more modes would not be particularly helpful in describing a location for the data.

Percentiles

A **percentile** provides information about how the data are spread over the interval from the smallest value to the largest value. For a data set containing n observations, the **pth percentile** divides the data into two parts: approximately $p\%$ of the observations are less than the pth percentile, and approximately $(100 - p)\%$ of the observations are greater than the pth percentile.

Colleges and universities frequently report admission test scores in terms of percentiles. For instance, suppose an applicant obtains a score of 630 on the math portion of an admission test. How this applicant performed in relation to others taking the same test may not be readily apparent from this score. However, if the score of 630 corresponds to the 82nd percentile, we know that approximately that 82% of the applicants scored lower than this individual and approximately 18% of the applicants scored higher than this individual.

To calculate the pth percentile for a data set containing n observations, we must first arrange the data in ascending order (smallest value to largest value). The smallest value is in position 1, the next smallest value is in position 2, and so on. The location of the pth percentile, denoted L_p, is computed using the following equation:

Several procedures can be used to compute the location of the pth percentile using sample data. All provide similar values, especially for large data sets. The procedure we show here is the procedure used by Excel's PERCENTILE.EXC function as well as several other statistical software packages.

LOCATION OF THE *P*TH PERCENTILE

$$L_p = \frac{p}{100}(n + 1) \tag{3.5}$$

Once we find the position of the value of the pth percentile, we have the information we need to calculate the pth percentile.

To illustrate the computation of the pth percentile, let us compute the 80th percentile for the starting salary data in Table 3.1. We begin by arranging the sample of 12 starting salaries in ascending order.

3710	3755	3850	3880	3880	3890	3920	3940	3950	4050	4130	4325
Position 1	2	3	4	5	6	7	8	9	10	11	12

The position of each observation in the sorted data is shown directly below its value. For instance, the smallest value (3710) is in position 1, the next smallest value (3755) is in position 2, and so on. Using equation (3.5) with $p = 80$ and $n = 12$, the location of the 80th percentile is

$$L_{80} = \frac{p}{100}(n + 1) = \left(\frac{80}{100}\right)(12 + 1) = 10.4$$

The interpretation of $L_{80} = 10.4$ is that the 80th percentile is 40% of the way between the value in position 10 and the value in position 11. In other words, the 80th percentile is the value in position 10 (4050) plus .4 times the difference between the value in position 11 (4130) and the value in position 10 (4050). Thus, the 80th percentile is

$$80\text{th percentile} = 4050 + .4(4130 - 4050) = 4050 + .4(80) = 4082$$

Let us now compute the 50th percentile for the starting salary data. With $p = 50$ and $n = 12$, the location of the 50th percentile is

$$L_{50} = \frac{p}{100}(n + 1) = \left(\frac{50}{100}\right)(12 + 1) = 6.5$$

With $L_{50} = 6.5$, we see that the 50th percentile is 50% of the way between the value in position 6 (3890) and the value in position 7 (3920). Thus, the 50th percentile is

$$\text{50th percentile} = 3890 + .5(3920 - 3890) = 3890 + .5(30) = 3905$$

Note that the *50th percentile is also the median.*

Quartiles

Quartiles are just specific percentiles; thus, the steps for computing percentiles can be applied directly in the computation of quartiles.

It is often desirable to divide a data set into four parts, with each part containing approximately one-fourth, or 25%, of the observations. These division points are referred to as the **quartiles** and are defined as follows.

$$Q_1 = \text{first quartile, or 25th percentile}$$
$$Q_2 = \text{second quartile, or 50th percentile (also the median)}$$
$$Q_3 = \text{third quartile, or 75th percentile}$$

Because quartiles are specific percentiles, the procedure for computing percentiles can be used to compute the quartiles.

To illustrate the computation of the quartiles for a data set consisting of n observations, we will compute the quartiles for the starting salary data in Table 3.1. Previously we showed that the 50th percentile for the starting salary data is 3905; thus, the second quartile (median) is $Q_2 = 3905$. To compute the first and third quartiles, we must find the 25th and 75th percentiles. The calculations follow.

For Q_1,

$$L_{25} = \frac{p}{100}(n + 1) = \left(\frac{25}{100}\right)(12 + 1) = 3.25$$

The first quartile, or 25th percentile, is .25 of the way between the value in position 3 (3850) and the value in position 4 (3880). Thus,

$$Q_1 = 3850 + .25(3880 - 3850) = 3850 + .25(30) = 3857.5$$

For Q_3,

$$L_{75} = \frac{p}{100}(n + 1) = \left(\frac{75}{100}\right)(12 + 1) = 9.75$$

The third quartile, or 75th percentile, is .75 of the way between the value in position 9 (3950) and the value in position 10 (4050). Thus,

$$Q_3 = 3950 + .75(4050 - 3950) = 3950 + .75(100) = 4025$$

The quartiles divide the starting salary data into four parts, with each part containing 25% of the observations.

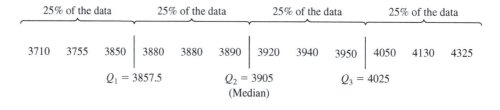

We defined the quartiles as the 25th, 50th, and 75th percentiles and then we computed the quartiles in the same way as percentiles. However, other conventions are sometimes used to compute quartiles, and the actual values reported for quartiles may vary slightly depending on the convention used. Nevertheless, the objective of all procedures for computing quartiles is to divide the data into four parts that contain equal numbers of observations.

NOTES AND COMMENTS

1. It is better to use the median than the mean as a measure of central location when a data set contains extreme values. Another measure that is sometimes used when extreme values are present is the trimmed mean. The trimmed mean is obtained by deleting a percentage of the smallest and largest values from a data set and then computing the mean of the remaining values. For example, the 5% trimmed mean is obtained by removing the smallest 5% and the largest 5% of the data values and then computing the mean of the remaining values. Using the sample with $n = 12$ starting salaries, $0.05(12) = 0.6$. Rounding this value to 1 indicates that the 5% trimmed mean is obtained by removing the smallest data value and the largest data value and then computing the mean of the remaining 10 values. For the starting salary data, the 5% trimmed mean is 3924.50.

2. Other commonly used percentiles are the quintiles (the 20th, 40th, 60th, and 80th percentiles) and the deciles (the 10th, 20th, 30th, 40th, 50th, 60th, 70th, 80th, and 90th percentiles).

Exercises

Methods

1. Consider a sample with data values of 10, 20, 12, 17, and 16. Compute the mean and median.

2. Consider a sample with data values of 10, 20, 21, 17, 16, and 12. Compute the mean and median.

3. Consider the following data and corresponding weights.

x_i	Weight (w_i)
3.2	6
2.0	3
2.5	2
5.0	8

a. Compute the weighted mean.
b. Compute the sample mean of the four data values without weighting. Note the difference in the results provided by the two computations.

4. Consider the following data.

Period	Rate of Return (%)
1	−6.0
2	−8.0
3	−4.0
4	2.0
5	5.4

What is the mean growth rate over these five periods?

5. Consider a sample with data values of 27, 25, 20, 15, 30, 34, 28, and 25. Compute the 20th, 25th, 65th, and 75th percentiles.

6. Consider a sample with data values of 53, 55, 70, 58, 64, 57, 53, 69, 57, 68, and 53. Compute the mean, median, and mode.

Applications

7. The average number of minutes Americans commute to work is 27.7 minutes (*Sterling's Best Places*, April 13, 2012). The average commute time in minutes for 48 cities are as follows:

CommuteTime

Albuquerque	23.3	Jacksonville	26.2	Phoenix	28.3
Atlanta	28.3	Kansas City	23.4	Pittsburgh	25.0
Austin	24.6	Las Vegas	28.4	Portland	26.4
Baltimore	32.1	Little Rock	20.1	Providence	23.6
Boston	31.7	Los Angeles	32.2	Richmond	23.4
Charlotte	25.8	Louisville	21.4	Sacramento	25.8
Chicago	38.1	Memphis	23.8	Salt Lake City	20.2
Cincinnati	24.9	Miami	30.7	San Antonio	26.1
Cleveland	26.8	Milwaukee	24.8	San Diego	24.8
Columbus	23.4	Minneapolis	23.6	San Francisco	32.6
Dallas	28.5	Nashville	25.3	San Jose	28.5
Denver	28.1	New Orleans	31.7	Seattle	27.3
Detroit	29.3	New York	43.8	St. Louis	26.8
El Paso	24.4	Oklahoma City	22.0	Tucson	24.0
Fresno	23.0	Orlando	27.1	Tulsa	20.1
Indianapolis	24.8	Philadelphia	34.2	Washington, D.C.	32.8

  a. What is the mean commute time for these 48 cities?
  b. Compute the median commute time.
  c. Compute the mode.
  d. Compute the third quartile.

8. *The Wall Street Journal* reported that the median salary for middle-level manager jobs was approximately $85,000 (*The Wall Street Journal*, August 6, 2013). Suppose that an independent study of middle-level managers employed at companies located in Atlanta, Georgia, was conducted to compare the salaries of managers working at firms in Atlanta to the national average. The following data show the salary, in thousands of dollars, for a sample of 15 middle-level managers.

  108   83   106   73   53   85   80   63   67   75   124   55   93   118   77

  a. Compute the median salary for the sample of 15 middle-level managers. How does the median for this group compare to the median reported by *The Wall Street Journal*?
  b. Compute the mean annual salary and discuss how and why it differs from the median computed in part (a).
  c. Compute the first and third quartiles.

9. Which companies spend the most money on advertising? *Business Insider* maintains a list of the top-spending companies. In 2014, Procter & Gamble spent more than any other company, a whopping $5 billion. In second place was Comcast, which spent $3.08 billion (*Business Insider* website, December 2014). The top 12 companies and the amount each spent on advertising in billions of dollars are as follows.

AdvertisingSpend

Company	Advertising ($billions)	Company	Advertising ($billions)
Procter & Gamble	$5.00	American Express	$2.19
Comcast	3.08	General Motors	2.15
AT&T	2.91	Toyota	2.09
Ford	2.56	Fiat Chrysler	1.97
Verizon	2.44	Walt Disney Company	1.96
L'Oreal	2.34	J.P Morgan	1.88

    a. What is the mean amount spent on advertising?

    b. What is the median amount spent on advertising?

    c. What are the first and third quartiles?

JacketRatings

10. Over a nine-month period, OutdoorGearLab tested hardshell jackets designed for ice climbing, mountaineering, and backpacking. Based on the breathability, durability, versatility, features, mobility, and weight of each jacket, an overall rating ranging from 0 (lowest) to 100 (highest) was assigned to each jacket tested. The following data show the results for 20 top-of-the-line jackets (OutdoorGearLab website, February 27, 2013).

42	66	67	71	78	62	61	76	71	67
61	64	61	54	83	63	68	69	81	53

    a. Compute the mean, median, and mode.

    b. Compute the first and third quartiles.

    c. Compute and interpret the 90th percentile.

11. According to the National Education Association (NEA), teachers generally spend more than 40 hours each week working on instructional duties (NEA website, April 2012). The following data show the number of hours worked per week for a sample of 13 high school science teachers and a sample of 11 high school English teachers.

    High School Science Teachers: 53 56 54 54 55 58 49 61 54 54 52 53 54

    High School English Teachers: 52 47 50 46 47 48 49 46 55 44 47

    a. What is the median number of hours worked per week for the sample of 13 high school science teachers?

    b. What is the median number of hours worked per week for the sample of 11 high school English teachers?

    c. Which group has the higher median number of hours worked per week? What is the difference between the median number of hours worked per week?

BigBangTheory

12. *The Big Bang Theory*, a situation comedy featuring Johnny Galecki, Jim Parsons, and Kaley Cuoco-Sweeting, is one of the most watched programs on network television. The first two episodes for the 2011–2012 season premiered on September 22, 2011; the first episode attracted 14.1 million viewers and the second episode attracted 14.7 million viewers. The following table shows the number of viewers in millions for the first 21 episodes of the 2011–2012 season (*The Big Bang Theory* website, April 17, 2012).

Air Date	Viewers (millions)	Air Date	Viewers (millions)
September 22, 2011	14.1	January 12, 2012	16.1
September 22, 2011	14.7	January 19, 2012	15.8
September 29, 2011	14.6	January 26, 2012	16.1
October 6, 2011	13.6	February 2, 2012	16.5
October 13, 2011	13.6	February 9, 2012	16.2
October 20, 2011	14.9	February 16, 2012	15.7
October 27, 2011	14.5	February 23, 2012	16.2
November 3, 2011	16.0	March 8, 2012	15.0
November 10, 2011	15.9	March 29, 2012	14.0
November 17, 2011	15.1	April 5, 2012	13.3
December 8, 2011	14.0		

    a. Compute the minimum and maximum number of viewers.

    b. Compute the mean, median, and mode.

    c. Compute the first and third quartiles.

    d. Has viewership grown or declined over the 2011–2012 season? Discuss.

13. In automobile mileage and gasoline-consumption testing, 13 automobiles were road tested for 300 miles in both city and highway driving conditions. The following data were recorded for miles-per-gallon performance.

City: 16.2 16.7 15.9 14.4 13.2 15.3 16.8 16.0 16.1 15.3 15.2 15.3 16.2
Highway: 19.4 20.6 18.3 18.6 19.2 17.4 17.2 18.6 19.0 21.1 19.4 18.5 18.7

Use the mean, median, and mode to make a statement about the difference in performance for city and highway driving.

StateUnemp

14. The data contained in the file named StateUnemp show the unemployment rate in March 2011 and the unemployment rate in March 2012 for every state and the District of Columbia (Bureau of Labor Statistics website, April 20, 2012). To compare unemployment rates in March 2011 with unemployment rates in March 2012, compute the first quartile, the median, and the third quartile for the March 2011 unemployment data and the March 2012 unemployment data. What do these statistics suggest about the change in unemployment rates across the states?

15. Martinez Auto Supplies has retail stores located in eight cities in California. The price they charge for a particular product in each city varies because of differing competitive conditions. For instance, the price they charge for a case of a popular brand of motor oil in each city follows. Also shown are the number of cases that Martinez Auto sold last quarter in each city.

City	Price ($)	Sales (cases)
Bakersfield	34.99	501
Los Angeles	38.99	1425
Modesto	36.00	294
Oakland	33.59	882
Sacramento	40.99	715
San Diego	38.59	1088
San Francisco	39.59	1644
San Jose	37.99	819

Compute the average sales price per case for this product during the last quarter.

16. The grade point average for college students is based on a weighted mean computation. For most colleges, the grades are given the following data values: A (4), B (3), C (2), D (1), and F (0). After 60 credit hours of course work, a student at State University earned 9 credit hours of A, 15 credit hours of B, 33 credit hours of C, and 3 credit hours of D.

    a. Compute the student's grade point average.
    b. Students at State University must maintain a 2.5 grade point average for their first 60 credit hours of course work in order to be admitted to the business college. Will this student be admitted?

17. The following table shows the total return and the number of funds for four categories of mutual funds.

Type of Fund	Number of Funds	Total Return (%)
Domestic Equity	9191	4.65
International Equity	2621	18.15
Specialty Stock	1419	11.36
Hybrid	2900	6.75

    a. Using the number of funds as weights, compute the weighted average total return for these mutual funds.

    b. Is there any difficulty associated with using the "number of funds" as the weights in computing the weighted average total return in part (a)? Discuss. What else might be used for weights?

    c. Suppose you invested $10,000 in this group of mutual funds and diversified the investment by placing $2000 in Domestic Equity funds, $4000 in International Equity funds, $3000 in Specialty Stock funds, and $1000 in Hybrid funds. What is the expected return on the portfolio?

18. Based on a survey of master's programs in business administration, magazines such as *U.S. News & World Report* rank U.S. business schools. These types of rankings are based in part on surveys of business school deans and corporate recruiters. Each survey respondent is asked to rate the overall academic quality of the master's program on a scale from 1 "marginal" to 5 "outstanding." Use the sample of responses shown below to compute the weighted mean score for the business school deans and the corporate recruiters. Discuss.

Quality Assessment	Business School Deans	Corporate Recruiters
5	44	31
4	66	34
3	60	43
2	10	12
1	0	0

19. Annual revenue for Corning Supplies grew by 5.5% in 2010, 1.1% in 2011, −3.5% in 2012, −1.1% in 2013, and 1.8% in 2014. What is the mean growth annual rate over this period?

20. Suppose that at the beginning of 2004 you invested $10,000 in the Stivers mutual fund and $5000 in the Trippi mutual fund. The value of each investment at the end of each subsequent year is provided in the table below. Which mutual fund performed better?

Year	Stivers	Trippi
2004	11,000	5,600
2005	12,000	6,300
2006	13,000	6,900
2007	14,000	7,600
2008	15,000	8,500
2009	16,000	9,200
2010	17,000	9,900
2011	18,000	10,600

21. If an asset declines in value from $5000 to $3500 over nine years, what is the mean annual growth rate in the asset's value over these nine years?

22. The current value of a company is $25 million. If the value of the company six year ago was $10 million, what is the company's mean annual growth rate over the past six years?

3.2 Measures of Variability

The variability in the delivery time creates uncertainty for production scheduling. Methods in this section help measure and understand variability.

In addition to measures of location, it is often desirable to consider measures of variability, or dispersion. For example, suppose that you are a purchasing agent for a large manufacturing firm and that you regularly place orders with two different suppliers. After several months of operation, you find that the mean number of days required to fill orders is 10 days for both of the suppliers. The histograms summarizing the number of working days required to fill orders from the suppliers are shown in Figure 3.2. Although the mean number of days is 10 for both suppliers, do the two suppliers demonstrate the same degree of reliability in terms of making deliveries on schedule? Note the dispersion, or variability, in delivery times indicated by the histograms. Which supplier would you prefer?

For most firms, receiving materials and supplies on schedule is important. The 7- or 8-day deliveries shown for J.C. Clark Distributors might be viewed favorably; however, a few of the slow 13- to 15-day deliveries could be disastrous in terms of keeping a workforce busy and production on schedule. This example illustrates a situation in which the variability in the delivery times may be an overriding consideration in selecting a supplier. For most purchasing agents, the lower variability shown for Dawson Supply, Inc., would make Dawson the preferred supplier.

We turn now to a discussion of some commonly used measures of variability.

Range

The simplest measure of variability is the **range**.

> RANGE
>
> $$\text{Range} = \text{Largest value} - \text{Smallest value}$$

Let us refer to the data on starting salaries for business school graduates in Table 3.1. The largest starting salary is 4325 and the smallest is 3710. The range is $4325 - 3710 = 615$.

FIGURE 3.2   HISTORICAL DATA SHOWING THE NUMBER OF DAYS REQUIRED TO FILL ORDERS

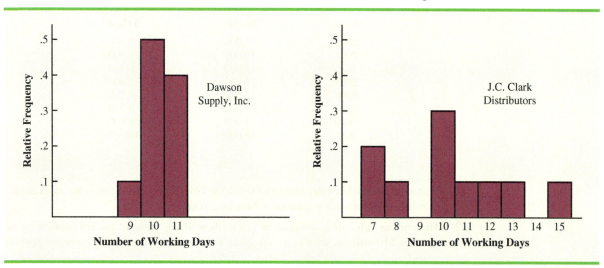

Although the range is the easiest of the measures of variability to compute, it is seldom used as the only measure. The reason is that the range is based on only two of the observations and thus is highly influenced by extreme values. Suppose the highest paid graduate received a starting salary of $10,000 per month. In this case, the range would be $10,000 - 3710 = 6290$ rather than 615. This large value for the range would not be especially descriptive of the variability in the data because 11 of the 12 starting salaries are closely grouped between 3710 and 4130.

Interquartile Range

A measure of variability that overcomes the dependency on extreme values is the **interquartile range (IQR)**. This measure of variability is the difference between the third quartile, Q_3, and the first quartile, Q_1. In other words, the interquartile range is the range for the middle 50% of the data.

> **INTERQUARTILE RANGE**
>
> $$IQR = Q_3 - Q_1 \tag{3.6}$$

For the data on monthly starting salaries, the quartiles are $Q_3 = 4000$ and $Q_1 = 3865$. Thus, the interquartile range is $4000 - 3865 = 135$.

Variance

The **variance** is a measure of variability that utilizes all the data. The variance is based on the difference between the value of each observation (x_i) and the mean. The difference between each x_i and the mean ($\bar{x}$ for a sample, μ for a population) is called a *deviation about the mean*. For a sample, a deviation about the mean is written ($x_i - \bar{x}$); for a population, it is written ($x_i - \mu$). In the computation of the variance, the deviations about the mean are *squared*.

If the data are for a population, the average of the squared deviations is called the *population variance*. The population variance is denoted by the Greek symbol σ^2. For a population of N observations and with μ denoting the population mean, the definition of the population variance is as follows.

> **POPULATION VARIANCE**
>
> $$\sigma^2 = \frac{\Sigma(x_i - \mu)^2}{N} \tag{3.7}$$

In most statistical applications, the data being analyzed are for a sample. When we compute a sample variance, we are often interested in using it to estimate the population variance σ^2. Although a detailed explanation is beyond the scope of this text, it can be shown that if the sum of the squared deviations about the sample mean is divided by $n - 1$, and not n, the resulting sample variance provides an unbiased estimate of the population variance. For this reason, the *sample variance,* denoted by s^2, is defined as follows.

The sample variance s^2 is a point estimator of the population variance σ^2.

> **SAMPLE VARIANCE**
>
> $$s^2 = \frac{\Sigma(x_i - \bar{x})^2}{n - 1} \tag{3.8}$$

TABLE 3.3   COMPUTATION OF DEVIATIONS AND SQUARED DEVIATIONS ABOUT
THE MEAN FOR THE CLASS SIZE DATA

Number of Students in Class (x_i)	Mean Class Size $(\bar{x})$	Deviation About the Mean $(x_i - \bar{x})$	Squared Deviation About the Mean $(x_i - \bar{x})^2$
46	44	2	4
54	44	10	100
42	44	−2	4
46	44	2	4
32	44	−12	144
		0	256
		$\Sigma(x_i - \bar{x})$	$\Sigma(x_i - \bar{x})^2$

To illustrate the computation of the sample variance, we will use the data on class size for the sample of five college classes as presented in Section 3.1. A summary of the data, including the computation of the deviations about the mean and the squared deviations about the mean, is shown in Table 3.3. The sum of squared deviations about the mean is $\Sigma(x_i - \bar{x})^2 = 256$. Hence, with $n - 1 = 4$, the sample variance is

$$s^2 = \frac{\Sigma(x_i - \bar{x})^2}{n - 1} = \frac{256}{4} = 64$$

Before moving on, let us note that the units associated with the sample variance often cause confusion. Because the values being summed in the variance calculation, $(x_i - \bar{x})^2$, are squared, the units associated with the sample variance are also *squared*. For instance, the sample variance for the class size data is $s^2 = 64$ (students)^2. The squared units associated with variance make it difficult to develop an intuitive understanding and interpretation of the numerical value of the variance. We recommend that you think of the variance as a measure useful in comparing the amount of variability for two or more variables. In a comparison of the variables, the one with the largest variance shows the most variability. Further interpretation of the value of the variance may not be necessary.

The variance is useful in comparing the variability of two or more variables.

As another illustration of computing a sample variance, consider the starting salaries listed in Table 3.1 for the 12 business school graduates. In Section 3.1, we showed that the sample mean starting salary was 3940. The computation of the sample variance ($s^2 = 27{,}440.91$) is shown in Table 3.4.

In Tables 3.3 and 3.4 we show both the sum of the deviations about the mean and the sum of the squared deviations about the mean. For any data set, the sum of the deviations about the mean will *always equal zero*. Note that in Tables 3.3 and 3.4, $\Sigma(x_i - \bar{x}) = 0$. The positive deviations and negative deviations cancel each other, causing the sum of the deviations about the mean to equal zero.

Standard Deviation

The **standard deviation** is defined to be the positive square root of the variance. Following the notation we adopted for a sample variance and a population variance, we use s to denote the sample standard deviation and σ to denote the population standard deviation. The standard deviation is derived from the variance in the following way.

TABLE 3.4 COMPUTATION OF THE SAMPLE VARIANCE FOR THE STARTING SALARY DATA

Monthly Salary (x_i)	Sample Mean ($\bar{x}$)	Deviation About the Mean ($x_i - \bar{x}$)	Squared Deviation About the Mean ($(x_i - \bar{x})^2$)
3850	3940	−90	8100
3950	3940	10	100
4050	3940	110	12,100
3880	3940	−60	3600
3755	3940	−185	34,225
3710	3940	−230	52,900
3890	3940	−50	2500
4130	3940	190	36,100
3940	3940	0	0
4325	3940	385	148,225
3920	3940	−20	400
3880	3940	−60	3600
		0	301,850
		$\Sigma(x_i - \bar{x})$	$\Sigma(x_i - \bar{x})^2$

Using equation (3.8),

$$s^2 = \frac{\Sigma(x_i - \bar{x})^2}{n - 1} = \frac{301,850}{11} = 27,440.91$$

The sample standard deviation s is a point estimator of the population standard deviation σ.

STANDARD DEVIATION

$$\text{Sample standard deviation} = s = \sqrt{s^2} \qquad (3.9)$$

$$\text{Population standard deviation} = \sigma = \sqrt{\sigma^2} \qquad (3.10)$$

Recall that the sample variance for the sample of class sizes in five college classes is $s^2 = 64$. Thus, the sample standard deviation is $s = \sqrt{64} = 8$. For the data on starting salaries, the sample standard deviation is $s = \sqrt{27,440.91} = 165.65$.

The standard deviation is easier to interpret than the variance because the standard deviation is measured in the same units as the data.

What is gained by converting the variance to its corresponding standard deviation? Recall that the units associated with the variance are squared. For example, the sample variance for the starting salary data of business school graduates is $s^2 = 27,440.91$ (dollars)^2. Because the standard deviation is the square root of the variance, the units of the variance, dollars squared, are converted to dollars in the standard deviation. Thus, the standard deviation of the starting salary data is $165.65. In other words, the standard deviation is measured in the same units as the original data. For this reason the standard deviation is more easily compared to the mean and other statistics that are measured in the same units as the original data.

Coefficient of Variation

The coefficient of variation is a relative measure of variability; it measures the standard deviation relative to the mean.

In some situations we may be interested in a descriptive statistic that indicates how large the standard deviation is relative to the mean. This measure is called the **coefficient of variation** and is usually expressed as a percentage.

COEFFICIENT OF VARIATION

$$\left(\frac{\text{Standard deviation}}{\text{Mean}} \times 100 \right)\% \qquad (3.11)$$

For the class size data, we found a sample mean of 44 and a sample standard deviation of 8. The coefficient of variation is $[(8/44) \times 100]\% = 18.2\%$. In words, the coefficient of variation tells us that the sample standard deviation is 18.2% of the value of the sample mean. For the starting salary data with a sample mean of 3940 and a sample standard deviation of 165.65, the coefficient of variation, $[(165.65/3940) \times 100]\% = 4.2\%$, tells us the sample standard deviation is only 4.2% of the value of the sample mean. In general, the coefficient of variation is a useful statistic for comparing the variability of variables that have different standard deviations and different means.

NOTES AND COMMENTS

1. Statistical software packages and spreadsheets can be used to develop the descriptive statistics presented in this chapter. After the data are entered into a worksheet, a few simple commands can be used to generate the desired output. In two chapter-ending appendixes we show how Minitab and Excel can be used to develop descriptive statistics.

2. The standard deviation is a commonly used measure of the risk associated with investing in stock and stock funds (*Morningstar* website, July 21, 2012). It provides a measure of how monthly returns fluctuate around the long-run average return.

3. Rounding the value of the sample mean $\bar{x}$ and the values of the squared deviations $(x_i - \bar{x})^2$ may introduce errors when a calculator is used in the computation of the variance and standard deviation. To reduce rounding errors, we recommend carrying at least six significant digits during intermediate calculations. The resulting variance or standard deviation can then be rounded to fewer digits.

4. An alternative formula for the computation of the sample variance is

$$s^2 = \frac{\sum x_i^2 - n\bar{x}^2}{n - 1}$$

where $\sum x_i^2 = x_1^2 + x_2^2 + \cdots + x_n^2$.

5. The mean absolute error (MAE) is another measure of variability that is computed by summing the absolute values of the deviations of the observations about the mean and dividing this sum by the number of observations. For a sample of size n, the MAE is computed as follows:

$$\text{MAE} = \frac{\sum |x_i - \bar{x}|}{n}$$

For the class size data presented in Section 3.1, $\bar{x} = 44$, $\sum |x_i - \bar{x}| = 28$, and the MAE $= 28/5 = 5.6$. You can learn more about the MAE and other measures of variability in Chapter 17.

Exercises

Methods

23. Consider a sample with data values of 10, 20, 12, 17, and 16. Compute the range and interquartile range.

24. Consider a sample with data values of 10, 20, 12, 17, and 16. Compute the variance and standard deviation.

 25. Consider a sample with data values of 27, 25, 20, 15, 30, 34, 28, and 25. Compute the range, interquartile range, variance, and standard deviation.

Applications

 26. Data collected by the Oil Price Information Service from more than 90,000 gasoline and convenience stores throughout the U.S. showed that the average price for a gallon of unleaded gasoline was $3.28 (MSN Auto website, February 2, 2014). The following data show the price per gallon ($) for a sample of 20 gasoline and convenience stores located in San Francisco.

3.59	3.59	4.79	3.56	3.55	3.71	3.65	3.60	3.75	3.56
3.57	3.59	3.55	3.99	4.15	3.66	3.63	3.73	3.61	3.57

a. Use the sample data to estimate the mean price for a gallon of unleaded gasoline in San Francisco.

b. Compute the sample standard deviation.

c. Compare the mean price per gallon for the sample data to the national average price. What conclusions can you draw about the cost living in San Francisco?

27. The results of a search to find the least expensive round-trip flights to Atlanta and Salt Lake City from 14 major U.S. cities are shown in the following table. The departure date was June 20, 2012, and the return date was June 27, 2012.

Flights

Departure City	Round-Trip Cost ($)	
	Atlanta	Salt Lake City
Cincinnati	340.10	570.10
New York	321.60	354.60
Chicago	291.60	465.60
Denver	339.60	219.60
Los Angeles	359.60	311.60
Seattle	384.60	297.60
Detroit	309.60	471.60
Philadelphia	415.60	618.40
Washington, D.C.	293.60	513.60
Miami	249.60	523.20
San Francisco	539.60	381.60
Las Vegas	455.60	159.60
Phoenix	359.60	267.60
Dallas	333.90	458.60

a. Compute the mean price for a round-trip flight into Atlanta and the mean price for a round-trip flight into Salt Lake City. Is Atlanta less expensive to fly into than Salt Lake City? If so, what could explain this difference?

b. Compute the range, variance, and standard deviation for the two samples. What does this information tell you about the prices for flights into these two cities?

28. The Australian Open is the first of the four Grand Slam professional tennis events held each year. Victoria Azarenka beat Maria Sharapova to win the 2012 Australian Open women's title (*Washington Post,* January 27, 2012). During the tournament Ms. Azarenka's serve speed reached 178 kilometers per hour. A list of the 20 Women's Singles serve speed leaders for the 2012 Australian Open is provided below.

AustralianOpen

Player	Serve Speed (km/h)	Player	Serve Speed (km/h)
S. Williams	191	G. Arn	179
S. Lisicki	190	V. Azarenka	178
M. Keys	187	A. Ivanovic	178
L. Hradecka	187	P. Kvitova	178
J. Gajdosova	187	M. Krajicek	178
J. Hampton	181	V. Dushevina	178
B. Mattek-Sands	181	S. Stosur	178
F. Schiavone	179	S. Cirstea	177
P. Parmentier	179	M. Barthel	177
N. Petrova	179	P. Ormaechea	177

a. Compute the mean, variance, and standard deviation for the serve speeds.

b. A similar sample of the 20 Women's Singles serve speed leaders for the 2011 Wimbledon tournament showed a sample mean serve speed of 182.5 kilometers per hour. The variance and standard deviation were 33.3 and 5.77, respectively. Discuss any difference between the serve speeds in the Australian Open and the Wimbledon women's tournaments.

29. The *Los Angeles Times* regularly reports the air quality index for various areas of Southern California. A sample of air quality index values for Pomona provided the following data: 28, 42, 58, 48, 45, 55, 60, 49, and 50.
    a. Compute the range and interquartile range.
    b. Compute the sample variance and sample standard deviation.
    c. A sample of air quality index readings for Anaheim provided a sample mean of 48.5, a sample variance of 136, and a sample standard deviation of 11.66. What comparisons can you make between the air quality in Pomona and that in Anaheim on the basis of these descriptive statistics?

30. The following data were used to construct the histograms of the number of days required to fill orders for Dawson Supply, Inc., and J.C. Clark Distributors (see Figure 3.2).

Dawson Supply Days for Delivery: 11   10   9   10   11   11   10   11   10   10
Clark Distributors Days for Delivery: 8   10   13   7   10   11   10   7   15   12

Use the range and standard deviation to support the previous observation that Dawson Supply provides the more consistent and reliable delivery times.

31. The results of Accounting Principals' latest Workonomix survey indicate the average American worker spends $1092 on coffee annually (*The Consumerist,* January 20, 2012). To determine if there are any differences in coffee expenditures by age group, samples of 10 consumers were selected for three age groups (18–34, 35–44, and 45 and Older). The dollar amount each consumer in the sample spent last year on coffee is provided below.

18–34	35–44	45 and Older
1355	969	1135
115	434	956
1456	1792	400
2045	1500	1374
1621	1277	1244
994	1056	825
1937	1922	763
1200	1350	1192
1567	1586	1305
1390	1415	1510

Coffee

a. Compute the mean, variance, and standard deviation for the each of these three samples.
b. What observations can be made based on these data?

Advertising

32. *Advertising Age* annually compiles a list of the 100 companies that spend the most on advertising. Consumer-goods company Procter & Gamble has often topped the list, spending billions of dollars annually (*Advertising Age* website, March 12, 2013). Consider the data found in the file Advertising. It contains annual advertising expenditures for a sample of 20 companies in the automotive sector and 20 companies in the department store sector.
    a. What is the mean advertising spent for each sector?
    b. What is the standard deviation for each sector?
    c. What is the range of advertising spent for each sector?
    d. What is the interquartile range for each sector?
    e. Based on this sample and your answers to parts (a) to (d), comment on any differences in the advertising spending in the automotive companies versus the department store companies.

33. Scores turned in by an amateur golfer at the Bonita Fairways Golf Course in Bonita Springs, Florida, during 2011 and 2012 are as follows:

2011 Season: 74   78   79   77   75   73   75   77
2012 Season: 71   70   75   77   85   80   71   79

a. Use the mean and standard deviation to evaluate the golfer's performance over the two-year period.

b. What is the primary difference in performance between 2011 and 2012? What improvement, if any, can be seen in the 2012 scores?

34. The following times were recorded by the quarter-mile and mile runners of a university track team (times are in minutes).

Quarter-Mile Times:	.92	.98	1.04	.90	.99
Mile Times:	4.52	4.35	4.60	4.70	4.50

After viewing this sample of running times, one of the coaches commented that the quarter-milers turned in the more consistent times. Use the standard deviation and the coefficient of variation to summarize the variability in the data. Does the use of the coefficient of variation indicate that the coach's statement should be qualified?

3.3 Measures of Distribution Shape, Relative Location, and Detecting Outliers

We have described several measures of location and variability for data. In addition, it is often important to have a measure of the shape of a distribution. In Chapter 2 we noted that a histogram provides a graphical display showing the shape of a distribution. An important numerical measure of the shape of a distribution is called **skewness**.

Distribution Shape

Figure 3.3 shows four histograms constructed from relative frequency distributions. The histograms in Panels A and B are moderately skewed. The one in Panel A is skewed to the left; its skewness is $-.85$. The histogram in Panel B is skewed to the right; its skewness is $+.85$. The histogram in Panel C is symmetric; its skewness is zero. The histogram in Panel D is highly skewed to the right; its skewness is 1.62. The formula used to compute skewness is somewhat complex.[1] However, the skewness can easily be computed using statistical software. For data skewed to the left, the skewness is negative; for data skewed to the right, the skewness is positive. If the data are symmetric, the skewness is zero.

For a symmetric distribution, the mean and the median are equal. When the data are positively skewed, the mean will usually be greater than the median; when the data are negatively skewed, the mean will usually be less than the median. The data used to construct the histogram in Panel D are customer purchases at a women's apparel store. The mean purchase amount is $77.60 and the median purchase amount is $59.70. The relatively few large purchase amounts tend to increase the mean, while the median remains unaffected by the large purchase amounts. The median provides the preferred measure of location when the data are highly skewed.

z-Scores

In addition to measures of location, variability, and shape, we are also interested in the relative location of values within a data set. Measures of relative location help us determine how far a particular value is from the mean.

---

[1]The formula for the skewness of sample data:

$$\text{Skewness} = \frac{n}{(n-1)(n-2)} \sum \left(\frac{x_i - \bar{x}}{s} \right)^3$$

FIGURE 3.3   HISTOGRAMS SHOWING THE SKEWNESS FOR FOUR DISTRIBUTIONS

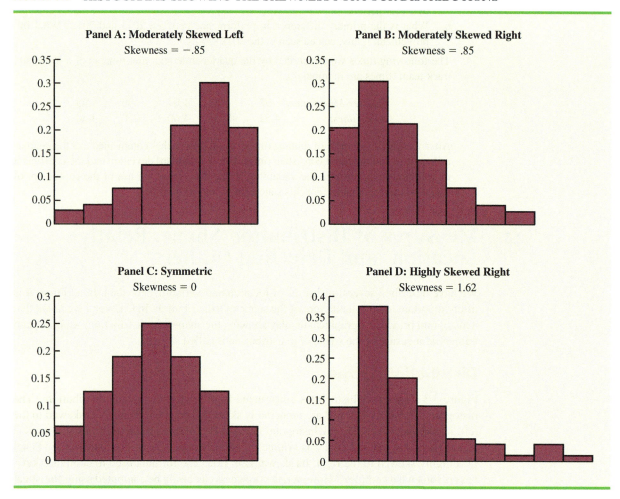

By using both the mean and standard deviation, we can determine the relative location of any observation. Suppose we have a sample of n observations, with the values denoted by $x_1, x_2, \ldots, x_n$. In addition, assume that the sample mean, $\bar{x}$, and the sample standard deviation, s, are already computed. Associated with each value, x_i, is another value called its **z-score**. Equation (3.12) shows how the z-score is computed for each x_i.

z-SCORE

$$z_i = \frac{x_i - \bar{x}}{s}$$
(3.12)

where

z_i = the z-score for x_i
$\bar{x}$ = the sample mean
s = the sample standard deviation

TABLE 3.5 z-SCORES FOR THE CLASS SIZE DATA

Number of Students in Class (x_i)	Deviation About the Mean ($x_i - \bar{x}$)	z-Score $\left(\dfrac{x_i - \bar{x}}{s}\right)$
46	2	2/8 = .25
54	10	10/8 = 1.25
42	−2	−2/8 = −.25
46	2	2/8 = .25
32	−12	−12/8 = −1.50

The z-score is often called the *standardized value*. The z-score, z_i, can be interpreted as the *number of standard deviations x_i is from the mean $\bar{x}$*. For example, $z_1 = 1.2$ would indicate that x_1 is 1.2 standard deviations greater than the sample mean. Similarly, $z_2 = -.5$ would indicate that x_2 is .5, or 1/2, standard deviation less than the sample mean. A z-score greater than zero occurs for observations with a value greater than the mean, and a z-score less than zero occurs for observations with a value less than the mean. A z-score of zero indicates that the value of the observation is equal to the mean.

The z-score for any observation can be interpreted as a measure of the relative location of the observation in a data set. Thus, observations in two different data sets with the same z-score can be said to have the same relative location in terms of being the same number of standard deviations from the mean.

The process of converting a value for a variable to a z-score is often referred to as a z transformation.

The z-scores for the class size data from Section 3.1 are computed in Table 3.5. Recall the previously computed sample mean, $\bar{x} = 44$, and sample standard deviation, $s = 8$. The z-score of -1.50 for the fifth observation shows it is farthest from the mean; it is 1.50 standard deviations below the mean. Figure 3.4 provides a dot plot of the class size data with a graphical representation of the associated z-scores on the axis below.

Chebyshev's Theorem

Chebyshev's theorem enables us to make statements about the proportion of data values that must be within a specified number of standard deviations of the mean.

FIGURE 3.4   DOT PLOT SHOWING CLASS SIZE DATA AND z-SCORES

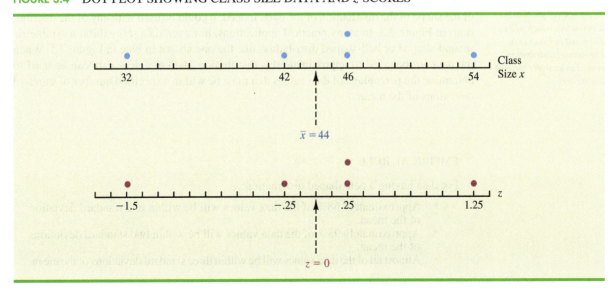

CHEBYSHEV'S THEOREM

At least $(1 - 1/z^2)$ of the data values must be within z standard deviations of the mean, where z is any value greater than 1.

Some of the implications of this theorem, with $z = 2, 3,$ and 4 standard deviations, follow.

- At least .75, or 75%, of the data values must be within $z = 2$ standard deviations of the mean.
- At least .89, or 89%, of the data values must be within $z = 3$ standard deviations of the mean.
- At least .94, or 94%, of the data values must be within $z = 4$ standard deviations of the mean.

For an example using Chebyshev's theorem, suppose that the midterm test scores for 100 students in a college business statistics course had a mean of 70 and a standard deviation of 5. How many students had test scores between 60 and 80? How many students had test scores between 58 and 82?

For the test scores between 60 and 80, we note that 60 is two standard deviations below the mean and 80 is two standard deviations above the mean. Using Chebyshev's theorem, we see that at least .75, or at least 75%, of the observations must have values within two standard deviations of the mean. Thus, at least 75% of the students must have scored between 60 and 80.

Chebyshev's theorem requires $z > 1$; but z need not be an integer.

For the test scores between 58 and 82, we see that $(58 - 70)/5 = -2.4$ indicates 58 is 2.4 standard deviations below the mean and that $(82 - 70)/5 = +2.4$ indicates 82 is 2.4 standard deviations above the mean. Applying Chebyshev's theorem with $z = 2.4$, we have

$$\left(1 - \frac{1}{z^2}\right) = \left(1 - \frac{1}{(2.4)^2}\right) = .826$$

At least 82.6% of the students must have test scores between 58 and 82.

Empirical Rule

The empirical rule is based on the normal probability distribution, which will be discussed in Chapter 6. The normal distribution is used extensively throughout the text.

One of the advantages of Chebyshev's theorem is that it applies to any data set regardless of the shape of the distribution of the data. Indeed, it could be used with any of the distributions in Figure 3.3. In many practical applications, however, data sets exhibit a symmetric mound-shaped or bell-shaped distribution like the one shown in blue in Figure 3.5. When the data are believed to approximate this distribution, the **empirical rule** can be used to determine the percentage of data values that must be within a specified number of standard deviations of the mean.

EMPIRICAL RULE

For data having a bell-shaped distribution:

- Approximately 68% of the data values will be within one standard deviation of the mean.
- Approximately 95% of the data values will be within two standard deviations of the mean.
- Almost all of the data values will be within three standard deviations of the mean.

FIGURE 3.5 A BELL-SHAPED DISTRIBUTION OF DETERGENT CARTON WEIGHTS WITH PERCENTAGE OF DATA VALUES WITHIN 1, 2, AND 3 STANDARD DEVIATIONS

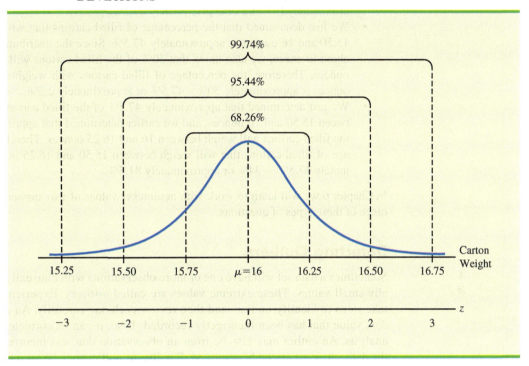

For example, liquid detergent cartons are filled automatically on a production line. Filling weights frequently have a bell-shaped distribution. If the mean filling weight is 16 ounces and the standard deviation is .25 ounces, we can use the empirical rule to draw the following conclusions.

- Approximately 68% of the filled cartons will have weights between 15.75 and 16.25 ounces (within one standard deviation of the mean).
- Approximately 95% of the filled cartons will have weights between 15.50 and 16.50 ounces (within two standard deviations of the mean).
- Almost all filled cartons will have weights between 15.25 and 16.75 ounces (within three standard deviations of the mean).

Use Figure 3.5 to help you answer these four questions.

Can we use this information to say anything about how many filled cartons will:

- weigh between 16 and 16.25 ounces?
- weigh between 15.50 and 16 ounces?
- weigh less than 15.50 ounces?
- weigh between 15.50 and 16.25 ounces?

If we recognize that the normal distribution is symmetric about its mean, we can answer each of the questions in the previous list, and we will be able to determine the following:

- Since the percentage of filled cartons that will weigh between 15.75 and 16.25 is approximately 68% and the mean 16 is at the midpoint between 15.75 and 16.25, the percentage of filled cartons that will weigh between 16 and 16.25 ounces is approximately (68%)/2 or approximately 34%.

- Since the percentage of filled cartons that will weigh between 15.50 and 16.50 is approximately 95% and the mean 16 is at the midpoint between 15.50 and 16.50, the percentage of filled cartons that will weigh between 15.50 and 16 ounces is approximately (95%)/2 or approximately 47.5%.
- We just determined that the percentage of filled cartons that will weigh between 15.50 and 16 ounces is approximately 47.5%. Since the distribution is symmetric about its mean, we also know that 50% of the filled cartons will weigh below 16 ounces. Therefore, the percentage of filled cartons with weights less than 15.50 ounces is approximately 50% – 47.5% or approximately 2.5%.
- We just determined that approximately 47.5% of the filled cartons will weigh between 15.50 and 16 ounces, and we earlier determined that approximately 34% of the filled cartons will weigh between 16 and 16.25 ounces. Therefore, the percentage of filled cartons that will weigh between 15.50 and 16.25 ounces is approximately 47.5% + 34% or approximately 81.5%.

In Chapter 6 we will learn to work with noninteger values of z to answer a much broader range of these types of questions.

Detecting Outliers

Sometimes a data set will have one or more observations with unusually large or unusually small values. These extreme values are called **outliers**. Experienced statisticians take steps to identify outliers and then review each one carefully. An outlier may be a data value that has been incorrectly recorded. If so, it can be corrected before further analysis. An outlier may also be from an observation that was incorrectly included in the data set; if so, it can be removed. Finally, an outlier may be an unusual data value that has been recorded correctly and belongs in the data set. In such cases it should remain.

It is a good idea to check for outliers before making decisions based on data analysis. Errors are often made in recording data and entering data into the computer. Outliers should not necessarily be deleted, but their accuracy and appropriateness should be verified.

Standardized values (z-scores) can be used to identify outliers. Recall that the empirical rule allows us to conclude that for data with a bell-shaped distribution, almost all the data values will be within three standard deviations of the mean. Hence, in using z-scores to identify outliers, we recommend treating any data value with a z-score less than -3 or greater than $+3$ as an outlier. Such data values can then be reviewed for accuracy and to determine whether they belong in the data set.

Refer to the z-scores for the class size data in Table 3.5. The z-score of -1.50 shows the fifth class size is farthest from the mean. However, this standardized value is well within the -3 to $+3$ guideline for outliers. Thus, the z-scores do not indicate that outliers are present in the class size data.

Another approach to identifying outliers is based upon the values of the first and third quartiles (Q_1 and Q_3) and the interquartile range (IQR). Using this method, we first compute the following lower and upper limits:

$$\text{Lower Limit} = Q_1 - 1.5(\text{IQR})$$
$$\text{Upper Limit} = Q_3 + 1.5(\text{IQR})$$

The approach that uses the first and third quartiles and the IQR to identify outliers does not necessarily provide the same results as the approach based upon a z-score less than -3 or greater than $+3$. Either or both procedures may be used.

An observation is classified as an outlier if its value is less than the lower limit or greater than the upper limit. For the monthly starting salary data shown in Table 3.1, $Q_1 = 3857.5$, $Q_3 = 4025$, IQR $= 167.5$, and the lower and upper limits are

$$\text{Lower Limit} = Q_1 - 1.5(\text{IQR}) = 3857.5 - 1.5(167.5) = 3606.25$$
$$\text{Upper Limit} = Q_3 + 1.5(\text{IQR}) = 4025 + 1.5(167.5) = 4276.25$$

Looking at the data in Table 3.1, we see that there are no observations with a starting salary less than the lower limit of 3606.25. But, there is one starting salary, 4325, that is greater than the upper limit of 4276.25. Thus, 4325 is considered to be an outlier using this alternate approach to identifying outliers.

NOTES AND COMMENTS

1. Chebyshev's theorem is applicable for any data set and can be used to state the minimum number of data values that will be within a certain number of standard deviations of the mean. If the data are known to be approximately bell-shaped, more can be said. For instance, the empirical rule allows us to say that *approximately* 95% of the data values will be within two standard deviations of the mean; Chebyshev's theorem allows us to conclude only that at least 75% of the data values will be in that interval.

2. Before analyzing a data set, statisticians usually make a variety of checks to ensure the validity of data. In a large study it is not uncommon for errors to be made in recording data values or in entering the values into a computer. Identifying outliers is one tool used to check the validity of the data.

Exercises

Methods

35. Consider a sample with data values of 10, 20, 12, 17, and 16. Compute the z-score for each of the five observations.

36. Consider a sample with a mean of 500 and a standard deviation of 100. What are the z-scores for the following data values: 520, 650, 500, 450, and 280?

 37. Consider a sample with a mean of 30 and a standard deviation of 5. Use Chebyshev's theorem to determine the percentage of the data within each of the following ranges:
   a.   20 to 40
   b.   15 to 45
   c.   22 to 38
   d.   18 to 42
   e.   12 to 48

38. Suppose the data have a bell-shaped distribution with a mean of 30 and a standard deviation of 5. Use the empirical rule to determine the percentage of data within each of the following ranges:
   a.   20 to 40
   b.   15 to 45
   c.   25 to 35

Applications

 39. The results of a national survey showed that on average, adults sleep 6.9 hours per night. Suppose that the standard deviation is 1.2 hours.
   a.   Use Chebyshev's theorem to calculate the percentage of individuals who sleep between 4.5 and 9.3 hours.
   b.   Use Chebyshev's theorem to calculate the percentage of individuals who sleep between 3.9 and 9.9 hours.

    c. Assume that the number of hours of sleep follows a bell-shaped distribution. Use the empirical rule to calculate the percentage of individuals who sleep between 4.5 and 9.3 hours per day. How does this result compare to the value that you obtained using Chebyshev's theorem in part (a)?

40. The Energy Information Administration reported that the mean retail price per gallon of regular grade gasoline was \$3.43 (Energy Information Administration, July 2012). Suppose that the standard deviation was \$.10 and that the retail price per gallon has a bell-shaped distribution.
    a. What percentage of regular grade gasoline sold between \$3.33 and \$3.53 per gallon?
    b. What percentage of regular grade gasoline sold between \$3.33 and \$3.63 per gallon?
    c. What percentage of regular grade gasoline sold for more than \$3.63 per gallon?

41. The Graduate Management Admission Test (GMAT) is a standardized exam used by many universities as part of the assessment for admission to graduate study in business. The average GMAT score is 547 (*Magoosh* website, January 5, 2015). Assume that GMAT scores are bell-shaped with a standard deviation of 100.
    a. What percentage of GMAT scores are 647 or higher?
    b. What percentage of GMAT scores are 747 or higher?
    c. What percentage of GMAT scores are between 447 and 547?
    d. What percentage of GMAT scores are between 347 and 647?

42. Many families in California are using backyard structures for home offices, art studios, and hobby areas as well as for additional storage. Suppose that the mean price for a customized wooden, shingled backyard structure is \$3100. Assume that the standard deviation is \$1200.
    a. What is the z-score for a backyard structure costing \$2300?
    b. What is the z-score for a backyard structure costing \$4900?
    c. Interpret the z-scores in parts (a) and (b). Comment on whether either should be considered an outlier.
    d. If the cost for a backyard shed-office combination built in Albany, California, is \$13,000, should this structure be considered an outlier? Explain.

43. According to a *Los Angeles Times* study of more than 1 million medical dispatches from 2007 to 2012, the 911 response time for medical aid varies dramatically across Los Angeles (*LA Times* website, November 2012). Under national standards adopted by the Los Angeles Fire Department, rescuers are supposed to arrive within six minutes to almost all medical emergencies. But the *Times* analysis found that in affluent hillside communities stretching from Griffith Park to Pacific Palisades, firefighters failed to hit that mark nearly 85% of the time.

    The following data show the response times, in minutes, for 10 emergency calls in the Griffith Park neighborhood.

11.8	10.3	10.7	10.6	11.5	8.3	10.5	10.9	10.7	11.2

    Based on this sample of ten response times, compute the descriptive statistics in parts (a) and (b) and then answer the questions in parts (c) and (d):
    a. Mean, median, and mode
    b. Range and standard deviation
    c. Should the response time of 8.3 minutes be considered an outlier in comparison to the other response times?
    d. Do the response times indicate that the city is meeting the national standards? Should the city consider making changes to its response strategies? Would adding more stations to areas in the city be a practical solution? Discuss.

44. A sample of 10 NCAA college basketball game scores provided the following data.

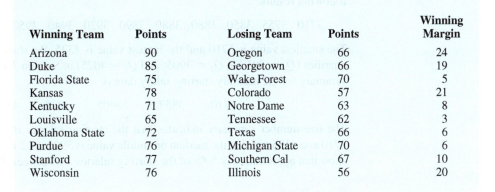

Winning Team	Points	Losing Team	Points	Winning Margin
Arizona	90	Oregon	66	24
Duke	85	Georgetown	66	19
Florida State	75	Wake Forest	70	5
Kansas	78	Colorado	57	21
Kentucky	71	Notre Dame	63	8
Louisville	65	Tennessee	62	3
Oklahoma State	72	Texas	66	6
Purdue	76	Michigan State	70	6
Stanford	77	Southern Cal	67	10
Wisconsin	76	Illinois	56	20

a. Compute the mean and standard deviation for the points scored by the winning team.
b. Assume that the points scored by the winning teams for all NCAA games follow a bell-shaped distribution. Using the mean and standard deviation found in part (a), estimate the percentage of all NCAA games in which the winning team scores 84 or more points. Estimate the percentage of NCAA games in which the winning team scores more than 90 points.
c. Compute the mean and standard deviation for the winning margin. Do the data contain outliers? Explain.

45. *The Wall Street Journal* reported that Walmart Stores Inc. is planning to lay off 2300 employees at its Sam's Club warehouse unit. Approximately half of the layoffs will be hourly employees (*The Wall Street Journal*, January 25–26, 2014). Suppose the following data represent the percentage of hourly employees laid off for 15 Sam's Club stores.

55   56   44   43   44   56   60   62   57   45   36   38   50   69   65

a. Compute the mean and median percentage of hourly employees being laid off at these stores.
b. Compute the first and third quartiles.
c. Compute the range and interquartile range.
d. Compute the variance and standard deviation.
e. Do the data contain any outliers?
f. Based on the sample data, does it appear that Walmart is meeting its goal for reducing the number of hourly employees?

Five-Number Summaries and Box Plots

Summary statistics and easy-to-draw graphs based on summary statistics can be used to quickly summarize large quantities of data. In this section we show how five-number summaries and box plots can be developed to identify several characteristics of a data set.

Five-Number Summary

In a **five-number summary**, five numbers are used to summarize the data:

1. Smallest value
2. First quartile (Q_1)
3. Median (Q_2)
4. Third quartile (Q_3)
5. Largest value

To illustrate the development of a five-number summary, we will use the monthly starting salary data shown in Table 3.1. Arranging the data in ascending order, we obtain the following results.

3710 3755 3850 3880 3880 3890 3920 3940 3950 4050 4130 4325

The smallest value is 3710 and the largest value is 4325. We showed how to compute the quartiles ($Q_1 = 3857.5$; $Q_2 = 3905$; and $Q_3 = 4025$) in Section 3.1. Thus, the five-number summary for the monthly starting salary data is

3710   3857.5   3905   4025   4325

The five-number summary indicates that the starting salaries in the sample are between 3710 and 4325 and that the median or middle value is 3905; and, the first and third quartiles show that approximately 50% of the starting salaries are between 3857.5 and 4025.

Box Plot

A box plot is a graphical display of data based on a five-number summary. A key to the development of a box plot is the computation of the interquartile range, $\text{IQR} = Q_3 - Q_1$. Figure 3.6 shows a box plot for the monthly starting salary data. The steps used to construct the box plot follow.

1. A box is drawn with the ends of the box located at the first and third quartiles. For the salary data, $Q_1 = 3857.5$ and $Q_2 = 4025$. This box contains the middle 50% of the data.
2. A vertical line is drawn in the box at the location of the median (3905 for the salary data).

Box plots provide another way to identify outliers. But they do not necessarily identify the same values as those with a z-score less than –3 or greater than +3. Either or both procedures may be used.

3. By using the interquartile range, $\text{IQR} = Q_3 - Q_1$, *limits* are located at 1.5(IQR) below Q_1 and 1.5(IQR) above Q_3. For the salary data, $\text{IQR} = Q_3 - Q_1 = 4025 - 3857.5 = 167.5$. Thus, the limits are $3857.5 - 1.5(167.5) = 3606.25$ and $4025 + 1.5(167.5) = 4276.25$. Data outside these limits are considered *outliers*.
4. The horizontal lines extending from each end of the box in Figure 3.6 are called *whiskers*. The whiskers are drawn from the ends of the box to the smallest and largest values *inside* the *limits* computed in step 3. Thus, the whiskers end at salary values of 3710 and 4130.
5. Finally, the location of each outlier is shown with a small asterisk. In Figure 3.6 we see one outlier, 4325.

FIGURE 3.6   BOX PLOT OF THE MONTHLY STARTING SALARY DATA WITH LINES SHOWING THE LOWER AND UPPER LIMITS

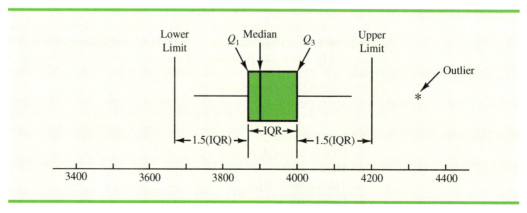

FIGURE 3.7 BOX PLOT OF THE MONTHLY STARTING SALARY DATA

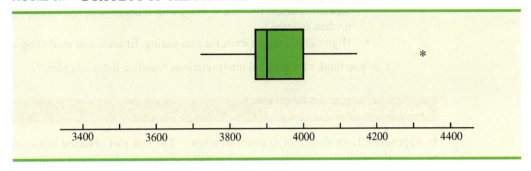

In Figure 3.6 we included lines showing the location of the upper and lower limits. These lines were drawn to show how the limits are computed and where they are located. Although the limits are always computed, generally they are not drawn on the box plots. Figure 3.7 shows the usual appearance of a box plot for the starting salary data.

Comparative Analysis Using Box Plots

Box plots can also be used to provide a graphical summary of two or more groups and facilitate visual comparisons among the groups. For example, suppose the placement office decided to conduct a follow-up study to compare monthly starting salaries by the graduate's major: accounting, finance, information systems, management, and marketing. The major and starting salary data for a new sample of 111 recent business school graduates are shown in the data set named 2012MajorSalary, and Figure 3.8 shows the box plots corresponding to each major. Note that major is shown on the horizontal axis, and each box plot is shown vertically above the corresponding major. Displaying box plots in this manner is an excellent graphical technique for making comparisons among two or more groups.

DATA *file*

2012MajorSalary

What interpretations can you make from the box plots in Figure 3.8? Specifically, we note the following:

- The higher salaries are in accounting; the lower salaries are in management and marketing.

FIGURE 3.8 MINITAB BOX PLOTS OF MONTHLY STARTING SALARY BY MAJOR

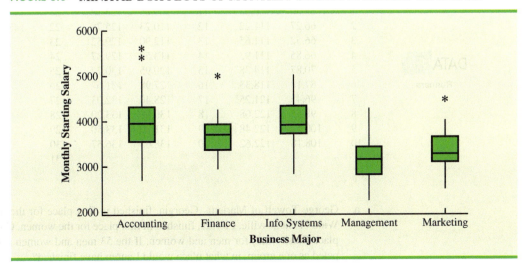

- Based on the medians, accounting and information systems have similar and higher median salaries. Finance is next, with management and marketing showing lower median salaries.
- High salary outliers exist for accounting, finance, and marketing majors.

Can you think of additional interpretations based on these box plots?

NOTES AND COMMENTS

In Appendix 3.1, we show how to construct a box plot for the starting salary data using Minitab. The box plot obtained looks just like the one in Figure 3.7, but turned on its side.

Exercises

Methods

46. Consider a sample with data values of 27, 25, 20, 15, 30, 34, 28, and 25. Provide the five-number summary for the data.

47. Show the box plot for the data in exercise 46.

 SELF*test* 48. Show the five-number summary and the box plot for the following data: 5, 15, 18, 10, 8, 12, 16, 10, 6.

49. A data set has a first quartile of 42 and a third quartile of 50. Compute the lower and upper limits for the corresponding box plot. Should a data value of 65 be considered an outlier?

Applications

50. Naples, Florida, hosts a half-marathon (13.1-mile race) in January each year. The event attracts top runners from throughout the United States as well as from around the world. In January 2009, 22 men and 31 women entered the 19–24 age class. Finish times in minutes are as follows (*Naples Daily News,* January 19, 2009). Times are shown in order of finish.

DATA *file*

Runners

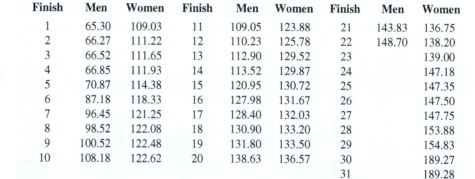

Finish	Men	Women	Finish	Men	Women	Finish	Men	Women
1	65.30	109.03	11	109.05	123.88	21	143.83	136.75
2	66.27	111.22	12	110.23	125.78	22	148.70	138.20
3	66.52	111.65	13	112.90	129.52	23		139.00
4	66.85	111.93	14	113.52	129.87	24		147.18
5	70.87	114.38	15	120.95	130.72	25		147.35
6	87.18	118.33	16	127.98	131.67	26		147.50
7	96.45	121.25	17	128.40	132.03	27		147.75
8	98.52	122.08	18	130.90	133.20	28		153.88
9	100.52	122.48	19	131.80	133.50	29		154.83
10	108.18	122.62	20	138.63	136.57	30		189.27
						31		189.28

a. George Towett of Marietta, Georgia, finished in first place for the men and Lauren Wald of Gainesville, Florida, finished in first place for the women. Compare the first-place finish times for men and women. If the 53 men and women runners had competed as one group, in what place would Lauren have finished?

b. What is the median time for men and women runners? Compare men and women runners based on their median times.

c. Provide a five-number summary for both the men and the women.

d. Are there outliers in either group?

e. Show the box plots for the two groups. Did men or women have the most variation in finish times? Explain.

 SELFtest

51. Annual sales, in millions of dollars, for 21 pharmaceutical companies follow.

8408	1374	1872	8879	2459	11413
608	14138	6452	1850	2818	1356
10498	7478	4019	4341	739	2127
3653	5794	8305			

a. Provide a five-number summary.

b. Compute the lower and upper limits.

c. Do the data contain any outliers?

d. Johnson & Johnson's sales are the largest on the list at $14,138 million. Suppose a data entry error (a transposition) had been made and the sales had been entered as $41,138 million. Would the method of detecting outliers in part (c) identify this problem and allow for correction of the data entry error?

e. Show a box plot.

52. *Consumer Reports* provided overall customer satisfaction scores for AT&T, Sprint, T-Mobile, and Verizon cell-phone services in major metropolitan areas throughout the United States. The rating for each service reflects the overall customer satisfaction considering a variety of factors such as cost, connectivity problems, dropped calls, static interference, and customer support. A satisfaction scale from 0 to 100 was used with 0 indicating completely dissatisfied and 100 indicating completely satisfied. The ratings for the four cell-phone services in 20 metropolitan areas are as shown (*Consumer Reports*, January 2009).

CellService

Metropolitan Area	AT&T	Sprint	T-Mobile	Verizon
Atlanta	70	66	71	79
Boston	69	64	74	76
Chicago	71	65	70	77
Dallas	75	65	74	78
Denver	71	67	73	77
Detroit	73	65	77	79
Jacksonville	73	64	75	81
Las Vegas	72	68	74	81
Los Angeles	66	65	68	78
Miami	68	69	73	80
Minneapolis	68	66	75	77
Philadelphia	72	66	71	78
Phoenix	68	66	76	81
San Antonio	75	65	75	80
San Diego	69	68	72	79
San Francisco	66	69	73	75
Seattle	68	67	74	77
St. Louis	74	66	74	79
Tampa	73	63	73	79
Washington	72	68	71	76

a. Consider T-Mobile first. What is the median rating?

b. Develop a five-number summary for the T-Mobile service.

c. Are there outliers for T-Mobile? Explain.

d. Repeat parts (b) and (c) for the other three cell-phone services.

e. Show the box plots for the four cell-phone services on one graph. Discuss what a comparison of the box plots tells about the four services. Which service did *Consumer Reports* recommend as being best in terms of overall customer satisfaction?

AdmiredCompanies

53. *Fortune* magazine's list of the world's most admired companies for 2014 is provided in the data contained in the DATAfile named AdmiredCompanies (*Fortune*, March 17, 2014). The data in the column labelled Return shows the one-year total return (%) for the top ranked 50 companies. For the same time period the S&P average return was 18.4%.

a. Compute the median return for the top ranked 50 companies.

b. What percentage of the top-ranked 50 companies had a one-year return greater than the S&P average return?

c. Develop the five-number summary for the data.

d. Are there any outliers?

e. Develop a box plot for the one-year total return.

BorderCrossings

54. The Bureau of Transportation Statistics keeps track of all border crossings through ports of entry along the U.S.-Canadian and U.S.-Mexican borders. The data contained in the DATAfile named BorderCrossings show the most recently published figures for the number of personal vehicle crossings (rounded to the nearest 1000) at the 50 busiest ports of entry during the month of August (U.S. Department of Transportation website, February 28, 2013).

a. What are the mean and median number of crossings for these ports of entry?

b. What are the first and third quartiles?

c. Provide a five-number summary.

d. Do the data contain any outliers? Show a box plot.

3.5   Measures of Association Between Two Variables

Thus far we have examined numerical methods used to summarize the data for *one variable at a time.* Often a manager or decision maker is interested in the *relationship between two variables.* In this section we present covariance and correlation as descriptive measures of the relationship between two variables.

We begin by reconsidering the application concerning a stereo and sound equipment store in San Francisco as presented in Section 2.4. The store's manager wants to determine the relationship between the number of weekend television commercials shown and the sales at the store during the following week. Sample data with sales expressed in hundreds of dollars are provided in Table 3.6. It shows 10 observations ($n = 10$), one for each week. The scatter diagram in Figure 3.9 shows a positive relationship, with higher sales (y) associated with a greater number of commercials (x). In fact, the scatter diagram suggests that a straight line could be used as an approximation of the relationship. In the following discussion, we introduce **covariance** as a descriptive measure of the linear association between two variables.

Covariance

For a sample of size n with the observations (x_1, y_1), (x_2, y_2), and so on, the sample covariance is defined as follows:

SAMPLE COVARIANCE

$$s_{xy} = \frac{\Sigma(x_i - \bar{x})(y_i - \bar{y})}{n - 1}$$ **(3.13)**

This formula pairs each x_i with a y_i. We then sum the products obtained by multiplying the deviation of each x_i from its sample mean $\bar{x}$ by the deviation of the corresponding y_i from its sample mean $\bar{y}$; this sum is then divided by $n - 1$.

To measure the strength of the linear relationship between the number of commercials x and the sales volume y in the stereo and sound equipment store problem, we use equation (3.13) to compute the sample covariance. The calculations in Table 3.7 show the computation of

TABLE 3.6   SAMPLE DATA FOR THE STEREO AND SOUND EQUIPMENT STORE

DATA *file*

Stereo

Week	Number of Commercials x	Sales Volume ($100s) y
1	2	50
2	5	57
3	1	41
4	3	54
5	4	54
6	1	38
7	5	63
8	3	48
9	4	59
10	2	46

FIGURE 3.9   SCATTER DIAGRAM FOR THE STEREO AND SOUND EQUIPMENT STORE

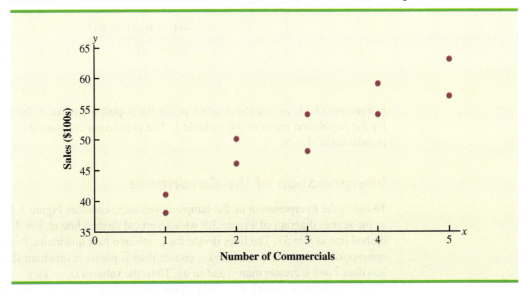

TABLE 3.7   CALCULATIONS FOR THE SAMPLE COVARIANCE

x_i	y_i	$x_i - \bar{x}$	$y_i - \bar{y}$	$(x_i - \bar{x})(y_i - \bar{y})$
2	50	-1	-1	1
5	57	2	6	12
1	41	-2	-10	20
3	54	0	3	0
4	54	1	3	3
1	38	-2	-13	26
5	63	2	12	24
3	48	0	-3	0
4	59	1	8	8
2	46	-1	-5	5
Totals 30	510	0	0	99

$$s_{xy} = \frac{\Sigma(x_i - \bar{x})(y_i - \bar{y})}{n - 1} = \frac{99}{10 - 1} = 11$$

$\Sigma(x_i - \bar{x})(y_i - \bar{y})$. Note that $\bar{x} = 30/10 = 3$ and $\bar{y} = 510/10 = 51$. Using equation (3.13), we obtain a sample covariance of

$$s_{xy} = \frac{\Sigma(x_i - \bar{x})(y_i - \bar{y})}{n - 1} = \frac{99}{9} = 11$$

The formula for computing the covariance of a population of size N is similar to equation (3.13), but we use different notation to indicate that we are working with the entire population.

POPULATION COVARIANCE

$$\sigma_{xy} = \frac{\Sigma(x_i - \mu_x)(y_i - \mu_y)}{N} \qquad \textbf{(3.14)}$$

In equation (3.14) we use the notation μ_x for the population mean of the variable x and μ_y for the population mean of the variable y. The population covariance σ_{xy} is defined for a population of size N.

Interpretation of the Covariance

To aid in the interpretation of the sample covariance, consider Figure 3.10. It is the same as the scatter diagram of Figure 3.9 with a vertical dashed line at $\bar{x} = 3$ and a horizontal dashed line at $\bar{y} = 51$. The lines divide the graph into four quadrants. Points in quadrant I correspond to x_i greater than $\bar{x}$ and y_i greater than $\bar{y}$, points in quadrant II correspond to x_i less than $\bar{x}$ and y_i greater than $\bar{y}$, and so on. Thus, the value of $(x_i - \bar{x})(y_i - \bar{y})$ must be positive for points in quadrant I, negative for points in quadrant II, positive for points in quadrant III, and negative for points in quadrant IV.

FIGURE 3.10   PARTITIONED SCATTER DIAGRAM FOR THE STEREO AND SOUND EQUIPMENT STORE

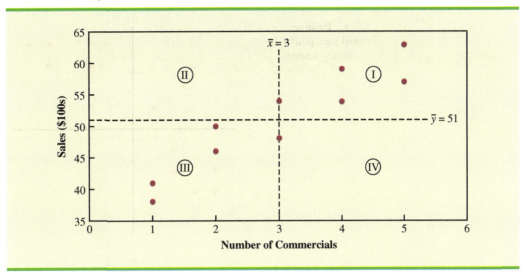

The covariance is a measure of the linear association between two variables.

If the value of s_{xy} is positive, the points with the greatest influence on s_{xy} must be in quadrants I and III. Hence, a positive value for s_{xy} indicates a positive linear association between x and y; that is, as the value of x increases, the value of y increases. If the value of s_{xy} is negative, however, the points with the greatest influence on s_{xy} are in quadrants II and IV. Hence, a negative value for s_{xy} indicates a negative linear association between x and y; that is, as the value of x increases, the value of y decreases. Finally, if the points are evenly distributed across all four quadrants, the value of s_{xy} will be close to zero, indicating no linear association between x and y. Figure 3.11 shows the values of s_{xy} that can be expected with three different types of scatter diagrams.

Referring again to Figure 3.10, we see that the scatter diagram for the stereo and sound equipment store follows the pattern in the top panel of Figure 3.11. As we should expect, the value of the sample covariance indicates a positive linear relationship with $s_{xy} = 11$.

From the preceding discussion, it might appear that a large positive value for the covariance indicates a strong positive linear relationship and that a large negative value indicates a strong negative linear relationship. However, one problem with using covariance as a measure of the strength of the linear relationship is that the value of the covariance depends on the units of measurement for x and y. For example, suppose we are interested in the relationship between height x and weight y for individuals. Clearly the strength of the relationship should be the same whether we measure height in feet or inches. Measuring the height in inches, however, gives us much larger numerical values for $(x_i - \bar{x})$ than when we measure height in feet. Thus, with height measured in inches, we would obtain a larger value for the numerator $\Sigma(x_i - \bar{x})(y_i - \bar{y})$ in equation (3.13)— and hence a larger covariance—when in fact the relationship does not change. A measure of the relationship between two variables that is not affected by the units of measurement for x and y is the **correlation coefficient**.

Correlation Coefficient

For sample data, the Pearson product moment correlation coefficient is defined as follows.

FIGURE 3.11 INTERPRETATION OF SAMPLE COVARIANCE

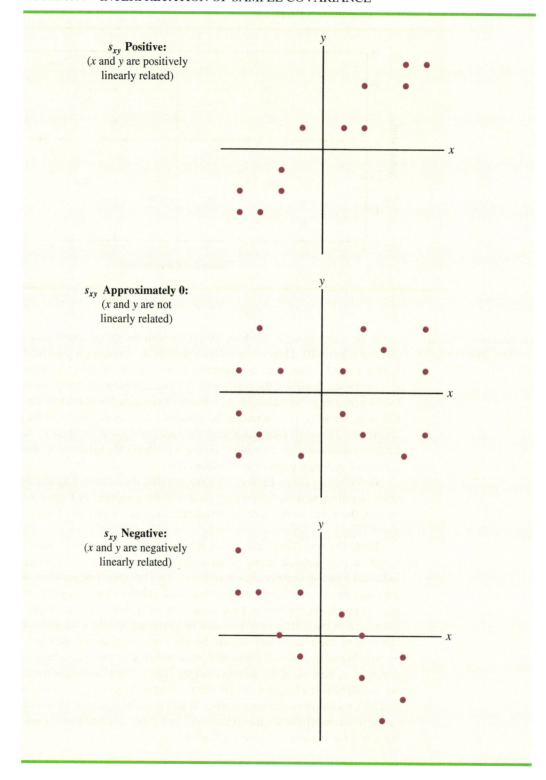

PEARSON PRODUCT MOMENT CORRELATION COEFFICIENT: SAMPLE DATA

$$r_{xy} = \frac{s_{xy}}{s_x s_y} \qquad \textbf{(3.15)}$$

where

r_{xy} = sample correlation coefficient

s_{xy} = sample covariance

s_x = sample standard deviation of x

s_y = sample standard deviation of y

Equation (3.15) shows that the Pearson product moment correlation coefficient for sample data (commonly referred to more simply as the *sample correlation coefficient*) is computed by dividing the sample covariance by the product of the sample standard deviation of x and the sample standard deviation of y.

Let us now compute the sample correlation coefficient for the stereo and sound equipment store. Using the data in Table 3.6, we can compute the sample standard deviations for the two variables:

$$s_x = \sqrt{\frac{\Sigma(x_i - \bar{x})^2}{n-1}} = \sqrt{\frac{20}{9}} = 1.49$$

$$s_y = \sqrt{\frac{\Sigma(y_i - \bar{y})^2}{n-1}} = \sqrt{\frac{566}{9}} = 7.93$$

Now, because $s_{xy} = 11$, the sample correlation coefficient equals

$$r_{xy} = \frac{s_{xy}}{s_x s_y} = \frac{11}{(1.49)(7.93)} = .93$$

The formula for computing the correlation coefficient for a population, denoted by the Greek letter ρ_{xy} (rho, pronounced "row"), follows.

PEARSON PRODUCT MOMENT CORRELATION COEFFICIENT:
POPULATION DATA

$$\rho_{xy} = \frac{\sigma_{xy}}{\sigma_x \sigma_y} \qquad \textbf{(3.16)}$$

The sample correlation coefficient r_{xy} is a point estimator of the population correlation coefficient ρ_{xy}.

where

ρ_{xy} = population correlation coefficient

σ_{xy} = population covariance

σ_x = population standard deviation for x

σ_y = population standard deviation for y

The sample correlation coefficient r_{xy} provides an estimate of the population correlation coefficient ρ_{xy}.

FIGURE 3.12   SCATTER DIAGRAM DEPICTING A PERFECT POSITIVE LINEAR
RELATIONSHIP

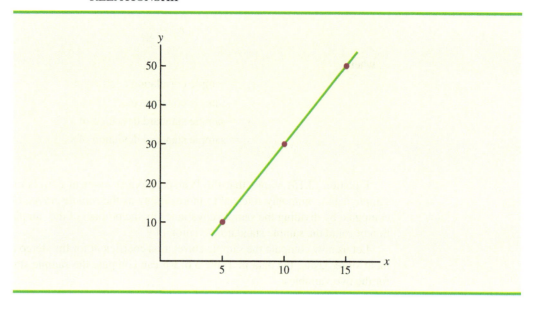

Interpretation of the Correlation Coefficient

First let us consider a simple example that illustrates the concept of a perfect positive linear relationship. The scatter diagram in Figure 3.12 depicts the relationship between x and y based on the following sample data.

x_i	y_i
5	10
10	30
15	50

The straight line drawn through each of the three points shows a perfect linear relationship between x and y. In order to apply equation (3.15) to compute the sample correlation we must first compute s_{xy}, s_x, and s_y. Some of the computations are shown in Table 3.8. Using the results in this table, we find

$$s_{xy} = \frac{\Sigma(x_i - \bar{x})(y_i - \bar{y})}{n - 1} = \frac{200}{2} = 100$$

$$s_x = \sqrt{\frac{\Sigma(x_i - \bar{x})^2}{n - 1}} = \sqrt{\frac{50}{2}} = 5$$

$$s_y = \sqrt{\frac{\Sigma(y_i - \bar{y})^2}{n - 1}} = \sqrt{\frac{800}{2}} = 20$$

$$r_{xy} = \frac{s_{xy}}{s_x s_y} = \frac{100}{5(20)} = 1$$

Thus, we see that the value of the sample correlation coefficient is 1.

TABLE 3.8 COMPUTATIONS USED IN CALCULATING THE SAMPLE CORRELATION COEFFICIENT

	x_i	y_i	$x_i - \bar{x}$	$(x_i - \bar{x})^2$	$y_i - \bar{y}$	$(y_i - \bar{y})^2$	$(x_i - \bar{x})(y_i - \bar{y})$
	5	10	−5	25	−20	400	100
	10	30	0	0	0	0	0
	15	50	5	25	20	400	100
Totals	30	90	0	50	0	800	200

$\bar{x} = 10 \quad \bar{y} = 30$

The correlation coefficient ranges from −1 to +1. Values close to −1 or +1 indicate a strong linear relationship. The closer the correlation is to zero, the weaker the relationship.

In general, it can be shown that if all the points in a data set fall on a positively-sloped straight line, the value of the sample correlation coefficient is +1; that is, a sample correlation coefficient of +1 corresponds to a perfect positive linear relationship between x and y. Moreover, if the points in the data set fall on a straight line having negative slope, the value of the sample correlation coefficient is −1; that is, a sample correlation coefficient of −1 corresponds to a perfect negative linear relationship between x and y.

Let us now suppose that a certain data set indicates a positive linear relationship between x and y but that the relationship is not perfect. The value of r_{xy} will be less than 1, indicating that the points in the scatter diagram are not all on a straight line. As the points deviate more and more from a perfect positive linear relationship, the value of r_{xy} becomes smaller and smaller. A value of r_{xy} equal to zero indicates no linear relationship between x and y, and values of r_{xy} near zero indicate a weak linear relationship.

For the data involving the stereo and sound equipment store, $r_{xy} = .93$. Therefore, we conclude that a strong positive linear relationship occurs between the number of commercials and sales. More specifically, an increase in the number of commercials is associated with an increase in sales.

In closing, we note that correlation provides a measure of linear association and not necessarily causation. A high correlation between two variables does not mean that changes in one variable will cause changes in the other variable. For example, we may find that the quality rating and the typical meal price of restaurants are positively correlated. However, simply increasing the meal price at a restaurant will not cause the quality rating to increase.

NOTES AND COMMENTS

1. Because the correlation coefficient measures only the strength of the linear relationship between two quantitative variables, it is possible for the correlation coefficient to be near zero, suggesting no linear relationship, when the relationship between the two variables is nonlinear. For example, the following scatter diagram shows the relationship between the amount spent by a small retail store for environmental control (heating and cooling) and the daily high outside temperature over 100 days.

    The sample correlation coefficient for these data is $r_{xy} = -.007$ and indicates there is no linear relationship between the two variables. However, the scatter diagram provides strong visual evidence of a nonlinear relationship. That is, we can see that as the daily high outside temperature increases, the money spent on environmental control first decreases as less heating is required and then increases as greater cooling is required.

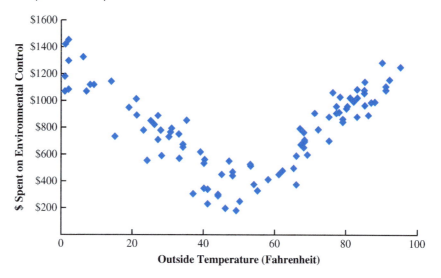

2. While the correlation coefficient is useful in assessing the relationship between two quantitative variables, other measures—such as the Spearman rank-correlation coefficient—can be used to assess a relationship between two variables when at least one of the variables is nominal or ordinal. We discuss the use of the Spearman rank-correlation coefficient in Chapter 18.

Exercises

Methods

SELF*test*

55. Five observations taken for two variables follow.

x_i	4	6	11	3	16
y_i	50	50	40	60	30

  a. Develop a scatter diagram with x on the horizontal axis.
  b. What does the scatter diagram developed in part (a) indicate about the relationship between the two variables?
  c. Compute and interpret the sample covariance.
  d. Compute and interpret the sample correlation coefficient.

56. Five observations taken for two variables follow.

x_i	6	11	15	21	27
y_i	6	9	6	17	12

  a. Develop a scatter diagram for these data.
  b. What does the scatter diagram indicate about a relationship between x and y?
  c. Compute and interpret the sample covariance.
  d. Compute and interpret the sample correlation coefficient.

Applications

57. Ten major college football bowl games were played in January 2010, with the University of Alabama beating the University of Texas 37 to 21 to become the national champion of college football. The results of the 10 bowl games follow (*USA Today,* January 8, 2010).

BowlGames

Bowl Game	Score	Predicted Point Margin	Actual Point Margin
Outback	Auburn 38 Northwestern 35	5	3
Gator	Florida State 33 West Virginia 21	1	12
Capital One	Penn State 19 LSU 17	3	2
Rose	Ohio State 26 Oregon 17	−2	9
Sugar	Florida 51 Cincinnati 24	14	27
Cotton	Mississippi State 21 Oklahoma State 7	3	14
Alamo	Texas Tech 41 Michigan State 31	9	10
Fiesta	Boise State 17 TCU 10	−4	7
Orange	Iowa 24 Georgia Tech 14	−3	10
Championship	Alabama 37 Texas 21	4	16

The predicted winning point margin was based on Las Vegas betting odds approximately one week before the bowl games were played. For example, Auburn was predicted to beat Northwestern in the Outback Bowl by five points. The actual winning point margin for Auburn was three points. A negative predicted winning point margin means that the team that won the bowl game was an underdog and expected to lose. For example, in the Rose Bowl, Ohio State was a two-point underdog to Oregon and ended up winning by nine points.

    a.   Develop a scatter diagram with predicted point margin on the horizontal axis.

    b.   What is the relationship between predicted and actual point margins?

    c.   Compute and interpret the sample covariance.

    d.   Compute the sample correlation coefficient. What does this value indicate about the relationship between the Las Vegas predicted point margin and the actual point margin in college football bowl games?

58.   A department of transportation's study on driving speed and miles per gallon for midsize automobiles resulted in the following data:

Speed (Miles per Hour)	30	50	40	55	30	25	60	25	50	55
Miles per Gallon	28	25	25	23	30	32	21	35	26	25

Compute and interpret the sample correlation coefficient.

SmokeDetectors

59.   Over the past 40 years, the percentage of homes in the United States with smoke detectors has risen steadily and has plateaued at about 96% (*National Fire Protection Association* website, January, 2015). With this increase in the use of home smoke detectors, what has happened to the death rate from home fires? The DATAfile *SmokeDetectors* contains 17 years of data on the estimated percentage of homes with smoke detectors and the estimated home fire deaths per million of population.

    a.   Do you expect a positive or negative relationship between smoke detector use and deaths from home fires? Why or why not?

    b.   Compute and report the correlation coefficient. Is there a positive or negative correlation between smoke detector use and deaths from home fires? Comment.

    c.   Show a scatter plot of the death rate per million of population and the percentage of homes with smoke detectors.

Russell

60.   The Russell 1000 is a stock market index consisting of the largest U.S. companies. The Dow Jones Industrial Average is based on 30 large companies. The DATAfile Russell gives the annual percentage returns for each of these stock indexes for the years 1988 to 2012 (1stock1 website).

    a.   Plot these percentage returns using a scatter plot.

    b.   Compute the sample mean and standard deviation for each index.

c. Compute the sample correlation.

d. Discuss similarities and differences in these two indexes.

BestPrivateColleges

61. A random sample of 30 colleges from Kiplinger's list of the best values in private college provided the data shown in the DATAfile named BestPrivateColleges (Kiplinger, October 2013). The variable named Admit Rate (%) shows the percentage of students that applied to the college and were admitted, and the variable named 4-yr Grad. Rate (%) shows the percentage of students that were admitted and graduated in four years.

a. Develop a scatter diagram with Admit Rate (%) as the independent variable. What does the scatter diagram indicate about the relationship between the two variables?

b. Compute the sample correlation coefficient. What does the value of the sample correlation coefficient indicate about the relationship between the Admit Rate (%) and the 4-yr Grad. Rate (%)?

3.6 Data Dashboards: Adding Numerical Measures to Improve Effectiveness

In Section 2.5 we provided an introduction to data visualization, a term used to describe the use of graphical displays to summarize and present information about a data set. The goal of data visualization is to communicate key information about the data as effectively and clearly as possible. One of the most widely used data visualization tools is a data dashboard, a set of visual displays that organizes and presents information that is used to monitor the performance of a company or organization in a manner that is easy to read, understand, and interpret. In this section we extend the discussion of data dashboards to show how the addition of numerical measures can improve the overall effectiveness of the display.

The addition of numerical measures, such as the mean and standard deviation of key performance indicators (KPIs) to a data dashboard is critical because numerical measures often provide benchmarks or goals by which KPIs are evaluated. In addition, graphical displays that include numerical measures as components of the display are also frequently included in data dashboards. We must keep in mind that the purpose of a data dashboard is to provide information on the KPIs in a manner that is easy to read, understand, and interpret. Adding numerical measures and graphs that utilize numerical measures can help us accomplish these objectives.

To illustrate the use of numerical measures in a data dashboard, recall the Grogan Oil Company application that we used in Section 2.5 to introduce the concept of a data dashboard. Grogan Oil has offices located in three Texas cities: Austin (its headquarters), Houston, and Dallas. Grogan's Information Technology (IT) call center, located in the Austin office, handles calls regarding computer-related problems (software, Internet, and email) from employees in the three offices. Figure 3.13 shows the data dashboard that Grogan developed to monitor the performance of the call center. The key components of this dashboard are as follows:

- The stacked bar chart in the upper left corner of the dashboard shows the call volume for each type of problem (software, Internet, or email) over time.
- The pie chart in the upper right corner of the dashboard shows the percentage of time that call center employees spent on each type of problem or not working on a call (idle).
- For each unresolved case that was received more than 15 minutes ago, the bar chart shown in the middle left portion of the dashboard shows the length of time that each of these cases has been unresolved.
- The bar chart in the middle right portion of the dashboard shows the call volume by office (Houston, Dallas, Austin) for each type of problem.

FIGURE 3.13   INITIAL GROGAN OIL INFORMATION TECHNOLOGY CALL CENTER DATA DASHBOARD

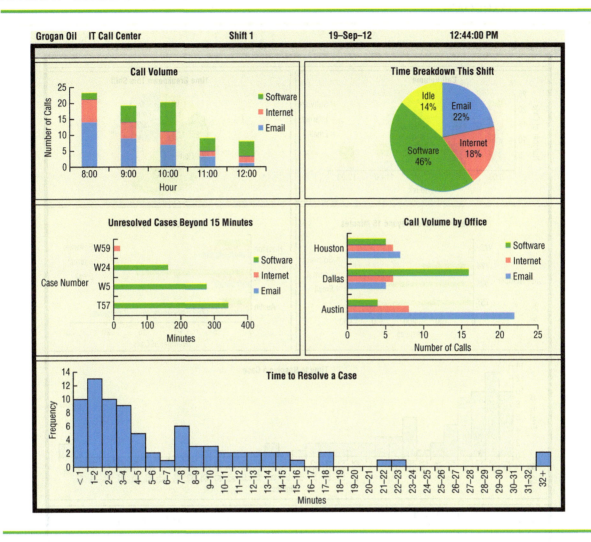

- The histogram at the bottom of the dashboard shows the distribution of the time to resolve a case for all resolved cases for the current shift.

In order to gain additional insight into the performance of the call center, Grogan's IT manager has decided to expand the current dashboard by adding box plots for the time required to resolve calls received for each type of problem (email, Internet, and software). In addition, a graph showing the time to resolve individual cases has been added in the lower left portion of the dashboard. Finally, the IT manager added a display of summary statistics for each type of problem and summary statistics for each of the first few hours of the shift. The updated dashboard is shown in Figure 3.14.

The IT call center has set a target performance level or benchmark of 10 minutes for the mean time to resolve a case. Furthermore, the center has decided it is undesirable for the time to resolve a case to exceed 15 minutes. To reflect these benchmarks, a black horizontal line at the mean target value of 10 minutes and a red horizontal line at the maximum acceptable level of 15 minutes have been added to both the graph showing the time to resolve cases and the box plots of the time required to resolve calls received for each type of problem.

FIGURE 3.14   UPDATED GROGAN OIL INFORMATION TECHNOLOGY CALL CENTER DATA
DASHBOARD

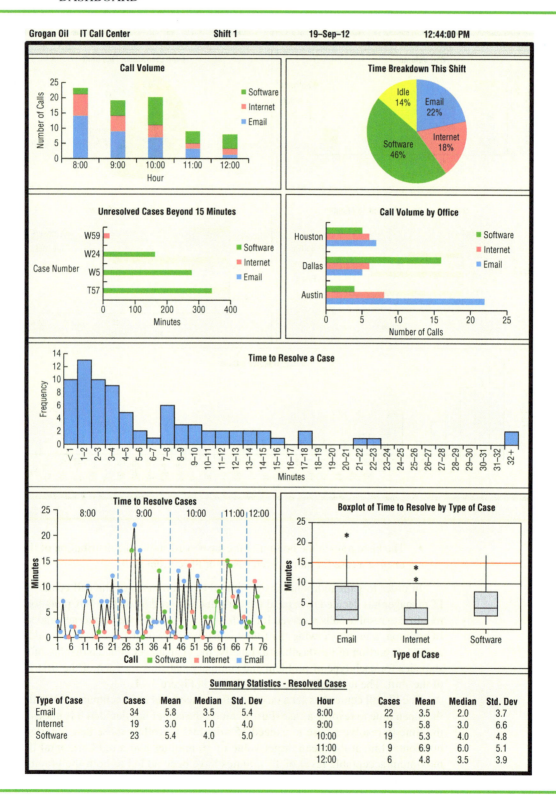

The summary statistics in the dashboard in Figure 3.21 show that the mean time to resolve an email case is 5.8 minutes, the mean time to resolve an Internet case is 3.0 minutes, and the mean time to resolve a software case is 5.4 minutes. Thus, the mean time to resolve each type of case is better than the target mean (10 minutes).

Reviewing the box plots, we see that the box associated with the email cases is "larger" than the boxes associated with the other two types of cases. The summary statistics also show that the standard deviation of the time to resolve email cases is larger than the standard deviations of the times to resolve the other types of cases. This leads us to take a closer look at the email cases in the two new graphs. The box plot for the email cases has a whisker that extends beyond 15 minutes and an outlier well beyond 15 minutes. The graph of the time to resolve individual cases (in the lower left position of the dashboard) shows that this is because of two calls on email cases during the 9:00 hour that took longer than the target maximum time (15 minutes) to resolve. This analysis may lead the IT call center manager to further investigate why resolution times are more variable for email cases than for Internet or software cases. Based on this analysis, the IT manager may also decide to investigate the circumstances that led to inordinately long resolution times for the two email cases that took longer than 15 minutes to resolve.

The graph of the time to resolve individual cases shows that most calls received during the first hour of the shift were resolved relatively quickly; the graph also shows that the time to resolve cases increased gradually throughout the morning. This could be due to a tendency for complex problems to arise later in the shift or possibly to the backlog of calls that accumulates over time. Although the summary statistics suggest that cases submitted during the 9:00 hour take the longest to resolve, the graph of time to resolve individual cases shows that two time-consuming email cases and one time-consuming software case were reported during that hour, and this may explain why the mean time to resolve cases during the 9:00 hour is larger than during any other hour of the shift. Overall, reported cases have generally been resolved in 15 minutes or less during this shift.

Drilling down refers to functionality in interactive data dashboards that allows the user to access information and analyses at an increasingly detailed level.

Dashboards such as the Grogan Oil data dashboard are often interactive. For instance, when a manager uses a mouse or a touch screen monitor to position the cursor over the display or point to something on the display, additional information, such as the time to resolve the problem, the time the call was received, and the individual and/or the location that reported the problem, may appear. Clicking on the individual item may also take the user to a new level of analysis at the individual case level.

Summary

In this chapter we introduced several descriptive statistics that can be used to summarize the location, variability, and shape of a data distribution. Unlike the tabular and graphical displays introduced in Chapter 2, the measures introduced in this chapter summarize the data in terms of numerical values. When the numerical values obtained are for a sample, they are called sample statistics. When the numerical values obtained are for a population, they are called population parameters. Some of the notation used for sample statistics and population parameters follow.

In statistical inference, a sample statistic is referred to as a point estimator of the population parameter.

	Sample Statistic	Population Parameter
Mean	$\bar{x}$	μ
Variance	s^2	σ^2
Standard deviation	s	σ
Covariance	s_{xy}	σ_{xy}
Correlation	r_{xy}	ρ_{xy}

As measures of location, we defined the mean, median, mode, weighted mean, geometric mean, percentiles, and quartiles. Next, we presented the range, interquartile range, variance, standard deviation, and coefficient of variation as measures of variability or dispersion. Our primary measure of the shape of a data distribution was the skewness. Negative values of skewness indicate a data distribution skewed to the left, and positive values of skewness indicate a data distribution skewed to the right. We then described how the mean and standard deviation could be used, applying Chebyshev's theorem and the empirical rule, to provide more information about the distribution of data and to identify outliers.

In Section 3.4 we showed how to develop a five-number summary and a box plot to provide simultaneous information about the location, variability, and shape of the distribution. In Section 3.5 we introduced covariance and the correlation coefficient as measures of association between two variables. In the final section, we showed how adding numerical measures can improve the effectiveness of data dashboards.

The descriptive statistics we discussed can be developed using statistical software packages and spreadsheets. In the chapter-ending appendixes we show how to use Minitab and Excel to develop the descriptive statistics introduced in this chapter.

Glossary

Box plot A graphical summary of data based on a five-number summary.

Chebyshev's theorem A theorem that can be used to make statements about the proportion of data values that must be within a specified number of standard deviations of the mean.

Coefficient of variation A measure of relative variability computed by dividing the standard deviation by the mean and multiplying by 100.

Correlation coefficient A measure of linear association between two variables that takes on values between -1 and $+1$. Values near $+1$ indicate a strong positive linear relationship; values near -1 indicate a strong negative linear relationship; and values near zero indicate the lack of a linear relationship.

Covariance A measure of linear association between two variables. Positive values indicate a positive relationship; negative values indicate a negative relationship.

Empirical rule A rule that can be used to compute the percentage of data values that must be within one, two, and three standard deviations of the mean for data that exhibit a bell-shaped distribution.

Five-number summary A technique that uses five numbers to summarize the data: smallest value, first quartile, median, third quartile, and largest value.

Geometric mean A measure of location that is calculated by finding the nth root of the product of n values.

Interquartile range (IQR) A measure of variability, defined to be the difference between the third and first quartiles.

Mean A measure of central location computed by summing the data values and dividing by the number of observations.

Median A measure of central location provided by the value in the middle when the data are arranged in ascending order.

Mode A measure of location, defined as the value that occurs with greatest frequency.

Outlier An unusually small or unusually large data value.

Percentile A value such that at least p percent of the observations are less than or equal to this value and at least $(100 - p)$ percent of the observations are greater than or equal to this value. The 50th percentile is the median.

Point estimator A sample statistic, such as $\bar{x}$, s^2, and s, used to estimate the corresponding population parameter.

Population parameter A numerical value used as a summary measure for a population (e.g., the population mean, μ, the population variance, σ^2, and the population standard deviation, σ).

Quartiles The 25th, 50th, and 75th percentiles, referred to as the first quartile, the second quartile (median), and third quartile, respectively. The quartiles can be used to divide a data set into four parts, with each part containing approximately 25% of the data.

Range A measure of variability, defined to be the largest value minus the smallest value.

Sample statistic A numerical value used as a summary measure for a sample (e.g., the sample mean, $\bar{x}$, the sample variance, s^2, and the sample standard deviation, s).

Skewness A measure of the shape of a data distribution. Data skewed to the left result in negative skewness; a symmetric data distribution results in zero skewness; and data skewed to the right result in positive skewness.

Standard deviation A measure of variability computed by taking the positive square root of the variance.

Variance A measure of variability based on the squared deviations of the data values about the mean.

Weighted mean The mean obtained by assigning each observation a weight that reflects its importance.

z-score A value computed by dividing the deviation about the mean $(x_i - \bar{x})$ by the standard deviation s. A z-score is referred to as a standardized value and denotes the number of standard deviations x_i is from the mean.

Key Formulas

Sample Mean

$$\bar{x} = \frac{\Sigma x_i}{n} \tag{3.1}$$

Population Mean

$$\mu = \frac{\Sigma x_i}{N} \tag{3.2}$$

Weighted Mean

$$\bar{x} = \frac{\Sigma w_i x_i}{\Sigma w_i} \tag{3.3}$$

Geometric Mean

$$\bar{x}_g = \sqrt[n]{(x_1)(x_2)\cdots(x_n)} = [(x_1)(x_2)\cdots(x_n)]^{1/n} \tag{3.4}$$

Location of the pth Percentile

$$L_p = \frac{p}{100}(n+1) \tag{3.5}$$

Interquartile Range

$$\text{IQR} = Q_3 - Q_1 \tag{3.6}$$

Population Variance

$$\sigma^2 = \frac{\Sigma(x_i - \mu)^2}{N} \tag{3.7}$$

Sample Variance

$$s^2 = \frac{\Sigma(x_i - \bar{x})^2}{n - 1} \tag{3.8}$$

Standard Deviation

$$\text{Sample standard deviation} = s = \sqrt{s^2} \tag{3.9}$$

$$\text{Population standard deviation} = \sigma = \sqrt{\sigma^2} \tag{3.10}$$

Coefficient of Variation

$$\left(\frac{\text{Standard deviation}}{\text{Mean}} \times 100\right)\% \tag{3.11}$$

z-Score

$$z_i = \frac{x_i - \bar{x}}{s} \tag{3.12}$$

Sample Covariance

$$s_{xy} = \frac{\Sigma(x_i - \bar{x})(y_i - \bar{y})}{n - 1} \tag{3.13}$$

Population Covariance

$$\sigma_{xy} = \frac{\Sigma(x_i - \mu_x)(y_i - \mu_y)}{N} \tag{3.14}$$

Pearson Product Moment Correlation Coefficient: Sample Data

$$r_{xy} = \frac{s_{xy}}{s_x s_y} \tag{3.15}$$

Pearson Product Moment Correlation Coefficient: Population Data

$$\rho_{xy} = \frac{\sigma_{xy}}{\sigma_x \sigma_y} \tag{3.16}$$

Supplementary Exercises

62. The average number of times Americans dine out in a week fell from 4.0 in 2008 to 3.8 in 2012 (Zagat.com, April, 2012). The number of times a sample of 20 families dined out last week provides the following data.

6	1	5	3	7	3	0	3	1	3
4	1	2	4	1	0	5	6	3	1

   a. Compute the mean and median.
   b. Compute the first and third quartiles.
   c. Compute the range and interquartile range.
   d. Compute the variance and standard deviation.
   e. The skewness measure for these data is 0.34. Comment on the shape of this distribution. Is it the shape you would expect? Why or why not?
   f. Do the data contain outliers?

Coaches

63. *USA Today* reports that NCAA colleges and universities are paying higher salaries to a newly recruited football coach compared to what they paid their previous football coach. (*USA Today*, February 12, 2013). The annual base salaries for the previous head football coach and the new head football coach at 23 schools are given in the DATAfile Coaches.
   a. Determine the median annual salary for a previous head football coach and a new head football coach.
   b. Compute the range for salaries for both previous and new head football coaches.
   c. Compute the standard deviation for salaries for both previous and new head football coaches.
   d. Based on your answers to (a) to (c), comment on any differences between the annual base salary a school pays a new head football coach compared to what it paid its previous head football coach.

64. The average waiting time for a patient at an El Paso physician's office is just over 29 minutes, well above the national average of 21 minutes. In fact, El Paso has the longest physician's office waiting times in the United States (*El Paso Times,* January 8, 2012). In order to address the issue of long patient wait times, some physician's offices are using wait tracking systems to notify patients of expected wait times. Patients can adjust their arrival times based on this information and spend less time in waiting rooms. The following data show wait times (minutes) for a sample of patients at offices that do not have an office tracking system and wait times for a sample of patients at offices with an office tracking system.

WaitTracking

Without Wait Tracking System	With Wait Tracking System
24	31
67	11
17	14
20	18
31	12
44	37
12	9
23	13
16	12
37	15

a. What are the mean and median patient wait times for offices with a wait tracking system? What are the mean and median patient wait times for offices without a wait tracking system?

b. What are the variance and standard deviation of patient wait times for offices with a wait tracking system? What are the variance and standard deviation of patient wait times for visits to offices without a wait tracking system?

c. Do offices with a wait tracking system have shorter patient wait times than offices without a wait tracking system? Explain.

d. Considering only offices without a wait tracking system, what is the z-score for the tenth patient in the sample?

e. Considering only offices with a wait tracking system, what is the z-score for the sixth patient in the sample? How does this z-score compare with the z-score you calculated for part (d)?

f. Based on z-scores, do the data for offices without a wait tracking system contain any outliers? Based on z-scores, do the data for offices with a wait tracking system contain any outliers?

Sleep

65. U.S. companies lose \$63.2 billion per year from workers with insomnia. Workers lose an average of 7.8 days of productivity per year due to lack of sleep (*Wall Street Journal*, January 23, 2013). The following data show the number of hours of sleep attained during a recent night for a sample of 20 workers.

| 6 | 5 | 10 | 5 | 6 | 9 | 9 | 5 | 9 | 5 |
| 8 | 7 | 8 | 6 | 9 | 8 | 9 | 6 | 10 | 8 |

a. What is the mean number of hours of sleep for this sample?

b. What is the variance? Standard deviation?

Smartphone

66. A study of smartphone users shows that 68% of smartphone use occurs at home and a user spends an average of 410 minutes per month using a smartphone to interact with other people (*Harvard Business Review*, January–February 2013). Consider the following data indicating the number of minutes in a month spent interacting with others via a smartphone for a sample of 50 smartphone users.

353	458	404	394	416
437	430	369	448	430
431	469	446	387	445
354	468	422	402	360
444	424	441	357	435
461	407	470	413	351
464	374	417	460	352
445	387	468	368	430
384	367	436	390	464
405	372	401	388	367

a. What is the mean number of minutes spent interacting with others for this sample? How does it compare to the mean reported in the study?

b. What is the standard deviation for this sample?

c. Are there any outliers in this sample?

67. Public transportation and the automobile are two methods an employee can use to get to work each day. Samples of times recorded for each method are shown. Times are in minutes.

| *Public Transportation:* | 28 | 29 | 32 | 37 | 33 | 25 | 29 | 32 | 41 | 34 |
| *Automobile:* | | 29 | 31 | 33 | 32 | 34 | 30 | 31 | 32 | 35 | 33 |

a. Compute the sample mean time to get to work for each method.
b. Compute the sample standard deviation for each method.
c. On the basis of your results from parts (a) and (b), which method of transportation should be preferred? Explain.
d. Develop a box plot for each method. Does a comparison of the box plots support your conclusion in part (c)?

68. In 2007 the *New York Times* reported that the median annual household income in the United States was $55,500 (*New York Times* website, August, 21, 2013). Answer the following questions based on the following sample of 14 household incomes for 2013 ($1000s).

49.4	52.4	53.4	51.3	52.1	48.7	52.1
52.2	64.5	51.6	46.5	52.9	52.5	51.2

a. What is the median household income for the sample data for 2013?
b. Based on the sample data, estimate the percentage change in the median household income from 2007 to 2013.
c. Compute the first and third quartiles.
d. Provide a five-number summary.
e. Using the z-score approach, do the data contain any outliers? Does the approach that uses the values of the first and third quartiles and the interquartile range to detect outliers provide the same results?

69. The data contained in the DATAfile named FoodIndustry show the company/chain name, the average sales per store ($1000s), and the food segment industry for 47 restaurant chains (*Quick Service Restaurant Magazine* website, August 2013).

FoodIndustry

a. What was the mean U.S. sales per store for the 47 restaurant chains?
b. What are the first and third quartiles? What is your interpretation of the quartiles?
c. Show a box plot for the level of sales and discuss if there are any outliers in terms of sales that would skew the results.
d. Develop a frequency distribution showing the average sales per store for each segment. Comment on the results obtained.

70. *Travel + Leisure* magazine provides an annual list of the 500 best hotels in the world. The magazine provides a rating for each hotel along with a brief description that includes the size of the hotel, amenities, and the cost per night for a double room. A sample of 12 of the top-rated hotels in the United States follows.

Travel

Hotel	Location	Rooms	Cost/Night
Boulders Resort & Spa	Phoenix, AZ	220	499
Disney's Wilderness Lodge	Orlando, FL	727	340
Four Seasons Hotel Beverly Hills	Los Angeles, CA	285	585
Four Seasons Hotel	Boston, MA	273	495
Hay-Adams	Washington, DC	145	495
Inn on Biltmore Estate	Asheville, NC	213	279
Loews Ventana Canyon Resort	Phoenix, AZ	398	279
Mauna Lani Bay Hotel	Island of Hawaii	343	455
Montage Laguna Beach	Laguna Beach, CA	250	595
Sofitel Water Tower	Chicago, IL	414	367
St. Regis Monarch Beach	Dana Point, CA	400	675
The Broadmoor	Colorado Springs, CO	700	420

a. What is the mean number of rooms?
b. What is the mean cost per night for a double room?

c. Develop a scatter diagram with the number of rooms on the horizontal axis and the cost per night on the vertical axis. Does there appear to be a relationship between the number of rooms and the cost per night? Discuss.

d. What is the sample correlation coefficient? What does it tell you about the relationship between the number of rooms and the cost per night for a double room? Does this appear reasonable? Discuss.

71. The 32 teams in the National Football League (NFL) are worth, on average, $1.17 billion, 5% more than last year. The following data show the annual revenue ($ millions) and the estimated team value ($ millions) for the 32 NFL teams (*Forbes* website, February 28, 2014).

NFLTeamValue

Team	Revenue ($ millions)	Current Value ($ millions)
Arizona Cardinals	253	961
Atlanta Falcons	252	933
Baltimore Ravens	292	1227
Buffalo Bills	256	870
Carolina Panthers	271	1057
Chicago Bears	298	1252
Cincinnati Bengals	250	924
Cleveland Browns	264	1005
Dallas Cowboys	539	2300
Denver Broncos	283	1161
Detroit Lions	248	900
Green Bay Packers	282	1183
Houston Texans	320	1450
Indianapolis Colts	276	1200
Jacksonville Jaguars	260	840
Kansas City Chiefs	245	1009
Miami Dolphins	268	1074
Minnesota Vikings	234	1007
New England Patriots	408	1800
New Orleans Saints	276	1004
New York Giants	338	1550
New York Jets	321	1380
Oakland Raiders	229	825
Philadelphia Eagles	306	1314
Pittsburgh Steelers	266	1118
San Diego Chargers	250	949
San Francisco 49ers	255	1224
Seattle Seahawks	270	1081
St. Louis Rams	239	875
Tampa Bay Buccaneers	267	1067
Tennessee Titans	270	1055
Washington Redskins	381	1700

a. Develop a scatter diagram with Revenue on the horizontal axis and Value on the vertical axis. Does there appear that there is any relationship between the two variables?

b. What is the sample correlation coefficient? What can you say about the strength of the relationship between Revenue and Value?

72. Does a major league baseball team's record during spring training indicate how the team will play during the regular season? Over a six-year period, the correlation coefficient between a team's winning percentage in spring training and its winning percentage in the regular season is .18. Shown are the winning percentages for the 14 American League teams during a previous season.

DATA *file*

SpringTraining

Team	Spring Training	Regular Season	Team	Spring Training	Regular Season
Baltimore Orioles	.407	.422	Minnesota Twins	.500	.540
Boston Red Sox	.429	.586	New York Yankees	.577	.549
Chicago White Sox	.417	.546	Oakland A's	.692	.466
Cleveland Indians	.569	.500	Seattle Mariners	.500	.377
Detroit Tigers	.569	.457	Tampa Bay Rays	.731	.599
Kansas City Royals	.533	.463	Texas Rangers	.643	.488
Los Angeles Angels	.724	.617	Toronto Blue Jays	.448	.531

a. What is the correlation coefficient between the spring training and the regular season winning percentages?

b. What is your conclusion about a team's record during spring training indicating how the team will play during the regular season? What are some of the reasons why this occurs? Discuss.

73. The days to maturity for a sample of five money market funds are shown here. The dollar amounts invested in the funds are provided. Use the weighted mean to determine the mean number of days to maturity for dollars invested in these five money market funds.

Days to Maturity	Dollar Value ($millions)
20	20
12	30
7	10
5	15
6	10

74. Automobiles traveling on a road with a posted speed limit of 55 miles per hour are checked for speed by a state police radar system. Following is a frequency distribution of speeds.

Speed (miles per hour)	Frequency
45–49	10
50–54	40
55–59	150
60–64	175
65–69	75
70–74	15
75–79	10
Total	475

a. What is the mean speed of the automobiles traveling on this road?

b. Compute the variance and the standard deviation.

75. The Panama Railroad Company was established in 1850 to construct a railroad across the isthmus that would allow fast and easy access between the Atlantic and Pacific Oceans. The following table (*The Big Ditch*, Mauer and Yu, 2011) provides annual returns for Panama Railroad stock from 1853 through 1880.

Year	Return on Panama Railroad Company Stock (%)
*1853	−1
1854	−9
1855	19
1856	2
1857	3
1858	36
1859	21
1860	16
1861	−5
1862	43
1863	44
1864	48
1865	7
1866	11
1867	23
1868	20
1869	−11
1870	−51
1871	−42
1872	39
1873	42
1874	12
1875	26
1876	9
1877	−6
1878	25
1879	31
1880	30

DATA file

PanamaRailroad

a. Create a graph of the annual returns on the stock. The New York Stock Exchange earned an annual average return of 8.4% from 1853 through 1880. Can you tell from the graph if the Panama Railroad Company stock outperformed the New York Stock Exchange?

b. Calculate the mean annual return on Panama Railroad Company stock from 1853 through 1880. Did the stock outperform the New York Stock Exchange over the same period?

Case Problem 1   Pelican Stores

Pelican Stores, a division of National Clothing, is a chain of women's apparel stores operating throughout the country. The chain recently ran a promotion in which discount coupons were sent to customers of other National Clothing stores. Data collected for a sample of 100 in-store credit card transactions at Pelican Stores during one day while the promotion was running are contained in the file named PelicanStores. Table 3.9 shows a portion of the data set. The proprietary card method of payment refers to charges made using a National Clothing charge card. Customers who made a purchase using a discount coupon are referred to as promotional customers and customers who made a purchase but did not use a discount coupon are referred to as regular customers. Because the promotional coupons were not sent to regular Pelican Stores customers, management considers the sales made to people presenting the promotional coupons as sales it would not otherwise make. Of course, Pelican also hopes that the promotional customers will continue to shop at its stores.

TABLE 3.9   SAMPLE OF 100 CREDIT CARD PURCHASES AT PELICAN STORES

PelicanStores

Customer	Type of Customer	Items	Net Sales	Method of Payment	Gender	Marital Status	Age
1	Regular	1	39.50	Discover	Male	Married	32
2	Promotional	1	102.40	Proprietary Card	Female	Married	36
3	Regular	1	22.50	Proprietary Card	Female	Married	32
4	Promotional	5	100.40	Proprietary Card	Female	Married	28
5	Regular	2	54.00	MasterCard	Female	Married	34
6	Regular	1	44.50	MasterCard	Female	Married	44
7	Promotional	2	78.00	Proprietary Card	Female	Married	30
8	Regular	1	22.50	Visa	Female	Married	40
9	Promotional	2	56.52	Proprietary Card	Female	Married	46
10	Regular	1	44.50	Proprietary Card	Female	Married	36
.	.	.	.	.	.	.	.
.	.	.	.	.	.	.	.
.	.	.	.	.	.	.	.
96	Regular	1	39.50	MasterCard	Female	Married	44
97	Promotional	9	253.00	Proprietary Card	Female	Married	30
98	Promotional	10	287.59	Proprietary Card	Female	Married	52
99	Promotional	2	47.60	Proprietary Card	Female	Married	30
100	Promotional	1	28.44	Proprietary Card	Female	Married	44

Most of the variables shown in Table 3.9 are self-explanatory, but two of the variables require some clarification.

Items   The total number of items purchased
Net Sales   The total amount ($) charged to the credit card

Pelican's management would like to use this sample data to learn about its customer base and to evaluate the promotion involving discount coupons.

Managerial Report

Use the methods of descriptive statistics presented in this chapter to summarize the data and comment on your findings. At a minimum, your report should include the following:

1. Descriptive statistics on net sales and descriptive statistics on net sales by various classifications of customers.
2. Descriptive statistics concerning the relationship between age and net sales.

Case Problem 2   Motion Picture Industry

The motion picture industry is a competitive business. More than 50 studios produce several hundred new motion pictures each year, and the financial success of the motion pictures varies considerably. The opening weekend gross sales, the total gross sales, the number of theaters the movie was shown in, and the number of weeks the motion picture was in release are common variables used to measure the success of a motion picture. Data on the top 100 grossing motion pictures released in 2011 (Box Office Mojo website, March 17, 2012) are contained in a file named 2011Movies. Table 3.10 shows the data for the first 10 motion pictures in this file. Note that some movies, such as *War Horse,* were released late in 2011 and continued to run in 2012.

TABLE 3.10   PERFORMANCE DATA FOR 10 MOTION PICTURES

Motion Picture	Opening Gross Sales ($millions)	Total Gross Sales ($millions)	Number of Theaters	Weeks in Release
Harry Potter and the Deathly Hallows Part 2	169.19	381.01	4375	19
Transformers: Dark of the Moon	97.85	352.39	4088	15
The Twilight Saga: Breaking Dawn Part 1	138.12	281.29	4066	14
The Hangover Part II	85.95	254.46	3675	16
Pirates of the Caribbean: On Stranger Tides	90.15	241.07	4164	19
Fast Five	86.20	209.84	3793	15
Mission: Impossible—Ghost Protocol	12.79	208.55	3555	13
Cars 2	66.14	191.45	4115	25
Sherlock Holmes: A Game of Shadows	39.64	186.59	3703	13
Thor	65.72	181.03	3963	16

2011Movies

Managerial Report

Use the numerical methods of descriptive statistics presented in this chapter to learn how these variables contribute to the success of a motion picture. Include the following in your report:

1. Descriptive statistics for each of the four variables along with a discussion of what the descriptive statistics tell us about the motion picture industry.
2. What motion pictures, if any, should be considered high-performance outliers? Explain.
3. Descriptive statistics showing the relationship between total gross sales and each of the other variables. Discuss.

Case Problem 3 # Business Schools of Asia-Pacific

Asian

The pursuit of a higher education degree in business is now international. A survey shows that more and more Asians choose the master of business administration (MBA) degree route to corporate success. As a result, the number of applicants for MBA courses at Asia-Pacific schools continues to increase.

Across the region, thousands of Asians show an increasing willingness to temporarily shelve their careers and spend two years in pursuit of a theoretical business qualification. Courses in these schools are notoriously tough and include economics, banking, marketing, behavioral sciences, labor relations, decision making, strategic thinking, business law, and more. The data set in Table 3.11 shows some of the characteristics of the leading Asia-Pacific business schools.

Managerial Report

Use the methods of descriptive statistics to summarize the data in Table 3.11. Discuss your findings.

1. Include a summary for each variable in the data set. Make comments and interpretations based on maximums and minimums, as well as the appropriate means and proportions. What new insights do these descriptive statistics provide concerning Asia-Pacific business schools?

TABLE 3.11 DATA FOR 25 ASIA-PACIFIC BUSINESS SCHOOLS

Business School	Full-Time Enrollment	Students per Faculty	Local Tuition ($)	Foreign Tuition ($)	Age	% Foreign	GMAT	English Test	Work Experience	Starting Salary ($)
Melbourne Business School	200	5	24,420	29,600	28	47	Yes	No	Yes	71,400
University of New South Wales (Sydney)	228	4	19,993	32,582	29	28	Yes	No	Yes	65,200
Indian Institute of Management (Ahmedabad)	392	5	4,300	4,300	22	0	No	No	No	7,100
Chinese University of Hong Kong	90	5	11,140	11,140	29	10	Yes	Yes	No	31,000
International University of Japan (Niigata)	126	4	33,060	33,060	28	60	Yes	Yes	No	87,000
Asian Institute of Management (Manila)	389	5	7,562	9,000	25	50	Yes	No	Yes	22,800
Indian Institute of Management (Bangalore)	380	5	3,935	16,000	23	1	Yes	No	No	7,500
National University of Singapore	147	6	6,146	7,170	29	51	Yes	Yes	Yes	43,300
Indian Institute of Management (Calcutta)	463	8	2,880	16,000	23	0	No	No	No	7,400
Australian National University (Canberra)	42	2	20,300	20,300	30	80	Yes	Yes	Yes	46,600
Nanyang Technological University (Singapore)	50	5	8,500	8,500	32	20	Yes	No	Yes	49,300
University of Queensland (Brisbane)	138	17	16,000	22,800	32	26	No	No	Yes	49,600
Hong Kong University of Science and Technology	60	2	11,513	11,513	26	37	Yes	No	Yes	34,000
Macquarie Graduate School of Management (Sydney)	12	8	17,172	19,778	34	27	No	No	Yes	60,100
Chulalongkorn University (Bangkok)	200	7	17,355	17,355	25	6	Yes	No	Yes	17,600
Monash Mt. Eliza Business School (Melbourne)	350	13	16,200	22,500	30	30	Yes	Yes	Yes	52,500
Asian Institute of Management (Bangkok)	300	10	18,200	18,200	29	90	No	Yes	Yes	25,000
University of Adelaide	20	19	16,426	23,100	30	10	No	No	Yes	66,000
Massey University (Palmerston North, New Zealand)	30	15	13,106	21,625	37	35	No	Yes	Yes	41,400
Royal Melbourne Institute of Technology Business Graduate School	30	7	13,880	17,765	32	30	No	Yes	Yes	48,900
Jamnalal Bajaj Institute of Management Studies (Mumbai)	240	9	1,000	1,000	24	0	No	No	Yes	7,000
Curtin Institute of Technology (Perth)	98	15	9,475	19,097	29	43	Yes	No	Yes	55,000
Lahore University of Management Sciences	70	14	11,250	26,300	23	2.5	No	No	No	7,500
Universiti Sains Malaysia (Penang)	30	5	2,260	2,260	32	15	No	Yes	Yes	16,000
De La Salle University (Manila)	44	17	3,300	3,600	28	3.5	Yes	No	Yes	13,100

2. Summarize the data to compare the following:
   a. Any difference between local and foreign tuition costs.
   b. Any difference between mean starting salaries for schools requiring and not requiring work experience.
   c. Any difference between starting salaries for schools requiring and not requiring English tests.
3. Do starting salaries appear to be related to tuition?
4. Present any additional graphical and numerical summaries that will be beneficial in communicating the data in Table 3.11 to others.

Case Problem 4   Heavenly Chocolates Website Transactions

Heavenly Chocolates manufactures and sells quality chocolate products at its plant and retail store located in Saratoga Springs, New York. Two years ago the company developed a website and began selling its products over the Internet. Website sales have exceeded the company's expectations, and management is now considering strategies to increase sales even further. To learn more about the website customers, a sample of 50 Heavenly Chocolate transactions was selected from the previous month's sales. Data showing the day of the week each transaction was made, the type of browser the customer used, the time spent on the website, the number of website pages viewed, and the amount spent by each of the 50 customers are contained in the file named Shoppers. A portion of the data are shown in Table 3.12.

Heavenly Chocolates would like to use the sample data to determine if online shoppers who spend more time and view more pages also spend more money during their visit to the website. The company would also like to investigate the effect that the day of the week and the type of browser have on sales.

Managerial Report

Use the methods of descriptive statistics to learn about the customers who visit the Heavenly Chocolates website. Include the following in your report.

1. Graphical and numerical summaries for the length of time the shopper spends on the website, the number of pages viewed, and the mean amount spent per transaction.

TABLE 3.12   A SAMPLE OF 50 HEAVENLY CHOCOLATES WEBSITE TRANSACTIONS

DATA *file*
Shoppers

Customer	Day	Browser	Time (min)	Pages Viewed	Amount Spent ($)
1	Mon	Internet Explorer	12.0	4	54.52
2	Wed	Other	19.5	6	94.90
3	Mon	Internet Explorer	8.5	4	26.68
4	Tue	Firefox	11.4	2	44.73
5	Wed	Internet Explorer	11.3	4	66.27
6	Sat	Firefox	10.5	6	67.80
7	Sun	Internet Explorer	11.4	2	36.04
.	.	.	.	.	.
.	.	.	.	.	.
.	.	.	.	.	.
48	Fri	Internet Explorer	9.7	5	103.15
49	Mon	Other	7.3	6	52.15
50	Fri	Internet Explorer	13.4	3	98.75

Discuss what you learn about Heavenly Cholcolates' online shoppers from these numerical summaries.

2. Summarize the frequency, the total dollars spent, and the mean amount spent per transaction for each day of week. What observations can you make about Heavenly Chocolates' business based on the day of the week? Discuss.

3. Summarize the frequency, the total dollars spent, and the mean amount spent per transaction for each type of browser. What observations can you make about Heavenly Chocolate's business based on the type of browser? Discuss.

4. Develop a scatter diagram and compute the sample correlation coefficient to explore the relationship between the time spent on the website and the dollar amount spent. Use the horizontal axis for the time spent on the website. Discuss.

5. Develop a scatter diagram and compute the sample correlation coefficient to explore the relationship between the number of website pages viewed and the amount spent. Use the horizontal axis for the number of website pages viewed. Discuss.

6. Develop a scatter diagram and compute the sample correlation coefficient to explore the relationship between the time spent on the website and the number of pages viewed. Use the horizontal axis to represent the number of pages viewed. Discuss.

Case Problem 5   African Elephant Populations

Although millions of elephants once roamed across Africa, by the mid-1980s elephant populations in African nations had been devastated by poaching. Elephants are important to African ecosystems. In tropical forests, elephants create clearings in the canopy that encourage new tree growth. In savannas, elephants reduce bush cover to create an environment that is favorable to browsing and grazing animals. In addition, the seeds of many plant species depend on passing through an elephant's digestive tract before germination.

The status of the elephant now varies greatly across the continent. In some nations, strong measures have been taken to effectively protect elephant populations; for example, Kenya has destroyed over five tons of elephant ivory confiscated from poachers in an attempt to deter the growth of illegal ivory trade (Associated Press, July 20, 2011). In other nations the elephant populations remain in danger due to poaching for meat and ivory, loss of habitat, and conflict with humans. Table 3.13 shows elephant populations for several African nations in 1979, 1989, and 2007 (ElephantDatabase.org website, December 15, 2014).

The David Sheldrick Wildlife Trust was established in 1977 to honor the memory of naturalist David Leslie William Sheldrick, who founded Warden of Tsavo East National Park in Kenya and headed the Planning Unit of the Wildlife Conservation and Management Department in that country. Management of the Sheldrick Trust would like to know what these data indicate about elephant populations in various African countries since 1979.

Managerial Report

Use methods of descriptive statistics to summarize the data and comment on changes in elephant populations in African nations since 1979. At a minimum your report should include the following.

1. The mean annual change in elephant population for each country in the 10 years from 1979 to 1989, and a discussion of which countries saw the largest changes in elephant population over this 10-year period.

2. The mean annual change in elephant population for each country from 1989 to 2007, and a discussion of which countries saw the largest changes in elephant population over this 18-year period.

TABLE 3.13   ELEPHANT POPULATIONS FOR SEVERAL AFRICAN NATIONS IN 1979, 1989, AND 2007

Country	1979 Elephant Population	Elephant Population 1989 Elephant Population	2007 Elephant Population	2012 Elephant Population
Angola	12,400	12,400	2,530	2,530
Botswana	20,000	51,000	175,487	175,454
Cameroon	16,200	21,200	15,387	14,049
Cen African Rep	63,000	19,000	3,334	2,285
Chad	15,000	3,100	6,435	3,004
Congo	10,800	70,000	22,102	49,248
Dem Rep of Congo	377,700	85,000	23,714	13,674
Gabon	13,400	76,000	70,637	77,252
Kenya	65,000	19,000	31,636	36,260
Mozambique	54,800	18,600	26,088	26,513
Somalia	24,300	6,000	70	70
Tanzania	316,300	80,000	167,003	117,456
Zambia	150,000	41,000	29,231	21,589
Zimbabwe	30,000	43,000	99,107	100,291

DATA *file*

2012African Eliphants

3. The mean annual change in elephant population for each country from 2007 to 2012, and a discussion of which countries saw the largest changes in elephant population over this 5-year period.

4. A comparison of your results from parts 1, 2, and 3, and a discussion of the conclusions you can draw from this comparison.

Appendix 3.1   Descriptive Statistics Using Minitab

In this appendix, we describe how Minitab can be used to compute a variety of descriptive statistics and display box plots. We then show how Minitab can be used to obtain covariance and correlation measures for two variables.

Descriptive Statistics

DATA *file*

2012StartSalary

Table 3.1 provided the starting salaries for 12 business school graduates. These data are in column C2 of the file 2012StartSalary. The following steps can be used to generate descriptive statistics for the starting salary data.

Step 1. Select the **Stat** menu
Step 2. Choose **Basic Statistics**
Step 3. Choose **Display Descriptive Statistics**
Step 4. When the Display Descriptive Statistics dialog box appears:
       Enter C2 in the **Variables** box
       Click **OK**

Figure 3.15 shows the descriptive statistics obtained using Minitab. Definitions of the headings follow.

N	number of data values	Minimum	minimum data value
N*	number of missing data values	Q1	first quartile
Mean	mean	Median	median
SE Mean	standard error of mean	Q3	third quartile
StDev	standard deviation	Maximum	maximum data value

FIGURE 3.15   DESCRIPTIVE STATISTICS PROVIDED BY MINITAB

N	N*	Mean	SEMean	StDev
12	0	3940.0	47.8	165.7
Minimum	**Q1**	**Median**	**Q3**	**Maximum**
3710.0	3857.5	3905.0	4025.0	4325.0

The label SE Mean refers to the *standard error of the mean.* It is computed by dividing the standard deviation by the square root of *N*. The interpretation and use of this measure are discussed in Chapter 7 when we introduce the topics of sampling and sampling distributions.

The 10 descriptive statistics shown in Figure 3.15 are the default descriptive statistics selected automatically by Minitab. These descriptive statistics are of interest to the majority of users. However, Minitab provides 15 additional descriptive statistics that may be selected depending upon the preferences of the user. The variance, coefficient of variation, range, interquartile range, mode, and skewness are among the additional descriptive statistics available. To select one or more of these additional descriptive statistics, modify step 4 as follows.

Step 4. When the Display Descriptive Statistics dialog box appears:
Enter C2 in the **Variables** box
Click **Statistics**
Select the **descriptive statistics** you wish to obtain or
choose **All** to obtain all 25 descriptive statistics
Click **OK**
Click **OK**

Box Plot

The following steps use the file 2012StartSalary to generate the box plot for the starting salary data.

Step 1. Select the **Graph** menu
Step 2. Choose **Boxplot**
Step 3. Under the heading **OneY** select **Simple** and click **OK**
Step 4. When the Boxplot: One Y, Simple dialog box appears:
Enter C2 in the **Graph variables** box
Click **OK**

Covariance and Correlation

Stereo

Table 3.6 provided the number of commercials and the sales volume for a stereo and sound equipment store. These data are available in the file Stereo, with the number of commercials in column C2 and the sales volume in column C3. The following steps show how Minitab can be used to compute the covariance for the two variables.

Step 1. Select the **Stat** menu
Step 2. Choose **Basic Statistics**
Step 3. Choose **Covariance**
Step 4. When the Covariance dialog box appears:
Enter C2 C3 in the **Variables** box
Click **OK**

To obtain the correlation coefficient for the number of commercials and the sales volume, only one change is necessary in the preceding procedure. In step 3, choose the **Correlation** option.

Appendix 3.2 Descriptive Statistics Using Excel

Excel can be used to generate the descriptive statistics discussed in this chapter. We show how Excel can be used to generate several measures of location and variability for a single variable and to generate the covariance and correlation coefficient as measures of association between two variables.

Using Excel Functions

2012StartSalary

Excel provides functions for computing the mean, median, mode, sample variance, and sample standard deviation. We illustrate the use of these Excel functions by computing the mean, median, mode, sample variance, and sample standard deviation for the starting salary data in Table 3.1. Refer to Figure 3.16 as we describe the steps involved. The data are entered in column B.

FIGURE 3.16 USING EXCEL FUNCTIONS FOR COMPUTING THE MEAN, MEDIAN, MODE, VARIANCE, AND STANDARD DEVIATION

	A	B	C	D	E
1	Graduate	Starting Salary		Mean	=AVERAGE(B2:B13)
2	1	3850		Median	=MEDIAN(B2:B13)
3	2	3950		Mode	=MODE.SNGL(B2:B13)
4	3	4050		Variance	=VAR.S(B2:B13)
5	4	3880		Standard Deviation	=STDEV.S(B2:B13)
6	5	3755			
7	6	3710			
8	7	3890			
9	8	4130			
10	9	3940			
11	10	4325			
12	11	3920			
13	12	3880			

	A	B	C	D	E
1	Graduate	Starting Salary		Mean	3940
2	1	3850		Median	3905
3	2	3950		Mode	3880
4	3	4050		Variance	27440.91
5	4	3880		Standard Deviation	165.65
6	5	3755			
7	6	3710			
8	7	3890			
9	8	4130			
10	9	3940			
11	10	4325			
12	11	3920			
13	12	3880			

Stereo

Excel's AVERAGE function can be used to compute the mean by entering the following formula into cell E1:

$$=AVERAGE(B2:B13)$$

To find the variance, standard deviation, and covariance for population data, follow the same steps but use the VAR.P, STDEV.P, and COV.P functions.

Similarly, the formulas =MEDIAN(B2:B13), =MODE.SNGL(B2:B13), =VAR.S(B2:B13), and =STDEV.S(B2:B13) are entered into cells E2:E5, respectively, to compute the median, mode, variance, and standard deviation for this sample. The worksheet in the foreground shows that the values computed using the Excel functions are the same as we computed earlier in the chapter.

Excel also provides functions that can be used to compute the sample covariance and the sample correlation coefficient. We show here how these functions can be used to compute the sample covariance and the sample correlation coefficient for the stereo and sound equipment store data in Table 3.6. Refer to Figure 3.17 as we present the steps involved.

Excel's sample covariance function, COVARIANCE.S, can be used to compute the sample covariance by entering the following formula into cell F1:

$$=COVARIANCE.S(B2:B11,C2:C11)$$

*If the **Analysis** tab doesn't appear on your ribbon or if the **Data Analysis** option doesn't appear in the **Data Analysis** tab, you need to activate the **Data Analysis ToolPak** by following these three steps:*

*1. Click the **File** tab, then click **Options**, and then click the **Add-Ins** category.*

*2. In the **Manage** box, click **Excel Add-ins**, and then click **Go**. The **Add-Ins** dialog box will then appear.*

*3. In the **Add-Ins available** box, select the check box next to the **Data Analysis ToolPak** add-in and click **OK**.*

*The **Analysis** tab will now be available with the **Data Analysis** option.*

Similarly, the formula =CORREL(B2:B11,C2:C11) is entered into cell F2 to compute the sample correlation coefficient. The worksheet in the foreground shows the values computed using the Excel functions. Note that the value of the sample covariance (11) is the same as computed using equation (3.13). And the value of the sample correlation coefficient (.93) is the same as computed using equation (3.15).

Using Excel's Descriptive Statistics Tool

As we already demonstrated, Excel provides statistical functions to compute descriptive statistics for a data set. These functions can be used to compute one statistic at a time (e.g., mean, variance, etc.). Excel also provides a variety of Data Analysis Tools. One of these tools, called Descriptive Statistics, allows the user to compute a variety of descriptive statistics at once. We show here how it can be used to compute descriptive statistics for the starting salary data in Table 3.1.

FIGURE 3.17   USING EXCEL FUNCTIONS FOR COMPUTING THE COVARIANCE AND CORRELATION

	A	B	C	D	E	F	G
1	Week	Commercials	Sales Volume		Sample Covariance	=COVARIANCE.S(B2:B11,C2:C11)	
2	1	2	50		Sample Correlation	=CORREL(B2:B11,C2:C11)	
3	2	5	57				
4	3	1	41				
5	4	3	54				
6	5	4	54				
7	6	1	38				
8	7	5	63				
9	8	3	48				
10	9	4	59				
11	10	2	46				
12							

	A	B	C	D	E	F	G
1	Week	Commercials	Sales Volume		Sample Covariance	11	
2	1	2	50		Sample Correlation	0.9305	
3	2	5	57				
4	3	1	41				
5	4	3	54				
6	5	4	54				
7	6	1	38				
8	7	5	63				
9	8	3	48				
10	9	4	59				
11	10	2	46				
12							

FIGURE 3.18 EXCEL'S DESCRIPTIVE STATISTICS TOOL OUTPUT

	A	B	C	D	E
1	**Graduate**	**Starting Salary**		*Starting Salary*	
2	1	3850			
3	2	3950		**Mean**	3940
4	3	4050		**Standard Error**	47.82
5	4	3880		**Median**	3905
6	5	3755		**Mode**	3880
7	6	3710		**Standard Deviation**	165.65
8	7	3890		**Sample Variance**	27440.91
9	8	4130		Kurtosis	1.72
10	9	3940		Skewness	1.09
11	10	4325		**Range**	615
12	11	3920		**Minimum**	3710
13	12	3880		**Maximum**	4325
14				**Sum**	47280
15				**Count**	12

2012StartSalary

Step 1. Click the **Data** tab on the Ribbon
Step 2. In the **Analysis** group, click **Data Analysis**
Step 3. When the Data Analysis dialog box appears:
    Choose **Descriptive Statistics**
    Click **OK**
Step 4. When the Descriptive Statistics dialog box appears:
    Enter B1:B13 in the **Input Range** box
    Select **Grouped By Columns**
    Select **Labels in First Row**
    Select **Output Range**
    Enter D1 in the **Output Range** box (to identify the upper left-hand corner
      of the section of the worksheet where the descriptive statistics will ap-
      pear)
    Select **Summary statistics**
    Click **OK**

Cells D1:E15 of Figure 3.18 show the descriptive statistics provided by Excel. The boldface entries are the descriptive statistics we covered in this chapter. The descriptive statistics that are not boldface are either covered subsequently in the text or discussed in more advanced texts.

CHAPTER 4

Linear Programming Applications in Marketing, Finance, and Operations Management

CONTENTS

Linear programming has proven to be one of the most successful quantitative approaches to decision making. Applications have been reported in almost every industry. These applications include production scheduling, media selection, financial planning, capital budgeting, transportation, distribution system design, product mix, staffing, and blending.

The wide variety of Management Science in Actions presented in Chapters 2 and 3 illustrated the use of linear programming as a flexible problem-solving tool. The Management Science in Action, A Marketing Planning Model at Marathon Oil Company, provides another example of the use of linear programming by showing how Marathon uses a large-scale linear programming model to solve a wide variety of planning problems. Later in the chapter other Management Science in Action vignettes illustrate how General Electric uses linear programming for making solar energy investment decisions; how Jeppesen Sanderson uses linear programming to optimize production of flight manuals; and how the Kellogg Company uses a large-scale linear programming model to integrate production, distribution, and inventory planning.

In this chapter we present a variety of applications from the traditional business areas of marketing, finance, and operations management. We emphasize modeling, computer solution, and interpretation of output. A mathematical model is developed for each problem studied, and solutions are presented for most of the applications. In the chapter appendix we illustrate the use of Excel Solver by solving a financial planning problem.

MANAGEMENT SCIENCE IN ACTION

A MARKETING PLANNING MODEL AT MARATHON OIL COMPANY*

Marathon Oil Company has four refineries within the United States, operates 50 light products terminals, and has product demand at more than 95 locations. The Supply and Transportation Division faces the problem of determining which refinery should supply which terminal and, at the same time, determining which products should be transported via pipeline, barge, or tanker to minimize cost. Product demand must be satisfied, and the supply capability of each refinery must not be exceeded. To help solve this difficult problem, Marathon Oil developed a marketing planning model.

The marketing planning model is a large-scale linear programming model that takes into account sales not only at Marathon product terminals but also at all exchange locations. An exchange contract is an agreement with other oil product marketers that involves exchanging or trading Marathon's products for theirs at different locations. All pipelines, barges, and tankers within Marathon's marketing area are also represented in the linear programming model.

The objective of the model is to minimize the cost of meeting a given demand structure, taking into account sales price, pipeline tariffs, exchange contract costs, product demand, terminal operating costs, refining costs, and product purchases.

The marketing planning model is used to solve a wide variety of planning problems that vary from evaluating gasoline blending economics to analyzing the economics of a new terminal or pipeline. With daily sales of about 10 million gallons of refined light product, a savings of even one-thousandth of a cent per gallon can result in significant long-term savings. At the same time, what may appear to be a savings in one area, such as refining or transportation, may actually add to overall costs when the effects are fully realized throughout the system. The marketing planning model allows a simultaneous examination of this total effect.

*Based on information provided by Robert W. Wernert at Marathon Oil Company, Findlay, Ohio.

4.1 MARKETING APPLICATIONS

Applications of linear programming in marketing are numerous. In this section we discuss applications in media selection and marketing research.

Media Selection

*In Section 2.1 we provided
some general guidelines
for modeling linear
programming problems.
You may want to review
Section 2.1 before pro-
ceeding with the linear
programming applications
in this chapter.*

Media selection applications of linear programming are designed to help marketing managers allocate a fixed advertising budget to various advertising media. Potential media include newspapers, magazines, radio, television, and direct mail. In these applications, the objective is to maximize reach, frequency, and quality of exposure. Restrictions on the allowable allocation usually arise during consideration of company policy, contract requirements, and media availability. In the application that follows, we illustrate how a media selection problem might be formulated and solved using a linear programming model.

Relax-and-Enjoy Lake Development Corporation is developing a lakeside community at a privately owned lake. The primary market for the lakeside lots and homes includes all middle- and upper-income families within approximately 100 miles of the development. Relax-and-Enjoy employed the advertising firm of Boone, Phillips, and Jackson (BP&J) to design the promotional campaign.

After considering possible advertising media and the market to be covered, BP&J recommended that the first month's advertising be restricted to five media. At the end of the month, BP&J will then reevaluate its strategy based on the month's results. BP&J collected data on the number of potential customers reached, the cost per advertisement, the maximum number of times each medium is available, and the exposure quality rating for each of the five media. The quality rating is measured in terms of an exposure quality unit, a measure of the relative value of one advertisement in each of the media. This measure, based on BP&J's experience in the advertising business, takes into account factors such as audience demographics (age, income, and education of the audience reached), image presented, and quality of the advertisement. The information collected is presented in Table 4.1.

Relax-and-Enjoy provided BP&J with an advertising budget of $30,000 for the first month's campaign. In addition, Relax-and-Enjoy imposed the following restrictions on how BP&J may allocate these funds: At least 10 television commercials must be used, at least 50,000 potential customers must be reached, and no more than $18,000 may be spent on television advertisements. What advertising media selection plan should be recommended?

TABLE 4.1   ADVERTISING MEDIA ALTERNATIVES FOR THE RELAX-AND-ENJOY LAKE
DEVELOPMENT CORPORATION

Advertising Media	Number of Potential Customers Reached	Cost ($) per Advertisement	Maximum Times Available per Month*	Exposure Quality Units
1. Daytime TV (1 min), station WKLA	1000	1500	15	65
2. Evening TV (30 sec), station WKLA	2000	3000	10	90
3. Daily newspaper (full page), *The Morning Journal*	1500	400	25	40
4. Sunday newspaper magazine (½ page color), *The Sunday Press*	2500	1000	4	60
5. Radio, 8:00 A.M. or 5:00 P.M. news (30 sec), station KNOP	300	100	30	20

*The maximum number of times the medium is available is either the maximum number of times the advertising medium occurs (e.g., four Sundays per month) or the maximum number of times BP&J recommends that the medium be used.

The decision to be made is how many times to use each medium. We begin by defining the decision variables:

$$DTV = \text{number of times daytime TV is used}$$
$$ETV = \text{number of times evening TV is used}$$
$$DN = \text{number of times daily newspaper is used}$$
$$SN = \text{number of times Sunday newspaper is used}$$
$$R = \text{number of times radio is used}$$

The data on quality of exposure in Table 4.1 show that each daytime TV (DTV) advertisement is rated at 65 exposure quality units. Thus, an advertising plan with DTV advertisements will provide a total of $65DTV$ exposure quality units. Continuing with the data in Table 4.1, we find evening TV (ETV) rated at 90 exposure quality units, daily newspaper (DN) rated at 40 exposure quality units, Sunday newspaper (SN) rated at 60 exposure quality units, and radio (R) rated at 20 exposure quality units. With the objective of maximizing the total exposure quality units for the overall media selection plan, the objective function becomes

Care must be taken to ensure the linear programming model accurately reflects the real problem. Always review your formulation thoroughly before attempting to solve the model.

$$\text{Max} \quad 65DTV + 90ETV + 40DN + 60SN + 20R \qquad \text{Exposure quality}$$

We now formulate the constraints for the model from the information given:

$$
\begin{array}{rcll}
DTV & \leq & 15 & \\
ETV & \leq & 10 & \\
DN & \leq & 25 & \left.\begin{array}{l}\\ \\ \\ \\ \\\end{array}\right\} \text{Availability of media}\\
SN & \leq & 4 & \\
R & \leq & 30 & \\
\end{array}
$$

$$1500DTV + 3000ETV + 400DN + 1000SN + 100R \leq 30{,}000 \qquad \text{Budget}$$

$$
\begin{array}{rcll}
DTV + ETV & \geq & 10 & \left.\begin{array}{l}\\ \\\end{array}\right\} \text{Television}\\
1500DTV + 3000ETV & \leq & 18{,}000 & \text{restrictions}\\
\end{array}
$$

$$1000DTV + 2000ETV + 1500DN + 2500SN + 300R \geq 50{,}000 \quad \text{Customers reached}$$
$$DTV, ETV, DN, SN, R \geq 0$$

Problem 1 provides practice at formulating a similar media selection model.

The optimal solution to this five-variable, nine-constraint linear programming model is shown in Figure 4.1; a summary is presented in Table 4.2.

The optimal solution calls for advertisements to be distributed among daytime TV, daily newspaper, Sunday newspaper, and radio. The maximum number of exposure quality units is 2370, and the total number of customers reached is 61,500. The Reduced Costs column in Figure 4.1 indicates that the number of exposure quality units for evening TV would have to increase by at least 65 before this media alternative could appear in the optimal solution. Note that the budget constraint (constraint 6) has a dual value of 0.06. Therefore, a $1.00 increase in the advertising budget will lead to an increase of 0.06 exposure quality units. The dual value of −25.000 for constraint 7 indicates that increasing the required number of television commercials by 1 will decrease the exposure quality of the advertising plan by 25 units. Alternatively, decreasing the required number of television commercials by 1 will increase the exposure quality of the advertising plan by 25 units.

FIGURE 4.1   THE SOLUTION FOR THE RELAX-AND-ENJOY LAKE DEVELOPMENT
CORPORATION PROBLEM

```
Optimal Objective Value =      2370.00000

      Variable            Value            Reduced Cost
    -------------      -------------      -----------------
        DTV               10.00000             0.00000
        ETV                0.00000           -65.00000
        DN                25.00000             0.00000
        SN                 2.00000             0.00000
        R                 30.00000             0.00000

      Constraint      Slack/Surplus         Dual Value
    -------------      -------------      -----------------
          1                5.00000             0.00000
          2               10.00000             0.00000
          3                0.00000            16.00000
          4                2.00000             0.00000
          5                0.00000            14.00000
          6                0.00000             0.06000
          7                0.00000           -25.00000
          8             3000.00000             0.00000
          9            11500.00000             0.00000
```

Media Availability

Budget

Television Restrictions

Audience Coverage

TABLE 4.2   ADVERTISING PLAN FOR THE RELAX-AND-ENJOY LAKE
DEVELOPMENT CORPORATION

Media	Frequency	Budget
Daytime TV	10	$15,000
Daily newspaper	25	10,000
Sunday newspaper	2	2,000
Radio	30	3,000
		$30,000

Exposure quality units = 2370
Total customers reached = 61,500

Thus, Relax-and-Enjoy should consider reducing the requirement of having at least 10 television commercials.

A possible shortcoming of this model is that, even if the exposure quality measure were not subject to error, it offers no guarantee that maximization of total exposure quality will lead to maximization of profit or of sales (a common surrogate for profit). However, this issue is not a shortcoming of linear programming; rather, it is a shortcoming of the use of exposure quality as a criterion. If we could directly measure the effect of an advertisement on profit, we could use total profit as the objective to be maximized.

NOTES AND COMMENTS

1. The media selection model required subjective evaluations of the exposure quality for the media alternatives. Marketing managers may have substantial data concerning exposure quality, but the final coefficients used in the objective function may also include considerations based primarily on managerial judgment. Judgment is an acceptable way of obtaining input for a linear programming model.

2. The media selection model presented in this section uses exposure quality as the objective function and places a constraint on the number of customers reached. An alternative formulation of this problem would be to use the number of customers reached as the objective function and add a constraint indicating the minimum total exposure quality required for the media plan.

Marketing Research

An organization conducts marketing research to learn about consumer characteristics, attitudes, and preferences. Marketing research firms that specialize in providing such information often do the actual research for client organizations. Typical services offered by a marketing research firm include designing the study, conducting market surveys, analyzing the data collected, and providing summary reports and recommendations for the client. In the research design phase, targets or quotas may be established for the number and types of respondents to be surveyed. The marketing research firm's objective is to conduct the survey so as to meet the client's needs at a minimum cost.

Market Survey, Inc. (MSI), specializes in evaluating consumer reaction to new products, services, and advertising campaigns. A client firm requested MSI's assistance in ascertaining consumer reaction to a recently marketed household product. During meetings with the client, MSI agreed to conduct door-to-door personal interviews to obtain responses from households with children and households without children. In addition, MSI agreed to conduct both day and evening interviews. Specifically, the client's contract called for MSI to conduct 1000 interviews under the following quota guidelines.

1. Interview at least 400 households with children.
2. Interview at least 400 households without children.
3. The total number of households interviewed during the evening must be at least as great as the number of households interviewed during the day.
4. At least 40% of the interviews for households with children must be conducted during the evening.
5. At least 60% of the interviews for households without children must be conducted during the evening.

Because the interviews for households with children take additional interviewer time and because evening interviewers are paid more than daytime interviewers, the cost varies with the type of interview. Based on previous research studies, estimates of the interview costs are as follows:

	Interview Cost	
Household	**Day**	**Evening**
Children	$20	$25
No children	$18	$20

What is the household, time-of-day interview plan that will satisfy the contract requirements at a minimum total interviewing cost?

In formulating the linear programming model for the MSI problem, we utilize the following decision-variable notation:

DC = the number of daytime interviews of households with children

EC = the number of evening interviews of households with children

DNC = the number of daytime interviews of households without children

ENC = the number of evening interviews of households without children

We begin the linear programming model formulation by using the cost-per-interview data to develop the objective function:

$$\text{Min} \quad 20DC + 25EC + 18DNC + 20ENC$$

The constraint requiring a total of 1000 interviews is

$$DC + EC + DNC + ENC = 1000$$

The five specifications concerning the types of interviews are as follows.

- Households with children:

$$DC + EC \geq 400$$

- Households without children:

$$DNC + ENC \geq 400$$

- At least as many evening interviews as day interviews:

$$EC + ENC \geq DC + DNC$$

- At least 40% of interviews of households with children during the evening:

$$EC \geq 0.4(DC + EC)$$

- At least 60% of interviews of households without children during the evening:

$$ENC \geq 0.6(DNC + ENC)$$

When we add the nonnegativity requirements, the four-variable and six-constraint linear programming model becomes

Min $20DC + 25EC + 18DNC + 20ENC$

s.t.

$DC +$	$EC +$	$DNC +$	$ENC = 1000$	Total interviews
$DC +$	EC		≥ 400	Households with children
		$DNC +$	$ENC \geq 400$	Households without children
	$EC + ENC \geq DC + DNC$			Evening interviews
	$EC \geq 0.4(DC + EC)$			Evening interviews in households with children
	$ENC \geq 0.6(DNC + ENC)$			Evening interviews in households without children

$DC, EC, DNC, ENC \geq 0$

The optimal solution to this linear program is shown in Figure 4.2. The solution reveals that the minimum cost of $20,320 occurs with the following interview schedule.

Household	Number of Interviews		Totals
	Day	Evening	
Children	240	160	400
No children	240	360	600
Totals	480	520	1000

Hence, 480 interviews will be scheduled during the day and 520 during the evening. Households with children will be covered by 400 interviews, and households without children will be covered by 600 interviews.

Selected sensitivity analysis information from Figure 4.2 shows a dual value of 19.200 for constraint 1. In other words, the value of the optimal solution will increase by $19.20 if the number of interviews is increased from 1000 to 1001. Thus, $19.20 is the incremental cost of obtaining additional interviews. It also is the savings that could be realized by reducing the number of interviews from 1000 to 999.

The surplus variable, with a value of 200.000, for constraint 3 shows that 200 more households without children will be interviewed than required. Similarly, the surplus variable, with a value of 40.000, for constraint 4 shows that the number of evening interviews exceeds the number of daytime interviews by 40. The zero values for the surplus variables in constraints 5 and 6 indicate that the more expensive evening interviews are being held at a minimum. Indeed, the dual value of 5.000 for constraint 5 indicates that if one more household (with children) than the minimum requirement must be interviewed during the evening, the total interviewing cost will go up by $5.00. Similarly, constraint 6 shows that requiring one more household (without children) to be interviewed during the evening will increase costs by $2.00.

FIGURE 4.2   THE SOLUTION FOR THE MARKET SURVEY PROBLEM

Market

```
Optimal Objective Value =              20320.00000

        Variable              Value              Reduced Cost
     --------------     ---------------     ------------------

          DC              240.00000                0.00000
          EC              160.00000                0.00000
          DNC             240.00000                0.00000
          ENC             360.00000                0.00000


        Constraint        Slack/Surplus           Dual Value
     --------------     ---------------     ----------------

           1                0.00000               19.20000
           2                0.00000                2.80000
           3              200.00000                0.00000
           4               40.00000                0.00000
           5                0.00000                5.00000
           6                0.00000                2.00000
```

4.2   FINANCIAL APPLICATIONS

In finance, linear programming can be applied in problem situations involving capital budgeting, asset allocation, portfolio selection, financial planning, and many others. In this section, we describe a portfolio selection problem and a problem involving funding of an early retirement program.

Portfolio Selection

Portfolio selection problems involve situations in which a financial manager must select specific investments—for example, stocks and bonds—from a variety of investment alternatives. Managers of mutual funds, credit unions, insurance companies, and banks frequently encounter this type of problem. The objective function for portfolio selection problems usually is maximization of expected return or minimization of risk. The constraints usually take the form of restrictions on the type of permissible investments, state laws, company policy, maximum permissible risk, and so on. Problems of this type have been formulated and solved using a variety of mathematical programming techniques. In this section we formulate and solve a portfolio selection problem as a linear program.

Consider the case of Welte Mutual Funds, Inc., located in New York City. Welte just obtained $100,000 by converting industrial bonds to cash and is now looking for other investment opportunities for these funds. Based on Welte's current investments, the firm's top financial analyst recommends that all new investments be made in the oil industry, steel industry, or in government bonds. Specifically, the analyst identified five investment opportunities and projected their annual rates of return. The investments and rates of return are shown in Table 4.3.

Management of Welte imposed the following investment guidelines.

1. Neither industry (oil or steel) should receive more than $50,000.
2. Government bonds should be at least 25% of the steel industry investments.
3. The investment in Pacific Oil, the high-return but high-risk investment, cannot be more than 60% of the total oil industry investment.

What portfolio recommendations—investments and amounts—should be made for the available $100,000? Given the objective of maximizing projected return subject to the budgetary and managerially imposed constraints, we can answer this question by formulating and solving a linear programming model of the problem. The solution will provide investment recommendations for the management of Welte Mutual Funds.

TABLE 4.3   INVESTMENT OPPORTUNITIES FOR WELTE MUTUAL FUNDS

Investment	Projected Rate of Return (%)
Atlantic Oil	7.3
Pacific Oil	10.3
Midwest Steel	6.4
Huber Steel	7.5
Government bonds	4.5

Let

$$A = \text{dollars invested in Atlantic Oil}$$
$$P = \text{dollars invested in Pacific Oil}$$
$$M = \text{dollars invested in Midwest Steel}$$
$$H = \text{dollars invested in Huber Steel}$$
$$G = \text{dollars invested in government bonds}$$

Using the projected rates of return shown in Table 4.3, we write the objective function for maximizing the total return for the portfolio as

$$\text{Max} \quad 0.073A + 0.103P + 0.064M + 0.075H + 0.045G$$

The constraint specifying investment of the available \$100,000 is

$$A + P + M + H + G = 100{,}000$$

The requirements that neither the oil nor the steel industry should receive more than \$50,000 are

$$A + P \leq 50{,}000$$
$$M + H \leq 50{,}000$$

The requirement that government bonds be at least 25% of the steel industry investment is expressed as

$$G \geq 0.25(M + H)$$

Finally, the constraint that Pacific Oil cannot be more than 60% of the total oil industry investment is

$$P \leq 0.60(A + P)$$

By adding the nonnegativity restrictions, we obtain the complete linear programming model for the Welte Mutual Funds investment problem:

Max $0.073A + 0.103P + 0.064M + 0.075H + 0.045G$

s.t.

$A +$	$P +$	$M +$	$H +$	$G = 100{,}000$	Available funds
$A +$	P			$\leq 50{,}000$	Oil industry maximum
		$M +$	H	$\leq 50{,}000$	Steel industry maximum
	$G \geq 0.25 (M + H)$				Government bonds minimum
	$P \leq 0.60 (A + P)$				Pacific Oil restriction

$$A, P, M, H, G \geq 0$$

The optimal solution to this linear program is shown in Figure 4.3. Table 4.4 shows how the funds are divided among the securities. Note that the optimal solution indicates that the portfolio should be diversified among all the investment opportunities except

FIGURE 4.3 THE SOLUTION FOR THE WELTE MUTUAL FUNDS PROBLEM

```
Optimal Objective Value =              8000.00000

     Variable            Value            Reduced Costs
   ------------      ------------        ---------------
        A            20000.00000              0.00000
        P            30000.00000              0.00000
        M                0.00000             -0.01100
        H            40000.00000              0.00000
        G            10000.00000              0.00000

    Constraint       Slack/Surplus          Dual Value
   ------------      ------------        ---------------
        1                0.00000              0.06900
        2                0.00000              0.02200
        3            10000.00000              0.00000
        4                0.00000             -0.02400
        5                0.00000              0.03000
```

Midwest Steel. The projected annual return for this portfolio is $8000, which is an overall return of 8%.

The optimal solution shows the dual value for constraint 3 is zero. The reason is that the steel industry maximum isn't a binding constraint; increases in the steel industry limit of $50,000 will not improve the value of the optimal solution. Indeed, the slack variable for this constraint shows that the current steel industry investment is $10,000 below its limit of $50,000. The dual values for the other constraints are nonzero, indicating that these constraints are binding.

The dual value for the available funds constraint provides information on the rate of return from additional investment funds.

The dual value of 0.069 for constraint 1 shows that the value of the optimal solution can be increased by 0.069 if one more dollar can be made available for the portfolio investment. If more funds can be obtained at a cost of less than 6.9%, management should consider obtaining them. However, if a return in excess of 6.9% can be obtained by investing funds elsewhere (other than in these five securities), management should question the wisdom of investing the entire $100,000 in this portfolio.

Similar interpretations can be given to the other dual values. Note that the dual value for constraint 4 is negative at –0.024. This result indicates that increasing the value on the

TABLE 4.4 OPTIMAL PORTFOLIO SELECTION FOR WELTE MUTUAL FUNDS

Investment	Amount	Expected Annual Return
Atlantic Oil	$ 20,000	$1460
Pacific Oil	30,000	3090
Huber Steel	40,000	3000
Government bonds	10,000	450
Totals	$100,000	$8000

Expected annual return of $8000
Overall rate of return = 8%

right-hand side of the constraint by one unit can be expected to decrease the objective function value of the optimal solution by 0.024. In terms of the optimal portfolio, then, if Welte invests one more dollar in government bonds (beyond the minimum requirement), the total return will decrease by $0.024. To see why this decrease occurs, note again from the dual value for constraint 1 that the marginal return on the funds invested in the portfolio is 6.9% (the average return is 8%). The rate of return on government bonds is 4.5%. Thus, the cost of investing one more dollar in government bonds is the difference between the marginal return on the portfolio and the marginal return on government bonds: 6.9% − 4.5% = 2.4%.

Note that the optimal solution shows that Midwest Steel should not be included in the portfolio ($M = 0$). The associated reduced cost for M of − 0.011 tells us that the objective function coefficient for Midwest Steel would have to increase by 0.011 before considering the Midwest Steel investment alternative would be advisable. With such an increase the Midwest Steel return would be 0.064 + 0.011 = 0.075, making this investment just as desirable as the currently used Huber Steel investment alternative.

Finally, a simple modification of the Welte linear programming model permits determining the fraction of available funds invested in each security. That is, we divide each of the right-hand-side values by 100,000. Then the optimal values for the variables will give the fraction of funds that should be invested in each security for a portfolio of any size.

NOTES AND COMMENTS

1. The optimal solution to the Welte Mutual Funds problem indicates that $20,000 is to be spent on the Atlantic Oil stock. If Atlantic Oil sells for $75 per share, we would have to purchase exactly 266⅔ shares in order to spend exactly $20,000. The difficulty of purchasing fractional shares can be handled by purchasing the largest possible integer number of shares with the allotted funds (e.g., 266 shares of Atlantic Oil). This approach guarantees that the budget constraint will not be violated. This approach, of course, introduces the possibility that the solution will no longer be optimal, but the danger is slight if a large number of securities are involved. In cases where the analyst believes that the decision variables *must* have integer values, the problem must be formulated as an integer linear programming model. Integer linear programming is the topic of Chapter 7.

2. Financial portfolio theory stresses obtaining a proper balance between risk and return. In the Welte problem, we explicitly considered return in the objective function. Risk is controlled by choosing constraints that ensure diversity among oil and steel stocks and a balance between government bonds and the steel industry investment.

Financial Planning

Linear programming has been used for a variety of financial planning applications. The Management Science in Action, General Electric Uses Linear Programming for Solar Energy Investment Decisions, describes how linear programming is used to evaluate various scenarios to guide capital investment strategy over a long-term horizon.

MANAGEMENT SCIENCE IN ACTION

GENERAL ELECTRIC USES LINEAR PROGRAMMING FOR SOLAR ENERGY INVESTMENT DECISIONS*

With growing concerns about the environment and our ability to continue to utilize limited non-renewable sources for energy, companies have begun to place much more emphasis on renewable forms of energy. Water, wind, and solar energy are renewable forms of energy that have become the focus of considerable investment by companies.

(continued)

General Electric (GE) has products in a variety of areas within the energy sector. One such area of interest to GE is solar energy. Solar energy is a relatively new concept with rapidly changing technologies; for example, solar cells and solar power systems. Solar cells can convert sunlight directly into electricity. Concentrating solar power systems focus a larger area of sunlight into a small beam that can be used as a heat source for conventional power generation. Solar cells can be placed on rooftops and hence can be used by both commercial and residential customers, whereas solar power systems are mostly used in commercial settings. In recent years, GE has invested in several solar cell technologies.

Determining the appropriate amount of production capacity in which to invest is a difficult problem due to the uncertainties in technology development, costs, and solar energy demand. GE uses a set of decision support tools to solve this problem. A detailed descriptive analytical model is used to estimate the cost of newly developed or proposed solar cells. Statistical models developed for new product introductions are used to estimate annual solar demand 10 to 15 years into the future. Finally, the cost and demand estimates are used in a multiperiod linear program to determine the best production capacity investment plan.

The linear program finds an optimal expansion plan by taking into account inventory, capacity, production, and budget constraints. Because of the high level of uncertainty, the linear program is solved over multiple future scenarios. A solution to each individual scenario is found and evaluated in the other scenarios to assess the risk associated with that plan. GE planning analysts have used these tools to support management's strategic investment decisions in the solar energy sector.

*Based on B. G. Thomas and S. Bollapragada, "General Electric Uses an Integrated Framework for Product Costing, Demand Forecasting and Capacity Planning for New Photovoltaic Technology Products," *Interfaces* 40, no. 5 (September/October 2010): 353–367.

In the rest of this section, we describe an application of linear programming to minimize the cost of satisfying a company's obligations to its early retirement program. Hewlitt Corporation established an early retirement program as part of its corporate restructuring. At the close of the voluntary sign-up period, 68 employees had elected early retirement. As a result of these early retirements, the company incurs the following obligations over the next eight years:

Year	1	2	3	4	5	6	7	8
Cash Requirement	430	210	222	231	240	195	225	255

The cash requirements (in thousands of dollars) are due at the beginning of each year.

The corporate treasurer must determine how much money must be set aside today to meet the eight yearly financial obligations as they come due. The financing plan for the retirement program includes investments in government bonds as well as savings. The investments in government bonds are limited to three choices:

Bond	Price	Rate (%)	Years to Maturity
1	$1150	8.875	5
2	1000	5.500	6
3	1350	11.750	7

The government bonds have a par value of $1000, which means that even with different prices each bond pays $1000 at maturity. The rates shown are based on the par value. For purposes of planning, the treasurer assumed that any funds not invested in bonds will be placed in savings and earn interest at an annual rate of 4%.

We define the decision variables as follows:

F = total dollars required to meet the retirement plan's eight-year obligation

B_1 = units of bond 1 purchased at the beginning of year 1

B_2 = units of bond 2 purchased at the beginning of year 1

B_3 = units of bond 3 purchased at the beginning of year 1

S_i = amount placed in savings at the beginning of year i for $i = 1, \ldots, 8$

The objective function is to minimize the total dollars needed to meet the retirement plan's eight-year obligation, or

$$\text{Min} \quad F$$

A key feature of this type of financial planning problem is that a constraint must be formulated for each year of the planning horizon. In general, each constraint takes the form:

$$\begin{pmatrix} \text{Funds available at} \\ \text{the beginning of the year} \end{pmatrix} - \begin{pmatrix} \text{Funds invested in bonds} \\ \text{and placed in savings} \end{pmatrix} = \begin{pmatrix} \text{Cash obligation for} \\ \text{the current year} \end{pmatrix}$$

The funds available at the beginning of year 1 are given by F. With a current price of $1150 for bond 1 and investments expressed in thousands of dollars, the total investment for B_1 units of bond 1 would be $1.15B_1$. Similarly, the total investment in bonds 2 and 3 would be $1B_2$ and $1.35B_3$, respectively. The investment in savings for year 1 is S_1. Using these results and the first-year obligation of 430, we obtain the constraint for year 1:

$$F - 1.15B_1 - 1B_2 - 1.35B_3 - S_1 = 430 \quad \text{year 1}$$

We do not consider future investments in bonds because the future price of bonds depends on interest rates and cannot be known in advance.

Investments in bonds can take place only in this first year, and the bonds will be held until maturity.

The funds available at the beginning of year 2 include the investment returns of 8.875% on the par value of bond 1, 5.5% on the par value of bond 2, 11.75% on the par value of bond 3, and 4% on savings. The new amount to be invested in savings for year 2 is S_2. With an obligation of 210, the constraint for year 2 is

$$0.08875B_1 + 0.055B_2 + 0.1175B_3 + 1.04S_1 - S_2 = 210 \quad \text{year 2}$$

Similarly, the constraints for Years 3 to 8 are

$$0.08875B_1 + 0.055B_2 + 0.1175B_3 + 1.04S_2 - S_3 = 222 \quad \text{year 3}$$
$$0.08875B_1 + 0.055B_2 + 0.1175B_3 + 1.04S_3 - S_4 = 231 \quad \text{year 4}$$
$$0.08875B_1 + 0.055B_2 + 0.1175B_3 + 1.04S_4 - S_5 = 240 \quad \text{year 5}$$
$$1.08875B_1 + 0.055B_2 + 0.1175B_3 + 1.04S_5 - S_6 = 195 \quad \text{year 6}$$
$$1.055B_2 + 0.1175B_3 + 1.04S_6 - S_7 = 225 \quad \text{year 7}$$
$$1.1175B_3 + 1.04S_7 - S_8 = 255 \quad \text{year 8}$$

Note that the constraint for year 6 shows that funds available from bond 1 are $1.08875B_1$. The coefficient of 1.08875 reflects the fact that bond 1 matures at the end of year 5. As a result, the par value plus the interest from bond 1 during year 5 is available at the beginning of year 6. Also, because bond 1 matures in year 5 and becomes available for use at the beginning of year 6, the variable B_1 does not appear in the constraints for years 7 and 8. Note the similar interpretation for bond 2, which matures at the end of year 6 and has the par value plus interest available at the beginning of year 7. In addition, bond 3 matures at the end of year 7 and has the par value plus interest available at the beginning of year 8.

Finally, note that a variable S_8 appears in the constraint for year 8. The retirement fund obligation will be completed at the beginning of year 8, so we anticipate that S_8 will be zero and no funds will be put into savings. However, the formulation includes S_8 in the event that the bond income plus interest from the savings in year 7 exceed the 255 cash requirement for year 8. Thus, S_8 is a surplus variable that shows any funds remaining after the eight-year cash requirements have been satisfied.

The optimal solution to this 12-variable, 8-constraint linear program is shown in Figure 4.4. With an objective function value of 1728.79385, the total investment required to meet the retirement plan's eight-year obligation is $1,728,794. Using the current prices of $1150, $1000, and $1350 for each of the bonds, respectively, we can summarize the initial investments in the three bonds as follows:

Bond	**Units Purchased**	**Investment Amount**
1	$B_1 = 144.988$	$1150(144.988) = \$166,736$
2	$B_2 = 187.856$	$1000(187.856) = \$187,856$
3	$B_3 = 228.188$	$1350(228.188) = \$308,054$

FIGURE 4.4   THE SOLUTION FOR THE HEWLITT CORPORATION CASH
REQUIREMENTS PROBLEM

```
Optimal Objective Value =            1728.79385

        Variable            Value             Reduced Cost
     --------------     --------------     -----------------

          F              1728.79385              0.00000
          B1              144.98815              0.00000
          B2              187.85585              0.00000
          B3              228.18792              0.00000
          S1              636.14794              0.00000
          S2              501.60571              0.00000
          S3              349.68179              0.00000
          S4              182.68091              0.00000
          S5                0.00000              0.06403
          S6                0.00000              0.01261
          S7                0.00000              0.02132
          S8                0.00000              0.67084


        Constraint       Slack/Surplus          Dual Value
     --------------     --------------     -----------------

           1                0.00000              1.00000
           2                0.00000              0.96154
           3                0.00000              0.92456
           4                0.00000              0.88900
           5                0.00000              0.85480
           6                0.00000              0.76036
           7                0.00000              0.71899
           8                0.00000              0.67084
```

The solution also shows that $636,148 (see S_1) will be placed in savings at the beginning of the first year. By starting with $1,728,794, the company can make the specified bond and savings investments and have enough left over to meet the retirement program's first-year cash requirement of $430,000.

The optimal solution in Figure 4.4 shows that the decision variables S_1, S_2, S_3, and S_4 all are greater than zero, indicating investments in savings are required in each of the first four years. However, interest from the bonds plus the bond maturity incomes will be sufficient to cover the retirement program's cash requirements in years 5 through 8.

In this application, the dual value can be thought of as the present value of each dollar in the cash requirement. For example, each dollar that must be paid in year 8 has a present value of $0.67084.

The dual values have an interesting interpretation in this application. Each right-hand-side value corresponds to the payment that must be made in that year. Note that the dual values are positive, indicating that increasing the required payment in any year by $1,000 would *increase* the total funds required for the retirement program's obligation by $1,000 times the dual value. Also note that the dual values show that increases in required payments in the early years have the largest impact. This makes sense in that there is little time to build up investment income in the early years versus the subsequent years. This suggests that if Hewlitt faces increases in required payments it would benefit by deferring those increases to later years if possible.

NOTES AND COMMENTS

1. The optimal solution for the Hewlitt Corporation problem shows fractional numbers of government bonds at 144.988, 187.856, and 228.188 units, respectively. However, fractional bond units usually are not available. If we were conservative and rounded up to 145, 188, and 229 units, respectively, the total funds required for the eight-year retirement program obligation would be approximately $1254 more than the total funds indicated by the objective function. Because of the magnitude of the funds involved, rounding up probably would provide a workable solution. If an optimal integer solution were required, the methods of integer linear programming covered in Chapter 7 would have to be used.

2. We implicitly assumed that interest from the government bonds is paid annually. Investments such as treasury notes actually provide interest payments every six months. In such cases, the model can be reformulated with six-month periods, with interest and/or cash payments occurring every six months.

4.3   OPERATIONS MANAGEMENT APPLICATIONS

Linear programming applications developed for production and operations management include scheduling, staffing, inventory control, and capacity planning. In this section we describe examples with make-or-buy decisions, production scheduling, and workforce assignments.

A Make-or-Buy Decision

We illustrate the use of a linear programming model to determine how much of each of several component parts a company should manufacture and how much it should purchase from an outside supplier. Such a decision is referred to as a make-or-buy decision.

The Janders Company markets various business and engineering products. Currently, Janders is preparing to introduce two new calculators: one for the business market called the Financial Manager and one for the engineering market called the Technician. Each calculator has three components: a base, an electronic cartridge, and a faceplate or top. The same base is used for both calculators, but the cartridges and tops are different. All components can be manufactured by the company or purchased from outside suppliers. The manufacturing costs and purchase prices for the components are summarized in Table 4.5.

TABLE 4.5   MANUFACTURING COSTS AND PURCHASE PRICES FOR JANDERS CALCULATOR COMPONENTS

	Cost per Unit	
Component	**Manufacture (regular time)**	**Purchase**
Base	$0.50	$0.60
Financial cartridge	$3.75	$4.00
Technician cartridge	$3.30	$3.90
Financial top	$0.60	$0.65
Technician top	$0.75	$0.78

Company forecasters indicate that 3000 Financial Manager calculators and 2000 Technician calculators will be needed. However, manufacturing capacity is limited. The company has 200 hours of regular manufacturing time and 50 hours of overtime that can be scheduled for the calculators. Overtime involves a premium at the additional cost of $9 per hour. Table 4.6 shows manufacturing times (in minutes) for the components.

The problem for Janders is to determine how many units of each component to manufacture and how many units of each component to purchase. We define the decision variables as follows:

$$BM = \text{number of bases manufactured}$$
$$BP = \text{number of bases purchased}$$
$$FCM = \text{number of Financial cartridges manufactured}$$
$$FCP = \text{number of Financial cartridges purchased}$$
$$TCM = \text{number of Technician cartridges manufactured}$$
$$TCP = \text{number of Technician cartridges purchased}$$
$$FTM = \text{number of Financial tops manufactured}$$
$$FTP = \text{number of Financial tops purchased}$$
$$TTM = \text{number of Technician tops manufactured}$$
$$TTP = \text{number of Technician tops purchased}$$

One additional decision variable is needed to determine the hours of overtime that must be scheduled:

$$OT = \text{number of hours of overtime to be scheduled}$$

TABLE 4.6   MANUFACTURING TIMES IN MINUTES PER UNIT FOR JANDERS CALCULATOR COMPONENTS

Component	**Manufacturing Time**
Base	1.0
Financial cartridge	3.0
Technician cartridge	2.5
Financial top	1.0
Technician top	1.5

The objective function is to minimize the total cost, including manufacturing costs, purchase costs, and overtime costs. Using the cost-per-unit data in Table 4.5 and the overtime premium cost rate of $9 per hour, we write the objective function as

$$\text{Min}\quad 0.5BM + 0.6BP + 3.75FCM + 4FCP + 3.3TCM + 3.9TCP + 0.6FTM$$
$$+ 0.65FTP + 0.75TTM + 0.78TTP + 9OT$$

The first five constraints specify the number of each component needed to satisfy the demand for 3000 Financial Manager calculators and 2000 Technician calculators. A total of 5000 base components are needed, with the number of other components depending on the demand for the particular calculator. The five demand constraints are

$$BM + BP = 5000 \quad \text{Bases}$$
$$FCM + FCP = 3000 \quad \text{Financial cartridges}$$
$$TCM + TCP = 2000 \quad \text{Technician cartridges}$$
$$FTM + FTP = 3000 \quad \text{Financial tops}$$
$$TTM + TTP = 2000 \quad \text{Technician tops}$$

Two constraints are needed to guarantee that manufacturing capacities for regular time and overtime cannot be exceeded. The first constraint limits overtime capacity to 50 hours, or

$$OT \le 50$$

The same units of measure must be used for both the left-hand side and right-hand side of the constraint. In this case, minutes are used.

The second constraint states that the total manufacturing time required for all components must be less than or equal to the total manufacturing capacity, including regular time plus overtime. The manufacturing times for the components are expressed in minutes, so we state the total manufacturing capacity constraint in minutes, with the 200 hours of regular time capacity becoming $60(200) = 12{,}000$ minutes. The actual overtime required is unknown at this point, so we write the overtime as $60OT$ minutes. Using the manufacturing times from Table 4.6, we have

$$BM + 3FCM + 2.5TCM + FTM + 1.5TTM \le 12{,}000 + 60OT$$

The complete formulation of the Janders make-or-buy problem with all decision variables greater than or equal to zero is

$$\text{Min}\quad 0.5BM + 0.6BP + 3.75FCM + 4FCP + 3.3TCM + 3.9TCP$$
$$+ 0.6FTM + 0.65FTP + 0.75TTM + 0.78TTP + 9OT$$

s.t.

BM				$+$	$BP = 5000$	Bases
	FCM			$+$	$FCP = 3000$	Financial cartridges
		TCM		$+$	$TCP = 2000$	Technician cartridges
			FTM	$+$	$FTP = 3000$	Financial tops
			$TTM +$		$TTP = 2000$	Technician tops
					$OT \le \quad 50$	Overtime hours
$BM + 3FCM + 2.5TCM + FTM + 1.5TTM$					$\le 12{,}000 + 60OT$	Manufacturing capacity

The optimal solution to this 11-variable, 7-constraint linear program is shown in Figure 4.5. The optimal solution indicates that all 5000 bases (BM), 667 Financial Manager cartridges (FCM), and 2000 Technician cartridges (TCM) should be manufactured. The remaining 2333 Financial Manager cartridges (FCP), all the Financial Manager tops (FTP),

FIGURE 4.5   THE SOLUTION FOR THE JANDERS MAKE-OR-BUY PROBLEM

Janders

```
Optimal Objective Value =        24443.33333
```

Variable	Value	Reduced Cost
BM	5000.00000	0.00000
BP	0.00000	0.01667
FCM	666.66667	0.00000
FCP	2333.33333	0.00000
TCM	2000.00000	0.00000
TCP	0.00000	0.39167
FTM	0.00000	0.03333
FTP	3000.00000	0.00000
TTM	0.00000	0.09500
TTP	2000.00000	0.00000
OT	0.00000	4.00000

Constraint	Slack/Surplus	Dual Value
1	0.00000	0.58333
2	0.00000	4.00000
3	0.00000	3.50833
4	0.00000	0.65000
5	0.00000	0.78000
6	50.00000	0.00000
7	0.00000	-0.08333

Variable	Objective Coefficient	Allowable Increase	Allowable Decrease
BM	0.50000	0.01667	Infinite
BP	0.60000	Infinite	0.01667
FCM	3.75000	0.10000	0.05000
FCP	4.00000	0.05000	0.10000
TCM	3.30000	0.39167	Infinite
TCP	3.90000	Infinite	0.39167
FTM	0.60000	Infinite	0.03333
FTP	0.65000	0.03333	Infinite
TTM	0.75000	Infinite	0.09500
TTP	0.78000	0.09500	Infinite
OT	9.00000	Infinite	4.00000

Constraint	RHS Value	Allowable Increase	Allowable Decrease
1	5000.00000	2000.00000	5000.00000
2	3000.00000	Infinite	2333.33333
3	2000.00000	800.00000	2000.00000
4	3000.00000	Infinite	3000.00000
5	2000.00000	Infinite	2000.00000
6	50.00000	Infinite	50.00000
7	12000.00000	7000.00000	2000.00000

and all Technician tops (*TTP*) should be purchased. No overtime manufacturing is necessary, and the total cost associated with the optimal make-or-buy plan is $24,443.33.

Sensitivity analysis provides some additional information about the unused overtime capacity. The Reduced Costs column shows that the overtime (*OT*) premium would have to decrease by $4 per hour before overtime production should be considered. That is, if the overtime premium is $9 − $4 = $5 or less, Janders may want to replace some of the purchased components with components manufactured on overtime.

The dual value for the manufacturing capacity constraint 7 is −0.083. This value indicates that an additional hour of manufacturing capacity is worth $0.083 per minute or ($0.083) (60) = $5 per hour. The right-hand-side range for constraint 7 shows that this conclusion is valid until the amount of regular time increases to 19,000 minutes, or 316.7 hours.

Sensitivity analysis also indicates that a change in prices charged by the outside suppliers can affect the optimal solution. For instance, the objective coefficient range for *BP* is 0.583 (0.600 − 0.017) to no upper limit. If the purchase price for bases remains at $0.583 or more, the number of bases purchased (*BP*) will remain at zero. However, if the purchase price drops below $0.583, Janders should begin to purchase rather than manufacture the base component. Similar sensitivity analysis conclusions about the purchase price ranges can be drawn for the other components.

NOTES AND COMMENTS

The proper interpretation of the dual value for manufacturing capacity (constraint 7) in the Janders problem is that an additional hour of manufacturing capacity is worth ($0.083)(60) = $5 per hour. Thus, the company should be willing to pay a premium of $5 per hour over and above the current regular time cost per hour, which is already included in the manufacturing cost of the product. Thus, if the regular time cost is $18 per hour, Janders should be willing to pay up to $18 + $5 = $23 per hour to obtain additional labor capacity.

Production Scheduling

One of the most important applications of linear programming deals with multiperiod planning such as production scheduling. The solution to a production scheduling problem enables the manager to establish an efficient low-cost production schedule for one or more products over several time periods (weeks or months). Essentially, a production scheduling problem can be viewed as a product-mix problem for each of several periods in the future. The manager must determine the production levels that will allow the company to meet product demand requirements, given limitations on production capacity, labor capacity, and storage space, while minimizing total production costs.

One advantage of using linear programming for production scheduling problems is that they recur. A production schedule must be established for the current month, then again for the next month, for the month after that, and so on. When looking at the problem each month, the production manager will find that, although demand for the products has changed, production times, production capacities, storage space limitations, and so on are roughly the same. Thus, the production manager is basically re-solving the same problem handled in previous months, and a general linear programming model of the production scheduling procedure may be applied frequently. Once the model has been formulated, the manager can simply supply the data—demand, capacities, and so on—for the given production period and use the linear programming model repeatedly to develop the production schedule. The Management Science in Action, Optimizing Production of Flight Manuals at

MANAGEMENT SCIENCE IN ACTION

OPTIMIZING PRODUCTION OF FLIGHT MANUALS AT JEPPESEN SANDERSON, INC.*

Jeppesen Sanderson, Inc., manufactures and distributes flight manuals that contain safety information to more than 300,000 pilots and 4000 airlines. Every week Jeppesen mails between 5 and 30 million pages of chart revisions to 200,000 customers worldwide, and the company receives about 1500 new orders each week. In the late 1990s, its customer service deteriorated as its existing production and supporting systems failed to keep up with this level of activity. To meet customer service goals, Jeppesen turned to optimization-based decision support tools for production planning.

Jeppesen developed a large-scale linear program called Scheduler to minimize the cost of producing the weekly revisions. Model constraints included capacity constraints and numerous internal business rules. The model includes 250,000

variables, and 40,000 to 50,000 constraints. Immediately after introducing the model, Jeppesen established a new record for the number of consecutive weeks with 100% on-time revisions. Scheduler decreased tardiness of revisions from approximately 9% to 3% and dramatically improved customer satisfaction. Even more importantly, Scheduler provided a model of the production system for Jeppesen to use in strategic economic analysis. Overall, the use of optimization techniques at Jeppesen resulted in cost reductions of nearly 10% and a 24% increase in profit.

*Based on E. Katok, W. Tarantino, and R. Tiedman, "Improving Performance and Flexibility at Jeppesen: The World's Leading Aviation-Information Company," *Interfaces* (January/February 2001): 7–29.

Jeppesen Sanderson, Inc., describes how linear programming is used to minimize the cost of producing weekly revisions to flight manuals.

Let us consider the case of the Bollinger Electronics Company, which produces two different electronic components for a major airplane engine manufacturer. The airplane engine manufacturer notifies the Bollinger sales office each quarter of its monthly requirements for components for each of the next three months. The monthly requirements for the components may vary considerably, depending on the type of engine the airplane engine manufacturer is producing. The order shown in Table 4.7 has just been received for the next three-month period.

After the order is processed, a demand statement is sent to the production control department. The production control department must then develop a three-month production plan for the components. In arriving at the desired schedule, the production manager will want to identify the following:

1. Total production cost
2. Inventory holding cost
3. Change-in-production-level costs

In the remainder of this section, we show how to formulate a linear programming model of the production and inventory process for Bollinger Electronics to minimize the total cost.

TABLE 4.7   THREE-MONTH DEMAND SCHEDULE FOR BOLLINGER
ELECTRONICS COMPANY

Component	April	May	June
322A	1000	3000	5000
802B	1000	500	3000

To develop the model, we let x_{im} denote the production volume in units for product i in month m. Here $i = 1, 2$, and $m = 1, 2, 3$; $i = 1$ refers to component 322A, $i = 2$ refers to component 802B, $m = 1$ refers to April, $m = 2$ refers to May, and $m = 3$ refers to June. The purpose of the double subscript is to provide a more descriptive notation. We could simply use x_6 to represent the number of units of product 2 produced in month 3, but x_{23} is more descriptive, identifying directly the product and month represented by the variable.

If component 322A costs \$20 per unit produced and component 802B costs \$10 per unit produced, the total production cost part of the objective function is

$$\text{Total production cost} = 20x_{11} + 20x_{12} + 20x_{13} + 10x_{21} + 10x_{22} + 10x_{23}$$

Because the production cost per unit is the same each month, we don't need to include the production costs in the objective function; that is, regardless of the production schedule selected, the total production cost will remain the same. In other words, production costs are not relevant costs for the production scheduling decision under consideration. In cases in which the production cost per unit is expected to change each month, the variable production costs per unit per month must be included in the objective function. The solution for the Bollinger Electronics problem will be the same regardless of whether these costs are included; therefore, we included them so that the value of the linear programming objective function will include all the costs associated with the problem.

To incorporate the relevant inventory holding costs into the model, we let s_{im} denote the inventory level for product i at the end of month m. Bollinger determined that on a monthly basis inventory holding costs are 1.5% of the cost of the product; that is, (0.015)(\$20) = \$0.30 per unit for component 322A and (0.015)(\$10) = \$0.15 per unit for component 802B. A common assumption made in using the linear programming approach to production scheduling is that monthly ending inventories are an acceptable approximation to the average inventory levels throughout the month. Making this assumption, we write the inventory holding cost portion of the objective function as

$$\text{Inventory holding cost} = 0.30s_{11} + 0.30s_{12} + 0.30s_{13} + 0.15s_{21} + 0.15s_{22} + 0.15s_{23}$$

To incorporate the costs of fluctuations in production levels from month to month, we need to define two additional variables:

$$I_m = \text{increase in the total production level necessary during month } m$$
$$D_m = \text{decrease in the total production level necessary during month } m$$

After estimating the effects of employee layoffs, turnovers, reassignment training costs, and other costs associated with fluctuating production levels, Bollinger estimates that the cost associated with increasing the production level for any month is \$0.50 per unit increase. A similar cost associated with decreasing the production level for any month is \$0.20 per unit. Thus, we write the third portion of the objective function as

$$\text{Change-in-production-level costs} = 0.50I_1 + 0.50I_2 + 0.50I_3$$
$$+ 0.20D_1 + 0.20D_2 + 0.20D_3$$

Note that the cost associated with changes in production level is a function of the change in the total number of units produced in month m compared to the total number of units produced in month $m - 1$. In other production scheduling applications, fluctuations in production level might be measured in terms of machine hours or labor-hours required rather than in terms of the total number of units produced.

Combining all three costs, the complete objective function becomes

$$\text{Min } 20x_{11} + 20x_{12} + 20x_{13} + 10x_{21} + 10x_{22} + 10x_{23} + 0.30s_{11}$$
$$+ 0.30s_{12} + 0.30s_{13} + 0.15s_{21} + 0.15s_{22} + 0.15s_{23} + 0.50I_1$$
$$+ 0.50I_2 + 0.50I_3 + 0.20D_1 + 0.20D_2 + 0.20D_3$$

We now consider the constraints. First, we must guarantee that the schedule meets customer demand. Because the units shipped can come from the current month's production or from inventory carried over from previous months, the demand requirement takes the form

$$\begin{pmatrix} \text{Ending} \\ \text{inventory} \\ \text{from previous} \\ \text{month} \end{pmatrix} + \begin{pmatrix} \text{Current} \\ \text{production} \end{pmatrix} - \begin{pmatrix} \text{Ending} \\ \text{inventory} \\ \text{for this} \\ \text{month} \end{pmatrix} = \begin{pmatrix} \text{This month's} \\ \text{demand} \end{pmatrix}$$

Suppose that the inventories at the beginning of the three-month scheduling period were 500 units for component 322A and 200 units for component 802B. The demand for both products in the first month (April) was 1000 units, so the constraints for meeting demand in the first month become

$$500 + x_{11} - s_{11} = 1000$$
$$200 + x_{21} - s_{21} = 1000$$

Moving the constants to the right-hand side, we have

$$x_{11} - s_{11} = 500$$
$$x_{21} - s_{21} = 800$$

Similarly, we need demand constraints for both products in the second and third months. We write them as follows:

Month 2

$$s_{11} + x_{12} - s_{12} = 3000$$
$$s_{21} + x_{22} - s_{22} = 500$$

Month 3

$$s_{12} + x_{13} - s_{13} = 5000$$
$$s_{22} + x_{23} - s_{23} = 3000$$

If the company specifies a minimum inventory level at the end of the three-month period of at least 400 units of component 322A and at least 200 units of component 802B, we can add the constraints

$$s_{13} \geq 400$$
$$s_{23} \geq 200$$

Suppose that we have the additional information on machine, labor, and storage capacity shown in Table 4.8. Machine, labor, and storage space requirements are given in Table 4.9. To reflect these limitations, the following constraints are necessary:

Machine Capacity

$$0.10x_{11} + 0.08x_{21} \leq 400 \quad \text{month 1}$$
$$0.10x_{12} + 0.08x_{22} \leq 500 \quad \text{month 2}$$
$$0.10x_{13} + 0.08x_{23} \leq 600 \quad \text{month 3}$$

Labor Capacity

$$0.05x_{11} + 0.07x_{21} \leq 300 \quad \text{month 1}$$
$$0.05x_{12} + 0.07x_{22} \leq 300 \quad \text{month 2}$$
$$0.05x_{13} + 0.07x_{23} \leq 300 \quad \text{month 3}$$

Storage Capacity

$$2s_{11} + 3s_{21} \leq 10,000 \quad \text{month 1}$$
$$2s_{12} + 3s_{22} \leq 10,000 \quad \text{month 2}$$
$$2s_{13} + 3s_{23} \leq 10,000 \quad \text{month 3}$$

One final set of constraints must be added to guarantee that I_m and D_m will reflect the increase or decrease in the total production level for month m. Suppose that the production levels for March, the month before the start of the current production scheduling period, had been 1500 units of component 322A and 1000 units of component 802B for a

TABLE 4.8   MACHINE, LABOR, AND STORAGE CAPACITIES
FOR BOLLINGER ELECTRONICS

Month	Machine Capacity (hours)	Labor Capacity (hours)	Storage Capacity (square feet)
April	400	300	10,000
May	500	300	10,000
June	600	300	10,000

TABLE 4.9   MACHINE, LABOR, AND STORAGE REQUIREMENTS FOR COMPONENTS
322A AND 802B

Component	Machine (hours/unit)	Labor (hours/unit)	Storage (square feet/unit)
322A	0.10	0.05	2
802B	0.08	0.07	3

total production level of $1500 + 1000 = 2500$ units. We can find the amount of the change in production for April from the relationship

$$\text{April production} - \text{March production} = \text{Change}$$

Using the April production variables, x_{11} and x_{21}, and the March production of 2500 units, we have

$$(x_{11} + x_{21}) - 2500 = \text{Change}$$

Note that the change can be positive or negative. A positive change reflects an increase in the total production level, and a negative change reflects a decrease in the total production level. We can use the increase in production for April, I_1, and the decrease in production for April, D_1, to specify the constraint for the change in total production for the month of April:

$$(x_{11} + x_{21}) - 2500 = I_1 - D_1$$

Of course, we cannot have an increase in production and a decrease in production during the same one-month period; thus, either, I_1 or D_1 will be zero. If April requires 3000 units of production, $I_1 = 500$ and $D_1 = 0$. If April requires 2200 units of production, $I_1 = 0$ and $D_1 = 300$. This approach of denoting the change in production level as the difference between two nonnegative variables, I_1 and D_1, permits both positive and negative changes in the total production level. If a single variable (say, c_m) had been used to represent the change in production level, only positive changes would be possible because of the non-negativity requirement.

Using the same approach in May and June (always subtracting the previous month's total production from the current month's total production), we obtain the constraints for the second and third months of the production scheduling period:

$$(x_{12} + x_{22}) - (x_{11} + x_{21}) = I_2 - D_2$$
$$(x_{13} + x_{23}) - (x_{12} + x_{22}) = I_3 - D_3$$

Linear programming models for production scheduling are often very large. Thousands of decision variables and constraints are necessary when the problem involves numerous products, machines, and time periods. Data collection for large-scale models can be more time-consuming than either the formulation of the model or the development of the computer solution.

The initially rather small, two-product, three-month scheduling problem has now developed into an 18-variable, 20-constraint linear programming problem. Note that in this problem we were concerned only with one type of machine process, one type of labor, and one type of storage area. Actual production scheduling problems usually involve several machine types, several labor grades, and/or several storage areas, requiring large-scale linear programs. For instance, a problem involving 100 products over a 12-month period could have more than 1000 variables and constraints.

Figure 4.6 shows the optimal solution to the Bollinger Electronics production scheduling problem. Table 4.10 contains a portion of the managerial report based on the optimal solution.

Consider the monthly variation in the production and inventory schedule shown in Table 4.10. Recall that the inventory cost for component 802B is one-half the inventory cost for component 322A. Therefore, as might be expected, component 802B is produced heavily in the first month (April) and then held in inventory for the demand that will occur in future months. Component 322A tends to be produced when needed, and only small amounts are carried in inventory.

FIGURE 4.6   THE SOLUTION FOR THE BOLLINGER ELECTRONICS PROBLEM

```
Optimal Objective Value =          225295.00000

        Variable              Value             Reduced Cost
    --------------       ---------------      -----------------
         X11               500.00000               0.00000
         X12              3200.00000               0.00000
         X13              5200.00000               0.00000
         S11                 0.00000               0.17222
         S12               200.00000               0.00000
         S12               400.00000               0.00000
         X21              2500.00000               0.00000
         X22              2000.00000               0.00000
         X23                 0.00000               0.12778
         S21              1700.00000               0.00000
         S22              3200.00000               0.00000
         S23               200.00000               0.00000
         I1                500.00000               0.00000
         I2               2200.00000               0.00000
         I3                  0.00000               0.07222
         D1                  0.00000               0.70000
         D2                  0.00000               0.70000
         D3                  0.00000               0.62778

       Constraint        Slack/Surplus           Dual Value
    --------------       ---------------      -----------------
          1                  0.00000              20.00000
          2                  0.00000              10.00000
          3                  0.00000              20.12778
          4                  0.00000              10.15000
          5                  0.00000              20.42778
          6                  0.00000              10.30000
          7                  0.00000              20.72778
          8                  0.00000              10.45000
          9                150.00000               0.00000
         10                 20.00000               0.00000
         11                 80.00000               0.00000
         12                100.00000               0.00000
         13                  0.00000              -1.11111
         14                 40.00000               0.00000
         15               4900.00000               0.00000
         16                  0.00000               0.00000
         17               8600.00000               0.00000
         18                  0.00000              -0.50000
         19                  0.00000              -0.50000
         20                  0.00000              -0.42778
```

TABLE 4.10 MINIMUM COST PRODUCTION SCHEDULE INFORMATION FOR THE BOLLINGER ELECTRONICS PROBLEM

Activity	April	May	June
Production			
Component 322A	500	3200	5200
Component 802B	2500	2000	0
Totals	3000	5200	5200
Ending inventory			
Component 322A	0	200	400
Component 802B	1700	3200	200
Machine usage			
Scheduled hours	250	480	520
Slack capacity hours	150	20	80
Labor usage			
Scheduled hours	200	300	260
Slack capacity hours	100	0	40
Storage usage			
Scheduled storage	5100	10,000	1400
Slack capacity	4900	0	8600
Total production, inventory, and production-smoothing cost = $225,295			

The costs of increasing and decreasing the total production volume tend to smooth the monthly variations. In fact, the minimum-cost schedule calls for a 500-unit increase in total production in April and a 2200-unit increase in total production in May. The May production level of 5200 units is then maintained during June.

The machine usage section of the report shows ample machine capacity in all three months. However, labor capacity is at full utilization (slack = 0 for constraint 13 in Figure 4.6) in the month of May. The dual value shows that an additional hour of labor capacity in May will decrease total cost by approximately $1.11.

A linear programming model of a two-product, three-month production system can provide valuable information in terms of identifying a minimum-cost production schedule. In larger production systems, where the number of variables and constraints is too large to track manually, linear programming models can provide a significant advantage in developing cost-saving production schedules. The Management Science in Action, Optimizing Production, Inventory, and Distribution at the Kellogg Company, illustrates the use of a large-scale multiperiod linear program for production planning and distribution.

Workforce Assignment

Workforce assignment problems frequently occur when production managers must make decisions involving staffing requirements for a given planning period. Workforce assignments often have some flexibility, and at least some personnel can be assigned to more than one department or work center. Such is the case when employees have been cross-trained on two or more jobs or, for instance, when sales personnel can be transferred between stores. In the following application, we show how linear programming

OPTIMIZING PRODUCTION, INVENTORY, AND DISTRIBUTION
AT THE KELLOGG COMPANY*

The Kellogg Company is the largest cereal producer in the world and a leading producer of convenience foods, such as Kellogg's Pop-Tarts and Nutri-Grain cereal bars. Kellogg produces more than 40 different cereals at plants in 19 countries, on six continents. The company markets its products in more than 160 countries and employs more than 15,600 people in its worldwide organization. In the cereal business alone, Kellogg coordinates the production of about 80 products using a total of approximately 90 production lines and 180 packaging lines.

Kellogg has a long history of using linear programming for production planning and distribution. The Kellogg Planning System (KPS) is a large-scale, multiperiod linear program. The operational version of KPS makes production, packaging, inventory, and distribution decisions on a weekly basis. The primary objective of the system is to minimize the total cost of meeting estimated demand; constraints involve processing line capacities, packaging line capacities, and satisfying safety stock requirements.

A tactical version of KPS helps to establish plant budgets and make capacity-expansion and consolidation decisions on a monthly basis. The tactical version was recently used to guide a consolidation of production capacity that resulted in projected savings of $35 to $40 million per year. Because of the success Kellogg has had using KPS in their North American operations, the company is now introducing KPS into Latin America, and is studying the development of a global KPS model.

*Based on G. Brown, J. Keegan, B. Vigus, and K. Wood, "The Kellogg Company Optimizes Production, Inventory, and Distribution," *Interfaces* (November/December 2001): 1–15.

can be used to determine not only an optimal product mix, but also an optimal workforce assignment.

McCormick Manufacturing Company produces two products with contributions to profit per unit of $10 and $9, respectively. The labor requirements per unit produced and the total hours of labor available from personnel assigned to each of four departments are shown in Table 4.11. Assuming that the number of hours available in each department is fixed, we can formulate McCormick's problem as a standard product-mix linear program with the following decision variables:

$$P_1 = \text{units of product 1}$$
$$P_2 = \text{units of product 2}$$

TABLE 4.11   DEPARTMENTAL LABOR-HOURS PER UNIT AND TOTAL HOURS
AVAILABLE FOR THE McCORMICK MANUFACTURING COMPANY

	Labor-Hours per Unit		
Department	**Product 1**	**Product 2**	**Total Hours Available**
1	0.65	0.95	6500
2	0.45	0.85	6000
3	1.00	0.70	7000
4	0.15	0.30	1400

The linear program is

$$\text{Max} \quad 10P_1 + 9P_2$$

s.t.

$$0.65P_1 + 0.95P_2 \leq 6500$$
$$0.45P_1 + 0.85P_2 \leq 6000$$
$$1.00P_1 + 0.70P_2 \leq 7000$$
$$0.15P_1 + 0.30P_2 \leq 1400$$
$$P_1, P_2 \geq 0$$

The optimal solution to the linear programming model is shown in Figure 4.7. After rounding, it calls for 5744 units of product 1, 1795 units of product 2, and a total profit of $73,590. With this optimal solution, departments 3 and 4 are operating at capacity, and departments 1 and 2 have a slack of approximately 1062 and 1890 hours, respectively. We would anticipate that the product mix would change and that the total profit would increase if the workforce assignment could be revised so that the slack, or unused hours, in departments 1 and 2 could be transferred to the departments currently working at capacity. However, the production manager may be uncertain as to how the workforce should be reallocated among the four departments. Let us expand the linear programming model to include decision variables that will help determine the optimal workforce assignment in addition to the profit-maximizing product mix.

Suppose that McCormick has a cross-training program that enables some employees to be transferred between departments. By taking advantage of the cross-training skills, a limited number of employees and labor-hours may be transferred from one department to another. For example, suppose that the cross-training permits transfers as shown in Table 4.12. Row 1 of this table shows that some employees assigned to department 1 have cross-training skills that permit them to be transferred to department 2 or 3. The right-hand column shows that, for the current production planning period, a maximum of 400 hours can be transferred from department 1. Similar cross-training transfer capabilities and capacities are shown for departments 2, 3, and 4.

FIGURE 4.7   THE SOLUTION FOR THE McCORMICK MANUFACTURING COMPANY
PROBLEM WITH NO WORKFORCE TRANSFERS PERMITTED

WEB file

McCormick

```
Optimal Objective Value =            73589.74359

        Variable            Value          Reduced Cost
      -------------      -------------    ----------------
           1               5743.58974           0.00000
           2               1794.87179           0.00000

        Constraint        Slack/Surplus       Dual Value
      -------------      -------------    ----------------
           1               1061.53846           0.00000
           2               1889.74359           0.00000
           3                  0.00000           8.46154
           4                  0.00000          10.25641
```

TABLE 4.12 CROSS-TRAINING ABILITY AND CAPACITY INFORMATION

From Department	Cross-Training Transfers Permitted to Department				Maximum Hours Transferable
	1	2	3	4	
1	—	yes	yes	—	400
2	—	—	yes	yes	800
3	—	—	—	yes	100
4	yes	yes	—	—	200

When workforce assignments are flexible, we do not automatically know how many hours of labor should be assigned to or be transferred from each department. We need to add decision variables to the linear programming model to account for such changes.

b_i = the labor-hours allocated to department i for i = 1, 2, 3, and 4

t_{ij} = the labor-hours transferred from department i to department j

The right-hand sides are now treated as decision variables. With the addition of decision variables b_1, b_2, b_3, and b_4, we write the capacity restrictions for the four departments as follows:

$$0.65P_1 + 0.95P_2 \le b_1$$
$$0.45P_1 + 0.85P_2 \le b_2$$
$$1.00P_1 + 0.70P_2 \le b_3$$
$$0.15P_1 + 0.30P_2 \le b_4$$

The labor-hours ultimately allocated to each department must be determined by a series of labor balance equations, or constraints, that include the number of hours initially assigned to each department plus the number of hours transferred into the department minus the number of hours transferred out of the department. Using department 1 as an example, we determine the workforce allocation as follows:

$$b_1 = \left(\begin{array}{c} \text{Hours} \\ \text{initially in} \\ \text{department 1} \end{array} \right) + \left(\begin{array}{c} \text{Hours} \\ \text{transferred into} \\ \text{department 1} \end{array} \right) - \left(\begin{array}{c} \text{Hours} \\ \text{transferred out of} \\ \text{department 1} \end{array} \right)$$

Table 4.11 shows 6500 hours initially assigned to department 1. We use the transfer decision variables t_{i1} to denote transfers into department 1 and t_{1j} to denote transfers from department 1. Table 4.12 shows that the cross-training capabilities involving department 1 are restricted to transfers from department 4 (variable t_{41}) and transfers to either department 2 or department 3 (variables t_{12} and t_{13}). Thus, we can express the total workforce allocation for department 1 as

$$b_1 = 6500 + t_{41} - t_{12} - t_{13}$$

Moving the decision variables for the workforce transfers to the left-hand side, we have the labor balance equation or constraint

$$b_1 - t_{41} + t_{12} + t_{13} = 6500$$

This form of constraint will be needed for each of the four departments. Thus, the following labor balance constraints for departments 2, 3, and 4 would be added to the model.

$$b_2 - t_{12} - t_{42} + t_{23} + t_{24} = 6000$$
$$b_3 - t_{13} - t_{23} + t_{34} = 7000$$
$$b_4 - t_{24} - t_{34} + t_{41} + t_{42} = 1400$$

Finally, Table 4.12 shows the number of hours that may be transferred from each department is limited, indicating that a transfer capacity constraint must be added for each of the four departments. The additional constraints are

$$t_{12} + t_{13} \leq 400$$
$$t_{23} + t_{24} \leq 800$$
$$t_{34} \leq 100$$
$$t_{41} + t_{42} \leq 200$$

The complete linear programming model has two product decision variables (P_1 and P_2), four department workforce assignment variables (b_1, b_2, b_3, and b_4), seven transfer variables (t_{12}, t_{13}, t_{23}, t_{24}, t_{34}, t_{41}, and t_{42}), and 12 constraints. Figure 4.8 shows the optimal solution to this linear program.

Variations in the workforce assignment model could be used in situations such as allocating raw material resources to products, allocating machine time to products, and allocating salesforce time to stores or sales territories.

McCormick's profit can be increased by $84,011 − $73,590 = $10,421 by taking advantage of cross-training and workforce transfers. The optimal product mix of 6825 units of product 1 and 1751 units of product 2 can be achieved if t_{13} = 400 hours are transferred from department 1 to department 3; t_{23} = 651 hours are transferred from department 2 to department 3; and t_{24} = 149 hours are transferred from department 2 to department 4. The resulting workforce assignments for departments 1 through 4 would provide 6100, 5200, 8051, and 1549 hours, respectively.

If a manager has the flexibility to assign personnel to different departments, reduced workforce idle time, improved workforce utilization, and improved profit should result. The linear programming model in this section automatically assigns employees and labor-hours to the departments in the most profitable manner.

Blending Problems

Blending problems arise whenever a manager must decide how to blend two or more resources to produce one or more products. In these situations, the resources contain one or more essential ingredients that must be blended into final products that will contain specific percentages of each. In most of these applications, then, management must decide how much of each resource to purchase to satisfy product specifications and product demands at minimum cost.

Blending problems occur frequently in the petroleum industry (e.g., blending crude oil to produce different octane gasolines), chemical industry (e.g., blending chemicals to produce fertilizers and weed killers), and food industry (e.g., blending ingredients to produce soft drinks and soups). In this section we illustrate how to apply linear programming to a blending problem in the petroleum industry.

The Grand Strand Oil Company produces regular and premium gasoline for independent service stations in the southeastern United States. The Grand Strand refinery manufactures the gasoline products by blending three petroleum components. The gasolines are sold at different prices, and the petroleum components have different costs. The firm wants

FIGURE 4.8 THE SOLUTION FOR THE McCORMICK MANUFACTURING
COMPANY PROBLEM

```
Optimal Objective Value =            84011.29945

     Variable              Value              Reduced Cost
   ------------        ---------------      ----------------
        P1                6824.85900             0.00000
        P2                1751.41200             0.00000
        B1                6100.00000             0.00000
        B2                5200.00000             0.00000
        B3                8050.84700             0.00000
        B4                1549.15300             0.00000
       T41                   0.00000             7.45763
       T12                   0.00000             8.24859
       T13                 400.00000             0.00000
       T42                   0.00000             8.24859
       T23                 650.84750             0.00000
       T24                 149.15250             0.00000
       T34                   0.00000             0.00000

    Constraint         Slack/Surplus            Dual Value
   ------------        ---------------      ----------------
         1                   0.00000             0.79096
         2                 640.11300             0.00000
         3                   0.00000             8.24859
         4                   0.00000             8.24859
         5                   0.00000             0.79096
         6                   0.00000             0.00000
         7                   0.00000             8.24859
         8                   0.00000             8.24859
         9                   0.00000             7.45763
        10                   0.00000             8.24859
        11                 100.00000             0.00000
        12                 200.00000             0.00000
```

WEB file

McCormick

to determine how to mix or blend the three components into the two gasoline products and maximize profits.

Data available show that regular gasoline can be sold for $2.90 per gallon and premium gasoline for $3.00 per gallon. For the current production planning period, Grand Strand can obtain the three petroleum components at the cost per gallon and in the quantities shown in Table 4.13.

Product specifications for the regular and premium gasolines restrict the amounts of each component that can be used in each gasoline product. Table 4.14 lists the product specifications. Current commitments to distributors require Grand Strand to produce at least 10,000 gallons of regular gasoline.

The Grand Strand blending problem is to determine how many gallons of each component should be used in the regular gasoline blend and how many should be used in the

TABLE 4.13 PETROLEUM COST AND SUPPLY FOR THE GRAND STRAND BLENDING PROBLEM

Petroleum Component	Cost per Gallon	Maximum Available
1	$2.50	5,000 gallons
2	$2.60	10,000 gallons
3	$2.84	10,000 gallons

TABLE 4.14 PRODUCT SPECIFICATIONS FOR THE GRAND STRAND BLENDING PROBLEM

Product	Specifications
Regular gasoline	At most 30% component 1
	At least 40% component 2
	At most 20% component 3
Premium gasoline	At least 25% component 1
	At most 45% component 2
	At least 30% component 3

premium gasoline blend. The optimal blending solution should maximize the firm's profit, subject to the constraints on the available petroleum supplies shown in Table 4.13, the product specifications shown in Table 4.14, and the required 10,000 gallons of regular gasoline.

We define the decision variables as

$$x_{ij} = \text{gallons of component } i \text{ used in gasoline } j,$$
$$\text{where } i = 1, 2, \text{ or } 3 \text{ for components } 1, 2, \text{ or } 3,$$
$$\text{and } j = r \text{ if regular or } j = p \text{ if premium}$$

The six decision variables are

x_{1r} = gallons of component 1 in regular gasoline

x_{2r} = gallons of component 2 in regular gasoline

x_{3r} = gallons of component 3 in regular gasoline

x_{1p} = gallons of component 1 in premium gasoline

x_{2p} = gallons of component 2 in premium gasoline

x_{3p} = gallons of component 3 in premium gasoline

The total number of gallons of each type of gasoline produced is the sum of the number of gallons produced using each of the three petroleum components.

Total Gallons Produced

$$\text{Regular gasoline} = x_{1r} + x_{2r} + x_{3r}$$
$$\text{Premium gasoline} = x_{1p} + x_{2p} + x_{3p}$$

The total gallons of each petroleum component are computed in a similar fashion.

Total Petroleum Component Use

$$\text{component 1} = x_{1r} + x_{1p}$$
$$\text{component 2} = x_{2r} + x_{2p}$$
$$\text{component 3} = x_{3r} + x_{3p}$$

We develop the objective function of maximizing the profit contribution by identifying the difference between the total revenue from both gasolines and the total cost of the three petroleum components. By multiplying the $2.90 per gallon price by the total gallons of regular gasoline, the $3.00 per gallon price by the total gallons of premium gasoline, and the component cost per gallon figures in Table 4.13 by the total gallons of each component used, we obtain the objective function:

$$\text{Max } 2.90(x_{1r} + x_{2r} + x_{3r}) + 3.00(x_{1p} + x_{2p} + x_{3p})$$
$$- 2.50(x_{1r} + x_{1p}) - 2.60(x_{2r} + x_{2p}) - 2.84(x_{3r} + x_{3p})$$

When we combine terms, the objective function becomes

$$\text{Max } 0.40x_{1r} + 0.30x_{2r} + 0.06x_{3r} + 0.50x_{1p} + 0.40x_{2p} + 0.16x_{3p}$$

The limitations on the availability of the three petroleum components are

$$x_{1r} + x_{1p} \leq 5{,}000 \quad \text{component 1}$$
$$x_{2r} + x_{2p} \leq 10{,}000 \quad \text{component 2}$$
$$x_{3r} + x_{3p} \leq 10{,}000 \quad \text{component 3}$$

Six constraints are now required to meet the product specifications stated in Table 4.14. The first specification states that component 1 can account for no more than 30% of the total gallons of regular gasoline produced. That is,

$$x_{1r} \leq 0.30(x_{1r} + x_{2r} + x_{3r})$$

The second product specification listed in Table 4.14 becomes

$$x_{2r} \geq 0.40(x_{1r} + x_{2r} + x_{3r})$$

Similarly, we write the four remaining blending specifications listed in Table 4.14 as

$$x_{3r} \leq 0.20(x_{1r} + x_{2r} + x_{3r})$$
$$x_{1p} \geq 0.25(x_{1p} + x_{2p} + x_{3p})$$
$$x_{2p} \leq 0.45(x_{1p} + x_{2p} + x_{3p})$$
$$x_{3p} \geq 0.30(x_{1p} + x_{2p} + x_{3p})$$

The constraint for at least 10,000 gallons of regular gasoline is

$$x_{1r} + x_{2r} + x_{3r} \geq 10{,}000$$

The complete linear programming model with six decision variables and 10 constraints is

Max $0.40x_{1r} + 0.30x_{2r} + 0.06x_{3r} + 0.50x_{1p} + 0.40x_{2p} + 0.16x_{3p}$

s.t.

$$
\begin{array}{rl}
x_{1r} \qquad\qquad\qquad + \quad x_{1p} \qquad\qquad\qquad & \le 5{,}000 \\
x_{2r} \qquad\qquad\qquad + \quad x_{2p} \qquad\qquad & \le 10{,}000 \\
x_{3r} \qquad\qquad\qquad + \quad x_{3p} & \le 10{,}000 \\
x_{1r} \qquad\qquad\qquad\qquad\qquad\qquad & \le 0.30(x_{1r} + x_{2r} + x_{3r}) \\
x_{2r} \qquad\qquad\qquad\qquad\qquad & \ge 0.40(x_{1r} + x_{2r} + x_{3r}) \\
x_{3r} \qquad\qquad\qquad\qquad & \le 0.20(x_{1r} + x_{2r} + x_{3r}) \\
x_{1p} \qquad\qquad\qquad & \ge 0.25(x_{1p} + x_{2p} + x_{3p}) \\
x_{2p} \qquad\qquad & \le 0.45(x_{1p} + x_{2p} + x_{3p}) \\
x_{3p} & \ge 0.30(x_{1p} + x_{2p} + x_{3p}) \\
\end{array}
$$

$$x_{1r} + \quad x_{2r} + \quad x_{2r} \qquad\qquad\qquad\qquad \ge 10{,}000$$

$$x_{1r},\, x_{2r},\, x_{3r},\, x_{1p},\, x_{2p},\, x_{3p} \ge 0$$

Try Problem 15 as another example of a blending model.

The optimal solution to the Grand Strand blending problem is shown in Figure 4.9. The optimal solution, which provides a profit of $7100, is summarized in Table 4.15. The optimal blending strategy shows that 10,000 gallons of regular gasoline should be produced. The regular gasoline will be manufactured as a blend of 1250 gallons of component 1, 6750 gallons of component 2, and 2000 gallons of component 3. The 15,000 gallons of premium gasoline will be manufactured as a blend of 3750 gallons of component 1, 3250 gallons of component 2, and 8000 gallons of component 3.

FIGURE 4.9   THE SOLUTION FOR THE GRAND STRAND BLENDING PROBLEM

Optimal Objective Value =   7100.00000

Variable	Value	Reduced Cost
X1R	1250.00000	0.00000
X2R	6750.00000	0.00000
X3R	2000.00000	0.00000
X1P	3750.00000	0.00000
X2P	3250.00000	0.00000
X3P	8000.00000	0.00000

Constraint	Slack/Surplus	Dual Value
1	0.00000	0.50000
2	0.00000	0.40000
3	0.00000	0.16000
4	1750.00000	0.00000
5	2750.00000	0.00000
6	0.00000	0.00000
7	0.00000	0.00000
8	3500.00000	0.00000
9	3500.00000	0.00000
10	0.00000	-0.10000

TABLE 4.15   GRAND STRAND GASOLINE BLENDING SOLUTION

Gasoline	Gallons of Component (percentage)			Total
	Component 1	Component 2	Component 3	
Regular	1250 (12.5%)	6750 (67.5%)	2000 (20%)	10,000
Premium	3750 (25%)	3250 (21⅔%)	8000 (53⅓%)	15,000

The interpretation of the slack and surplus variables associated with the product specification constraints (constraints 4–9) in Figure 4.9 needs some clarification. If the constraint is a $\leq$ constraint, the value of the slack variable can be interpreted as the gallons of component use below the maximum amount of the component use specified by the constraint. For example, the slack of 1750.000 for constraint 4 shows that component 1 use is 1750 gallons below the maximum amount of component 1 that could have been used in the production of 10,000 gallons of regular gasoline. If the product specification constraint is a $\geq$ constraint, a surplus variable shows the gallons of component use above the minimum amount of component use specified by the blending constraint. For example, the surplus of 2750.000 for constraint 5 shows that component 2 use is 2750 gallons above the minimum amount of component 2 that must be used in the production of 10,000 gallons of regular gasoline.

NOTES AND COMMENTS

A convenient way to define the decision variables in a blending problem is to use a matrix in which the rows correspond to the raw materials and the columns correspond to the final products. For example, in the Grand Strand blending problem, we define the decision variables as follows:

This approach has two advantages: (1) it provides a systematic way to define the decision variables for any blending problem; and (2) it provides a visual image of the decision variables in terms of how they are related to the raw materials, products, and each other.

		Final Products	
		Regular Gasoline	Premium Gasoline
	Component 1	x_{1r}	x_{1p}
Raw Materials	Component 2	x_{2r}	x_{2p}
	Component 3	x_{3r}	x_{3p}

SUMMARY

In this chapter we presented a broad range of applications that demonstrate how to use linear programming to assist in the decision-making process. We formulated and solved problems from marketing, finance, and operations management, and interpreted the computer output.

Many of the illustrations presented in this chapter are scaled-down versions of actual situations in which linear programming has been applied. In real-world applications, the problem may not be so concisely stated, the data for the problem may not be as readily available, and the problem most likely will involve numerous decision variables and/or constraints. However, a thorough study of the applications in this chapter is a good place to begin in applying linear programming to real problems.

PROBLEMS

Note: The following problems have been designed to give you an understanding and appreciation of the broad range of problems that can be formulated as linear programs. You should be able to formulate a linear programming model for each of the problems. However, you will need access to a linear programming computer package to develop the solutions and make the requested interpretations.

1. The Westchester Chamber of Commerce periodically sponsors public service seminars and programs. Currently, promotional plans are under way for this year's program. Advertising alternatives include television, radio, and newspaper. Audience estimates, costs, and maximum media usage limitations are as shown.

Constraint	Television	Radio	Newspaper
Audience per advertisement	100,000	18,000	40,000
Cost per advertisement	$2000	$300	$600
Maximum media usage	10	20	10

   To ensure a balanced use of advertising media, radio advertisements must not exceed 50% of the total number of advertisements authorized. In addition, television should account for at least 10% of the total number of advertisements authorized.

   a. If the promotional budget is limited to $18,200, how many commercial messages should be run on each medium to maximize total audience contact? What is the allocation of the budget among the three media, and what is the total audience reached?

   b. By how much would audience contact increase if an extra $100 were allocated to the promotional budget?

2. The management of Hartman Company is trying to determine the amount of each of two products to produce over the coming planning period. The following information concerns labor availability, labor utilization, and product profitability.

Department	Product (hours/unit) 1	Product (hours/unit) 2	Labor-Hours Available
A	1.00	0.35	100
B	0.30	0.20	36
C	0.20	0.50	50
Profit contribution/unit	$30.00	$15.00	

   a. Develop a linear programming model of the Hartman Company problem. Solve the model to determine the optimal production quantities of Products 1 and 2.

   b. In computing the profit contribution per unit, management doesn't deduct labor costs because they are considered fixed for the upcoming planning period. However, suppose that overtime can be scheduled in some of the departments. Which departments would you recommend scheduling for overtime? How much would you be willing to pay per hour of overtime in each department?

   c. Suppose that 10, 6, and 8 hours of overtime may be scheduled in departments A, B, and C, respectively. The cost per hour of overtime is $18 in department A, $22.50 in department B, and $12 in department C. Formulate a linear programming model that can be used to determine the optimal production quantities if overtime is made available. What are the optimal production quantities, and what is the revised total contribution to profit? How much overtime do you recommend using in each department? What is the increase in the total contribution to profit if overtime is used?

3. The employee credit union at State University is planning the allocation of funds for the coming year. The credit union makes four types of loans to its members. In addition, the credit union invests in risk-free securities to stabilize income. The various revenue-producing investments together with annual rates of return are as follows:

Type of Loan/Investment	Annual Rate of Return (%)
Automobile loans	8
Furniture loans	10
Other secured loans	11
Signature loans	12
Risk-free securities	9

The credit union will have $2 million available for investment during the coming year. State laws and credit union policies impose the following restrictions on the composition of the loans and investments.

- Risk-free securities may not exceed 30% of the total funds available for investment.
- Signature loans may not exceed 10% of the funds invested in all loans (automobile, furniture, other secured, and signature loans).
- Furniture loans plus other secured loans may not exceed the automobile loans.
- Other secured loans plus signature loans may not exceed the funds invested in risk-free securities.

How should the $2 million be allocated to each of the loan/investment alternatives to maximize total annual return? What is the projected total annual return?

4. Hilltop Coffee manufactures a coffee product by blending three types of coffee beans. The cost per pound and the available pounds of each bean are as follows:

Bean	Cost per Pound	Available Pounds
1	$0.50	500
2	$0.70	600
3	$0.45	400

Consumer tests with coffee products were used to provide ratings on a scale of 0–100, with higher ratings indicating higher quality. Product quality standards for the blended coffee require a consumer rating for aroma to be at least 75 and a consumer rating for taste to be at least 80. The individual ratings of the aroma and taste for coffee made from 100% of each bean are as follows.

Bean	Aroma Rating	Taste Rating
1	75	86
2	85	88
3	60	75

Assume that the aroma and taste attributes of the coffee blend will be a weighted average of the attributes of the beans used in the blend.

   a. What is the minimum-cost blend that will meet the quality standards and provide 1000 pounds of the blended coffee product?

   b. What is the cost per pound for the coffee blend?

   c. Determine the aroma and taste ratings for the coffee blend.

   d. If additional coffee were to be produced, what would be the expected cost per pound?

5. Kilgore's Deli is a small delicatessen located near a major university. Kilgore's does a large walk-in carry-out lunch business. The deli offers two luncheon chili specials, Wimpy and Dial 911. At the beginning of the day, Kilgore needs to decide how much of each special to make (he always sells out of whatever he makes). The profit on one serving of Wimpy is $.45, on one serving of Dial 911, $.58. Each serving of Wimpy requires .25 pound of beef, .25 cup of onions, and 5 ounces of Kilgore's special sauce. Each serving of Dial 911 requires .25 pound of beef, .4 cup of onions, 2 ounces of Kilgore's special sauce, and 5 ounces of hot sauce. Today, Kilgore has 20 pounds of beef, 15 cups of onions, 88 ounces of Kilgore's special sauce, and 60 ounces of hot sauce on hand.

   a. Develop an LP model that will tell Kilgore how many servings of Wimpy and Dial 911 to make in order to maximize his profit today.

   b. Find an optimal solution.

   c. What is the dual value for special sauce? Interpret the dual value.

   d. Increase the amount of special sauce available by 1 ounce and re-solve. Does the solution confirm the answer to part (c)? Give the new solution.

6. G. Kunz and Sons, Inc., manufactures two products used in the heavy equipment industry. Both products require manufacturing operations in two departments. The following are the production time (in hours) and profit contribution figures for the two products.

Product	Profit per Unit	Labor-Hours	
		Dept. A	Dept. B
1	$25	6	12
2	$20	8	10

For the coming production period, Kunz has available a total of 900 hours of labor that can be allocated to either of the two departments. Find the production plan and labor allocation (hours assigned in each department) that will maximize the total contribution to profit.

7. As part of the settlement for a class action lawsuit, Hoxworth Corporation must provide sufficient cash to make the following annual payments (in thousands of dollars).

Year	1	2	3	4	5	6
Payment	190	215	240	285	315	460

The annual payments must be made at the beginning of each year. The judge will approve an amount that, along with earnings on its investment, will cover the annual payments. Investment of the funds will be limited to savings (at 4% annually) and government securities, at prices and rates currently quoted in *The Wall Street Journal*.

Hoxworth wants to develop a plan for making the annual payments by investing in the following securities (par value = $1000). Funds not invested in these securities will be placed in savings.

Security	Current Price	Rate (%)	Years to Maturity
1	$1055	6.750	3
2	$1000	5.125	4

Assume that interest is paid annually. The plan will be submitted to the judge and, if approved, Hoxworth will be required to pay a trustee the amount that will be required to fund the plan.

a. Use linear programming to find the minimum cash settlement necessary to fund the annual payments.

b. Use the dual value to determine how much more Hoxworth should be willing to pay now to reduce the payment at the beginning of year 6 to $400,000.

c. Use the dual value to determine how much more Hoxworth should be willing to pay to reduce the year 1 payment to $150,000.

d. Suppose that the annual payments are to be made at the end of each year. Reformulate the model to accommodate this change. How much would Hoxworth save if this change could be negotiated?

8. The Clark County Sheriff's Department schedules police officers for 8-hour shifts. The beginning times for the shifts are 8:00 A.M., noon, 4:00 P.M., 8:00 P.M., midnight, and 4:00 A.M. An officer beginning a shift at one of these times works for the next 8 hours. During normal weekday operations, the number of officers needed varies depending on the time of day. The department staffing guidelines require the following minimum number of officers on duty:

Time of Day	Minimum Officers on Duty
8:00 A.M.–Noon	5
Noon–4:00 P.M.	6
4:00 P.M.–8:00 P.M.	10
8:00 P.M.–Midnight	7
Midnight–4:00 A.M.	4
4:00 A.M.–8:00 A.M.	6

Determine the number of police officers that should be scheduled to begin the 8-hour shifts at each of the six times (8:00 A.M., noon, 4:00 P.M., 8:00 P.M., midnight, and 4:00 A.M.) to minimize the total number of officers required. (*Hint:* Let x_1 = the number of officers beginning work at 8:00 A.M., x_2 = the number of officers beginning work at noon, and so on.)

9. Epsilon Airlines services predominately the eastern and southeastern United States. The vast majority of Epsilon's customers make reservations through Epsilon's website, but a small percentage of customers make reservations via phone. Epsilon employs call-center personnel to handle these reservations along with any problems with the website reservation system and for the rebooking of flights for customers if their plans change or their travel is disrupted. Staffing the call center appropriately is a challenge for Epsilon's

management team. Having too many employees on hand is a waste of money, but having too few results in very poor customer service and the potential loss of customers.

Epsilon analysts have estimated the minimum number of call-center employees needed by day of week for the upcoming vacation season (June, July, and the first two weeks of August). These estimates are as follows:

Day	Minimum Number of Employees Needed
Monday	75
Tuesday	50
Wednesday	45
Thursday	60
Friday	90
Saturday	75
Sunday	45

The call-center employees work five consecutive days and then have two consecutive days off. An employee may start work any day of the week. Each call-center employee receives the same salary. Assume that the schedule cycles and ignore start-up and stopping of the schedule. Develop a model that will minimize the total number of call-center employees needed to meet the minimum requirements. Find the optimal solution. Give the number of call-center employees that exceed the minimum required.

10. An investment advisor at Shore Financial Services wants to develop a model that can be used to allocate investment funds among four alternatives: stocks, bonds, mutual funds, and cash. For the coming investment period, the company developed estimates of the annual rate of return and the associated risk for each alternative. Risk is measured using an index between 0 and 1, with higher risk values denoting more volatility and thus more uncertainty.

Investment	Annual Rate of Return (%)	Risk
Stocks	10	0.8
Bonds	3	0.2
Mutual funds	4	0.3
Cash	1	0.0

Because cash is held in a money market fund, the annual return is lower, but it carries essentially no risk. The objective is to determine the portion of funds allocated to each investment alternative in order to maximize the total annual return for the portfolio subject to the risk level the client is willing to tolerate.

Total risk is the sum of the risk for all investment alternatives. For instance, if 40% of a client's funds are invested in stocks, 30% in bonds, 20% in mutual funds, and 10% in cash, the total risk for the portfolio would be $0.40(0.8) + 0.30(0.2) + 0.20(0.3) + 0.10(0.0) = 0.44$. An investment advisor will meet with each client to discuss the client's investment objectives and to determine a maximum total risk value for the client. A maximum total risk value of less than 0.3 would be assigned to a conservative investor; a maximum total risk value of between 0.3 and 0.5 would be assigned to a moderate tolerance to risk; and a maximum total risk value greater than 0.5 would be assigned to a more aggressive investor.

Shore Financial Services specified additional guidelines that must be applied to all clients. The guidelines are as follows:

- No more than 75% of the total investment may be in stocks.
- The amount invested in mutual funds must be at least as much as invested in bonds.
- The amount of cash must be at least 10%, but no more than 30% of the total investment funds.

a. Suppose the maximum risk value for a particular client is 0.4. What is the optimal allocation of investment funds among stocks, bonds, mutual funds, and cash? What is the annual rate of return and the total risk for the optimal portfolio?

b. Suppose the maximum risk value for a more conservative client is 0.18. What is the optimal allocation of investment funds for this client? What is the annual rate of return and the total risk for the optimal portfolio?

c. Another more aggressive client has a maximum risk value of 0.7. What is the optimal allocation of investment funds for this client? What is the annual rate of return and the total risk for the optimal portfolio?

d. Refer to the solution for the more aggressive client in part (c). Would this client be interested in having the investment advisor increase the maximum percentage allowed in stocks or decrease the requirement that the amount of cash must be at least 10% of the funds invested? Explain.

e. What is the advantage of defining the decision variables as is done in this model rather than stating the amount to be invested and expressing the decision variables directly in dollar amounts?

11. Edwards Manufacturing Company purchases two component parts from three different suppliers. The suppliers have limited capacity, and no one supplier can meet all the company's needs. In addition, the suppliers charge different prices for the components. Component price data (in price per unit) are as follows:

| | | Supplier | |
Component	1	2	3
1	$12	$13	$14
2	$10	$11	$10

Each supplier has a limited capacity in terms of the total number of components it can supply. However, as long as Edwards provides sufficient advance orders, each supplier can devote its capacity to component 1, component 2, or any combination of the two components, if the total number of units ordered is within its capacity. Supplier capacities are as follows:

Supplier	1	2	3
Capacity	600	1000	800

If the Edwards production plan for the next period includes 1000 units of component 1 and 800 units of component 2, what purchases do you recommend? That is, how many units of each component should be ordered from each supplier? What is the total purchase cost for the components?

12. The Atlantic Seafood Company (ASC) is a buyer and distributor of seafood products that are sold to restaurants and specialty seafood outlets throughout the Northeast. ASC has a frozen storage facility in New York City that serves as the primary distribution point for all products. One of the ASC products is frozen large black tiger shrimp, which are sized at 16–20 pieces per pound. Each Saturday ASC can purchase more tiger shrimp or sell the tiger shrimp at the existing New York City warehouse market price. The ASC goal is to buy tiger shrimp at a low weekly price and sell it later at a higher price. ASC currently has 20,000 pounds of tiger shrimp in storage. Space is available to store a maximum of 100,000 pounds of tiger shrimp each week. In addition, ASC developed the following estimates of tiger shrimp prices for the next four weeks:

Week	Price/lb
1	$6.00
2	$6.20
3	$6.65
4	$5.55

ASC would like to determine the optimal buying-storing-selling strategy for the next four weeks. The cost to store a pound of shrimp for one week is $0.15, and to account for unforeseen changes in supply or demand, management also indicated that 25,000 pounds of tiger shrimp must be in storage at the end of week 4. Determine the optimal buying-storing-selling strategy for ASC. What is the projected four-week profit?

13. Romans Food Market, located in Saratoga, New York, carries a variety of specialty foods from around the world. Two of the store's leading products use the Romans Food Market name: Romans Regular Coffee and Romans DeCaf Coffee. These coffees are blends of Brazilian Natural and Colombian Mild coffee beans, which are purchased from a distributor located in New York City. Because Romans purchases large quantities, the coffee beans may be purchased on an as-needed basis for a price 10% higher than the market price the distributor pays for the beans. The current market price is $0.47 per pound for Brazilian Natural and $0.62 per pound for Colombian Mild. The compositions of each coffee blend are as follows:

	Blend	
Bean	**Regular**	**DeCaf**
Brazilian Natural	75%	40%
Colombian Mild	25%	60%

Romans sells the Regular blend for $3.60 per pound and the DeCaf blend for $4.40 per pound. Romans would like to place an order for the Brazilian and Colombian coffee beans that will enable the production of 1000 pounds of Romans Regular coffee and 500 pounds of Romans DeCaf coffee. The production cost is $0.80 per pound for the Regular blend. Because of the extra steps required to produce DeCaf, the production cost for the DeCaf blend is $1.05 per pound. Packaging costs for both products are $0.25 per pound. Formulate a linear programming model that can be used to determine the pounds of Brazilian Natural and Colombian Mild that will maximize the total contribution to profit. What is the optimal solution and what is the contribution to profit?

14. The production manager for the Classic Boat Corporation must determine how many units of the Classic 21 model to produce over the next four quarters. The company has a beginning inventory of 100 Classic 21 boats, and demand for the four quarters is 2000 units in quarter 1, 4000 units in quarter 2, 3000 units in quarter 3, and 1500 units in quarter 4. The firm has limited production capacity in each quarter. That is, up to 4000 units can be produced in quarter 1, 3000 units in quarter 2, 2000 units in quarter 3, and 4000 units in quarter 4. Each boat held in inventory in quarters 1 and 2 incurs an inventory holding cost of $250 per unit; the holding cost for quarters 3 and 4 is $300 per unit. The production costs for the first quarter are $10,000 per unit; these costs are expected to increase by 10% each quarter because of increases in labor and material costs. Management specified that the ending inventory for quarter 4 must be at least 500 boats.

   a. Formulate a linear programming model that can be used to determine the production schedule that will minimize the total cost of meeting demand in each quarter subject to the production capacities in each quarter and also to the required ending inventory in quarter 4.
   b. Solve the linear program formulated in part (a). Then develop a table that will show for each quarter the number of units to manufacture, the ending inventory, and the costs incurred.
   c. Interpret each of the dual values corresponding to the constraints developed to meet demand in each quarter. Based on these dual values, what advice would you give the production manager?
   d. Interpret each of the dual values corresponding to the production capacity in each quarter. Based on each of these dual values, what advice would you give the production manager?

15. Seastrand Oil Company produces two grades of gasoline: regular and high octane. Both gasolines are produced by blending two types of crude oil. Although both types of crude oil contain the two important ingredients required to produce both gasolines, the percentage of important ingredients in each type of crude oil differs, as does the cost per gallon. The percentage of ingredients A and B in each type of crude oil and the cost per gallon are shown.

Crude Oil	Cost	Ingredient A	Ingredient B	
1	$0.10	20%	60%	Crude oil 1 is 60% ingredient B
2	$0.15	50%	30%	

Each gallon of regular gasoline must contain at least 40% of ingredient A, whereas each gallon of high octane can contain at most 50% of ingredient B. Daily demand for regular and high-octane gasoline is 800,000 and 500,000 gallons, respectively. How many gallons of each type of crude oil should be used in the two gasolines to satisfy daily demand at a minimum cost?

16. The Ferguson Paper Company produces rolls of paper for use in adding machines, desk calculators, and cash registers. The rolls, which are 200 feet long, are produced in widths of 1½, 2½, and 3½ inches. The production process provides 200-foot rolls in 10-inch widths only. The firm must therefore cut the rolls to the desired final product sizes. The seven cutting alternatives and the amount of waste generated by each are as follows:

Cutting Alternative	Number of Rolls			Waste (inches)
	1½ in.	2½ in.	3½ in.	
1	6	0	0	1
2	0	4	0	0
3	2	0	2	0
4	0	1	2	½
5	1	3	0	1
6	1	2	1	0
7	4	0	1	½

The minimum requirements for the three products are

Roll Width (inches)	1½	2½	3½
Units	1000	2000	4000

a. If the company wants to minimize the number of 10-inch rolls that must be manufactured, how many 10-inch rolls will be processed on each cutting alternative? How many rolls are required, and what is the total waste (inches)?

b. If the company wants to minimize the waste generated, how many 10-inch rolls will be processed on each cutting alternative? How many rolls are required, and what is the total waste (inches)?

c. What are the differences in parts (a) and (b) to this problem? In this case, which objective do you prefer? Explain. What types of situations would make the other objective more desirable?

17. Frandec Company manufactures, assembles, and rebuilds material handling equipment used in warehouses and distribution centers. One product, called a Liftmaster, is assembled from four components: a frame, a motor, two supports, and a metal strap. Frandec's production schedule calls for 5000 Liftmasters to be made next month. Frandec purchases the motors from an outside supplier, but the frames, supports, and straps may be either manufactured by the company or purchased from an outside supplier. Manufacturing and purchase costs per unit are shown.

Component	Manufacturing Cost	Purchase Cost
Frame	$38.00	$51.00
Support	$11.50	$15.00
Strap	$ 6.50	$ 7.50

Three departments are involved in the production of these components. The time (in minutes per unit) required to process each component in each department and the available capacity (in hours) for the three departments are as follows:

Component	Department		
	Cutting	Milling	Shaping
Frame	3.5	2.2	3.1
Support	1.3	1.7	2.6
Strap	0.8	—	1.7
Capacity (hours)	350	420	680

a. Formulate and solve a linear programming model for this make-or-buy application. How many of each component should be manufactured and how many should be purchased?

b. What is the total cost of the manufacturing and purchasing plan?

c. How many hours of production time are used in each department?

d. How much should Frandec be willing to pay for an additional hour of time in the shaping department?

e. Another manufacturer has offered to sell frames to Frandec for $45 each. Could Frandec improve its position by pursuing this opportunity? Why or why not?

18. The Two-Rivers Oil Company near Pittsburgh transports gasoline to its distributors by truck. The company recently contracted to supply gasoline distributors in southern Ohio, and it has $600,000 available to spend on the necessary expansion of its fleet of gasoline tank trucks. Three models of gasoline tank trucks are available.

Truck Model	Capacity (gallons)	Purchase Cost	Monthly Operating Cost, Including Depreciation
Super Tanker	5000	$67,000	$550
Regular Line	2500	$55,000	$425
Econo-Tanker	1000	$46,000	$350

The company estimates that the monthly demand for the region will be 550,000 gallons of gasoline. Because of the size and speed differences of the trucks, the number of deliveries or round trips possible per month for each truck model will vary. Trip capacities are estimated at 15 trips per month for the Super Tanker, 20 trips per month for the Regular Line, and 25 trips per month for the Econo-Tanker. Based on maintenance and driver availability, the firm does not want to add more than 15 new vehicles to its fleet. In addition, the company has decided to purchase at least three of the new Econo-Tankers for use on short-run, low-demand routes. As a final constraint, the company does not want more than half the new models to be Super Tankers.

a. If the company wishes to satisfy the gasoline demand with a minimum monthly operating expense, how many models of each truck should be purchased?

b. If the company did not require at least three Econo-Tankers and did not limit the number of Super Tankers to at most half the new models, how many models of each truck should be purchased?

19. The Silver Star Bicycle Company will be manufacturing both men's and women's models for its Easy-Pedal 10-speed bicycles during the next two months. Management wants to develop a production schedule indicating how many bicycles of each model should be produced in each month. Current demand forecasts call for 150 men's and 125 women's models to be shipped during the first month and 200 men's and 150 women's models to be shipped during the second month. Additional data are shown:

Model	Production Costs	Labor Requirements (hours)		Current Inventory
		Manufacturing	**Assembly**	
Men's	$120	2.0	1.5	20
Women's	$ 90	1.6	1.0	30

Last month the company used a total of 1000 hours of labor. The company's labor relations policy will not allow the combined total hours of labor (manufacturing plus assembly) to increase or decrease by more than 100 hours from month to month. In addition, the company charges monthly inventory at the rate of 2% of the production cost based on the inventory levels at the end of the month. The company would like to have at least 25 units of each model in inventory at the end of the two months.

a. Establish a production schedule that minimizes production and inventory costs and satisfies the labor-smoothing, demand, and inventory requirements. What inventories will be maintained and what are the monthly labor requirements?

b. If the company changed the constraints so that monthly labor increases and decreases could not exceed 50 hours, what would happen to the production schedule? How much will the cost increase? What would you recommend?

20. Filtron Corporation produces filtration containers used in water treatment systems. Although business has been growing, the demand each month varies considerably. As a result, the company utilizes a mix of part-time and full-time employees to meet production demands. Although this approach provides Filtron with great flexibility, it has resulted in increased costs and morale problems among employees. For instance, if Filtron needs to increase production from one month to the next, additional part-time employees have to be hired and trained, and costs go up. If Filtron has to decrease production, the workforce has to be reduced and Filtron incurs additional costs in terms of unemployment benefits and decreased morale. Best estimates are that increasing the number of units produced from one month to the next will increase production costs by $1.25 per unit, and that decreasing the number of units produced will increase production costs by $1.00 per unit. In February Filtron produced 10,000 filtration containers but only sold 7500 units; 2500 units are currently in inventory. The sales forecasts for March, April, and May are for 12,000 units, 8000 units, and 15,000 units, respectively. In addition, Filtron has the capacity to store up to 3000 filtration containers at the end of any month. Management would like to determine the number of units to be produced in March, April, and May that will minimize the total cost of the monthly production increases and decreases.

21. Greenville Cabinets received a contract to produce speaker cabinets for a major speaker manufacturer. The contract calls for the production of 3300 bookshelf speakers and 4100 floor speakers over the next two months, with the following delivery schedule:

Model	Month 1	Month 2
Bookshelf	2100	1200
Floor	1500	2600

Greenville estimates that the production time for each bookshelf model is 0.7 hour and the production time for each floor model is 1 hour. The raw material costs are $10 for each bookshelf model and $12 for each floor model. Labor costs are $22 per hour using regular production time and $33 using overtime. Greenville has up to 2400 hours of regular production time available each month and up to 1000 additional hours of overtime available each month. If production for either cabinet exceeds demand in month 1, the cabinets can be stored at a cost of $5 per cabinet. For each product, determine the number of units that should be manufactured each month on regular time and on overtime to minimize total production and storage costs.

22. TriCity Manufacturing (TCM) makes Styrofoam cups, plates, and sandwich and meal containers. Next week's schedule calls for the production of 80,000 small sandwich containers, 80,000 large sandwich containers, and 65,000 meal containers. To make these

containers, Styrofoam sheets are melted and formed into final products using three machines: M1, M2, and M3. Machine M1 can process Styrofoam sheets with a maximum width of 12 inches. The width capacity of machine M2 is 16 inches, and the width capacity of machine M3 is 20 inches. The small sandwich containers require 10-inch-wide Styrofoam sheets; thus, these containers can be produced on each of the three machines. The large sandwich containers require 12-inch-wide sheets; thus, these containers can also be produced on each of the three machines. However, the meal containers require 16-inch-wide Styrofoam sheets, so the meal containers cannot be produced on machine M1. Waste is incurred in the production of all three containers because Styrofoam is lost in the heating and forming process as well as in the final trimming of the product. The amount of waste generated varies depending upon the container produced and the machine used. The following table shows the waste in square inches for each machine and product combination. The waste material is recycled for future use.

Machine	Small Sandwich	Large Sandwich	Meal
M1	20	15	—
M2	24	28	18
M3	32	35	36

Production rates also depend upon the container produced and the machine used. The following table shows the production rates in units per minute for each machine and product combination. Machine capacities are limited for the next week. Time available is 35 hours for machine M1, 35 hours for machine M2, and 40 hours for machine M3.

Machine	Small Sandwich	Large Sandwich	Meal
M1	30	25	—
M2	45	40	30
M3	60	52	44

a. Costs associated with reprocessing the waste material have been increasing. Thus, TCM would like to minimize the amount of waste generated in meeting next week's production schedule. Formulate a linear programming model that can be used to determine the best production schedule.

b. Solve the linear program formulated in part (a) to determine the production schedule. How much waste is generated? Which machines, if any, have idle capacity?

23. EZ-Windows, Inc., manufactures replacement windows for the home remodeling business. In January, the company produced 15,000 windows and ended the month with 9000 windows in inventory. EZ-Windows' management team would like to develop a production schedule for the next three months. A smooth production schedule is obviously desirable because it maintains the current workforce and provides a similar month-to-month operation. However, given the sales forecasts, the production capacities, and the storage capabilities as shown, the management team does not think a smooth production schedule with the same production quantity each month possible.

	February	March	April
Sales forecast	15,000	16,500	20,000
Production capacity	14,000	14,000	18,000
Storage capacity	6,000	6,000	6,000

The company's cost accounting department estimates that increasing production by one window from one month to the next will increase total costs by $1.00 for each unit increase in the production level. In addition, decreasing production by one unit from one month to the next will increase total costs by $0.65 for each unit decrease in the production level. Ignoring production and inventory carrying costs, formulate and solve a linear programming model that will minimize the cost of changing production levels while still satisfying the monthly sales forecasts.

24. Morton Financial must decide on the percentage of available funds to commit to each of two investments, referred to as A and B, over the next four periods. The following table shows the amount of new funds available for each of the four periods, as well as the cash expenditure required for each investment (negative values) or the cash income from the investment (positive values). The data shown (in thousands of dollars) reflect the amount of expenditure or income if 100% of the funds available in any period are invested in either A or B. For example, if Morton decides to invest 100% of the funds available in any period in investment A, it will incur cash expenditures of $1000 in period 1, $800 in period 2, $200 in period 3, and income of $200 in period 4. Note, however, if Morton made the decision to invest 80% in investment A, the cash expenditures or income would be 80% of the values shown.

Period	New Investment Funds Available	Investment A	Investment B
1	1500	-1000	-800
2	400	-800	-500
3	500	-200	-300
4	100	200	300

The amount of funds available in any period is the sum of the new investment funds for the period, the new loan funds, the savings from the previous period, the cash income from investment A, and the cash income from investment B. The funds available in any period can be used to pay the loan and interest from the previous period, placed in savings, used to pay the cash expenditures for investment A, or used to pay the cash expenditures for investment B.

Assume an interest rate of 10% per period for savings and an interest rate of 18% per period on borrowed funds. Let

$$S(t) = \text{the savings for period } t$$
$$L(t) = \text{the new loan funds for period } t$$

Then, in any period t, the savings income from the previous period is $1.1S(t - 1)$, and the loan and interest expenditure from the previous period is $1.18L(t - 1)$.

At the end of period 4, investment A is expected to have a cash value of $3200 (assuming a 100% investment in A), and investment B is expected to have a cash value of $2500 (assuming a 100% investment in B). Additional income and expenses at the end of period 4 will be income from savings in period 4 less the repayment of the period 4 loan plus interest.

Suppose that the decision variables are defined as

$$x_1 = \text{the proportion of investment A undertaken}$$
$$x_2 = \text{the proportion of investment B undertaken}$$

For example, if $x_1 = 0.5$, $500 would be invested in investment A during the first period, and all remaining cash flows and ending investment A values would be multiplied by 0.5. The same holds for investment B. The model must include constraints $x_1 \leq 1$ and $x_2 \leq 1$ to make sure that no more than 100% of the investments can be undertaken.

If no more than $200 can be borrowed in any period, determine the proportions of investments A and B and the amount of savings and borrowing in each period that will maximize the cash value for the firm at the end of the four periods.

25. Western Family Steakhouse offers a variety of low-cost meals and quick service. Other than management, the steakhouse operates with two full-time employees who work 8 hours per day. The rest of the employees are part-time employees who are scheduled for 4-hour shifts during peak meal times. On Saturdays the steakhouse is open from 11:00 A.M. to 10:00 P.M. Management wants to develop a schedule for part-time employees that will minimize labor costs and still provide excellent customer service. The average wage rate for the part-time employees is $7.60 per hour. The total number of full-time and part-time employees needed varies with the time of day as shown.

Time	Total Number of Employees Needed
11:00 A.M.–Noon	9
Noon–1:00 P.M.	9
1:00 P.M.–2:00 P.M.	9
2:00 P.M.–3:00 P.M.	3
3:00 P.M.–4:00 P.M.	3
4:00 P.M.–5:00 P.M.	3
5:00 P.M.–6:00 P.M.	6
6:00 P.M.–7:00 P.M.	12
7:00 P.M.–8:00 P.M.	12
8:00 P.M.–9:00 P.M.	7
9:00 P.M.–10:00 P.M.	7

One full-time employee comes on duty at 11:00 A.M., works 4 hours, takes an hour off, and returns for another 4 hours. The other full-time employee comes to work at 1:00 P.M. and works the same 4-hours-on, 1-hour-off, 4-hours-on pattern.

a. Develop a minimum-cost schedule for part-time employees.

b. What is the total payroll for the part-time employees? How many part-time shifts are needed? Use the surplus variables to comment on the desirability of scheduling at least some of the part-time employees for 3-hour shifts.

c. Assume that part-time employees can be assigned either a 3-hour or a 4-hour shift. Develop a minimum-cost schedule for the part-time employees. How many part-time shifts are needed, and what is the cost savings compared to the previous schedule?

Case Problem 1   PLANNING AN ADVERTISING CAMPAIGN

The Flamingo Grill is an upscale restaurant located in St. Petersburg, Florida. To help plan an advertising campaign for the coming season, Flamingo's management team hired the advertising firm of Haskell & Johnson (HJ). The management team requested HJ's recommendation concerning how the advertising budget should be distributed across television, radio, and newspaper advertisements. The budget has been set at $279,000.

In a meeting with Flamingo's management team, HJ consultants provided the following information about the industry exposure effectiveness rating per ad, their estimate of the number of potential new customers reached per ad, and the cost for each ad.

Advertising Media	Exposure Rating per Ad	New Customers per Ad	Cost per Ad
Television	90	4000	$10,000
Radio	25	2000	$ 3,000
Newspaper	10	1000	$ 1,000

The exposure rating is viewed as a measure of the value of the ad to both existing customers and potential new customers. It is a function of such things as image, message recall, visual and audio appeal, and so on. As expected, the more expensive television advertisement has the highest exposure effectiveness rating along with the greatest potential for reaching new customers.

At this point, the HJ consultants pointed out that the data concerning exposure and reach were only applicable to the first few ads in each medium. For television, HJ stated that the exposure rating of 90 and the 4000 new customers reached per ad were reliable for the first 10 television ads. After 10 ads, the benefit is expected to decline. For planning purposes, HJ recommended reducing the exposure rating to 55 and the estimate of the potential new customers reached to 1500 for any television ads beyond 10. For radio ads, the preceding data are reliable up to a maximum of 15 ads. Beyond 15 ads, the exposure rating declines to 20 and the number of new customers reached declines to 1200 per ad. Similarly, for newspaper ads, the preceding data are reliable up to a maximum of 20; the exposure rating declines to 5 and the potential number of new customers reached declines to 800 for additional ads.

Flamingo's management team accepted maximizing the total exposure rating, across all media, as the objective of the advertising campaign. Because of management's concern with attracting new customers, management stated that the advertising campaign must reach at least 100,000 new customers. To balance the advertising campaign and make use of all advertising media, Flamingo's management team also adopted the following guidelines.

- Use at least twice as many radio advertisements as television advertisements.
- Use no more than 20 television advertisements.
- The television budget should be at least $140,000.
- The radio advertising budget is restricted to a maximum of $99,000.
- The newspaper budget is to be at least $30,000.

HJ agreed to work with these guidelines and provide a recommendation as to how the $279,000 advertising budget should be allocated among television, radio, and newspaper advertising.

Managerial Report

Develop a model that can be used to determine the advertising budget allocation for the Flamingo Grill. Include a discussion of the following in your report.

1. A schedule showing the recommended number of television, radio, and newspaper advertisements and the budget allocation for each medium. Show the total exposure and indicate the total number of potential new customers reached.
2. How would the total exposure change if an additional $10,000 were added to the advertising budget?
3. A discussion of the ranges for the objective function coefficients. What do the ranges indicate about how sensitive the recommended solution is to HJ's exposure rating coefficients?
4. After reviewing HJ's recommendation, the Flamingo's management team asked how the recommendation would change if the objective of the advertising campaign was to maximize the number of potential new customers reached. Develop the media schedule under this objective.
5. Compare the recommendations from parts 1 and 4. What is your recommendation for the Flamingo Grill's advertising campaign?

Case Problem 2   SCHNEIDER'S SWEET SHOP

Schneider's Sweet Shop specializes in homemade candies and ice cream. Schneider produces its ice cream in-house, in batches of 50 pounds. The first stage in ice cream making is the blending of ingredients to obtain a mix which meets pre-specified requirements on the percentages of certain constituents of the mix. The desired composition is as follows:

1.	Fat	16.00%
2.	Serum solids	8.00%
3.	Sugar solids	16.00%
4.	Egg solids	.35%
5.	Stabilizer	.25%
6.	Emulsifier	.15%
7.	Water	59.25%

The mix can be composed of ingredients from the following list:

Ingredient Cost ($/lb.)		
1.	40% Cream	$1.19
2.	23% Cream	.70
3.	Butter	2.32
4.	Plastic cream	2.30
5.	Butter oil	2.87
6.	4% Milk	.25
7.	Skim condensed milk	.35
8.	Skim milk powder	.65
9.	Liquid sugar	.25
10.	Sugared frozen fresh egg yolk	1.75
11.	Powdered egg yolk	4.45
12.	Stabilizer	2.45
13.	Emulsifier	1.68
14.	Water	.00

The number of pounds of a constituent found in a pound of an ingredient is shown below. Note that a pound of stabilizer contributes only to the stabilizer requirement (one pound), one pound of emulsifier contributes only to the emulsifier requirement (one pound), and that water contributes only to the water requirement (one pound).

Constituent							Ingredient							
PRIVATE	1	2	3	4	5	6	7	8	9	10	11	12	13	14
1	.4	.2	.8	.8	.9	.1				.5	.6			
2	.1			.1		.1	.3	1						
3									.7	.1				
4										.4	.4			
5												1		
6													1	
7	.5	.8	.2	.1	.1	.8	.7		.3					1

Young Jack Schneider has recently acquired the shop from his father. Jack's father has in the past used the following mixture: 9.73 pounds of plastic cream, 3.03 pounds of skim milk powder, 11.37 pounds of liquid sugar, .44 pounds of sugared frozen fresh egg yolk, .12 pounds of stabilizer, .07 pounds of emulsifier, and 25.24 pounds of water. (The scale at Schneider's is only accurate to 100th of a pound). Jack feels that perhaps it is possible to produce the ice cream in a more cost-effective manner. He would like to find the cheapest mix for producing a batch of ice cream, which meets the requirements specified above.

Jack is also curious about the cost effect of being a little more flexible in the requirements listed above. He wants to know the cheapest mix if the composition meets the following tolerances:

1.	Fat	15.00–17.00%
2.	Serum solids	7.00–9.00%
3.	Sugar solids	15.50–16.50%
4.	Egg solids	.30–.40%
5.	Stabilizer	.20–.30%
6.	Emulsifier	.10–.20%
7.	Water	58.00–59.50%

Managerial Report

Write a managerial report which compares the cost of Papa Jack's approach to (a) the cost-minimized approach using the desired composition and (b) the cost-minimized approach with the more flexible requirements. Include in your report the following:

1. The cost of 50 pounds of ice cream under each of the three approaches
2. The amount of each ingredient used in the mix for each of the three approaches
3. A recommendation as to which approach should be used

Case Problem 3   TEXTILE MILL SCHEDULING

The Scottsville Textile Mill* produces five different fabrics. Each fabric can be woven on one or more of the mill's 38 looms. The sales department's forecast of demand for the next month is shown in Table 4.16, along with data on the selling price per yard, variable cost

---

*This case is based on the Calhoun Textile Mill Case by Jeffrey D. Camm, P. M. Dearing, and Suresh K. Tadisnia, 1987.

TABLE 4.16 MONTHLY DEMAND, SELLING PRICE, VARIABLE COST, AND PURCHASE PRICE DATA FOR SCOTTSVILLE TEXTILE MILL FABRICS

Fabric	Demand (yards)	Selling Price ($/yard)	Variable Cost ($/yard)	Purchase Price ($/yard)
1	16,500	0.99	0.66	0.80
2	22,000	0.86	0.55	0.70
3	62,000	1.10	0.49	0.60
4	7,500	1.24	0.51	0.70
5	62,000	0.70	0.50	0.70

TABLE 4.17 LOOM PRODUCTION RATES FOR THE SCOTTSVILLE TEXTILE MILL

Fabric	Loom Rate (yards/hour)	
	Dobbie	Regular
1	4.63	—
2	4.63	—
3	5.23	5.23
4	5.23	5.23
5	4.17	4.17

Note: Fabrics 1 and 2 can be manufactured only on the dobbie loom.

per yard, and purchase price per yard. The mill operates 24 hours a day and is scheduled for 30 days during the coming month.

The mill has two types of looms: dobbie and regular. The dobbie looms are more versatile and can be used for all five fabrics. The regular looms can produce only three of the fabrics. The mill has a total of 38 looms: 8 are dobbie and 30 are regular. The rate of production for each fabric on each type of loom is given in Table 4.17. The time required to change over from producing one fabric to another is negligible and does not have to be considered.

The Scottsville Textile Mill satisfies all demand with either its own fabric or fabric purchased from another mill. Fabrics that cannot be woven at the Scottsville Mill because of limited loom capacity will be purchased from another mill. The purchase price of each fabric is also shown in Table 4.16.

Managerial Report

Develop a model that can be used to schedule production for the Scottsville Textile Mill, and at the same time, determine how many yards of each fabric must be purchased from another mill. Include a discussion and analysis of the following items in your report:

1. The final production schedule and loom assignments for each fabric.
2. The projected total contribution to profit.
3. A discussion of the value of additional loom time. (The mill is considering purchasing a ninth dobbie loom. What is your estimate of the monthly profit contribution of this additional loom?)
4. A discussion of the objective coefficients' ranges.

5. A discussion of how the objective of minimizing total costs would provide a different model than the objective of maximizing total profit contribution. (How would the interpretation of the objective coefficients' ranges differ for these two models?)

Case Problem 4   WORKFORCE SCHEDULING

Davis Instruments has two manufacturing plants located in Atlanta, Georgia. Product demand varies considerably from month to month, causing Davis extreme difficulty in workforce scheduling. Recently Davis started hiring temporary workers supplied by WorkForce Unlimited, a company that specializes in providing temporary employees for firms in the greater Atlanta area. WorkForce Unlimited offered to provide temporary employees under three contract options that differ in terms of the length of employment and the cost. The three options are summarized:

Option	Length of Employment	Cost
1	One month	$2000
2	Two months	$4800
3	Three months	$7500

The longer contract periods are more expensive because WorkForce Unlimited experiences greater difficulty finding temporary workers who are willing to commit to longer work assignments.

Over the next six months, Davis projects the following needs for additional employees:

Month	January	February	March	April	May	June
Employees Needed	10	23	19	26	20	14

Each month, Davis can hire as many temporary employees as needed under each of the three options. For instance, if Davis hires five employees in January under Option 2, WorkForce Unlimited will supply Davis with five temporary workers who will work for two months: January and February. For these workers, Davis will have to pay 5($4800) = $24,000. Because of some merger negotiations under way, Davis does not want to commit to any contractual obligations for temporary employees that extend beyond June.

Davis's quality control program requires each temporary employee to receive training at the time of hire. The training program is required even if the person worked for Davis Instruments in the past. Davis estimates that the cost of training is $875 each time a temporary employee is hired. Thus, if a temporary employee is hired for one month, Davis will incur a training cost of $875, but will incur no additional training cost if the employee is on a two- or three-month contract.

Managerial Report

Develop a model that can be used to determine the number of temporary employees Davis should hire each month under each contract plan in order to meet the projected needs at a minimum total cost. Include the following items in your report:

1. A schedule that shows the number of temporary employees that Davis should hire each month for each contract option.

2. A summary table that shows the number of temporary employees that Davis should hire under each contract option, the associated contract cost for each option, and the associated training cost for each option. Provide summary totals showing the total number of temporary employees hired, total contract costs, and total training costs.

3. If the cost to train each temporary employee could be reduced to $700 per month, what effect would this change have on the hiring plan? Explain. Discuss the implications that this effect on the hiring plan has for identifying methods for reducing training costs. How much of a reduction in training costs would be required to change the hiring plan based on a training cost of $875 per temporary employee?

4. Suppose that Davis hired 10 full-time employees at the beginning of January in order to satisfy part of the labor requirements over the next six months. If Davis can hire full-time employees for $16.50 per hour, including fringe benefits, what effect would it have on total labor and training costs over the six-month period as compared to hiring only temporary employees? Assume that full-time and temporary employees both work approximately 160 hours per month. Provide a recommendation regarding the decision to hire additional full-time employees.

Case Problem 5   DUKE ENERGY COAL ALLOCATION*

Duke Energy manufactures and distributes electricity to customers in the United States and Latin America. Duke recently purchased Cinergy Corporation, which has generating facilities and energy customers in Indiana, Kentucky, and Ohio. For these customers Cinergy has been spending $725 to $750 million each year for the fuel needed to operate its coal-fired and gas-fired power plants; 92% to 95% of the fuel used is coal. In this region, Duke Energy uses 10 coal-burning generating plants: five located inland and five located on the Ohio River. Some plants have more than one generating unit. Duke Energy uses 28–29 million tons of coal per year at a cost of approximately $2 million every day in this region.

The company purchases coal using fixed-tonnage or variable-tonnage contracts from mines in Indiana (49%), West Virginia (20%), Ohio (12%), Kentucky (11%), Illinois (5%), and Pennsylvania (3%). The company must purchase all of the coal contracted for on fixed-tonnage contracts, but on variable-tonnage contracts it can purchase varying amounts up to the limit specified in the contract. The coal is shipped from the mines to Duke Energy's generating facilities in Ohio, Kentucky, and Indiana. The cost of coal varies from $19 to $35 per ton and transportation/delivery charges range from $1.50 to $5.00 per ton.

A model is used to determine the megawatt-hours (mWh) of electricity that each generating unit is expected to produce and to provide a measure of each generating unit's efficiency, referred to as the heat rate. The heat rate is the total BTUs required to produce 1 kilowatt-hour (kWh) of electrical power.

Coal Allocation Model

Duke Energy uses a linear programming model, called the coal allocation model, to allocate coal to its generating facilities. The objective of the coal allocation model is to determine the lowest-cost method for purchasing and distributing coal to the generating units. The supply/availability of the coal is determined by the contracts with the various mines,

---

*The authors are indebted to Thomas Mason and David Bossee of Duke Energy Corporation, formerly Cinergy Corp., for their contribution to this case problem.

and the demand for coal at the generating units is determined indirectly by the megawatt-hours of electricity each unit must produce.

The cost to process coal, called the add-on cost, depends upon the characteristics of the coal (moisture content, ash content, BTU content, sulfur content, and grindability) and the efficiency of the generating unit. The add-on cost plus the transportation cost are added to the purchase cost of the coal to determine the total cost to purchase and use the coal.

Current Problem

Duke Energy signed three fixed-tonnage contracts and four variable-tonnage contracts. The company would like to determine the least-cost way to allocate the coal available through these contracts to five generating units. The relevant data for the three fixed-tonnage contracts are as follows:

Supplier	Number of Tons Contracted For	Cost ($/ton)	BTUs/lb
RAG	350,000	22	13,000
Peabody Coal Sales	300,000	26	13,300
American Coal Sales	275,000	22	12,600

For example, the contract signed with RAG requires Duke Energy to purchase 350,000 tons of coal at a price of $22 per ton; each pound of this particular coal provides 13,000 BTUs.

The data for the four variable-tonnage contracts follow:

Supplier	Number of Tons Available	Cost ($/ton)	BTUs/lb
Consol, Inc.	200,000	32	12,250
Cyprus Amax	175,000	35	12,000
Addington Mining	200,000	31	12,000
Waterloo	180,000	33	11,300

For example, the contract with Consol, Inc., enables Duke Energy to purchase up to 200,000 tons of coal at a cost of $32 per ton; each pound of this coal provides 12,250 BTUs.

The number of megawatt-hours of electricity that each generating unit must produce and the heat rate provided are as follows:

Generating Unit	Electricity Produced (mWh)	Heat Rate (BTUs per kWh)
Miami Fort Unit 5	550,000	10,500
Miami Fort Unit 7	500,000	10,200
Beckjord Unit 1	650,000	10,100
East Bend Unit 2	750,000	10,000
Zimmer Unit 1	1,100,000	10,000

For example, Miami Fort Unit 5 must produce 550,000 megawatt-hours of electricity, and 10,500 BTUs are needed to produce each kilowatt-hour.

The transportation cost and the add-on cost in dollars per ton are shown here:

	Transportation Cost ($/ton)				
Supplier	**Miami Fort Unit 5**	**Miami Fort Unit 7**	**Beckjord Unit 1**	**East Bend Unit 2**	**Zimmer Unit 1**
RAG	5.00	5.00	4.75	5.00	4.75
Peabody	3.75	3.75	3.50	3.75	3.50
American	3.00	3.00	2.75	3.00	2.75
Consol	3.25	3.25	2.85	3.25	2.85
Cyprus	5.00	5.00	4.75	5.00	4.75
Addington	2.25	2.25	2.00	2.25	2.00
Waterloo	2.00	2.00	1.60	2.00	1.60

	Add-On Cost ($/ton)				
Supplier	**Miami Fort Unit 5**	**Miami Fort Unit 7**	**Beckjord Unit 1**	**East Bend Unit 2**	**Zimmer Unit 1**
RAG	10.00	10.00	10.00	5.00	6.00
Peabody	10.00	10.00	11.00	6.00	7.00
American	13.00	13.00	15.00	9.00	9.00
Consol	10.00	10.00	11.00	7.00	7.00
Cyprus	10.00	10.00	10.00	5.00	6.00
Addington	5.00	5.00	6.00	4.00	4.00
Waterloo	11.00	11.00	11.00	7.00	9.00

Managerial Report

Prepare a report that summarizes your recommendations regarding Duke Energy's coal allocation problem. Be sure to include information and analysis for the following issues:

1. Determine how much coal to purchase from each of the mining companies and how it should be allocated to the generating units. What is the cost to purchase, deliver, and process the coal?
2. Compute the average cost of coal in cents per million BTUs for each generating unit (a measure of the cost of fuel for the generating units).
3. Compute the average number of BTUs per pound of coal received at each generating unit (a measure of the energy efficiency of the coal received at each unit).
4. Suppose that Duke Energy can purchase an additional 80,000 tons of coal from American Coal Sales as an "all or nothing deal" for $30 per ton. Should Duke Energy purchase the additional 80,000 tons of coal?
5. Suppose that Duke Energy learns that the energy content of the coal from Cyprus Amax is actually 13,000 BTUs per pound. Should Duke Energy revise its procurement plan?
6. Duke Energy has learned from its trading group that Duke Energy can sell 50,000 megawatt-hours of electricity over the grid (to other electricity suppliers) at a price of $30 per megawatt-hour. Should Duke Energy sell the electricity? If so, which generating units should produce the additional electricity?

Appendix 4.1   EXCEL SOLUTION OF HEWLITT CORPORATION FINANCIAL PLANNING PROBLEM

In Appendix 2.2 we showed how Excel could be used to solve the Par Inc.'s linear programming problem. To illustrate the use of Excel in solving a more complex linear programming problem, we show the solution to the Hewlitt Corporation financial planning problem presented in Section 4.2.

The spreadsheet formulation and solution of the Hewlitt Corporation problem are shown in Figure 4.10. As described in Appendix 2.2, our practice is to put the data required for the problem in the top part of the worksheet and build the model in the bottom part of the worksheet. The model consists of a set of cells for the decision variables, a cell for the objective function, a set of cells for the left-hand-side functions, and a set of cells for the right-hand sides of the constraints. The cells for each of these model components are screened; the cells for the decision variables are also enclosed by a boldface line. Descriptive labels are used to make the spreadsheet easy to read.

Formulation

The data and descriptive labels are contained in cells A1:G12. The screened cells in the bottom portion of the spreadsheet contain the key elements of the model required by the Excel Solver.

WEB file

Hewlitt

FIGURE 4.10   EXCEL SOLUTION FOR THE HEWLITT CORPORATION PROBLEM

	A	B	C	D	E	F	G	H	I	J	K	L
1	**Hewlitt Corporation Cash Requirements**											
2												
3		**Cash**										
4	**Year**	**Rqmt.**				**Bond**						
5	1	430			1	2	3					
6	2	210		**Price ($1000)**	1.15	1	1.35					
7	3	222		**Rate**	0.08875	0.055	0.1175					
8	4	231		**Years to Maturity**	5	6	7					
9	5	240										
10	6	195		**Annual Savings Multiple**		1.04						
11	7	225										
12	8	255										
13												
14	**Model**											
15												
16	F	B1	B2	B3	S1	S2	S3	S4	S5	S6	S7	S8
17	1728.794	144.988	187.856	228.188	636.148	501.606	349.682	182.681	0	0	0	0
18												
19					**Cash Flow**		**Net Cash**		**Cash**			
20	**Min Funds**	1728.7939		**Constraints**	**In**	**Out**	**Flow**		**Rqmt.**			
21				Year 1	1728.794	1298.794	430	=	430			
22				Year 2	711.6057	501.6057	210	=	210			
23				Year 3	571.6818	349.6818	222	=	222			
24				Year 4	413.6809	182.6809	231	=	231			
25				Year 5	240	0	240	=	240			
26				Year 6	195	0	195	=	195			
27				Year 7	225	0	225	=	225			
28				Year 8	255	0	255	=	255			

Decision Variables Cells A17:L17 are reserved for the decision variables. The optimal values (rounded to three places) are shown to be $F = 1728.794$, $B_1 = 144.988$, $B_2 = 187.856$, $B_3 = 228.188$, $S_1 = 636.148$, $S_2 = 501.606$, $S_3 = 349.682$, $S_4 = 182.681$, and $S_5 = S_6 = S_7 = S_8 = 0$.

Objective Function The formula =A17 has been placed into cell B20 to reflect the total funds required. It is simply the value of the decision variable, F. The total funds required by the optimal solution is shown to be $1,728,794.

Left-Hand Sides The left-hand sides for the eight constraints represent the annual net cash flow. They are placed into cells G21:G28.
Cell G21 = E21 – F21 (Copy to G22:G28)

For this problem, some of the left-hand-side cells reference other cells that contain formulas. These referenced cells provide Hewlitt's cash flow in and cash flow out for each of the eight years.* The cells and their formulas are as follows:

Cell E21 = A17

Cell E22 = SUMPRODUCT($E$7:$G$7,$B$17:$D$17)+$F$10*E17

Cell E23 = SUMPRODUCT($E$7:$G$7,$B$17:$D$17)+$F$10*F17

Cell E24 = SUMPRODUCT($E$7:$G$7,$B$17:$D$17)+$F$10*G17

Cell E25 = SUMPRODUCT($E$7:$G$7,$B$17:$D$17)+$F$10*H17

Cell E26 = (1+E7)*B17+F7*C17+G7*D17+F10*I17

Cell E27 = (1+F7)*C17+G7*D17+F10*J17

Cell E28 = (1+G7)*D17+F10*K17

Cell F21 = SUMPRODUCT(E6:G6,B17:D17)+E17

Cell F22 = F17

Cell F23 = G17

Cell F24 = H17

Cell F25 = I17

Cell F26 = J17

Cell F27 = K17

Cell F28 = L17

Right-Hand Sides The right-hand sides for the eight constraints represent the annual cash requirements. They are placed into cells I21:I28.
Cell I21 = B5 (Copy to I22:I28)

Excel Solution

We are now ready to use the information in the worksheet to determine the optimal solution to the Hewlitt Corporation problem. The following steps describe how to use Excel to obtain the optimal solution.

---

*The cash flow in is the sum of the positive terms in each constraint equation in the mathematical model, and the cash flow out is the sum of the negative terms in each constraint equation.

FIGURE 4.11   SOLVER PARAMETERS DIALOG BOX FOR THE HEWLITT
CORPORATION PROBLEM

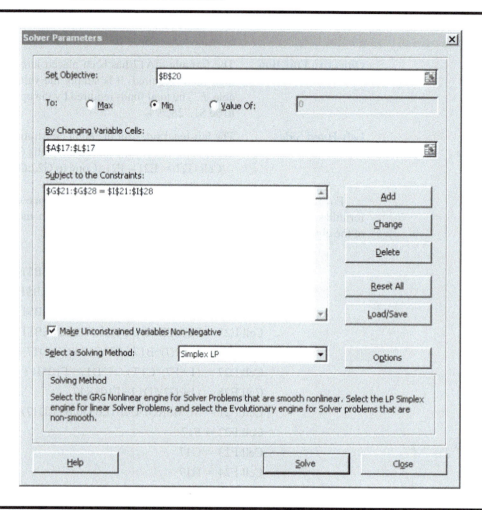

Step 1.   Select the **Data** tab
Step 2.   Select **Solver** from the **Analysis** group
Step 3.   When the **Solver Parameters** dialog box appears (see Figure 4.11):
            Enter B20 in the **Set Objective** box
            Select the **To: Min** option
            Enter A17:L17 in the **By Changing Variable Cells** box
Step 4.   Choose **Add**
            When the **Add Constraint** dialog box appears:
            Enter G21:G28 in the left-hand box of the **Cell Reference** area
            Select = from the middle drop-down button
            Enter I21:I28 in the **Constraint** area
            Click **OK**
Step 5.   When the **Solver Parameters** dialog box reappears (see Figure 4.11):
            Select **Make Unconstrained Variables Non-Negative**

Step 6. Select the **Select a Solving Method** drop-down button
Select **Simplex LP**

Step 7. Choose **Solve**

Step 8. When the **Solver Results** dialog box appears:
Select **Keep Solver Solution**
Select **Sensitivity** in the **Reports** box
Click **OK**

The Solver Parameters dialog box is shown in Figure 4.11. The optimal solution is shown in Figure 4.10; the accompanying sensitivity report is shown in Figure 4.12.

Discussion

Figures 4.10 and 4.12 contain essentially the same information as that provided in Figure 4.4. Recall that the Excel sensitivity report uses the term *shadow price* to describe the *change* in value of the solution per unit increase in the right-hand side of a constraint. This is the same as the Dual Value in Figure 4.4.

FIGURE 4.12   EXCEL'S SENSITIVITY REPORT FOR THE HEWLITT
CORPORATION PROBLEM

Adjustable Cells

Cell	Name	Final Value	Reduced Cost	Objective Coefficient	Allowable Increase	Allowable Decrease
$A$17	F	1728.793855	0	1	1E + 30	1
$B$17	B1	144.9881496	0	0	0.067026339	0.013026775
$C$17	B2	187.8558478	0	0	0.012795531	0.020273774
$D$17	B3	228.1879195	0	0	0.022906851	0.749663022
$E$17	S1	636.1479438	0	0	0.109559907	0.05507386
$F$17	S2	501.605712	0	0	0.143307365	0.056948823
$G$17	S3	349.681791	0	0	0.210854199	0.059039182
$H$17	S4	182.680913	0	0	0.413598622	0.061382404
$I$17	S5	0	0.064025159	0	1E + 30	0.064025159
$J$17	S6	0	0.012613604	0	1E + 30	0.012613604
$K$17	S7	0	0.021318233	0	1E + 30	0.021318233
$L$17	S8	0	0.670839393	0	1E + 30	0.670839393

Constraints

Cell	Name	Final Value	Shadow Price	Constraint R.H. Side	Allowable Increase	Allowable Decrease
$G$21	Year 1 Flow	430	1	430	1E + 30	1728.793855
$G$22	Year 2 Flow	210	0.961538462	210	1E + 30	661.5938616
$G$23	Year 3 Flow	222	0.924556213	222	1E + 30	521.6699405
$G$24	Year 4 Flow	231	0.888996359	231	1E + 30	363.6690626
$G$25	Year 5 Flow	240	0.854804191	240	1E + 30	189.9881496
$G$26	Year 6 Flow	195	0.760364454	195	2149.927647	157.8558478
$G$27	Year 7 Flow	225	0.718991202	225	3027.962172	198.1879195
$G$28	Year 8 Flow	255	0.670839393	255	1583.881915	255

CHAPTER 5

Distribution and Network Models

CONTENTS

The models discussed in this chapter belong to a special class of linear programming problems called *network flow* problems. We begin by discussing models commonly encountered when dealing with problems related to supply chains, specifically transportation and transshipment problems. We then consider three other types of network problems: assignment problems, shortest-route problems, and maximal flow problems.

In each case, we present a graphical representation of the problem in the form of a *network*. We then show how the problem can be formulated and solved as a linear program. In the last section of the chapter we present a production and inventory problem that is an interesting application of the transshipment problem.

6.1 SUPPLY CHAIN MODELS

A **supply chain** describes the set of all interconnected resources involved in producing and distributing a product. For instance, a supply chain for automobiles could include raw material producers, automotive-parts suppliers, distribution centers for storing automotive parts, assembly plants, and car dealerships. All the materials needed to produce a finished automobile must flow through the supply chain. In general, supply chains are designed to satisfy customer demand for a product at minimum cost. Those that control the supply chain must make decisions such as where to produce the product, how much should be produced, and where it should be sent. We will look at two specific types of problems common in supply chain models that can be solved using linear programing: transportation problems and transshipment problems.

Transportation Problem

The **transportation problem** arises frequently in planning for the distribution of goods and services from several supply locations to several demand locations. Typically, the quantity of goods available at each supply location (origin) is limited, and the quantity of goods needed at each of several demand locations (destinations) is known. The usual objective in a transportation problem is to minimize the cost of shipping goods from the origins to the destinations.

Let us illustrate by considering a transportation problem faced by Foster Generators. This problem involves the transportation of a product from three plants to four distribution centers. Foster Generators operates plants in Cleveland, Ohio; Bedford, Indiana; and York, Pennsylvania. Production capacities over the next three-month planning period for one particular type of generator are as follows:

Origin	Plant	Three-Month Production Capacity (units)
1	Cleveland	5,000
2	Bedford	6,000
3	York	2,500
	Total	13,500

The firm distributes its generators through four regional distribution centers located in Boston, Chicago, St. Louis, and Lexington; the three-month forecast of demand for the distribution centers is as follows:

Destination	Distribution Center	Three-Month Demand Forecast (units)
1	Boston	6,000
2	Chicago	4,000
3	St. Louis	2,000
4	Lexington	1,500
	Total	13,500

Management would like to determine how much of its production should be shipped from each plant to each distribution center. Figure 6.1 shows graphically the 12 distribution routes Foster can use. Such a graph is called a **network**; the circles are referred to as **nodes**

FIGURE 6.1   THE NETWORK REPRESENTATION OF THE FOSTER GENERATORS TRANSPORTATION PROBLEM

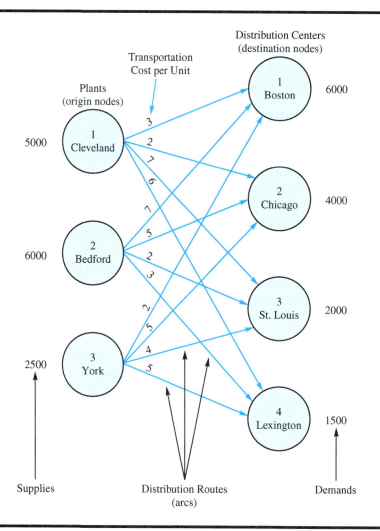

TABLE 6.1 TRANSPORTATION COST PER UNIT FOR THE FOSTER GENERATORS TRANSPORTATION PROBLEM

Origin	Destination			
	Boston	**Chicago**	**St. Louis**	**Lexington**
Cleveland	3	2	7	6
Bedford	7	5	2	3
York	2	5	4	5

and the lines connecting the nodes as **arcs**. Each origin and destination is represented by a node, and each possible shipping route is represented by an arc. The amount of the supply is written next to each origin node, and the amount of the demand is written next to each destination node. The goods shipped from the origins to the destinations represent the flow in the network. Note that the direction of flow (from origin to destination) is indicated by the arrows.

Try Problem 1 for practice in developing a network model of a transportation problem.

For Foster's transportation problem, the objective is to determine the routes to be used and the quantity to be shipped via each route that will provide the minimum total transportation cost. The cost for each unit shipped on each route is given in Table 6.1 and is shown on each arc in Figure 6.1.

A linear programming model can be used to solve this transportation problem. We use double-subscripted decision variables, with x_{11} denoting the number of units shipped from origin 1 (Cleveland) to destination 1 (Boston), x_{12} denoting the number of units shipped from origin 1 (Cleveland) to destination 2 (Chicago), and so on. In general, the decision variables for a transportation problem having m origins and n destinations are written as follows:

The first subscript identifies the "from" node of the corresponding arc and the second subscript identifies the "to" node of the arc.

$$x_{ij} = \text{number of units shipped from origin } i \text{ to destination } j$$
$$\text{where } i = 1, 2, \ldots, m \text{ and } j = 1, 2, \ldots, n$$

Because the objective of the transportation problem is to minimize the total transportation cost, we can use the cost data in Table 6.1 or on the arcs in Figure 6.1 to develop the following cost expressions:

Transportation costs for
units shipped from Cleveland $= 3x_{11} + 2x_{12} + 7x_{13} + 6x_{14}$

Transportation costs for
units shipped from Bedford $= 7x_{21} + 5x_{22} + 2x_{23} + 3x_{24}$

Transportation costs for
units shipped from York $= 2x_{31} + 5x_{32} + 4x_{33} + 5x_{34}$

The sum of these expressions provides the objective function showing the total transportation cost for Foster Generators.

Transportation problems need constraints because each origin has a limited supply and each destination has a demand requirement. We consider the supply constraints first. The capacity at the Cleveland plant is 5000 units. With the total number of units shipped from the Cleveland plant expressed as $x_{11} + x_{12} + x_{13} + x_{14}$, the supply constraint for the Cleveland plant is

$$x_{11} + x_{12} + x_{13} + x_{14} \leq 5000 \quad \text{Cleveland supply}$$

With three origins (plants), the Foster transportation problem has three supply constraints. Given the capacity of 6000 units at the Bedford plant and 2500 units at the York plant, the two additional supply constraints are

$$x_{21} + x_{22} + x_{23} + x_{24} \leq 6000 \quad \text{Bedford supply}$$
$$x_{31} + x_{32} + x_{33} + x_{34} \leq 2500 \quad \text{York supply}$$

With the four distribution centers as the destinations, four demand constraints are needed to ensure that destination demands will be satisfied:

To obtain a feasible solution, the total supply must be greater than or equal to the total demand.

$$x_{11} + x_{21} + x_{31} = 6000 \quad \text{Boston demand}$$
$$x_{12} + x_{22} + x_{32} = 4000 \quad \text{Chicago demand}$$
$$x_{13} + x_{23} + x_{33} = 2000 \quad \text{St. Louis demand}$$
$$x_{14} + x_{24} + x_{34} = 1500 \quad \text{Lexington demand}$$

Combining the objective function and constraints into one model provides a 12-variable, 7-constraint linear programming formulation of the Foster Generators transportation problem:

$$\text{Min } 3x_{11} + 2x_{12} + 7x_{13} + 6x_{14} + 7x_{21} + 5x_{22} + 2x_{23} + 3x_{24} + 2x_{31} + 5x_{32} + 4x_{33} + 5x_{34}$$

s.t.

$$
\begin{aligned}
x_{11} + x_{12} + x_{13} + x_{14} & & & \leq 5000 \\
x_{21} + x_{22} + x_{23} + x_{24} & & & \leq 6000 \\
x_{31} + x_{32} + x_{33} + x_{34} & \leq 2500 \\
x_{11} \qquad\qquad + x_{21} \qquad\qquad + x_{31} & = 6000 \\
x_{12} \qquad\qquad + x_{22} \qquad\qquad + x_{32} & = 4000 \\
x_{13} \qquad\qquad + x_{23} \qquad\qquad + x_{33} & = 2000 \\
x_{14} \qquad\qquad + x_{24} \qquad\qquad + x_{34} & = 1500 \\
\end{aligned}
$$

$$x_{ij} \geq 0 \quad \text{for } i = 1, 2, 3 \text{ and } j = 1, 2, 3, 4$$

Comparing the linear programming formulation to the network in Figure 6.1 leads to several observations: All the information needed for the linear programming formulation is on the network. Each node has one constraint and each arc has one variable. The sum of the variables corresponding to arcs from an origin node must be less than or equal to the origin's supply, and the sum of the variables corresponding to the arcs into a destination node must be equal to the destination's demand.

The optimal objective function values and optimal decision variable values for the Foster Generators problem are shown in Figure 6.2, which indicates that the minimum total transportation cost is $39,500. The values for the decision variables show the optimal amounts to ship over each route. For example, 3500 units should be shipped from Cleveland to Boston, and 1500 units should be shipped from Cleveland to Chicago. Other values of the decision variables indicate the remaining shipping quantities and routes. Table 6.2 shows the minimum cost transportation schedule, and Figure 6.3 summarizes the optimal solution on the network.

Problem Variations

The Foster Generators problem illustrates use of the basic transportation model. Variations of the basic transportation model may involve one or more of the following situations:

1. Total supply not equal to total demand
2. Maximization objective function
3. Route capacities or route minimums
4. Unacceptable routes

FIGURE 6.2 OPTIMAL SOLUTION FOR THE FOSTER GENERATORS TRANSPORTATION PROBLEM

WEB file

Foster

```
Optimal Objective Value = 39500.00000

      Variable            Value          Reduced Costs
    -------------     ---------------    ---------------
        X11             3500.00000          0.00000
        X12             1500.00000          0.00000
        X13                0.00000          8.00000
        X14                0.00000          6.00000
        X21                0.00000          1.00000
        X22             2500.00000          0.00000
        X23             2000.00000          0.00000
        X24             1500.00000          0.00000
        X31             2500.00000          0.00000
        X32                0.00000          4.00000
        X33                0.00000          6.00000
        X34                0.00000          6.00000
```

TABLE 6.2 OPTIMAL SOLUTION TO THE FOSTER GENERATORS TRANSPORTATION PROBLEM

| Route | | Units | Cost | Total |
From	To	Shipped	per Unit	Cost
Cleveland	Boston	3500	$3	$10,500
Cleveland	Chicago	1500	$2	$ 3,000
Bedford	Chicago	2500	$5	$12,500
Bedford	St. Louis	2000	$2	$ 4,000
Bedford	Lexington	1500	$3	$ 4,500
York	Boston	2500	$2	$ 5,000
				$39,500

With slight modifications in the linear programming model, we can easily accommodate these situations.

Total Supply Not Equal to Total Demand Often *the total supply is not equal to the total demand.* If total supply exceeds total demand, no modification in the linear programming formulation is necessary. Excess supply will appear as slack in the linear programming solution. Slack for any particular origin can be interpreted as the unused supply or amount not shipped from the origin.

Whenever total supply is less than total demand, the model does not determine how the unsatisfied demand is handled (e.g., backorders). The manager must handle this aspect of the problem.

If total supply is less than total demand, the linear programming model of a transportation problem will not have a feasible solution. In this case, we modify the network representation by adding a **dummy origin** with a supply equal to the difference between the total demand and the total supply. With the addition of the dummy origin and an arc from the

FIGURE 6.3   NETWORK DIAGRAM FOR THE OPTIMAL SOLUTION TO THE FOSTER GENERATORS TRANSPORTATION PROBLEM

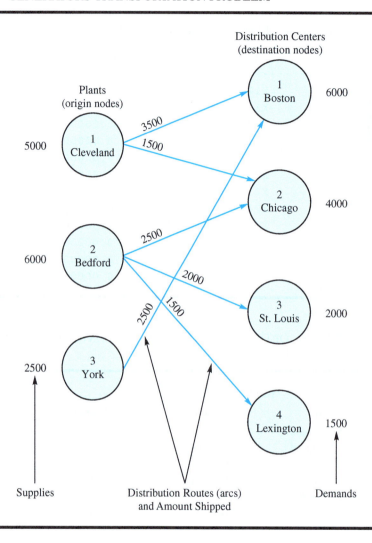

dummy origin to each destination, the linear programming model will have a feasible solution. A zero cost per unit is assigned to each arc leaving the dummy origin so that the value of the optimal solution for the revised problem will represent the shipping cost for the units actually shipped (no shipments actually will be made from the dummy origin). When the optimal solution is implemented, the destinations showing shipments being received from the dummy origin will be the destinations experiencing a shortfall or unsatisfied demand.

Try Problem 6 for practice with a case in which demand is greater than supply with a maximization objective.

Maximization Objective Function   In some transportation problems, the objective is to find a solution that maximizes profit or revenue. Using the values for profit or revenue per unit as coefficients in the objective function, we simply solve a maximization rather than a minimization linear program. This change does not affect the constraints.

Route Capacities or Route Minimums   The linear programming formulation of the transportation problem also can accommodate capacities or minimum quantities for one or more of the routes. For example, suppose that in the Foster Generators problem the York–Boston route (origin 3 to destination 1) had a capacity of 1000 units because of limited space availability on its normal mode of transportation. With x_{31} denoting the amount shipped from York to Boston, the route capacity constraint for the York–Boston route would be

$$x_{31} \leq 1000$$

Similarly, route minimums can be specified. For example,

$$x_{22} \geq 2000$$

would guarantee that a previously committed order for a Bedford–Chicago delivery of at least 2000 units would be maintained in the optimal solution.

Unacceptable Routes   Finally, establishing a route from every origin to every destination may not be possible. To handle this situation, we simply drop the corresponding arc from the network and remove the corresponding variable from the linear programming formulation. For example, if the Cleveland–St. Louis route were unacceptable or unusable, the arc from Cleveland to St. Louis could be dropped in Figure 6.1, and x_{13} could be removed from the linear programming formulation. Solving the resulting 11-variable, 7-constraint model would provide the optimal solution while guaranteeing that the Cleveland–St. Louis route is not used.

A General Linear Programming Model

To show the general linear programming model for a transportation problem with m origins and n destinations, we use the following notation:

$$x_{ij} = \text{number of units shipped from origin } i \text{ to destination } j$$
$$c_{ij} = \text{cost per unit of shipping from origin } i \text{ to destination } j$$
$$s_i = \text{supply or capacity in units at origin } i$$
$$d_j = \text{demand in units at destination } j$$

The general linear programming model is as follows:

$$\text{Min} \quad \sum_{i=1}^{n} \sum_{j=1}^{n} c_{ij} x_{ij}$$

s.t.

$$\sum_{j=1}^{n} x_{ij} \leq s_i \qquad i = 1, 2, \ldots, m \quad \text{Supply}$$

$$\sum_{i=1}^{m} x_{ij} = d_j \qquad j = 1, 2, \ldots, n \quad \text{Demand}$$

$$x_{ij} \geq 0 \qquad \text{for all } i \text{ and } j$$

As mentioned previously, we can add constraints of the form $x_{ij} \leq L_{ij}$ if the route from origin i to destination j has capacity L_{ij}. A transportation problem that includes constraints of this type is called a **capacitated transportation problem**. Similarly, we can add route minimum constraints of the form $x_{ij} \geq M_{ij}$ if the route from origin i to destination j must handle at least M_{ij} units.

The Management Science in Action, Optimizing Freight Car Assignments at Union Pacific, describes how Union Pacific railroad used an optimization model to solve a transportation problem of assigning empty freight cars to customer requests.

OPTIMIZING FREIGHT CAR ASSIGNMENTS AT UNION PACIFIC*

Union Pacific (UP) is one of the largest railroads in North America. It owns over 100,000 freight cars, which it uses to service its customers via a network of over 30,000 miles of railroad track. In response to customer demand, UP moves empty freight cars to its customer locations, where the cars are loaded. UP then transports the loaded cars to destinations designated by the customers.

At any point in time, Union Pacific may have hundreds of customer requests for empty freight cars to transport their products. Empty freight cars are typically scattered throughout UP's rail network at previous delivery destinations. A day-to-day decision faced by UP operations managers is how to assign these empty freight cars to current freight car requests from its customers. The assignments need to be cost effective but also must meet the customers' needs in terms of service time.

UP partnered with researchers from Purdue University to develop an optimization model to assist with the empty freight car assignment problem. In order to be useful, the model had to be simple enough to be solved quickly and had to run within UP's existing information systems. A transportation model was developed, with supply being the empty freight cars at their current locations and demand being the current and forecasted requests at the customer locations. The objective function includes not just the cost of transporting the cars, but other factors such as early and late delivery penalties and customer priority. This allows the managers to trade off a variety of factors with the cost of assignments to ensure that the proper level of service is achieved. The model outputs the number of empty cars to move from each current location to the locations of customers requesting cars. The model is used on a daily basis for operations planning and is also used to study the potential impact of changes in operational policies.

*Based on A. Narisetty et al., "An Optimization Model for Empty Freight Car Assignment at Union Pacific Railroad," *Interfaces* 38, no. 2 (March/April 2008): 89–102.

Transshipment Problem

The **transshipment problem** is an extension of the transportation problem in which intermediate nodes, referred to as *transshipment nodes*, are added to account for locations such as warehouses. In this more general type of distribution problem, shipments may be made between any pair of the three general types of nodes: origin nodes, transshipment nodes, and destination nodes. For example, the transshipment problem permits shipments of goods from origins to intermediate nodes and on to destinations, from one origin to another origin, from one intermediate location to another, from one destination location to another, and directly from origins to destinations.

As was true for the transportation problem, the supply available at each origin is limited, and the demand at each destination is specified. The objective in the transshipment problem is to determine how many units should be shipped over each arc in the network so that all destination demands are satisfied with the minimum possible transportation cost.

Try Problem 11, part (a), for practice in developing a network representation of a transshipment problem.

Let us consider the transshipment problem faced by Ryan Electronics. Ryan is an electronics company with production facilities in Denver and Atlanta. Components produced at either facility may be shipped to either of the firm's regional warehouses, which are located in Kansas City and Louisville. From the regional warehouses, the firm supplies retail outlets in Detroit, Miami, Dallas, and New Orleans. The key features of the problem are shown in the network model depicted in Figure 6.4. Note that the supply at each origin and demand at each destination are shown in the left and right margins, respectively. nodes 1 and 2 are the origin nodes; nodes 3 and 4 are the transshipment nodes; and nodes 5, 6, 7, and 8 are the destination nodes. The transportation cost per unit for each distribution route is shown in Table 6.3 and on the arcs of the network model in Figure 6.4.

FIGURE 6.4   NETWORK REPRESENTATION OF THE RYAN ELECTRONICS
TRANSSHIPMENT PROBLEM

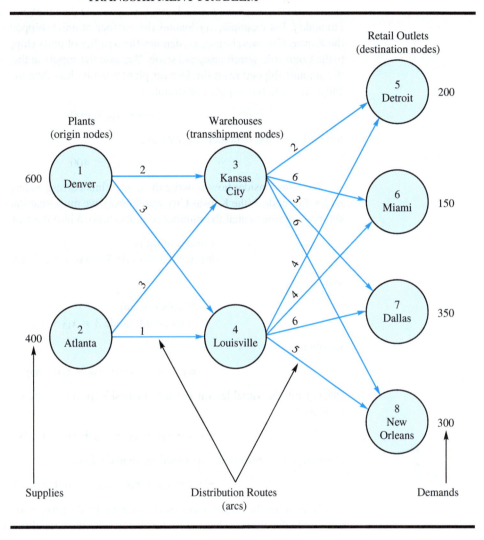

TABLE 6.3   TRANSPORTATION COST PER UNIT FOR THE RYAN ELECTRONICS
TRANSSHIPMENT PROBLEM

	Warehouse	
Plant	**Kansas City**	**Louisville**
Denver	2	3
Atlanta	3	1

	Retail Outlet			
Warehouse	**Detroit**	**Miami**	**Dallas**	**New Orleans**
Kansas City	2	6	3	6
Louisville	4	4	6	5

As with the transportation problem, we can formulate a linear programming model of the transshipment problem from a network representation. Again, we need a constraint for each node and a variable for each arc. Let x_{ij} denote the number of units shipped from node i to node j. For example, x_{13} denotes the number of units shipped from the Denver plant to the Kansas City warehouse, x_{14} denotes the number of units shipped from the Denver plant to the Louisville warehouse, and so on. Because the supply at the Denver plant is 600 units, the amount shipped from the Denver plant must be less than or equal to 600. Mathematically, we write this supply constraint as

$$x_{13} + x_{14} \leq 600$$

Similarly, for the Atlanta plant we have

$$x_{23} + x_{24} \leq 400$$

We now consider how to write the constraints corresponding to the two transshipment nodes. For node 3 (the Kansas City warehouse), we must guarantee that the number of units shipped out must equal the number of units shipped into the warehouse. If

$$\text{Number of units} \atop \text{shipped out of node } 3 = x_{35} + x_{36} + x_{37} + x_{38}$$

and

$$\text{Number of units} \atop \text{shipped into node } 3 = x_{13} + x_{23}$$

we obtain

$$x_{35} + x_{36} + x_{37} + x_{38} = x_{13} + x_{23}$$

Placing all the variables on the left-hand side provides the constraint corresponding to node 3 as

$$-x_{13} - x_{23} + x_{35} + x_{36} + x_{37} + x_{38} = 0$$

Similarly, the constraint corresponding to node 4 is

$$-x_{14} - x_{24} + x_{45} + x_{46} + x_{47} + x_{48} = 0$$

To develop the constraints associated with the destination nodes, we recognize that for each node the amount shipped to the destination must equal the demand. For example, to satisfy the demand for 200 units at node 5 (the Detroit retail outlet), we write

$$x_{35} + x_{45} = 200$$

Similarly, for nodes 6, 7, and 8, we have

$$x_{36} + x_{46} = 150$$
$$x_{37} + x_{47} = 350$$
$$x_{38} + x_{48} = 300$$

Try Problem 11, parts (b) and (c), for practice in developing the linear programming model and in solving a transshipment problem on the computer.

As usual, the objective function reflects the total shipping cost over the 12 shipping routes. Combining the objective function and constraints leads to a 12-variable, 8-constraint linear programming model of the Ryan Electronics transshipment problem (see Figure 6.5). Figure 6.6 shows the optimal solution and Table 6.4 summarizes the optimal solution.

As mentioned at the beginning of this section, in the transshipment problem, arcs may connect any pair of nodes. All such shipping patterns are possible in a transshipment

FIGURE 6.5 LINEAR PROGRAMMING FORMULATION OF THE RYAN ELECTRONICS TRANSSHIPMENT PROBLEM

$$\text{Min } 2x_{13} + 3x_{14} + 3x_{23} + 1x_{24} + 2x_{35} + 6x_{36} + 3x_{37} + 6x_{38} + 4x_{45} + 4x_{46} + 6x_{47} + 5x_{48}$$

s.t.

$$
\begin{array}{llll}
x_{13} + x_{14} & & \leq 600 & \text{Origin node} \\
\quad x_{23} + x_{24} & & \leq 400 & \text{constraints} \\
-x_{13} \quad - x_{23} \quad + x_{35} + x_{36} + x_{37} + x_{38} & = 0 & \text{Transshipment node} \\
\quad - x_{14} \quad - x_{24} \quad + x_{45} + x_{46} + x_{47} + x_{48} = 0 & \text{constraints} \\
x_{35} \quad + x_{45} & = 200 & \\
x_{36} \quad + x_{46} & = 150 & \text{Destination node} \\
x_{37} \quad + x_{47} & = 350 & \text{constraints} \\
x_{38} \quad + x_{48} = 300 &
\end{array}
$$

$x_{ij} \geq 0$ for all i and j

FIGURE 6.6 OPTIMAL SOLUTION FOR THE RYAN ELECTRONICS TRANSSHIPMENT PROBLEM

WEB file

Ryan

```
Optimal Objective Value = 5200.00000

        Variable              Value          Reduced Costs
      --------------      ---------------    -----------------
          X13              550.00000             0.00000
          X14               50.00000             0.00000
          X23                0.00000             3.00000
          X24              400.00000             0.00000
          X35              200.00000             0.00000
          X36                0.00000             1.00000
          X37              350.00000             0.00000
          X38                0.00000             0.00000
          X45                0.00000             3.00000
          X46              150.00000             0.00000
          X47                0.00000             4.00000
          X48              300.00000             0.00000
```

problem. We still require only one constraint per node, but the constraint must include a variable for every arc entering or leaving the node. For origin nodes, the sum of the shipments out minus the sum of the shipments in must be less than or equal to the origin supply. For destination nodes, the sum of the shipments in minus the sum of the shipments out must equal demand. For transshipment nodes, the sum of the shipments out must equal the sum of the shipments in, as before.

For an illustration of this more general type of transshipment problem, let us modify the Ryan Electronics problem. Suppose that it is possible to ship directly from Atlanta to New Orleans at $4 per unit and from Dallas to New Orleans at $1 per unit. The network model corresponding to this modified Ryan Electronics problem is shown in Figure 6.7, the

TABLE 6.4   OPTIMAL SOLUTION TO THE RYAN ELECTRONICS TRANSSHIPMENT
PROBLEM

Route				
From	**To**	**Units Shipped**	**Cost per Unit**	**Total Cost**
Denver	Kansas City	550	$2	$1100
Denver	Louisville	50	$3	$ 150
Atlanta	Louisville	400	$1	$ 400
Kansas City	Detroit	200	$2	$ 400
Kansas City	Dallas	350	$3	$1050
Louisville	Miami	150	$4	$ 600
Louisville	New Orleans	300	$5	$1500
				$5200

FIGURE 6.7   NETWORK REPRESENTATION OF THE MODIFIED RYAN ELECTRONICS
TRANSSHIPMENT PROBLEM

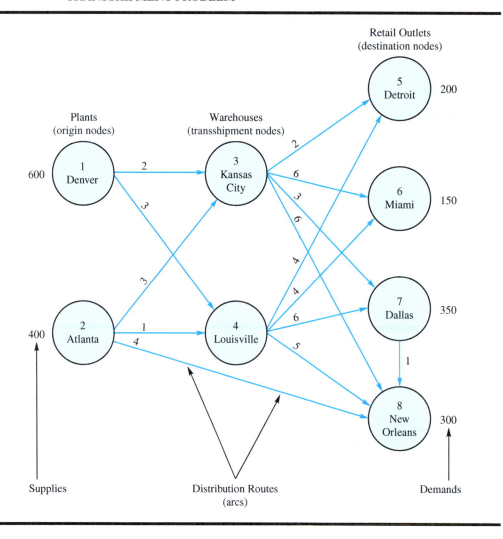

FIGURE 6.8 LINEAR PROGRAMMING FORMULATION OF THE MODIFIED RYAN ELECTRONICS TRANSSHIPMENT PROBLEM

$$\text{Min} \quad 2x_{13} + 3x_{14} + 3x_{23} + 1x_{24} + 2x_{35} + 6x_{36} + 3x_{37} + 6x_{38} + 4x_{45} + 4x_{46} + 6x_{47} + 5x_{48} + 4x_{28} + 1x_{78}$$

s.t.

$x_{13} + x_{14}$				≤ 600	Origin node constraints
$x_{23} + x_{24}$			$+ x_{28}$	≤ 400	
$-x_{13} \quad - x_{23} \quad + x_{35} + x_{36} + x_{37} + x_{38}$				$= 0$	Transshipment node
$- x_{14} \quad - x_{24}$		$+ x_{45} + x_{46} + x_{47} + x_{48}$		$= 0$	constraints
x_{35}		$+ x_{45}$		$= 200$	
x_{36}		$+ x_{46}$		$= 150$	Destination node
x_{37}		$+ x_{47}$	$- x_{78} = 350$		constraints
x_{38}		$+ x_{48} + x_{28} + x_{78} = 300$			

$$x_{ij} \geq 0 \quad \text{for all } i \text{ and } j$$

FIGURE 6.9 OPTIMAL SOLUTION FOR THE MODIFIED RYAN ELECTRONICS TRANSSHIPMENT PROBLEM

```
Optimal objective Value = 4600.00000
```

Variable	Value	Reducec Costs
X13	550.000	0.00000
X14	50.000	0.00000
X23	0.000	3.00000
X24	100.000	0.00000
X35	200.000	0.00000
X36	0.000	1.00000
X37	350.000	0.00000
X38	0.000	2.00000
X45	0.000	3.00000
X46	150.000	0.00000
X47	0.000	4.00000
X48	0.000	2.00000
X28	300.000	0.00000
X78	0.000	0.00000

WEB file

ModifiedRyan

linear programming formulation is shown in Figure 6.8, and the optimal solution is shown in Figure 6.9.

Try Problem 12 for practice working with transshipment problems with this more general structure.

In Figure 6.7 we added two new arcs to the network model. Thus, two new variables are necessary in the linear programming formulation. Figure 6.8 shows that the new variables x_{28} and x_{78} appear in the objective function and in the constraints corresponding to the nodes to which the new arcs are connected. Figure 6.9 shows that the value of the optimal solution has been reduced $600 by allowing these additional shipping routes. The value of $x_{28} = 300$ indicates that 300 units are being shipped directly from Atlanta to New Orleans.

The value of $x_{78} = 0$ indicates that no units are shipped from Dallas to New Orleans in this solution.[1]

Problem Variations

As with transportation problems, transshipment problems may be formulated with several variations, including

1. Total supply not equal to total demand
2. Maximization objective function
3. Route capacities or route minimums
4. Unacceptable routes

The linear programming model modifications required to accommodate these variations are identical to the modifications required for the transportation problem. When we add one or more constraints of the form $x_{ij} \le L_{ij}$ to show that the route from node i to node j has capacity L_{ij}, we refer to the transshipment problem as a **capacitated transshipment problem**.

A General Linear Programming Model

To show the general linear programming model for the transshipment problem, we use the following notation:

$$x_{ij} = \text{number of units shipped from node } i \text{ to node } j$$
$$c_{ij} = \text{cost per unit of shipping from node } i \text{ to node } j$$
$$s_i = \text{supply at origin node } i$$
$$d_j = \text{demand at destination node } j$$

The general linear programming model for the transshipment problem is as follows:

$$\text{Min} \sum_{\text{all arcs}} c_{ij} x_{ij}$$

s.t.

$$\sum_{\text{arcs out}} x_{ij} - \sum_{\text{arcs in}} x_{ij} \le s_i \quad \text{Origin nodes } i$$

$$\sum_{\text{arcs out}} x_{ij} - \sum_{\text{arcs in}} x_{ij} = 0 \quad \text{Transshipment nodes}$$

$$\sum_{\text{arcs in}} x_{ij} - \sum_{\text{arcs out}} x_{ij} = d_j \quad \text{Destination nodes } j$$

$$x_{ij} \ge 0 \text{ for all } i \text{ and } j$$

The Management Science in Action, Product Sourcing Heuristic at Procter & Gamble, describes a transshipment model used by Procter & Gamble to help make strategic decisions related to sourcing and distribution.

---

[1]This is an example of a linear programming with alternate optimal solutions. The solution $x_{13} = 600, x_{14} = 0, x_{23} = 0,$ $x_{24} = 150, x_{28} = 250, x_{35} = 200, x_{36} = 0, x_{37} = 400, x_{38} = 0, x_{45} = 0, x_{46} = 150, x_{47} = 0, x_{48} = 0, x_{78} = 50$ is also optimal. Thus, in this solution both new routes are used: $x_{28} = 250$ units are shipped from Atlanta to New Orleans and $x_{78} = 50$ units are shipped from Dallas to New Orleans.

NOTES AND COMMENTS

1. Supply chain models used in practice usually lead to large linear programs. Problems with 100 origins and 100 destinations are not unusual. Such a problem would involve (100)(100) = 10,000 variables.

2. To handle a situation in which some routes may be unacceptable, we stated that you could drop the corresponding arc from the network and remove the corresponding variable from the linear programming formulation. Another approach often used is to assign an extremely large objective function cost coefficient to any unacceptable arc. If the problem has already been formulated, another option is to add a constraint to the formulation that sets the variable you want to remove equal to zero.

3. The optimal solution to a transportation model will consist of integer values for the decision variables as long as all supply and demand values are integers. The reason is the special mathematical structure of the linear programming model. Each variable appears in exactly one supply and one demand constraint, and all coefficients in the constraint equations are 1 or 0.

4. In the general linear programming formulation of the transshipment problem, the constraints for the destination nodes are often written as

$$\sum_{\text{arcs out}} x_{ij} - \sum_{\text{arcs in}} x_{ij} = -d_j$$

The advantage of writing the constraints this way is that the left-hand side of each constraint then represents the flow out of the node minus the flow in.

MANAGEMENT SCIENCE IN ACTION

PRODUCT SOURCING HEURISTIC AT PROCTER & GAMBLE*

A few years ago Procter & Gamble (P&G) embarked on a major strategic planning initiative called the North American Product Sourcing Study. P&G wanted to consolidate its product sources and optimize its distribution system design throughout North America. A decision support system used to aid in this project was called the Product Sourcing Heuristic (PSH) and was based on a transshipment model much like the ones described in this chapter.

In a preprocessing phase, the many P&G products were aggregated into groups that shared the same technology and could be made at the same plant. The PSH employing the transshipment model was then used by product strategy teams responsible for developing product sourcing options for these product groups. The various plants that could produce the product group were the source nodes, the company's regional distribution centers were the transshipment nodes, and P&G's customer zones were the destinations. Direct shipments to customer zones as well as shipments through distribution centers were employed.

The product strategy teams used the heuristic interactively to explore a variety of questions concerning product sourcing and distribution. For instance, the team might be interested in the impact of closing two of five plants and consolidating production in the three remaining plants. The product sourcing heuristic would then delete the source nodes corresponding to the two closed plants, make any capacity modifications necessary to the sources corresponding to the remaining three plants, and re-solve the transshipment problem. The product strategy team could then examine the new solution, make some more modifications, solve again, and so on.

The Product Sourcing Heuristic was viewed as a valuable decision support system by all who used it. When P&G implemented the results of the study, it realized annual savings in the $200 million range. The PSH proved so successful in North America that P&G used it in other markets around the world.

*Based on information provided by Franz Dill and Tom Chorman of Procter & Gamble.

6.2 ASSIGNMENT PROBLEM

The **assignment problem** arises in a variety of decision-making situations; typical assignment problems involve assigning jobs to machines, agents to tasks, sales personnel to sales territories, contracts to bidders, and so on. A distinguishing feature of the assignment problem is that *one* agent is assigned to *one and only one* task. Specifically, we look for the set of assignments that will optimize a stated objective, such as minimize cost, minimize time, or maximize profits.

To illustrate the assignment problem, let us consider the case of Fowle Marketing Research, which has just received requests for market research studies from three new clients. The company faces the task of assigning a project leader (agent) to each client (task). Currently, three individuals have no other commitments and are available for the project leader assignments. Fowle's management realizes, however, that the time required to complete each study will depend on the experience and ability of the project leader assigned. The three projects have approximately the same priority, and management wants to assign project leaders to minimize the total number of days required to complete all three projects. If a project leader is to be assigned to one client only, which assignments should be made?

Try Problem 17, part (a), for practice in developing a network model for an assignment problem.

To answer the assignment question, Fowle's management must first consider all possible project leader–client assignments and then estimate the corresponding project completion times. With three project leaders and three clients, nine assignment alternatives are possible. The alternatives and the estimated project completion times in days are summarized in Table 6.5.

Figure 6.10 shows the network representation of Fowle's assignment problem. The nodes correspond to the project leaders and clients, and the arcs represent the possible assignments of project leaders to clients. The supply at each origin node and the demand at each destination node are 1; the cost of assigning a project leader to a client is the time it takes that project leader to complete the client's task. Note the similarity between the network models of the assignment problem (Figure 6.10) and the transportation problem (Figure 6.1). The assignment problem is a special case of the transportation problem in which all supply and demand values equal 1, and the amount shipped over each arc is either 0 or 1.

Because the assignment problem is a special case of the transportation problem, we can use the linear programming formulation for the transportation problem to solve the assignment problem. Again, we need a constraint for each node and a variable for each arc. Recall that in the transportation problem the double-subscripted decision variables x_{ij} denoted the number of units shipped from node i to node j. In the assignment problem, the value of each x_{ij} variable will either be 0 or 1 due to the structure of the problem. Therefore, if $x_{11} = 1$ we interpret this as "project leader 1 (Terry) is assigned to client 1," or if $x_{11} = 0$ we interpret

TABLE 6.5 ESTIMATED PROJECT COMPLETION TIMES (DAYS) FOR THE FOWLE MARKETING RESEARCH ASSIGNMENT PROBLEM

		Client	
Project Leader	**1**	**2**	**3**
1. Terry	10	15	9
2. Carle	9	18	5
3. McClymonds	6	14	3

FIGURE 6.10   A NETWORK MODEL OF THE FOWLE MARKETING RESEARCH
ASSIGNMENT PROBLEM

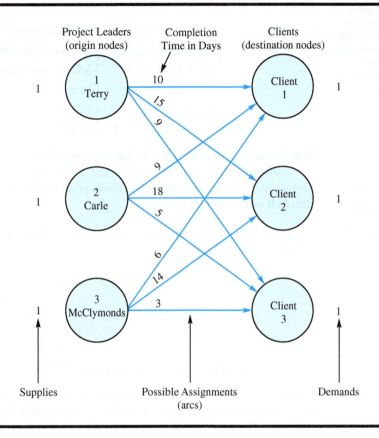

this as "project leader 1 (Terry) is not assigned to client 1." In general, we interpret the decision variables for Fowle's assignment problem as

$$x_{ij} = \begin{cases} 1 & \text{if project leader } i \text{ is assigned to client } j \\ 0 & \text{otherwise} \end{cases}$$

where $i = 1, 2, 3$, and $j = 1, 2, 3$

Using this notation and the completion time data in Table 6.5, we develop completion time expressions:

Days required for Terry's assignment $= 10x_{11} + 15x_{12} + 9x_{13}$
Days required for Carle's assignment $= 9x_{21} + 18x_{22} + 5x_{23}$
Days required for McClymonds's assignment $= 6x_{31} + 14x_{32} + 3x_{33}$

The sum of the completion times for the three project leaders will provide the total days required to complete the three assignments. Thus, the objective function is

$$\text{Min } 10x_{11} + 15x_{12} + 9x_{13} + 9x_{21} + 18x_{22} + 5x_{23} + 6x_{31} + 14x_{32} + 3x_{33}$$

Due to the special structure of the assignment problem, the x_{ij} variables will either be 0 or 1 and not any value in between, e.g., 0.6. In Chapter 7, we discuss optimization problems which represent discrete choices with 0-1 (or binary) variables that must be explicitly constrained to avoid fractional values.

Because the number of project leaders equals the number of clients, all the constraints could be written as equalities. But when the number of project leaders exceeds the number of clients, less-than-or-equal-to constraints must be used for the project leader constraints.

The constraints for the assignment problem reflect the conditions that each project leader can be assigned to at most one client and that each client must have one assigned project leader. These constraints are written as follows:

$$x_{11} + x_{12} + x_{13} \leq 1 \quad \text{Terry's assignment}$$
$$x_{21} + x_{22} + x_{23} \leq 1 \quad \text{Carle's assignment}$$
$$x_{31} + x_{32} + x_{33} \leq 1 \quad \text{McClymonds's assignment}$$
$$x_{11} + x_{21} + x_{31} = 1 \quad \text{Client 1}$$
$$x_{12} + x_{22} + x_{32} = 1 \quad \text{Client 2}$$
$$x_{13} + x_{23} + x_{33} = 1 \quad \text{Client 3}$$

Note that each node in Figure 6.10 has one constraint.

Combining the objective function and constraints into one model provides the following nine-variable, six-constraint linear programming model of the Fowle Marketing Research assignment problem:

Try Problem 17, part (b), for practice in formulating and solving a linear programming model for an assignment problem on the computer.

$$
\begin{aligned}
\text{Min} \quad & 10x_{11} + 15x_{12} + 9x_{13} + 9x_{21} + 18x_{22} + 5x_{23} + 6x_{31} + 14x_{32} + 3x_{33} \\
\text{s.t.} \quad & \\
& x_{11} + x_{12} + x_{13} && \leq 1 \\
& x_{21} + x_{22} + x_{23} && \leq 1 \\
& x_{31} + x_{32} + x_{33} \leq 1 \\
& x_{11} + x_{21} + x_{31} && = 1 \\
& x_{12} + x_{22} + x_{32} && = 1 \\
& x_{13} + x_{23} + x_{33} = 1 \\
& x_{ij} \geq 0 \quad \text{for } i = 1, 2, 3 \text{ and } j = 1, 2, 3
\end{aligned}
$$

Figure 6.11 shows the optimal solution for this model. Terry is assigned to client 2 ($x_{12} = 1$), Carle is assigned to client 3 ($x_{23} = 1$), and McClymonds is assigned to client 1 ($x_{31} = 1$). The total completion time required is 26 days. This solution is summarized in Table 6.6.

FIGURE 6.11   OPTIMAL SOLUTION FOR THE FOWLE MARKETING RESEARCH ASSIGNMENT PROBLEM

```
Optimal Objective Value = 26.00000

          Variable            Value            Reduced Costs
        -------------     ---------------     ------------------
            X11             0.00000               0.00000
            X12             1.00000               0.00000
            X13             0.00000               2.00000
            X21             0.00000               1.00000
            X22             0.00000               5.00000
            X23             1.00000               0.00000
            X31             1.00000               0.00000
            X32             0.00000               3.00000
            X33             0.00000               0.00000
```

WEB file

Fowle

TABLE 6.6 OPTIMAL PROJECT LEADER ASSIGNMENTS FOR THE FOWLE
MARKETING RESEARCH ASSIGNMENT PROBLEM

Project Leader	Assigned Client	Days
Terry	2	15
Carle	3	5
McClymonds	1	6
	Total	26

Problem Variations

Because the assignment problem can be viewed as a special case of the transportation problem, the problem variations that may arise in an assignment problem parallel those for the transportation problem. Specifically, we can handle

1. Total number of agents (supply) not equal to the total number of tasks (demand)
2. A maximization objective function
3. Unacceptable assignments

The situation in which the number of agents does not equal the number of tasks is analogous to total supply not equaling total demand in a transportation problem. If the number of agents exceeds the number of tasks, the extra agents simply remain unassigned in the linear programming solution. If the number of tasks exceeds the number of agents, the linear programming model will not have a feasible solution. In this situation, a simple modification is to add enough dummy agents to equalize the number of agents and the number of tasks. For instance, in the Fowle problem we might have had five clients (tasks) and only three project leaders (agents). By adding two dummy project leaders, we can create a new assignment problem with the number of project leaders equal to the number of clients. The objective function coefficients for the assignment of dummy project leaders would be zero so that the value of the optimal solution would represent the total number of days required by the assignments actually made (no assignments will actually be made to the clients receiving dummy project leaders).

If the assignment alternatives are evaluated in terms of revenue or profit rather than time or cost, the linear programming formulation can be solved as a maximization rather than a minimization problem. In addition, if one or more assignments are unacceptable, the corresponding decision variable can be removed from the linear programming formulation. This situation could happen, for example, if an agent did not have the experience necessary for one or more of the tasks.

A General Linear Programming Model

In the general linear programming model for an assignment problem with m agents and n tasks, c_{ij} represents the cost of assigning agent i to task j and the value of x_{ij} represents whether (1) or not (0) agent i is assigned to task j. We express the formulation as:

$$\text{Min} \quad \sum_{i=1}^{m} \sum_{j=1}^{n} c_{ij}x_{ij}$$

s.t.

$$\sum_{j=1}^{n} x_{ij} \leq 1 \quad i = 1, 2, \ldots, m \quad \text{Agents}$$

$$\sum_{i=1}^{m} x_{ij} = 1 \quad j = 1, 2, \ldots, n \quad \text{Tasks}$$

$$x_{ij} \geq 0 \quad \text{for all } i \text{ and } j$$

At the beginning of this section, we indicated that a distinguishing feature of the assignment problem is that *one* agent is assigned to *one and only one* task. In generalizations of the assignment problem where one agent can be assigned to two or more tasks, the linear programming formulation of the problem can be easily modified. For example, let us assume that in the Fowle Marketing Research problem Terry could be assigned up to two clients; in this case, the constraint representing Terry's assignment would be $x_{11} + x_{12} + x_{13} \leq 2$. In general, if a_i denotes the upper limit for the number of tasks to which agent i can be assigned, we write the agent constraints as

$$\sum_{j=1}^{n} x_{ij} \leq a_i \quad i = 1, 2, \ldots, m$$

If some tasks require more than one agent, the linear programming formulation can also accommodate the situation. Use the number of agents required as the right-hand side of the appropriate task constraint.

NOTES AND COMMENTS

1. As noted, the assignment model is a special case of the transportation model. We stated in the Notes and Comments at the end of the preceding section that the optimal solution to the transportation problem will consist of integer values for the decision variables as long as the supplies and demands are integers. For the assignment problem, all supplies and demands equal 1; thus, the optimal solution must be integer valued and the integer values must be 0 or 1.
2. Combining the method for handling multiple assignments with the notion of a dummy agent provides another means of dealing with

situations when the number of tasks exceeds the number of agents. That is, we add one dummy agent but provide the dummy agent with the capability to handle multiple tasks. The number of tasks the dummy agent can handle is equal to the difference between the number of tasks and the number of agents.
3. The Management Science in Action, Assigning Consultants to Clients at Energy Education, Inc. describes how a consulting company uses an assignment problem as part of an innovative model to minimize the travel costs for their clients.

MANAGEMENT SCIENCE IN ACTION

ASSIGNING CONSULTANTS TO CLIENTS AT ENERGY EDUCATION, INC.*

Energy Education, Inc. (EEI) is a consulting firm that provides experts to schools, universities, and other organizations to implement energy

conservation programs. It is estimated that EEI has helped more than 1100 clients save in excess of $2.3 billion in energy costs over the course of the 25 years in which EEI has provided consulting services. EEI consultants spend almost all of their time working at the client location which results in frequent travel and high travel costs for the company. On average, a consultant for EEI spends about $1,000 per week for air travel costs alone.

Because of the large expense associated with consultant travel, EEI seeks to minimize travel costs whenever possible. To help minimize consultant-travel cost, EEI created models that assign consultants to clients. The objective of these models is to minimize the total number of flights required each week while meeting all client needs. These models include an assignment-type problem similar to those described in this chapter as part of a more complicated framework that also considers the optimal routing of consultants among client locations.

The models developed by EEI are solved using dedicated optimization software, and the output of the models provides a weekly assignment and travel route for each consultant. The new models resulted in a 44% reduction in flight costs for EEI over a 12-week period in comparison to the consultant assignments and travel plans used previously. The number of consultants required to meet all client demand was also reduced using the new models, leading to a direct labor cost reduction of 15%. In total, EEI realized an annual cost savings of nearly $500,000 from implementing their models for assigning consultants to clients and optimizing consultant travel.

*Based on Junfang Yu and Randy Hoff, "Optimal Routing and Assignment of Consultants for Energy Education, Inc.," *Interfaces* 43, no. 2 (March–April 2013): 142–151.

6.3   SHORTEST-ROUTE PROBLEM

In this section we consider a problem in which the objective is to determine the **shortest route**, or *path*, between two nodes in a network. We will demonstrate the shortest-route problem by considering the situation facing the Gorman Construction Company. Gorman has several construction sites located throughout a three-county area. With multiple daily trips carrying personnel, equipment, and supplies from Gorman's office to the construction sites, the costs associated with transportation activities are substantial. The travel alternatives between Gorman's office and each construction site can be described by the road network shown in Figure 6.12. The road distances in miles between the nodes are shown above the corresponding arcs. In this application, Gorman would like to determine the route that will minimize the total travel distance between Gorman's office (located at node 1) and the construction site located at node 6.

A key to developing a model for the shortest-route problem is to understand that the problem is a special case of the transshipment problem. Specifically, the Gorman shortest-route problem can be viewed as a transshipment problem with one origin node (node 1), one destination node (node 6), and four transshipment nodes (nodes 2, 3, 4, and 5). The transshipment network for the Gorman shortest-route problem is shown in Figure 6.13. Arrows added to the arcs show the direction of flow, which is always *out* of the origin node and *into* the destination node. Note also that two directed arcs are shown between the pairs of transshipment nodes. For example, one arc going from node 2 to node 3 indicates that the shortest route may go from node 2 to node 3, and one arc going from node 3 to node 2 indicates that the shortest route may go from node 3 to node 2. The distance between two transshipment nodes is the same in either direction.

To find the shortest route between node 1 and node 6, think of node 1 as having a supply of 1 unit and node 6 as having a demand of 1 unit. Let x_{ij} denote the number of units that flow or are shipped from node i to node j. Because only 1 unit will be shipped from node 1 to node 6, the value of x_{ij} will be either 1 or 0. Thus, if $x_{ij} = 1$, the arc from node i to

FIGURE 6.12   ROAD NETWORK FOR THE GORMAN COMPANY SHORTEST-ROUTE PROBLEM

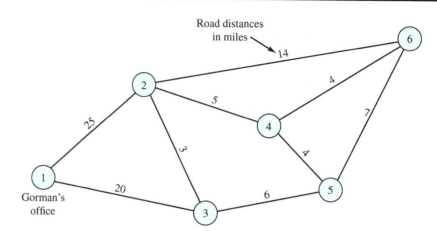

Note: (1) The length of each arc is not necessarily proportional to the travel distance it represents.

(2) All roads are two-way; thus, flow may be in either direction.

FIGURE 6.13   TRANSSHIPMENT NETWORK FOR THE GORMAN SHORTEST-ROUTE PROBLEM

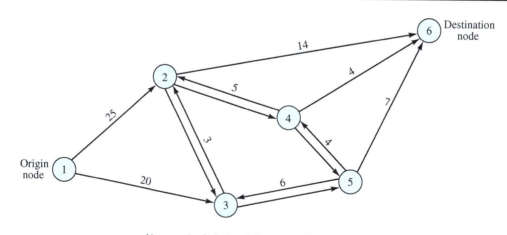

Note: nodes 2, 3, 4, and 5 are transshipment nodes.

node j is on the shortest route from node 1 to node 6; if $x_{ij} = 0$, the arc from node i to node j is not on the shortest route. Because we are looking for the shortest route between node 1 and node 6, the objective function for the Gorman problem is

$$\text{Min} \quad 25x_{12} + 20x_{13} + 3x_{23} + 3x_{32} + 5x_{24} + 5x_{42} + 14x_{26} + 6x_{35} + 6x_{53}$$
$$+ 4x_{45} + 4x_{54} + 4x_{46} + 7x_{56}$$

To develop the constraints for the model, we begin with node 1. Because the supply at node 1 is 1 unit, the flow out of node 1 must equal 1. Thus, the constraint for node 1 is written

$$x_{12} + x_{13} = 1$$

For transshipment nodes 2, 3, 4, and 5, the flow out of each node must equal the flow into each node; thus, the flow out minus the flow in must be 0. The constraints for the four transshipment nodes are as follows:

	Flow Out	Flow In
Node 2	$x_{23} + x_{24} + x_{26}$	$-x_{12} - x_{32} - x_{42} = 0$
Node 3	$x_{32} + x_{35}$	$-x_{13} - x_{23} - x_{53} = 0$
Node 4	$x_{42} + x_{45} + x_{46}$	$-x_{24} - x_{54} \quad\;\; = 0$
Node 5	$x_{53} + x_{54} + x_{56}$	$-x_{35} - x_{45} \quad\;\; = 0$

Because node 6 is the destination node with a demand of 1 unit, the flow into node 6 must equal 1. Thus, the constraint for node 6 is written as

$$x_{26} + x_{46} + x_{56} = 1$$

Including the negative constraints $x_{ij} \geq 0$ for all i and j, the linear programming model for the Gorman shortest-route problem is shown in Figure 6.14.

The optimal solution for the Gorman shortest-route problem is shown in Figure 6.15. The objective function value of 32 indicates that the shortest route between Gorman's office located at node 1 to the construction site located at node 6 is 32 miles. With $x_{13} = 1$, $x_{32} = 1$, $x_{24} = 1$, and $x_{46} = 1$, the shortest route from node 1 to node 6 is 1–3–2–4–6; in

FIGURE 6.14 LINEAR PROGRAMMING FORMULATION OF THE GORMAN SHORTEST-ROUTE PROBLEM

$$\text{Min } 25x_{12} + 20x_{13} + 3x_{23} + 3x_{32} + 5x_{24} + 5x_{42} + 14x_{26} + 6x_{35} + 6x_{53} + 4x_{45} + 4x_{54} + 4x_{46} + 7x_{56}$$

s.t.

$$
\begin{aligned}
x_{12} + x_{13} &= 1 \quad &\text{Origin node} \\
-x_{12} + x_{23} - x_{32} + x_{24} - x_{42} + x_{26} &= 0 \\
-x_{13} - x_{23} + x_{32} + x_{35} - x_{53} &= 0 \\
-x_{24} + x_{42} + x_{45} - x_{54} + x_{46} &= 0 \\
-x_{35} + x_{53} - x_{45} + x_{54} + x_{56} &= 0 \\
x_{26} + x_{46} + x_{56} &= 1 \quad &\text{Destination node}
\end{aligned}
$$

Transshipment nodes

$$x_{ij} \geq 0 \text{ for all } i \text{ and } j$$

FIGURE 6.15   OPTIMAL SOLUTION FOR THE GORMAN SHORTEST-ROUTE PROBLEM

Optimal Objective Value = 32.00000

Gorman

Variable	Value	Reduced Cost
X12	0.00000	2.00000
X13	1.00000	0.00000
X23	0.00000	6.00000
X32	1.00000	0.00000
X24	1.00000	0.00000
X42	0.00000	10.00000
X26	0.00000	5.00000
X35	0.00000	0.00000
X53	0.00000	12.00000
X45	0.00000	7.00000
X54	0.00000	1.00000
X46	1.00000	0.00000
X56	0.00000	0.00000

Try Problem 23 to practice solving a shortest-route problem.

other words, the shortest route takes us from node 1 to node 3; then from node 3 to node 2; then from node 2 to node 4; and finally from node 4 to node 6.

A General Linear Programming Model

Due to the special structure of the shortest-route problem, the x_{ij} variables will either be 0 or 1 and not any value in between, such as 0.6. In Chapter 7, we discuss optimization problems which represent discrete choices with 0-1 (or binary) variables that must be explicitly constrained to avoid fractional values.

The general linear programming model for the shortest-route problem is as follows:

$$\text{Min} \quad \sum_{\text{all arcs}} c_{ij} x_{ij}$$

s.t.

$$\sum_{\text{arcs out}} x_{ij} = 1 \quad \text{Origin node } i$$

$$\sum_{\text{arcs out}} x_{ij} - \sum_{\text{arcs in}} x_{ij} = 0 \quad \text{Transshipment nodes}$$

$$\sum_{\text{arcs in}} x_{ij} = 1 \quad \text{Destination node } j$$

In this linear programming model, c_{ij} represents the distance, time, or cost associated with the arc from node i to node j, and the value of x_{ij} represents whether (1) or not (0) the arc from node i to node j is on the shortest route. If $x_{ij} = 1$, the arc from node i to node j is on the shortest route. If $x_{ij} = 0$, the arc from node i to node j is note on the shortest route.

NOTES AND COMMENTS

1. In the Gorman problem we assumed that all roads in the network are two-way. As a result, the road connecting nodes 2 and 3 in the road network resulted in the creation of two corresponding arcs in the transshipment network. Two decision variables, x_{23} and x_{32}, were required to show that the shortest route might go from node 2 to node 3 or from node 3 to node 2. If the road connecting nodes 2 and 3 had been a one-way road allowing flow only from node 2 to node 3, decision variable x_{32} would not have been included in the model.

6.4   MAXIMAL FLOW PROBLEM

The objective in a **maximal flow** problem is to determine the maximum amount of flow (vehicles, messages, fluid, etc.) that can enter and exit a network system in a given period of time. In this problem, we attempt to transmit flow through all arcs of the network as efficiently as possible. The amount of flow is limited due to capacity restrictions on the various arcs of the network. For example, highway types limit vehicle flow in a transportation system, while pipe sizes limit oil flow in an oil distribution system. The maximum or upper limit on the flow in an arc is referred to as the **flow capacity** of the arc. Even though we do not specify capacities for the nodes, we do assume that the flow out of a node is equal to the flow into the node.

As an example of the maximal flow problem, consider the north–south interstate highway system passing through Cincinnati, Ohio. The north–south vehicle flow reaches a level of 15,000 vehicles per hour at peak times. Due to a summer highway maintenance program, which calls for the temporary closing of lanes and lower speed limits, a network of alternate routes through Cincinnati has been proposed by a transportation planning committee. The alternate routes include other highways as well as city streets. Because of differences in speed limits and traffic patterns, flow capacities vary depending on the particular streets and roads used. The proposed network with arc flow capacities is shown in Figure 6.16.

FIGURE 6.16   NETWORK OF HIGHWAY SYSTEM AND FLOW CAPACITIES (1000S/HOUR) FOR CINCINNATI

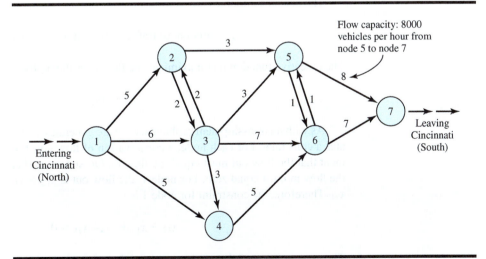

FIGURE 6.17   FLOW OVER ARC FROM NODE 7 TO NODE 1 TO REPRESENT
TOTAL FLOW THROUGH THE CINCINNATI HIGHWAY
SYSTEM

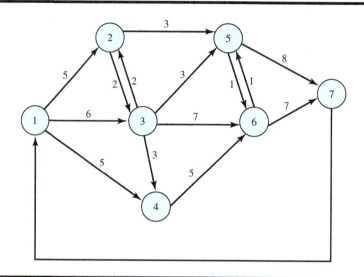

The direction of flow for each arc is indicated, and the arc capacity is shown next to each arc. Note that most of the streets are one-way. However, a two-way street can be found between nodes 2 and 3 and between nodes 5 and 6. In both cases, the capacity is the same in each direction.

We will show how to develop a capacitated transshipment model for the maximal flow problem. First, we will add an arc from node 7 back to node 1 to represent the total flow through the highway system. Figure 6.17 shows the modified network. The newly added arc shows no capacity; indeed, we will want to maximize the flow over that arc. Maximizing the flow over the arc from node 7 to node 1 is equivalent to maximizing the number of cars that can get through the north–south highway system passing through Cincinnati.

The decision variables are as follows:

$$x_{ij} = \text{amount of traffic flow from node } i \text{ to node } j$$

The objective function that maximizes the flow over the highway system is

$$\text{Max } x_{71}$$

As with all transshipment problems, each arc generates a variable and each node generates a constraint. For each node, a conservation of flow constraint represents the requirement that the flow out must equal the flow in. Or, stated another way, the flow out minus the flow in must equal zero. For node 1, the flow out is $x_{12} + x_{13} + x_{14}$, and the flow in is x_{71}. Therefore, the constraint for node 1 is

$$x_{12} + x_{13} + x_{14} - x_{71} = 0$$

The conservation of flow constraints for the other six nodes are developed in a similar fashion.

	Flow Out	**Flow In**	
Node 2	$x_{23} + x_{25}$	$-x_{12} - x_{32}$	$= 0$
Node 3	$x_{32} + x_{34} + x_{35} + x_{36}$	$-x_{13} - x_{23}$	$= 0$
Node 4	x_{46}	$-x_{14} - x_{34}$	$= 0$
Node 5	$x_{56} + x_{57}$	$-x_{25} - x_{35} - x_{65}$	$= 0$
Node 6	$x_{65} + x_{67}$	$-x_{36} - x_{46} - x_{56}$	$= 0$
Node 7	x_{71}	$-x_{57} - x_{67}$	$= 0$

Additional constraints are needed to enforce the capacities on the arcs. These 14 simple upper-bound constraints are given.

$$x_{12} \leq 5 \quad x_{13} \leq 6 \quad x_{14} \leq 5$$
$$x_{23} \leq 2 \quad x_{25} \leq 3$$
$$x_{32} \leq 2 \quad x_{34} \leq 3 \quad x_{35} \leq 5 \quad x_{36} \leq 7$$
$$x_{46} \leq 5$$
$$x_{56} \leq 1 \quad x_{57} \leq 8$$
$$x_{65} \leq 1 \quad x_{67} \leq 7$$

Note that the only arc without a capacity is the one we added from node 7 to node 1.

The optimal solution for this 15-variable, 21-constraint linear programming problem is shown in Figure 6.18. We note that the value of the optimal solution is 14. This result

FIGURE 6.18 OPTIMAL SOLUTION FOR THE CINCINNATI HIGHWAY SYSTEM MAXIMAL FLOW PROBLEM

WEB file

Cincinnati

```
Optimal Objective Value = 14.00000
```

Variable	Value	Reduced Cost
X12	3.00000	0.00000
X13	6.00000	0.00000
X14	5.00000	0.00000
X23	0.00000	0.00000
X25	3.00000	0.00000
X34	0.00000	0.00000
X35	3.00000	0.00000
X36	3.00000	0.00000
X32	0.00000	0.00000
X46	5.00000	0.00000
X56	0.00000	1.00000
X57	7.00000	0.00000
X65	1.00000	0.00000
X67	7.00000	0.00000
X71	14.00000	0.00000

FIGURE 6.19   MAXIMAL FLOW PATTERN FOR THE CINCINNATI HIGHWAY
SYSTEM NETWORK

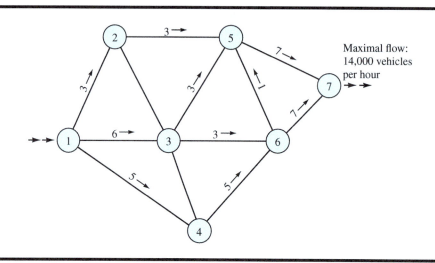

Try Problem 29 for practice in solving a maximal flow problem.

implies that the maximal flow over the highway system is 14,000 vehicles. Figure 6.19 shows how the vehicle flow is routed through the original highway network. We note, for instance, that 3000 vehicles per hour are routed between nodes 1 and 2, 6000 vehicles per hour are routed between nodes 1 and 3, 0 vehicles are routed between nodes 2 and 3, and so on.

The results of the maximal flow analysis indicate that the planned highway network system will not handle the peak flow of 15,000 vehicles per hour. The transportation planners will have to expand the highway network, increase current arc flow capacities, or be prepared for serious traffic problems. If the network is extended or modified, another maximal flow analysis will determine the extent of any improved flow. The Management Science in Action, Finding the Shortest Paths for Containerships, describes how Danaos Corporation computes shortest path routes for their containerships to save millions of dollars in reduced fuel costs.

NOTES AND COMMENTS

1. The maximal flow problem of this section can also be solved with a slightly different formulation if the extra arc between nodes 7 and 1 is not used. The alternate approach is to maximize the flow into node 7 ($x_{57} + x_{67}$) and drop the conservation of flow constraints for nodes 1 and 7. However, the formulation used in this section is most common in practice.

2. Network models can be used to describe a variety of management science problems. Unfortunately, no one network solution algorithm can be used to solve every network problem. It is important to recognize the specific type of problem being modeled in order to select the correct specialized solution algorithm.

FINDING THE SHORTEST PATHS FOR CONTAINERSHIPS*

Danaos Corporation is an international shipping company based in Greece that owns more than 60 containerships. Danaos' containerships travel millions of miles each year to transport millions of containers all around the world. Danaos has developed a powerful tool to improve shipping operations known as the Operations Research in Ship Management (ORISMA) tool. Part of this tool involves the solving of shortest-path problems to determine a containership's optimal route.

Optimizing the travel route for a containership generates substantial savings through the use of less fuel and because it allows the ship to generate more revenue in less time by visiting additional ports to pickup and deliver containers. A subcomponent of ORISMA determines the shortest-path route between two given waypoints (intermediate points of a ship's complete voyage) by defining nodes in the feasible sailing space for the containership.

Danaos determined that it generated $1.3 million in additional revenue in a single year by using ORISMA to reduce the amount of time containerships spent traveling between ports. Furthermore, it saved $3.2 million in reduced fuel costs during the same year. Danaos estimates that further use of ORISMA will increase profitability by 7–10% annually in the future. As a nice byproduct of Danaos' reduced travel times and decreased fuel usage, carbon emissions have been cut substantially and customers are happier to get their products with less lead time.

*Based on Takis Varelas, Sofia Archontaki, John Dimotikalis, Osman Turan, Iraklis Lazakis, and Orestis Varelas, "Optimizing Ship Routing to Maximize Fleet Revenue at Danaos," *Interfaces* 43, no. 1 (January–February 2013): 37–47.

6.5   A PRODUCTION AND INVENTORY APPLICATION

The introduction to supply chain models in Section 6.1 involved applications for the shipment of goods from several supply locations or origins to several demand sites or destinations. Although the shipment of goods is the subject of many supply chain problems, supply chain models can be developed for applications that have nothing to do with the physical shipment of goods from origins to destinations. In this section we show how to use a transshipment model to solve a production and inventory problem.

Contois Carpets is a small manufacturer of carpeting for home and office installations. Production capacity, demand, production cost per square yard, and inventory holding cost per square yard for the next four quarters are shown in Table 6.7. Note that production capacity, demand, and production costs vary by quarter, whereas the cost of carrying inventory from one quarter to the next is constant at $0.25 per yard. Contois wants to

TABLE 6.7   PRODUCTION, DEMAND, AND COST ESTIMATES FOR CONTOIS CARPETS

Quarter	Production Capacity (square yards)	Demand (square yards)	Production Cost ($/square yard)	Inventory Cost ($/square yard)
1	600	400	2	0.25
2	300	500	5	0.25
3	500	400	3	0.25
4	400	400	3	0.25

determine how many yards of carpeting to manufacture each quarter to minimize the total production and inventory cost for the four-quarter period.

The network flows into and out of demand nodes are what make the model a transshipment model.

We begin by developing a network representation of the problem. First, we create four nodes corresponding to the production in each quarter and four nodes corresponding to the demand in each quarter. Each production node is connected by an outgoing arc to the demand node for the same period. The flow on the arc represents the number of square yards of carpet manufactured for the period. For each demand node, an outgoing arc represents the amount of inventory (square yards of carpet) carried over to the demand node for the next period. Figure 6.20 shows the network model. Note that nodes 1–4 represent the production for each quarter and that nodes 5–8 represent the demand for each quarter. The quarterly production capacities are shown in the left margin, and the quarterly demands are shown in the right margin.

FIGURE 6.20   NETWORK REPRESENTATION OF THE CONTOIS CARPETS PROBLEM

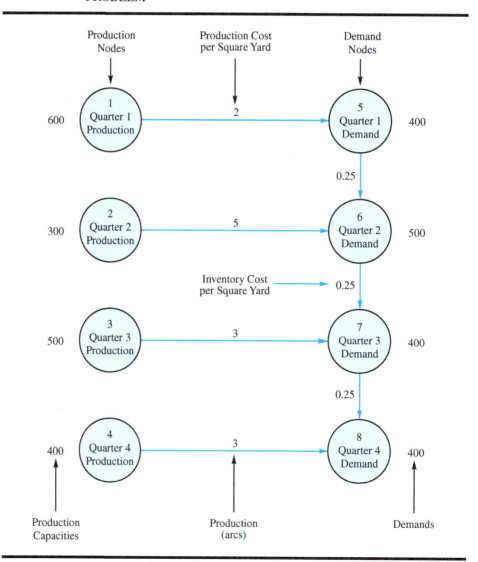

The objective is to determine a production scheduling and inventory policy that will minimize the total production and inventory cost for the four quarters. Constraints involve production capacity and demand in each quarter. As usual, a linear programming model can be developed from the network by establishing a constraint for each node and a variable for each arc.

Let x_{15} denote the number of square yards of carpet manufactured in quarter 1. The capacity of the facility is 600 square yards in quarter 1, so the production capacity constraint is

$$x_{15} \leq 600$$

Using similar decision variables, we obtain the production capacities for quarters 2–4:

$$x_{26} \leq 300$$
$$x_{37} \leq 500$$
$$x_{48} \leq 400$$

We now consider the development of the constraints for each of the demand nodes. For node 5, one arc enters the node, which represents the number of square yards of carpet produced in quarter 1, and one arc leaves the node, which represents the number of square yards of carpet that will not be sold in quarter 1 and will be carried over for possible sale in quarter 2. In general, for each quarter the beginning inventory plus the production minus the ending inventory must equal demand. However, because quarter 1 has no beginning inventory, the constraint for node 5 is

$$x_{15} - x_{56} = 400$$

The constraints associated with the demand nodes in quarters 2, 3, and 4 are

$$x_{56} + x_{26} - x_{67} = 500$$
$$x_{67} + x_{37} - x_{78} = 400$$
$$x_{78} + x_{48} = 400$$

Note that the constraint for node 8 (fourth-quarter demand) involves only two variables because no provision is made for holding inventory for a fifth quarter.

The objective is to minimize total production and inventory cost, so we write the objective function as

$$\text{Min} \quad 2x_{15} + 5x_{26} + 3x_{37} + 3x_{48} + 0.25x_{56} + 0.25x_{67} + 0.25x_{78}$$

The complete linear programming formulation of the Contois Carpets problem is

$$\text{Min} \quad 2x_{15} + 5x_{26} + 3x_{37} + 3x_{48} + 0.25x_{56} + 0.25x_{67} + 0.25x_{78}$$

s.t.

x_{15}							≤ 600
	x_{26}						≤ 300
		x_{37}					≤ 500
			x_{48}				≤ 400
x_{15}				$- x_{56}$			$= 400$
	x_{26}			$+ x_{56}$	$- x_{67}$		$= 500$
		x_{37}			$+ x_{67}$	$- x_{78}$	$= 400$
			x_{48}			$+ x_{78}$	$= 400$

$$x_{ij} \geq 0 \quad \text{for all } i \text{ and } j$$

FIGURE 6.21   OPTIMAL SOLUTION FOR THE CONTOIS CARPETS PROBLEM

Contois

```
Optimal Objective Value = 5150.00000

       Variable            Value            Reduced Cost
     --------------    ---------------    -----------------
        X15              600.00000            0.00000
        X26              300.00000            0.00000
        X37              400.00000            0.00000
        X48              400.00000            0.00000
        X56              200.00000            0.00000
        X67                0.00000            2.25000
        X78                0.00000            0.00000
```

Figure 6.21 shows the optimal solution for this problem. Contois Carpets should manufacture 600 square yards of carpet in quarter 1, 300 square yards in quarter 2, 400 square yards in quarter 3, and 400 square yards in quarter 4. Note also that 200 square yards will be carried over from quarter 1 to quarter 2. The total production and inventory cost is $5150.

NOTES AND COMMENTS

1. For the network models presented in this chapter, the amount leaving the starting node for an arc is always equal to the amount entering the ending node for that arc. An extension of such a network model is the case where a gain or a loss occurs as an arc is traversed. The amount entering the destination node may be greater or smaller than the amount leaving the origin node. For instance, if cash is the commodity flowing across an arc, the cash earns interest from one period to the next. Thus, the amount of cash entering the next period is greater than the amount leaving the previous period by the amount of interest earned. Networks with gains or losses are treated in more advanced texts on network flow programming.

SUMMARY

In this chapter we introduced models related to supply chain problems—specifically, transportation and transshipment problems—as well as assignment, shortest-route, and maximal flow problems. All of these types of problems belong to the special category of linear programs called *network flow problems*. In general, the network model for these problems consists of nodes representing origins, destinations, and, if necessary, transshipment points in the network system. Arcs are used to represent the routes for shipment, travel, or flow between the various nodes.

Transportation problems and transshipment problems are commonly encountered when dealing with supply chains. The general transportation problem has m origins and n destinations. Given the supply at each origin, the demand at each destination, and unit shipping cost between each origin and each destination, the transportation model determines the optimal amounts to ship from each origin to each destination. The transshipment problem is an extension of the transportation problem involving transfer points referred to as transshipment nodes. In this more general model, we allow arcs between any pair of nodes in the network.

The assignment problem is a special case of the transportation problem in which all supply and all demand values are 1. We represent each agent as an origin node and each task as a destination node. The assignment model determines the minimum cost or maximum profit assignment of agents to tasks.

The shortest-route problem finds the shortest route or path between two nodes of a network. Distance, time, and cost are often the criteria used for this model. The shortest-route problem can be expressed as a transshipment problem with one origin and one destination. By shipping one unit from the origin to the destination, the solution will determine the shortest route through the network.

The maximal flow problem can be used to allocate flow to the arcs of the network so that flow through the network system is maximized. Arc capacities determine the maximum amount of flow for each arc. With these flow capacity constraints, the maximal flow problem is expressed as a capacitated transshipment problem.

In the last section of the chapter, we showed how a variation of the transshipment problem could be used to solve a production and inventory problem. In the chapter appendix we show how to use Excel to solve three of the distribution and network problems presented in the chapter.

GLOSSARY

Arcs   The lines connecting the nodes in a network.

Assignment problem   A network flow problem that often involves the assignment of agents to tasks; it can be formulated as a linear program and is a special case of the transportation problem.

Capacitated transportation problem   A variation of the basic transportation problem in which some or all of the arcs are subject to capacity restrictions.

Capacitated transshipment problem   A variation of the transshipment problem in which some or all of the arcs are subject to capacity restrictions.

Dummy origin   An origin added to a transportation problem to make the total supply equal to the total demand. The supply assigned to the dummy origin is the difference between the total demand and the total supply.

Flow capacity   The maximum flow for an arc of the network. The flow capacity in one direction may not equal the flow capacity in the reverse direction.

Maximal flow   The maximum amount of flow that can enter and exit a network system during a given period of time.

Network   A graphical representation of a problem consisting of numbered circles (nodes) interconnected by a series of lines (arcs); arrowheads on the arcs show the direction of flow. Transportation, assignment, and transshipment problems are network flow problems.

Nodes   The intersection or junction points of a network.

Shortest route   Shortest path between two nodes in a network.

Supply chain   The set of all interconnected resources involved in producing and distributing a product.

Transportation problem   A network flow problem that often involves minimizing the cost of shipping goods from a set of origins to a set of destinations; it can be formulated and solved as a linear program by including a variable for each arc and a constraint for each node.

Transshipment problem   An extension of the transportation problem to distribution problems involving transfer points and possible shipments between any pair of nodes.

PROBLEMS

1. A company imports goods at two ports: Philadelphia and New Orleans. Shipments of one product are made to customers in Atlanta, Dallas, Columbus, and Boston. For the next planning period, the supplies at each port, customer demands, and shipping costs per case from each port to each customer are as follows:

Port	Atlanta	Dallas	Columbus	Boston	Port Supply
			Customers		
Philadelphia	2	6	6	2	5000
New Orleans	1	2	5	7	3000
Demand	1400	3200	2000	1400	

Develop a network representation of the distribution system (transportation problem).

2. Consider the following network representation of a transportation problem:

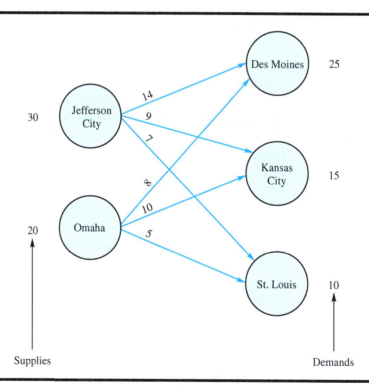

The supplies, demands, and transportation costs per unit are shown on the network.
a. Develop a linear programming model for this problem; be sure to define the variables in your model.
b. Solve the linear program to determine the optimal solution.

3. Tri-County Utilities, Inc., supplies natural gas to customers in a three-county area. The company purchases natural gas from two companies: Southern Gas and Northwest Gas. Demand forecasts for the coming winter season are as follows: Hamilton County, 400 units; Butler County, 200 units; and Clermont County, 300 units. Contracts to provide the following quantities have been written: Southern Gas, 500 units; and Northwest Gas, 400 units. Distribution costs for the counties vary, depending upon the location of the suppliers. The distribution costs per unit (in thousands of dollars) are as follows:

	To		
From	**Hamilton**	**Butler**	**Clermont**
Southern Gas	10	20	15
Northwest Gas	12	15	18

a. Develop a network representation of this problem.
b. Develop a linear programming model that can be used to determine the plan that will minimize total distribution costs.
c. Describe the distribution plan and show the total distribution cost.
d. Recent residential and industrial growth in Butler County has the potential for increasing demand by as much as 100 units. Which supplier should Tri-County contract with to supply the additional capacity?

4. GloFish, Inc., has genetically engineered a species of fish that glows in normal lighting conditions. The company believes the new fish will be a huge success as a new pet option for children and adults alike. GloFish, Inc. has developed two varieties of its glowing fish: one that glows red and one that glows blue. GloFish currently "grows" its fish at two different fish farms in the United States: one in Michigan and one in Texas. The Michigan farm can produce up to 1 million red and 1 million blue GloFish per year; the Texas farm can produce up to 600,000 GloFish, but only in the blue variety. GloFish ships its fish between the fish farms and its three retail stores using a third-party shipper. The shipment rates between origins and destinations are shown in the following table. These costs are per fish and do not depend on the color of the fish being shipped.

	Cost of Shipping GloFish		
	Retailer 1	**Retailer 2**	**Retailer 3**
Michigan	$1.00	$2.50	$0.50
Texas	$2.00	$1.50	$2.80

Estimated demands by each retailer for each color of fish are shown in the following table:

	Demand for GloFish		
	Retailer 1	**Retailer 2**	**Retailer 3**
Red	320,000	300,000	160,000
Blue	380,000	450,000	290,000

a. What is the optimal policy for the fish farms? How many red and blue fish should be produced in Michigan and shipped to each retailer? How many blue fish should be produced in Texas and shipped to each retailer?

b. What is the minimum shipping cost that can be incurred and still meet demand requirements at retailers 1, 2, and 3?

c. How much should GloFish be willing to invest to enable the Texas farm to produce both red and blue GloFish while maintaining the maximum of 600,000 total fish produced at the Texas farm?

5. Premier Consulting's two consultants, Avery and Baker, can be scheduled to work for clients up to a maximum of 160 hours each over the next four weeks. A third consultant, Campbell, has some administrative assignments already planned and is available for clients up to a maximum of 140 hours over the next four weeks. The company has four clients with projects in process. The estimated hourly requirements for each of the clients over the four-week period are as follows:

Client	Hours
A	180
B	75
C	100
D	85

Hourly rates vary for the consultant–client combination and are based on several factors, including project type and the consultant's experience. The rates (dollars per hour) for each consultant–client combination are as follows:

	Client			
Consultant	**A**	**B**	**C**	**D**
Avery	100	125	115	100
Baker	120	135	115	120
Campbell	155	150	140	130

a. Develop a network representation of the problem.

b. Formulate the problem as a linear program, with the optimal solution providing the hours each consultant should be scheduled for each client to maximize the consulting firm's billings. What is the schedule and what is the total billing?

c. New information shows that Avery doesn't have the experience to be scheduled for client B. If this consulting assignment is not permitted, what impact does it have on total billings? What is the revised schedule?

6. Klein Chemicals, Inc., produces a special oil-based material that is currently in short supply. Four of Klein's customers have already placed orders that together exceed the combined capacity of Klein's two plants. Klein's management faces the problem of deciding how many units it should supply to each customer. Because the four customers are in different industries, different prices can be charged because of the various industry pricing structures. However, slightly different production costs at the two plants and varying transportation costs between the plants and customers make a "sell to the highest bidder"

strategy unacceptable. After considering price, production costs, and transportation costs, Klein established the following profit per unit for each plant–customer alternative:

Plant	Customer			
	D_1	D_2	D_3	D_4
Clifton Springs	$32	$34	$32	$40
Danville	$34	$30	$28	$38

The plant capacities and customer orders are as follows:

Plant	Capacity (units)	Distributor Orders (units)
Clifton Springs	5000	D_1 2000
		D_2 5000
Danville	3000	D_3 3000
		D_4 2000

How many units should each plant produce for each customer to maximize profits? Which customer demands will not be met? Show your network model and linear programming formulation.

7. Aggie Power Generation supplies electrical power to residential customers for many U.S. cities. Its main power generation plants are located in Los Angeles, Tulsa, and Seattle. The following table shows Aggie Power Generation's major residential markets, the annual demand in each market (in megawatts or MW), and the cost to supply electricity to each market from each power generation plant (prices are in $/MW).

City	Distribution Costs			
	Los Angeles	Tulsa	Seattle	Demand (MW)
Seattle	$356.25	$593.75	$59.38	950.00
Portland	$356.25	$593.75	$178.13	831.25
San Francisco	$178.13	$475.00	$296.88	2375.00
Boise	$356.25	$475.00	$296.88	593.75
Reno	$237.50	$475.00	$356.25	950.00
Bozeman	$415.63	$415.63	$296.88	593.75
Laramie	$356.25	$415.63	$356.25	1187.50
Park City	$356.25	$356.25	$475.00	712.50
Flagstaff	$178.13	$475.00	$593.75	1187.50
Durango	$356.25	$296.88	$593.75	1543.75

a. If there are no restrictions on the amount of power that can be supplied by any of the power plants, what is the optimal solution to this problem? Which cities should be supplied by which power plants? What is the total annual power distribution cost for this solution?

b. If at most 4000 MW of power can be supplied by any one of the power plants, what is the optimal solution? What is the annual increase in power distribution cost that results from adding these constraints to the original formulation?

8. Forbelt Corporation has a one-year contract to supply motors for all refrigerators produced by the Ice Age Corporation. Ice Age manufactures the refrigerators at four locations around the country: Boston, Dallas, Los Angeles, and St. Paul. Plans call for the following number (in thousands) of refrigerators to be produced at each location:

Boston	50
Dallas	70
Los Angeles	60
St. Paul	80

Forbelt's three plants are capable of producing the motors. The plants and production capacities (in thousands) are as follows:

Denver	100
Atlanta	100
Chicago	150

Because of varying production and transportation costs, the profit that Forbelt earns on each lot of 1000 units depends on which plant produced the lot and which destination it was shipped to. The following table gives the accounting department estimates of the profit per unit (shipments will be made in lots of 1000 units):

	Shipped To			
Produced At	**Boston**	**Dallas**	**Los Angeles**	**St. Paul**
Denver	7	11	8	13
Atlanta	20	17	12	10
Chicago	8	18	13	16

With profit maximization as a criterion, Forbelt's management wants to determine how many motors should be produced at each plant and how many motors should be shipped from each plant to each destination.
a. Develop a network representation of this problem.
b. Find the optimal solution.

9. The Ace Manufacturing Company has orders for three similar products:

Product	Orders (units)
A	2000
B	500
C	1200

Three machines are available for the manufacturing operations. All three machines can produce all the products at the same production rate. However, due to varying defect percentages of each product on each machine, the unit costs of the products vary depending on the machine used. Machine capacities for the next week and the unit costs are as follows:

Machine	Capacity (units)
1	1500
2	1500
3	1000

Machine	Product A	B	C
1	$1.00	$1.20	$0.90
2	$1.30	$1.40	$1.20
3	$1.10	$1.00	$1.20

Use the transportation model to develop the minimum cost production schedule for the products and machines. Show the linear programming formulation.

10. Hatcher Enterprises uses a chemical called Rbase in production operations at five divisions. Only six suppliers of Rbase meet Hatcher's quality control standards. All six suppliers can produce Rbase in sufficient quantities to accommodate the needs of each division. The quantity of Rbase needed by each Hatcher division and the price per gallon charged by each supplier are as follows:

Division	Demand (1000s of gallons)
1	40
2	45
3	50
4	35
5	45

Supplier	Price per Gallon ($)
1	12.60
2	14.00
3	10.20
4	14.20
5	12.00
6	13.00

The cost per gallon ($) for shipping from each supplier to each division is provided in the following table:

Division	Supplier 1	2	3	4	5	6
1	2.75	2.50	3.15	2.80	2.75	2.75
2	0.80	0.20	5.40	1.20	3.40	1.00
3	4.70	2.60	5.30	2.80	6.00	5.60
4	2.60	1.80	4.40	2.40	5.00	2.80
5	3.40	0.40	5.00	1.20	2.60	3.60

Hatcher believes in spreading its business among suppliers so that the company will be less affected by supplier problems (e.g., labor strikes or resource availability). Company policy requires that each division have a separate supplier.

a. For each supplier–division combination, compute the total cost of supplying the division's demand.

b. Determine the optimal assignment of suppliers to divisions.

11. The distribution system for the Herman Company consists of three plants, two warehouses, and four customers. Plant capacities and shipping costs per unit (in $) from each plant to each warehouse are as follows:

| | Warehouse | | |
Plant	1	2	Capacity
1	4	7	450
2	8	5	600
3	5	6	380

Customer demand and shipping costs per unit (in $) from each warehouse to each customer are as follows:

a. Develop a network representation of this problem.
b. Formulate a linear programming model of the problem.
c. Solve the linear program to determine the optimal shipping plan.

| | Customer | | | |
Warehouse	1	2	3	4
1	6	4	8	4
2	3	6	7	7
Demand	300	300	300	400

12. Refer to Problem 11. Suppose that shipments between the two warehouses are permitted at $2 per unit and that direct shipments can be made from Plant 3 to Customer 4 at a cost of $7 per unit.

a. Develop a network representation of this problem.
b. Formulate a linear programming model of this problem.
c. Solve the linear program to determine the optimal shipping plan.

13. Sports of All Sorts produces, distributes, and sells high-quality skateboards. Its supply chain consists of three factories (located in Detroit, Los Angeles, and Austin) that produce skateboards. The Detroit and Los Angeles facilities can produce 350 skateboards per week, but the Austin plant is larger and can produce up to 700 skateboards per week. Skateboards must be shipped from the factories to one of four distribution centers, or DCs (located in Iowa, Maryland, Idaho, and Arkansas). Each distribution center can process (repackage, mark for sale, and ship) at most 500 skateboards per week.

Skateboards are then shipped from the distribution centers to retailers. Sports of All Sorts supplies three major U.S. retailers: Just Sports, Sports 'N Stuff, and The Sports Dude. The weekly demands are 200 skateboards at Just Sports, 500 skateboards at Sports 'N Stuff, and 650 skateboards at The Sports Dude. The following tables display the per-unit costs for shipping skateboards between the factories and DCs and for shipping between the DCs and the retailers.

Shipping Costs ($ per skateboard)

Factory/DCs	Iowa	Maryland	Idaho	Arkansas
Detroit	$25.00	$25.00	$35.00	$40.00
Los Angeles	$35.00	$45.00	$35.00	$42.50
Austin	$40.00	$40.00	$42.50	$32.50

Retailers/DCs	Iowa	Maryland	Idaho	Arkansas
Just Sports	$30.00	$20.00	$35.00	$27.50
Sports 'N Stuff	$27.50	$32.50	$40.00	$25.00
The Sports Dude	$30.00	$40.00	$32.50	$42.50

    a. Draw the network representation for this problem.

    b. Build a model to minimize the transportation cost of a logistics system that will deliver skateboards from the factories to the distribution centers and from the distribution centers to the retailers. What is the optimal production strategy and shipping pattern for Sports of All Sorts? What is the minimum attainable transportation cost?

    c. Sports of All Sorts is considering expansion of the Iowa DC capacity to 800 units per week. The annual amortized cost of expansion is $40,000. Should the company expand the Iowa DC capacity so that it can process 800 skateboards per week? (Assume 50 operating weeks per year.)

14. The Moore & Harman Company is in the business of buying and selling grain. An important aspect of the company's business is arranging for the purchased grain to be shipped to customers. If the company can keep freight costs low, profitability will improve.

    The company recently purchased three rail cars of grain at Muncie, Indiana; six rail cars at Brazil, Indiana; and five rail cars at Xenia, Ohio. Twelve carloads of grain have been sold. The locations and the amount sold at each location are as follows:

Location	Number of Rail Car Loads
Macon, GA	2
Greenwood, SC	4
Concord, SC	3
Chatham, NC	3

All shipments must be routed through either Louisville or Cincinnati. Shown are the shipping costs per bushel (in cents) from the origins to Louisville and Cincinnati and the costs per bushel to ship from Louisville and Cincinnati to the destinations.

	To	
From	**Louisville**	**Cincinnati**
Muncie	8	6
Brazil	3	8
Xenia	9	3

Cost per bushel from Muncie to Cincinnati is 6¢

		To		
From	**Macon**	**Greenwood**	**Concord**	**Chatham**
Louisville	44	34	34	32
Cincinnati	57	35	28	24

Cost per bushel from
Cincinnati to Greenwood is 35¢

Determine a shipping schedule that will minimize the freight costs necessary to satisfy demand. Which (if any) rail cars of grain must be held at the origin until buyers can be found?

15. The following linear programming formulation is for a transshipment problem:

$$\text{Min} \quad 11x_{13} + 12x_{14} + 10x_{21} + 8x_{34} + 10x_{35} + 11x_{42} + 9x_{45} + 12x_{52}$$

s.t.

$$
\begin{aligned}
x_{13} + x_{14} - x_{21} && &&&&&&\leq 5 \\
x_{21} && &- x_{42} && - x_{52} &&\leq 3 \\
x_{13} && - x_{34} - x_{35} && &&&&\leq 6 \\
- x_{14} && - x_{34} && + x_{42} + x_{45} &&&&\leq 2 \\
&& x_{35} && + x_{45} - x_{52} &&\leq 4
\end{aligned}
$$

$$x_{ij} \geq 0 \quad \text{for all } i, j$$

Show the network representation of this problem.

16. A rental car company has an imbalance of cars at seven of its locations. The following network shows the locations of concern (the nodes) and the cost to move a car between locations. A positive number by a node indicates an excess supply at the node, and a negative number indicates an excess demand.

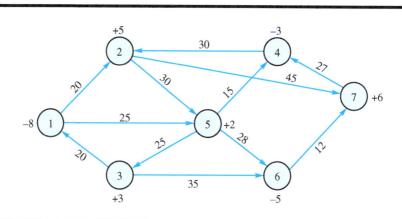

a. Develop a linear programming model of this problem.
b. Solve the model formulated in part (a) to determine how the cars should be redistributed among the locations.

17. Scott and Associates, Inc., is an accounting firm that has three new clients. Project leaders will be assigned to the three clients. Based on the different backgrounds and experiences of the leaders, the various leader–client assignments differ in terms of projected completion times. The possible assignments and the estimated completion times in days are as follows:

	Client		
Project Leader	**1**	**2**	**3**
Jackson	10	16	32
Ellis	14	22	40
Smith	22	24	34

a. Develop a network representation of this problem.
b. Formulate the problem as a linear program, and solve. What is the total time required?

18. CarpetPlus sells and installs floor covering for commercial buildings. Brad Sweeney, a CarpetPlus account executive, was just awarded the contract for five jobs. Brad must now assign a CarpetPlus installation crew to each of the five jobs. Because the commission Brad will earn depends on the profit CarpetPlus makes, Brad would like to determine an assignment that will minimize total installation costs. Currently, five installation crews are available for assignment. Each crew is identified by a color code, which aids in tracking of job progress on a large white board. The following table shows the costs (in hundreds of dollars) for each crew to complete each of the five jobs:

	Job				
Crew	**1**	**2**	**3**	**4**	**5**
Red	30	44	38	47	31
White	25	32	45	44	25
Blue	23	40	37	39	29
Green	26	38	37	45	28
Brown	26	34	44	43	28

a. Develop a network representation of the problem.
b. Formulate and solve a linear programming model to determine the minimum cost assignment.

19. A local television station plans to drop four Friday evening programs at the end of the season. Steve Botuchis, the station manager, developed a list of six potential replacement programs. Estimates of the advertising revenue ($) that can be expected for each of the new programs in the four vacated time slots are as follows. Mr. Botuchis asked you to find the assignment of programs to time slots that will maximize total advertising revenue.

	5:00–5:30 P.M.	5:30–6:00 P.M.	7:00–7:30 P.M.	8:00–8:30 P.M.
Home Improvement	5000	3000	6000	4000
World News	7500	8000	7000	5500
NASCAR Live	8500	5000	6500	8000
Wall Street Today	7000	6000	6500	5000
Hollywood Briefings	7000	8000	3000	6000
Ramundo & Son	6000	4000	4500	7000

20. The U.S. Cable Company uses a distribution system with five distribution centers and eight customer zones. Each customer zone is assigned a sole source supplier; each customer zone receives all of its cable products from the same distribution center. In an effort to balance demand and workload at the distribution centers, the company's vice president of logistics specified that distribution centers may not be assigned more than three customer zones. The following table shows the five distribution centers and cost of supplying each customer zone (in thousands of dollars):

Customer Zones

Distribution Centers	Los Angeles	Chicago	Columbus	Atlanta	Newark	Kansas City	Denver	Dallas
Plano	70	47	22	53	98	21	27	13
Nashville	75	38	19	58	90	34	40	26
Flagstaff	15	78	37	82	111	40	29	32
Springfield	60	23	8	39	82	36	32	45
Boulder	45	40	29	75	86	25	11	37

a. Determine the assignment of customer zones to distribution centers that will minimize cost.

b. Which distribution centers, if any, are not used?

c. Suppose that each distribution center is limited to a maximum of two customer zones. How does this constraint change the assignment and the cost of supplying customer zones?

21. United Express Service (UES) uses large quantities of packaging materials at its four distribution hubs. After screening potential suppliers, UES identified six vendors that can provide packaging materials that will satisfy its quality standards. UES asked each of the six vendors to submit bids to satisfy annual demand at each of its four distribution hubs over the next year. The following table lists the bids received (in thousands of dollars). UES wants to ensure that each of the distribution hubs is serviced by a different vendor. Which bids should UES accept, and which vendors should UES select to supply each distribution hub?

Distribution Hub

Bidder	1	2	3	4
Martin Products	190	175	125	230
Schmidt Materials	150	235	155	220
Miller Containers	210	225	135	260
D&J Burns	170	185	190	280
Larbes Furnishings	220	190	140	240
Lawler Depot	270	200	130	260

22. The quantitative methods department head at a major midwestern university will be scheduling faculty to teach courses during the coming autumn term. Four core courses need to be covered. The four courses are at the undergraduate (UG), master of business administration (MBA), master of science (MS), and doctor of philosophy (Ph.D.) levels. Four professors will be assigned to the courses, with each professor receiving one of the courses. Student evaluations of professors are available from previous terms. Based on a rating scale of 4 (excellent), 3 (very good), 2 (average), 1 (fair), and 0 (poor), the average student evaluations for each professor are shown. Professor D does not have a Ph.D. and cannot be assigned to teach the Ph.D. level course. If the department head makes teaching assignments based on maximizing the student evaluation ratings over all four courses, what staffing assignments should be made?

	Course			
Professor	**UG**	**MBA**	**MS**	**Ph.D.**
A	2.8	2.2	3.3	3.0
B	3.2	3.0	3.6	3.6
C	3.3	3.2	3.5	3.5
D	3.2	2.8	2.5	—

23. Find the shortest route from node 1 to node 7 in the network shown.

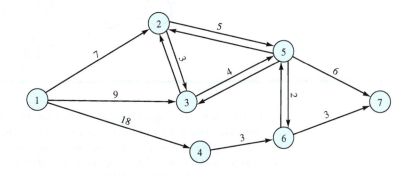

24. In the original Gorman Construction Company problem, we found the shortest distance from the office (node 1) to the construction site located at node 6. Because some of the roads are highways and others are city streets, the shortest-distance routes between the office and the construction site may not necessarily provide the quickest or shortest-time route. Shown here is the Gorman road network with travel time rather than distance. Find the shortest route from Gorman's office to the construction site at node 6 if the objective is to minimize travel time rather than distance.

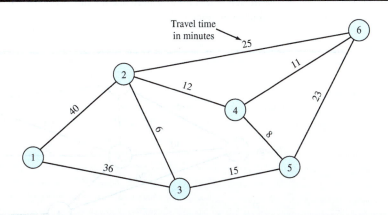

25. Cleveland Area Rapid Delivery (CARD) operates a delivery service in the Cleveland metropolitan area. Most of CARD's business involves rapid delivery of documents and

parcels between offices during the business day. CARD promotes its ability to make fast and on-time deliveries anywhere in the metropolitan area. When a customer calls with a delivery request, CARD quotes a guaranteed delivery time. The following network shows the street routes available. The numbers above each arc indicate the travel time in minutes between the two locations.

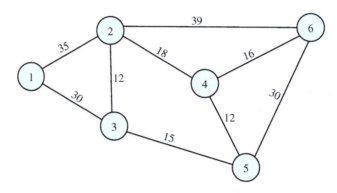

a. Develop a linear programming model that can be used to find the minimum time required to make a delivery from location 1 to location 6.
b. How long does it take to make a delivery from location 1 to location 6?
c. Assume that it is now 1:00 P.M. and that CARD just received a request for a pickup at location 1. The closest CARD courier is 8 minutes away from location 1. If CARD provides a 20% safety margin in guaranteeing a delivery time, what is the guaranteed delivery time if the package picked up at location 1 is to be delivered to location 6?

26. Morgan Trucking Company operates a special pickup and delivery service between Chicago and six other cities located in a four-state area. When Morgan receives a request for service, it dispatches a truck from Chicago to the city requesting service as soon as possible. With both fast service and minimum travel costs as objectives for Morgan, it is important that the dispatched truck take the shortest route from Chicago to the specified city. Assume that the following network (not drawn to scale) with distances given in miles represents the highway network for this problem. Find the shortest-route distances from Chicago to node 6.

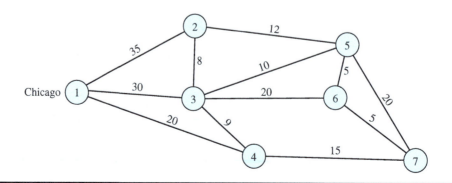

27. City Cab Company identified 10 primary pickup and drop locations for cab riders in New York City. In an effort to minimize travel time and improve customer service and the utilization of the company's fleet of cabs, management would like the cab drivers to take the shortest route between locations whenever possible. Using the following network of roads and streets, what is the route a driver beginning at location 1 should take to reach location 10? The travel times in minutes are shown on the arcs of the network. Note that there are two one-way streets and that the direction is shown by the arrows.

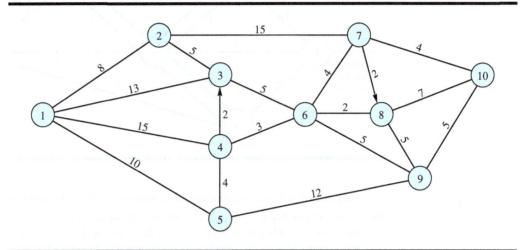

28. The five nodes in the following network represent points one year apart over a four-year period. Each node indicates a time when a decision is made to keep or replace a firm's computer equipment. If a decision is made to replace the equipment, a decision must also be made as to how long the new equipment will be used. The arc from node 0 to node 1 represents the decision to keep the current equipment one year and replace it at the end of the year. The arc from node 0 to node 2 represents the decision to keep the current equipment two years and replace it at the end of year 2. The numbers above the arcs indicate the total cost associated with the equipment replacement decisions. These costs include discounted purchase price, trade-in value, operating costs, and maintenance costs. Use a shortest-route model to determine the minimum cost equipment replacement policy for the four-year period.

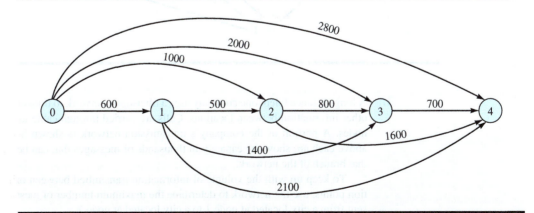

29. The north–south highway system passing through Albany, New York, can accommodate the capacities shown.

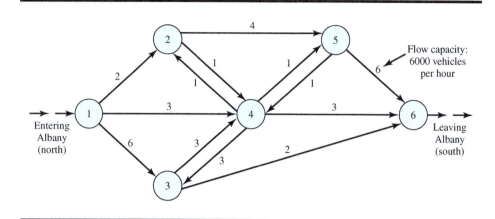

Can the highway system accommodate a north–south flow of 10,000 vehicles per hour?

30. If the Albany highway system described in Problem 29 has revised flow capacities as shown in the following network, what is the maximal flow in vehicles per hour through the system? How many vehicles per hour must travel over each road (arc) to obtain this maximal flow?

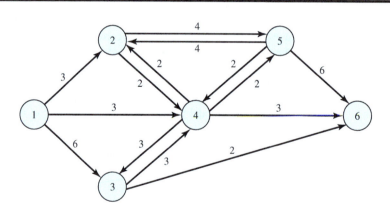

31. A long-distance telephone company uses a fiber-optic network to transmit phone calls and other information between locations. Calls are carried through cable lines and switching nodes. A portion of the company's transmission network is shown here. The numbers above each arc show the capacity in thousands of messages that can be transmitted over that branch of the network.

To keep up with the volume of information transmitted between origin and destination points, use the network to determine the maximum number of messages that may be sent from a city located at node 1 to a city located at node 7.

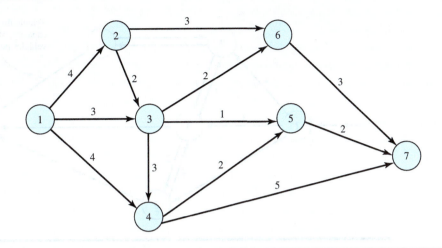

32. The High-Price Oil Company owns a pipeline network that is used to convey oil from its source to several storage locations. A portion of the network is as follows:

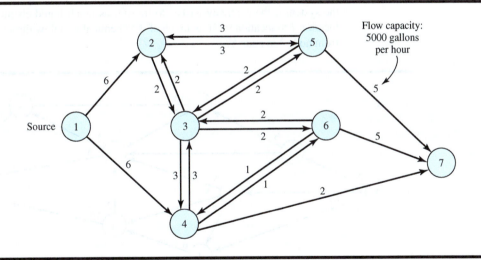

Due to the varying pipe sizes, the flow capacities vary. By selectively opening and closing sections of the pipeline network, the firm can supply any of the storage locations.

a. If the firm wants to fully utilize the system capacity to supply location 7, how long will it take to satisfy a location 7 demand of 100,000 gallons? What is the maximal flow for this pipeline system?

b. If a break occurs on line 2–3 and that line is closed down, what is the maximal flow for the system? How long will it take to transmit 100,000 gallons to location 7?

33. For the following highway network system, determine the maximal flow in vehicles per hour:

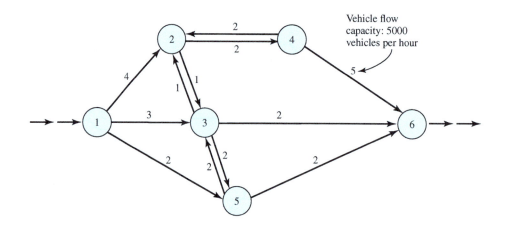

The highway commission is considering adding segment 3–4 to permit a flow of 2000 vehicles per hour or, at an additional cost, a flow of 3000 vehicles per hour. What is your recommendation for the proposed segment 3–4 of the highway network?

34. A chemical processing plant has a network of pipes that are used to transfer liquid chemical products from one part of the plant to another. The following pipe network has pipe flow capacities in gallons per minute as shown. What is the maximum flow capacity for the system if the company wishes to transfer as much liquid chemical as possible from location 1 to location 9? How much of the chemical will flow through the section of pipe from node 3 to node 5?

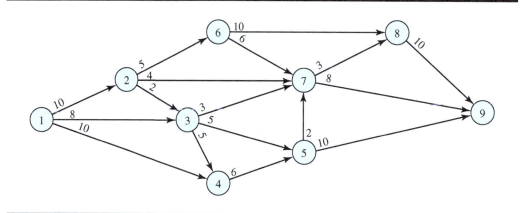

35. Refer to the Contois Carpets problem, for which the network representation is shown in Figure 6.20. Suppose that Contois has a beginning inventory of 50 yards of carpet and requires an inventory of 100 yards at the end of quarter 4.
   a. Develop a network representation of this modified problem.
   b. Develop a linear programming model and solve for the optimal solution.

36. Sanders Fishing Supply of Naples, Florida, manufactures a variety of fishing equipment that it sells throughout the United States. For the next three months, Sanders estimates demand for a particular product at 150, 250, and 300 units, respectively. Sanders can

supply this demand by producing on regular time or overtime. Because of other commitments and anticipated cost increases in month 3, the production capacities in units and the production costs per unit are as follows:

Production	Capacity (units)	Cost per Unit
Month 1—Regular	275	$ 50
Month 1—Overtime	100	$ 80
Month 2—Regular	200	$ 50
Month 2—Overtime	50	$ 80
Month 3—Regular	100	$ 60
Month 3—Overtime	50	$100

Inventory may be carried from one month to the next, but the cost is $20 per unit per month. For example, regular production from month 1 used to meet demand in month 2 would cost Sanders $50 + $20 = $70 per unit. This same month 1 production used to meet demand in month 3 would cost Sanders $50 + 2($20) = $90 per unit.

a. Develop a network representation of this production scheduling problem as a transportation problem. (*Hint*: Use six origin nodes; the supply for origin node 1 is the maximum that can be produced in month 1 on regular time, and so on.)
b. Develop a linear programming model that can be used to schedule regular and overtime production for each of the three months.
c. What is the production schedule, how many units are carried in inventory each month, and what is the total cost?
d. Is there any unused production capacity? If so, where?

Case Problem 1   SOLUTIONS PLUS

Solutions Plus is an industrial chemicals company that produces specialized cleaning fluids and solvents for a wide variety of applications. Solutions Plus just received an invitation to submit a bid to supply Great North American railroad with a cleaning fluid for locomotives. Great North American needs the cleaning fluid at 11 locations (railway stations); it provided the following information to Solutions Plus regarding the number of gallons of cleaning fluid required at each location (see Table 6.8).

Solutions Plus can produce the cleaning fluid at its Cincinnati plant for $1.20 per gallon. Even though the Cincinnati location is its only plant, Solutions Plus has negotiated

TABLE 6.8   GALLONS OF CLEANING FLUID REQUIRED AT EACH LOCATION

Location	Gallons Required	Location	Gallons Required
Santa Ana	22,418	Glendale	33,689
El Paso	6,800	Jacksonville	68,486
Pendleton	80,290	Little Rock	148,586
Houston	100,447	Bridgeport	111,475
Kansas City	24,570	Sacramento	112,000
Los Angeles	64,761		

TABLE 6.9   FREIGHT COST ($ PER GALLON)

	Cincinnati	Oakland
Santa Ana	—	0.22
El Paso	0.84	0.74
Pendleton	0.83	0.49
Houston	0.45	—
Kansas City	0.36	—
Los Angeles	—	0.22
Glendale	—	0.22
Jacksonville	0.34	—
Little Rock	0.34	—
Bridgeport	0.34	—
Sacramento	—	0.15

with an industrial chemicals company located in Oakland, California, to produce and ship up to 500,000 gallons of the locomotive cleaning fluid to selected Solutions Plus customer locations. The Oakland company will charge Solutions Plus $1.65 per gallon to produce the cleaning fluid, but Solutions Plus thinks that the lower shipping costs from Oakland to some customer locations may offset the added cost to produce the product.

The president of Solutions Plus, Charlie Weaver, contacted several trucking companies to negotiate shipping rates between the two production facilities (Cincinnati and Oakland) and the locations where the railroad locomotives are cleaned. Table 6.9 shows the quotes received in terms of dollars per gallon. The "—" entries in Table 6.9 identify shipping routes that will not be considered because of the large distances involved. These quotes for shipping rates are guaranteed for one year.

To submit a bid to the railroad company, Solutions Plus must determine the price per gallon it will charge. Solutions Plus usually sells its cleaning fluids for 15% more than its cost to produce and deliver the product. For this big contract, however, Fred Roedel, the director of marketing, suggested that maybe the company should consider a smaller profit margin. In addition, to ensure that if Solutions Plus wins the bid, it will have adequate capacity to satisfy existing orders as well as accept orders for other new business, the management team decided to limit the number of gallons of the locomotive cleaning fluid produced in the Cincinnati plant to 500,000 gallons at most.

Managerial Report

You are asked to make recommendations that will help Solutions Plus prepare a bid. Your report should address, but not be limited to, the following issues:

1. If Solutions Plus wins the bid, which production facility (Cincinnati or Oakland) should supply the cleaning fluid to the locations where the railroad locomotives are cleaned? How much should be shipped from each facility to each location?
2. What is the breakeven point for Solutions Plus? That is, how low can the company go on its bid without losing money?
3. If Solutions Plus wants to use its standard 15% markup, how much should it bid?
4. Freight costs are significantly affected by the price of oil. The contract on which Solutions Plus is bidding is for two years. Discuss how fluctuation in freight costs might affect the bid Solutions Plus submits.

Case Problem 2   SUPPLY CHAIN DESIGN

The Darby Company manufactures and distributes meters used to measure electric power consumption. The company started with a small production plant in El Paso and gradually built a customer base throughout Texas. A distribution center was established in Fort Worth, Texas, and later, as business expanded, a second distribution center was established in Santa Fe, New Mexico.

The El Paso plant was expanded when the company began marketing its meters in Arizona, California, Nevada, and Utah. With the growth of the West Coast business, the Darby Company opened a third distribution center in Las Vegas and just two years ago opened a second production plant in San Bernardino, California.

Manufacturing costs differ between the company's production plants. The cost of each meter produced at the El Paso plant is $10.50. The San Bernardino plant utilizes newer and more efficient equipment; as a result, manufacturing costs are $0.50 per meter less than at the El Paso plant.

Due to the company's rapid growth, not much attention had been paid to the efficiency of its supply chain, but Darby's management decided that it is time to address this issue. The cost of shipping a meter from each of the two plants to each of the three distribution centers is shown in Table 6.10.

The quarterly production capacity is 30,000 meters at the older El Paso plant and 20,000 meters at the San Bernardino plant. Note that no shipments are allowed from the San Bernardino plant to the Fort Worth distribution center.

The company serves nine customer zones from the three distribution centers. The forecast of the number of meters needed in each customer zone for the next quarter is shown in Table 6.11.

TABLE 6.10   SHIPPING COST PER UNIT FROM PRODUCTION PLANTS TO DISTRIBUTION CENTERS (IN $)

	Distribution Center		
Plant	**Fort Worth**	**Santa Fe**	**Las Vegas**
El Paso	3.20	2.20	4.20
San Bernardino	—	3.90	1.20

TABLE 6.11   QUARTERLY DEMAND FORECAST

Customer Zone	**Demand (meters)**
Dallas	6300
San Antonio	4880
Wichita	2130
Kansas City	1210
Denver	6120
Salt Lake City	4830
Phoenix	2750
Los Angeles	8580
San Diego	4460

TABLE 6.12   SHIPPING COST FROM THE DISTRIBUTION CENTERS TO THE CUSTOMER ZONES

Distribution Center		Customer Zone							
	Dallas	San Antonio	Wichita	Kansas City	Denver	Salt Lake City	Phoenix	Los Angeles	San Diego
Fort Worth	0.3	2.1	3.1	4.4	6.0	—	—	—	—
Santa Fe	5.2	5.4	4.5	6.0	2.7	4.7	3.4	3.3	2.7
Las Vegas	—	—	—	—	5.4	3.3	2.4	2.1	2.5

The cost per unit of shipping from each distribution center to each customer zone is given in Table 6.12; note that some distribution centers cannot serve certain customer zones. These are indicated by a dash, "—".

In its current supply chain, demand at the Dallas, San Antonio, Wichita, and Kansas City customer zones is satisfied by shipments from the Fort Worth distribution center. In a similar manner, the Denver, Salt Lake City, and Phoenix customer zones are served by the Santa Fe distribution center, and the Los Angeles and San Diego customer zones are served by the Las Vegas distribution center. To determine how many units to ship from each plant, the quarterly customer demand forecasts are aggregated at the distribution centers, and a transportation model is used to minimize the cost of shipping from the production plants to the distribution centers.

Managerial Report

You are asked to make recommendations for improving Darby Company's supply chain. Your report should address, but not be limited to, the following issues:

1. If the company does not change its current supply chain, what will its distribution costs be for the following quarter?
2. Suppose that the company is willing to consider dropping the distribution center limitations; that is, customers could be served by any of the distribution centers for which costs are available. Can costs be reduced? If so, by how much?
3. The company wants to explore the possibility of satisfying some of the customer demand directly from the production plants. In particular, the shipping cost is $0.30 per unit from San Bernardino to Los Angeles and $0.70 from San Bernardino to San Diego. The cost for direct shipments from El Paso to San Antonio is $3.50 per unit. Can distribution costs be further reduced by considering these direct plant-to-customer shipments?
4. Over the next five years, Darby is anticipating moderate growth (5000 meters) to the north and west. Would you recommend that Darby consider plant expansion at this time?

Appendix 6.1   EXCEL SOLUTION OF TRANSPORTATION, TRANSSHIPMENT, AND ASSIGNMENT PROBLEMS

In this appendix we will use an Excel worksheet to solve transportation, transshipment, and assignment problems. We start with the Foster Generators transportation problem (see Section 6.1).

Transportation Problem

The first step is to enter the data for the transportation costs, the origin supplies, and the destination demands in the top portion of the worksheet. Then the linear programming model is developed in the bottom portion of the worksheet. As with all linear programs, the worksheet model has four key elements: the decision variables, the objective function, the constraint left-hand sides, and the constraint right-hand sides. For a transportation problem, the decision variables are the amounts shipped from each origin to each destination; the objective function is the total transportation cost; the left-hand sides are the number of units shipped from each origin and the number of units shipped into each destination; and the right-hand sides are the origin supplies and the destination demands.

The formulation and solution of the Foster Generators problem are shown in Figure 6.22. The data are in the top portion of the worksheet. The model appears in the bottom portion of the worksheet.

FIGURE 6.22   EXCEL SOLUTION OF THE FOSTER GENERATORS PROBLEM

WEB file

Foster

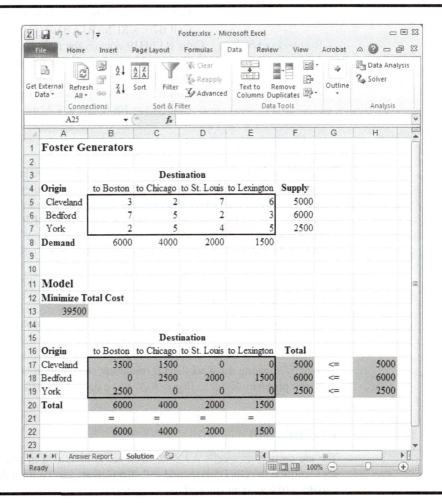

Formulation

The data and descriptive labels are contained in cells A1:F8. The transportation costs are in cells B5:E7. The origin supplies are in cells F5:F7, and the destination demands are in cells B8:E8. The key elements of the model required by the Excel Solver are the decision variables, the objective function, the constraint left-hand sides, and the constraint right-hand sides.

Decision Variables   Cells B17:E19 are reserved for the decision variables. The optimal values are shown to be $x_{11} = 3500$, $x_{12} = 1500$, $x_{22} = 2500$, $x_{23} = 2000$, $x_{24} = 1500$, and $x_{41} = 2500$. All other decision variables equal zero, indicating that nothing will be shipped over the corresponding routes.

Objective Function   The formula SUMPRODUCT(B5:E7,B17:E19) has been placed into cell A13 to compute the cost of the solution. The minimum cost solution is shown to have a value of \$39,500.

Left-Hand Sides   Cells F17:F19 contain the left-hand sides for the supply constraints, and cells B20:E20 contain the left-hand sides for the demand constraints.
   Cell F17 = SUM(B17:E17) (Copy to F18:F19)
   Cell B20 = SUM(B17:B19) (Copy to C20:E20)

Right-Hand Sides   Cells H17:H19 contain the right-hand sides for the supply constraints, and cells B22:E22 contain the right-hand sides for the demand constraints.
   Cell H17 = F5 (Copy to H18:H19)
   Cell B22 = B8 (Copy to C22:E22)

Excel Solution

The solution shown in Figure 6.22 can be obtained by selecting **Solver** from the **Analysis Group** in the **Data Ribbon**. The Data Ribbon is displayed at the top of the worksheet in Figure 6.22. When the **Solver Parameters** dialog box appears, enter the proper values for the constraints and the objective function, select **Simplex LP,** and click the checkbox for **Make Unconstrained Variables Non-negative.** Then click **Solve.** The information entered into the **Solver Parameters** dialog box is shown in Figure 6.23.

Transshipment Problem

The worksheet model we present for the transshipment problem can be used for all the network flow problems (transportation, transshipment, and assignment) in this chapter. We organize the worksheet into two sections: an arc section and a node section. Let us illustrate by showing the worksheet formulation and solution of the Ryan Electronics transshipment problem. Refer to Figure 6.24 as we describe the steps involved.

Formulation

The arc section uses cells A4:C16. Each arc is identified in cells A5:A16. The arc costs are identified in cells B5:B16, and cells C5:C16 are reserved for the values of the decision variables (the amount shipped over the arcs).

FIGURE 6.23   EXCEL SOLVER PARAMETERS DIALOG BOX FOR THE FOSTER
GENERATORS PROBLEM

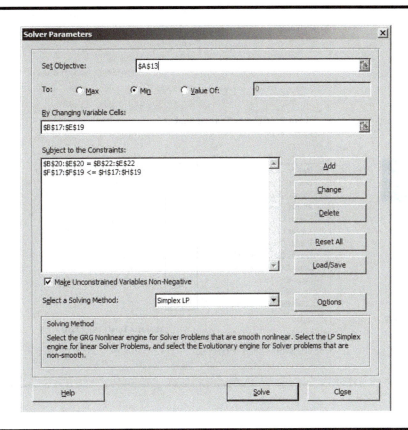

The node section uses cells F5:K14. Each of the nodes is identified in cells F7:F14. The
following formulas are entered into cells G7:H14 to represent the flow out and the flow in
for each node:

Units shipped in:	Cell G9 = C5+C7
	Cell G10 = C6+C8
	Cell G11 = C9+C13
	Cell G12 = C10+C14
	Cell G13 = C11+C15
	Cell G14 = C12+C16

Units shipped out:	Cell H7 = SUM(C5:C6)
	Cell H8 = SUM(C7:C8)
	Cell H9 = SUM(C9:C12)
	Cell H10 = SUM(C13:C16)

The net shipments in cells I7:I14 are the flows out minus the flows in for each node. For
supply nodes, the flow out will exceed the flow in, resulting in positive net shipments.
For demand nodes, the flow out will be less than the flow in, resulting in negative net

FIGURE 6.24   EXCEL SOLUTION FOR THE RYAN ELECTRONICS PROBLEM

Ryan

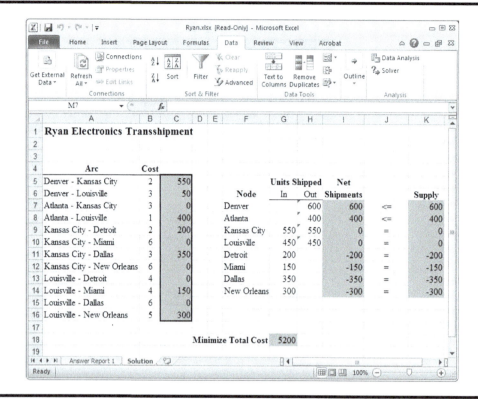

shipments. The "net" supply appears in cells K7:K14. Note that the net supply is negative for demand nodes.

Decision Variables	Cells C5:C16 are reserved for the decision variables. The optimal number of units to ship over each arc is shown.
Objective Function	The formula =SUMPRODUCT(B5:B16,C5:C16) is placed into cell G18 to show the total cost associated with the solution. As shown, the minimum total cost is $5200.
Left-Hand Sides	The left-hand sides of the constraints represent the net shipments for each node. Cells I7:I14 are reserved for these constraints. Cell I7 = H7-G7 (Copy to I8:I14)
Right-Hand Sides	The right-hand sides of the constraints represent the supply at each node. Cells K7:K14 are reserved for these values. (Note the negative supply at the four demand nodes.)

Excel Solution

The solution can be obtained by selecting **Solver** from the **Analysis Group** in the **Data Ribbon**. The Data Ribbon is displayed at the top of the worksheet in Figure 6.24. When the

FIGURE 6.25   EXCEL SOLVER PARAMETERS DIALOG BOX FOR THE RYAN ELECTRONICS PROBLEM

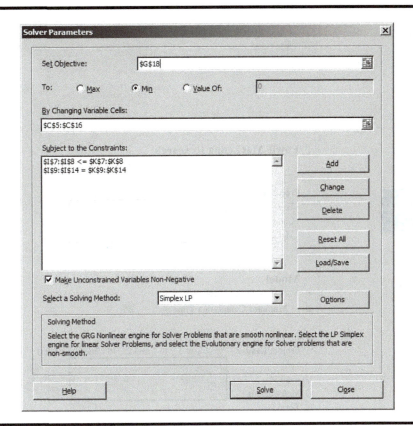

Solver Parameters dialog box appears, enter the proper values for the constraints and the objective function, select **Simplex LP**, and click the checkbox for **Make Unconstrained Variables Non-negative.** Then click **Solve.** The information entered into the **Solver Parameters** dialog box is shown in Figure 6.25.

Assignment Problem

The first step is to enter the data for the assignment costs in the top portion of the worksheet. Even though the assignment model is a special case of the transportation model, it is not necessary to enter values for origin supplies and destination demands because they are always equal to 1.

The linear programming model is developed in the bottom portion of the worksheet. As with all linear programs, the model has four key elements: the decision variables, the objective function, the constraint left-hand sides, and the constraint right-hand sides. For an assignment problem the decision variables indicate whether an agent is assigned to a task (with a 1 for yes or 0 for no); the objective function is the total cost of all assignments; the constraint left-hand sides are the number of tasks that are assigned to each agent and the number of agents that are assigned to each task; and the right-hand sides are the number of tasks each agent can handle (1) and the number of agents each task requires (1). The worksheet formulation and solution for the Fowle marketing research problem are shown in Figure 6.26.

FIGURE 6.26   EXCEL SOLUTION OF THE FOWLE MARKETING RESEARCH
PROBLEM

Fowle

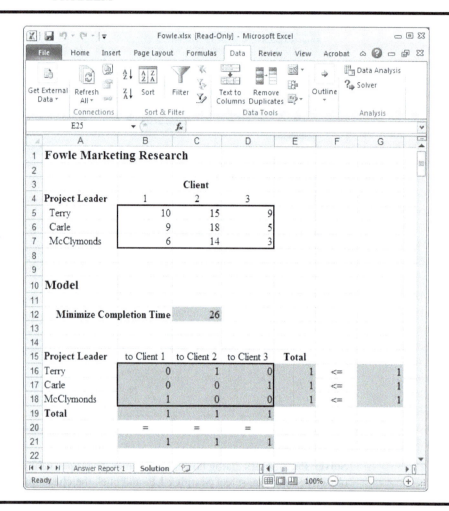

Formulation

The data and descriptive labels are contained in cells A3:D7. Note that we have not inserted supply and demand values because they are always equal to 1 in an assignment
problem. The model appears in the bottom portion of the worksheet.

Decision Variables	Cells B16:D18 are reserved for the decision variables. The optimal values are shown to be $x_{12} = 1$, $x_{23} = 1$, and $x_{31} = 1$, with all other variables $= 0$.
Objective Function	The formula =SUMPRODUCT(B5:D7,B16:D18) has been placed into cell C12 to compute the number of days required to complete all the jobs. The minimum time solution has a value of 26 days.
Left-Hand Sides	Cells E16:E18 contain the left-hand sides of the constraints for the number of clients each project leader can handle. Cells

B19:D19 contain the left-hand sides of the constraints requiring that each client must be assigned a project leader.

   Cell E16 = SUM(B16:D16) (Copy to E17:E18)
   Cell B19 = SUM(B16:B18) (Copy to C19:D19)

Right-Hand Sides   Cells G16:G18 contain the right-hand sides for the project leader constraints, and cells B21:D21 contain the right-hand sides for the client constraints. All right-hand-side cell values are 1.

Excel Solution

The solution shown in Figure 6.26 can be obtained by selecting **Solver** from the **Analysis Group** in the **Data Ribbon**. The Data Ribbon is displayed at the top of the worksheet in Figure 6.26. When the **Solver Parameters** dialog box appears, enter the proper values for the constraints and the objective function, select **Simplex LP,** and click the checkbox for **Make Unconstrained Variables Non-negative.** Then click **Solve.** The information entered into the **Solver Parameters** dialog box is shown in Figure 6.27.

FIGURE 6.27   EXCEL SOLVER PARAMETERS DIALOG BOX FOR THE FOWLE MARKETING RESEARCH PROBLEM

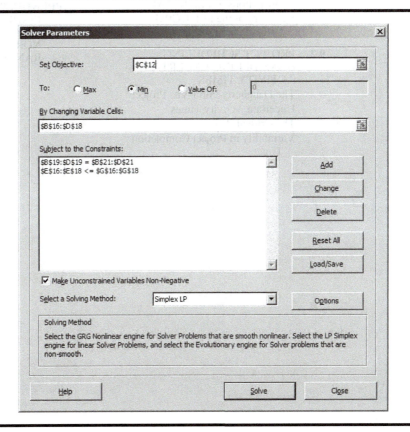

CHAPTER 6

Project Scheduling: PERT/CPM

CONTENTS

In many situations managers are responsible for planning, scheduling, and controlling projects that consist of numerous separate jobs or tasks performed by a variety of departments and individuals. Often these projects are so large or complex that the manager cannot possibly remember all the information pertaining to the plan, schedule, and progress of the project. In these situations the **program evaluation and review technique (PERT)** and the **critical path method (CPM)** have proven to be extremely valuable.

PERT and CPM can be used to plan, schedule, and control a wide variety of projects. Common applications include:

1. Research and development of new products and processes
2. Construction of plants, buildings, and highways
3. Maintenance of large and complex equipment
4. Design and installation of new systems

Henry L. Gantt developed the Gantt Chart as a graphical aid to scheduling jobs on machines. This application was the first of what has become known as project scheduling techniques.

In these types of projects, project managers must schedule and coordinate the various jobs or **activities** so that the entire project is completed on time. A complicating factor in carrying out this task is the interdependence of the activities; for example, some activities depend on the completion of other activities before they can be started. Because projects may comprise as many as several thousand activities, project managers look for procedures that will help them answer questions such as the following:

1. What is the total time to complete the project?
2. What are the scheduled start and finish dates for each specific activity?
3. Which activities are "critical" and must be completed *exactly* as scheduled to keep the project on schedule?
4. How long can "noncritical" activities be delayed before they cause an increase in the total project completion time?

PERT and CPM can help answer these questions.

Although PERT and CPM have the same general purpose and utilize much of the same terminology, the techniques were developed independently. PERT was developed in the late 1950s by the Navy specifically for the Polaris missile project. Many activities associated with this project had never been attempted previously, so PERT was developed to handle uncertain activity times. CPM was developed originally by DuPont and Remington Rand primarily for industrial projects for which activity times were certain and variability was not a concern. CPM offered the option of reducing activity times by adding more workers and/or resources, usually at an increased cost. Thus, a distinguishing feature of CPM was that it identified trade-offs between time and cost for various project activities.

Today's computerized versions of PERT and CPM combine the best features of both approaches. Thus, the distinction between the two techniques is no longer necessary. As a result, we refer to the project scheduling procedures covered in this chapter as PERT/CPM. We begin the discussion of PERT/CPM by considering a project for the expansion of the Western Hills Shopping Center. At the end of the section, we describe how the investment securities firm of Seasongood & Mayer used PERT/CPM to schedule a $31 million hospital revenue bond project.

9.1   PROJECT SCHEDULING BASED ON EXPECTED ACTIVITY TIMES

The owner of the Western Hills Shopping Center plans to modernize and expand the current 32-business shopping center complex. The project is expected to provide room for 8 to 10 new businesses. Financing has been arranged through a private investor. All that

TABLE 9.1   LIST OF ACTIVITIES FOR THE WESTERN HILLS SHOPPING CENTER PROJECT

Activity	Activity Description	Immediate Predecessor	Expected Activity Time
A	Prepare architectural drawings	—	5
B	Identify potential new tenants	—	6
C	Develop prospectus for tenants	A	4
D	Select contractor	A	3
E	Prepare building permits	A	1
F	Obtain approval for building permits	E	4
G	Perform construction	D, F	14
H	Finalize contracts with tenants	B, C	12
I	Tenants move in	G, H	2
		Total	51

The effort that goes into identifying activities, determining interrelationships among activities, and estimating activity times is crucial to the success of PERT/ CPM. A substantial amount of time may be needed to complete this initial phase of the project scheduling process.

Immediate predecessor information determines whether activities can be completed in parallel (worked on simultaneously) or in series (one completed before another begins). Generally, a project with more series relationships will take longer to complete.

A project network is extremely helpful in visualizing the interrelationships among the activities. No rules guide the conversion of a list of activities and immediate predecessor information into a project network. The process of constructing a project network generally improves with practice and experience.

remains is for the owner of the shopping center to plan, schedule, and complete the expansion project. Let us show how PERT/CPM can help.

The first step in the PERT/CPM scheduling process is to develop a list of the activities that make up the project. Table 9.1 shows the list of activities for the Western Hills Shopping Center expansion project. Nine activities are described and denoted A through I for later reference. Table 9.1 also shows the immediate predecessor(s) and the activity time (in weeks) for each activity. For a given activity, the **immediate predecessor** column identifies the activities that must be completed *immediately prior* to the start of that activity. Activities A and B do not have immediate predecessors and can be started as soon as the project begins; thus, a dash is written in the immediate predecessor column for these activities. The other entries in the immediate predecessor column show that activities C, D, and E cannot be started until activity A has been completed; activity F cannot be started until activity E has been completed; activity G cannot be started until both activities D and F have been completed; activity H cannot be started until both activities B and C have been completed; and, finally, activity I cannot be started until both activities G and H have been completed. The project is finished when activity I is completed.

The last column in Table 9.1 shows the expected number of weeks required to complete each activity. For example, activity A is expected to take 5 weeks, activity B is expected to take 6 weeks, and so on. The sum of expected activity times is 51. As a result, you may think that the total time required to complete the project is 51 weeks. However, as we show, two or more activities often may be scheduled concurrently (assuming sufficient availability of other required resources, such as labor and equipment), thus shortening the completion time for the project. Ultimately, PERT/CPM will provide a detailed activity schedule for completing the project in the shortest time possible.

Using the immediate predecessor information in Table 9.1, we can construct a graphical representation of the project, or the **project network**. Figure 9.1 depicts the project network for Western Hills Shopping Center. The activities correspond to the *nodes* of the network (drawn as rectangles), and the *arcs* (the lines with arrows) show the precedence relationships among the activities. In addition, nodes have been added to the network to denote the start and the finish of the project. A project network will help a manager visualize the activity relationships and provide a basis for carrying out the PERT/CPM computations.

FIGURE 9.1   PROJECT NETWORK FOR THE WESTERN HILLS SHOPPING CENTER

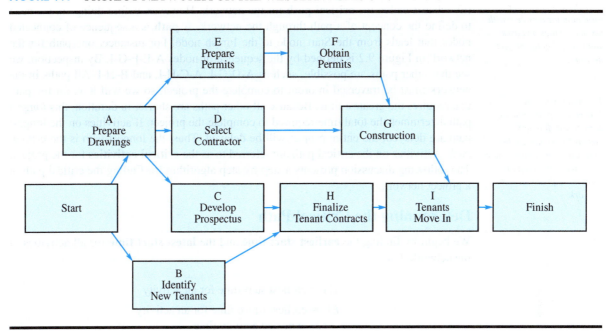

FIGURE 9.2   WESTERN HILLS SHOPPING CENTER PROJECT NETWORK WITH ACTIVITY TIMES

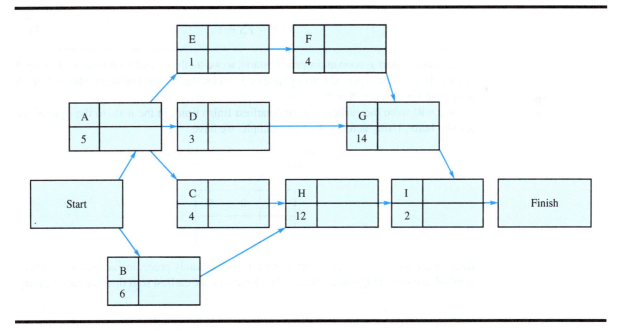

The Concept of a Critical Path

To facilitate the PERT/CPM computations, we modified the project network as shown in Figure 9.2. Note that the upper left-hand corner of each node contains the corresponding activity letter. The activity time appears immediately below the letter.

Problem 3 provides the immediate predecessor information for a project with seven activities and asks you to develop the project network.

For convenience, we use the convention of referencing activities with letters. Generally, we assign the letters in approximate order as we move from left to right through the project network.

To determine the project completion time, we have to analyze the network and identify what is called the **critical path** for the network. However, before doing so, we need to define the concept of a path through the network. A **path** is a sequence of connected nodes that leads from the Start node to the Finish node. For instance, one path for the network in Figure 9.2 is defined by the sequence of nodes A-E-F-G-I. By inspection, we see that other paths are possible, such as A-D-G-I, A-C-H-I, and B-H-I. All paths in the network must be traversed in order to complete the project, so we will look for the path that requires the greatest time. Because all other paths are shorter in duration, this *longest* path determines the total time required to complete the project. If activities on the longest path are delayed, the entire project will be delayed. Thus, the longest path is the *critical path*. Activities on the critical path are referred to as the **critical activities** for the project. The following discussion presents a step-by-step algorithm for finding the critical path in a project network.

Determining the Critical Path

We begin by finding the **earliest start time** and the **latest start time** for all activities in the network. Let

$$ES = \text{earliest start time for an activity}$$
$$EF = \text{earliest finish time for an activity}$$
$$t = \text{expected activity time}$$

The **earliest finish time** for any activity is

$$EF = ES + t \qquad (9.1)$$

Activity A can start as soon as the project starts, so we set the earliest start time for activity A equal to 0. With an expected activity time of 5 weeks, the earliest finish time for activity A is $EF = ES + t = 0 + 5 = 5$.

We will write the earliest start and earliest finish times in the node to the right of the activity letter. Using activity A as an example, we have

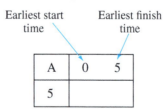

Because an activity cannot be started until *all* immediately preceding activities have been finished, the following rule can be used to determine the earliest start time for each activity:

The earliest start time for an activity is equal to the *largest* (i.e., *latest*) of the earliest finish times for all its immediate predecessors.

Let us apply the earliest start time rule to the portion of the network involving nodes A, B, C, and H, as shown in Figure 9.3. With an earliest start time of 0 and an activity time of 6 for activity B, we show $ES = 0$ and $EF = ES + t = 0 + 6 = 6$ in the node for

FIGURE 9.3 A PORTION OF THE WESTERN HILLS SHOPPING CENTER PROJECT
NETWORK, SHOWING ACTIVITIES A, B, C, AND H

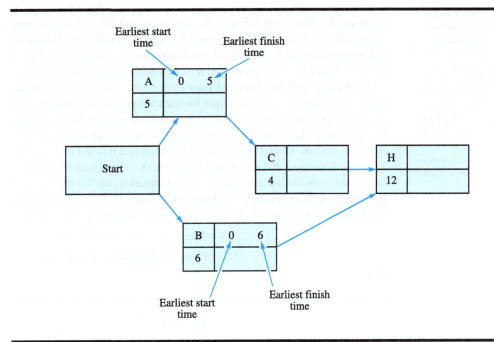

FIGURE 9.4 DETERMINING THE EARLIEST START TIME FOR ACTIVITY H

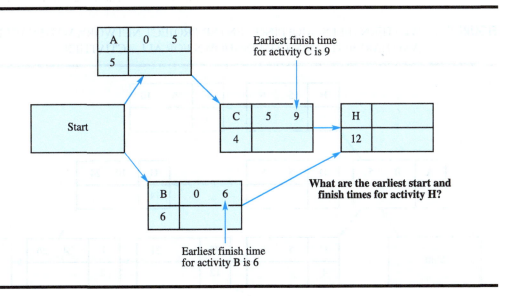

activity B. Looking at node C, we note that activity A is the only immediate predecessor for activity C. The earliest finish time for activity A is 5, so the earliest start time for activity C must be $ES = 5$. Thus, with an activity time of 4, the earliest finish time for activity C is $EF = ES + t = 5 + 4 = 9$. Both the earliest start time and the earliest finish time can be shown in the node for activity C (see Figure 9.4).

Determining the expected completion time of a project via critical path calculations implicitly assumes that sufficient resources (labor, equipment, supplies, etc.) are available to execute activities in parallel. If the resources available are insufficient to support the schedule generated by PERT/CPM, then more advanced techniques such as an integer linear programming model (Chapter 7) can be applied.

Continuing with Figure 9.4, we move on to activity H and apply the earliest start time rule for this activity. With both activities B and C as immediate predecessors, the earliest start time for activity H must be equal to the largest of the earliest finish times for activities B and C. Thus, with $EF = 6$ for activity B and $EF = 9$ for activity C, we select the largest value, 9, as the earliest start time for activity H ($ES = 9$). With an activity time of 12 as shown in the node for activity H, the earliest finish time is $EF = ES + t = 9 + 12 = 21$. The $ES = 9$ and $EF = 21$ values can now be entered in the node for activity H in Figure 9.4.

Continuing with this **forward pass** through the network, we can establish the earliest start time and the earliest finish time for each activity in the network. Figure 9.5 shows the Western Hills Shopping Center project network with the ES and EF values for each activity. Note that the earliest finish time for activity I, the last activity in the project, is 26 weeks. Therefore, we now know that the expected completion time for the entire project is 26 weeks.

We now continue the algorithm for finding the critical path by making a **backward pass** through the network. Because the expected completion time for the entire project is 26 weeks, we begin the backward pass with a **latest finish time** of 26 for activity I. Once the latest finish time for an activity is known, the *latest start time* for an activity can be computed as follows. Let

$$LS = \text{latest start time for an activity}$$

$$LF = \text{latest finish time for an activity}$$

Then

$$LS = LF - t \tag{9.2}$$

Beginning the backward pass with activity I, we know that the latest finish time is $LF = 26$ and that the activity time is $t = 2$. Thus, the latest start time for activity I is

FIGURE 9.5   WESTERN HILLS SHOPPING CENTER PROJECT NETWORK WITH EARLIEST START AND EARLIEST FINISH TIMES SHOWN FOR ALL ACTIVITIES

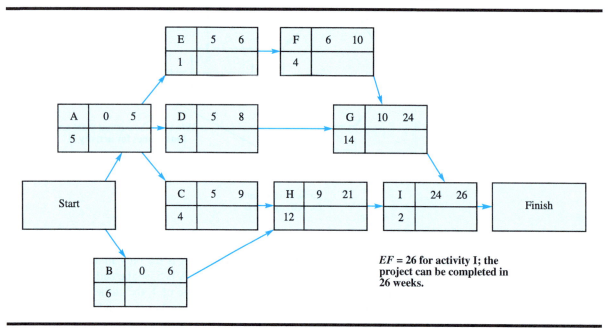

$LS = LF - t = 26 - 2 = 24$. We will write the LS and LF values in the node directly below the earliest start (ES) and earliest finish (EF) times. Thus, for node I, we have

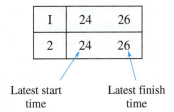

Latest start   Latest finish
time   time

The following rule can be used to determine the latest finish time for each activity in the network:

> The latest finish time for an activity is the *smallest (i.e., earliest)* of the latest start times for all activities that immediately follow the activity.

Logically, this rule states that the latest time an activity can be finished equals the earliest (smallest) value for the latest start time of following activities. Figure 9.6 shows the complete project network with the LS and LF backward pass results. We can use the latest finish time rule to verify the LS and LF values shown for activity H. The latest finish time for activity H must be the latest start time for activity I. Thus, we set $LF = 24$ for activity H. Using equation (9.2), we find that $LS = LF - t = 24 - 12 = 12$ as the latest start time for activity H. These values are shown in the node for activity H in Figure 9.6.

FIGURE 9.6   WESTERN HILLS SHOPPING CENTER PROJECT NETWORK WITH LATEST START AND LATEST FINISH TIMES SHOWN IN EACH NODE

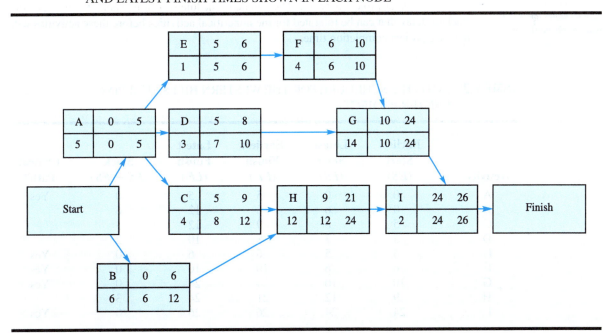

Activity A requires a more involved application of the latest start time rule. First, note that three activities (C, D, and E) immediately follow activity A. Figure 9.6 shows that the latest start times for activities C, D, and E are $LS = 8$, $LS = 7$, and $LS = 5$, respectively. The latest finish time rule for activity A states that the LF for activity A is the smallest of the latest start times for activities C, D, and E. With the smallest value being 5 for activity E, we set the latest finish time for activity A to $LF = 5$. Verify this result and the other latest start times and latest finish times shown in the nodes in Figure 9.6.

After we complete the forward and backward passes, we can determine the amount of slack associated with each activity. **Slack** is the length of time an activity can be delayed without increasing the project completion time. The amount of slack for an activity is computed as follows:

$$\text{Slack} = LS - ES = LF - EF \qquad (9.3)$$

One of the primary contributions of PERT/CPM is the identification of the critical activities. The project manager will want to monitor critical activities closely because a delay in any one of these activities will lengthen the project completion time.

For example, the slack associated with activity C is $LS - ES = 8 - 5 = 3$ weeks. Hence, activity C can be delayed up to 3 weeks, and the entire project can still be completed in 26 weeks. In this sense, activity C is not critical to the completion of the entire project in 26 weeks. Next, we consider activity E. Using the information in Figure 9.6, we find that the slack is $LS - ES = 5 - 5 = 0$. Thus, activity E has zero, or no, slack. Consequently, this activity cannot be delayed without increasing the completion time for the entire project. In other words, completing activity E exactly as scheduled is critical in terms of keeping the project on schedule, and so activity E is a critical activity. In general, the *critical activities* are the activities with zero slack.

The critical path algorithm is a longest path algorithm. From the start node to the finish node, the critical path identifies the path that requires the most time.

The start and finish times shown in Figure 9.6 can be used to develop a detailed start time and finish time schedule for all activities. Putting this information in tabular form provides the activity schedule shown in Table 9.2. Note that the slack column shows that activities A, E, F, G, and I have zero slack. Hence, these activities are the critical activities for the project; the path formed by nodes A-E-F-G-I is the *critical path* in the Western Hills Shopping Center project network. The detailed schedule shown in Table 9.2 indicates the slack or delay that can be tolerated for the noncritical activities before these activities will increase project completion time.

TABLE 9.2   ACTIVITY SCHEDULE FOR THE WESTERN HILLS SHOPPING CENTER PROJECT

Activity	Earliest Start (ES)	Latest Start (LS)	Earliest Finish (EF)	Latest Finish (LF)	Slack ($LS - ES$)	Critical Path?
A	0	0	5	5	0	Yes
B	0	6	6	12	6	
C	5	8	9	12	3	
D	5	7	8	10	2	
E	5	5	6	6	0	Yes
F	6	6	10	10	0	Yes
G	10	10	24	24	0	Yes
H	9	12	21	24	3	
I	24	24	26	26	0	Yes

Contributions of PERT/CPM

We previously stated that project managers look for procedures that will help answer important questions regarding the planning, scheduling, and controlling of projects. Let us reconsider these questions in light of the information that the critical path calculations have given us.

1. How long will the project take to complete?
    Answer: The project can be completed in 26 weeks if each activity is completed on schedule.
2. What are the scheduled start and completion times for each activity?
    Answer: The activity schedule (see Table 9.2) shows the earliest start, latest start, earliest finish, and latest finish times for each activity.
3. Which activities are critical and must be completed *exactly* as scheduled to keep the project on schedule?
    Answer: A, E, F, G, and I are the critical activities.
4. How long can noncritical activities be delayed before they cause an increase in the completion time for the project?
    Answer: The activity schedule (see Table 9.2) shows the slack associated with each activity.

Such information is valuable in managing any project. Although the effort required to develop the immediate predecessor relationships and the activity time estimates generally increases with the size of the project, the procedure and contribution of PERT/CPM to larger projects are identical to those shown for the shopping center expansion project. The Management Science in Action, Hospital Revenue Bond at Seasongood & Mayer, describes a 23-activity project that introduced a $31 million hospital revenue bond. PERT/CPM was used to identify the critical activities, the expected project completion time of 29 weeks, and the activity start times and finish times necessary to keep the entire project on schedule.

Summary of the PERT/CPM Critical Path Procedure

Before leaving this section, let us summarize the PERT/CPM critical path procedure.

Step 1. Develop a list of the activities that make up the project.
Step 2. Determine the immediate predecessor(s) for each activity in the project.
Step 3. Estimate the expected completion time for each activity.
Step 4. Draw a project network depicting the activities and immediate predecessors listed in steps 1 and 2.
Step 5. Use the project network and the activity time estimates to determine the earliest start and the earliest finish time for each activity by making a forward pass through the network. The earliest finish time for the last activity in the project identifies the expected time required to complete the entire project.
Step 6. Use the expected project completion time identified in step 5 as the latest finish time for the last activity and make a backward pass through the network to identify the latest start and latest finish time for each activity.
Step 7. Use the difference between the latest start time and the earliest start time for each activity to determine the slack for each activity.
Step 8. Find the activities with zero slack; these are the critical activities.
Step 9. Use the information from steps 5 and 6 to develop the activity schedule for the project.

MANAGEMENT SCIENCE IN ACTION

HOSPITAL REVENUE BOND AT SEASONGOOD & MAYER

Seasongood & Mayer is an investment securities firm located in Cincinnati, Ohio. The firm engages in municipal financing, including the underwriting of new issues of municipal bonds, acting as a market maker for previously issued bonds, and performing other investment banking services.

Seasongood & Mayer provided the underwriting for a $31 million issue of hospital facilities revenue bonds for Providence Hospital in Hamilton County, Ohio. The project of underwriting this municipal bond issue began with activities such as drafting the legal documents, drafting a description of the existing hospital facilities, and completing a feasibility study. A total of 23 activities defined the project that would be completed when the hospital

signed the construction contract and then made the bond proceeds available. The immediate predecessor relationships for the activities and the activity times were developed by a project management team.

PERT/CPM analysis of the project network identified the 10 critical path activities. The analysis also provided the expected completion time of 29 weeks, or approximately seven months. The activity schedule showed the start time and finish time for each activity and provided the information necessary to monitor the project and keep it on schedule. PERT/CPM was instrumental in helping Seasongood & Mayer obtain the financing for the project within the time specified in the construction bid.

NOTES AND COMMENTS

1. Software packages such as Microsoft Project perform the critical path calculations quickly and efficiently. Program inputs include the activities, their immediate predecessors, and expected activity times. The project manager can modify any aspect of the project and quickly determine how the modification affects the activity schedule and the expected time required to complete the project.
2. Suppose that, after analyzing a PERT/CPM network, the project manager finds that the project completion time is unacceptable (i.e.,

the project is going to take too long). In this case, the manager must take one or both of the following steps. First, review the original PERT/CPM network to see whether any immediate predecessor relationships can be modified so that at least some of the critical path activities can be done simultaneously. Second, consider adding resources to critical path activities in an attempt to shorten the critical path; we discuss this alternative, referred to as *crashing,* in Section 9.3.

9.2   PROJECT SCHEDULING CONSIDERING UNCERTAIN ACTIVITY TIMES

In this section we consider the details of project scheduling for a problem involving new-product research and development. Because many of the activities in such a project have never been attempted by this organization, the project manager wants to account for uncertainties in the activity times. Let us show how project scheduling can be conducted with uncertain activity times.

The Daugherty Porta-Vac Project

The H. S. Daugherty Company has manufactured industrial vacuum cleaning systems for many years. Recently, a member of the company's new-product research team submitted a report suggesting that the company consider manufacturing a cordless vacuum cleaner. The new product, referred to as Porta-Vac, could contribute to Daugherty's expansion into the household market. Management hopes that the Porta-Vac can be manufactured at a reasonable cost and that its portability and no-cord convenience will make it extremely attractive to potential consumers.

Daugherty's management wants to study the feasibility of manufacturing the Porta-Vac product. The feasibility study will provide a recommendation on the action to be taken. To complete this study, information must be obtained from the firm's research and development (R&D), product testing, manufacturing, cost estimating, and market research groups. How long will it take to complete this feasibility study? In the following discussion, we show how to answer this question and provide an activity schedule for the project.

Again, the first step in the project scheduling process is to identify all activities that make up the project and determine the immediate predecessor(s) for each activity. Table 9.3 shows this information for the Porta-Vac project.

The Porta-Vac project network is shown in Figure 9.7. Verify that the network does in fact maintain the immediate predecessor relationships shown in Table 9.3.

TABLE 9.3   ACTIVITY LIST FOR THE PORTA-VAC PROJECT

Activity	Description	Immediate Predecessor
A	Develop product design	—
B	Plan market research	—
C	Prepare routing (manufacturing engineering)	A
D	Build prototype model	A
E	Prepare marketing brochure	A
F	Prepare cost estimates (industrial engineering)	C
G	Do preliminary product testing	D
H	Complete market survey	B, E
I	Prepare pricing and forecast report	H
J	Prepare final report	F, G, I

FIGURE 9.7   PORTA-VAC CORDLESS VACUUM CLEANER PROJECT NETWORK

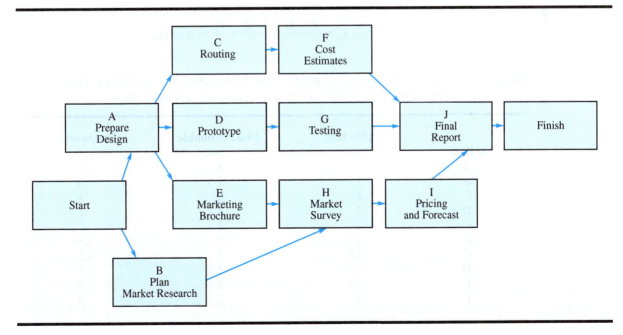

Uncertain Activity Times

Once we develop the project network, we will need information on the time required to complete each activity. This information is used in calculating the total time required to complete the project and in scheduling of specific activities. For repeat projects, such as construction and maintenance projects, managers may have the experience and historical data necessary to provide accurate activity time estimates. However, for new or unique projects, estimating the time for each activity may be quite difficult. In fact, in many cases activity times are uncertain and are best described by a range of possible values rather than by one specific time estimate. In these instances, the uncertain activity times are treated as random variables with associated probability distributions. As a result, probability statements will be provided about the ability to meet a specific project completion date.

To incorporate uncertain activity times into the analysis, we need to obtain three time estimates for each activity:

Optimistic time a = the minimum activity time if everything progresses ideally

Most probable time m = the most probable activity time under normal conditions

Pessimistic time b = the maximum activity time if substantial delays are encountered

To illustrate the PERT/CPM procedure with uncertain activity times, let us consider the optimistic, most probable, and pessimistic time estimates for the Porta-Vac activities as presented in Table 9.4. Using activity A as an example, we see that the most probable time is 5 weeks, with a range from 4 weeks (optimistic) to 12 weeks (pessimistic). If the activity could be repeated a large number of times, what is the average time for the activity? This average or **expected time** (t) is as follows:

$$t = \frac{a + 4m + b}{6} \tag{9.4}$$

For activity A we have an average or expected time of

$$t_A = \frac{4 + 4(5) + 12}{6} = \frac{36}{6} = 6 \text{ weeks}$$

TABLE 9.4   OPTIMISTIC, MOST PROBABLE, AND PESSIMISTIC ACTIVITY TIME
ESTIMATES (IN WEEKS) FOR THE PORTA-VAC PROJECT

Activity	Optimistic (a)	Most Probable (m)	Pessimistic (b)
A	4	5	12
B	1	1.5	5
C	2	3	4
D	3	4	11
E	2	3	4
F	1.5	2	2.5
G	1.5	3	4.5
H	2.5	3.5	7.5
I	1.5	2	2.5
J	1	2	3

With uncertain activity times, we can use the *variance* to describe the dispersion or variation in the activity time values. The variance of the activity time is given by the formula[1]

$$\sigma^2 = \left(\frac{b-a}{6}\right)^2 \tag{9.5}$$

The difference between the pessimistic (*b*) and optimistic (*a*) time estimates greatly affects the value of the variance. Large differences in these two values reflect a high degree of uncertainty in the activity time. Using equation (9.5), we obtain the measure of uncertainty—that is, the variance—of activity A, denoted σ_A^2:

$$\sigma_A^2 = \left(\frac{12-4}{6}\right)^2 = \left(\frac{8}{6}\right)^2 = 1.78$$

Equations (9.4) and (9.5) are based on the assumption that the activity time distribution can be described by a **beta probability distribution**.[2] With this assumption, the probability distribution for the time to complete activity A is as shown in Figure 9.8. Using equations (9.4) and (9.5) and the data in Table 9.4, we calculated the expected time and variance for each Porta-Vac activity; the results are summarized in Table 9.5. The Porta-Vac project network with expected activity times is shown in Figure 9.9.

FIGURE 9.8   ACTIVITY TIME DISTRIBUTION FOR PRODUCT DESIGN (ACTIVITY A) FOR THE PORTA-VAC PROJECT

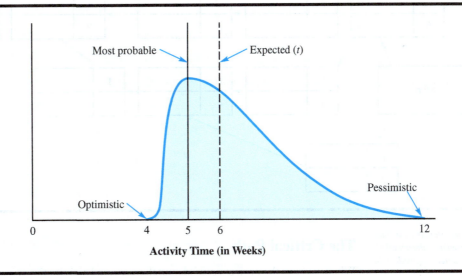

[1]The variance equation is based on the notion that a standard deviation is approximately $\frac{1}{6}$ of the difference between the extreme values of the distribution: $(b - a)/6$. The variance is the square of the standard deviation.

[2]The equations for *t* and σ^2 require additional assumptions about the parameters of the beta probability distribution. However, even when these additional assumptions are not made, the equations still provide good approximations of *t* and σ^2.

TABLE 9.5   EXPECTED TIMES AND VARIANCES FOR THE PORTA-VAC
PROJECT ACTIVITIES

Activity	Expected Time (weeks)	Variance
A	6	1.78
B	2	0.44
C	3	0.11
D	5	1.78
E	3	0.11
F	2	0.03
G	3	0.25
H	4	0.69
I	2	0.03
J	2	0.11
	Total 32	

FIGURE 9.9   PORTA-VAC PROJECT NETWORK WITH EXPECTED ACTIVITY TIMES

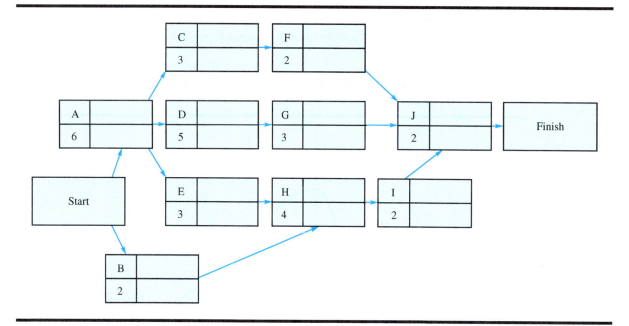

The Critical Path

When uncertain activity times are considered, the actual time required to complete the project may differ from the expected time to complete the project provided by the critical path calculations. However, for planning purposes, the expected time provides valuable information for the project manager.

When we have the project network and the expected activity times, we are ready to proceed with the critical path calculations necessary to determine the expected time required to complete the project and determine the activity schedule. In these calculations, we find the critical path for the Porta-Vac project by applying the critical path procedure introduced in Section 9.1 to the expected activity times (Table 9.5). After the critical activities and the expected time to complete the project have been determined, we analyze the effect of the activity time variability.

Proceeding with a forward pass through the network shown in Figure 9.9, we can establish the earliest start (*ES*) and earliest finish (*EF*) times for each activity. Figure 9.10 shows the project network with the *ES* and *EF* values. Note that the earliest finish time for activity J, the last activity, is 17 weeks. Thus, the expected completion time for the project is 17 weeks. Next, we make a backward pass through the network. The backward pass provides the latest start (*LS*) and latest finish (*LF*) times shown in Figure 9.11.

FIGURE 9.10 PORTA-VAC PROJECT NETWORK WITH EARLIEST START AND EARLIEST FINISH TIMES

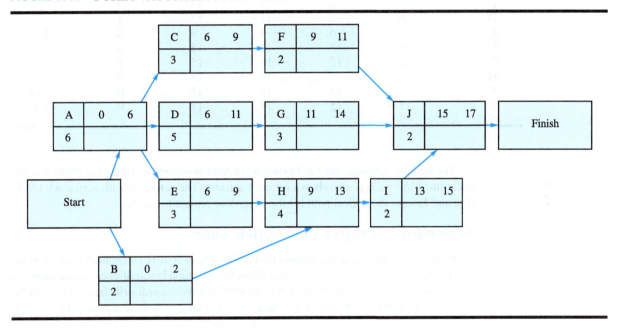

FIGURE 9.11 PORTA-VAC PROJECT NETWORK WITH LATEST START AND LATEST FINISH TIMES

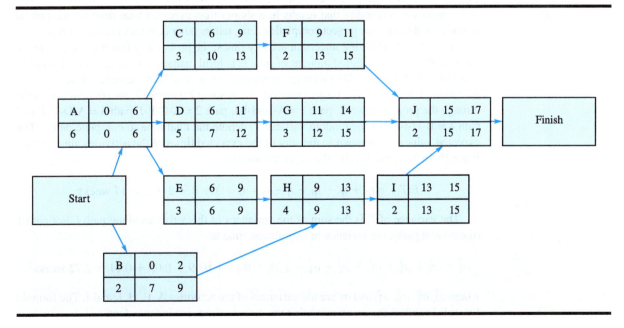

TABLE 9.6   ACTIVITY SCHEDULE FOR THE PORTA-VAC PROJECT

Activity	Earliest Start (ES)	Latest Start (LS)	Earliest Finish (EF)	Latest Finish (LF)	Slack (LS − ES)	Critical Path?
A	0	0	6	6	0	Yes
B	0	7	2	9	7	
C	6	10	9	13	4	
D	6	7	11	12	1	
E	6	6	9	9	0	Yes
F	9	13	11	15	4	
G	11	12	14	15	1	
H	9	9	13	13	0	Yes
I	13	13	15	15	0	Yes
J	15	15	17	17	0	Yes

The activity schedule for the Porta-Vac project is shown in Table 9.6. Note that the slack time $(LS - ES)$ is also shown for each activity. The activities with zero slack (A, E, H, I, and J) form the critical path for the Porta-Vac project network.

Variability in Project Completion Time

We know that for the Porta-Vac project the critical path of A-E-H-I-J resulted in an expected total project completion time of 17 weeks. However, variation in activities can cause variation in the project completion time. Variation in noncritical activities ordinarily has no effect on the project completion time because of the slack time associated with these activities. However, if a noncritical activity is delayed long enough to expend its slack time, it becomes part of a new critical path and may affect the project completion time. Variability leading to a longer-than-expected total time for the critical activities will always extend the project completion time, and, conversely, variability that results in a shorter-than-expected total time for the critical activities will reduce the project completion time, unless other activities become critical.

For a project involving uncertain activity times, the probability that the project can be completed within a specified amount of time is helpful managerial information. To understand the effect of variability on project management, we consider the variation along every path through the Porta-Vac project network. Examining Figure 9.11, we observe four paths through the project network: path 1 = A-E-H-I-J, path 2 = A-C-F-J, path 3 = A-D-G-J, and path 4 = B-H-I-J. Let the random variable T_i denote the total time to complete path i. The expected value of T_i is equal to the sum of the expected times of the activities along path i. For path 1 (the critical path), the expected time is

$$E(T_1) = t_A + t_E + t_H + t_I + t_J = 6 + 3 + 4 + 2 + 2 = 17 \text{ weeks}$$

The variance of T_i is the sum of the variances of the activities along path i. For path 1 (the critical path), the variance in completion time is

$$\sigma_1^2 = \sigma_A^2 + \sigma_E^2 + \sigma_H^2 + \sigma_I^2 + \sigma_J^2 = 1.78 + 0.11 + 0.69 + 0.03 + 0.11 = 2.72 \text{ weeks}^2$$

where $\sigma_A^2, \sigma_E^2, \sigma_H^2, \sigma_I^2,$ and σ_J^2 are the variances of the activities A, E, H, I, and J. The formula for σ_1^2 is based on the assumption that the activity times are independent.

If two or more activities are dependent, the formula provides only an approximation of the variance of the path completion time. The closer the activities are to being independent, the better the approximation.

Knowing that the standard deviation is the square root of the variance, we compute the standard deviation σ_1 for the path 1 completion time as

$$\sigma_1 = \sqrt{\sigma_1^2} = \sqrt{2.72} = 1.65$$

Assuming that the distribution of the path completion time T_1 follows a normal or bellshaped distribution[3] allows us to draw the distribution shown in Figure 9.12. With this distribution, we can compute the probability that a path of activities will meet be completed within a specified time. For example, suppose that management allotted 20 weeks for the Porta-Vac project. What is the probability that path 1 will be completed within 20 weeks? We are asking for the probability that $T_1 \leq 20$, which corresponds graphically to the shaded area in Figure 9.13. The z-score for the normal probability distribution at $T_1 = 20$ is

$$z_1 = \frac{20 - 17}{1.65} = 1.82$$

The normal distribution tends to be a better approximation of the distribution of completion time for larger projects.

Using $z = 1.82$ and the table for the normal distribution (see Appendix B), we find that the probability of path 1 meeting the 20-week deadline is 0.9656.

In Table 9.7, we repeat the calculation of the expected completion time and variance in completion time for the other paths through the project network (including path 1 again for completeness). As Table 9.7 shows, path 2 and path 4 are virtually guaranteed to be completed by the 20-week deadline and path 3 has a probability of 0.9783 of meeting the 20-week deadline.

Appendix 9.1 describes how to compute cumulative probabilities for normal random variables in Excel.

One method for estimating the probability that the entire Porta-Vac project will be completed by the 20-week deadline is to consider only the path with the smallest completion probability. As is often the case, the critical path (path 1) has the smallest completion probability. So a simple estimate of the probability that the entire Porta-Vac project will be complete within 20 weeks is 0.9656.

FIGURE 9.12   NORMAL DISTRIBUTION OF THE CRITICAL PATH COMPLETION TIME FOR THE PORTA-VAC PROJECT

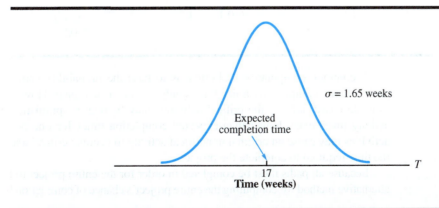

---

[3]Use of the normal distribution as an approximation is based on the central limit theorem, which indicates that the sum of independent activity times follows a normal distribution as the number of activity times becomes large.

FIGURE 9.13   PROBABILITY THE CRITICAL PATH WILL BE COMPLETED BY THE
20-WEEK DEADLINE

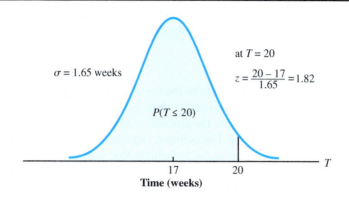

TABLE 9.7   COMPUTING THE PROBABILITY OF EACH PROJECT PATH MEETING
THE 20-WEEK DEADLINE

Expected Path Completion Time	Standard Deviation of Path Completion Time	z-Score	Probability of Meeting Deadline
$E(T_1) = 6 + 3 + 4 + 2$ $+ 2 = 17$	$\sigma_1^2 = 1.78 + 0.11 + 0.69$ $+ 0.03 + 0.11$ $= 2.72$	$z_1 = \dfrac{20 - 17}{\sqrt{2.72}}$ $= 1.82$	0.9656
$E(T_2) = 6 + 3 + 2 + 2$ $= 13$	$\sigma_2^2 = 1.78 + 0.11 + 0.03$ $+ 0.11 = 2.03$	$z_2 = \dfrac{20 - 13}{\sqrt{2.03}}$ $= 4.91$	> 0.9999
$E(T_3) = 6 + 5 + 3 + 2$ $= 16$	$\sigma_3^2 = 1.78 + 1.78 + 0.25$ $+ 0.11 = 3.92$	$z_3 = \dfrac{20 - 16}{\sqrt{3.92}}$ $= 2.02$	0.9783
$E(T_4) = 2 + 4 + 2 + 2$ $= 10$	$\sigma_4^2 = 0.44 + 0.69 + 0.03$ $+ 0.11 = 1.27$	$z_4 = \dfrac{20 - 10}{\sqrt{1.27}}$ $= 7.02$	> 0.9999

A common computational shortcut is to base the probability estimate of the entire project being complete by a deadline solely on the critical path. However, a probability estimate based only on the critical activities may be overly optimistic. When uncertain activity times exist, longer-than-expected completion times for one or more noncritical activities may cause an original noncritical activity to become critical and hence increase the time required to complete the project.

Because all paths must be completed in order for the entire project to be completed, an alternative method for computing the entire project's chance of completion by the deadline is

P (*path* 1 *completed by deadline*) $\times$ P (*path* 2 *completed by deadline*)
$\times P$ (*path* 3 *completed by deadline*) $\times P$(*path* 4 *completed by deadline*)
$0.9656 \times 1.0 \times 0.9783 \times 1.0 = 0.9446$

Simulation is another technique used in project management and is particularly useful for estimating the probability of an extremely complex project being completed by a specified deadline.

This calculation assumes that each path is independent. As all of these paths share at least one common activity, this assumption is violated. Consequentially, this estimate will be a pessimistic estimate of the likelihood of meeting the project deadline.

Regardless of the method to estimate the completion probability, a project manager should frequently monitor the progress of the project. In particular, the project manager should monitor activities with large variances in their activity times. The Management Science in Action, Project Management Helps the U.S. Air Force Reduce Maintenance Time, describes how closely managing the progress of individual activities and the assignment of resources led to dramatic improvements in the maintenance of military aircraft.

MANAGEMENT SCIENCE IN ACTION

PROJECT MANAGEMENT HELPS THE U.S. AIR FORCE REDUCE MAINTENANCE TIME*

Warner Robins Air Logistics Center (WR-ALC) provides maintenance and repair services for U.S. Air Force aircraft and ground equipment. To support combat zone efforts, the U.S. Air Force requested that WR-ALC reduce the amount of time it took to complete maintenance service on its C-5 transporter aircraft.

To identify ways to improve the management of its repair and overhaul process, WR-ALC adopted the method of critical chain project management (CCPM) by viewing each aircraft at its facility as a project with a series of tasks, precedence dependencies between these tasks, and resource requirements. Identifying tasks at a level of detail that allowed supervisors to clearly assign mechanics, maintenance tools, and facilities resulted in a project network of approximately 450 activities.

By explicitly accounting for each task's resource requirements (mechanics, aircraft parts, maintenance tools, etc.), CCPM identifies a "critical chain" of activities. Efforts to reduce the critical chain led to the insight that a task should not be started until all resources needed to complete the task are available. While this approach, called "pipelining," often results in an initial delay to the start of a task, it allows for the quicker completion of the task by eliminating delays after the task's launch and by reducing efficiency-robbing multitasking (across tasks) by the mechanics.

*Based on M. M. Srinivasan, W. D. Best, and S. Chandrasekaran, "Warner Robins Air Logistics Center Streamlines Aircraft Repair and Overhaul," *Interfaces* 37, no. 1 (2007), pp. 7–21.

9.3 CONSIDERING TIME–COST TRADE-OFFS

Using additional resources to reduce activity times was proposed by the developers of CPM. The shortening of activity times is referred to as crashing.

When determining the time estimates for activities in a project, the project manager bases these estimates on the amount of resources (workers, equipment, etc.) that will be assigned to an activity. The original developers of CPM provided the project manager with the option of adding resources to selected activities to reduce project completion time. Added resources (such as more workers, overtime, and so on) generally increase project costs, so the decision to reduce activity times must take into consideration the additional cost involved. In effect, the project manager must make a decision that involves trading additional project costs for reduced activity time.

Table 9.8 defines a two-machine maintenance project consisting of five activities. Management has substantial experience with similar projects and the times for maintenance activities have very little variability; hence, a single time estimate is given for each activity. The project network is shown in Figure 9.14.

The procedure for making critical path calculations for the maintenance project network is the same one that was used to find the critical path in the networks for both the Western Hills Shopping Center expansion project and the Porta-Vac project. Making the forward pass and backward pass calculations for the network in Figure 9.14, we obtained

TABLE 9.8   ACTIVITY LIST FOR THE TWO-MACHINE MAINTENANCE PROJECT

Activity	Description	Immediate Predecessor	Expected Time (days)
A	Overhaul machine I	—	7
B	Adjust machine I	A	3
C	Overhaul machine II	—	6
D	Adjust machine II	C	3
E	Test system	B, D	2

FIGURE 9.14   TWO-MACHINE MAINTENANCE PROJECT NETWORK

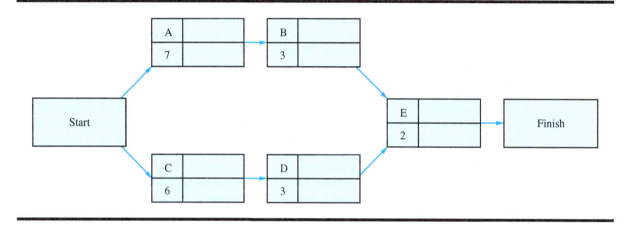

TABLE 9.9   ACTIVITY SCHEDULE FOR THE TWO-MACHINE MAINTENANCE PROJECT

Activity	Earliest Start (ES)	Latest Start (LS)	Earliest Finish (EF)	Latest Finish (LF)	Slack (LS − ES)	Critical Path?
A	0	0	7	7	0	Yes
B	7	7	10	10	0	Yes
C	0	1	6	7	1	
D	6	7	9	10	1	
E	10	10	12	12	0	Yes

the activity schedule shown in Table 9.9. The zero slack times, and thus the critical path, are associated with activities A-B-E. The length of the critical path, and thus the total time required to complete the project, is 12 days.

Crashing Activity Times

Now suppose that current production levels make completing the maintenance project within 10 days imperative. By looking at the length of the critical path of the network (12 days), we realize that meeting the desired project completion time is impossible unless we can shorten selected activity times. This shortening of activity times, which usually can be achieved by adding resources, is referred to as **crashing**. Because the added resources associated with crashing activity times usually result in added project costs, we will want to identify the activities that cost the least to crash and then crash those activities by only the amount necessary to meet the desired project completion time.

To determine where and how much to crash activity times, we need information on how much each activity can be crashed and how much the crashing process costs. Hence, we must ask for the following information:

1. Activity cost under the normal or expected activity time
2. Time to complete the activity under maximum crashing (i.e., the shortest possible activity time)
3. Activity cost under maximum crashing

Let

$$\tau_i = \text{expected time for activity } i$$

$$\tau'_i = \text{time for activity } i \text{ under maximum crashing}$$

$$M_i = \text{maximum possible reduction in time for activity } i \text{ due to crashing}$$

Given τ_i and τ'_i, we can compute M_i:

$$M_i = \tau_i - \tau'_i \qquad (9.6)$$

This assumes that each unit of time gained by crashing an activity has the same associated cost. It is possible that the first few units of time gained by crashing an activity cost less than ensuing units of time gained by crashing the activity.

Next, let C_i denote the cost for activity i under the normal or expected activity time and let C_i' denote the cost for activity i under maximum crashing. Thus, per unit of time (e.g., per day), the crashing cost K_i for each activity is given by

$$K_i = \frac{C'_i - C_i}{M_i} \qquad (9.7)$$

For example, if the normal or expected time for activity A is 7 days at a cost of $C_A = \$500$ and the time under maximum crashing is 4 days at a cost of $C_A = \$800$, equations (9.6) and (9.7) show that the maximum possible reduction in time for activity A is

$$M_A = 7 - 4 = 3 \text{ days}$$

with a crashing cost of

$$K_A = \frac{C'_A - C_A}{M_A} = \frac{800 - 500}{3} = \frac{300}{3} = \$100 \text{ per day}$$

We make the assumption that any portion or fraction of the activity crash time can be achieved for a corresponding portion of the activity crashing cost. For example, if we decided to crash activity A by only 1.5 days, the added cost would be 1.5 (\$100) = \$150, which results in a total activity cost of \$500 + \$150 = \$650. Figure 9.15 shows the graph

FIGURE 9.15   TIME–COST RELATIONSHIP FOR ACTIVITY A

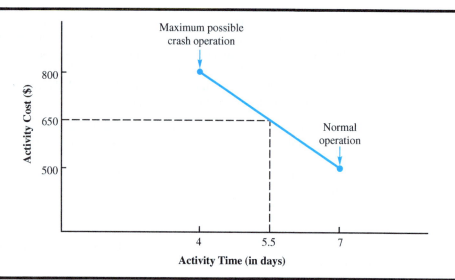

TABLE 9.10   NORMAL AND CRASH ACTIVITY DATA FOR THE TWO-MACHINE MAINTENANCE
PROJECT

| Activity | Time (days) | | Total Cost | | Maximum Reduction in Time (M_i) | Crash Cost per Day $\left(K_i = \dfrac{C_i' - C_i}{M_i}\right)$ |
	Normal	Crash	Normal (C_i)	Crash (C_i')		
A	7	4	$ 500	$ 800	3	$100
B	3	2	200	350	1	150
C	6	4	500	900	2	200
D	3	1	200	500	2	150
E	2	1	300	550	1	250
			$1700	$3100		

of the time–cost relationship for activity A. The complete normal and crash activity data for the two-machine maintenance project are given in Table 9.10.

Which activities should be crashed—and by how much—to meet the 10-day project completion deadline at minimum cost? Your first reaction to this question may be to consider crashing the critical activities—A, B, or E. Activity A has the lowest crashing cost per day of the three, and crashing this activity by 2 days will reduce the A-B-E path to the desired 10 days. Keep in mind, however, that as you crash the current critical activities, other paths may become critical. Thus, you will need to check the critical path in the revised network and perhaps either identify additional activities to crash or modify your initial crashing decision. For a small network, this trial-and-error approach can be used to make crashing decisions; in larger networks, however, a mathematical procedure is required to determine the optimal crashing decisions.

Linear Programming Model for Crashing

Let us describe how linear programming can be used to solve the network crashing problem. With PERT/CPM, we know that when an activity starts at its earliest start time, then

$$\text{Finish time} = \text{Earliest start time} + \text{Activity time}$$

However, if slack time is associated with an activity, then the activity need not start at its earliest start time. In this case, we may have

$$\text{Finish time} > \text{Earliest start time} + \text{Activity time}$$

Because we do not know ahead of time whether an activity will start at its earliest start time, we use the following inequality to show the general relationship among finish time, earliest start time, and activity time for each activity:

$$\text{Finish time} \geq \text{Earliest start time} + \text{Activity time}$$

Consider activity A, which has an expected time of 7 days. Let x_A = finish time for activity A, and y_A = amount of time activity A is crashed. If we assume that the project begins at time 0, the earliest start time for activity A is 0. Because the time for activity A is reduced by the amount of time that activity A is crashed, the finish time for activity A must satisfy the relationship

$$x_A \geq 0 + (7 - y_A)$$

Moving y_A to the left side

$$x_A + y_A \geq 7$$

In general, let

$$x_i = \text{the finish time for activity } i \qquad\qquad i = A, B, C, D, E$$

$$y_i = \text{the amount of time activity } i \text{ is crashed} \qquad i = A, B, C, D, E$$

If we follow the same approach that we used for activity A, the constraint corresponding to the finish time for activity C (expected time = 6 days) is

$$x_C \geq 0 + (6 - y_C) \quad \text{or} \quad x_C + y_C \geq 6$$

Continuing with the forward pass of the PERT/CPM procedure, we see that the earliest start time for activity B is x_A, the finish time for activity A. Thus, the constraint corresponding to the finish time for activity B is

$$x_B \geq x_A + (3 - y_B) \quad \text{or} \quad x_B + y_B - x_A \geq 3$$

Similarly, we obtain the constraint for the finish time for activity D:

$$x_D \geq x_C + (3 - y_D) \quad \text{or} \quad x_D + y_D - x_C \geq 3$$

Finally, we consider activity E. The earliest start time for activity E equals the *largest* of the finish times for activities B and D. Because the finish times for both activities B and D will be determined by the crashing procedure, we must write two constraints for activity E, one based on the finish time for activity B and one based on the finish time for activity D:

$$x_E + y_E - x_B \geq 2 \quad \text{and} \quad x_E + y_E - x_D \geq 2$$

Recall that current production levels made completing the maintenance project within 10 days imperative. Thus, the constraint for the finish time for activity E is

$$x_E \leq 10$$

In addition, we must add the following five constraints corresponding to the maximum allowable crashing time for each activity:

$$y_A \leq 3, \quad y_B \leq 1, \quad y_C \leq 2, \quad y_D \leq 2, \quad \text{and} \quad y_E \leq 1$$

As with all linear programs, we add the usual nonnegativity requirements for the decision variables.

All that remains is to develop an objective function for the model. Because the total project cost for a normal completion time is fixed at $1700 (see Table 9.10), we can minimize the total project cost (normal cost plus crashing cost) by minimizing the total crashing costs. Thus, the linear programming objective function becomes

$$\text{Min } 100y_A + 150y_B + 200y_C + 150y_D + 250y_E$$

Thus, to determine the optimal crashing for each of the activities, we must solve a 10-variable, 12-constraint linear programming model. Optimization software, such as Excel Solver, provides the optimal solution of crashing activity A by 1 day and activity E by 1 day, with a total crashing cost of $100 + $250 = $350. With the minimum cost crashing solution, the activity times are as follows:

Activity	Time in Days	
A	6	(Crash 1 day)
B	3	
C	6	
D	3	
E	1	(Crash 1 day)

The linear programming solution provided the revised activity times, but not the revised earliest start time, latest start time, and slack information. The revised activity times and the usual PERT/CPM procedure must be used to develop the activity schedule for the project.

NOTES AND COMMENTS

1. Note that the two-machine maintenance project network for the crashing illustration (see Figure 9.14) has only one activity, activity E, leading directly to the Finish node. As a result, the project completion time is equal to the completion time for activity E. Thus, the linear programming constraint requiring the project completion in 10 days or less could be written $x_E \leq 10$.

If two or more activities lead directly to the Finish node of a project network, a slight modification is required in the linear programming model for crashing. Consider the portion of the project network shown here. In this case, we suggest creating an additional variable, x_{FIN},

which indicates the finish or completion time for the entire project. The fact that the project cannot be finished until both activities E and G are completed can be modeled by the two constraints

$$x_{FIN} \geq x_E \quad \text{or} \quad x_{FIN} - x_E \geq 0$$

$$x_{FIN} \geq x_G \quad \text{or} \quad x_{FIN} - x_G \geq 0$$

The constraint that the project must be finished by time T can be added as $x_{FIN} \leq T$. Problem 22 gives you practice with this type of project network.

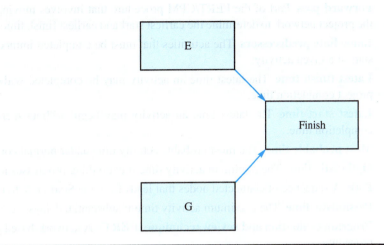

SUMMARY

In this chapter we showed how PERT/CPM can be used to plan, schedule, and control a wide variety of projects. The key to this approach to project scheduling is the development of a PERT/CPM project network that depicts the activities and their precedence relationships. From this project network and activity time estimates, the critical path for the network and the associated critical activities can be identified. In the process, an activity schedule showing the earliest start and earliest finish times, the latest start and latest finish times, and the slack for each activity can be identified.

We showed how we can include capabilities for handling variable or uncertain activity times and how to use this information to provide a probability statement about the chances the project can be completed in a specified period of time. We introduced crashing as a procedure for reducing activity times to meet project completion deadlines, and we showed how a linear programming model can be used to determine the crashing decisions that will minimize the cost of reducing the project completion time.

GLOSSARY

Activities Specific jobs or tasks that are components of a project. Activities are represented by nodes in a project network.

Backward pass Part of the PERT/CPM procedure that involves moving backward through the network to determine the latest start and latest finish times for each activity.

Beta probability distribution A probability distribution used to describe activity times.

Crashing The shortening of activity times by adding resources and hence usually increasing cost.

Critical activities The activities on the critical path.

Critical path The longest path in a project network.

Critical path method (CPM) A network-based project scheduling procedure.

Earliest finish time The earliest time an activity may be completed.

Earliest start time The earliest time an activity may begin.

Expected time The average activity time.

Forward pass Part of the PERT/CPM procedure that involves moving forward through the project network to determine the earliest start and earliest finish times for each activity.

Immediate predecessors The activities that must be completed immediately prior to the start of a given activity.

Latest finish time The latest time an activity may be completed without increasing the project completion time.

Latest start time The latest time an activity may begin without increasing the project completion time.

Most probable time The most probable activity time under normal conditions.

Optimistic time The minimum activity time if everything progresses ideally.

Path A sequence of connected nodes that leads from the Start node to the Finish node.

Pessimistic time The maximum activity time if substantial delays are encountered.

Program evaluation and review technique (PERT) A network-based project scheduling procedure.

Project network A graphical representation of a project that depicts the activities and shows the predecessor relationships among the activities.

Slack The length of time an activity can be delayed without affecting the project completion time.

PROBLEMS

1. The Mohawk Discount Store is designing a management training program for individuals at its corporate headquarters. The company wants to design the program so that trainees can complete it as quickly as possible. Important precedence relationships must be maintained between assignments or activities in the program. For example, a trainee cannot serve as an assistant to the store manager until the trainee has obtained experience in the credit department and at least one sales department. The following activities are the assignments that must be completed by each trainee in the program. Construct a project network for this problem. Do not perform any further analysis.

Activity	A	B	C	D	E	F	G	H
Immediate Predecessor	—	—	A	A, B	A, B	C	D, F	E, G

2. Bridge City Developers is coordinating the construction of an office complex. As part of the planning process, the company generated the following activity list. Draw a project network that can be used to assist in the scheduling of the project activities.

Activity	A	B	C	D	E	F	G	H	I	J
Immediate Predecessor	—	—	—	A, B	A, B	D	E	C	C	F, G, H, I

3. Construct a project network for the following project. The project is completed when activities F and G are both complete.

Activity	A	B	C	D	E	F	G
Immediate Predecessor	—	—	A	A	C, B	C, B	D, E

4. Assume that the project in Problem 3 has the following activity times (in months):

Activity	A	B	C	D	E	F	G
Time	4	6	2	6	3	3	5

   a. Find the critical path.

   b. The project must be completed in 1.5 years. Do you anticipate difficulty in meeting the deadline? Explain.

5. Consider the Western Hills Shopping Center project summarized by Figure 9.6 and Table 9.2. Suppose the project has been underway for seven weeks. Activities A and E have been completed. Activity F has commenced but has three weeks remaining. Activities C and D have not started yet. Activity B has one week remaining (it was not started until week 2). Update the activity schedule for the project. In particular, how has the slack for each activity changed?

6. Consider the following project network and activity times (in weeks):

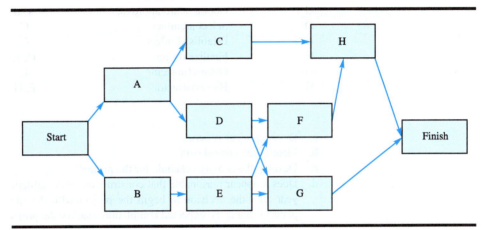

Activity	A	B	C	D	E	F	G	H
Time	5	3	7	6	7	3	10	8

   a. Identify the critical path.

   b. How much time will be needed to complete this project?

   c. Can activity D be delayed without delaying the entire project? If so, by how many weeks?

   d. Can activity C be delayed without delaying the entire project? If so, by how many weeks?

   e. What is the schedule for activity E?

7. Embassy Club Condominium, located on the west coast of Florida, is undertaking a summer renovation of its main building. The project is scheduled to begin May 1, and a September 1 (17-week) completion date is desired. The condominium manager identified the following renovation activities and their estimated times:

Activity	Immediate Predecessor	Time
A	—	3
B	—	1
C	—	2
D	A, B, C	4
E	C, D	5
F	A	3
G	D, F	6
H	E	4

   a. Draw a project network.

   b. What are the critical activities?

   c. What activity has the most slack time?

   d. Will the project be completed by September 1?

8. Colonial State College is considering building a new multipurpose athletic complex on campus. The complex would provide a new gymnasium for intercollegiate basketball games, expanded office space, classrooms, and intramural facilities. The following activities would have to be undertaken before construction can begin:

Activity	Description	Immediate Predecessor	Time (weeks)
A	Survey building site	—	6
B	Develop initial design	—	8
C	Obtain board approval	A, B	12
D	Select architect	C	4
E	Establish budget	C	6
F	Finalize design	D, E	15
G	Obtain financing	E	12
H	Hire contractor	F, G	8

a. Draw a project network.
b. Identify the critical path.
c. Develop the activity schedule for the project.
d. Does it appear reasonable that construction of the athletic complex could begin one year after the decision to begin the project with the site survey and initial design plans? What is the expected completion time for the project?

9. At a local university, the Student Commission on Programming and Entertainment (SCOPE) is preparing to host its first rock concert of the school year. To successfully produce this rock concert, SCOPE has listed the requisite activities and related information in the following table (duration estimates measured in days).

Activity	Immediate Predecessor(s)	Optimistic	Most Probable	Pessimistic
A: Negotiate contract with selected musicians	—	8	10	15
B: Reserve site	—	7	8	9
C: Manage travel logistics for music group	A	5	6	10
D: Screen & hire security personnel	B	3	3	3
E: Arrange advertising & ticketing	B, C	1	5	9
F: Hire parking staff	D	4	7	10
G: Arrange concession sales	E	3	8	10

a. Draw the project network.
b. Compute the expected duration and variance of each activity.
c. Determine the critical path in the project network.
d. What is the expected duration and variance of the critical path?
e. What is the likelihood that the project will be completed within 30 days?
f. If activity B is delayed by six days beyond its early start time, how does this affect the expected project duration?

10. The following estimates of activity times (in days) are available for a small project:

Activity	Optimistic	Most Probable	Pessimistic
A	4	5.0	6
B	8	9.0	10
C	7	7.5	11
D	7	9.0	10
E	6	7.0	9
F	5	6.0	7

    a. Compute the expected activity completion times and the variance for each activity.
    b. An analyst determined that the critical path consists of activities B-D-F. Compute the expected project completion time and the variance of this path.

11. Building a backyard swimming pool consists of nine major activities. The activities and their immediate predecessors are shown. Develop the project network.

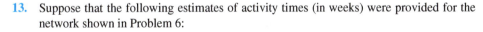

Activity	A	B	C	D	E	F	G	H	I
Immediate Predecessor	—	—	A, B	A, B	B	C	D	D, F	E, G, H

12. Assume that the activity time estimates (in days) for the swimming pool construction project in Problem 11 are as follows:

Activity	Optimistic	Most Probable	Pessimistic
A	3	5	6
B	2	4	6
C	5	6	7
D	7	9	10
E	2	4	6
F	1	2	3
G	5	8	10
H	6	8	10
I	3	4	5

    a. What are the critical activities?
    b. What is the expected time to complete the project?
    c. Based only on the critical path, what is the estimated probability that the project can be completed in 25 or fewer days?

13. Suppose that the following estimates of activity times (in weeks) were provided for the network shown in Problem 6:

Activity	Optimistic	Most Probable	Pessimistic
A	4.0	5.0	6.0
B	2.5	3.0	3.5
C	6.0	7.0	8.0
D	5.0	5.5	9.0
E	5.0	7.0	9.0
F	2.0	3.0	4.0
G	8.0	10.0	12.0
H	6.0	7.0	14.0

Based only on the critical path, what is the estimated probability that the project will be completed

a. Within 21 weeks?
b. Within 22 weeks?
c. Within 25 weeks?

14. Davison Construction Company is building a luxury lakefront home in the Finger Lakes region of New York. Coordination of the architect and subcontractors will require a major effort to meet the 44-week (approximately 10-month) completion date requested by the owner. The Davison project manager prepared the following project network:

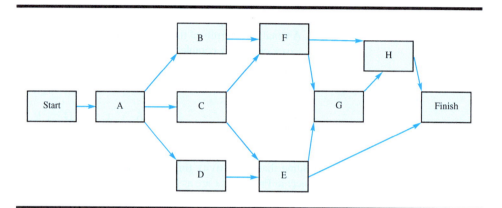

Estimates of the optimistic, most probable, and pessimistic times (in weeks) for the activities are as follows:

Activity	Optimistic	Most Probable	Pessimistic
A	4	8	12
B	6	7	8
C	6	12	18
D	3	5	7
E	6	9	18
F	5	8	17
G	10	15	20
H	5	6	13

a. Find the critical path.
b. What is the expected project completion time?
c. Based only on the critical path, what is the estimated probability the project can be completed in the 44 weeks as requested by the owner?
d. Based only on the critical path, what is the estimated probability the building project could run more than 3 months late? Use 57 weeks for this calculation.
e. What should the construction company tell the owner?

15. Doug Casey is in charge of planning and coordinating next spring's sales management training program for his company. Doug listed the following activity information for this project:

Activity	Description	Immediate Predecessor	Time (weeks)		
			Optimistic	Most Probable	Pessimistic
A	Plan topic	—	1.5	2.0	2.5
B	Obtain speakers	A	2.0	2.5	6.0
C	List meeting locations	—	1.0	2.0	3.0
D	Select location	C	1.5	2.0	2.5
E	Finalize speaker travel plans	B, D	0.5	1.0	1.5
F	Make final check with speakers	E	1.0	2.0	3.0
G	Prepare and mail brochure	B, D	3.0	3.5	7.0
H	Take reservations	G	3.0	4.0	5.0
I	Handle last-minute details	F, H	1.5	2.0	2.5

    a. Draw a project network.

    b. Prepare an activity schedule.

    c. What are the critical activities and what is the expected project completion time?

    d. If Doug wants a 0.99 probability of completing the project on time, how far ahead of the scheduled meeting date should he begin working on the project?

16. Management Decision Systems (MDS) is a consulting company that specializes in the development of decision support systems. MDS has a four-person team working on a current project with a small company to set up a system that scrapes data from a collection of websites and then automatically generates a report for management on a daily basis.

Activity	Description	Immediate Predecessor	Time (Weeks)		
			Optimistic	Most Probable	Pessimistic
A	Report generation	—	1	7	11
B	Web scraping	—	3	8	10
C	Testing	A, B	1	1	1

    a. Construct the project network.

    b. Based solely on the critical path, estimate the probability that the project will be complete within 10 weeks.

    c. Using all paths through project network, estimate the probability that the project will be complete within 10 weeks.

    d. Should you use the estimate in (b) or (c)?

17. The Porsche Shop, founded in 1985 by Dale Jensen, specializes in the restoration of vintage Porsche automobiles. One of Jensen's regular customers asked him to prepare an estimate for the restoration of a 1964 model 356SC Porsche. To estimate the time and cost to perform such a restoration, Jensen broke the restoration process into four separate activities: disassembly and initial preparation work (A), body restoration (B), engine restoration (C), and final assembly (D). Once activity A has been completed, activities B and C can be performed independently of each other; however, activity D can be started only if both activities B and C have been completed. Based on his

inspection of the car, Jensen believes that the following time estimates (in days) are applicable:

Activity	Optimistic	Most Probable	Pessimistic
A	3	4	8
B	5	8	11
C	2	4	6
D	4	5	12

Jensen estimates that the parts needed to restore the body will cost $3000 and that the parts needed to restore the engine will cost $5000. His current labor costs are $400 a day.

a. Develop a project network.
b. What is the expected project completion time?
c. Jensen's business philosophy is based on making decisions using a best- and worst-case scenario. Develop cost estimates for completing the restoration based on both a best- and worst-case analysis. Assume that the total restoration cost is the sum of the labor cost plus the material cost.
d. If Jensen obtains the job with a bid that is based on the costs associated with an expected completion time, what is the probability that he will lose money on the job?
e. If Jensen obtains the job based on a bid of $16,800, what is the probability that he will lose money on the job?

18. The manager of the Oak Hills Swimming Club is planning the club's swimming team program. The first team practice is scheduled for May 1. The activities, their immediate predecessors, and the activity time estimates (in weeks) are as follows:

Activity	Description	Immediate Predecessor	Time (weeks) Optimistic	Most Probable	Pessimistic
A	Meet with board	—	1	1	2
B	Hire coaches	A	4	6	8
C	Reserve pool	A	2	4	6
D	Announce program	B, C	1	2	3
E	Meet with coaches	B	2	3	4
F	Order team suits	A	1	2	3
G	Register swimmers	D	1	2	3
H	Collect fees	G	1	2	3
I	Plan first practice	E, H, F	1	1	1

a. Draw a project network.
b. Develop an activity schedule.
c. What are the critical activities, and what is the expected project completion time?
d. If the club manager plans to start the project on February 1, what is the probability the swimming program will be ready by the scheduled May 1 date (13 weeks)? Should the manager begin planning the swimming program before February 1?

19. The product development group at Landon Corporation has been working on a new computer software product that has the potential to capture a large market share. Through outside sources, Landon's management learned that a competitor is working to introduce a similar product. As a result, Landon's top management increased its pressure on the product development group. The group's leader turned to PERT/CPM as an aid to scheduling the activities remaining before the new product can be brought to the market. The project network is as follows:

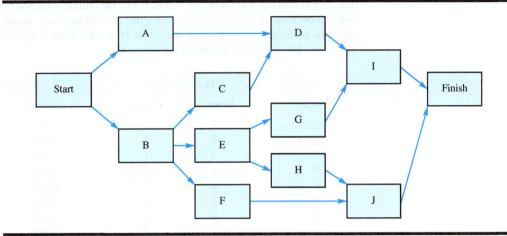

The activity time estimates (in weeks) are as follows:

Activity	Optimistic	Most Probable	Pessimistic
A	3.0	4.0	5.0
B	3.0	3.5	7.0
C	4.0	5.0	6.0
D	2.0	3.0	4.0
E	6.0	10.0	14.0
F	7.5	8.5	12.5
G	4.5	6.0	7.5
H	5.0	6.0	13.0
I	2.0	2.5	6.0
J	4.0	5.0	6.0

a. Develop an activity schedule for this project and identify the critical path activities.
b. What is the probability that the project will be completed so that Landon Corporation may introduce the new product within 25 weeks? Within 30 weeks?

20. Norton Industries is installing a new computer system. The activities, the activity times, and the project network are as follows:

Activity	Time	Activity	Time
A	3	E	4
B	6	F	3
C	2	G	9
D	5	H	3

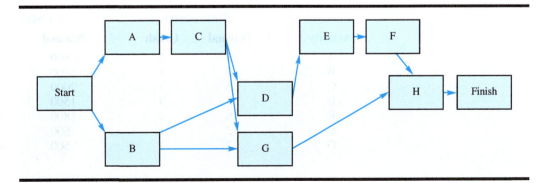

The critical path calculation shows B-D-E-F-H is the critical path, and the expected project completion time is 21 weeks. After viewing this information, management requested overtime be used to complete the project in 16 weeks. Thus, crashing of the project is necessary. The following information is relevant:

Activity	Time (weeks) Normal	Time (weeks) Crash	Cost ($) Normal	Cost ($) Crash
A	3	1	900	1700
B	6	3	2000	4000
C	2	1	500	1000
D	5	3	1800	2400
E	4	3	1500	1850
F	3	1	3000	3900
G	9	4	8000	9800
H	3	2	1000	2000

a. Formulate a linear programming model that can be used to make the crashing decisions for this project.
b. Solve the linear programming model and make the minimum cost crashing decisions. What is the added cost of meeting the 16-week completion time?
c. Develop a complete activity schedule based on the crashed activity times.

21. Consider the following project network and activity times (in days):

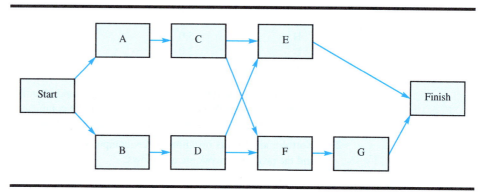

Activity	A	B	C	D	E	F	G
Time	3	2	5	5	6	2	2

The crashing data for this project are as follows:

Activity	Time (days) Normal	Time (days) Crash	Cost ($) Normal	Cost ($) Crash
A	3	2	800	1400
B	2	1	1200	1900
C	5	3	2000	2800
D	5	3	1500	2300
E	6	4	1800	2800
F	2	1	600	1000
G	2	1	500	1000

a. Find the critical path and the expected project completion time.
b. What is the total project cost using the normal times?

22. Refer to Problem 21. Assume that management desires a 12-day project completion time.
  a. Formulate a linear programming model that can be used to assist with the crashing decisions.
  b. What activities should be crashed?
  c. What is the total project cost for the 12-day completion time?

23. Consider the following project network. Note that the normal or expected activity times are denoted τ_i, i = A, B, ..., I. Let x_i = the earliest finish time for activity i. Formulate a linear programming model that can be used to determine the length of the critical path.

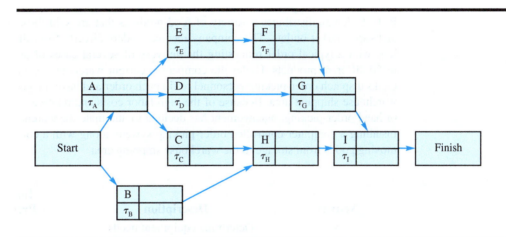

24. Office Automation, Inc., developed a proposal for introducing a new computerized office system that will standardize the electronic archiving of invoices for a particular company. Contained in the proposal is a list of activities that must be accomplished to complete the new office system project. Use the following relevant information about the activities:

Activity	Description	Immediate Predecessor	Time (weeks) Normal	Time (weeks) Crash	Cost ($1000s) Normal	Cost ($1000s) Crash
A	Plan needs	—	10	8	30	70
B	Order equipment	A	8	6	120	150
C	Install equipment	B	10	7	100	160
D	Set up training lab	A	7	6	40	50
E	Conduct training course	D	10	8	50	75
F	Test system	C, E	3	3	60	—

a. Develop a project network.
b. Develop an activity schedule.
c. What are the critical activities, and what is the expected project completion time?
d. Assume that the company wants to complete the project in six months or 26 weeks. What crashing decisions do you recommend to meet the desired completion time at the least possible cost? Work through the network and attempt to make the crashing decisions by inspection.

    e. Develop an activity schedule for the crashed project.
    f. What added project cost is required to meet the six-month completion time?

25. Because Landon Corporation (see Problem 19) is being pressured to complete the product development project at the earliest possible date, the project leader requested that the possibility of crashing the project be evaluated.

    a. Formulate a linear programming model that could be used in making the crashing decisions.
    b. What information would have to be provided before the linear programming model could be implemented?

Case Problem 1   R. C. COLEMAN

R. C. Coleman distributes a variety of food products that are sold through grocery store and supermarket outlets. The company receives orders directly from the individual outlets, with a typical order requesting the delivery of several cases of anywhere from 20 to 50 different products. Under the company's current warehouse operation, warehouse clerks dispatch order-picking personnel to fill each order and have the goods moved to the warehouse shipping area. Because of the high labor costs and relatively low productivity of hand order-picking, management has decided to automate the warehouse operation by installing a computer-controlled order-picking system, along with a conveyor system for moving goods from storage to the warehouse shipping area.

Activity	Description	Immediate Predecessor
A	Determine equipment needs	—
B	Obtain vendor proposals	—
C	Select vendor	A, B
D	Order system	C
E	Design new warehouse layout	C
F	Design warehouse	E
G	Design computer interface	C
H	Interface computer	D, F, G
I	Install system	D, F
J	Train system operators	H
K	Test system	I, J

Activity	Optimistic	Most Probable	Pessimistic
		Time (weeks)	
A	4	6	8
B	6	8	16
C	2	4	6
D	8	10	24
E	7	10	13
F	4	6	8
G	4	6	20
H	4	6	8
I	4	6	14
J	3	4	5
K	2	4	6

R. C. Coleman's director of material management has been named the project manager in charge of the automated warehouse system. After consulting with members of the engineering staff and warehouse management personnel, the director compiled a list of activities associated with the project. The optimistic, most probable, and pessimistic times (in weeks) have also been provided for each activity.

Managerial Report

Develop a report that presents the activity schedule and expected project completion time for the warehouse expansion project. Include a project network in the report. In addition, take into consideration the following issues:

1. R. C. Coleman's top management established a required 40-week completion time for the project. Can this completion time be achieved? Include probability information in your discussion. What recommendations do you have if the 40-week completion time is required?
2. Suppose that management requests that activity times be shortened to provide an 80% chance of meeting the 40-week completion time. If the variance in the project completion time is the same as you found in part (1), how much should the expected project completion time be shortened to achieve the goal of an 80% chance of completion within 40 weeks?
3. Using the expected activity times as the normal times and the following crashing information, determine the activity crashing decisions and revised activity schedule for the warehouse expansion project:

Activity	Crashed Activity Time (weeks)	Cost ($) Normal	Cost ($) Crashed
A	4	1,000	1,900
B	7	1,000	1,800
C	2	1,500	2,700
D	8	2,000	3,200
E	7	5,000	8,000
F	4	3,000	4,100
G	5	8,000	10,250
H	4	5,000	6,400
I	4	10,000	12,400
J	3	4,000	4,400
K	3	5,000	5,500

Appendix 9.1 FINDING CUMULATIVE PROBABILITIES FOR NORMALLY DISTRIBUTED RANDOM VARIABLES

Excel can be used to find the probability a project with uncertain activity times will be completed in some given completion time (assuming the project completion time is normally distributed). We demonstrate this on the Porta-Vac Project we considered in Section 9.2. Recall that management allotted 20 days to complete the project. We have found the z value that corresponds to $T = 20$:

$$z = \frac{20 - 17}{1.65} = 1.82$$

The Excel function NORM.S.DIST is only recognized by Excel 2013. Earlier versions of Excel use the function name NORMSDIST to compute the same value.

Now we will make use of the Excel function

$$=\text{NORM.S.DIST}(z, \text{TRUE})$$

by substituting the value of z we have found into the function (entering "TRUE" for the second argument signifies that we desire the cumulative probability associated with z). Enter the following function into any empty cell in an Excel worksheet:

$$=\text{NORM.S.DIST}(1.82, \text{TRUE})$$

The resulting value is 0.96562, which is the probability that the completion time for the Porta-Vac project will be no more than 20 days.

CHAPTER 7

Inventory Models

CONTENTS

Inventory refers to idle goods or materials held by an organization for use sometime in the future. Items carried in inventory include raw materials, purchased parts, components, subassemblies, work-in-process, finished goods, and supplies. Two primary reasons organizations stock inventory are: (1) to take advantage of economies-of-scale that exist due to the fixed cost of ordering items, and (2) to buffer against uncertainty in customer demand or disruptions in supply. Even though inventory serves an important and essential role, the expense associated with financing and maintaining inventories is a substantial part of the cost of doing business. In large organizations, the cost associated with inventory can run into the millions of dollars.

In applications involving inventory, managers must answer two important questions.

1. *How much* should be ordered when the inventory is replenished?
2. *When* should the inventory be replenished?

The inventory procedure described for the drugstore industry is discussed in detail in Section 10.7.

Virtually every business uses some sort of inventory management model or system to address the preceding questions. Hewlett-Packard works with its retailers to help determine the retailer's inventory replenishment strategies for the printers and other HP products. IBM developed inventory management policies for a range of microelectronic parts that are used in IBM plants as well as sold to a number of outside customers. The Management Science in Action, Inventory Management at CVS Corporation, describes an inventory system used to determine order quantities in the drugstore industry.

The purpose of this chapter is to show how quantitative models can assist in making the how-much-to-order and when-to-order inventory decisions. We will first consider *deterministic* inventory models, for which we assume that the rate of demand for the item is constant or nearly constant. Later we will consider *probabilistic* inventory models, for which the demand for the item fluctuates and can be described only in probabilistic terms.

MANAGEMENT SCIENCE IN ACTION

INVENTORY MANAGEMENT AT CVS CORPORATION*

CVS is one of the largest drugstore chains in the United States. The primary inventory management area in the drugstore involves the numerous basic products that are carried in inventory on an everyday basis. For these items, the most important issue is the replenishment quantity or order size each time an order is placed. In most drugstore chains, basic products are ordered under a periodic review inventory system, with the review period being one week.

The weekly review system uses electronic ordering equipment that scans an order label affixed to the shelf directly below each item. Among other information on the label is the item's replenishment level or order-to-quantity. The store employee placing the order determines the weekly order quantity by counting the number of units of the product on the shelf and subtracting this quantity from the replenishment level. A computer program determines the replenishment quantity for each item in each individual store, based on each store's movement rather than on the company movement. To minimize stock-outs the replenishment quantity is set equal to the store's three-week demand or movement for the product.

*Based on information provided by Bob Carver. (The inventory system described was originally implemented in the CVS stores formerly known as SupeRX.)

10.1   ECONOMIC ORDER QUANTITY (EOQ) MODEL

The cost associated with developing and maintaining inventory is larger than many people think. Models such as the ones presented in this chapter can be used to develop cost-effective inventory management decisions.

The **economic order quantity (EOQ)** model is applicable when the demand for an item shows a constant, or nearly constant, rate and when the entire quantity ordered arrives in inventory at one point in time. The **constant demand rate** assumption means that the same number of units is taken from inventory each period of time such as 5 units every day, 25 units every week, 100 units every four-week period, and so on.

To illustrate the EOQ model, let us consider the situation faced by the R&B Beverage Company. R&B Beverage is a distributor of beer, wine, and soft drink products. From a main warehouse located in Columbus, Ohio, R&B supplies nearly 1000 retail stores with beverage products. The beer inventory, which constitutes about 40% of the company's total inventory, averages approximately 50,000 cases. With an average cost per case of approximately $8, R&B estimates the value of its beer inventory to be $400,000.

One of the most criticized assumptions of the EOQ model is the constant demand rate. Obviously, the model would be inappropriate for items with widely fluctuating and variable demand rates. However, as this example shows, the EOQ model can provide a realistic approximation of the optimal order quantity when demand is relatively stable and occurs at a nearly constant rate.

The warehouse manager decided to conduct a detailed study of the inventory costs associated with Bub Beer, the number-one-selling R&B beer. The purpose of the study is to establish the how-much-to-order and the when-to-order decisions for Bub Beer that will result in the lowest possible total cost. As the first step in the study, the warehouse manager obtained the following demand data for the past 10 weeks:

Week	Demand (cases)
1	2000
2	2025
3	1950
4	2000
5	2100
6	2050
7	2000
8	1975
9	1900
10	2000
Total cases	20,000
Average cases per week	2000

Strictly speaking, these weekly demand figures do not show a constant demand rate. However, given the relatively low variability exhibited by the weekly demand, inventory planning with a constant demand rate of 2000 cases per week appears acceptable. In practice, you will find that the actual inventory situation seldom, if ever, satisfies the assumptions of the model exactly. Thus, in any particular application, the manager must determine whether the model assumptions are close enough to reality for the model to be useful. In this situation, because demand varies from a low of 1900 cases to a high of 2100 cases, the assumption of constant demand of 2000 cases per week appears to be a reasonable approximation.

The how-much-to-order decision involves selecting an order quantity that draws a compromise between (1) keeping small inventories and ordering frequently, and (2) keeping large inventories and ordering infrequently. The first alternative can result in undesirably high ordering costs, while the second alternative can result in undesirably high inventory holding costs. To find an optimal compromise between these conflicting alternatives, let us consider a mathematical model that shows the total cost as the sum of the holding cost and the ordering cost.[1]

As with other quantitative models, accurate estimates of cost parameters are critical. In the EOQ model, estimates of both the inventory holding cost and the ordering cost are needed. Also see footnote 1, which refers to relevant costs.

Holding costs are the costs associated with maintaining or carrying a given level of inventory; these costs depend on the size of the inventory. The first holding cost to consider is the cost of financing the inventory investment. When a firm borrows money, it incurs an interest charge. If the firm uses its own money, it experiences an opportunity cost associated with not being able to use the money for other investments. In either case, an interest cost exists for the capital tied up in inventory. This **cost of capital** is usually expressed as a percentage of the amount invested. R&B estimates its cost of capital at an annual rate of 18%.

A number of other holding costs, such as insurance, taxes, breakage, pilferage, and warehouse overhead, also depend on the value of the inventory. R&B estimates these other costs at an annual rate of approximately 7% of the value of its inventory. Thus, the total holding cost for the R&B beer inventory is 18% + 7% = 25% of the value of the inventory. The cost of one case of Bub Beer is $8. With an annual holding cost rate of 25%, the cost of holding one case of Bub Beer in inventory for 1 year is 0.25($8) = $2.00.

The next step in the inventory analysis is to determine the **ordering cost**. This cost, which is considered fixed regardless of the order quantity, covers the preparation of the voucher; and the processing of the order, including payment, postage, telephone, transportation, invoice verification, receiving, and so on. For R&B Beverage, the largest portion of the ordering cost involves the salaries of the purchasers. An analysis of the purchasing process showed that a purchaser spends approximately 45 minutes preparing and processing an order for Bub Beer. With a wage rate and fringe benefit cost for purchasers of $20 per hour, the labor portion of the ordering cost is $15. Making allowances for paper, postage, telephone, transportation, and receiving costs at $17 per order, the manager estimates that the ordering cost is $32 per order. That is, R&B is paying $32 per order regardless of the quantity requested in the order.

The holding cost, ordering cost, and demand information are the three data items that must be known prior to the use of the EOQ model. After developing these data for the R&B problem, we can look at how they are used to develop a total cost model. We begin by defining Q as the order quantity. Thus, the how-much-to-order decision involves finding the value of Q that will minimize the sum of holding and ordering costs.

The inventory for Bub Beer will have a maximum value of Q units when an order of size Q is received from the supplier. R&B will then satisfy customer demand from inventory until the inventory is depleted, at which time another shipment of Q units will be received. Thus, assuming a constant demand, the graph of the inventory for Bub Beer is as shown in Figure 10.1. Note that the graph indicates an average inventory of $\frac{1}{2}Q$ for the period in question. This level should appear reasonable because the maximum inventory is Q, the minimum is zero, and the inventory declines at a constant rate over the period.

Figure 10.1 shows the inventory pattern during one order cycle of length T. As time goes on, this pattern will repeat. The complete inventory pattern is shown in Figure 10.2. If the average inventory during each cycle is $\frac{1}{2}Q$, the average inventory over any number of cycles is also $\frac{1}{2}Q$.

Most inventory cost models use an annual cost. Thus, demand should be expressed in units per year, and inventory holding cost should be based on an annual rate.

The holding cost can be calculated using the average inventory. That is, we can calculate the holding cost by multiplying the average inventory by the cost of carrying one unit in inventory for the stated period. The period selected for the model is up to you; it could be one week, one month, one year, or more. However, because the holding cost for many

---

[1] Even though analysts typically refer to "total cost" models for inventory systems, often these models describe only the total variable or total relevant costs for the decision being considered. Costs that are not affected by the how-much-to-order decision are considered fixed or constant and are not included in the model.

FIGURE 10.1   INVENTORY FOR BUB BEER

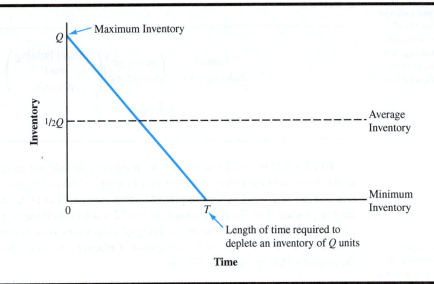

FIGURE 10.2   INVENTORY PATTERN FOR THE EOQ INVENTORY MODEL

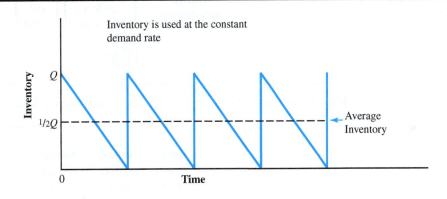

industries and businesses is expressed as an *annual* percentage, most inventory models are developed on an *annual* cost basis.

Let

$$I = \text{annual holding cost rate}$$

$$C = \text{unit cost of the inventory item}$$

$$C_h = \text{annual cost of holding one unit in inventory}$$

The annual cost of holding one unit in inventory is

$$C_h = IC \tag{10.1}$$

C_h *is the cost of holding one unit in inventory for one year. Because smaller order quantities Q will result in lower inventory, total annual holding cost can be reduced by using smaller order quantities.*

The general equation for the annual holding cost for the average inventory of $\frac{1}{2}Q$ units is as follows:

$$\begin{pmatrix} \text{Annual} \\ \text{holding cost} \end{pmatrix} = \begin{pmatrix} \text{Average} \\ \text{inventory} \end{pmatrix} \begin{pmatrix} \text{Annual holding} \\ \text{cost} \\ \text{per unit} \end{pmatrix}$$

$$= \frac{1}{2} Q C_h \qquad (10.2)$$

To complete the total cost model, we must now include the annual ordering cost. The goal is to express the annual ordering cost in terms of the order quantity Q. The first question is, How many orders will be placed during the year? Let D denote the annual demand for the product. For R&B Beverage, D = (52 weeks)(2000 cases per week) = 104,000 cases per year. We know that by ordering Q units every time we order, we will have to place D/Q orders per year. If C_o is the cost of placing one order, the general equation for the annual ordering cost is as follows:

C_o, *the fixed cost per order, is independent of the amount ordered. For a given annual demand of D units, the total annual ordering cost can be reduced by using larger order quantities.*

$$\begin{pmatrix} \text{Annual} \\ \text{ordering cost} \end{pmatrix} = \begin{pmatrix} \text{Number of} \\ \text{orders} \\ \text{per year} \end{pmatrix} \begin{pmatrix} \text{Cost} \\ \text{per} \\ \text{order} \end{pmatrix}$$

$$= \left(\frac{D}{Q} \right) C_o \qquad (10.3)$$

Thus, the total annual cost, denoted TC, can be expressed as follows:

$$\begin{matrix} \text{Total} & \text{Annual} & \text{Annual} \\ \text{annual} = & \text{holding} + & \text{ordering} \\ \text{cost} & \text{cost} & \text{cost} \end{matrix}$$

$$TC = \frac{1}{2} Q C_h + \frac{D}{Q} C_o \qquad (10.4)$$

Using the Bub Beer data [$C_h = IC = (0.25)(\$8) = \$2$, $C_o = \$32$, and $D = 104,000$], the total annual cost model is

$$TC = \frac{1}{2} Q(\$2) + \frac{104,000}{Q} (\$32) = Q + \frac{3,328,000}{Q}$$

The development of the total cost model goes a long way toward solving the inventory problem. We now are able to express the total annual cost as a function of *how much* should be ordered. The development of a realistic total cost model is perhaps the most important part of the application of quantitative methods to inventory decision making. Equation (10.4) is the general total cost equation for inventory situations for which the assumptions of the economic order quantity model are valid.

The How-Much-to-Order Decision

The next step is to find the order quantity Q that will minimize the total annual cost for Bub Beer. Using a trial-and-error approach, we can compute the total annual cost for several possible order quantities. As a starting point, let us consider $Q = 8000$. The total annual cost for Bub Beer is

$$TC = Q + \frac{3{,}328{,}000}{Q}$$

$$= 8000 + \frac{3{,}328{,}000}{8000} = \$8416$$

A trial order quantity of 5000 gives

$$TC = 5000 + \frac{3{,}328{,}000}{5000} = \$5666$$

The results of several other trial order quantities are shown in Table 10.1. It shows the lowest cost solution to be about 2000 cases. Graphs of the annual holding and ordering costs and total annual costs are shown in Figure 10.3.

The advantage of the trial-and-error approach is that it is rather easy to do and provides the total annual cost for a number of possible order quantity decisions. In this case, the minimum cost order quantity appears to be approximately 2000 cases. The disadvantage of this approach, however, is that it does not provide the exact minimum cost order quantity.

Refer to Figure 10.3. The minimum total cost order quantity is denoted by an order size of Q^*. By using differential calculus, it can be shown (see Appendix 10.1) that the value of Q^* that minimizes the total annual cost is given by the formula

The EOQ formula determines the optimal order quantity by balancing the annual holding cost and the annual ordering cost.

$$Q^* = \sqrt{\frac{2DC_o}{C_h}} \qquad (10.5)$$

This formula is referred to as the *economic order quantity (EOQ) formula*.

Using equation (10.5), the minimum total annual cost order quantity for Bub Beer is

$$Q^* = \sqrt{\frac{2(104{,}000)32}{2}} = 1824 \text{ cases}$$

TABLE 10.1 ANNUAL HOLDING, ORDERING, AND TOTAL COSTS FOR VARIOUS ORDER QUANTITIES OF BUB BEER

	Annual Cost		
Order Quantity	**Holding**	**Ordering**	**Total**
5000	$5000	$ 666	$5666
4000	$4000	$ 832	$4832
3000	$3000	$1109	$4109
2000	$2000	$1664	$3664
1000	$1000	$3328	$4328

FIGURE 10.3   ANNUAL HOLDING, ORDERING, AND TOTAL COSTS FOR BUB BEER

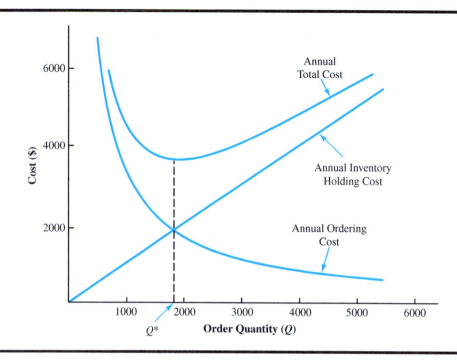

Problem 2 at the end of the chapter asks you to show that equal holding and ordering costs is a property of the EOQ model.

The reorder point is expressed in terms of inventory position, the amount of inventory on hand plus the amount on order. With short lead times, inventory position is usually the same as the inventory on hand. However, with long lead times, inventory position may be larger than inventory on hand.

The use of an order quantity of 1824 in equation (10.4) shows that the minimum cost inventory policy for Bub Beer has a total annual cost of $3649. Note that $Q^* = 1824$ balances the holding and ordering costs. Check for yourself to see that these costs are equal.[2]

The When-to-Order Decision

Now that we know how much to order, we want to address the question of *when* to order. To answer this question, we need to introduce the concept of inventory position. The **inventory position** is defined as the amount of inventory on hand plus the amount of inventory on order. The when-to-order decision is expressed in terms of a **reorder point**—the inventory position at which a new order should be placed.

The manufacturer of Bub Beer guarantees a two-day delivery on any order placed by R&B Beverage. Hence, assuming R&B Beverage operates 250 days per year, the annual demand of 104,000 cases implies a daily demand of $104,000/250 = 416$ cases. Thus, we expect (2 days)(416 cases per day) = 832 cases of Bub to be sold during the two days it takes a new order to reach the R&B warehouse. In inventory terminology, the two-day delivery period is referred to as the **lead time** for a new order, and the 832-case demand anticipated during this period is referred to as the **lead-time demand**. Thus, R&B should order a new shipment of Bub Beer from the manufacturer when the inventory reaches 832 cases. For inventory systems using the constant demand rate assumption and a fixed

---

[2]Actually, Q^* from equation (10.5) is 1824.28, but because we cannot order fractional cases of beer, a Q^* of 1824 is shown. This value of Q^* may cause a few cents deviation between the two costs. If Q^* is used at its exact value, the holding and ordering costs will be exactly the same.

lead time, the reorder point is the same as the lead-time demand. For these systems, the general expression for the reorder point is as follows:

$$r = dm \qquad (10.6)$$

where

$$r = \text{reorder point}$$
$$d = \text{demand per day}$$
$$m = \text{lead time for a new order in days}$$

The question of how frequently the order will be placed can now be answered. The period between orders is referred to as the **cycle time**. Previously in equation (10.3), we defined D/Q as the number of orders that will be placed in a year. Thus, $D/Q^* = 104,000/1824 = 57$ is the number of orders R&B Beverage will place for Bub Beer each year. If R&B places 57 orders over 250 working days, it will order approximately every $250/57 = 4.39$ working days. Thus, the cycle time is 4.39 working days. The general expression for a cycle time[3] of T days is given by

$$T = \frac{250}{D/Q^*} = \frac{250Q^*}{D} \qquad (10.7)$$

Sensitivity Analysis for the EOQ Model

Even though substantial time may have been spent in arriving at the cost per order (\$32) and the holding cost rate (25%), we should realize that these figures are at best good estimates. Thus, we may want to consider how much the recommended order quantity would change with different estimated ordering and holding costs. To determine the effects of various cost scenarios, we can calculate the recommended order quantity under several different cost conditions. Table 10.2 shows the minimum total cost order quantity for several cost possibilities. As you can see from the table, the value of Q^* appears relatively stable, even with some variations in the cost estimates. Based on these results, the best order quantity for Bub Beer is in the range of 1700–2000 cases. If operated properly, the total cost for the Bub Beer inventory system should be close to \$3400–\$3800 per year. We also note that little risk is associated with implementing the calculated order quantity of 1824. For example, if R&B implements an order quantity of 1824 cases (using cost estimates based on \$32 per order and 25% annual holding rate), but the actual cost per order turns out to be \$34 and the actual annual holding rate turns out to be 24%, then R&B experiences only a \$5 increase (\$3690–\$3685) in the total annual cost.

From the preceding analysis, we would say that this EOQ model is insensitive to small variations or errors in the cost estimates. This insensitivity is a property of EOQ models in general, which indicates that if we have at least reasonable estimates of ordering cost and holding cost, we can expect to obtain a good approximation of the true minimum cost order quantity.

---

[3]This general expression for cycle time is based on 250 working days per year. If the firm operated 300 working days per year and wanted to express cycle time in terms of working days, the cycle time would be given by $T = 300Q^*/D$.

TABLE 10.2   OPTIMAL ORDER QUANTITIES FOR SEVERAL COST POSSIBILITIES

Possible Inventory Holding Cost (%)	Possible Cost per Order	Optimal Order Quantity (Q*)	Projected Total Annual Cost	
			Using Q*	Using Q = 1824
24	$30	1803	$3461	$3462
24	34	1919	3685	3690
26	30	1732	3603	3607
26	34	1844	3835	3836

Excel Solution of the EOQ Model

Inventory models such as the EOQ model are easily implemented with the aid of spreadsheets. The Excel EOQ worksheet for Bub Beer is shown in Figure 10.4. The worksheet view of the formulas is on the left and the worksheet view of the values is on the right. Data on annual demand, ordering cost, annual inventory holding cost rate, cost per unit, working days per year, and lead time in days are input in cells B3 to B8. The appropriate EOQ model formulas, which determine the optimal inventory policy, are placed in cells B13 to B21. For example, cell B13 computes the optimal economic order quantity 1824.28, and

FIGURE 10.4   WORKSHEET FOR THE BUB BEER EOQ INVENTORY MODEL

WEB file

EOQ

	A	B
1	**Economic Order Quantity**	
2		
3	Annual Demand	104000
4	Ordering Cost	32
5	Annual Inventory Holding Rate %	25
6	Cost per Unit	8
7	Working Days per Year	250
8	Lead Time (Days)	2
9		
10		
11	**Optimal Inventory Policy**	
12		
13	Economic Order Quantity	=SQRT(2*B3*B4/(B5/100*B6))
14	Annual Inventory Holding Cost	=(1/2)*B13*(B5/100*B6)
15	Annual Ordering Cost	=(B3/B13)*B4
16	Total Annual Cost	=B14+B15
17	Maximum Inventory Level	=B13
18	Average Inventory Level	=B17/2
19	Reorder Point	=(B3/B7)*B8
20	Number of Orders per Year	=B3/B13
21	Cycle Time (Days)	=B7/B20

	A	B
1	**Economic Order Quantity**	
2		
3	Annual Demand	104,000
4	Ordering Cost	$32.00
5	Annual Inventory Holding Rate %	25
6	Cost per Unit	$8.00
7	Working Days per Year	250
8	Lead Time (Days)	2
9		
10		
11	**Optimal Inventory Policy**	
12		
13	Economic Order Quantity	1824.28
14	Annual Inventory Holding Cost	$1,824.28
15	Annual Ordering Cost	$1,824.28
16	Total Annual Cost	$3,648.56
17	Maximum Inventory Level	1,824.28
18	Average Inventory Level	912.14
19	Reorder Point	832.00
20	Number of Orders per Year	57.01
21	Cycle Time (Days)	4.39

TABLE 10.3   THE EOQ MODEL ASSUMPTIONS

1. Demand D is deterministic and occurs at a constant rate.
2. The order quantity Q is the same for each order. The inventory level increases by Q units each time an order is received.
3. The cost per order, C_o, is constant and does not depend on the quantity ordered.
4. The purchase cost per unit, C, is constant and does not depend on the quantity ordered.
5. The inventory holding cost per unit per time period, C_h, is constant. The total inventory holding cost depends on both C_h and the size of the inventory.
6. Shortages such as stock-outs or backorders are not permitted.
7. The lead time for an order is constant.
8. The inventory position is reviewed continuously. As a result, an order is placed as soon as the inventory position reaches the reorder point.

cell B16 computes the total annual cost $3648.56. If sensitivity analysis is desired, one or more of the input data values can be modified. The impact of any change or changes on the optimal inventory policy will then appear in the worksheet.

The Excel worksheet in Figure 10.4 is a template that can be used for the EOQ model. This worksheet and similar Excel worksheets for the other inventory models presented in this chapter are available at the WEBfiles link on the website that accompanies this text.

Summary of the EOQ Model Assumptions

You should carefully review the assumptions of the inventory model before applying it in an actual situation. Several inventory models discussed later in this chapter alter one or more of the assumptions of the EOQ model.

To use the optimal order quantity and reorder point model described in this section, an analyst must make assumptions about how the inventory system operates. The EOQ model with its economic order quantity formula is based on some specific assumptions about the R&B inventory system. A summary of the assumptions for this model is provided in Table 10.3. Before using the EOQ formula, carefully review these assumptions to ensure that they are applicable to the inventory system being analyzed. If the assumptions are not reasonable, seek a different inventory model.

Various types of inventory systems are used in practice, and the inventory models presented in the following sections alter one or more of the EOQ model assumptions shown in Table 10.3. When the assumptions change, a different inventory model with different optimal operating policies becomes necessary.

NOTES AND COMMENTS

1. With relatively long lead times, the lead-time demand and the resulting reorder point r, determined by equation (10.6), may exceed Q^*. If this condition occurs, at least one order will be outstanding when a new order is placed. For example, assume that Bub Beer has a lead time of $m = 6$ days. With a daily demand of $d = 432$ cases, equation (10.6) shows that the reorder point would be $r = dm = 6 \times 432 = 2592$ cases. Note that this reorder point exceeds $Q^* = 1824$ which also corresponds to the maximum inventory level (see Figure 10.1). At first glance, this seems impossible—how can we order when inventory drops to 2592 cases when the maximum inventory level is 1824? The key is to remember that the reorder point is expressed in terms of inventory position which equals cases "on-hand" + cases "on the way." Thus, to interpret the $r = 2592$, realize that 2592 total cases = will occur when there are 1824 cases on the way (from a previous order) and 768 on-hand. So, the model states that we should place another order when the on-hand inventory level is 768 cases. That is, because the lead time is so long (6 days), we have to place an order of Q units before the last order of Q units has even arrived!

10.2   ECONOMIC PRODUCTION LOT SIZE MODEL

The inventory model presented in this section is similar to the EOQ model in that we are attempting to determine *how much* we should order and *when* the order should be placed. We again assume a constant demand rate. However, instead of assuming that the order arrives in a shipment of size Q^*, as in the EOQ model, we assume that units are supplied to inventory at a constant rate over several days or several weeks. The **constant supply rate** assumption implies that the same number of units is supplied to inventory each period of time (e.g., 10 units every day or 50 units every week). This model is designed for production situations for which, once an order is placed, production begins and a constant number of units is added to inventory each day until the production run has been completed.

The inventory model in this section alters assumption 2 of the EOQ model (see Table 10.3). The assumption concerning the arrival of Q units each time an order is received is changed to a constant production supply rate.

If we have a production system that produces 50 units per day and we decide to schedule 10 days of production, we have a 50(10) = 500-unit production lot size. The **lot size** is the number of units in an order. In general, if we let Q indicate the production lot size, the approach to the inventory decisions is similar to the EOQ model; that is, we build a holding and ordering cost model that expresses the total cost as a function of the production lot size. Then we attempt to find the production lot size that minimizes the total cost.

One other condition that should be mentioned at this time is that the model only applies to situations where the production rate is greater than the demand rate; the production system must be able to satisfy demand. For instance, if the constant demand rate is 400 units per day, the production rate must be at least 400 units per day to satisfy demand.

During the production run, demand reduces the inventory while production adds to inventory. Because we assume that the production rate exceeds the demand rate, each day during a production run we produce more units than are demanded. Thus, the excess production causes a gradual inventory buildup during the production period. When the production run is completed, the continuing demand causes the inventory to gradually decline until a new production run is started. The inventory pattern for this system is shown in Figure 10.5.

This model differs from the EOQ model in that a setup cost replaces the ordering cost, and the saw-tooth inventory pattern shown in Figure 10.5 differs from the inventory pattern shown in Figure 10.2.

As in the EOQ model, we are now dealing with two costs, the holding cost and the ordering cost. Here the holding cost is identical to the definition in the EOQ model, but the interpretation of the ordering cost is slightly different. In fact, in a production situation the ordering cost is more correctly referred to as the production **setup cost**. This cost, which includes labor, material, and lost production costs incurred while preparing

FIGURE 10.5   INVENTORY PATTERN FOR THE PRODUCTION LOT SIZE
INVENTORY MODEL

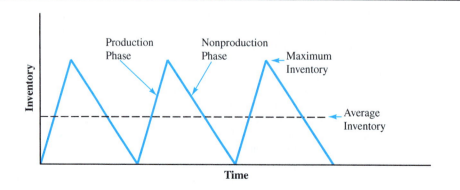

the production system for operation, is a fixed cost that occurs for every production run regardless of the production lot size.

Total Cost Model

Let us begin building the production lot size model by writing the holding cost in terms of the production lot size Q. Again, the approach is to develop an expression for average inventory and then establish the holding costs associated with the average inventory. We use a one-year time period and an annual cost for the model.

In the EOQ model the average inventory is one-half the maximum inventory, or $\frac{1}{2}Q$. Figure 10.5 shows that for a production lot size model, a constant inventory buildup rate occurs during the production run, and a constant inventory depletion rate occurs during the nonproduction period; thus, the average inventory will be one-half the maximum inventory. However, in this inventory system the production lot size Q does not go into inventory at one point in time, and thus the inventory never reaches a level of Q units.

To show how we can compute the maximum inventory, let

$$d = \text{daily demand rate}$$
$$p = \text{daily production rate}$$
$$t = \text{number of days for a production run}$$

At this point, the logic of the production lot size model is easier to follow using a daily demand rate d and a daily production rate p. However, when the total annual cost model is eventually developed, we recommend that inputs to the model be expressed in terms of the annual demand rate D and the annual production rate P.

Because we are assuming that p will be larger than d, the daily inventory buildup rate during the production phase is $p - d$. If we run production for t days and place $p - d$ units in inventory each day, the inventory at the end of the production run will be $(p - d)t$. From Figure 10.5 we can see that the inventory at the end of the production run is also the maximum inventory. Thus,

$$\text{Maximum inventory} = (p - d)t \qquad (10.8)$$

If we know we are producing a production lot size of Q units at a daily production rate of p units, then $Q = pt$, and the length of the production run t must be

$$t = \frac{Q}{p} \text{ days} \qquad (10.9)$$

Thus,

$$\text{Maximum inventory} = (p - d)t = (p - d)\left(\frac{Q}{p}\right)$$
$$= \left(1 - \frac{d}{p}\right)Q \qquad (10.10)$$

The average inventory, which is one-half the maximum inventory, is given by

$$\text{Average inventory} = \frac{1}{2}\left(1 - \frac{d}{p}\right)Q \qquad (10.11)$$

With an annual per-unit holding cost of C_h, the general equation for annual holding cost is as follows:

$$\text{Annual} \atop \text{holding cost} = \left(\text{Average} \atop \text{inventory}\right)\left(\text{Annual} \atop \text{cost} \atop \text{per unit}\right)$$

$$= \frac{1}{2}\left(1 - \frac{d}{p}\right)QC_h \qquad (10.12)$$

If D is the annual demand for the product and C_o is the setup cost for a production run, then the annual setup cost, which takes the place of the annual ordering cost in the EOQ model, is as follows:

$$\text{Annual setup cost} = \left(\text{Number of production} \atop \text{runs per year}\right)\left(\text{Setup cost} \atop \text{per run}\right)$$

$$= \frac{D}{Q}C_o \qquad (10.13)$$

Thus, the total annual cost (TC) model is

$$TC = \frac{1}{2}\left(1 - \frac{d}{p}\right)QC_h + \frac{D}{Q}C_o \qquad (10.14)$$

Suppose that a production facility operates 250 days per year. Then we can write daily demand d in terms of annual demand D as follows:

$$d = \frac{D}{250}$$

Now let P denote the annual production for the product if the product were produced every day. Then

$$P = 250p \quad \text{and} \quad p = \frac{P}{250}$$

Thus,[4]

$$\frac{d}{p} = \frac{D/250}{P/250} = \frac{D}{P}$$

Therefore, we can write the total annual cost model as follows:

$$TC = \frac{1}{2}\left(1 - \frac{D}{P}\right)QC_h + \frac{D}{Q}C_o \qquad (10.15)$$

---

[4]The ratio $d/p = D/P$ holds regardless of the number of days of operation; 250 days is used here merely as an illustration.

Equations (10.14) and (10.15) are equivalent. However, equation (10.15) may be used more frequently because an *annual* cost model tends to make the analyst think in terms of collecting *annual* demand data (*D*) and *annual* production data (*P*) rather than daily data.

Economic Production Lot Size

As the production rate P approaches infinity, D/P approaches zero. In this case, equation (10.16) is equivalent to the EOQ model in equation (10.5).

Given estimates of the holding cost (C_h), setup cost (C_o), annual demand rate (*D*), and annual production rate (*P*), we could use a trial-and-error approach to compute the total annual cost for various production lot sizes (*Q*). However, trial and error is not necessary; we can use the minimum cost formula for Q^* that has been developed using differential calculus (see Appendix 10.2). The equation is as follows:

$$Q^* = \sqrt{\frac{2DC_o}{(1 - D/P)C_h}} \qquad (10.16)$$

LotSize

An Example Beauty Bar Soap is produced on a production line that has an annual capacity of 60,000 cases. The annual demand is estimated at 26,000 cases, with the demand rate essentially constant throughout the year. The cleaning, preparation, and setup of the production line cost approximately $135. The manufacturing cost per case is $4.50, and the annual holding cost is figured at a 24% rate. Thus, $C_h = IC = 0.24(\$4.50) = \$1.08$. What is the recommended production lot size?

Using equation (10.16), we have

$$Q^* = \sqrt{\frac{2(26,000)(135)}{(1 - 26,000/60,000)(1.08)}} = 3387$$

Work Problem 13 as an example of an economic production lot size model.

The total annual cost using equation (10.15) and $Q^* = 3387$ is $2073.

Other relevant data include a five-day lead time to schedule and set up a production run and 250 working days per year. Thus, the lead-time demand of $(26,000/250)(5) = 520$ cases is the reorder point. The cycle time is the time between production runs. Using equation (10.7), the cycle time is $T = 250Q^*/D = [(250)(3387)]/26,000$, or 33 working days. Thus, we should plan a production run of 3387 units every 33 working days.

10.3   INVENTORY MODEL WITH PLANNED SHORTAGES

A **shortage** or **stock-out** occurs when demand exceeds the amount of inventory on hand. In many situations, shortages are undesirable and should be avoided if at all possible. However, in other cases it may be desirable—from an economic point of view—to plan for and allow shortages. In practice, these types of situations are most commonly found where the value of the inventory per unit is high and hence the holding cost is high. An example of this type of situation is a new car dealer's inventory. Often a specific car that a customer wants is not in stock. However, if the customer is willing to wait a few weeks, the dealer is usually able to order the car.

The assumptions of the EOQ model in Table 10.3 apply to this inventory model with the exception that shortages, referred to as backorders, are now permitted.

The model developed in this section takes into account a type of shortage known as a **backorder**. In a backorder situation, we assume that when a customer places an order and discovers that the supplier is out of stock, the customer waits until the new shipment arrives, and then the order is filled. Frequently, the waiting period in backorder situations is relatively short. Thus, by promising the customer top priority and immediate delivery when the goods become available, companies may be able to convince the customer to wait until the order arrives. In these cases, the backorder assumption is valid.

The backorder model that we develop is an extension of the EOQ model presented in Section 10.1. We use the EOQ model for which all goods arrive in inventory at one time and are subject to a constant demand rate. If we let S indicate the number of backorders that have accumulated by the time a new shipment of size Q is received, then the inventory system for the backorder case has the following characteristics:

- If S backorders exist when a new shipment of size Q arrives, then S backorders are shipped to the appropriate customers, and the remaining $Q - S$ units are placed in inventory. Therefore, $Q - S$ is the maximum inventory.
- The inventory cycle of T days is divided into two distinct phases: t_1 days when inventory is on hand and orders are filled as they occur, and t_2 days when stock-outs occur and all new orders are placed on backorder.

The inventory pattern for the inventory model with backorders, where negative inventory represents the number of backorders, is shown in Figure 10.6.

With the inventory pattern now defined, we can proceed with the basic step of all inventory models—namely, the development of a total cost model. For the inventory model with backorders, we encounter the usual holding costs and ordering costs. We also incur a backorder cost in terms of the labor and special delivery costs directly associated with the handling of the backorders. Another portion of the backorder cost accounts for the loss of goodwill because some customers will have to wait for their orders. Because the **goodwill cost** depends on how long a customer has to wait, it is customary to adopt the convention of expressing backorder cost in terms of the cost of having a unit on backorder for a stated period of time. This method of costing backorders on a time basis is similar to the method used to compute the inventory holding cost, and we can use it to compute a total annual cost of backorders once the average backorder level and the backorder cost per unit per period are known.

Let us begin the development of a total cost model by calculating the average inventory for a hypothetical problem. If we have an average inventory of two units for three days and no inventory on the fourth day, what is the average inventory over the four-day period? It is

$$\frac{2 \text{ units (3 days)} + 0 \text{ units (1 day)}}{4 \text{ days}} = \frac{6}{4} = 1.5 \text{ units}$$

FIGURE 10.6   INVENTORY PATTERN FOR AN INVENTORY MODEL WITH BACKORDERS

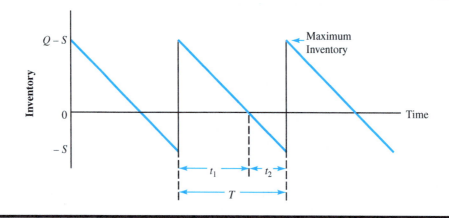

Refer to Figure 10.6. You can see that this situation is what happens in the backorder model. With a maximum inventory of $Q - S$ units, the t_1 days we have inventory on hand will have an average inventory of $(Q - S)/2$. No inventory is carried for the t_2 days in which we experience backorders. Thus, over the total cycle time of $T = t_1 + t_2$ days, we can compute the average inventory as follows:

$$\text{Average inventory} = \frac{\frac{1}{2}(Q - S)t_1 + 0t_2}{t_1 + t_2} = \frac{\frac{1}{2}(Q - S)t_1}{T} \qquad (10.17)$$

Can we find other ways of expressing t_1 and T? Because we know that the maximum inventory is $Q - S$ and that d represents the constant daily demand, we have

$$t_1 = \frac{Q - S}{d} \text{ days} \qquad (10.18)$$

That is, the maximum inventory of $Q - S$ units will be used up in $(Q - S)/d$ days. Because Q units are ordered for each cycle, we know the length of a cycle must be

$$T = \frac{Q}{d} \text{ days} \qquad (10.19)$$

Combining equations (10.18) and (10.19) with equation (10.17), we can compute the average inventory as follows:

$$\text{Average inventory} = \frac{\frac{1}{2}(Q - S)[(Q - S)/d]}{Q/d} = \frac{(Q - S)^2}{2Q} \qquad (10.20)$$

Thus, the average inventory is expressed in terms of two inventory decisions: how much we will order (Q) and the maximum number of backorders (S).

The formula for the annual number of orders placed using this model is identical to that for the EOQ model. With D representing the annual demand, we have

$$\text{Annual number of orders} = \frac{D}{Q} \qquad (10.21)$$

The next step is to develop an expression for the average backorder level. Because we know the maximum for backorders is S, we can use the same logic we used to establish average inventory in finding the average number of backorders. We have an average number of backorders during the period t_2 of $\frac{1}{2}$ the maximum number of backorders or $\frac{1}{2}S$. We do not have any backorders during the t_1 days we have inventory; therefore we can calculate the average backorders in a manner similar to equation (10.17). Using this approach, we have

$$\text{Average backorders} = \frac{0t_1 + (S/2)t_2}{T} = \frac{(S/2)t_2}{T} \qquad (10.22)$$

When we let the maximum number of backorders reach an amount S at a daily rate of d, the length of the backorder portion of the inventory cycle is

$$t_2 = \frac{S}{d} \qquad (10.23)$$

Using equations (10.23) and (10.19) in equation (10.22), we have

$$\text{Average backorders} = \frac{(S/2)(S/d)}{Q/d} = \frac{S^2}{2Q} \qquad (10.24)$$

Let

The backorder cost C_b is one of the most difficult costs to estimate in inventory models. The reason is that it attempts to measure the cost associated with the loss of goodwill when a customer must wait for an order. Expressing this cost on an annual basis adds to the difficulty.

C_h = cost to hold one unit in inventory for one year

C_o = cost per order

C_b = cost to maintain one unit on backorder for one year

The total annual cost (TC) for the inventory model with backorders becomes

$$TC = \frac{(Q - S)^2}{2Q} C_h + \frac{D}{Q} C_o + \frac{S^2}{2Q} C_b \qquad (10.25)$$

Given C_h, C_o, and C_b and the annual demand D, differential calculus can be used to show that the minimum cost values for the order quantity Q^* and the planned backorders S^* are as follows:

$$Q^* = \sqrt{\frac{2DC_o}{C_h}\left(\frac{C_h + C_b}{C_b}\right)} \qquad (10.26)$$

$$S^* = Q^*\left(\frac{C_h}{C_h + C_b}\right) \qquad (10.27)$$

Shortage

An Example   Suppose that the Higley Radio Components Company has a product for which the assumptions of the inventory model with backorders are valid. Information obtained by the company is as follows:

$$D = 2000 \text{ units per year}$$
$$I = 20\%$$
$$C = \$50 \text{ per unit}$$
$$C_h = IC = (0.20)(\$50) = \$10 \text{ per unit per year}$$
$$C_o = \$25 = \text{ per order}$$

An inventory situation that incorporates backorder costs is considered in Problem 15.

The company is considering the possibility of allowing some backorders to occur for the product. The annual backorder cost is estimated to be \$30 per unit per year. Using equations (10.26) and (10.27), we have

$$Q^* = \sqrt{\frac{2(2000)(25)}{10}\left(\frac{10+30}{30}\right)} = 115$$

and

$$S^* = 115\left(\frac{10}{10+30}\right) = 29$$

If this solution is implemented, the system will operate with the following properties:

$$\text{Maximum inventory} = Q - S = 115 - 29 = 86$$

$$\text{Cycle time} = T = \frac{Q}{D}(250) = \frac{115}{2000}(250) = 14 \text{ working days}$$

The total annual cost is

If backorders can be tolerated, the total cost including the backorder cost will be less than the total cost of the EOQ model. Some people think the model with backorders will have a greater cost because it includes a backorder cost in addition to the usual inventory holding and ordering costs. You can point out the fallacy in this thinking by noting that the backorder model leads to lower inventory and hence lower inventory holding costs.

$$\text{Holding cost} = \frac{(86)^2}{2(115)}(10) = \$322$$

$$\text{Ordering cost} = \frac{2000}{115}(25) = \$435$$

$$\text{Backorder cost} = \frac{(29)^2}{2(115)}(30) = \$110$$

$$\text{Total cost} = \$867$$

If the company chooses to prohibit backorders and adopts the regular EOQ model, the recommended inventory decision would be

$$Q^* = \sqrt{\frac{2(2000)(25)}{10}} = \sqrt{10,000} = 100$$

This order quantity would result in a holding cost and an ordering cost of \$500 each or a total annual cost of \$1000. Thus, in this problem, allowing backorders is projecting a \$1000 − \$867 = \$133, or 13.3%, savings in cost from the no-stock-out EOQ model. The preceding comparison and conclusion are based on the assumption that the backorder model with an annual cost per backordered unit of \$30 is a valid model for the actual inventory situation. If the company is concerned that stock-outs might lead to lost sales, then the savings might not be enough to warrant switching to an inventory policy that allows for planned shortages.

NOTES AND COMMENTS

1. Equation (10.27) shows that the optimal number of planned backorders S^* is proportional to the ratio $C_h/(C_h + C_b)$, where C_h is the annual holding cost per unit and C_b is the annual backorder cost per unit. Whenever C_h increases, this ratio becomes larger, and the number of planned backorders increases. This relationship explains why items that have a high per-unit cost and a correspondingly high annual holding cost are more economically handled on a backorder basis. On the other hand, whenever the backorder cost C_b increases, the ratio becomes smaller, and the number of planned backorders decreases. Thus, the model provides the intuitive result that items with high backorder costs will be handled with few backorders. In fact, with high backorder costs, the backorder model and the EOQ model with no backordering allowed provide similar inventory policies.

10.4   QUANTITY DISCOUNTS FOR THE EOQ MODEL

In the quantity discount model, assumption 4 of the EOQ model in Table 10.3 is altered. The cost per unit varies depending on the quantity ordered.

Quantity discounts occur in numerous situations for which suppliers provide an incentive for large order quantities by offering a lower purchase cost when items are ordered in larger quantities. In this section we show how the EOQ model can be used when quantity discounts are available.

Assume that we have a product for which the basic EOQ model (see Table 10.3) is applicable. Instead of a fixed unit cost, the supplier quotes the following discount schedule:

Discount Category	Order Size	Discount (%)	Unit Cost
1	0 to 999	0	$5.00
2	1000 to 2499	3	4.85
3	2500 and over	5	4.75

The 5% discount for the 2500-unit minimum order quantity looks tempting. However, realizing that higher order quantities result in higher inventory holding costs, we should prepare a thorough cost analysis before making a final ordering and inventory policy recommendation.

Suppose that the data and cost analyses show an annual holding cost rate of 20%, an ordering cost of $49 per order, and an annual demand of 5000 units; what order quantity should we select? The following three-step procedure shows the calculations necessary to make this decision. In the preliminary calculations, we use Q_1 to indicate the order quantity for discount category 1, Q_2 for discount category 2, and Q_3 for discount category 3.

Step 1. For each discount category, compute a Q^* using the EOQ formula based on the unit cost associated with the discount category.

Recall that the EOQ model provides $Q^* = \sqrt{2DC_o/C_h}$, where $C_h = IC = (0.20)C$. With three discount categories providing three different unit costs C, we obtain

WEB file

Discount

$$Q_1^* = \sqrt{\frac{2(5000)49}{(0.20)(5.00)}} = 700$$

$$Q_2^* = \sqrt{\frac{2(5000)49}{(0.20)(4.85)}} = 711$$

$$Q_3^* = \sqrt{\frac{2(5000)49}{(0.20)(4.75)}} = 718$$

Because the only differences in the EOQ formulas come from slight differences in the holding cost, the economic order quantities resulting from this step will be approximately the same. However, these order quantities will usually not all be of the size necessary to qualify for the discount price assumed. In the preceding case, both Q_2^* and Q_3^* are insufficient order quantities to obtain their assumed discounted costs of $4.85 and $4.75, respectively. For those order quantities for which the assumed price cannot be obtained, the following procedure must be used:

Step 2. For the Q^* that is too small to qualify for the assumed discount price, adjust the order quantity upward to the nearest order quantity that will allow the product to be purchased at the assumed price.

In our example, this adjustment causes us to set

$$Q_2^* = 1000$$

and

$$Q_3^* = 2500$$

If a calculated Q^* for a given discount price is large enough to qualify for a bigger discount, that value of Q^* cannot lead to an optimal solution. Although the reason may not be obvious, it does turn out to be a property of the EOQ quantity discount model.

In the previous inventory models considered, the annual purchase cost of the item was not included because it was constant and never affected by the inventory order policy decision. However, in the quantity discount model, the annual purchase cost depends on the order quantity and the associated unit cost. Thus, annual purchase cost (annual demand $D \times$ unit cost C) is included in the equation for total cost as shown here.

In the EOQ model with quantity discounts, the annual purchase cost must be included because purchase cost depends on the order quantity. Thus, it is a relevant cost.

$$TC = \frac{Q}{2} C_h + \frac{D}{Q} C_o + DC \qquad (10.28)$$

Using this total cost equation, we can determine the optimal order quantity for the EOQ discount model in step 3.

Problem 21 will give you practice in applying the EOQ model to situations with quantity discounts.

Step 3. For each order quantity resulting from steps 1 and 2, compute the total annual cost using the unit price from the appropriate discount category and equation (10.28). The order quantity yielding the minimum total annual cost is the optimal order quantity.

The step 3 calculations for the example problem are summarized in Table 10.4. As you can see, a decision to order 1000 units at the 3% discount rate yields the minimum cost solution. Even though the 2500-unit order quantity would result in a 5% discount, its excessive holding cost makes it the second-best solution. Figure 10.7 shows the total cost curve for each of the three discount categories. Note that $Q^* = 1000$ provides the minimum cost order quantity.

TABLE 10.4 TOTAL ANNUAL COST CALCULATIONS FOR THE EOQ MODEL WITH QUANTITY DISCOUNTS

Discount Category	Unit Cost	Order Quantity	Annual Cost			
			Holding	Ordering	Purchase	Total
1	$5.00	700	$ 350	$350	$25,000	$25,700
2	4.85	1000	$ 485	$245	$24,250	$24,980
3	4.75	2500	$1188	$ 98	$23,750	$25,036

FIGURE 10.7   TOTAL COST CURVES FOR THE THREE DISCOUNT CATEGORIES

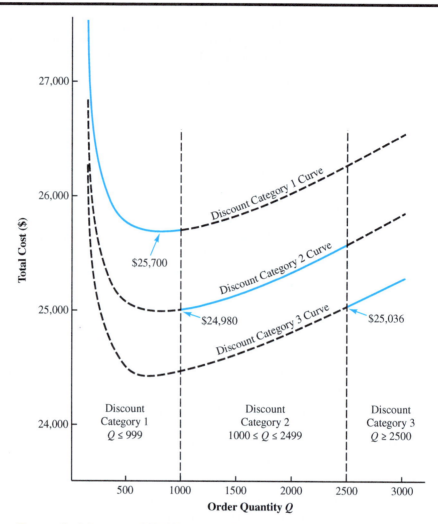

The overall minimum cost of $24,980 occurs at $Q^* = 1000$.

10.5   SINGLE-PERIOD INVENTORY MODEL WITH PROBABILISTIC DEMAND

The inventory models discussed thus far were based on the assumption that the demand rate is constant and **deterministic** throughout the year. We developed minimum cost order quantity and reorder point policies based on this assumption. In situations for which the demand rate is not deterministic, other models treat demand as **probabilistic** and best described by a probability distribution. In this section we consider a single-period inventory model with probabilistic demand.

The single-period inventory model refers to inventory situations for which *one* order is placed for the product; at the end of the period, the product has either sold out, or a surplus of unsold items will be sold for a salvage value. The single-period inventory model is applicable

*This inventory model is
the first in the chapter
that explicitly treats
probabilistic demand.
Unlike the EOQ model,
it is for a single period,
and unused inventory is
not carried over to future
periods.*

in situations involving seasonal or perishable items that cannot be carried in inventory and sold in future periods. Seasonal clothing (such as bathing suits and winter coats) are typically handled in a single-period manner. In these situations, a buyer places one preseason order for each item and then experiences a stock-out or holds a clearance sale on the surplus stock at the end of the season. No items are carried in inventory and sold the following year. Newspapers are another example of a product that is ordered one time and is either sold or not sold during the single period. Although newspapers are ordered daily, they cannot be carried in inventory and sold in later periods. Thus, newspaper orders may be treated as a sequence of single-period models; that is, each day or period is separate, and a single-period inventory decision must be made each period (day). Because we order only once for the period, the only inventory decision we must make is *how much* of the product to order at the start of the period.

Obviously, if the demand were known for a single-period inventory situation, the solution would be easy; we would simply order the amount we knew would be demanded. However, in most single-period models, the exact demand is not known. In fact, forecasts may show that demand can have a wide variety of values. If we are going to analyze this type of inventory problem in a quantitative manner, we need information about the probabilities associated with the various demand values. Thus, the single-period model presented in this section is based on probabilistic demand.

Neiman Marcus

Let us consider a single-period inventory model that could be used to make a how-much-to-order decision for Neiman Marcus, a high-end fashion store. The buyer for Neiman Marcus decided to order Manolo Blahnik heels shown at a buyers' meeting in New York City. The shoe will be part of the company's spring–summer promotion and will be sold through nine retail stores in the Chicago area. Because the shoe is designed for spring and summer months, it cannot be expected to sell in the fall. Neiman Marcus plans to hold a special August clearance sale in an attempt to sell all shoes not sold by July 31. The shoes cost $700 a pair and retail for $900 a pair. At the sale price of $600 a pair, all surplus shoes can be expected to sell during the August sale. If you were the buyer for Neiman Marcus, how many pairs of the shoes would you order?

To answer the question of how much to order, we need information on the demand for the shoe. Specifically, we would need to construct a probability distribution for the possible values of demand. Let us suppose that the uniform probability distribution shown in Figure 10.8 can be used to describe the demand for the Manolo Blahnik heels. In particular,

FIGURE 10.8   UNIFORM PROBABILITY DISTRIBUTION OF DEMAND FOR
NEIMAN MARCUS PROBLEM

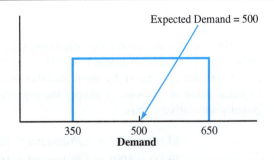

note that the range of demand is from 350 to 650 pairs of shoes, with an average, or expected, demand of 500 pairs of shoes.

Incremental analysis is a method that can be used to determine the optimal order quantity for a single-period inventory model. Incremental analysis addresses the how-much-to-order question by comparing the cost or loss of *ordering one additional unit* with the cost or loss of *not ordering one additional unit*. The costs involved are defined as follows:

c_o = cost per unit of *overestimating* demand. This cost represents the loss of ordering one additional unit and finding that it cannot be sold.

c_u = cost per unit of *underestimating* demand. This cost represents the opportunity loss of not ordering one additional unit and finding that it could have been sold.

In the Neiman Marcus problem, the company will incur the cost of overestimating demand whenever it orders too many pairs and has to sell the extra shoes during the August clearance sale. Thus, the cost per unit of overestimating demand is equal to the purchase cost per unit minus the August sales price per unit; that is, $c_o = \$700 - \$600 = \$100$. Therefore, Neiman Marcus will lose $100 for each pair of shoes that it orders over the quantity demanded. The cost of underestimating demand is the lost profit (often referred to as an opportunity cost) because a pair of shoes that could have been sold was not available in inventory. Thus, the per-unit cost of underestimating demand is the difference between the regular selling price per unit and the purchase cost per unit; that is, $c_u = \$900 - \$700 = \$200$.

The cost of underestimating demand is usually harder to determine than the cost of overestimating demand. The reason is that the cost of underestimating demand includes a lost profit and may include a customer loss of goodwill cost because the customer is unable to purchase the item when desired.

Because the exact level of demand for the Manolo Blahnik heels is unknown, we have to consider the probability of demand and thus the probability of obtaining the associated costs or losses. For example, let us assume that Neiman Marcus management wishes to consider an order quantity equal to the average or expected demand for 500 pairs of shoes. In incremental analysis, we consider the possible losses associated with an order quantity of 501 (ordering one additional unit) and an order quantity of 500 (not ordering one additional unit). The order quantity alternatives and the possible losses are summarized here.

The key to incremental analysis is to focus on the costs that are different when comparing an order quantity Q + 1 to an order quantity Q.

Order Quantity Alternatives	Loss Occurs If	Possible Loss	Probability Loss Occurs
$Q = 501$	Demand overestimated; the additional unit *cannot* be sold	$c_o = \$100$	$P(\text{demand} \leq 500)$
$Q = 500$	Demand underestimated; an additional unit *could have* been sold	$c_u = \$200$	$P(\text{demand} > 500)$

Using the demand probability distribution in Figure 10.8, we see that $P(\text{demand} \leq 500) = 0.50$ and that $P(\text{demand} > 500) = 0.50$. By multiplying the possible losses, $c_o = \$100$ and $c_u = \$200$, by the probability of obtaining the loss, we can compute the expected value of the loss, or simply the *expected loss* (EL), associated with the order quantity alternatives. Thus,

$$EL(Q = 501) = c_o P(\text{demand} \leq 500) = \$100(0.50) = \$50$$
$$EL(Q = 500) = c_u P(\text{demand} > 500) = \$200(0.50) = \$100$$

Based on these expected losses, do you prefer an order quantity of 501 or 500 pairs of shoes? Because the expected loss is greater for $Q = 500$, and because we want to avoid this higher cost or loss, we should make $Q = 501$ the preferred decision. We could now consider incrementing the order quantity one additional unit to $Q = 502$ and repeating the expected loss calculations.

Although we could continue this unit-by-unit analysis, it would be time-consuming and cumbersome. We would have to evaluate $Q = 502$, $Q = 503$, $Q = 504$, and so on until we found the value of Q where the expected loss of ordering one incremental unit is equal to the expected loss of not ordering one incremental unit; that is, the optimal order quantity Q^* occurs when the incremental analysis shows that

$$\text{EL}(Q^* + 1) = \text{EL}(Q^*) \tag{10.29}$$

When this relationship holds, increasing the order quantity by one additional unit has no economic advantage. Using the logic with which we computed the expected losses for the order quantities of 501 and 500, the general expressions for $\text{EL}(Q^* + 1)$ and $\text{EL}(Q^*)$ can be written as

$$\text{EL}(Q^* + 1) = c_o P(\text{demand} \leq Q^*) \tag{10.30}$$

$$\text{EL}(Q^*) = c_u P(\text{demand} > Q^*) \tag{10.31}$$

Because demand $\leq Q^*$ and demand $> Q^*$ are complementary events, we know from basic probability that

$$P(\text{demand} \leq Q^*) + P(\text{demand} > Q^*) = 1 \tag{10.32}$$

and we can write

$$P(\text{demand} > Q^*) = 1 - P(\text{demand} \leq Q^*) \tag{10.33}$$

Using this expression, equation (10.31) can be rewritten as

$$\text{EL}(Q^*) = c_u[1 - P(\text{demand} \leq Q^*)] \tag{10.34}$$

Equations (10.30) and (10.34) can be used to show that $\text{EL}(Q^* + 1) = \text{EL}(Q^*)$ whenever

$$c_o P(\text{demand} \leq Q^*) = c_u[1 - P(\text{demand} \leq Q^*)] \tag{10.35}$$

Solving for $P(\text{demand} \leq Q^*)$, we have

$$P(\text{demand} \leq Q^*) = \frac{c_u}{c_u + c_o} \tag{10.36}$$

This expression provides the general condition for the optimal order quantity Q^* in the single-period inventory model.

In the Neiman Marcus problem, $c_o = \$100$ and $c_u = \$200$. Thus, equation (10.36) shows that the optimal order size for the Manolo Blahnik heels must satisfy the following condition:

$$P(\text{demand} \leq Q^*) = \frac{c_u}{c_u + c_o} = \frac{200}{200 + 100} = \frac{200}{300} = \frac{2}{3}$$

We can find the optimal order quantity Q^* by referring to the probability distribution shown in Figure 10.8 and finding the value of Q that will provide $P(\text{demand} \leq Q^*) = \frac{2}{3}$. To find this solution, we note that in the uniform distribution the probability is evenly distributed over the entire range of 350–650 pairs of shoes. Thus, we can satisfy the expression for Q^* by moving two-thirds of the way from 350 to 650. Because this range is $650 - 350 = 300$, we move 200 units from 350 toward 650.

Doing so provides the optimal order quantity of 550 pairs of shoes.

In summary, the key to establishing an optimal order quantity for single-period inventory models is to identify the probability distribution that describes the demand for the item and to calculate the per-unit costs of overestimation and underestimation. Then, using the information for the per-unit costs of overestimation and underestimation, equation (10.36) can be used to find the location of Q^* in the probability distribution.

Nationwide Car Rental

As another example of a single-period inventory model with probabilistic demand, consider the situation faced by Nationwide Car Rental. Nationwide must decide how many automobiles to have available at each car rental location at specific points in time throughout the year. Using the Myrtle Beach, South Carolina, location as an example, management would like to know the number of full-sized automobiles to have available for the Labor Day weekend. Based on previous experience, customer demand for full-sized automobiles for the Labor Day weekend has a normal distribution with a mean of 150 automobiles and a standard deviation of 14 automobiles.

The Nationwide Car Rental situation can benefit from use of a single-period inventory model. The company must establish the number of full-sized automobiles to have available prior to the weekend. Customer demand over the weekend will then result in either a stock-out or a surplus. Let us denote the number of full-sized automobiles available by Q. If Q is greater than customer demand, Nationwide will have a surplus of cars. The cost of a surplus is the cost of overestimating demand. This cost is set at \$80 per car, which reflects, in part, the opportunity cost of not having the car available for rent elsewhere.

If Q is less than customer demand, Nationwide will rent all available cars and experience a stock-out or shortage. A shortage results in an underestimation cost of \$200 per car. This figure reflects the cost due to lost profit and the lost goodwill of not having a car available for a customer. Given this information, how many full-sized automobiles should Nationwide make available for the Labor Day weekend?

Using the cost of underestimation, $c_u = \$200$, and the cost of overestimation, $c_o = \$80$, equation (10.36) indicates that the optimal order quantity must satisfy the following condition:

$$P(\text{demand} \leq Q^*) = \frac{c_u}{(c_u + c_o)} = \frac{200}{200 + 80} = 0.7143$$

FIGURE 10.9   PROBABILITY DISTRIBUTION OF DEMAND FOR THE NATIONWIDE
CAR RENTAL PROBLEM SHOWING THE LOCATION OF Q^*

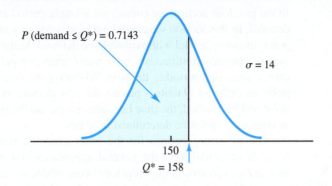

We can use the normal probability distribution for demand as shown in Figure 10.9
to find the order quantity that satisfies the condition that $P(\text{demand} \leq Q^*) = 0.7143$.
From Appendix B, we see that 0.7143 of the area in the left tail of the normal probability
distribution occurs at $z = 0.57$ standard deviations *above* the mean. With a mean demand
of $\mu = 150$ automobiles and a standard deviation of $\sigma = 14$ automobiles, we have

SinglePeriod

$$Q^* = \mu + 0.57\sigma$$
$$= 150 + 0.57(14) = 158$$

*An example of a single-
period inventory model
with probabilistic demand
described by a normal
probability distribution is
considered in Problem 25.*

Thus, Nationwide Car Rental should plan to have 158 full-sized automobiles available in
Myrtle Beach for the Labor Day weekend. Note that in this case the cost of overestimation is less than the cost of underestimation. Thus, Nationwide is willing to risk a higher
probability of overestimating demand and hence a higher probability of a surplus. In fact,
Nationwide's optimal order quantity has a 0.7143 probability of a surplus and a $1 - 0.7143 =$
0.2857 probability of a stock-out. As a result, the probability is 0.2857 that all 158 full-sized
automobiles will be rented during the Labor Day weekend.

NOTES AND COMMENTS

1. In any probabilistic inventory model, the assumption about the probability distribution for
   demand is critical and can affect the recommended inventory decision. In the problems
   presented in this section, we used the uniform
   and the normal probability distributions to describe demand. In some situations, other probability distributions may be more appropriate. In
   using probabilistic inventory models, we must
   exercise care in selecting the probability distribution that most realistically describes demand.
2. In the single-period inventory model, the value
   of $c_u/(c_u + c_o)$ plays a critical role in selecting the order quantity [see equation (10.36)].
   Whenever $c_u = c_o$, $c_u/(c_u + c_o)$ equals 0.50;

in this case, we should select an order quantity
corresponding to the median demand. With this
choice, a stock-out is just as likely as a surplus because the two costs are equal. However,
whenever $c_u < c_o$, a smaller order quantity will
be recommended. In this case, the smaller order
quantity will provide a higher probability of a
stock-out; however, the more expensive cost
of overestimating demand and having a surplus
will tend to be avoided. Finally, whenever $c_u >$
c_o, a larger order quantity will be recommended.
In this case, the larger order quantity provides a
lower probability of a stock-out in an attempt to
avoid the more expensive cost of underestimating demand and experiencing a stock-out.

10.6   ORDER-QUANTITY, REORDER POINT MODEL WITH PROBABILISTIC DEMAND

In the previous section we considered a single-period inventory model with probabilistic demand. In this section we extend our discussion to a multiperiod order-quantity, reorder point inventory model with probabilistic demand. In the multiperiod model, the inventory system operates continuously with many repeating periods or cycles; inventory can be carried from one period to the next. Whenever the inventory position reaches the reorder point, an order for Q units is placed. Because demand is probabilistic, the time the reorder point will be reached, the time between orders, and the time the order of Q units will arrive in inventory cannot be determined in advance.

The inventory model in this section is based on the assumptions of the EOQ model shown in Table 10.3, with the exception that demand is probabilistic rather than deterministic. With probabilistic demand, occasional shortages may occur.

The inventory pattern for the order-quantity, reorder point model with probabilistic demand will have the general appearance shown in Figure 10.10. Note that the increases, or jumps, in the inventory occur whenever an order of Q units arrives. The inventory decreases at a nonconstant rate based on the probabilistic demand. A new order is placed whenever the reorder point is reached. At times, the order quantity of Q units will arrive before inventory reaches zero. However, at other times, higher demand will cause a stock-out before a new order is received. As with other order-quantity, reorder point models, the manager must determine the order quantity Q and the reorder point r for the inventory system.

The exact mathematical formulation of an order-quantity, reorder point inventory model with probabilistic demand is beyond the scope of this text. However, we present a procedure that can be used to obtain good, workable order-quantity and reorder point inventory policies. The solution procedure can be expected to provide only an approximation of the optimal solution, but it can yield good solutions in many practical situations.

Let us consider the inventory problem of Dabco Industrial Lighting Distributors. Dabco purchases a special high-intensity lightbulb for industrial lighting systems from a well-known lightbulb manufacturer. Dabco would like a recommendation on how much to

FIGURE 10.10   INVENTORY PATTERN FOR AN ORDER-QUANTITY, REORDER POINT MODEL WITH PROBABILISTIC DEMAND

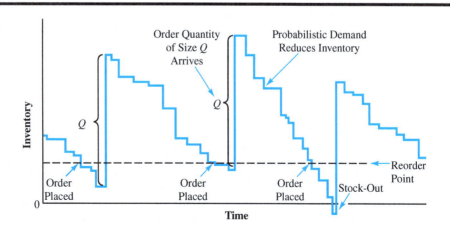

FIGURE 10.11 LEAD-TIME DEMAND PROBABILITY DISTRIBUTION FOR DABCO LIGHTBULBS

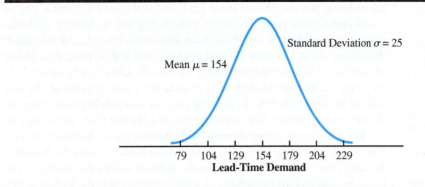

order and when to order so that a low-cost inventory policy can be maintained. Pertinent facts are that the ordering cost is $12 per order, one bulb costs $6, and Dabco uses a 20% annual holding cost rate for its inventory ($C_h = IC = 0.20 \times \$6 = \$1.20$). Dabco, which has more than 1000 customers, experiences a probabilistic demand; in fact, the number of units demanded varies considerably from day to day and from week to week. The lead time for a new order of lightbulbs is one week. Historical sales data indicate that demand during a one-week lead time can be described by a normal probability distribution with a mean of 154 lightbulbs and a standard deviation of 25 lightbulbs. The normal distribution of demand during the lead time is shown in Figure 10.11. Because the mean demand during one week is 154 units, Dabco can anticipate a mean or expected annual demand of 154 units per week × 52 weeks per year = 8008 units per year.

The How-Much-to-Order Decision

Although we are in a probabilistic demand situation, we have an estimate of the expected annual demand of 8008 units. We can apply the EOQ model from Section 10.1 as an approximation of the best order quantity, with the expected annual demand used for D. In Dabco's case

ProbDemandQ

$$Q^* = \sqrt{\frac{2DC_o}{C_h}} = \sqrt{\frac{2(8008)(12)}{(1.20)}} = 400 \text{ units}$$

When we studied the sensitivity of the EOQ model, we learned that the total cost of operating an inventory system was relatively insensitive to order quantities that were in the neighborhood of Q^*. Using this knowledge, we expect 400 units per order to be a good approximation of the optimal order quantity. Even if annual demand were as low as 7000 units or as high as 9000 units, an order quantity of 400 units should be a relatively good low-cost order size. Thus, given our best estimate of annual demand at 8008 units, we will use $Q^* = 400$.

We have established the 400-unit order quantity by ignoring the fact that demand is probabilistic. Using $Q^* = 400$, Dabco can anticipate placing approximately $D/Q^* = 8008/400 = 20$ orders per year with an average of approximately $250/20 = 12.5$ working days between orders.

The When-to-Order Decision

The probability of a stock-out during any one inventory cycle is easiest to estimate by first determining the number of orders that are expected during the year. The inventory manager can usually state a willingness to allow perhaps one, two, or three stock-outs during the year. The allowable stock-outs per year divided by the number of orders per year will provide the desired probability of a stock-out.

We now want to establish a when-to-order decision rule or reorder point that will trigger the ordering process. With a mean lead-time demand of 154 units, you might first suggest a 154-unit reorder point. However, considering the probability of demand now becomes extremely important. If 154 is the mean lead-time demand, and if demand is symmetrically distributed about 154, then the lead-time demand will be more than 154 units roughly 50% of the time. When the demand during the one-week lead time exceeds 154 units, Dabco will experience a shortage or stock-out. Thus, using a reorder point of 154 units, approximately 50% of the time (10 of the 20 orders a year, on average) Dabco will be short of bulbs before the new supply arrives. This shortage rate would most likely be viewed as unacceptable.

Refer to the **lead-time demand distribution** shown in Figure 10.11. Given this distribution, we can now determine how the reorder point r affects the probability of a stock-out. Because stock-outs occur whenever the demand during the lead time exceeds the reorder point, we can find the probability of a stock-out by using the lead-time demand distribution to compute the probability that demand will exceed r.

We could now approach the when-to-order problem by defining a cost per stock-out and then attempting to include this cost in a total cost equation. Alternatively, we can ask management to specify the average number of stock-outs that can be tolerated per year. If demand for a product is probabilistic, a manager who will never tolerate a stock-out is being somewhat unrealistic because attempting to avoid stock-outs completely will require high reorder points, high inventory, and an associated high holding cost.

Suppose in this case that Dabco management is willing to tolerate an average of one stock-out per year. Because Dabco places 20 orders per year, this decision implies that management is willing to allow demand during lead time to exceed the reorder point one time in 20, or 5% of the time. The reorder point r can be found by using the lead-time demand distribution to find the value of r with a 5% chance of having a lead-time demand that will exceed it. This situation is shown graphically in Figure 10.12.

From the standard normal probability distribution table in Appendix B, we see that $1 - 0.05 = 0.95$ of the area in the left tail of the normal probability distribution occurs at $z = 1.645$ standard deviations above the mean. Therefore, for the assumed normal distribution for lead-time demand with $\mu = 154$ and $\sigma = 25$, the reorder point r is

$$r = 154 + 1.645(25) = 195$$

FIGURE 10.12   REORDER POINT r THAT ALLOWS A 5% CHANCE OF A STOCK-OUT FOR DABCO LIGHTBULBS

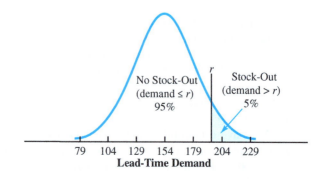

If a normal distribution is used for lead-time demand, the general equation for r is

$$r = \mu + z\sigma \qquad (10.37)$$

where z is the number of standard deviations necessary to obtain the acceptable stock-out probability.

Try Problem 29 as an example of an order-quantity, reorder point model with probabilistic demand.

Thus, the recommended inventory decision is to order 400 units whenever the inventory reaches the reorder point of 195. Because the mean or expected demand during the lead time is 154 units, the $195 - 154 = 41$ units serve as a **safety stock**, which absorbs higher-than-usual demand during the lead time. Roughly 95% of the time, the 195 units will be able to satisfy demand during the lead time. The anticipated annual cost for this system is as follows:

Holding cost, normal inventory $(Q/2)C_h$	$= (400/2)(1.20)$	$= \$240$
Holding cost, safety stock	$(41)C_h = 41(1.20)$	$= \$\ 49$
Ordering cost	$(D/Q)C_o = (8008/400)12$	$= \underline{\$240}$
	Total	$\$529$

If Dabco could assume that a known, constant demand rate of 8008 units per year existed for the lightbulbs, then $Q^* = 400$, $r = 154$, and a total annual cost of $\$240 + \$240 = \$480$ would be optimal. When demand is uncertain and can only be expressed in probabilistic terms, a larger total cost can be expected. The larger cost occurs in the form of larger holding costs because more inventory must be maintained to limit the number of stock-outs. For Dabco, this additional inventory or safety stock was 41 units, with an additional annual holding cost of \$49. The Management Science in Action, Inventory Models at Microsoft, describes how Microsoft has employed inventory models to increase customer service levels as well as reduce inventory costs.

MANAGEMENT SCIENCE IN ACTION

INVENTORY MODELS AT MICROSOFT*

While known more for its operating system software, Microsoft has steadily increased its presence in consumer electronics. Microsoft produces Xbox video game consoles and a variety of personal-computer accessories such as mice and keyboards. In 2008 the consumer-electronics division of Microsoft generated over \$8 billion in revenue compared to \$52 billion in revenue from software. While products such as the Xbox are sold year-round, approximately 40% of annual sales occur in October, November, and December. Therefore, it is critical that Microsoft has sufficient inventory available to meet demand for the holiday season.

In conjunction with the supply-chain-services company Optiant, Microsoft began an ambitious effort in 2005 to improve its inventory management systems. Microsoft developed new forecasting techniques to better estimate future demand for its products. It then set service-level requirements for each product based on profit margins and demand forecasts. These service levels were used in safety-stock model calculations to determine target inventory levels that drove production plans. The new safety-stock models were used for more than 10,000 different consumer-electronics products sold by Microsoft.

Microsoft has experienced substantial inventory level reductions since implementing its new models and policies. Corporate-wide, Microsoft has reduced its inventories by \$1.5 billion (60%). The consumer-electronics division of Microsoft posted its first ever profitable year in 2008. Microsoft largely credits these cost savings and profitability to superior forecasting and inventory models.

*Based on J.J. Neale and S.P. Willems, "Managing Inventory in Supply Chains with Nonstationary Demand," *Interfaces* 39, no. 5 (September 2009): 388–399.

NOTES AND COMMENTS

1. The safety stock required at Microsoft in the Management Science in Action, Inventory Models at Microsoft, was based on a service level defined by the probability of being able to satisfy all customer demand during an order cycle. If Microsoft wanted to guarantee that it would be able to meet all demand in 95% of all order cycles, then we would say that Microsoft has a 95% service level. This is sometimes referred to as a *Type-I* service level or a *cycle service level*. However, other definitions of *service level* may include the percentage of all customer demand that can be satisfied from inventory. Thus, when an inventory manager expresses a desired service level, it is a good idea to clarify exactly what the manager means by the term *service level*.

10.7   PERIODIC REVIEW MODEL WITH PROBABILISTIC DEMAND

Up to this point, we have assumed that the inventory position is reviewed continuously so that an order can be placed as soon as the inventory position reaches the reorder point. The inventory model in this section assumes probabilistic demand and a periodic review of the inventory position.

The order-quantity, reorder point inventory models previously discussed require a **continuous review inventory system**. In a continuous review inventory system, the inventory position is monitored continuously so that an order can be placed whenever the reorder point is reached. Computerized inventory systems can easily provide the continuous review required by the order-quantity, reorder point models.

An alternative to the continuous review system is the **periodic review inventory system**. With a periodic review system, the inventory is checked and reordering is done only at specified points in time. For example, inventory may be checked and orders placed on a weekly, biweekly, monthly, or some other periodic basis. When a firm or business handles multiple products, the periodic review system offers the advantage of requiring that orders for several items be placed at the same preset periodic review time. With this type of inventory system, the shipping and receiving of orders for multiple products are easily coordinated. Under the previously discussed order-quantity, reorder point systems, the reorder points for various products can be encountered at substantially different points in time, making the coordination of orders for multiple products more difficult.

To illustrate this system, let us consider Dollar Discounts, a firm with several retail stores that carry a wide variety of products for household use. The company operates its inventory system with a two-week periodic review. Under this system, a retail store manager may order any number of units of any product from the Dollar Discounts central warehouse every two weeks. Orders for all products going to a particular store are combined into one shipment. When making the order quantity decision for each product at a given review period, the store manager knows that a reorder for the product cannot be made until the next review period.

Assuming that the lead time is less than the length of the review period, an order placed at a review period will be received prior to the next review period. In this case, the how-much-to-order decision at any review period is determined using the following:

$$Q = M - H \qquad (10.38)$$

where

$$Q = \text{the order quantity}$$
$$M = \text{the replenishment level}$$
$$H = \text{the inventory on hand at the review period}$$

FIGURE 10.13   INVENTORY PATTERN FOR PERIODIC REVIEW MODEL
WITH PROBABILISTIC DEMAND

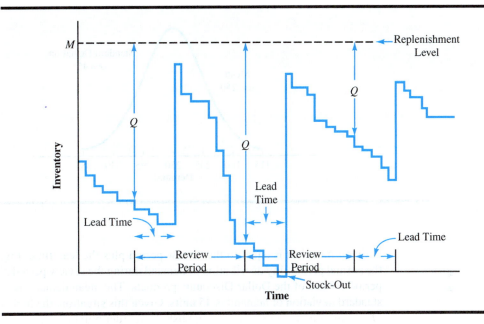

Because the demand is probabilistic, the inventory on hand at the review period, H, will vary. Thus, the order quantity that must be sufficient to bring the inventory position back to its maximum or replenishment level M can be expected to vary each period. For example, if the replenishment level for a particular product is 50 units and the inventory on hand at the review period is $H = 12$ units, an order of $Q = M - H = 50 - 12 = 38$ units should be made. Thus, under the periodic review model, enough units are ordered each review period to bring the inventory position back up to the replenishment level.

A typical inventory pattern for a periodic review system with probabilistic demand is shown in Figure 10.13. Note that the time between periodic reviews is predetermined and fixed. The order quantity Q at each review period can vary and is shown to be the difference between the replenishment level and the inventory on hand. Finally, as with other probabilistic models, an unusually high demand can result in an occasional stock-out.

The decision variable in the periodic review model is the replenishment level M. To determine M, we could begin by developing a total cost model, including holding, ordering, and stock-out costs. Instead, we describe an approach that is often used in practice. In this approach, the objective is to determine a replenishment level that will meet a desired performance level, such as a reasonably low probability of stock-out or a reasonably low number of stock-outs per year.

In the Dollar Discounts problem, we assume that management's objective is to determine the replenishment level with only a 1% chance of a stock-out. In the periodic review model, the order quantity at each review period must be sufficient to cover *demand for the review period plus the demand for the following lead time*. Suppose that an order is to be placed at time t. To determine this order quantity, we must realize that the quantity ordered at time t must last until the next time inventory is replenished, which will be time (t + review period + lead time). Thus, the total length of time that the order quantity

FIGURE 10.14   PROBABILITY DISTRIBUTION OF DEMAND DURING THE REVIEW
PERIOD AND LEAD TIME FOR THE DOLLAR DISCOUNTS PROBLEM

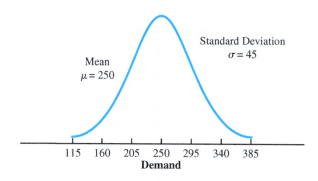

at time t must last is equal to the review period plus the lead time. Figure 10.14 shows
the normal probability distribution of demand during the review period plus the lead-time
period for one of the Dollar Discounts products. The mean demand is 250 units, and the
standard deviation of demand is 45 units. Given this situation, the logic used to establish
M is similar to the logic used to establish the reorder point in Section 10.6. Figure 10.15
shows the replenishment level M with a 1% chance that demand will exceed that replenishment level. In other words, Figure 10.15 shows the replenishment level that allows a
1% chance of a stock-out associated with the replenishment decision. Using the normal
probability distribution table in Appendix B, we see that $1 - 0.01 = 0.99$ of the area in
the left tail of the normal probability distribution occurs at $z = 2.33$ standard deviations
above the mean. Therefore, for the assumed normal probability distribution with $\mu = 250$
and $\sigma = 45$, the replenishment level is determined by

Periodic

$$M = 250 + 2.33(45) = 355$$

FIGURE 10.15   REPLENISHMENT LEVEL M THAT ALLOWS A 1% CHANCE
OF A STOCK-OUT FOR THE DOLLAR DISCOUNTS PROBLEM

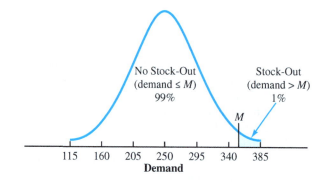

Problem 33 gives you practice in computing the replenishment level for a periodic review model with probabilistic demand.

Although other probability distributions can be used to express the demand during the review period plus the lead-time period, if the normal probability distribution is used, the general expression for M is

$$M = \mu + z\sigma \qquad (10.39)$$

where z is the number of standard deviations necessary to obtain the acceptable stock-out probability.

Periodic review systems provide advantages of coordinated orders for multiple items. However, periodic review systems require larger safety-stock levels than corresponding continuous review systems.

If demand had been deterministic rather than probabilistic, the replenishment level would have been the demand during the review period plus the demand during the lead-time period. In this case, the replenishment level would have been 250 units, and no stock-out would have occurred. However, with the probabilistic demand, we have seen that higher inventory is necessary to allow for uncertain demand and to control the probability of a stock-out. In the Dollar Discounts problem, $355 - 250 = 105$ is the safety stock that is necessary to absorb any higher-than-usual demand during the review period plus the demand during the lead-time period. This safety stock limits the probability of a stock-out to 1%.

More Complex Periodic Review Models

The periodic review model just discussed is one approach to determining a replenishment level for the periodic review inventory system with probabilistic demand. More complex versions of the periodic review model incorporate a reorder point as another decision variable; that is, instead of ordering at every periodic review, a reorder point is established. If the inventory on hand at the periodic review is at or below the reorder point, a decision is made to order up to the replenishment level. However, if the inventory on hand at the periodic review is greater than the reorder level, such an order is not placed, and the system continues until the next periodic review. In this case, the cost of ordering is a relevant cost and can be included in a cost model along with holding and stock-out costs. Optimal policies can be reached based on minimizing the expected total cost. Situations with lead times longer than the review period add to the complexity of the model. The mathematical level required to treat these more extensive periodic review models is beyond the scope of this text.

NOTES AND COMMENTS

1. The periodic review model presented in this section is based on the assumption that the lead time for an order is less than the periodic review period. Most periodic review systems operate under this condition. However, the case for which the lead time is longer than the review period can be handled by defining H in equation (10.38) as the inventory position, where H includes the inventory on hand plus the inventory on order. In this case, the order quantity at any review period is the amount needed for the inventory on hand plus all outstanding orders needed to reach the replenishment level.

2. In the order-quantity, reorder point model discussed in Section 10.6, a continuous review was used to initiate an order whenever the reorder point was reached. The safety stock for this model was based on the probabilistic demand during the lead time. The periodic review model presented in this section also determined a recommended safety stock. However, because the inventory review was only periodic, the safety stock was based on the probabilistic demand during the review period plus the lead-time period. This longer period for the safety stock computation means that periodic review systems tend to require a larger safety stock than do continuous review systems.

SUMMARY

In this chapter we presented some of the approaches used to assist managers in establishing low-cost inventory policies. We first considered cases for which the demand rate for the product is constant. In analyzing these inventory systems, total cost models were developed; these models included ordering costs, holding costs, and, in some cases, backorder costs. Then minimum cost formulas for the order quantity Q were presented. A reorder point r can be established by considering the lead-time demand.

In addition, we discussed inventory models for which a deterministic and constant rate could not be assumed, and thus demand was described by a probability distribution. A critical issue with these probabilistic inventory models is obtaining a probability distribution that most realistically approximates the demand distribution. We first described a single-period model where only one order is placed for the product and, at the end of the period, either the product has sold out or a surplus remains of unsold products that will be sold for a salvage value. Solution procedures were then presented for multiperiod models based on either an order-quantity, reorder point, continuous review system or a replenishment-level, periodic review system.

In closing this chapter, we reemphasize that inventory and inventory systems can be an expensive phase of a firm's operation. It is important for managers to be aware of the cost of inventory systems and to make the best possible operating policy decisions for the inventory system. Inventory models, as presented in this chapter, can help managers to develop good inventory policies.

GLOSSARY

Backorder The receipt of an order for a product when no units are in inventory. These backorders are eventually satisfied when a new supply of the product becomes available.

Constant demand rate An assumption of many inventory models that states that the same number of units are taken from inventory each period of time.

Constant supply rate A situation in which the inventory is built up at a constant rate over a period of time.

Continuous review inventory system A system in which the inventory position is monitored or reviewed on a continuous basis so that a new order can be placed as soon as the reorder point is reached.

Cost of capital The cost a firm incurs to obtain capital for investment. It may be stated as an annual percentage rate, and it is part of the holding cost associated with maintaining inventory.

Cycle time The length of time between the placing of two consecutive orders.

Deterministic inventory model A model where demand is considered known and not subject to uncertainty.

Economic order quantity (EOQ) The order quantity that minimizes the annual holding cost plus the annual ordering cost.

Goodwill cost A cost associated with a backorder, a lost sale, or any form of stock-out or unsatisfied demand. This cost may be used to reflect the loss of future profits because a customer experienced an unsatisfied demand.

Holding cost The cost associated with maintaining an inventory investment, including the cost of the capital investment in the inventory, insurance, taxes, warehouse overhead, and so on. This cost may be stated as a percentage of the inventory investment or as a cost per unit.

Incremental analysis A method used to determine an optimal order quantity by comparing the cost of ordering an additional unit with the cost of not ordering an additional unit.

Inventory position The inventory on hand plus the inventory on order.

Lead time The time between the placing of an order and its receipt in the inventory system.

Lead-time demand The number of units demanded during the lead-time period.

Lead-time demand distribution The distribution of demand that occurs during the lead-time period.

Lot size The order quantity in the production inventory model.

Ordering cost The fixed cost (salaries, paper, transportation, etc.) associated with placing an order for an item.

Periodic review inventory system A system in which the inventory position is checked or reviewed at predetermined periodic points in time. Reorders are placed only at periodic review points.

Probabilistic inventory model A model where demand is not known exactly; probabilities must be associated with the possible values for demand.

Quantity discounts Discounts or lower unit costs offered by the manufacturer when a customer purchases larger quantities of the product.

Reorder point The inventory position at which a new order should be placed.

Safety stock Inventory maintained in order to reduce the number of stock-outs resulting from higher-than-expected demand.

Setup cost The fixed cost (labor, materials, lost production) associated with preparing for a new production run.

Shortage or stock-out Occurrence when demand cannot be supplied from inventory.

Single-period inventory model An inventory model in which only one order is placed for the product, and at the end of the period either the item has sold out or a surplus of unsold items will be sold for a salvage value.

PROBLEMS

1. Suppose that the R&B Beverage Company has a soft drink product that shows a constant annual demand rate of 3600 cases. A case of the soft drink costs R&B $3. Ordering costs are $20 per order and holding costs are 25% of the value of the inventory. R&B has 250 working days per year, and the lead time is 5 days. Identify the following aspects of the inventory policy:
   a. Economic order quantity
   b. Reorder point
   c. Cycle time
   d. Total annual cost

2. A general property of the EOQ inventory model is that total inventory holding and total ordering costs are equal at the optimal solution. Use the data in Problem 1 to show that this result is true. Use equations (10.1), (10.2), and (10.3) to show that, in general, total holding costs and total ordering costs are equal whenever Q^* is used.

3. The reorder point [see equation (10.6)] is defined as the lead-time demand for an item. In cases of long lead times, the lead-time demand and thus the reorder point may exceed the economic order quantity Q^*. In such cases, the inventory position will not equal the inventory on hand when an order is placed, and the reorder point may be expressed in terms of either the inventory position or the inventory on hand. Consider the economic order quantity model with $D = 5000$, $C_o = \$32$, $C_h = \$2$, and 250 working days per year. Identify the reorder point in terms of the inventory position and in terms of the inventory on hand for each of the following lead times:
    a. 5 days
    b. 15 days
    c. 25 days
    d. 45 days

4. Westside Auto purchases a component used in the manufacture of automobile generators directly from the supplier. Westside's generator production operation, which is operated at a constant rate, will require 1000 components per month throughout the year (12,000 units annually). Assume that the ordering costs are $25 per order, the unit cost is $2.50 per component, and annual holding costs are 20% of the value of the inventory. Westside has 250 working days per year and a lead time of 5 days. Answer the following inventory policy questions:
    a. What is the EOQ for this component?
    b. What is the reorder point?
    c. What is the cycle time?
    d. What are the total annual holding and ordering costs associated with your recommended EOQ?

5. The Metropolitan Bus Company (MBC) purchases diesel fuel from American Petroleum Supply. In addition to the fuel cost, American Petroleum Supply charges MBC $250 per order to cover the expenses of delivering and transferring the fuel to MBC's storage tanks. The lead time for a new shipment from American Petroleum is 10 days; the cost of holding a gallon of fuel in the storage tanks is $0.04 per month, or $0.48 per year; and annual fuel usage is 150,000 gallons. MBC buses operate 300 days a year.
    a. What is the optimal order quantity for MBC?
    b. How frequently should MBC order to replenish the gasoline supply?
    c. The MBC storage tanks have a capacity of 15,000 gallons. Should MBC consider expanding the capacity of its storage tanks?
    d. What is the reorder point?

6. The manager at a local university bookstore wishes to apply the EOQ model to determine the respective order quantities for two products: ballpoint pens and mechanical pencils. The annual demand for pens and pencils is 1500 and 400, respectively. The ordering cost for each product is $20 per order and the wholesale price of a pen and pencil is $1.50 and $4, respectively. Assume the bookstore's annual holding rate is 10% and that the bookstore operates 240 days per year.
    a. Determine the optimal order quantity and the order cycle time for each product. What is the total cost (summed over both products)?
    b. The bookstore orders the pens and pencils from the same supplier. If these two products had the same cycle time, the corresponding shipment consolidation would reduce the ordering cost to $15. How much money does the bookstore save by consolidating the orders for these two products? (*Hint:* By setting the cycle times equal, we have

$Q_{pens}/(1500/240) = Q_{pencils}/(400/240)$ or $Q_{pens} = 3.75Q_{pencils}$). Make this substitution into the combined cost equation so that it is a function only of $Q_{pencils}$ and apply equation (10.5) with the appropriate values to determine $Q_{pencils}$ (and subsequently Q_{pens}).

7. A large distributor of oil-well drilling equipment operated over the past two years with EOQ policies based on an annual holding cost rate of 22%. Under the EOQ policy, a particular product has been ordered with a $Q^* = 80$. A recent evaluation of holding costs shows that because of an increase in the interest rate associated with bank loans, the annual holding cost rate should be 27%.
    a. What is the new economic order quantity for the product?
    b. Develop a general expression showing how the economic order quantity changes when the annual holding cost rate is changed from I to I'.

8. Nation-Wide Bus Lines is proud of its six-week bus driver–training program that it conducts for all new Nation-Wide drivers. As long as the class size remains less than or equal to 35, a six-week training program costs Nation-Wide $22,000 for instructors, equipment, and so on. The Nation-Wide training program must provide the company with approximately five new drivers per month. After completing the training program, new drivers are paid $1600 per month but do not work until a full-time driver position is open. Nation-Wide views the $1600 per month paid to each idle new driver as a holding cost necessary to maintain a supply of newly trained drivers available for immediate service. Viewing new drivers as inventory-type units, how large should the training classes be to minimize Nation-Wide's total annual training and new driver idle-time costs? How many training classes should the company hold each year? What is the total annual cost associated with your recommendation?

9. Cress Electronic Products manufactures components used in the automotive industry. Cress purchases parts for use in its manufacturing operation from a variety of different suppliers. One particular supplier provides a part where the assumptions of the EOQ model are realistic. The annual demand is 5000 units, the ordering cost is $80 per order, and the annual holding cost rate is 25%.
    a. If the cost of the part is $20 per unit, what is the economic order quantity?
    b. Assume 250 days of operation per year. If the lead time for an order is 12 days, what is the reorder point?
    c. If the lead time for the part is seven weeks (35 days), what is the reorder point? Compare this with the economic order quantity from part (a). Explain the relative size of these two quantities. Hint: Remember that the reorder point is expressed in terms of inventory position.
    d. What is the reorder point for part (c) if the reorder point is expressed in terms of the inventory on hand rather than the inventory position?

10. All-Star Bat Manufacturing, Inc., supplies baseball bats to major and minor league baseball teams. After an initial order in January, demand over the six-month baseball season is approximately constant at 1000 bats per month. Assuming that the bat production process can handle up to 4000 bats per month, the bat production setup costs are $150 per setup, the production cost is $10 per bat, and the holding costs have a monthly rate of 2%, what production lot size would you recommend to meet the demand during the baseball season? If All-Star operates 20 days per month, how often will the production process operate, and what is the length of a production run?

11. Assume that a production line operates such that the production lot size model of Section 10.2 is applicable. Given $D = 6400$ units per year, $C_o = \$100$, and $C_h = \$2$ per unit per year, compute the minimum cost production lot size for each of the following production rates:
    a. 8000 units per year
    b. 10,000 units per year
    c. 32,000 units per year
    d. 100,000 units per year

Compute the EOQ recommended lot size using equation (10.5). What two observations can you make about the relationship between the EOQ model and the production lot size model?

12. EL Computer produces its multimedia notebook computer on a production line that has an annual capacity of 16,000 units. EL Computer estimates the annual demand for this model at 6000 units. The cost to set up the production line is $2345, and the annual holding cost is $20 per unit. Current practice calls for production runs of 500 notebook computers each month.
    a. What is the optimal production lot size?
    b. How many production runs should be made each year? What is the recommended cycle time?
    c. Would you recommend changing the current production lot size policy from the monthly 500-unit production runs? Why or why not? What is the projected savings of your recommendation?

13. Wilson Publishing Company produces books for the retail market. Demand for a current book is expected to occur at a constant annual rate of 7200 copies. The cost of one copy of the book is $14.50. The holding cost is based on an 18% annual rate, and production setup costs are $150 per setup. The equipment with which the book is produced has an annual production volume of 25,000 copies. Wilson has 250 working days per year, and the lead time for a production run is 15 days. Use the production lot size model to compute the following values:
    a. Minimum cost production lot size
    b. Number of production runs per year
    c. Cycle time
    d. Length of a production run
    e. Maximum inventory
    f. Total annual cost
    g. Reorder point

14. A well-known manufacturer of several brands of toothpaste uses the production lot size model to determine production quantities for its various products. The product known as Extra White is currently being produced in production lot sizes of 5000 units. The length of the production run for this quantity is 10 days. Because of a recent shortage of a particular raw material, the supplier of the material announced that a cost increase will be passed along to the manufacturer of Extra White. Current estimates are that the new raw material cost will increase the manufacturing cost of the toothpaste products by 23% per unit. What will be the effect of this price increase on the production lot sizes for Extra White?

15. Suppose that Westside Auto of Problem 4, with $D = 12,000$ units per year, $C_h = (2.50)(0.20) = \$0.50$, and $C_o = \$25$, decided to operate with a backorder inventory policy. Backorder costs are estimated to be $5 per unit per year. Identify the following:
    a. Minimum cost order quantity
    b. Maximum number of backorders
    c. Maximum inventory
    d. Cycle time
    e. Total annual cost

16. Assuming 250 days of operation per year and a lead time of five days, what is the reorder point for Westside Auto in Problem 15? Show the general formula for the reorder point for the EOQ model with backorders. In general, is the reorder point when backorders are allowed greater than or less than the reorder point when backorders are not allowed? Explain.

17. A manager of an inventory system believes that inventory models are important decision-making aids. The manager has experience with the EOQ policy, but has never considered a backorder model because of the assumption that backorders were "bad" and should be avoided. However, with upper management's continued pressure for cost reduction, you have been asked to analyze the economics of a backorder policy for some products that can possibly be backordered. For a specific product with $D = 800$ units per year, $C_o = \$150$, $C_h = \$3$, and $C_b = \$20$, what is the difference in total annual cost between the EOQ model and the planned shortage or backorder model? If the manager adds constraints that no more than 25% of the units can be backordered and that no customer will have to wait more than 15 days for an order, should the backorder inventory policy be adopted? Assume 250 working days per year.

18. If the lead time for new orders is 20 days for the inventory system discussed in Problem 17, find the reorder point for both the EOQ and the backorder models.

19. The A&M Hobby Shop carries a line of radio-controlled model racing cars. Demand for the cars is assumed to be constant at a rate of 40 cars per month. The cars cost $60 each, and ordering costs are approximately $15 per order, regardless of the order size. The annual holding cost rate is 20%.
    a. Determine the economic order quantity and total annual cost under the assumption that no backorders are permitted.
    b. Using a $45 per-unit per-year backorder cost, determine the minimum cost inventory policy and total annual cost for the model racing cars.
    c. What is the maximum number of days a customer would have to wait for a backorder under the policy in part (b)? Assume that the Hobby Shop is open for business 300 days per year.
    d. Would you recommend a no-backorder or a backorder inventory policy for this product? Explain.
    e. If the lead time is six days, what is the reorder point for both the no-backorder and backorder inventory policies?

20. Assume that the following quantity discount schedule is appropriate. If annual demand is 120 units, ordering costs are $20 per order, and the annual holding cost rate is 25%, what order quantity would you recommend?

Order Size	Discount (%)	Unit Cost
0 to 49	0	$30.00
50 to 99	5	$28.50
100 or more	10	$27.00

21. Apply the EOQ model to the following quantity discount situation for which $D = 500$ units per year, $C_o = \$40$, and the annual holding cost rate is 20%. What order quantity do you recommend?

Discount Category	Order Size	Discount (%)	Unit Cost
1	0 to 99	0	$10.00
2	100 or more	3	$ 9.70

22. Keith Shoe Stores carries a basic black dress shoe for men that sells at an approximately constant rate of 500 pairs of shoes every three months. Keith's current buying policy is to order 500 pairs each time an order is placed. It costs Keith $30 to place an order. The annual holding cost rate is 20%. With the order quantity of 500, Keith obtains the shoes at the lowest possible unit cost of $28 per pair. Other quantity discounts offered by the manufacturer are as follows. What is the minimum cost order quantity for the shoes? What are the annual savings of your inventory policy over the policy currently being used by Keith?

Order Quantity	Price per Pair
0–99	$36
100–199	$32
200–299	$30
300 or more	$28

23. In the EOQ model with quantity discounts, we stated that if the Q^* for a price category is larger than necessary to qualify for the category price, the category cannot be optimal. Use the two discount categories in Problem 21 to show that this statement is true. That is, plot total cost curves for the two categories and show that if the category 2 minimum cost Q is an acceptable solution, we do not have to consider category 1.

24. University of Iowa Sports Information (UISI) procures its game-day football magazines from a publishing company at a price of $9.00 per magazine. UISI sells the magazines on the day of the corresponding football game at a retail price of $10.00. To sell these magazines, UISI hires vendors and pays them $0.50 for each program that they sell. For the first game of the season, UISI has determined that demand for the game-day football magazines is normally distributed with a mean of 9000 magazines and a standard deviation of 400 magazines. Any magazines that are not sold on the day of the game are worthless and UISI recycles them.
   a. What is UISI's optimal order quantity of game-day football magazines for the first game of the season?
   b. Instead of recycling the unsold programs, suppose the publisher offers to buy back any unsold programs for $8.00. Under this scenario, what is UISI's optimal order quantity?

25. The Gilbert Air-Conditioning Company is considering the purchase of a special shipment of portable air conditioners manufactured in Japan. Each unit will cost Gilbert $80, and it will be sold for $125. Gilbert does not want to carry surplus air conditioners over until the following year. Thus, all surplus air conditioners will be sold to a wholesaler for $50 per unit. Assume that the air conditioner demand follows a normal probability distribution with $\mu = 20$ and $\sigma = 8$.
   a. What is the recommended order quantity?
   b. What is the probability that Gilbert will sell all units it orders?

26. The Bridgeport city manager and the chief of police agreed on the size of the police force necessary for normal daily operations. However, they need assistance in determining the number of additional police officers needed to cover daily absences due to injuries, sickness, vacations, and personal leave. Records over the past three years show that the daily demand for additional police officers is normally distributed with a mean of 50 officers and a standard deviation of 10 officers. The cost of an additional police officer is based on the average pay rate of $150 per day. If the daily demand for additional police officers exceeds the number of additional officers available, the excess demand will be covered by overtime at the pay rate of $240 per day for each overtime officer.

a. If the number of additional police officers available is greater than demand, the city will have to pay for more additional police officers than needed. What is the cost of overestimating demand?

b. If the number of additional police officers available is less than demand, the city will have to use overtime to meet the demand. What is the cost of underestimating demand?

c. What is the optimal number of additional police officers that should be included in the police force?

d. On a typical day, what is the probability that overtime will be necessary?

27. A perishable dairy product is ordered daily at a particular supermarket. The product costs $1.19 per unit and sells for $1.65 per unit. If units are unsold at the end of the day, the supplier takes them back at a rebate of $1 per unit. Assume that daily demand is approximately normally distributed with $\mu = 150$ and $\sigma = 30$.

a. What is your recommended daily order quantity for the supermarket?

b. What is the probability that the supermarket will sell all the units it orders?

c. In problems such as these, why would the supplier offer a rebate as high as $1? For example, why not offer a nominal rebate of, say, 25¢ per unit? What happens to the supermarket order quantity as the rebate is reduced?

28. A retail outlet sells holiday candy for $10 per bag. The cost of the product is $8 per bag. All units not sold during the selling season prior to the holiday are sold for half the retail price in a postholiday clearance sale. Assume that demand for bags of holiday candy during the selling season is uniformly distributed between 200 and 800.

a. What is the recommended order quantity?

b. What is the probability that at least some customers will ask to purchase the product after the outlet is sold out? That is, what is the probability of a stock-out using your order quantity in part (a)?

c. To keep customers happy and returning to the store later, the owner feels that stockouts should be avoided if at all possible. What is your recommended order quantity if the owner is willing to tolerate a 0.15 probability of a stock-out?

d. Using your answer to part (c), what is the goodwill cost you are assigning to a stock-out?

29. Floyd Distributors, Inc., provides a variety of auto parts to small local garages. Floyd purchases parts from manufacturers according to the EOQ model and then ships the parts from a regional warehouse direct to its customers. For a particular type of muffler, Floyd's EOQ analysis recommends orders with $Q^* = 25$ to satisfy an annual demand of 200 mufflers. Floyd's has 250 working days per year, and the lead time averages 15 days.

a. What is the reorder point if Floyd assumes a constant demand rate?

b. Suppose that an analysis of Floyd's muffler demand shows that the lead-time demand follows a normal probability distribution with $\mu = 12$ and $\sigma = 2.5$. If Floyd's management can tolerate one stock-out per year, what is the revised reorder point?

c. What is the safety stock for part (b)? If $C_h = \$5$/unit/year, what is the extra cost due to the uncertainty of demand?

30. To serve "to-go" orders, Terrapin Coffeehouse faces normally distributed weekly demand with an average of 300 paper cups and a standard deviation of 75 cups per week. Terrapin orders cups by the box. Each box costs $10 and contains 100 cups. For each order placed, Terrapin pays a fixed $15 shipping fee (regardless of the number of boxes ordered) and the order arrives one week after Terrapin places it with the cup supplier. Terrapin estimates that holding costs are 15% per dollar per year. Due to the importance of cups to business,

Terrapin wants no more than a 1% chance of a stock-out during the one-week lead time for cup replenishment. Assume that there are 52 weeks in a year.

a.   What is the optimal order quantity (in terms of number of boxes)?

b.   What is the optimal reorder point (in terms of number of cups)?

31.   A product with an annual demand of 1000 units has C_o = $25.50 and C_h = $8. The demand exhibits some variability such that the lead-time demand follows a normal probability distribution with μ = 25 and σ = 5.

a.   What is the recommended order quantity?

b.   What are the reorder point and safety stock if the firm desires at most a 2% probability of stock-out on any given order cycle?

c.   If a manager sets the reorder point at 30, what is the probability of a stock-out on any given order cycle? How many times would you expect a stock-out during the year if this reorder point were used?

32.   The B&S Novelty and Craft Shop in Bennington, Vermont, sells a variety of quality hand-made items to tourists. B&S will sell 300 hand-carved miniature replicas of a Colonial soldier each year, but the demand pattern during the year is uncertain. The replicas sell for $20 each, and B&S uses a 15% annual inventory holding cost rate. Ordering costs are $5 per order, and demand during the lead time follows a normal probability distribution with μ = 15 and σ = 6.

a.   What is the recommended order quantity?

b.   If B&S is willing to accept a stock-out roughly twice a year, what reorder point would you recommend? What is the probability that B&S will have a stock-out in any one order cycle?

c.   What are the safety stock and annual safety stock costs for this product?

33.   A firm uses a one-week periodic review inventory system. A two-day lead time is needed for any order, and the firm is willing to tolerate an average of one stock-out per year.

a.   Using the firm's service guideline, what is the probability of a stock-out associated with each replenishment decision?

b.   What is the replenishment level if demand during the review period plus lead-time period is normally distributed with a mean of 60 units and a standard deviation of 12 units?

c.   What is the replenishment level if demand during the review period plus lead-time period is uniformly distributed between 35 and 85 units?

34.   Foster Drugs, Inc., handles a variety of health and beauty aid products. A particular hair conditioner product costs Foster Drugs $2.95 per unit. The annual holding cost rate is 20%. An order-quantity, reorder point inventory model recommends an order quantity of 300 units per order.

a.   Lead time is one week, and the lead-time demand is normally distributed with a mean of 150 units and a standard deviation of 40 units. What is the reorder point if the firm is willing to tolerate a 1% chance of stock-out on any one cycle?

b.   What safety stock and annual safety stock costs are associated with your recommendation in part (a)?

c.   The order-quantity, reorder point model requires a continuous review system. Management is considering making a transition to a periodic review system in an attempt to coordinate ordering for many of its products. The demand during the proposed two-week review period and the one-week lead-time period is normally distributed with a mean of 450 units and a standard deviation of 70 units. What is the recommended replenishment level for this periodic review system if the firm is willing to tolerate the same 1% chance of stock-out associated with any replenishment decision?

d.   What safety stock and annual safety stock costs are associated with your recommendation in part (c)?

e. Compare your answers to parts (b) and (d). The company is seriously considering the periodic review system. Would you support this decision? Explain.

f. Would you tend to favor the continuous review system for more expensive items? For example, assume that the product in the preceding example sold for $295 per unit. Explain.

35. Statewide Auto Parts uses a four-week periodic review system to reorder parts for its inventory stock. A one-week lead time is required to fill the order. Demand for one particular part during the five-week replenishment period is normally distributed with a mean of 18 units and a standard deviation of 6 units.

a. At a particular periodic review, 8 units are in inventory. The parts manager places an order for 16 units. What is the probability that this part will have a stock-out before an order that is placed at the next four-week review period arrives?

b. Assume that the company is willing to tolerate a 2.5% chance of a stock-out associated with a replenishment decision. How many parts should the manager have ordered in part (a)? What is the replenishment level for the four-week periodic review system?

36. Rose Office Supplies, Inc., which is open six days a week, uses a two-week periodic review for its store inventory. On alternating Monday mornings, the store manager fills out an order sheet requiring a shipment of various items from the company's warehouse. A particular three-ring notebook sells at an average rate of 16 notebooks per week. The standard deviation in sales is 5 notebooks per week. The lead time for a new shipment is three days. The mean lead-time demand is 8 notebooks with a standard deviation of 3.5.

a. What is the mean or expected demand during the review period plus the lead-time period?

b. Under the assumption of independent demand from week to week, the variances in demands are additive. Thus, the variance of the demand during the review period plus the lead-time period is equal to the variance of demand during the first week plus the variance of demand during the second week plus the variance of demand during the lead-time period. What is the variance of demand during the review period plus the lead-time period? What is the standard deviation of demand during the review period plus the lead-time period?

c. Assuming that demand has a normal probability distribution, what is the replenishment level that will provide an expected stock-out rate of one per year?

d. On Monday, March 22, 18 notebooks remain in inventory at the store. How many notebooks should the store manager order?

Case Problem 1   WAGNER FABRICATING COMPANY

Managers at Wagner Fabricating Company are reviewing the economic feasibility of manufacturing a part that the company currently purchases from a supplier. Forecasted annual demand for the part is 3200 units. Wagner operates 250 days per year.

Wagner's financial analysts established a cost of capital of 14% for the use of funds for investments within the company. In addition, over the past year $600,000 was the average investment in the company's inventory. Accounting information shows that a total of $24,000 was spent on taxes and insurance related to the company's inventory. In addition, an estimated $9000 was lost due to inventory shrinkage, which included damaged goods as well as pilferage. A remaining $15,000 was spent on warehouse overhead, including utility expenses for heating and lighting.

An analysis of the purchasing operation shows that approximately two hours are required to process and coordinate an order for the part regardless of the quantity ordered. Purchasing salaries average $28 per hour, including employee benefits. In addition, a detailed analysis of 125 orders showed that $2375 was spent on telephone, paper, and postage directly related to the ordering process.

A one-week lead time is required to obtain the part from the supplier. An analysis of demand during the lead time shows it is approximately normally distributed with a mean of 64 units and a standard deviation of 10 units. Service level guidelines indicate that one stock-out per year is acceptable.

Currently, the company has a contract to purchase the part from a supplier at a cost of $18 per unit. However, over the past few months, the company's production capacity has been expanded. As a result, excess capacity is now available in certain production departments, and the company is considering the alternative of producing the parts itself.

Forecasted utilization of equipment shows that production capacity will be available for the part being considered. The production capacity is available at the rate of 1000 units per month, with up to five months of production time available. Management believes that with a two-week lead time, schedules can be arranged so that the part can be produced whenever needed. The demand during the two-week lead time is approximately normally distributed, with a mean of 128 units and a standard deviation of 20 units. Production costs are expected to be $17 per part.

A concern of management is that setup costs will be substantial. The total cost of labor and lost production time is estimated to be $50 per hour, and a full eight-hour shift will be needed to set up the equipment for producing the part.

Managerial Report

Develop a report for management of Wagner Fabricating that will address the question of whether the company should continue to purchase the part from the supplier or begin to produce the part itself. Include the following factors in your report:

1. An analysis of the holding costs, including the appropriate annual holding cost rate
2. An analysis of ordering costs, including the appropriate cost per order from the supplier
3. An analysis of setup costs for the production operation
4. A development of the inventory policy for the following two alternatives:
   a. Ordering a fixed quantity Q from the supplier
   b. Ordering a fixed quantity Q from in-plant production
5. Include the following in the policies of parts 4(a) and 4(b):
   a. Optimal quantity $Q*$
   b. Number of order or production runs per year
   c. Cycle time
   d. Reorder point
   e. Amount of safety stock
   f. Expected maximum inventory
   g. Average inventory
   h. Annual holding cost
   i. Annual ordering cost
   j. Annual cost of the units purchased or manufactured

  k. Total annual cost of the purchase policy and the total annual cost of the production policy
6. Make a recommendation as to whether the company should purchase or manufacture the part. What savings are associated with your recommendation as compared with the other alternative?

Case Problem 2   RIVER CITY FIRE DEPARTMENT

The River City Fire Department (RCFD) fights fires and provides a variety of rescue operations in the River City metropolitan area. The RCFD staffs 13 ladder companies, 26 pumper companies, and several rescue units and ambulances. Normal staffing requires 186 firefighters to be on duty every day.

RCFD is organized with three firefighting units. Each unit works a full 24-hour day and then has two days (48 hours) off. For example, Unit 1 covers Monday, Unit 2 covers Tuesday, and Unit 3 covers Wednesday. Then Unit 1 returns on Thursday, and so on. Over a three-week (21-day) scheduling period, each unit will be scheduled for seven days. On a rotational basis, firefighters within each unit are given one of the seven regularly scheduled days off. This day off is referred to as a Kelley day. Thus, over a three-week scheduling period, each firefighter in a unit works six of the seven scheduled unit days and gets one Kelley day off.

Determining the number of firefighters to be assigned to each unit includes the 186 firefighters who must be on duty plus the number of firefighters in the unit who are off for a Kelley day. Furthermore, each unit needs additional staffing to cover firefighter absences due to injury, sick leave, vacations, or personal time. This additional staffing involves finding the best mix of adding full-time firefighters to each unit and the selective use of overtime. If the number of absences on a particular day brings the number of available firefighters below the required 186, firefighters who are currently off (e.g., on a Kelley day) must be scheduled to work overtime. Overtime is compensated at 1.55 times the regular pay rate.

Analysis of the records maintained over the last several years concerning the number of daily absences shows a normal probability distribution. A mean of 20 and a standard deviation of 5 provides a good approximation of the probability distribution for the number of daily absences.

Managerial Report

Develop a report that will enable Fire Chief O. E. Smith to determine the necessary numbers for the Fire Department. Include, at a minimum, the following items in your report:

1. Assuming no daily absences and taking into account the need to staff Kelley days, determine the base number of firefighters needed by each unit.
2. Using a minimum cost criterion, how many additional firefighters should be added to each unit in order to cover the daily absences? These extra daily needs will be filled by the additional firefighters and, when necessary, the more expensive use of overtime by off-duty firefighters.
3. On a given day, what is the probability that Kelley-day firefighters will be called in to work overtime?
4. Based on the three-unit organization, how many firefighters should be assigned to each unit? What is the total number of full-time firefighters required for the River City Fire Department?

Appendix 10.1   DEVELOPMENT OF THE OPTIMAL ORDER QUANTITY (Q) FORMULA FOR THE EOQ MODEL

Given equation (10.4) as the total annual cost for the EOQ model,

$$TC = \frac{1}{2}QC_h + \frac{D}{Q}C_o \tag{10.4}$$

we can find the order quantity Q that minimizes the total cost by setting the derivative, dTC/dQ, equal to zero and solving for Q^*.

$$\frac{dTC}{dQ} = \frac{1}{2}C_h - \frac{D}{Q^2}C_o = 0$$

$$\frac{1}{2}C_h = \frac{D}{Q^2}C_o$$

$$C_hQ^2 = 2DC_o$$

$$Q^2 = \frac{2DC_o}{C_h}$$

Hence,

$$Q^* = \sqrt{\frac{2DC_o}{C_h}} \tag{10.5}$$

The second derivative is

$$\frac{d^2TC}{dQ^2} = \frac{2D}{Q^3}C_o$$

Because the value of the second derivative is greater than zero, Q^* from equation (10.5) is the minimum-cost solution.

Appendix 10.2   DEVELOPMENT OF THE OPTIMAL LOT SIZE (Q^*) FORMULA FOR THE PRODUCTION LOT SIZE MODEL

Given equation (10.15) as the total annual cost for the production lot size model,

$$TC = \frac{1}{2}\left(1 - \frac{D}{P}\right)QC_h + \frac{D}{Q}C_o \tag{10.15}$$

we can find the order quantity Q that minimizes the total cost by setting the derivative, dTC/dQ, equal to zero and solving for Q^*.

$$\frac{dTC}{dQ} = \frac{1}{2}\left(1 - \frac{D}{P}\right)C_h - \frac{D}{Q^2}C_o = 0$$

Solving for Q^*, we have

$$\frac{1}{2}\left(1 - \frac{D}{P}\right)C_h = \frac{D}{Q^2}\,C_o$$

$$\left(1 - \frac{D}{P}\right)C_h Q^2 = 2DC_o$$

$$Q^2 = \frac{2DC_o}{(1 - D/P)C_h}$$

Hence,

$$Q^* = \sqrt{\frac{2DC_o}{(1 - D/P)C_h}} \tag{10.16}$$

The second derivative is

$$\frac{d^2TC}{dQ^2} = \frac{2DC_o}{Q^3}$$

Because the value of the second derivative is greater than zero, Q^* from equation (10.16) is a minimum-cost solution.

CHAPTER 8

Decision Analysis

CONTENTS

Decision analysis can be used to develop an optimal strategy when a decision maker is faced with several decision alternatives and an uncertain or risk-filled pattern of future events. For example, Ohio Edison used decision analysis to choose the best type of particulate control equipment for coal-fired generating units when it faced future uncertainties concerning sulfur content restrictions, construction costs, and so on. The State of North Carolina used decision analysis in evaluating whether to implement a medical screening test to detect metabolic disorders in newborns. The Management Science in Action, Natural Resource Management, discusses the use of decision analysis to evaluate alternative actions to protect endangered species.

Even when a careful decision analysis has been conducted, the uncertain future events make the final consequence uncertain. In some cases, the selected decision alternative may provide good or excellent results. In other cases, a relatively unlikely future event may occur, causing the selected decision alternative to provide only fair or even poor results. The risk associated with any decision alternative is a direct result of the uncertainty associated with the final consequence. A good decision analysis includes careful consideration of risk. Through risk analysis the decision maker is provided with probability information about the favorable as well as the unfavorable consequences that may occur.

We begin the study of decision analysis by considering problems that involve reasonably few decision alternatives and reasonably few possible future events. Influence diagrams and payoff tables are introduced to provide a structure for the decision problem

MANAGEMENT SCIENCE IN ACTION

NATURAL RESOURCE MANAGEMENT*

Caution must be exercised when making decisions on what measures are taken to protect an endangered or threatened species. A conservative action may not be sufficient to save the species, while an aggressive action may have serious economic consequences, and decision analysis has long been used to strike a balance of these two concerns. However, in recent years policy analysts have been giving increasing consideration to another issue—the potential deleterious long-run effects—the decision ultimately may have on the endangered or threatened species' ecosystem. Conservationists and policy analysts are now recognizing that the resilience of an ecological system, or the degree of disturbance that an ecological system can absorb without changing substantially, must be an important consideration when making these decisions.

In research funded by the U.S. Geological Survey and the U.S. Fish and Wildlife Service, B. Ken Williams of the Wildlife Society and Fred A. Johnson and James D. Nichols of the U.S. Geological Survey have developed a means for using decision analysis that considers resilience of an ecological system when assessing alternative strategies for protecting an endangered or threatened species. Although the resilience of the ecological system and the intended ecological and social benefits of various strategies for protecting a species are difficult to measure, this approach strives to consider them when selecting from various alternative strategies. Incorporating the resilience of the ecological system into decision analysis of alternative strategies for protecting endangered and threatened species promises to lead to actions that simultaneously enhance the probability of the species' survival and reduce the risk to the ecological system.

*Based on Fred A. Johnson, B. Ken Williams, and James D. Nichols, "Resilience Thinking and a Decision-Analytic Approach to Conservation: Strange Bedfellows or Essential Partners?" *Ecology and Society* 17, no. 4 (2013): 28.

and to illustrate the fundamentals of decision analysis. We then introduce decision trees to show the sequential nature of decision problems. Decision trees are used to analyze more complex problems and to identify an optimal sequence of decisions, referred to as an optimal decision strategy. Sensitivity analysis shows how changes in various aspects of the problem affect the recommended decision alternative.

13.1   PROBLEM FORMULATION

The first step in the decision analysis process is problem formulation. We begin with a verbal statement of the problem. We then identify the **decision alternatives**; the uncertain future events, referred to as **chance events**; and the **consequences** associated with each combination of decision alternative and chance event outcome. Let us begin by considering a construction project of the Pittsburgh Development Corporation.

Pittsburgh Development Corporation (PDC) purchased land that will be the site of a new luxury condominium complex. The location provides a spectacular view of downtown Pittsburgh and the Golden Triangle, where the Allegheny and Monongahela Rivers meet to form the Ohio River. PDC plans to price the individual condominium units between $300,000 and $1,400,000.

PDC commissioned preliminary architectural drawings for three different projects: one with 30 condominiums, one with 60 condominiums, and one with 90 condominiums. The financial success of the project depends upon the size of the condominium complex and the chance event concerning the demand for the condominiums. The statement of the PDC decision problem is to select the size of the new luxury condominium project that will lead to the largest profit given the uncertainty concerning the demand for the condominiums.

Given the statement of the problem, it is clear that the decision is to select the best size for the condominium complex. PDC has the following three decision alternatives:

$$d_1 = \text{a small complex with 30 condominiums}$$

$$d_2 = \text{a medium complex with 60 condominiums}$$

$$d_3 = \text{a large complex with 90 condominiums}$$

A factor in selecting the best decision alternative is the uncertainty associated with the chance event concerning the demand for the condominiums. When asked about the possible demand for the condominiums, PDC's president acknowledged a wide range of possibilities but decided that it would be adequate to consider two possible chance event outcomes: a strong demand and a weak demand.

In decision analysis, the possible outcomes for a chance event are referred to as the **states of nature**. The states of nature are defined so they are mutually exclusive (no more than one can occur) and collectively exhaustive (at least one must occur); thus one and only one of the possible states of nature will occur. For the PDC problem, the chance event concerning the demand for the condominiums has two states of nature:

$$s_1 = \text{strong demand for the condominiums}$$

$$s_2 = \text{weak demand for the condominiums}$$

Management must first select a decision alternative (complex size); then a state of nature follows (demand for the condominiums) and finally a consequence will occur. In this case, the consequence is PDC's profit.

Influence Diagrams

An **influence diagram** is a graphical device that shows the relationships among the decisions, the chance events, and the consequences for a decision problem. The **nodes** in an influence diagram represent the decisions, chance events, and consequences. Rectangles or squares depict **decision nodes**, circles or ovals depict **chance nodes**, and diamonds depict **consequence nodes**. The lines connecting the nodes, referred to as *arcs,* show the direction of influence that the nodes have on one another. Figure 13.1 shows the influence diagram for the PDC problem. The complex size is the decision node, demand is the chance node, and profit is the consequence node. The arcs connecting the nodes show that both the complex size and the demand influence PDC's profit.

Payoff Tables

Given the three decision alternatives and the two states of nature, which complex size should PDC choose? To answer this question, PDC will need to know the consequence associated with each decision alternative and each state of nature. In decision analysis, we refer to the consequence resulting from a specific combination of a decision alternative and a state of nature as a **payoff**. A table showing payoffs for all combinations of decision alternatives and states of nature is a **payoff table**.

Payoffs can be expressed in terms of profit, cost, time, distance, or any other measure appropriate for the decision problem being analyzed.

Because PDC wants to select the complex size that provides the largest profit, profit is used as the consequence. The payoff table with profits expressed in millions of dollars is shown in Table 13.1. Note, for example, that if a medium complex is built and demand turns out to be strong, a profit of \$14 million will be realized. We will use the notation V_{ij} to denote the payoff associated with decision alternative i and state of nature j. Using Table 13.1, $V_{31} = 20$ indicates a payoff of \$20 million occurs if the decision is to build a large complex (d_3) and the strong demand state of nature (s_1) occurs. Similarly, $V_{32} = -9$ indicates a loss of \$9 million if the decision is to build a large complex (d_3) and the weak demand state of nature (s_2) occurs.

FIGURE 13.1   INFLUENCE DIAGRAM FOR THE PDC PROJECT

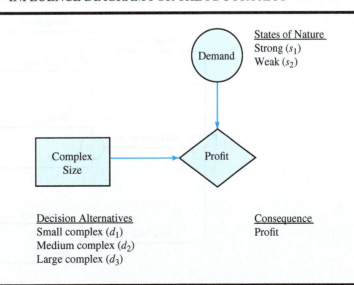

TABLE 13.1   PAYOFF TABLE FOR THE PDC CONDOMINIUM PROJECT (PAYOFFS IN $ MILLIONS)

	State of Nature	
Decision Alternative	**Strong Demand s_1**	**Weak Demand s_2**
Small complex, d_1	8	7
Medium complex, d_2	14	5
Large complex, d_3	20	−9

Decision Trees

A **decision tree** provides a graphical representation of the decision-making process. Figure 13.2 presents a decision tree for the PDC problem. Note that the decision tree shows the natural or logical progression that will occur over time. First, PDC must make a decision regarding the size of the condominium complex (d_1, d_2, or d_3). Then, after the decision is implemented, either state of nature s_1 or s_2 will occur. The number at each endpoint of the tree indicates the payoff associated with a particular sequence. For example, the topmost payoff of 8 indicates that an $8 million profit is anticipated if PDC constructs a small condominium complex (d_1) and demand turns out to be strong (s_1). The next payoff of 7 indicates an anticipated profit of $7 million if PDC constructs a small condominium complex (d_1) and demand turns out to be weak (s_2). Thus, the decision tree provides a graphical depiction of the sequences of decision alternatives and states of nature that provide the six possible payoffs for PDC.

If you have a payoff table, you can develop a decision tree. Try Problem 1, part (a).

The decision tree in Figure 13.2 shows four nodes, numbered 1−4. Squares are used to depict decision nodes and circles are used to depict chance nodes. Thus, node 1 is a decision node, and nodes 2, 3, and 4 are chance nodes. The **branches** connect the nodes; those

FIGURE 13.2   DECISION TREE FOR THE PDC CONDOMINIUM PROJECT (PAYOFFS IN $ MILLIONS)

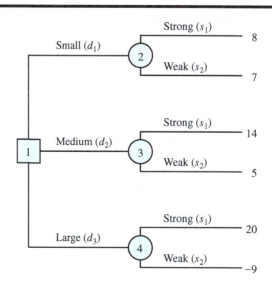

leaving the decision node correspond to the decision alternatives. The branches leaving each chance node correspond to the states of nature. The payoffs are shown at the end of the states-of-nature branches. We now turn to the question: How can the decision maker use the information in the payoff table or the decision tree to select the best decision alternative? Several approaches may be used.

NOTES AND COMMENTS

1. The first step in solving a complex problem is to decompose the problem into a series of smaller subproblems. Decision trees provide a useful way to decompose a problem and illustrate the sequential nature of the decision process.

2. People often view the same problem from different perspectives. Thus, the discussion regarding the development of a decision tree may provide additional insight about the problem.

13.2 DECISION MAKING WITHOUT PROBABILITIES

In this section we consider approaches to decision making that do not require knowledge of the probabilities of the states of nature. These approaches are appropriate in situations in which the decision maker has little confidence in his or her ability to assess the probabilities, or in which a simple best-case and worst-case analysis is desirable. Because different approaches sometimes lead to different decision recommendations, the decision maker must understand the approaches available and then select the specific approach that, according to the judgment of the decision maker, is the most appropriate.

Many people think of a good decision as one in which the consequence is good. However, in some instances, a good, well-thought-out decision may still lead to a bad or undesirable consequence while a poor, ill-conceived decision may still lead to a good or desirable consequence.

Optimistic Approach

The **optimistic approach** evaluates each decision alternative in terms of the *best* payoff that can occur. The decision alternative that is recommended is the one that provides the best possible payoff. For a problem in which maximum profit is desired, as in the PDC problem, the optimistic approach would lead the decision maker to choose the alternative corresponding to the largest profit. For problems involving minimization, this approach leads to choosing the alternative with the smallest payoff.

For a maximization problem, the optimistic approach often is referred to as the maximax approach; for a minimization problem, the corresponding terminology is minimin.

To illustrate the optimistic approach, we use it to develop a recommendation for the PDC problem. First, we determine the maximum payoff for each decision alternative; then we select the decision alternative that provides the overall maximum payoff. These steps systematically identify the decision alternative that provides the largest possible profit. Table 13.2 illustrates these steps.

TABLE 13.2   MAXIMUM PAYOFF FOR EACH PDC DECISION ALTERNATIVE

Decision Alternative	Maximum Payoff	
Small complex, d_1	8	
Medium complex, d_2	14	
Large complex, d_3	20	← Maximum of the maximum payoff values

Because 20, corresponding to d_3, is the largest payoff, the decision to construct the large condominium complex is the recommended decision alternative using the optimistic approach.

Conservative Approach

For a maximization problem, the conservative approach is often referred to as the maximin approach; for a minimization problem, the corresponding terminology is minimax.

The **conservative approach** evaluates each decision alternative in terms of the *worst* payoff that can occur. The decision alternative recommended is the one that provides the best of the worst possible payoffs. For a problem in which the output measure is profit, as in the PDC problem, the conservative approach would lead the decision maker to choose the alternative that maximizes the minimum possible profit that could be obtained. For problems involving minimization, this approach identifies the alternative that will minimize the maximum payoff.

To illustrate the conservative approach, we use it to develop a recommendation for the PDC problem. First, we identify the minimum payoff for each of the decision alternatives; then we select the decision alternative that maximizes the minimum payoff. Table 13.3 illustrates these steps for the PDC problem.

Because 7, corresponding to d_1, yields the maximum of the minimum payoffs, the decision alternative of a small condominium complex is recommended. This decision approach is considered conservative because it identifies the worst possible payoffs and then recommends the decision alternative that avoids the possibility of extremely "bad" payoffs. In the conservative approach, PDC is guaranteed a profit of at least $7 million. Although PDC may make more, it *cannot* make less than $7 million.

Minimax Regret Approach

In decision analysis, **regret** is the difference between the payoff associated with a particular decision alternative and the payoff associated with the decision that would yield the most desirable payoff for a given state of nature. Thus, regret represents how much potential payoff one would forgo by selecting a particular decision alternative given that a specific state of nature will occur. This is why regret is often referred to as **opportunity loss**.

As its name implies, under the **minimax regret approach** to decision making one would choose the decision alternative that minimizes the maximum state of regret that could occur over all possible states of nature. This approach is neither purely optimistic nor purely conservative. Let us illustrate the minimax regret approach by showing how it can be used to select a decision alternative for the PDC problem.

Suppose that PDC constructs a small condominium complex (d_1) and demand turns out to be strong (s_1). Table 13.1 showed that the resulting profit for PDC would be $8 million. However, given that the strong demand state of nature (s_1) has occurred, we realize

TABLE 13.3   MINIMUM PAYOFF FOR EACH PDC DECISION ALTERNATIVE

Decision Alternative	Minimum Payoff	
Small complex, d_1	7	← Maximum of the minimum payoff values
Medium complex, d_2	5	
Large complex, d_3	−9	

TABLE 13.4   OPPORTUNITY LOSS, OR REGRET, TABLE FOR THE PDC CONDOMINIUM
PROJECT ($ MILLIONS)

	State of Nature	
Decision Alternative	**Strong Demand s_1**	**Weak Demand s_2**
Small complex, d_1	12	0
Medium complex, d_2	6	2
Large complex, d_3	0	16

that the decision to construct a large condominium complex (d_3), yielding a profit of
$20 million, would have been the best decision. The difference between the payoff for the
best decision alternative ($20 million) and the payoff for the decision to construct a small
condominium complex ($8 million) is the regret or opportunity loss associated with deci-
sion alternative d_1 when state of nature s_1 occurs; thus, for this case, the opportunity loss
or regret is $20 million − $8 million = $12 million. Similarly, if PDC makes the decision
to construct a medium condominium complex (d_2) and the strong demand state of nature
(s_1) occurs, the opportunity loss, or regret, associated with d_2 would be $20 million −
$14 million = $6 million.

In general, the following expression represents the opportunity loss, or regret:

$$R_{ij} = |V_j^* - V_{ij}| \tag{13.1}$$

where

R_{ij} = the regret associated with decision alternative d_i and state of nature s_j

V_j^* = the payoff value[1] corresponding to the best decision for the state of nature s_j

V_{ij} = the payoff corresponding to decision alternative d_i and state of nature s_j

Note the role of the absolute value in equation (13.1). For minimization problems, the
best payoff, V_j^*, is the smallest entry in column j. Because this value always is less than or
equal to V_{ij}, the absolute value of the difference between V_j^* and V_{ij} ensures that the regret
is always the magnitude of the difference.

Using equation (13.1) and the payoffs in Table 13.1, we can compute the regret associated with each combination of decision alternative d_i and state of nature s_j. Because the
PDC problem is a maximization problem, V_j^* will be the largest entry in column j of the
payoff table. Thus, to compute the regret, we simply subtract each entry in a column from
the largest entry in the column. Table 13.4 shows the opportunity loss, or regret, table for
the PDC problem.

The next step in applying the minimax regret approach is to list the maximum regret
for each decision alternative; Table 13.5 shows the results for the PDC problem. Selecting
the decision alternative with the *minimum* of the *maximum* regret values—hence, the name
minimax regret—yields the minimax regret decision. For the PDC problem, the alternative
to construct the medium condominium complex, with a corresponding maximum regret of
$6 million, is the recommended minimax regret decision.

---

[1]In maximization problems, V_j^* will be the largest entry in column j of the payoff table. In minimization problems, V_j^*
will be the smallest entry in column j of the payoff table.

TABLE 13.5   MAXIMUM REGRET FOR EACH PDC DECISION ALTERNATIVE

Decision Alternative	Maximum Regret	
Small complex, d_1	12	
Medium complex, d_2	6	← Minimum of the maximum regret
Large complex, d_3	16	

For practice in developing a decision recommendation using the optimistic, conservative, and minimax regret approaches, try Problem 1, part (b).

Note that the three approaches discussed in this section provide different recommendations, which in itself isn't bad. It simply reflects the difference in decision-making philosophies that underlie the various approaches. Ultimately, the decision maker will have to choose the most appropriate approach and then make the final decision accordingly. The main criticism of the approaches discussed in this section is that they do not consider any information about the probabilities of the various states of nature. In the next section we discuss an approach that utilizes probability information in selecting a decision alternative.

13.3   DECISION MAKING WITH PROBABILITIES

In many decision-making situations, we can obtain probability assessments for the states of nature. When such probabilities are available, we can use the **expected value approach** to identify the best decision alternative. Let us first define the expected value of a decision alternative and then apply it to the PDC problem.

Let

$$N = \text{the number of states of nature}$$

$$P(s_j) = \text{the probability of state of nature } s_j$$

Because one and only one of the N states of nature can occur, the probabilities must satisfy two conditions:

$$P(s_j) \geq 0 \qquad \text{for all states of nature} \tag{13.2}$$

$$\sum_{j=1}^{N} P(s_j) = P(s_1) + P(s_2) + \cdots + P(s_N) = 1 \tag{13.3}$$

The **expected value (EV)** of decision alternative d_i is defined as follows:

$$\text{EV}(d_i) = \sum_{j=1}^{N} P(s_j)V_{ij} \tag{13.4}$$

In words, the expected value of a decision alternative is the sum of weighted payoffs for the decision alternative. The weight for a payoff is the probability of the associated state of nature and therefore the probability that the payoff will occur. Let us return to the PDC problem to see how the expected value approach can be applied.

PDC is optimistic about the potential for the luxury high-rise condominium complex. Suppose that this optimism leads to an initial subjective probability assessment of 0.8 that demand will be strong (s_1) and a corresponding probability of 0.2 that demand will be

Can you now use the expected value approach to develop a decision recommendation? Try Problem 5.

weak (s_2). Thus, $P(s_1) = 0.8$ and $P(s_2) = 0.2$. Using the payoff values in Table 13.1 and equation (13.4), we compute the expected value for each of the three decision alternatives as follows:

$$EV(d_1) = 0.8(8) + 0.2(7) \quad = 7.8$$
$$EV(d_2) = 0.8(14) + 0.2(5) \quad = 12.2$$
$$EV(d_3) = 0.8(20) + 0.2(-9) = 14.2$$

Thus, using the expected value approach, we find that the large condominium complex, with an expected value of $14.2 million, is the recommended decision.

The calculations required to identify the decision alternative with the best expected value can be conveniently carried out on a decision tree. Figure 13.3 shows the decision tree for the PDC problem with state-of-nature branch probabilities. Working backward through the decision tree, we first compute the expected value at each chance node. That is, at each chance node, we weight each possible payoff by its probability of occurrence. By doing so, we obtain the expected values for nodes 2, 3, and 4, as shown in Figure 13.4.

Computer packages are available to help in constructing more complex decision trees. See Appendices 13.1 and 13.2.

Because the decision maker controls the branch leaving decision node 1 and because we are trying to maximize the expected profit, the best decision alternative at node 1 is d_3. Thus, the decision tree analysis leads to a recommendation of d_3, with an expected value of $14.2 million. Note that this recommendation is also obtained with the expected value approach in conjunction with the payoff table.

Other decision problems may be substantially more complex than the PDC problem, but if a reasonable number of decision alternatives and states of nature are present, you can use the decision tree approach outlined here. First, draw a decision tree consisting of decision nodes, chance nodes, and branches that describe the sequential nature of the problem. If you use the expected value approach, the next step is to determine the probabilities for each of the states of nature and compute the expected value at each chance node. Then select the decision branch leading to the chance node with the best expected value. The decision alternative associated with this branch is the recommended decision.

FIGURE 13.3 PDC DECISION TREE WITH STATE-OF-NATURE BRANCH PROBABILITIES

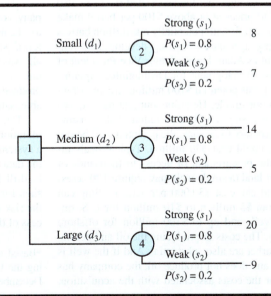

FIGURE 13.4   APPLYING THE EXPECTED VALUE APPROACH USING A DECISION TREE

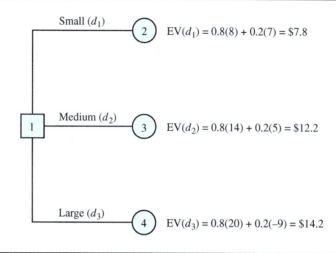

The Management Science in Action, Gushers, Dry Wells, and Decision Analysis, describes the importance of using data in the oil and natural gas industry to accurately estimate the likelihoods and the profit associated with possible outcomes in order to make wise development decisions.

MANAGEMENT SCIENCE IN ACTION

GUSHERS, DRY WELLS, AND DECISION ANALYSIS*

Oil and natural gas are big businesses; nine of the top ten organizations in Fortune's Global 500 are oil and gas companies. The rewards in these industries can be high, but the associated risks are also great. Oil prices at or above $100 per barrel make an oil reservoir with potentially one million barrels of supply appears an enticing development venture. But as Adam Farris, Senior Vice President of Business Development for Drillinginfo, explains, realizing this potential $100 million stream of revenue is not simple. He points out that the acquisition, processing, and interpretation of the seismic data necessary to evaluate the potential well before drilling could cost $30 million. Typical deals involve the procurement of access to thousands of acres of land (a single well may require 120 acres) and land can cost $30,000 per acre. Drilling can cost from $5 million to $10 million for U.S. on-shore wells and up to $100 million for offshore drilling. The costs of producing the oil and getting it to market are also substantial. And if the well is drilled and does not produce oil, the company has to incur the costs associated with the acquisition,

processing, and interpretation of the seismic data, obtaining access to the land, and drilling with no resulting revenue.

"If you are a major integrated oil and gas company, your profit on $100 million will be $1 million to $12 million (a bit higher for independent operators)," states Farris. "Many will lose money overall. Analytical approaches that impact the success rate of finding or reducing the cost to develop and produce oil and gas can make energy more affordable, safer and environmentally conscious."

Decision analysis provides a means for oil exploration companies to assess the complex data in a systematic manner and extract information from the data that ultimately are used to decide whether to drill in a potential well site. Identifying well sites for which the potential gains exceed justify the risk of drilling is critical to the economic success of these firms.

*Based on Adam Farris, "How Big Data Is Changing the Oil & Gas Industry," *Analytics* (November/ December 2012).

Expected Value of Perfect Information

Suppose that PDC has the opportunity to conduct a market research study that would help evaluate buyer interest in the condominium project and provide information that management could use to improve the probability assessments for the states of nature. To determine the potential value of this information, we begin by supposing that the study could provide *perfect information* regarding the states of nature; that is, we assume for the moment that PDC could determine with certainty, prior to making a decision, which state of nature is going to occur. To make use of this perfect information, we will develop a decision strategy that PDC should follow once it knows which state of nature will occur. A decision strategy is simply a decision rule that specifies the decision alternative to be selected after new information becomes available.

To help determine the decision strategy for PDC, we reproduced PDC's payoff table as Table 13.6. Note that, if PDC knew for sure that state of nature s_1 would occur, the best decision alternative would be d_3, with a payoff of \$20 million. Similarly, if PDC knew for sure that state of nature s_2 would occur, the best decision alternative would be d_1, with a payoff of \$7 million. Thus, we can state PDC's optimal decision strategy when the perfect information becomes available as follows:

> If s_1, select d_3 and receive a payoff of \$20 million.
>
> If s_2, select d_1 and receive a payoff of \$7 million.

What is the expected value for this decision strategy? To compute the expected value with perfect information, we return to the original probabilities for the states of nature: $P(s_1) = 0.8$ and $P(s_2) = 0.2$. Thus, there is a 0.8 probability that the perfect information will indicate state of nature s_1, and the resulting decision alternative d_3 will provide a \$20 million profit. Similarly, with a 0.2 probability for state of nature s_2, the optimal decision alternative d_1 will provide a \$7 million profit. Thus, from equation (13.4) the expected value of the decision strategy that uses perfect information is $0.8(20) + 0.2(7) = 17.4$.

We refer to the expected value of \$17.4 million as the *expected value with perfect information* (EVwPI).

Earlier in this section we showed that the recommended decision using the expected value approach is decision alternative d_3, with an expected value of \$14.2 million. Because this decision recommendation and expected value computation were made without the benefit of perfect information, \$14.2 million is referred to as the *expected value without perfect information* (EVwoPI).

The expected value with perfect information is \$17.4 million, and the expected value without perfect information is \$14.2; therefore, the expected value of the perfect information (EVPI) is $\$17.4 - \$14.2 = \$3.2$ million. In other words, \$3.2 million represents the additional expected value that can be obtained if perfect information were available about the states of nature.

TABLE 13.6 PAYOFF TABLE FOR THE PDC CONDOMINIUM PROJECT (\$ MILLIONS)

	State of Nature	
Decision Alternative	**Strong Demand s_1**	**Weak Demand s_2**
Small complex, d_1	8	7
Medium complex, d_2	14	5
Large complex, d_3	20	-9

It would be worth $3.2 million for PDC to learn the level of market acceptance before selecting a decision alternative.

Generally speaking, a market research study will not provide "perfect" information; however, if the market research study is a good one, the information gathered might be worth a sizable portion of the $3.2 million. Given the EVPI of $3.2 million, PDC might seriously consider a market survey as a way to obtain more information about the states of nature.

In general, the **expected value of perfect information (EVPI)** is computed as follows:

$$EVPI = |EVwPI - EVwoPI| \qquad (13.5)$$

where

$$EVPI = \text{expected value of perfect information}$$
$$EVwPI = \text{expected value } with \text{ perfect information about the states of nature}$$
$$EVwoPI = \text{expected value } without \text{ perfect information about the states of nature}$$

For practice in determining the expected value of perfect information, try Problem 14.

Note the role of the absolute value in equation (13.5). For minimization problems, the expected value with perfect information is always less than or equal to the expected value without perfect information. In this case, EVPI is the magnitude of the difference between EVwPI and EVwoPI, or the absolute value of the difference as shown in equation (13.5).

NOTES AND COMMENTS

1. We restate the *opportunity loss,* or *regret,* table for the PDC problem (see Table 13.4) as follows:

	State of Nature	
	Strong Demand	**Weak Demand**
Decision	s_1	s_2
Small complex, d_1	12	0
Medium complex, d_2	6	2
Large complex, d_3	0	16

Using $P(s_1)$, $P(s_2)$, and the opportunity loss values, we can compute the *expected opportunity loss* (EOL) for each decision alternative. With $P(s_1) = 0.8$ and $P(s_2) = 0.2$, the expected

opportunity loss for each of the three decision alternatives is

$$EOL(d_1) = 0.8(12) + 0.2(0) \quad = 9.6$$
$$EOL(d_2) = 0.8(6) \quad + 0.2(2) \quad = 5.2$$
$$EOL(d_3) = 0.8(0) \quad + 0.2(16) = 3.2$$

Regardless of whether the decision analysis involves maximization or minimization, the *minimum* expected opportunity loss always provides the best decision alternative. Thus, with $EOL(d_3) = 3.2$, d_3 is the recommended decision. In addition, the minimum expected opportunity loss always is *equal to the expected value of perfect information.* That is, EOL(best decision) = EVPI; for the PDC problem, this value is $3.2 million.

13.4   RISK ANALYSIS AND SENSITIVITY ANALYSIS

Risk analysis helps the decision maker recognize the difference between the expected value of a decision alternative and the payoff that may actually occur. **Sensitivity analysis** also helps the decision maker by describing how changes in the state-of-nature probabilities and/or changes in the payoffs affect the recommended decision alternative.

Risk Analysis

A decision alternative and a state of nature combine to generate the payoff associated with a decision. The **risk profile** for a decision alternative shows the possible payoffs along with their associated probabilities.

FIGURE 13.5   RISK PROFILE FOR THE LARGE COMPLEX DECISION ALTERNATIVE
FOR THE PDC CONDOMINIUM PROJECT

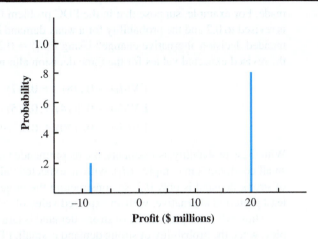

Let us demonstrate risk analysis and the construction of a risk profile by returning to the PDC condominium construction project. Using the expected value approach, we identified the large condominium complex (d_3) as the best decision alternative. The expected value of $14.2 million for d_3 is based on a 0.8 probability of obtaining a $20 million profit and a 0.2 probability of obtaining a $9 million loss. The 0.8 probability for the $20 million payoff and the 0.2 probability for the $-$9 million payoff provide the risk profile for the large complex decision alternative. This risk profile is shown graphically in Figure 13.5.

Sometimes a review of the risk profile associated with an optimal decision alternative may cause the decision maker to choose another decision alternative even though the expected value of the other decision alternative is not as good. For example, the risk profile for the medium complex decision alternative (d_2) shows a 0.8 probability for a $14 million payoff and a 0.2 probability for a $5 million payoff. Because no probability of a loss is associated with decision alternative d_2, the medium complex decision alternative would be judged less risky than the large complex decision alternative. As a result, a decision maker might prefer the less risky medium complex decision alternative even though it has an expected value of $2 million less than the large complex decision alternative.

Sensitivity Analysis

Sensitivity analysis can be used to determine how changes in the probabilities for the states of nature or changes in the payoffs affect the recommended decision alternative. In many cases, the probabilities for the states of nature and the payoffs are based on subjective assessments. Sensitivity analysis helps the decision maker understand which of these inputs are critical to the choice of the best decision alternative. If a small change in the value of one of the inputs causes a change in the recommended decision alternative, the solution to the decision analysis problem is sensitive to that particular input. Extra effort and care should be taken to make sure the input value is as accurate as possible. On the other hand, if a modest-to-large change in the value of one of the inputs does not cause a change in the recommended decision alternative, the solution to the decision analysis problem is not sensitive to that particular input. No extra time or effort would be needed to refine the estimated input value.

One approach to sensitivity analysis is to select different values for the probabilities of the states of nature and the payoffs and then resolve the decision analysis problem. If the recommended decision alternative changes, we know that the solution is sensitive to the changes made. For example, suppose that in the PDC problem the probability for a strong demand is revised to 0.2 and the probability for a weak demand is revised to 0.8. Would the recommended decision alternative change? Using $P(s_1) = 0.2$, $P(s_2) = 0.8$, and equation (13.4), the revised expected values for the three decision alternatives are

$$EV(d_1) = 0.2(8) + 0.8(7) = 7.2$$
$$EV(d_2) = 0.2(14) + 0.8(5) = 6.8$$
$$EV(d_3) = 0.2(20) + 0.8(-9) = -3.2$$

With these probability assessments, the recommended decision alternative is to construct a small condominium complex (d_1), with an expected value of $7.2 million. The probability of strong demand is only 0.2, so constructing the large condominium complex (d_3) is the least preferred alternative, with an expected value of $-$3.2 million (a loss).

Thus, when the probability of strong demand is large, PDC should build the large complex; when the probability of strong demand is small, PDC should build the small complex. Obviously, we could continue to modify the probabilities of the states of nature and learn even more about how changes in the probabilities affect the recommended decision alternative. The drawback to this approach is the numerous calculations required to evaluate the effect of several possible changes in the state-of-nature probabilities.

Computer software packages for decision analysis make it easy to calculate these revised scenarios.

For the special case of two states of nature, a graphical procedure can be used to determine how changes for the probabilities of the states of nature affect the recommended decision alternative. To demonstrate this procedure, we let p denote the probability of state of nature s_1; that is, $P(s_1) = p$. With only two states of nature in the PDC problem, the probability of state of nature s_2 is

$$P(s_2) = 1 - P(s_1) = 1 - p$$

Using equation (13.4) and the payoff values in Table 13.1, we determine the expected value for decision alternative d_1 as follows:

$$
\begin{aligned}
EV(d_1) &= P(s_1)(8) + P(s_2)(7) \\
&= p(8) + (1 - p)(7) \\
&= 8p + 7 - 7p = p + 7
\end{aligned}
\tag{13.6}
$$

Repeating the expected value computations for decision alternatives d_2 and d_3, we obtain expressions for the expected value of each decision alternative as a function of p:

$$EV(d_2) = 9p + 5 \tag{13.7}$$

$$EV(d_3) = 29p - 9 \tag{13.8}$$

Thus, we have developed three equations that show the expected value of the three decision alternatives as a function of the probability of state of nature s_1.

We continue by developing a graph with values of p on the horizontal axis and the associated EVs on the vertical axis. Because equations (13.6), (13.7), and (13.8) are linear equations, the graph of each equation is a straight line. For each equation, we can obtain

FIGURE 13.6 EXPECTED VALUE FOR THE PDC DECISION ALTERNATIVES AS A FUNCTION OF p

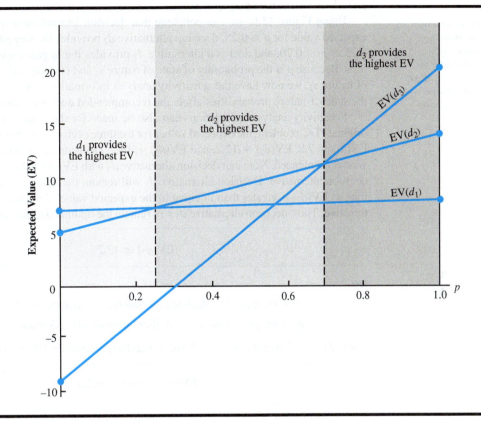

the line by identifying two points that satisfy the equation and drawing a line through the points. For instance, if we let $p = 0$ in equation (13.6), $EV(d_1) = 7$. Then, letting $p = 1$, $EV(d_1) = 8$. Connecting these two points, (0,7) and (1,8), provides the line labeled $EV(d_1)$ in Figure 13.6. Similarly, we obtain the lines labeled $EV(d_2)$ and $EV(d_3)$; these lines are the graphs of equations (13.7) and (13.8), respectively.

Figure 13.6 shows how the recommended decision changes as p, the probability of the strong demand state of nature (s_1), changes. Note that for small values of p, decision alternative d_1 (small complex) provides the largest expected value and is thus the recommended decision. When the value of p increases to a certain point, decision alternative d_2 (medium complex) provides the largest expected value and is the recommended decision. Finally, for large values of p, decision alternative d_3 (large complex) becomes the recommended decision.

The value of p for which the expected values of d_1 and d_2 are equal is the value of p corresponding to the intersection of the $EV(d_1)$ and the $EV(d_2)$ lines. To determine this value, we set $EV(d_1) = EV(d_2)$ and solve for the value of p:

$$p + 7 = 9p + 5$$
$$8p = 2$$
$$p = \frac{2}{8} = 0.25$$

Hence, when $p = 0.25$, decision alternatives d_1 and d_2 provide the same expected value. Repeating this calculation for the value of p corresponding to the intersection of the EV(d_2) and EV(d_3) lines, we obtain $p = 0.70$.

Graphical sensitivity analysis shows how changes in the probabilities for the states of nature affect the recommended decision alternative. Try Problem 8.

Using Figure 13.6, we can conclude that decision alternative d_1 provides the largest expected value for $p \le 0.25$, decision alternative d_2 provides the largest expected value for $0.25 \le p \le 0.70$, and decision alternative d_3 provides the largest expected value for $p \ge 0.70$. Because p is the probability of state of nature s_1 and $(1 - p)$ is the probability of state of nature s_2, we now have the sensitivity analysis information that tells us how changes in the state-of-nature probabilities affect the recommended decision alternative.

Sensitivity analysis calculations can also be made for the values of the payoffs. In the original PDC problem, the expected values for the three decision alternatives were as follows: EV(d_1) = 7.8, EV(d_2) = 12.2, and EV(d_3) = 14.2. Decision alternative d_3 (large complex) was recommended. Note that decision alternative d_2 with EV(d_2) = 12.2 was the second best decision alternative. Decision alternative d_3 will remain the optimal decision alternative as long as EV(d_3) is greater than or equal to the expected value of the second best decision alternative. Thus, decision alternative d_3 will remain the optimal decision alternative as long as

$$\text{EV}(d_3) \ge 12.2 \tag{13.9}$$

Let

$$S = \text{the payoff of decision alternative } d_3 \text{ when demand is strong}$$

$$W = \text{the payoff of decision alternative } d_3 \text{ when demand is weak}$$

Using $P(s_1) = 0.8$ and $P(s_2) = 0.2$, the general expression for EV(d_3) is

$$\text{EV}(d_3) = 0.8S + 0.2W \tag{13.10}$$

Assuming that the payoff for d_3 stays at its original value of $-\$9$ million when demand is weak, the large complex decision alternative will remain optimal as long as

$$\text{EV}(d_3) = 0.8S + 0.2(-9) \ge 12.2 \tag{13.11}$$

Solving for S, we have

$$0.8S - 1.8 \ge 12.2$$
$$0.8S \ge 14$$
$$S \ge 17.5$$

Recall that when demand is strong, decision alternative d_3 has an estimated payoff of $\$20$ million. The preceding calculation shows that decision alternative d_3 will remain optimal as long as the payoff for d_3 when demand is strong is at least $\$17.5$ million.

Assuming that the payoff for d_3 when demand is strong stays at its original value of $\$20$ million, we can make a similar calculation to learn how sensitive the optimal solution is with regard to the payoff for d_3 when demand is weak. Returning to the expected value calculation of equation (13.10), we know that the large complex decision alternative will remain optimal as long as

$$\text{EV}(d_3) = 0.8(20) + 0.2W \ge 12.2 \tag{13.12}$$

Solving for W, we have

$$16 + 0.2 \geq 12.2$$
$$0.2W \geq -3.8$$
$$W \geq -19$$

Recall that when demand is weak, decision alternative d_3 has an estimated payoff of $-\$9$ million. The preceding calculation shows that decision alternative d_3 will remain optimal as long as the payoff for d_3 when demand is weak is at least $-\$19$ million.

Based on this sensitivity analysis, we conclude that the payoffs for the large complex decision alternative (d_3) could vary considerably, and d_3 would remain the recommended decision alternative. Thus, we conclude that the optimal solution for the PDC decision problem is not particularly sensitive to the payoffs for the large complex decision alternative. We note, however, that this sensitivity analysis has been conducted based on only one change at a time. That is, only one payoff was changed and the probabilities for the states of nature remained $P(s_1) = 0.8$ and $P(s_2) = 0.2$. Note that similar sensitivity analysis calculations can be made for the payoffs associated with the small complex decision alternative d_1 and the medium complex decision alternative d_2. However, in these cases, decision alternative d_3 remains optimal only if the changes in the payoffs for decision alternatives d_1 and d_2 meet the requirements that $EV(d_1) \leq 14.2$ and $EV(d_2) \leq 14.2$.

Sensitivity analysis can assist management in deciding whether more time and effort should be spent obtaining better estimates of payoffs and probabilities.

NOTES AND COMMENTS

1. Some decision analysis software automatically provides the risk profiles for the optimal decision alternative. These packages also allow the user to obtain the risk profiles for other decision alternatives. After comparing the risk profiles, a decision maker may decide to select a decision alternative with a good risk profile even though the expected value of the decision alternative is not as good as the optimal decision alternative.

2. A *tornado diagram*, a graphical display, is particularly helpful when several inputs combine to determine the value of the optimal solution. By varying each input over its range of values, we obtain information about how each input affects the value of the optimal solution. To display this information, a bar is constructed for the input, with the width of the bar showing how the input affects the value of the optimal solution. The widest bar corresponds to the input that is most sensitive. The bars are arranged in a graph with the widest bar at the top, resulting in a graph that has the appearance of a tornado.

13.5   DECISION ANALYSIS WITH SAMPLE INFORMATION

In applying the expected value approach, we showed how probability information about the states of nature affects the expected value calculations and thus the decision recommendation. Frequently, decision makers have preliminary or **prior probability** assessments for the states of nature that are the best probability values available at that time. However, to make the best possible decision, the decision maker may want to seek additional information about the states of nature. This new information can be used to revise or update the prior probabilities so that the final decision is based on more accurate probabilities for the states of nature. Most often, additional information is obtained through experiments designed to provide **sample information** about the states of nature. Raw material sampling, product testing, and market research studies are examples of experiments (or studies) that may enable management to revise or update the state-of-nature probabilities. These revised probabilities are called **posterior probabilities**.

Let us return to the PDC problem and assume that management is considering a 6-month market research study designed to learn more about potential market acceptance of the PDC condominium project. Management anticipates that the market research study will provide one of the following two results:

1. Favorable report: A substantial number of the individuals contacted express interest in purchasing a PDC condominium.
2. Unfavorable report: Very few of the individuals contacted express interest in purchasing a PDC condominium.

Influence Diagram

By introducing the possibility of conducting a market research study, the PDC problem becomes more complex. The influence diagram for the expanded PDC problem is shown in Figure 13.7. Note that the two decision nodes correspond to the research study and the complex-size decisions. The two chance nodes correspond to the research study results and demand for the condominiums. Finally, the consequence node is the profit. From the arcs of the influence diagram, we see that demand influences both the research study results and profit. Although demand is currently unknown to PDC, some level of demand for the condominiums already exists in the Pittsburgh area. If existing demand is strong, the research study is likely to find a substantial number of individuals who express an interest in purchasing a condominium. However, if the existing demand is weak, the research study is more likely to find a substantial number of individuals who express little interest in purchasing a condominium. In this sense, existing demand for the condominiums will influence the research study results, and clearly, demand will have an influence upon PDC's profit.

The arc from the research study decision node to the complex-size decision node indicates that the research study decision precedes the complex-size decision. No arc spans from the research study decision node to the research study results node because the decision to conduct the research study does not actually influence the research study results. The decision to conduct the research study makes the research study results available, but it does not influence the results of the research study. Finally, the complex-size node and the

FIGURE 13.7   INFLUENCE DIAGRAM FOR THE PDC PROBLEM WITH SAMPLE INFORMATION

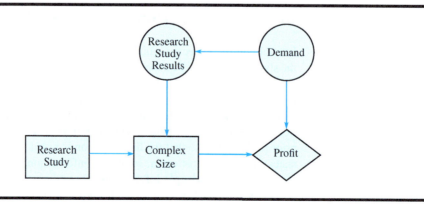

demand node both influence profit. Note that if a stated cost to conduct the research study were given, the decision to conduct the research study would also influence profit. In such a case, we would need to add an arc from the research study decision node to the profit node to show the influence that the research study cost would have on profit.

Decision Tree

The decision tree for the PDC problem with sample information shows the logical sequence for the decisions and the chance events in Figure 13.8.

First, PDC's management must decide whether the market research should be conducted. If it is conducted, PDC's management must be prepared to make a decision about the size of the condominium project if the market research report is favorable and, possibly, a different decision about the size of the condominium project if the market research report is unfavorable. In Figure 13.8, the squares are decision nodes and the circles are chance nodes. At each decision node, the branch of the tree that is taken is based on the decision made. At each chance node, the branch of the tree that is taken is based on probability or chance. For example, decision node 1 shows that PDC must first make the decision of whether to conduct the market research study. If the market research study is undertaken, chance node 2 indicates that both the favorable report branch and the unfavorable report branch are not under PDC's control and will be determined by chance. Node 3 is a decision node, indicating that PDC must make the decision to construct the small, medium, or large complex if the market research report is favorable. Node 4 is a decision node showing that PDC must make the decision to construct the small, medium, or large complex if the market research report is unfavorable. Node 5 is a decision node indicating that PDC must make the decision to construct the small, medium, or large complex if the market research is not undertaken. Nodes 6 to 14 are chance nodes indicating that the strong demand or weak demand state-of-nature branches will be determined by chance.

Analysis of the decision tree and the choice of an optimal strategy require that we know the branch probabilities corresponding to all chance nodes. PDC has developed the following branch probabilities:

If the market research study is undertaken

In Section 13.6 we explain how the branch probabilities for P(Favorable report) and P(Unfavorable report) can be developed.

$$P(\text{Favorable report}) = 0.77$$
$$P(\text{Unfavorable report}) = 0.23$$

If the market research report is favorable

$$P(\text{Strong demand given a favorable report}) = 0.94$$
$$P(\text{Weak demand given a favorable report}) = 0.06$$

If the market research report is unfavorable

$$P(\text{Strong demand given an unfavorable report}) = 0.35$$
$$P(\text{Weak demand given an unfavorable report}) = 0.65$$

If the market research report is not undertaken, the prior probabilities are applicable.

$$P(\text{Strong demand}) = 0.80$$
$$P(\text{Weak demand}) = 0.20$$

The branch probabilities are shown on the decision tree in Figure 13.9.

FIGURE 13.8   THE PDC DECISION TREE INCLUDING THE MARKET RESEARCH STUDY

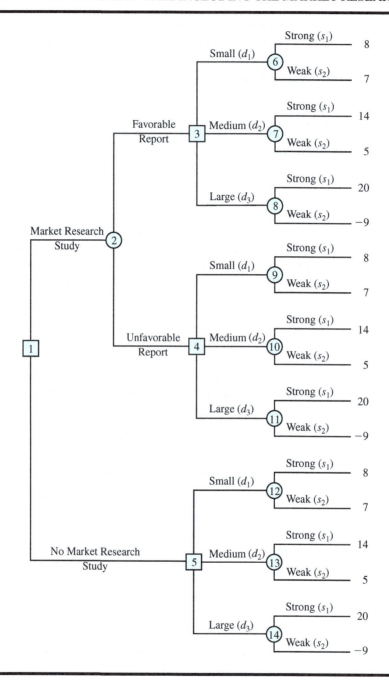

FIGURE 13.9   **THE PDC DECISION TREE WITH BRANCH PROBABILITIES**

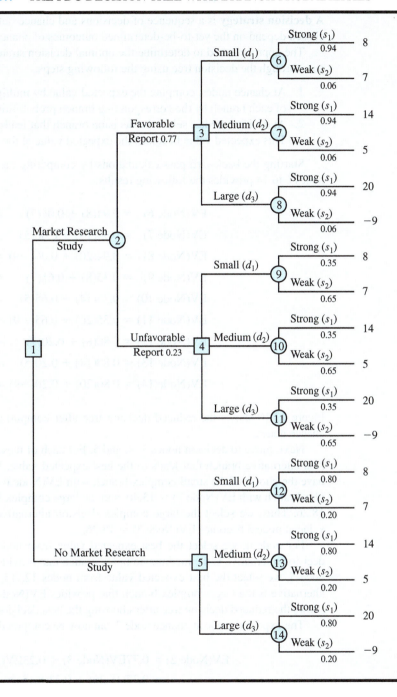

Decision Strategy

A **decision strategy** is a sequence of decisions and chance outcomes where the decisions chosen depend on the yet-to-be-determined outcomes of chance events.

The approach used to determine the optimal decision strategy is based on a backward pass through the decision tree using the following steps:

1. At chance nodes, compute the expected value by multiplying the payoff at the end of each branch by the corresponding branch probabilities.
2. At decision nodes, select the decision branch that leads to the best expected value. This expected value becomes the expected value at the decision node.

Starting the backward pass calculations by computing the expected values at chance nodes 6 to 14 provides the following results:

$$
\begin{aligned}
\text{EV(Node 6)} &= 0.94(8) + 0.06(7)   &&= 7.94 \\
\text{EV(Node 7)} &= 0.94(14) + 0.06(5) &&= 13.46 \\
\text{EV(Node 8)} &= 0.94(20) + 0.06(-9) &&= 18.26 \\
\text{EV(Node 9)} &= 0.35(8) + 0.65(7)   &&= 7.35 \\
\text{EV(Node 10)} &= 0.35(14) + 0.65(5) &&= 8.15 \\
\text{EV(Node 11)} &= 0.35(20) + 0.65(-9) &&= 1.15 \\
\text{EV(Node 12)} &= 0.80(8) + 0.20(7) &&= 7.80 \\
\text{EV(Node 13)} &= 0.80(14) + 0.20(5) &&= 12.20 \\
\text{EV(Node 14)} &= 0.80(20) + 0.20(-9) &&= 14.20
\end{aligned}
$$

Figure 13.10 shows the reduced decision tree after computing expected values at these chance nodes.

Next, move to decision nodes 3, 4, and 5. For each of these nodes, we select the decision alternative branch that leads to the best expected value. For example, at node 3 we have the choice of the small complex branch with EV(Node 6) = 7.94, the medium complex branch with EV(Node 7) = 13.46, and the large complex branch with EV(Node 8) = 18.26. Thus, we select the large complex decision alternative branch and the expected value at node 3 becomes EV(Node 3) = 18.26.

For node 4, we select the best expected value from nodes 9, 10, and 11. The best decision alternative is the medium complex branch that provides EV(Node 4) = 8.15. For node 5, we select the best expected value from nodes 12, 13, and 14. The best decision alternative is the large complex branch that provides EV(Node 5) = 14.20. Figure 13.11 shows the reduced decision tree after choosing the best decisions at nodes 3, 4, and 5.

The expected value at chance node 2 can now be computed as follows:

$$
\begin{aligned}
\text{EV(Node 2)} &= 0.77\text{EV(Node 3)} + 0.23\text{EV(Node 4)} \\
&= 0.77(18.26) + 0.23(8.15) = 15.93
\end{aligned}
$$

This calculation reduces the decision tree to one involving only the two decision branches from node 1 (see Figure 13.12).

Finally, the decision can be made at decision node 1 by selecting the best expected values from nodes 2 and 5. This action leads to the decision alternative to conduct the market research study, which provides an overall expected value of 15.93.

FIGURE 13.10 PDC DECISION TREE AFTER COMPUTING EXPECTED VALUES
AT CHANCE NODES 6 TO 14

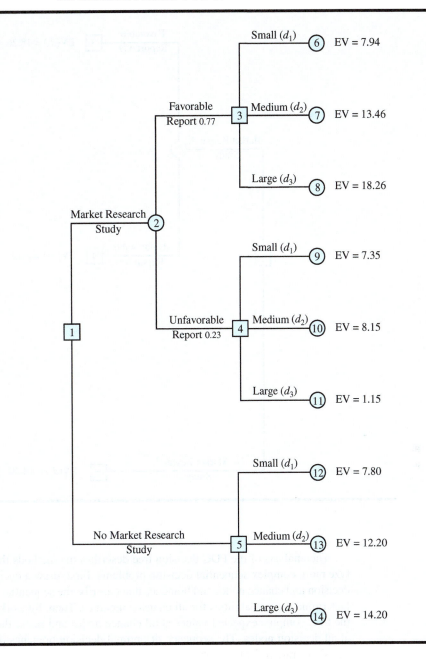

Problem 16 will test your ability to develop an optimal decision strategy.

The optimal decision for PDC is to conduct the market research study and then carry out the following decision strategy:

If the market research is favorable, construct the large condominium complex.

If the market research is unfavorable, construct the medium condominium complex.

FIGURE 13.11   PDC DECISION TREE AFTER CHOOSING BEST DECISIONS AT NODES 3, 4, AND 5

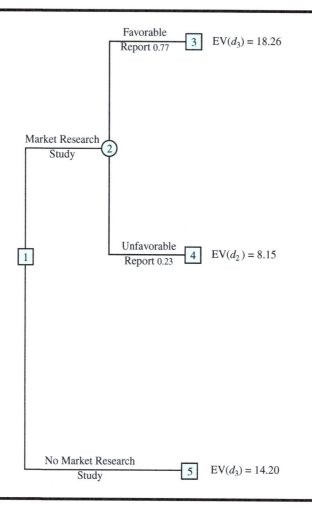

The analysis of the PDC decision tree describes the methods that can be used to analyze more complex sequential decision problems. First, draw a decision tree consisting of decision and chance nodes and branches that describe the sequential nature of the problem. Determine the probabilities for all chance outcomes. Then, by working backward through the tree, compute expected values at all chance nodes and select the best decision branch at all decision nodes. The sequence of optimal decision branches determines the optimal decision strategy for the problem.

The Management Science in Action, Decision Analysis At Bat, describes the application of decision analysis to guide a batter's strategy during an at-bat in a baseball game.

Risk Profile

Figure 13.13 provides a reduced decision tree showing only the sequence of decision alternatives and chance events for the PDC optimal decision strategy. By implementing the optimal decision strategy, PDC will obtain one of the four payoffs shown at the terminal

FIGURE 13.12 PDC DECISION TREE REDUCED TO TWO DECISION BRANCHES

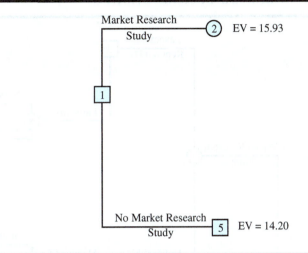

MANAGEMENT SCIENCE IN ACTION

DECISION ANALYSIS AT BAT*

Evan Gattis took a circuitous route to major league baseball. His path to becoming a 26-year-old rookie on the 2013 Atlanta Braves' roster has earned comparisons to Roy Hobbs, the mythical baseball player central to the novel and movie *The Natural*. As in the story of Roy Hobbs, Gattis dropped completely out of baseball for several years before returning in a big way. In his first month in the major leagues, he hit six home runs and was named the National League's Rookie of the Month. He duplicated both feats in his second month—he hit six more home runs and was again named the National League's Rookie of the Month. But what is most unusual about Gattis is that he may be the first major league baseball player to give credit to management science and decision analysis for his success.

While in the minor leagues Gattis began reading the work of University of Texas Professor J. Eric Bickel, who has used decision analysis to determine the optimal decisions for a hitter to make in each count. "One paper I wrote was how to act on different pitch counts," Bickel said. "Sometimes the batter will just let a pitch go by on purpose. If it's three balls, no strikes, a lot of times the coach will say, 'Don't swing at the pitch, no matter what.'"

What Bickel said is that most people don't understand why a batter would take a pitch on a 3-0 count. Because one more ball will result in a walk and put the batter on first base, under these circumstances the opposing pitcher will usually put a very hittable fastball through the heart of the

strike zone on the next pitch. However, Bickel's research demonstrates why taking a pitch when the count is three balls and no strikes rather than swinging at what will likely be a very hittable pitch increases the probability the batter will ultimately get on base.

"About 38 percent of all batters eventually get on base," Bickel said. "At 3-0, 77 percent of batters eventually get on base. Suppose you're sitting there with a 3-0 count. If you let the pitch go by, and the pitcher throws a strike, you're down to a 63 percent chance of getting on. If you instead put that ball in play, you only have a one-third chance of getting on base. Your choice is to put the ball in play and have a one-third chance of getting on base, or take a strike and still have a 63 percent chance of getting on base. That's why you take it."

Bickel has used decision analysis to determine a batter's optimal strategies for all ball-strike counts. His decision analysis and his lucid explanation of the resulting optimal strategies for various ball/strike counts have helped shape the way Gattis approaches each pitch when he is at bat.

*Based on Joe Lemire, "This Photo Is Just One Good Reason You Need to Know the Story of Evan Gattis," *Sports Illustrated* (June 10, 2013) and "Mastering the Numbers Game—Sports Illustrated Coverage," *Petroleum and Geosystems Engineering News*, University of Texas at Austin, http://www.pge.utexas.edu/news/136-eric-bickel.

FIGURE 13.13   PDC DECISION TREE SHOWING ONLY BRANCHES ASSOCIATED WITH OPTIMAL DECISION STRATEGY

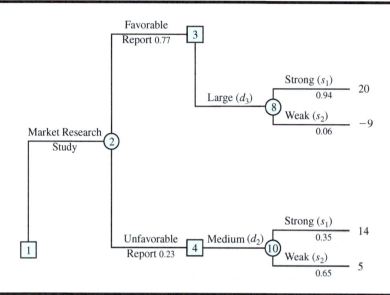

branches of the decision tree. Recall that a risk profile shows the possible payoffs with their associated probabilities. Thus, in order to construct a risk profile for the optimal decision strategy, we will need to compute the probability for each of the four payoffs.

Note that each payoff results from a sequence of branches leading from node 1 to the payoff. For instance, the payoff of $20 million is obtained by following the upper branch from node 1, the upper branch from node 2, the lower branch from node 3, and the upper branch from node 8. The probability of following that sequence of branches can be found by multiplying the probabilities for the branches from the chance nodes in the sequence. Thus, the probability of the $20 million payoff is $(0.77)(0.94) = 0.72$. Similarly, the probabilities for each of the other payoffs are obtained by multiplying the probabilities for the branches from the chance nodes leading to the payoffs. By doing so, we find the probability of the −$9 million payoff is $(0.77)(0.06) = 0.05$; the probability of the $14 million payoff is $(0.23)(0.35) = 0.08$; and the probability of the $5 million payoff is $(0.23)(0.65) = 0.15$. The following table showing the probability distribution for the payoffs for the PDC optimal decision strategy is the tabular representation of the risk profile for the optimal decision strategy.

Payoff ($ millions)	Probability
−9	0.05
5	0.15
14	0.08
20	0.72
	1.00

Figure 13.14 provides a graphical representation of the risk profile. Comparing Figures 13.5 and 13.14, we see that the PDC risk profile is changed by the strategy to conduct

FIGURE 13.14 RISK PROFILE FOR PDC CONDOMINIUM PROJECT WITH SAMPLE INFORMATION SHOWING PAYOFFS ASSOCIATED WITH OPTIMAL DECISION STRATEGY

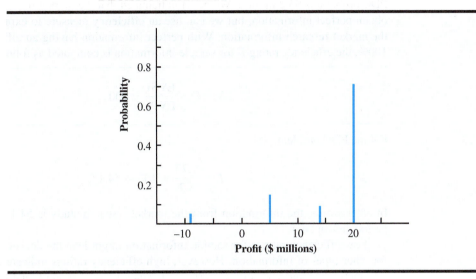

the market research study. In fact, the use of the market research study lowered the probability of the $9 million loss from 0.20 to 0.05. PDC's management would most likely view that change as a considerable reduction in the risk associated with the condominium project.

Expected Value of Sample Information

In the PDC problem, the market research study is the sample information used to determine the optimal decision strategy. The expected value associated with the market research study is $15.93. In Section 13.3 we showed that the best expected value if the market research study is *not* undertaken is $14.20. Thus, we can conclude that the difference, $15.93 − $14.20 = $1.73, is the **expected value of sample information (EVSI)**. In other words, conducting the market research study adds $1.73 million to the PDC expected value. In general, the expected value of sample information is as follows:

$$\text{EVSI} = \left| \text{EVwSI} - \text{EVwoSI} \right| \tag{13.13}$$

where

EVSI = expected value of sample information

EVwSI = expected value *with* sample information about the states of nature

EVwoSI = expected value *without* sample information about the states of nature

The EVSI = $1.73 million suggests PDC should be willing to pay up to $1.73 million to conduct the market research study.

Note the role of the absolute value in equation (13.13). For minimization problems, the expected value with sample information is always less than or equal to the expected value without sample information. In this case, EVSI is the magnitude of the difference between EVwSI and EVwoSI; thus, by taking the absolute value of the difference as shown in equation (13.13), we can handle both the maximization and minimization cases with one equation.

Efficiency of Sample Information

In Section 13.3 we showed that the expected value of perfect information (EVPI) for the PDC problem is $3.2 million. We never anticipated that the market research report would obtain perfect information, but we can use an **efficiency** measure to express the value of the market research information. With perfect information having an efficiency rating of 100%, the efficiency rating E for sample information is computed as follows:

$$E = \frac{\text{EVSI}}{\text{EVPI}} \times 100 \qquad (13.14)$$

For the PDC problem,

$$E = \frac{1.73}{3.2} \times 100 = 54.1\%$$

In other words, the information from the market research study is 54.1% as efficient as perfect information.

Low efficiency ratings for sample information might lead the decision maker to look for other types of information. However, high efficiency ratings indicate that the sample information is almost as good as perfect information and that additional sources of information would not yield substantially better results.

13.6   COMPUTING BRANCH PROBABILITIES WITH BAYES' THEOREM

In Section 13.5 the branch probabilities for the PDC decision tree chance nodes were specified in the problem description. No computations were required to determine these probabilities. In this section we show how **Bayes' theorem** can be used to compute branch probabilities for decision trees.

The PDC decision tree is shown again in Figure 13.15:

$$F = \text{Favorable market research report}$$
$$U = \text{Unfavorable market research report}$$
$$s_1 = \text{Strong demand (state of nature 1)}$$
$$s_2 = \text{Weak demand (state of nature 2)}$$

At chance node 2, we need to know the branch probabilities $P(F)$ and $P(U)$. At chance nodes 6, 7, and 8, we need to know the branch probabilities $P(s_1 \mid F)$, the probability of state of nature 1 given a favorable market research report, and $P(s_2 \mid F)$, the probability of state of nature 2 given a favorable market research report. $P(s_1 \mid F)$ and $P(s_2 \mid F)$ are referred to as *posterior probabilities* because they are conditional probabilities based on the outcome of the sample information. At chance nodes 9, 10, and 11, we need to know the branch probabilities $P(s_1 \mid U)$ and $P(s_2 \mid U)$; note that these are also posterior probabilities, denoting the probabilities of the two states of nature *given* that the market research report is unfavorable. Finally, at chance nodes 12, 13, and 14, we need the probabilities for the states of nature, $P(s_1)$ and $P(s_2)$, if the market research study is not undertaken.

In performing the probability computations, we need to know PDC's assessment of the probabilities for the two states of nature, $P(s_1)$ and $P(s_2)$, which are the prior probabilities as discussed earlier. In addition, we must know the **conditional probability** of the market

FIGURE 13.15   THE PDC DECISION TREE

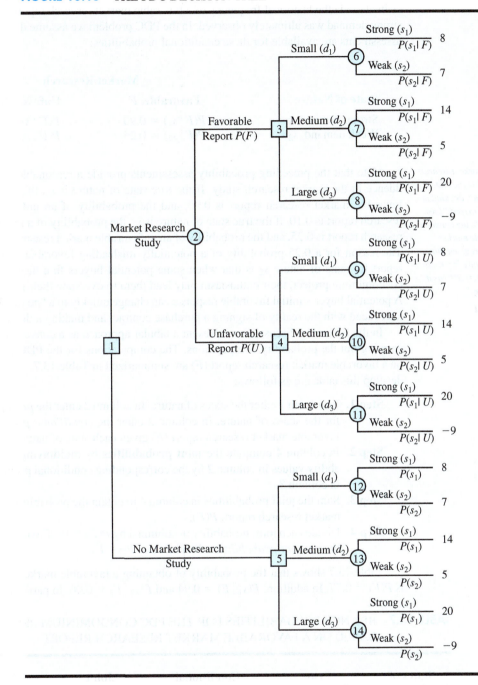

research outcomes (the sample information) *given* each state of nature. For example, we need to know the conditional probability of a favorable market research report given that the state of nature is strong demand for the PDC project; note that this conditional probability of F given state of nature s_1 is written $P(F \mid s_1)$. To carry out the probability calculations, we will need conditional probabilities for all sample outcomes given all states of nature, that is, $P(F \mid s_1)$, $P(F \mid s_2)$, $P(U \mid s_1)$, and $P(U \mid s_2)$. For example, $P(F \mid s_1)$ may be estimated via the historical frequency of a favorable market research report in cases where strong demand was ultimately observed. In the PDC problem we assume that the following assessments are available for these conditional probabilities:

	Market Research	
State of Nature	**Favorable, F**	**Unfavorable, U**
Strong demand, s_1	$P(F \mid s_1) = 0.90$	$P(U \mid s_1) = 0.10$
Weak demand, s_2	$P(F \mid s_2) = 0.25$	$P(U \mid s_2) = 0.75$

A favorable market research report given that the state of nature is weak demand is often referred to as a "false positive," while the converse (an unfavorable market research report given that the state of nature is strong demand) is referred to as a "false negative."

Note that the preceding probability assessments provide a reasonable degree of confidence in the market research study. If the true state of nature is s_1, the probability of a favorable market research report is 0.90, and the probability of an unfavorable market research report is 0.10. If the true state of nature is s_2, the probability of a favorable market research report is 0.25, and the probability of an unfavorable market research report is 0.75. The reason for a 0.25 probability of a potentially misleading favorable market research report for state of nature s_2 is that when some potential buyers first hear about the new condominium project, their enthusiasm may lead them to overstate their real interest in it. A potential buyer's initial favorable response can change quickly to a "no thank you" when later faced with the reality of signing a purchase contract and making a down payment.

In the following discussion we present a tabular approach as a convenient method for carrying out the probability computations. The computations for the PDC problem based on a favorable market research report (F) are summarized in Table 13.7. The steps used to develop this table are as follows:

Step 1. In column 1 enter the states of nature. In column 2 enter the *prior probabilities* for the states of nature. In column 3 enter the *conditional probabilities* of a favorable market research report (F) given each state of nature.

Step 2. In column 4 compute the **joint probabilities** by multiplying the prior probability values in column 2 by the corresponding conditional probability values in column 3.

Step 3. Sum the joint probabilities in column 4 to obtain the probability of a favorable market research report, $P(F)$.

Step 4. Divide each joint probability in column 4 by $P(F) - 0.77$ to obtain the revised or *posterior probabilities,* $P(s_1 \mid F)$ and $P(s_2 \mid F)$.

Table 13.7 shows that the probability of obtaining a favorable market research report is $P(F) = 0.77$. In addition, $P(s_1 \mid F) = 0.94$ and $P(s_2 \mid F) = 0.06$. In particular, note that a

TABLE 13.7   BRANCH PROBABILITIES FOR THE PDC CONDOMINIUM PROJECT
BASED ON A FAVORABLE MARKET RESEARCH REPORT

States of Nature s_j	Prior Probabilities $P(s_j)$	Conditional Probabilities $P(F \mid s_j)$	Joint Probabilities $P(F \cap s_j)$	Posterior Probabilities $P(s_j \mid F)$
s_1	0.8	0.90	0.72	0.94
s_2	0.2	0.25	0.05	0.06
	1.0		$P(F) = 0.77$	1.00

TABLE 13.8   BRANCH PROBABILITIES FOR THE PDC CONDOMINIUM PROJECT BASED ON AN UNFAVORABLE MARKET RESEARCH REPORT

States of Nature s_j	Prior Probabilities $P(s_j)$	Conditional Probabilities $P(U \mid s_j)$	Joint Probabilities $P(U \cap s_j)$	Posterior Probabilities $P(s_j \mid U)$
s_1	0.8	0.10	0.08	0.35
s_2	0.2	0.75	0.15	0.65
	1.0		$P(U) = 0.23$	1.00

favorable market research report will prompt a revised or posterior probability of 0.94 that the market demand of the condominium will be strong, s_1.

The tabular probability computation procedure must be repeated for each possible sample information outcome. Table 13.8 shows the computations of the branch probabilities of the PDC problem based on an unfavorable market research report. Note that the probability of obtaining an unfavorable market research report is $P(U) = 0.23$. If an unfavorable report is obtained, the posterior probability of a strong market demand, s_1, is 0.35 and of a weak market demand, s_2, is 0.65. The branch probabilities from Tables 13.7 and 13.8 were shown on the PDC decision tree in Figure 13.9.

Problem 23 asks you to compute the posterior probabilities.

The tabular method can be used directly to compute the branch probabilities in the decision tree. Alternatively, equation (13.15) provides a general formula for Bayes' theorem for computing posterior probabilities.

BAYES' THEOREM

$$P(A_i \mid B) = \frac{P(B \mid A_i)P(A_i)}{\Sigma_j P(B \mid A_j) P(A_j)} \qquad (13.15)$$

To perform the Bayes' theorem calculations for $P(s_1 \mid U)$ with equation (13.15), we replace B with U (unfavorable report) and A_i with s_1 in (13.15) so that we have,

$$P(s_1 \mid U) = \frac{P(U \mid s_1)P(s_1)}{\Sigma_j P(U \mid s_j) P(s_j)}$$

$$= \frac{0.10 \times 0.80}{(0.10 \times 0.80) + (0.20 \times 0.75)} = 0.35$$

which provides the same value as the tabular approach used to generate the values in Table 13.7.

The discussion in this section shows an underlying relationship between the probabilities on the various branches in a decision tree. It would be inappropriate to assume different prior probabilities, $P(s_1)$ and $P(s_2)$, without determining how these changes would alter $P(F)$ and $P(U)$, as well as the posterior probabilities $P(s_1 \mid F)$, $P(s_2 \mid F)$, $P(s_1 \mid U)$, and $P(s_2 \mid U)$.

MANAGEMENT SCIENCE IN ACTION

DECISION ANALYSIS HELPS TREAT AND PREVENT HEPATITIS B*

Hepatitis B is a viral disease that left untreated can lead to fatal liver conditions such as cirrhosis and cancer. The hepatitis B virus can be treated, and there exists a vaccine to prevent it. However, in order to make economically prudent allocations of their limited health care budgets, public health officials require analysis on the cost effectiveness (health benefit per dollar investment) of any potential health program. Unfortunately, since hepatitis B is a slow-progressing condition whose victims are often unaware of their potentially fatal infection, gathering data on the benefits of any public health policy addressing hepatitis B would take decades.

A multidisciplinary team consisting of management science researchers and a liver transplant surgeon from Stanford University applied decision analysis techniques to determine which combination of hepatitis B screening, treatment, and vaccination would be appropriate in the United States. Their decision tree contained the sequential decisions of (1) whether or not to perform a blood test to screen an individual for a hepatitis B infection, (2) whether or not to treat infected individuals, and (3) whether or not to vaccinate a noninfected (or nonscreened) individual.

For each policy, composed of a sequence of screening, treatment, and vaccination decisions, the researchers utilized existing infection and treatment knowledge to model future disease progression. Implementing their decision model in an Excel spreadsheet, the researchers concluded that it is cost effective to screen adult Asian and Pacific Islanders so that infected individuals can be treated (these individuals are genetically at a high risk for hepatitis B infection). Although it is not cost effective to universally vaccinate all U.S. adult Asian and Pacific Islanders, it proves to be cost effective to vaccinate people in close contact with infected individuals. Influenced by these findings, the Centers for Disease Control and Prevention updated its official policy in 2008 to recommend screening all adult Asian and Pacific Islanders and all adults in areas of intermediate (2% to 7%) hepatitis B prevalence.

*Based on David W. Hutton, Margaret L. Brandeau, and Samuel K. So, "Doing Good With Good OR: Supporting Cost-Effective Hepatitis B Interventions," *Interfaces* 41(May/June 2011): 289–300.

The Management Science in Action, Decision Analysis Helps Treat and Prevent Hepatitis B, discusses how medical researchers use posterior probability information and decision analysis to understand the risks and costs associated with treatment and screening procedures.

13.7   UTILITY THEORY

The decision analysis situations presented so far in this chapter expressed outcomes (payoffs) in terms of monetary values. With probability information available about the outcomes of the chance events, we defined the optimal decision alternative as the one that provided the best expected value. However, in some situations the decision alternative with the best expected value may not be the preferred alternative. A decision maker may also wish to consider intangible factors such as risk, image, or other nonmonetary criteria in order to evaluate the decision alternatives. When monetary value does not necessarily lead to the most preferred decision, expressing the value (or worth) of a consequence in terms of its utility will permit the use of expected utility to identify the most desirable decision alternative. The discussion of utility and its application in decision analysis is presented in this section.

Utility is a measure of the total worth or relative desirability of a particular outcome; it reflects the decision maker's attitude toward a collection of factors such as profit, loss, and risk. Researchers have found that as long as the monetary value of payoffs stays within a range that the decision maker considers reasonable, selecting the decision alternative with the best expected value usually leads to selection of the most preferred decision. However, when the payoffs are extreme, decision makers are often unsatisfied or uneasy with the decision that simply provides the best expected value.

As an example of a situation in which utility can help in selecting the best decision alternative, let us consider the problem faced by Swofford, Inc., a relatively small real estate investment firm located in Atlanta, Georgia. Swofford currently has two investment opportunities that require approximately the same cash outlay. The cash requirements necessary prohibit Swofford from making more than one investment at this time. Consequently, three possible decision alternatives may be considered.

The three decision alternatives, denoted d_1, d_2, and d_3, are

$$d_1 = \text{make investment A}$$
$$d_2 = \text{make investment B}$$
$$d_3 = \text{do not invest}$$

The monetary payoffs associated with the investment opportunities depend on the investment decision and on the direction of the real estate market during the next six months (the chance event). Real estate prices will go up, remain stable, or go down. Thus the states of nature, denoted s_1, s_2, and s_3, are

$$s_1 = \text{real estate prices go up}$$
$$s_2 = \text{real estate prices remain stable}$$
$$s_3 = \text{real estate prices go down}$$

Using the best information available, Swofford has estimated the profits, or payoffs, associated with each decision alternative and state-of-nature combination. The resulting payoff table is shown in Table 13.9.

The best estimate of the probability that real estate prices will go up is 0.3; the best estimate of the probability that prices will remain stable is 0.5; and the best estimate of the probability that prices will go down is 0.2. Thus the expected values for the three decision alternatives are

$$\text{EV}(d_1) = 0.3(30,000) + 0.5(20,000) \ \ + 0.2(-50,000) = \ \ \ \ 9000$$
$$\text{EV}(d_2) = 0.3(50,000) + 0.5(-20,000) + 0.2(-30,000) = -11,000$$
$$\text{EV}(d_3) = 0.3(0) \ \ \ \ \ \ \ + 0.5(0) \ \ \ \ \ \ \ \ + 0.2(0) \ \ \ \ \ \ \ \ \ \ = \ \ \ \ \ \ \ \ 0$$

Using the expected value approach, the optimal decision is to select investment A with an expected value of $9,000. Is it really the best decision alternative? Let us consider some other relevant factors that relate to Swofford's capability for absorbing the loss of $50,000 if investment A is made and prices actually go down.

TABLE 13.9   PAYOFF TABLE FOR SWOFFORD, INC.

	State of Nature		
Decision Alternative	**Prices Go Up s_1**	**Prices Stable s_2**	**Prices Go Down s_3**
Investment A, d_1	$30,000	$20,000	-$50,000
Investment B, d_2	$50,000	-$20,000	-$30,000
Do Not Invest, d_3	0	0	0

Actually, Swofford's current financial position is weak. This condition is partly reflected in Swofford's ability to make only one investment. More important, however, the firm's president believes that, if the next investment results in a substantial loss, Swofford's future will be in jeopardy. Although the expected value approach leads to a recommendation for d_1, do you think the firm's president would prefer this decision? We suspect that the president would select d_2 or d_3 to avoid the possibility of incurring a $50,000 loss. In fact, a reasonable conclusion is that, if a loss of even $30,000 could drive Swofford out of business, the president would select d_3, believing that both investments A and B are too risky for Swofford's current financial position.

The way we resolve Swofford's dilemma is first to determine Swofford's utility for the various outcomes. Recall that the utility of any outcome is the total worth of that outcome, taking into account all risks and consequences involved. If the utilities for the various consequences are assessed correctly, the decision alternative with the highest expected utility is the most preferred, or best, alternative. We next show how to determine the utility of the outcomes so that the alternative with the highest expected utility can be identified.

Utility and Decision Analysis

The procedure we use to establish a utility for each of the payoffs in Swofford's situation requires that we first assign a utility to the best and worst possible payoffs. Any values will work as long as the utility assigned to the best payoff is greater than the utility assigned to the worst payoff. In this case, $50,000 is the best payoff and −$50,000 is the worst. Suppose, then, that we arbitrarily make assignments to these two payoffs as follows:

Utility values of 0 and 1 could have been selected here; we selected 0 and 10 to avoid any possible confusion between the utility value for a payoff and the probability p.

p *is often referred to as the* indifference probability.

$$\text{Utility of } -\$50,000 = U(-50,000) = 0$$
$$\text{Utility of } \$50,000 = U(50,000) = 10$$

Let us now determine the utility associated with every other payoff.

Consider the process of establishing the utility of a payoff of $30,000. First we ask Swofford's president to state a preference between a guaranteed $30,000 payoff and an opportunity to engage in the following lottery, or bet, for some probability of p that we select:

Lottery: Swofford obtains a payoff of $50,000 with probability p and a payoff of −$50,000 with probability $(1 - p)$.

Obviously, if p is very close to 1, Swofford's president would prefer the lottery to the guaranteed payoff of $30,000 because the firm would virtually ensure itself a payoff of $50,000. If p is very close to 0, Swofford's president would clearly prefer the guarantee of $30,000. In any event, as p increases continuously from 0 to 1, the preference for the guaranteed payoff of $30,000 decreases and at some point is equal to the preference for the lottery. At this value of p, Swofford's president would have equal preference for the guaranteed payoff of $30,000 and the lottery; at greater values of p, Swofford's president would prefer the lottery to the guaranteed $30,000 payoff. For example, let us assume that when $p = 0.95$, Swofford's president is indifferent between the guaranteed payoff of $30,000 and the lottery. For this value of p, we can compute the utility of a $30,000 payoff as follows:

$$U(30,000) = pU(50,000) + (1 - p)U(-50,000)$$
$$= 0.95(10) + (0.05)(0)$$
$$= 9.5$$

Obviously, if we had started with a different assignment of utilities for a payoff of $50,000 and −$50,000, the result would have been a different utility for $30,000. For example, if we had started with an assignment of 100 for $50,000 and 10 for $-$50,000, the utility of a $30,000 payoff would be

$$U(30,000) = 0.95(100) + 0.05(10)$$
$$= 95.0 + 0.5$$
$$= 95.5$$

Hence, we must conclude that the utility assigned to each payoff is not unique but merely depends on the initial choice of utilities for the best and worst payoffs.

Before computing the utility for the other payoffs, let us consider the implication of Swofford's president assigning a utility of 9.5 to a payoff of $30,000. Clearly, when $p = 0.95$, the expected value of the lottery is

$$\text{EV(lottery)} = 0.95(\$50,000) + 0.05(-\$50,000)$$
$$= \$47,500 - \$2,500$$
$$= \$45,000$$

The difference between the expected value of the lottery and the guaranteed payoff can be viewed as the risk premium the decision maker is willing to pay.

Although the expected value of the lottery when $p = 0.95$ is $45,000, Swofford's president is indifferent between the lottery (and its associated risk) and a guaranteed payoff of $30,000. Thus, Swofford's president is taking a conservative, or risk-avoiding, viewpoint. A decision maker who would choose a guaranteed payoff over a lottery with a superior expected payoff is a **risk avoider** (or is said to be risk averse). The president would rather have $30,000 for certain than risk anything greater than a 5 percent chance of incurring a loss of $50,000. In other words, the difference between the EV of $45,000 and the guaranteed payoff of $30,000 is the risk premium that Swofford's president would be willing to pay to avoid the 5 percent chance of losing $50,000.

To compute the utility associated with a payoff of $-$20,000, we must ask Swofford's president to state a preference between a guaranteed $-$20,000 payoff and an opportunity to engage again in the following lottery:

Lottery: Swofford obtains a payoff of $50,000 with probability p and a payoff of $-$50,000 with probability $(1 - p)$.

Note that this lottery is exactly the same as the one we used to establish the utility of a payoff of $30,000 (in fact, we can use this lottery to establish the utility for any value in the Swofford payoff table). We need to determine the value of p that would make the president indifferent between a guaranteed payoff of $-$20,000 and the lottery. For example, we might begin by asking the president to choose between a certain loss of $20,000 and the lottery with a payoff of $50,000 with probability $p = 0.90$ and a payoff of $-$50,000 with probability $(1 - p) = 0.10$. What answer do you think we would get? Surely, with this high probability of obtaining a payoff of $50,000, the president would elect the lottery. Next, we might ask whether $p = 0.85$ would result in indifference between the loss of $20,000 for certain and the lottery. Again the president might prefer the lottery. Suppose that we continue until we get to $p = 0.55$, at which point the president is indifferent between the payoff of $-$20,000 and the lottery. In other words, for any value of p less than 0.55, the president would take a loss of $20,000 for certain rather than risk the potential loss of $50,000 with the lottery; and for any value of p above 0.55, the president would choose the lottery. Thus, the utility assigned to a payoff of $-$20,000 is

$$U(-\$20,000) = pU(50,000) + (1 - p)U(-\$50,000)$$
$$= 0.55(10) + 0.45(0)$$
$$= 5.5$$

Again let us assess the implication of this assignment by comparing it to the expected value approach. When $p = 0.55$, the expected value of the lottery is

$$EV(\text{lottery}) = 0.55(\$50,000) + 0.45(-\$50,000)$$
$$= \$27,500 - \$22,500$$
$$= \$5,000$$

Thus, Swofford's president would just as soon absorb a certain loss of $20,000 as take the lottery and its associated risk, even though the expected value of the lottery is $5,000. Once again this preference demonstrates the conservative, or risk-avoiding, point of view of Swofford's president.

In these two examples, we computed the utility for the payoffs of $30,000 and $-$20,000$. We can determine the utility for any payoff M in a similar fashion. First, we must find the probability p for which the decision maker is indifferent between a guaranteed payoff of M and a lottery with a payoff of $50,000 with probability p and $-$50,000$ with probability $(1 - p)$. The utility of M is then computed as follows:

$$U(M) = pU(\$50,000) + (1 - p)U(-\$50,000)$$
$$= p(10) + (1 - p)0$$
$$= 10p$$

Using this procedure we developed a utility for each of the remaining payoffs in Swofford's problem. The results are presented in Table 13.10.

Now that we have determined the utility of each of the possible monetary values, we can write the original payoff table in terms of utility. Table 13.11 shows the utility for the various outcomes in the Swofford problem. The notation we use for the entries in the utility table is U_{ij}, which denotes the utility associated with decision alternative d_i and state of nature s_j. Using this notation, we see that $U_{23} = 4.0$.

We can now compute the **expected utility (EU)** of the utilities in Table 13.11 in a similar fashion as we computed expected value in Section 13.3. In other words, to identify

TABLE 13.10   UTILITY OF MONETARY PAYOFFS FOR SWOFFORD, INC.

Monetary Value	Indifference Value of p	Utility
$50,000	Does not apply	10.0
30,000	0.95	9.5
20,000	0.90	9.0
0	0.75	7.5
$-20,000$	0.55	5.5
$-30,000$	0.40	4.0
$-50,000$	Does not apply	0

TABLE 13.11   UTILITY TABLE FOR SWOFFORD, INC.

| Decision Alternative | State of Nature | | |
	Prices Up s_1	Prices Stable s_2	Prices Down s_3
Investment A, d_1	9.5	9.0	0
Investment B, d_2	10.0	5.5	4.0
Do Not Invest, d_3	7.5	7.5	7.5

an optimal decision alternative for Swofford, Inc., the expected utility approach requires the analyst to compute the expected utility for each decision alternative and then select the alternative yielding the highest expected utility. With N possible states of nature, the expected utility of a decision alternative d_i is given by

---

EXPECTED UTILITY (EU)

$$EU(d_i) = \sum_{j=1}^{N} P(s_j)U_{ij}$$

(13.16)

The expected utility for each of the decision alternatives in the Swofford problem is

$$EU(d_1) = 0.3(9.5) + 0.5(9.0) + 0.2(0) = 7.35$$
$$EU(d_2) = 0.3(10) + 0.5(5.5) + 0.2(4.0) = 6.55$$
$$EU(d_3) = 0.3(7.5) + 0.5(7.5) + 0.2(7.5) = 7.50$$

Note that the optimal decision using the expected utility approach is d_3, do not invest. The ranking of alternatives according to the president's utility assignments and the associated monetary values are as follows:

Ranking of Decision Alternatives	Expected Utility	Expected Value
Do Not Invest	7.50	0
Investment A	7.35	9000
Investment B	6.55	−1000

Note that, although investment A had the highest expected value of $9,000, the analysis indicates that Swofford should decline this investment. The rationale behind not selecting investment A is that the 0.20 probability of a $50,000 loss was considered to involve a serious risk by Swofford's president. The seriousness of this risk and its associated impact on the company were not adequately reflected by the expected value of investment A. We assessed the utility for each payoff to assess this risk adequately.

The following steps state in general terms the procedure used to solve the Swofford, Inc., investment problem:

Step 1. Develop a payoff table using monetary values
Step 2. Identify the best and worst payoff values in the table and assign each a utility, with U(best payoff) > U(worst payoff)
Step 3. For every other monetary value M in the original payoff table, do the following to determine its utility:
    a. Define the lottery such that there is a probability p of the best payoff and a probability $(1 - p)$ of the worst payoff
    b. Determine the value of p such that the decision maker is indifferent between a guaranteed payoff of M and the lottery defined in step 3(a)
    c. Calculate the utility of M as follows:

$$U(M) = pU(\text{best payoff}) + (1 - p)U(\text{worst payoff})$$

Step 4. Convert each monetary value in the payoff table to a utility
Step 5. Apply the expected utility approach to the utility table developed in step 4 and select the decision alternative with the highest expected utility

The procedure we described for determining the utility of monetary consequences can also be used to develop a utility measure for nonmonetary consequences. Assign the best consequence a utility of 10 and the worst a utility of 0. Then create a lottery with a probability of p for the best consequence and $(1 - p)$ for the worst consequence. For each of the other consequences, find the value of p that makes the decision maker indifferent between the lottery and the consequence. Then calculate the utility of the consequence in question as follows:

$$U(\text{consequence}) = pU(\text{best consequence}) + (1 - p)U(\text{worst consequence})$$

Utility Functions

Next we describe how different decision makers may approach risk in terms of their assessment of utility. The financial position of Swofford, Inc., was such that the firm's president evaluated investment opportunities from a conservative, or risk-avoiding, point of view. However, if the firm had a surplus of cash and a stable future, Swofford's president might have been looking for investment alternatives that, although perhaps risky, contained a potential for substantial profit. That type of behavior would demonstrate that the president is a risk taker with respect to this decision.

A **risk taker** is a decision maker who would choose a lottery over a guaranteed payoff when the expected value of the lottery is inferior to the guaranteed payoff. In this section, we analyze the decision problem faced by Swofford from the point of view of a decision maker who would be classified as a risk taker. We then compare the conservative point of view of Swofford's president (a risk avoider) with the behavior of a decision maker who is a risk taker.

For the decision problem facing Swofford, Inc., using the general procedure for developing utilities as discussed previously, a risk taker might express the utility for the various payoffs shown in Table 13.12. As before, $U(50,000) = 10$ and $U(-50,000) = 0$. Note the difference in behavior reflected in Table 13.12 and Table 13.10. In other words, in determining the value of p at which the decision maker is indifferent between a guaranteed payoff of M and a lottery in which \$50,000 is obtained with probability p and $-\$50,000$ with probability $(1 - p)$, the risk taker is willing to accept a greater risk of incurring a loss of \$50,000 in order to gain the opportunity to realize a profit of \$50,000.

To help develop the utility table for the risk taker, we have reproduced the Swofford, Inc. payoff table in Table 13.13. Using these payoffs and the risk taker's utilities given in Table 13.12, we can write the risk taker's utility table as shown in Table 13.14. Using the

TABLE 13.12   REVISED UTILITIES FOR SWOFFORD, INC., ASSUMING A RISK TAKER

Monetary Value	Indifference Value of p	Utility
\$50,000	Does not apply	10.0
30,000	0.50	5.0
20,000	0.40	4.0
0	0.25	2.5
−20,000	0.15	1.5
−30,000	0.10	1.0
−50,000	Does not apply	0

TABLE 13.13 PAYOFF TABLE FOR SWOFFORD, INC.

Decision Alternative	State of Nature		
	Prices Up s_1	Prices Stable s_2	Prices Down s_3
Investment A, d_1	$30,000	$20,000	−$50,000
Investment B, d_2	$50,000	−$20,000	−$30,000
Do Not Invest, d_3	0	0	0

TABLE 13.14 UTILITY TABLE OF A RISK TAKER FOR SWOFFORD, INC.

Decision Alternative	State of Nature		
	Prices Up s_1	Prices Stable s_2	Prices Down s_3
Investment A, d_1	5.0	4.0	0
Investment B, d_2	10.0	1.5	1.0
Do Not Invest, d_3	2.5	2.5	2.5

state-of-nature probabilities $P(s_1) = 0.3$, $P(s_2) = 0.5$, and $P(s_3) = 0.2$, the expected utility for each decision alternative is

$$EU(d_1) = 0.3(5.0) + 0.5(4.0) + 0.2(0) = 3.50$$
$$EU(d_2) = 0.3(10) + 0.5(1.5) + 0.2(1.0) = 3.95$$
$$EU(d_3) = 0.3(2.5) + 0.5(2.5) + 0.2(2.5) = 2.50$$

What is the recommended decision? Perhaps somewhat to your surprise, the analysis recommends investment B, with the highest expected utility of 3.95. Recall that this investment has a −$1,000 expected value. Why is it now the recommended decision? Remember that the decision maker in this revised problem is a risk taker. Thus, although the expected value of investment B is negative, utility analysis has shown that this decision maker is enough of a risk taker to prefer investment B and its potential for the $50,000 profit.

Ranking by the expected utilities generates the following order of preference of the decision alternatives for the risk taker and the associated expected values:

Ranking of Decision Alternatives	Expected Utility	Expected Value
Investment B	3.95	−$1,000
Investment A	3.50	$9,000
Do Not Invest	2.50	0

Comparing the utility analysis for a risk taker with the more conservative preferences of the president of Swofford, Inc., who is a risk avoider, we see that, even with the same decision problem, different attitudes toward risk can lead to different recommended decisions. The utilities established by Swofford's president indicated that the firm should not invest at this time, whereas the utilities established by the risk taker showed a preference for investment B. Note that both of these decisions differ from the best expected value decision, which was investment A.

FIGURE 13.16   UTILITY FUNCTION FOR MONEY FOR RISK-AVOIDER, RISK-TAKER, AND RISK-NEUTRAL DECISION MAKERS

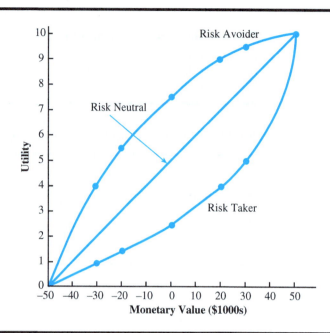

We can obtain another perspective of the difference between behaviors of a risk avoider and a risk taker by developing a graph that depicts the relationship between monetary value and utility. We use the horizontal axis of the graph to represent monetary values and the vertical axis to represent the utility associated with each monetary value. Now, consider the data in Table 13.10, with a utility corresponding to each monetary value for the original Swofford, Inc., problem. These values can be plotted on a graph to produce the top curve in Figure 13.16. The resulting curve is the **utility function for money** for Swofford's president. Recall that these points reflected the conservative, or risk-avoiding, nature of Swofford's president. Hence, we refer to the top curve in Figure 13.16 as a utility function for a risk avoider. Using the data in Table 13.12 developed for a risk taker, we can plot these points to produce the bottom curve in Figure 13.16. The resulting curve depicts the utility function for a risk taker.

By looking at the utility functions in Figure 13.16, we can begin to generalize about the utility functions for risk avoiders and risk takers. Although the exact shape of the utility function will vary from one decision maker to another, we can see the general shape of these two types of utility functions. The utility function for a risk avoider shows a diminishing marginal return for money. For example, the increase in utility going from a monetary value of −$30,000 to $0 is 7.5 − 4.0 = 3.5, whereas the increase in utility in going from $0 to $30,000 is only 9.5 − 7.5 = 2.0.

However, the utility function for a risk taker shows an increasing marginal return for money. For example, in Figure 13.16, the increase in utility for the risk taker in going from −$30,000 to $0 is 2.5 − 1.0 = 1.5, whereas the increase in utility in going from $0 to $30,000 for the risk taker is 5.0 − 2.5 = 2.5. Note also that in either case the utility function is always increasing; that is, more money leads to more utility. All utility functions possess this property.

We concluded that the utility function for a risk avoider shows a diminishing marginal return for money and that the utility function for a risk taker shows an increasing marginal return. When the marginal return for money is neither decreasing nor increasing but remains constant, the corresponding utility function describes the behavior of a decision maker who is neutral to risk. The following characteristics are associated with a **risk-neutral** decision maker:

1. The utility function can be drawn as a straight line connecting the "best" and the "worst" points.
2. The expected utility approach and the expected value approach applied to monetary payoffs result in the same action.

The straight, diagonal line in Figure 13.16 depicts the utility function of a risk-neutral decision maker using the Swofford, Inc., problem data.

Generally, when the payoffs for a particular decision-making problem fall into a reasonable range—the best is not too good and the worst is not too bad—decision makers tend to express preferences in agreement with the expected value approach. Thus, we suggest asking the decision maker to consider the best and worst possible payoffs for a problem and assess their reasonableness. If the decision maker believes that they are in the reasonable range, the decision alternative with the best expected value can be used. However, if the payoffs appear unreasonably large or unreasonably small (for example, a huge loss) and if the decision maker believes that monetary values do not adequately reflect her or his true preferences for the payoffs, a utility analysis of the problem should be considered.

Exponential Utility Function

Having a decision maker provide enough indifference values to create a utility function can be time consuming. An alternative is to assume that the decision maker's utility is defined by an exponential function. Figure 13.17 shows examples of different exponential utility

FIGURE 13.17   EXPONENTIAL UTILITY FUNCTIONS WITH DIFFERENT RISK
TOLERANCE (R) VALUES

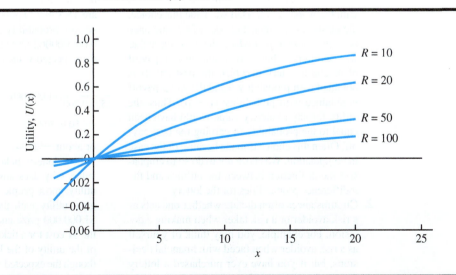

functions. Note that all the exponential utility functions indicate that the decision maker is risk averse. The form of the exponential utility function is as follows:

In equation (13.17), the number e ≈ 2.718282 . . . *is a mathematical constant corresponding to the base of the natural logarithm. In Excel,* e^x *can be evaluated for any power* x *using the function EXP(x).*

EXPONENTIAL UTILITY FUNCTION

$$U(x) = 1 - e^{-x/R} \qquad (13.17)$$

The R parameter in equation (13.17) represents the decision maker's risk tolerance; it controls the shape of the exponential utility function. Larger R values create flatter exponential functions, indicating that the decision maker is less risk averse (closer to risk neutral). Smaller R values indicate that the decision maker has less risk tolerance (is more risk averse). A common method to determine an approximate risk tolerance is to ask the decision maker to consider a scenario where he or she could win $\$R$ with probability 0.5 and lose $\$R/2$ with probability 0.5. The R value to use in equation (13.17) is the largest $\$R$ for which the decision maker would accept this gamble. For instance, if the decision maker is comfortable accepting a gamble with a 50 percent chance of winning $\$2,000$ and a 50 percent chance of losing $\$1,000$, but not with a gamble with a 50 percent chance of winning $\$3,000$ and a 50 percent chance of losing $\$1,500$ then we would use $R = \$2,000$ in equation (13.17). Determining the maximum gamble that a decision maker is willing to take and then using this value in the exponential utility function can be much less time-consuming than generating a complete table of indifference probabilities. One should remember that using an exponential utility function assumes that the decision maker is risk averse; however, this is often true in practice for business decisions.

NOTES AND COMMENTS

1. In the Swofford problem, we have been using a utility of 10 for the best payoff and 0 for the worst. We could have chosen any values as long as the utility associated with the best payoff exceeds the utility associated with the worst payoff. Alternatively, a utility of 1 can be associated with the best payoff and a utility of 0 associated with the worst payoff. Had we made this choice, the utility for any monetary value M would have been the value of p at which the decision maker was indifferent between a guaranteed payoff of M and a lottery in which the best payoff is obtained with probability p and the worst payoff is obtained with probability $(1 - p)$. Thus, the utility for any monetary value would have been equal to the probability of earning the best payoff. Often this choice is made because of the ease in computation. We chose not to do so to emphasize the distinction between the utilities and the indifference probabilities for the lottery.

2. Circumstances often dictate whether one acts as a risk avoider or a risk taker when making a decision. For example, you may think of yourself as a risk avoider when faced with financial decisions, but if you have ever purchased a lottery ticket, you have actually acted as a risk taker. For example, suppose you purchase a $\$1$ lottery ticket for a simple lottery in which the object is to pick the six numbers that will be drawn from 50 potential numbers. Also suppose that the winner (who correctly choses all six numbers that are drawn) will receive $\$1,000,000$. There are 15,890,700 possible winning combinations, so your probability of winning is $1/15890700 = 0.000000062929889809763$ (i.e., *very low*) and the expected value of your ticket is

$$\frac{1}{15,890,700}(\$1,000,000 - \$1) + \left(1 - \frac{1}{15,890,700}\right)(-\$1)$$

$$= -\$0.93707$$

or about $-\$0.94$.

If a lottery ticket has a negative expected value, why does anyone play? The answer is in utility; most people who play lotteries associate great utility with the possiblity of winning the $\$1,000,000$ prize and relatively little utility with the $\$1$ cost for a ticket, and so the expected value of the utility of the lottery ticket is positive even though the expected value of the ticket is negative.

SUMMARY

Decision analysis can be used to determine a recommended decision alternative or an optimal decision strategy when a decision maker is faced with an uncertain and risk-filled pattern of future events. The goal of decision analysis is to identify the best decision alternative or the optimal decision strategy given information about the uncertain events and the possible consequences or payoffs. The uncertain future events are called chance events, and the outcomes of the chance events are called states of nature. The "best" decision should consider the risk preference of the decision maker in evaluating outcomes.

We showed how influence diagrams, payoff tables, and decision trees could be used to structure a decision problem and describe the relationships among the decisions, the chance events, and the consequences. We presented three approaches to decision making without probabilities: the optimistic approach, the conservative approach, and the minimax regret approach. When probability assessments are provided for the states of nature, the expected value approach can be used to identify the recommended decision alternative or decision strategy.

Even though the expected value approach can be used to obtain a recommended decision alternative or optimal decision strategy, the payoff that actually occurs will usually have a value different from the expected value. A risk profile provides a probability distribution for the possible payoffs and can assist the decision maker in assessing the risks associated with different decision alternatives. Finally, sensitivity analysis can be conducted to determine the effect changes in the probabilities for the states of nature and changes in the values of the payoffs have on the recommended decision alternative.

In cases where sample information about the chance events is available, a sequence of decisions has to be made. First we must decide whether to obtain the sample information. If the answer to this decision is yes, an optimal decision strategy based on the specific sample information must be developed. In this situation, decision trees and the expected value approach can be used to determine the optimal decision strategy.

Bayes' theorem can be used to compute branch probabilities for decision trees. Bayes' theorem updates a decision maker's prior probabilities regarding the states of nature using sample information to compute revised posterior probabilities.

We showed how utility could be used in decision-making situations in which monetary value did not provide an adequate measure of the payoffs. Utility is a measure of the total worth of an outcome. As such, utility takes into account the decision maker's assessment of all aspects of a consequence, including profit, loss, risk, and perhaps additional nonmonetary factors. The examples showed how the use of expected utility can lead to decision recommendations that differ from those based on expected value.

A decision maker's judgment must be used to establish the utility for each consequence. We presented a step-by-step procedure to determine a decision maker's utility for monetary payoffs. We also discussed how conservative, risk-avoiding decision makers assess utility differently from more aggressive, risk-taking decision makers.

GLOSSARY

Bayes' theorem A theorem that enables the use of sample information to revise prior probabilities.

Branch Lines showing the alternatives from decision nodes and the outcomes from chance nodes.

Chance event An uncertain future event affecting the consequence, or payoff, associated with a decision.

Chance nodes Nodes indicating points where an uncertain event will occur.

Conditional probabilities The probability of one event given the known outcome of a (possibly) related event.

Consequence The result obtained when a decision alternative is chosen and a chance event occurs. A measure of the consequence is often called a payoff.

Consequence nodes Nodes of an influence diagram indicating points where a payoff will occur.

Conservative approach An approach to choosing a decision alternative without using probabilities. For a maximization problem, it leads to choosing the decision alternative that maximizes the minimum payoff; for a minimization problem, it leads to choosing the decision alternative that minimizes the maximum payoff.

Decision alternatives Options available to the decision maker.

Decision nodes Nodes indicating points where a decision is made.

Decision strategy A strategy involving a sequence of decisions and chance outcomes to provide the optimal solution to a decision problem.

Decision tree A graphical representation of the decision problem that shows the sequential nature of the decision-making process.

Efficiency The ratio of EVSI to EVPI as a percentage; perfect information is 100% efficient.

Expected utility (EU) The weighted average of the utilities associated with a decision alternative. The weights are the state-of-nature probabilities.

Expected value (EV) For a chance node, it is the weighted average of the payoffs. The weights are the state-of-nature probabilities.

Expected value approach An approach to choosing a decision alternative based on the expected value of each decision alternative. The recommended decision alternative is the one that provides the best expected value.

Expected value of perfect information (EVPI) The expected value of information that would tell the decision maker exactly which state of nature is going to occur (i.e., perfect information).

Expected value of sample information (EVSI) The difference between the expected value of an optimal strategy based on sample information and the "best" expected value without any sample information.

Influence diagram A graphical device that shows the relationship among decisions, chance events, and consequences for a decision problem.

Joint probabilities The probabilities of both sample information and a particular state of nature occurring simultaneously.

Minimax regret approach An approach to choosing a decision alternative without using probabilities. For each alternative, the maximum regret is computed, which leads to choosing the decision alternative that minimizes the maximum regret.

Node An intersection or junction point of an influence diagram or a decision tree.

Opportunity loss, or regret The amount of loss (lower profit or higher cost) from not making the best decision for each state of nature.

Optimistic approach An approach to choosing a decision alternative without using probabilities. For a maximization problem, it leads to choosing the decision alternative corresponding to the largest payoff; for a minimization problem, it leads to choosing the decision alternative corresponding to the smallest payoff.

Payoff A measure of the consequence of a decision such as profit, cost, or time. Each combination of a decision alternative and a state of nature has an associated payoff (consequence).

Payoff table A tabular representation of the payoffs for a decision problem.

Posterior (revised) probabilities The probabilities of the states of nature after revising the prior probabilities based on sample information.

Prior probabilities The probabilities of the states of nature prior to obtaining sample information.

Risk-neutral A decision maker who is neutral to risk. For this decision maker the decision alternative with the best expected value is identical to the alternative with the highest expected utility.

Risk analysis The study of the possible payoffs and probabilities associated with a decision alternative or a decision strategy.

Risk avoider A decision maker who would choose a guaranteed payoff over a lottery with a better expected payoff.

Risk profile The probability distribution of the possible payoffs associated with a decision alternative or decision strategy.

Risk taker A decision maker who would choose a lottery over a better guaranteed payoff.

Sample information New information obtained through research or experimentation that enables an updating or revision of the state-of-nature probabilities.

Sensitivity analysis The study of how changes in the probability assessments for the states of nature or changes in the payoffs affect the recommended decision alternative.

States of nature The possible outcomes for chance events that affect the payoff associated with a decision alternative.

Utility A measure of the total worth of a consequence reflecting a decision maker's attitude toward considerations such as profit, loss, and risk.

Utility function for money A curve that depicts the relationship between monetary value and utility.

PROBLEMS

1. The following payoff table shows profit for a decision analysis problem with two decision alternatives and three states of nature:

	State of Nature		
Decision Alternative	s_1	s_2	s_3
d_1	250	100	25
d_2	100	100	75

a. Construct a decision tree for this problem.
b. If the decision maker knows nothing about the probabilities of the three states of nature, what is the recommended decision using the optimistic, conservative, and minimax regret approaches?

2. Suppose that a decision maker faced with four decision alternatives and four states of nature develops the following profit payoff table:

| | State of Nature | | | |
Decision Alternative	s_1	s_2	s_3	s_4
d_1	14	9	10	5
d_2	11	10	8	7
d_3	9	10	10	11
d_4	8	10	11	13

a. If the decision maker knows nothing about the probabilities of the four states of nature, what is the recommended decision using the optimistic, conservative, and minimax regret approaches?
b. Which approach do you prefer? Explain. Is establishing the most appropriate approach before analyzing the problem important for the decision maker? Explain.
c. Assume that the payoff table provides *cost* rather than profit payoffs. What is the recommended decision using the optimistic, conservative, and minimax regret approaches?

3. Southland Corporation's decision to produce a new line of recreational products resulted in the need to construct either a small plant or a large plant. The best selection of plant size depends on how the marketplace reacts to the new product line. To conduct an analysis, marketing management has decided to view the possible long-run demand as low, medium, or high. The following payoff table shows the projected profit in millions of dollars:

| | Long-Run Demand | | |
Plant Size	Low	Medium	High
Small	150	200	200
Large	50	200	500

a. What is the decision to be made, and what is the chance event for Southland's problem?
b. Construct an influence diagram.
c. Construct a decision tree.
d. Recommend a decision based on the use of the optimistic, conservative, and minimax regret approaches.

4. Amy Lloyd is interested in leasing a new Honda and has contacted three automobile dealers for pricing information. Each dealer offered Amy a closed-end 36-month lease with no down payment due at the time of signing. Each lease includes a monthly charge and a mileage allowance. Additional miles receive a surcharge on a per-mile basis. The monthly lease cost, the mileage allowance, and the cost for additional miles follow:

Dealer	Monthly Cost	Mileage Allowance	Cost per Additional Mile
Hepburn Honda	$299	36,000	$0.15
Midtown Motors	$310	45,000	$0.20
Hopkins Automotive	$325	54,000	$0.15

Amy decided to choose the lease option that will minimize her total 36-month cost. The difficulty is that Amy is not sure how many miles she will drive over the next three years. For purposes of this decision, she believes it is reasonable to assume that she will drive 12,000 miles per year, 15,000 miles per year, or 18,000 miles per year. With this assumption Amy estimated her total costs for the three lease options. For example, she figures that the Hepburn Honda lease will cost her $10,764 if she drives 12,000 miles per year, $12,114 if she drives 15,000 miles per year, or $13,464 if she drives 18,000 miles per year.

a. What is the decision, and what is the chance event?

b. Construct a payoff table for Amy's problem.

c. If Amy has no idea which of the three mileage assumptions is most appropriate, what is the recommended decision (leasing option) using the optimistic, conservative, and minimax regret approaches?

d. Suppose that the probabilities that Amy drives 12,000, 15,000, and 18,000 miles per year are 0.5, 0.4, and 0.1, respectively. What option should Amy choose using the expected value approach?

e. Develop a risk profile for the decision selected in part (d). What is the most likely cost, and what is its probability?

f. Suppose that after further consideration Amy concludes that the probabilities that she will drive 12,000, 15,000, and 18,000 miles per year are 0.3, 0.4, and 0.3, respectively. What decision should Amy make using the expected value approach?

5. The following profit payoff table was presented in Problem 1. Suppose that the decision maker obtained the probability assessments $P(s_1) = 0.65$, $P(s_2) = 0.15$, and $P(s_3) = 0.20$. Use the expected value approach to determine the optimal decision.

	State of Nature		
Decision Alternative	s_1	s_2	s_3
d_1	250	100	25
d_2	100	100	75

6. Investment advisors estimated the stock market returns for four market segments: computers, financial, manufacturing, and pharmaceuticals. Annual return projections vary depending on whether the general economic conditions are improving, stable, or declining. The anticipated annual return percentages for each market segment under each economic condition are as follows:

	Economic Condition		
Market Segment	**Improving**	**Stable**	**Declining**
Computers	10	2	−4
Financial	8	5	−3
Manufacturing	6	4	−2
Pharmaceuticals	6	5	−1

a. Assume that an individual investor wants to select one market segment for a new investment. A forecast shows stable to declining economic conditions with the following probabilities: improving (0.2), stable (0.5), and declining (0.3). What is the preferred market segment for the investor, and what is the expected return percentage?

b. At a later date, a revised forecast shows a potential for an improvement in economic conditions. New probabilities are as follows: improving (0.4), stable (0.4), and declining (0.2). What is the preferred market segment for the investor based on these new probabilities? What is the expected return percentage?

7. Hudson Corporation is considering three options for managing its data processing operation: continuing with its own staff, hiring an outside vendor to do the managing (referred to as *outsourcing*), or using a combination of its own staff and an outside vendor. The cost

of the operation depends on future demand. The annual cost of each option (in thousands of dollars) depends on demand as follows:

Staffing Options	Demand		
	High	Medium	Low
Own staff	650	650	600
Outside vendor	900	600	300
Combination	800	650	500

a. If the demand probabilities are 0.2, 0.5, and 0.3, which decision alternative will minimize the expected cost of the data processing operation? What is the expected annual cost associated with that recommendation?

b. Construct a risk profile for the optimal decision in part (a). What is the probability of the cost exceeding $700,000?

8. The following payoff table shows the profit for a decision problem with two states of nature and two decision alternatives:

Decision Alternative	State of Nature	
	s_1	s_2
d_1	10	1
d_2	4	3

a. Use graphical sensitivity analysis to determine the range of probabilities of state of nature s_1 for which each of the decision alternatives has the largest expected value.

b. Suppose $P(s_1) = 0.2$ and $P(s_2) = 0.8$. What is the best decision using the expected value approach?

c. Perform sensitivity analysis on the payoffs for decision alternative d_1. Assume the probabilities are as given in part (b), and find the range of payoffs under states of nature s_1 and s_2 that will keep the solution found in part (b) optimal. Is the solution more sensitive to the payoff under state of nature s_1 or s_2?

9. Myrtle Air Express decided to offer direct service from Cleveland to Myrtle Beach. Management must decide between a full-price service using the company's new fleet of jet aircraft and a discount service using smaller capacity commuter planes. It is clear that the best choice depends on the market reaction to the service Myrtle Air offers. Management developed estimates of the contribution to profit for each type of service based upon two possible levels of demand for service to Myrtle Beach: strong and weak. The following table shows the estimated quarterly profits (in thousands of dollars):

Service	Demand for Service	
	Strong	Weak
Full price	$960	−$490
Discount	$670	$320

a. What is the decision to be made, what is the chance event, and what is the consequence for this problem? How many decision alternatives are there? How many outcomes are there for the chance event?

b. If nothing is known about the probabilities of the chance outcomes, what is the recommended decision using the optimistic, conservative, and minimax regret approaches?

c. Suppose that management of Myrtle Air Express believes that the probability of strong demand is 0.7 and the probability of weak demand is 0.3. Use the expected value approach to determine an optimal decision.

d. Suppose that the probability of strong demand is 0.8 and the probability of weak demand is 0.2. What is the optimal decision using the expected value approach?

e. Use graphical sensitivity analysis to determine the range of demand probabilities for which each of the decision alternatives has the largest expected value.

10. Video Tech is considering marketing one of two new video games for the coming holiday season: Battle Pacific or Space Pirates. Battle Pacific is a unique game and appears to have no competition. Estimated profits (in thousands of dollars) under high, medium, and low demand are as follows:

	Demand		
Battle Pacific	**High**	**Medium**	**Low**
Profit	$1000	$700	$300
Probability	0.2	0.5	0.3

Video Tech is optimistic about its Space Pirates game. However, the concern is that profitability will be affected by a competitor's introduction of a video game viewed as similar to Space Pirates. Estimated profits (in thousands of dollars) with and without competition are as follows:

| **Space Pirates** | **Demand** | | |
with Competition	**High**	**Medium**	**Low**
Profit	$800	$400	$200
Probability	0.3	0.4	0.3

| **Space Pirates** | **Demand** | | |
without Competition	**High**	**Medium**	**Low**
Profit	$1600	$800	$400
Probability	0.5	0.3	0.2

a. Develop a decision tree for the Video Tech problem.

b. For planning purposes, Video Tech believes there is a 0.6 probability that its competitor will produce a new game similar to Space Pirates. Given this probability of competition, the director of planning recommends marketing the Battle Pacific video game. Using expected value, what is your recommended decision?

c. Show a risk profile for your recommended decision.

d. Use sensitivity analysis to determine what the probability of competition for Space Pirates would have to be for you to change your recommended decision alternative.

11. For the Pittsburgh Development Corporation problem in Section 13.3, the decision alternative to build the large condominium complex was found to be optimal using the expected value approach. In Section 13.4 we conducted a sensitivity analysis for the payoffs associated with this decision alternative. We found that the large complex remained optimal as long as the payoff for the strong demand was greater than or equal to $17.5 million and as long as the payoff for the weak demand was greater than or equal to −$19 million.

a. Consider the medium complex decision. How much could the payoff under strong demand increase and still keep decision alternative d_3 the optimal solution?

b. Consider the small complex decision. How much could the payoff under strong demand increase and still keep decision alternative d_3 the optimal solution?

12. The distance from Potsdam to larger markets and limited air service have hindered the town in attracting new industry. Air Express, a major overnight delivery service, is considering establishing a regional distribution center in Potsdam. However, Air Express will not establish the center unless the length of the runway at the local airport is increased. Another candidate for new development is Diagnostic Research, Inc. (DRI), a leading producer of medical testing equipment. DRI is considering building a new manufacturing plant. Increasing the length of the runway is not a requirement for DRI, but the planning commission feels that doing so will help convince DRI to locate its new plant in Potsdam. Assuming that the town lengthens the runway, the Potsdam planning commission believes that the probabilities shown in the following table are applicable:

	DRI Plant	No DRI Plant
Air Express Center	0.30	0.10
No Air Express Center	0.40	0.20

For instance, the probability that Air Express will establish a distribution center and DRI will build a plant is 0.30.

The estimated annual revenue to the town, after deducting the cost of lengthening the runway, is as follows:

	DRI Plant	No DRI Plant
Air Express Center	$600,000	$150,000
No Air Express Center	$250,000	−$200,000

If the runway expansion project is not conducted, the planning commission assesses the probability that DRI will locate its new plant in Potsdam at 0.6; in this case, the estimated annual revenue to the town will be $450,000. If the runway expansion project is not conducted and DRI does not locate in Potsdam, the annual revenue will be $0 because no cost will have been incurred and no revenues will be forthcoming.

a. What is the decision to be made, what is the chance event, and what is the consequence?

b. Compute the expected annual revenue associated with the decision alternative to lengthen the runway.

c. Compute the expected annual revenue associated with the decision alternative not to lengthen the runway.

d. Should the town elect to lengthen the runway? Explain.

e. Suppose that the probabilities associated with lengthening the runway were as follows:

	DRI Plant	No DRI Plant
Air Express Center	0.40	0.10
No Air Express Center	0.30	0.20

What effect, if any, would this change in the probabilities have on the recommended decision?

13. Seneca Hill Winery recently purchased land for the purpose of establishing a new vineyard. Management is considering two varieties of white grapes for the new vineyard: Chardonnay and Riesling. The Chardonnay grapes would be used to produce a dry Chardonnay wine, and the Riesling grapes would be used to produce a semidry Riesling wine. It takes approximately four years from the time of planting before new grapes can be harvested. This length

of time creates a great deal of uncertainty concerning future demand and makes the decision about the type of grapes to plant difficult. Three possibilities are being considered: Chardonnay grapes only; Riesling grapes only; and both Chardonnay and Riesling grapes. Seneca management decided that for planning purposes it would be adequate to consider only two demand possibilities for each type of wine: strong or weak. With two possibilities for each type of wine, it was necessary to assess four probabilities. With the help of some forecasts in industry publications, management made the following probability assessments:

	Riesling Demand	
Chardonnay Demand	**Weak**	**Strong**
Weak	0.05	0.50
Strong	0.25	0.20

Revenue projections show an annual contribution to profit of $20,000 if Seneca Hill only plants Chardonnay grapes and demand is weak for Chardonnay wine, and $70,000 if Seneca only plants Chardonnay grapes and demand is strong for Chardonnay wine. If Seneca only plants Riesling grapes, the annual profit projection is $25,000 if demand is weak for Riesling grapes and $45,000 if demand is strong for Riesling grapes. If Seneca plants both types of grapes, the annual profit projections are shown in the following table:

	Riesling Demand	
Chardonnay Demand	**Weak**	**Strong**
Weak	$22,000	$40,000
Strong	$26,000	$60,000

a. What is the decision to be made, what is the chance event, and what is the consequence? Identify the alternatives for the decisions and the possible outcomes for the chance events.
b. Develop a decision tree.
c. Use the expected value approach to recommend which alternative Seneca Hill Winery should follow in order to maximize expected annual profit.
d. Suppose management is concerned about the probability assessments when demand for Chardonnay wine is strong. Some believe it is likely for Riesling demand to also be strong in this case. Suppose the probability of strong demand for Chardonnay and weak demand for Riesling is 0.05 and that the probability of strong demand for Chardonnay and strong demand for Riesling is 0.40. How does this change the recommended decision? Assume that the probabilities when Chardonnay demand is weak are still 0.05 and 0.50.
e. Other members of the management team expect the Chardonnay market to become saturated at some point in the future, causing a fall in prices. Suppose that the annual profit projections fall to $50,000 when demand for Chardonnay is strong and Chardonnay grapes only are planted. Using the original probability assessments, determine how this change would affect the optimal decision.

14. The following profit payoff table was presented in Problem 1:

	State of Nature		
Decision Alternative	s_1	s_2	s_3
d_1	250	100	25
d_2	100	100	75

The probabilities for the states of nature are $P(s_1) = 0.65$, $P(s_2) = 0.15$, and $P(s_3) = 0.20$.

a. What is the optimal decision strategy if perfect information were available?

b. What is the expected value for the decision strategy developed in part (a)?

c. Using the expected value approach, what is the recommended decision without perfect information? What is its expected value?

d. What is the expected value of perfect information?

15. The Lake Placid Town Council decided to build a new community center to be used for conventions, concerts, and other public events, but considerable controversy surrounds the appropriate size. Many influential citizens want a large center that would be a showcase for the area. But the mayor feels that if demand does not support such a center, the community will lose a large amount of money. To provide structure for the decision process, the council narrowed the building alternatives to three sizes: small, medium, and large. Everybody agreed that the critical factor in choosing the best size is the number of people who will want to use the new facility. A regional planning consultant provided demand estimates under three scenarios: worst case, base case, and best case. The worst-case scenario corresponds to a situation in which tourism drops substantially; the base-case scenario corresponds to a situation in which Lake Placid continues to attract visitors at current levels; and the best-case scenario corresponds to a substantial increase in tourism. The consultant has provided probability assessments of 0.10, 0.60, and 0.30 for the worst-case, base-case, and best-case scenarios, respectively.

The town council suggested using net cash flow over a 5-year planning horizon as the criterion for deciding on the best size. The following projections of net cash flow (in thousands of dollars) for a 5-year planning horizon have been developed. All costs, including the consultant's fee, have been included.

| | **Demand Scenario** | | |
Center Size	**Worst Case**	**Base Case**	**Best Case**
Small	400	500	660
Medium	−250	650	800
Large	−400	580	990

a. What decision should Lake Placid make using the expected value approach?

b. Construct risk profiles for the medium and large alternatives. Given the mayor's concern over the possibility of losing money and the result of part (a), which alternative would you recommend?

c. Compute the expected value of perfect information. Do you think it would be worth trying to obtain additional information concerning which scenario is likely to occur?

d. Suppose the probability of the worst-case scenario increases to 0.2, the probability of the base-case scenario decreases to 0.5, and the probability of the best-case scenario remains at 0.3. What effect, if any, would these changes have on the decision recommendation?

e. The consultant has suggested that an expenditure of $150,000 on a promotional campaign over the planning horizon will effectively reduce the probability of the worst-case scenario to zero. If the campaign can be expected to also increase the probability of the best-case scenario to 0.4, is it a good investment?

16. Consider a variation of the PDC decision tree shown in Figure 13.9. The company must first decide whether to undertake the market research study. If the market research study is conducted, the outcome will either be favorable (F) or unfavorable (U). Assume there are only two decision alternatives, d_1 and d_2, and two states of nature, s_1 and s_2. The payoff table showing profit is as follows:

Decision Alternative	State of Nature	
	s_1	s_2
d_1	100	300
d_2	400	200

a. Show the decision tree.
b. Using the following probabilities, what is the optimal decision strategy?

$$P(F) = 0.56 \qquad P(s_1 \mid F) = 0.57 \qquad P(s_1 \mid U) = 0.18 \qquad P(s_1) = 0.40$$

$$P(U) = 0.44 \qquad P(s_2 \mid F) = 0.43 \qquad P(s_2 \mid U) = 0.82 \qquad P(s_2) = 0.60$$

17. Hemmingway, Inc., is considering a $5 million research and development (R&D) project. Profit projections appear promising, but Hemmingway's president is concerned because the probability that the R&D project will be successful is only 0.50. Furthermore, the president knows that even if the project is successful, it will require that the company build a new production facility at a cost of $20 million in order to manufacture the product. If the facility is built, uncertainty remains about the demand and thus uncertainty about the profit that will be realized. Another option is that if the R&D project is successful, the company could sell the rights to the product for an estimated $25 million. Under this option, the company would not build the $20 million production facility.

The decision tree is shown in Figure 13.18. The profit projection for each outcome is shown at the end of the branches. For example, the revenue projection for the high demand outcome is $59 million. However, the cost of the R&D project ($5 million) and the cost of the production facility ($20 million) show the profit of this outcome to be $59 − $5 − $20 = $34 million. Branch probabilities are also shown for the chance events.

a. Analyze the decision tree to determine whether the company should undertake the R&D project. If it does, and if the R&D project is successful, what should the company do? What is the expected value of your strategy?
b. What must the selling price be for the company to consider selling the rights to the product?
c. Develop a risk profile for the optimal strategy.

FIGURE 13.18   DECISION TREE FOR HEMMINGWAY, INC.

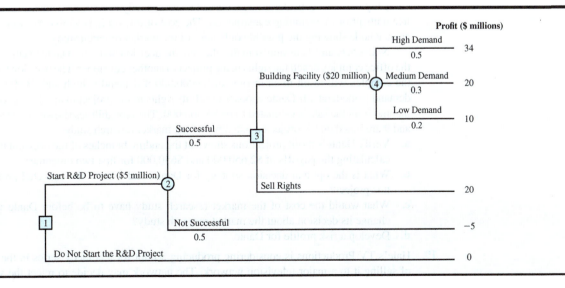

FIGURE 13.19   DECISION TREE FOR THE DANTE DEVELOPMENT CORPORATION

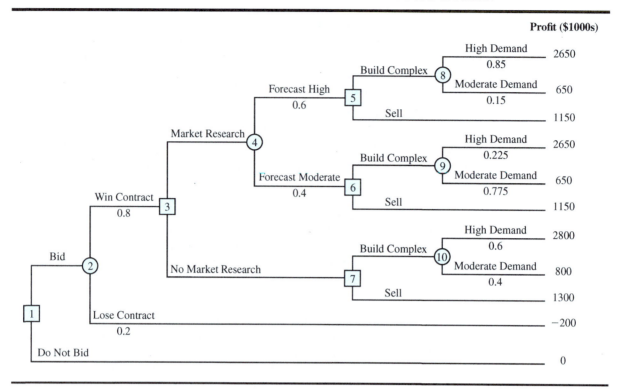

Profit ($1000s)

18. Dante Development Corporation is considering bidding on a contract for a new office building complex. Figure 13.19 shows the decision tree prepared by one of Dante's analysts. At node 1, the company must decide whether to bid on the contract. The cost of preparing the bid is $200,000. The upper branch from node 2 shows that the company has a 0.8 probability of winning the contract if it submits a bid. If the company wins the bid, it will have to pay $2,000,000 to become a partner in the project. Node 3 shows that the company will then consider doing a market research study to forecast demand for the office units prior to beginning construction. The cost of this study is $150,000. Node 4 is a chance node showing the possible outcomes of the market research study.

   Nodes 5, 6, and 7 are similar in that they are the decision nodes for Dante to either build the office complex or sell the rights in the project to another developer. The decision to build the complex will result in an income of $5,000,000 if demand is high and $3,000,000 if demand is moderate. If Dante chooses to sell its rights in the project to another developer, income from the sale is estimated to be $3,500,000. The probabilities shown at nodes 4, 8, and 9 are based on the projected outcomes of the market research study.

   a. Verify Dante's profit projections shown at the ending branches of the decision tree by calculating the payoffs of $2,650,000 and $650,000 for first two outcomes.

   b. What is the optimal decision strategy for Dante, and what is the expected profit for this project?

   c. What would the cost of the market research study have to be before Dante would change its decision about the market research study?

   d. Develop a risk profile for Dante.

19. Hale's TV Productions is considering producing a pilot for a comedy series in the hope of selling it to a major television network. The network may decide to reject the series,

but it may also decide to purchase the rights to the series for either one or two years. At this point in time, Hale may either produce the pilot and wait for the network's decision or transfer the rights for the pilot and series to a competitor for $100,000. Hale's decision alternatives and profits (in thousands of dollars) are as follows:

Decision Alternative	State of Nature		
	Reject, s_1	1 Year, s_2	2 Years, s_3
Produce pilot, d_1	-100	50	150
Sell to competitor, d_2	100	100	100

The probabilities for the states of nature are $P(s_1) = 0.20$, $P(s_2) = 0.30$, and $P(s_3) = 0.50$. For a consulting fee of $5000, an agency will review the plans for the comedy series and indicate the overall chances of a favorable network reaction to the series. Assume that the agency review will result in a favorable (F) or an unfavorable (U) review and that the following probabilities are relevant:

$$P(F) = 0.69 \qquad P(s_1 \mid F) = 0.09 \qquad P(s_1 \mid U) = 0.45$$
$$P(U) = 0.31 \qquad P(s_2 \mid F) = 0.26 \qquad P(s_2 \mid U) = 0.39$$
$$P(s_3 \mid F) = 0.65 \qquad P(s_3 \mid U) = 0.16$$

a. Construct a decision tree for this problem.
b. What is the recommended decision if the agency opinion is not used? What is the expected value?
c. What is the expected value of perfect information?
d. What is Hale's optimal decision strategy assuming the agency's information is used?
e. What is the expected value of the agency's information?
f. Is the agency's information worth the $5000 fee? What is the maximum that Hale should be willing to pay for the information?
g. What is the recommended decision?

20. Embassy Publishing Company received a six-chapter manuscript for a new college textbook. The editor of the college division is familiar with the manuscript and estimated a 0.65 probability that the textbook will be successful. If successful, a profit of $750,000 will be realized. If the company decides to publish the textbook and it is unsuccessful, a loss of $250,000 will occur.

Before making the decision to accept or reject the manuscript, the editor is considering sending the manuscript out for review. A review process provides either a favorable (F) or unfavorable (U) evaluation of the manuscript. Past experience with the review process suggests that probabilities $P(F) = 0.7$ and $P(U) = 0.3$ apply. Let $s_1 =$ the textbook is successful, and $s_2 =$ the textbook is unsuccessful. The editor's initial probabilities of s_1 and s_2 will be revised based on whether the review is favorable or unfavorable. The revised probabilities are as follows:

$$P(s_1 \mid F) = 0.75 \qquad P(s_1 \mid U) = 0.417$$
$$P(s_2 \mid F) = 0.25 \qquad P(s_2 \mid U) = 0.583$$

a. Construct a decision tree assuming that the company will first make the decision of whether to send the manuscript out for review and then make the decision to accept or reject the manuscript.
b. Analyze the decision tree to determine the optimal decision strategy for the publishing company.
c. If the manuscript review costs $5000, what is your recommendation?

d. What is the expected value of perfect information? What does this EVPI suggest for the company?

21. A real estate investor has the opportunity to purchase land currently zoned residential. If the county board approves a request to rezone the property as commercial within the next year, the investor will be able to lease the land to a large discount firm that wants to open a new store on the property. However, if the zoning change is not approved, the investor will have to sell the property at a loss. Profits (in thousands of dollars) are shown in the following payoff table:

	State of Nature	
	Rezoning Approved	**Rezoning Not Approved**
Decision Alternative	s_1	s_2
Purchase, d_1	600	-200
Do not purchase, d_2	0	0

a. If the probability that the rezoning will be approved is 0.5, what decision is recommended? What is the expected profit?

b. The investor can purchase an option to buy the land. Under the option, the investor maintains the rights to purchase the land anytime during the next three months while learning more about possible resistance to the rezoning proposal from area residents. Probabilities are as follows:

Let H = High resistance to rezoning

L = Low resistance to rezoning

$P(H) = 0.55$	$P(s_1 \mid H) = 0.18$	$P(s_2 \mid H) = 0.82$
$P(L) = 0.45$	$P(s_1 \mid L) = 0.89$	$P(s_2 \mid L) = 0.11$

What is the optimal decision strategy if the investor uses the option period to learn more about the resistance from area residents before making the purchase decision?

c. If the option will cost the investor an additional $10,000, should the investor purchase the option? Why or why not? What is the maximum that the investor should be willing to pay for the option?

22. Lawson's Department Store faces a buying decision for a seasonal product for which demand can be high, medium, or low. The purchaser for Lawson's can order one, two, or three lots of the product before the season begins but cannot reorder later. Profit projections (in thousands of dollars) are shown.

	State of Nature		
	High Demand	**Medium Demand**	**Low Demand**
Decision Alternative	s_1	s_2	s_3
Order 1 lot, d_1	60	60	50
Order 2 lots, d_2	80	80	30
Order 3 lots, d_3	100	70	10

a. If the prior probabilities for the three states of nature are 0.3, 0.3, and 0.4, respectively, what is the recommended order quantity?

b. At each preseason sales meeting, the vice president of sales provides a personal opinion regarding potential demand for this product. Because of the vice president's enthusiasm and optimistic nature, the predictions of market conditions have always been either "excellent" (E) or "very good" (V). Probabilities are as follows:

$P(E) = 0.70$	$P(s_1 \mid E) = 0.34$	$P(s_1 \mid V) = 0.20$
$P(V) = 0.30$	$P(s_2 \mid E) = 0.32$	$P(s_2 \mid V) = 0.26$
	$P(s_3 \mid E) = 0.34$	$P(s_3 \mid V) = 0.54$

What is the optimal decision strategy?

c. Use the efficiency of sample information and discuss whether the firm should consider a consulting expert who could provide independent forecasts of market conditions for the product.

23. Suppose that you are given a decision situation with three possible states of nature: s_1, s_2, and s_3. The prior probabilities are $P(s_1) = 0.2$, $P(s_2) = 0.5$, and $P(s_3) = 0.3$. With sample information I, $P(I \mid s_1) = 0.1$, $P(I \mid s_2) = 0.05$, and $P(I \mid s_3) = 0.2$. Compute the revised or posterior probabilities: $P(s_1 \mid I)$, $P(s_2 \mid I)$, and $P(s_3 \mid I)$.

24. To save on expenses, Rona and Jerry agreed to form a carpool for traveling to and from work. Rona preferred to use the somewhat longer but more consistent Queen City Avenue. Although Jerry preferred the quicker expressway, he agreed with Rona that they should take Queen City Avenue if the expressway had a traffic jam. The following payoff table provides the one-way time estimate in minutes for traveling to or from work:

	State of Nature	
	Expressway Open	**Expressway Jammed**
Decision Alternative	s_1	s_2
Queen City Avenue, d_1	30	30
Expressway, d_2	25	45

Based on their experience with traffic problems, Rona and Jerry agreed on a 0.15 probability that the expressway would be jammed.

In addition, they agreed that weather seemed to affect the traffic conditions on the expressway. Let

$$C = \text{clear}$$
$$O = \text{overcast}$$
$$R = \text{rain}$$

The following conditional probabilities apply:

$P(C \mid s_1) = 0.8$	$P(O \mid s_1) = 0.2$	$P(R \mid s_1) = 0.0$
$P(C \mid s_2) = 0.1$	$P(O \mid s_2) = 0.3$	$P(R \mid s_2) = 0.6$

a. Use Bayes' theorem for probability revision to compute the probability of each weather condition and the conditional probability of the expressway open, s_1, or jammed, s_2, given each weather condition.
b. Show the decision tree for this problem.
c. What is the optimal decision strategy, and what is the expected travel time?

25. The Gorman Manufacturing Company must decide whether to manufacture a component part at its Milan, Michigan, plant or purchase the component part from a supplier. The

resulting profit is dependent upon the demand for the product. The following payoff table shows the projected profit (in thousands of dollars):

| Decision Alternative | State of Nature | | |
	Low Demand s_1	Medium Demand s_2	High Demand s_3
Manufacture, d_1	-20	40	100
Purchase, d_2	10	45	70

The state-of-nature probabilities are $P(s_1) = 0.35$, $P(s_2) = 0.35$, and $P(s_3) = 0.30$.

a. Use a decision tree to recommend a decision.

b. Use EVPI to determine whether Gorman should attempt to obtain a better estimate of demand.

c. A test market study of the potential demand for the product is expected to report either a favorable (F) or unfavorable (U) condition. The relevant conditional probabilities are as follows:

$$P(F \mid s_1) = 0.10 \qquad P(U \mid s_1) = 0.90$$
$$P(F \mid s_2) = 0.40 \qquad P(U \mid s_2) = 0.60$$
$$P(F \mid s_3) = 0.60 \qquad P(U \mid s_3) = 0.40$$

What is the probability that the market research report will be favorable?

d. What is Gorman's optimal decision strategy?

e. What is the expected value of the market research information?

f. What is the efficiency of the information?

26. Alexander Industries is considering purchasing an insurance policy for its new office building in St. Louis, Missouri. The policy has an annual cost of $10,000. If Alexander Industries doesn't purchase the insurance and minor fire damage occurs, a cost of $100,000 is anticipated; the cost if major or total destruction occurs is $200,000. The costs, including the state-of-nature probabilities, are as follows:

| Decision Alternative | Damage | | |
	None s_1	Minor s_2	Major s_3
Purchase Insurance, d_1	10,000	10,000	10,000
Do Not Purchase Insurance, d_2	0	100,000	200,000
Probabilities	0.96	0.03	0.01

a. Using the expected value approach, what decision do you recommend?

b. What lottery would you use to assess utilities? (*Note:* Because the data are costs, the best payoff is $0.)

c. Assume that you found the following indifference probabilities for the lottery defined in part (b). What decision would you recommend?

Cost	Indifference Probability
10,000	$p = 0.99$
100,000	$p = 0.60$

   d. Do you favor using expected value or expected utility for this decision problem? Why?

27. In a certain state lottery, a lottery ticket costs $2. In terms of the decision to purchase or not to purchase a lottery ticket, suppose that the following payoff table applies:

	State of Nature	
	Win	Lose
Decision Alternatives	s_1	s_2
Purchase Lottery Ticket, d_1	300,000	-2
Do Not Purchase Lottery Ticket, d_2	0	0

   a. A realistic estimate of the chances of winning is 1 in 250,000. Use the expected value approach to recommend a decision.
   b. If a particular decision maker assigns an indifference probability of 0.000001 to the $0 payoff, would this individual purchase a lottery ticket? Use expected utility to justify your answer.

28. Three decision makers have assessed utilities for the following decision problem (payoff in dollars):

	State of Nature		
Decision Alternative	s_1	s_2	s_3
d_1	20	50	-20
d_2	80	100	-100

   The indifference probabilities are as follows:

	Indifference Probability (p)		
Payoff	**Decision Maker A**	**Decision Maker B**	**Decision Maker C**
100	1.00	1.00	1.00
80	0.95	0.70	0.90
50	0.90	0.60	0.75
20	0.70	0.45	0.60
-20	0.50	0.25	0.40
-100	0.00	0.00	0.00

   a. Plot the utility function for money for each decision maker.
   b. Classify each decision maker as a risk avoider, a risk taker, or risk neutral.
   c. For the payoff of 20, what is the premium that the risk avoider will pay to avoid risk? What is the premium that the risk taker will pay to have the opportunity of the high payoff?

29. In Problem 28, if $P(s_1) = 0.25$, $P(s_2) = 0.50$, and $P(s_3) = 0.25$, find a recommended decision for each of the three decision makers. (*Note:* For the same decision problem, different utilities can lead to different decisions.)

30. Translate the following monetary payoffs into utilities for a decision maker whose utility function is described by an exponential function with $R = 250$: $-$200, $-$100, $0, $100, $200, $300, $400, $500.

31. Consider a decision maker who is comfortable with an investment decision that has a 50 percent chance of earning $25,000 and a 50 percent chance of losing $12,500, but not with any larger investments that have the same relative payoffs.
    a. Write the equation for the exponential function that approximates this decision maker's utility function.
    b. Plot the exponential utility function for this decision maker for x values between $-20,000$ and 35,000. Is this decision maker risk seeking, risk neutral, or risk averse?
    c. Suppose the decision maker decides that she would actually be willing to make an investment that has a 50 percent chance of earning $30,000 and a 50 percent chance of losing $15,000. Plot the exponential function that approximates this utility function and compare it to the utility function from part (b). Is the decision maker becoming more risk seeking or more risk averse?

Case Problem 1   PROPERTY PURCHASE STRATEGY

Glenn Foreman, president of Oceanview Development Corporation, is considering submitting a bid to purchase property that will be sold by sealed bid at a county tax foreclosure. Glenn's initial judgment is to submit a bid of $5 million. Based on his experience, Glenn estimates that a bid of $5 million will have a 0.2 probability of being the highest bid and securing the property for Oceanview. The current date is June 1. Sealed bids for the property must be submitted by August 15. The winning bid will be announced on September 1.

If Oceanview submits the highest bid and obtains the property, the firm plans to build and sell a complex of luxury condominiums. However, a complicating factor is that the property is currently zoned for single-family residences only. Glenn believes that a referendum could be placed on the voting ballot in time for the November election. Passage of the referendum would change the zoning of the property and permit construction of the condominiums.

The sealed-bid procedure requires the bid to be submitted with a certified check for 10% of the amount bid. If the bid is rejected, the deposit is refunded. If the bid is accepted, the deposit is the down payment for the property. However, if the bid is accepted and the bidder does not follow through with the purchase and meet the remainder of the financial obligation within six months, the deposit will be forfeited. In this case, the county will offer the property to the next highest bidder.

To determine whether Oceanview should submit the $5 million bid, Glenn conducted some preliminary analysis. This preliminary work provided an assessment of 0.3 for the probability that the referendum for a zoning change will be approved and resulted in the following estimates of the costs and revenues that will be incurred if the condominiums are built:

Cost and Revenue Estimates

Revenue from condominium sales	$15,000,000
Cost	
Property	$5,000,000
Construction expenses	$8,000,000

If Oceanview obtains the property and the zoning change is rejected in November, Glenn believes that the best option would be for the firm not to complete the purchase of the property. In this case, Oceanview would forfeit the 10% deposit that accompanied the bid.

Because the likelihood that the zoning referendum will be approved is such an important factor in the decision process, Glenn suggested that the firm hire a market research service to conduct a survey of voters. The survey would provide a better estimate of the likelihood that the referendum for a zoning change would be approved. The market research firm that Oceanview Development has worked with in the past has agreed to do the study for $15,000. The results of the study will be available August 1, so that Oceanview will have this information before the August 15 bid deadline. The results of the survey will be either a prediction that the zoning change will be approved or a prediction that the zoning change will be rejected. After considering the record of the market research service in previous studies conducted for Oceanview, Glenn developed the following probability estimates concerning the accuracy of the market research information:

$$P(A \mid s_1) = 0.9 \qquad P(N \mid s_1) = 0.1$$
$$P(A \mid s_2) = 0.2 \qquad P(N \mid s_2) = 0.8$$

where

A = prediction of zoning change approval

N = prediction that zoning change will not be approved

s_1 = the zoning change is approved by the voters

s_2 = the zoning change is rejected by the voters

Managerial Report

Perform an analysis of the problem facing the Oceanview Development Corporation, and prepare a report that summarizes your findings and recommendations. Include the following items in your report:

1. A decision tree that shows the logical sequence of the decision problem
2. A recommendation regarding what Oceanview should do if the market research information is not available
3. A decision strategy that Oceanview should follow if the market research is conducted
4. A recommendation as to whether Oceanview should employ the market research firm, along with the value of the information provided by the market research firm

Include the details of your analysis as an appendix to your report.

Case Problem 2   LAWSUIT DEFENSE STRATEGY

John Campbell, an employee of Manhattan Construction Company, claims to have injured his back as a result of a fall while repairing the roof at one of the Eastview apartment buildings. He filed a lawsuit against Doug Reynolds, the owner of Eastview Apartments, asking for damages of $1,500,000. John claims that the roof had rotten sections and that his fall could have been prevented if Mr. Reynolds had told Manhattan Construction about the problem. Mr. Reynolds notified his insurance company, Allied Insurance, of the lawsuit. Allied must defend Mr. Reynolds and decide what action to take regarding the lawsuit.

Some depositions and a series of discussions took place between both sides. As a result, John Campbell offered to accept a settlement of $750,000. Thus, one option is for Allied to pay John $750,000 to settle the claim. Allied is also considering making John a counteroffer of $400,000 in the hope that he will accept a lesser amount to avoid the time and cost of going to trial. Allied's preliminary investigation shows that John's case is strong; Allied is concerned that John may reject its counteroffer and request a jury trial. Allied's lawyers spent some time exploring John's likely reaction if they make a counteroffer of $400,000.

The lawyers concluded that it is adequate to consider three possible outcomes to represent John's possible reaction to a counteroffer of $400,000: (1) John will accept the counteroffer and the case will be closed; (2) John will reject the counteroffer and elect to have a jury decide the settlement amount; or (3) John will make a counteroffer to Allied of $600,000. If John does make a counteroffer, Allied decided that it will not make additional counteroffers. It will either accept John's counteroffer of $600,000 or go to trial.

If the case goes to a jury trial, Allied considers three outcomes possible: (1) the jury may reject John's claim and Allied will not be required to pay any damages; (2) the jury will find in favor of John and award him $750,000 in damages; or (3) the jury will conclude that John has a strong case and award him the full amount of $1,500,000.

Key considerations as Allied develops its strategy for disposing of the case are the probabilities associated with John's response to an Allied counteroffer of $400,000 and the probabilities associated with the three possible trial outcomes. Allied's lawyers believe that the probability that John will accept a counteroffer of $400,000 is 0.10, the probability that John will reject a counteroffer of $400,000 is 0.40, and the probability that John will, himself, make a counteroffer to Allied of $600,000 is 0.50. If the case goes to court, they believe that the probability that the jury will award John damages of $1,500,000 is 0.30, the probability that the jury will award John damages of $750,000 is 0.50, and the probability that the jury will award John nothing is 0.20.

Managerial Report

Perform an analysis of the problem facing Allied Insurance and prepare a report that summarizes your findings and recommendations. Be sure to include the following items:

1. A decision tree
2. A recommendation regarding whether Allied should accept John's initial offer to settle the claim for $750,000
3. A decision strategy that Allied should follow if they decide to make John a counteroffer of $400,000
4. A risk profile for your recommended strategy

Appendix 13.1   USING ANALYTIC SOLVER PLATFORM TO CREATE DECISION TREES

In this appendix, we describe how Analytic Solver Platform can be used to develop a decision tree for the PDC problem presented in Section 13.3. The decision tree for the PDC problem is shown in Figure 13.20.

Getting Started: An Initial Decision Tree

To build a decision tree for the PDC problem using Analytic Solver Platform, follow these steps in a blank workbook in Excel:

Step 1. Select cell A1
Step 2. Click the **ANALYTIC SOLVER PLATFORM** tab on the Ribbon
Step 3. Click **Decision Tree** in the **Tools** group
        Select **Node**, and click **Add Node**

FIGURE 13.20   DECISION TREE FOR THE PDC CONDOMINIUM PROJECT
(PAYOFFS IN $ MILLIONS)

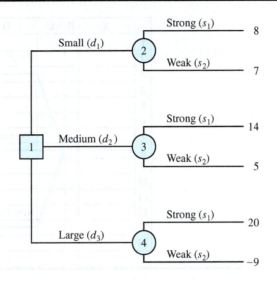

FIGURE 13.21   DECISION TREE WITH ONE DECISION NODE AND TWO
BRANCHES CREATED WITH ANALYTIC SOLVER PLATFORM

	A	B	C	D	E	F	G	H
1								
2				Decision 1				
3							0	
4					0	0		
5			1					
6		0						
7				Decision 2				
8							0	
9					0	0		

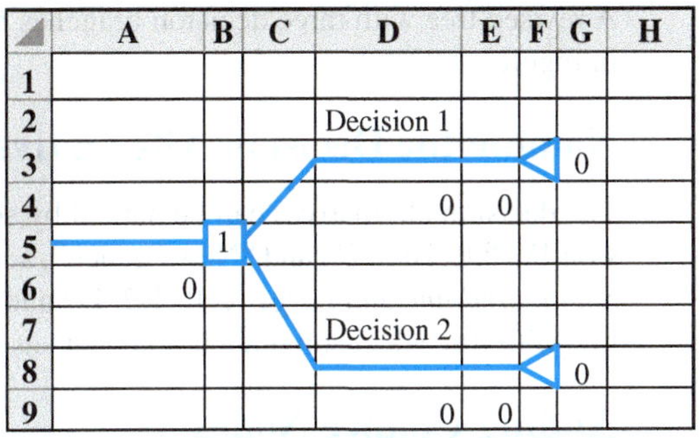

> **Step 4.** When the **Decision Tree** dialog box appears, verify that **Decision** is selected
> for **Node Type**, and click **OK**

A decision tree with one decision node and two branches (initially labeled as "Decision 1" and "Decision 2") appears, as shown in Figure 13.21.

Adding a Branch

The PDC problem has three decision alternatives (small, medium, and large condominium complexes), so we must add another decision branch to the tree.

> **Step 1.** Select cell B5
> **Step 2.** Click the **ANALYTIC SOLVER PLATFORM** tab in the Ribbon

FIGURE 13.22   DECISION TREE FOR THE PDC PROBLEM WITH THREE
BRANCHES CREATED WITH ANALYTIC SOLVER PLATFORM

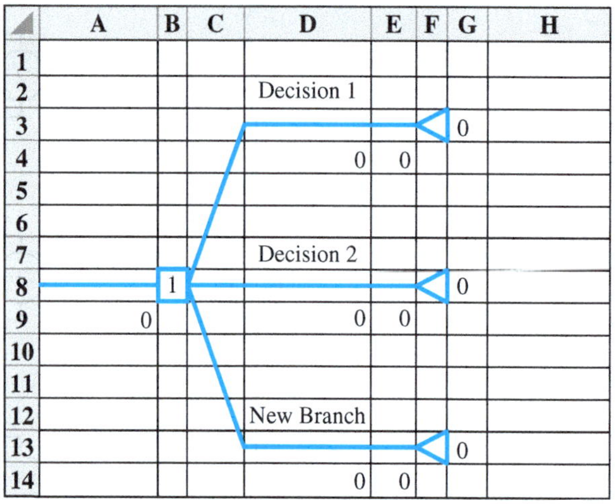

Step 3. Click **Decision Tree** in the **Tools** group
Select **Branch**, and click **Add Branch**
Step 4. When the **Decision Tree** dialog box appears, verify that **Decision** is selected
for **Node Type**, and click **OK**

A revised tree with three decision branches now appears in the Excel worksheet as shown
in Figure 13.22.

Naming the Decision Alternatives

The decision alternatives can be named by selecting the cells containing the labels "Decision 1", "Decision 2", and "New Branch", and then entering the corresponding PDC names
Small, *Medium*, and *Large* (cells D2, D7 and D12). After naming the alternatives, the PDC
tree with three decision branches appears as shown in Figure 13.23.

Adding Chance Nodes

The chance event for the PDC problem is the demand for the condominiums, which may
be either strong or weak. Thus, a chance node with two branches must be added at the end
of each decision alternative branch. To add a chance node with two branches to the top
decision alternative branch:

Step 1. Select cell F3
Step 2. Click the **ANALYTIC SOLVER PLATFORM** tab in the Ribbon
Step 3. Select **Decision Tree** from the **Tools** group
Select **Node**, and click **Add Node**
Step 4. When the **Decision Tree** dialog box appears, select **Event/Chance** in the **Node
Type** area
Click **OK**

The tree now appears as shown in Figure 13.24.

FIGURE 13.23   DECISION TREE FOR THE PDC PROBLEM WITH RENAMED BRANCHES CREATED WITH ANALYTIC SOLVER PLATFORM

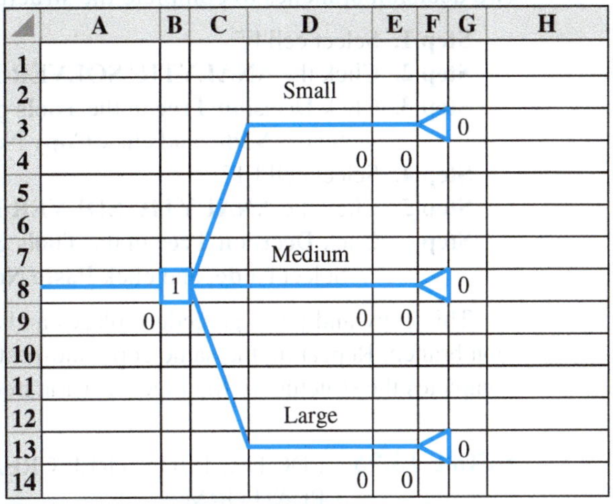

FIGURE 13.24   DECISION TREE FOR THE PDC PROBLEM WITH AN ADDED CHANCE NODE CREATED WITH ANALYTIC SOLVER PLATFORM

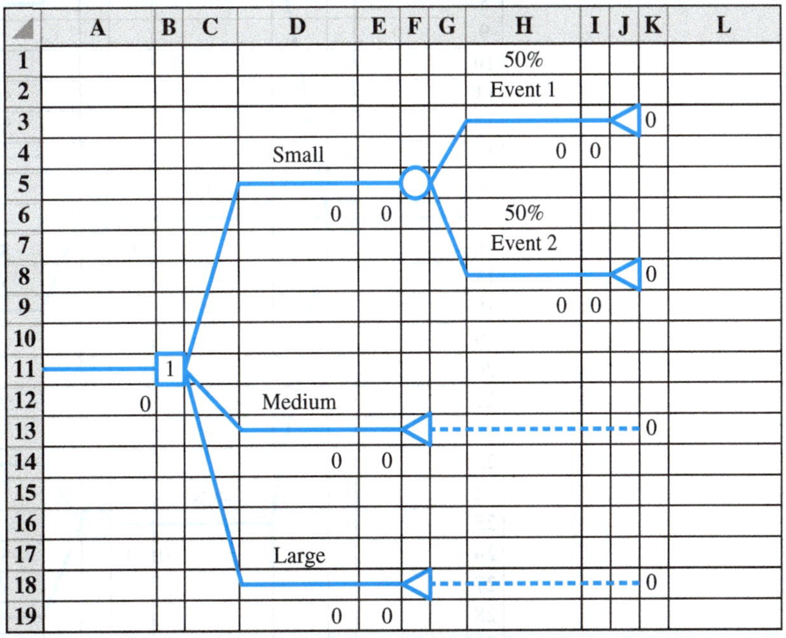

We next select the cells containing "Event 1" and "Event 2" (cells H2 and H7) and rename them *Strong* and *Weak* to provide the proper names for the PDC states of nature. After doing so, we can copy the subtree for the chance node in cell F5 to the other two decision branches to complete the structure of the PDC decision tree as follows:

Step 1. Select cell F5
Step 2. Click the **ANALYTIC SOLVER PLATFORM** tab in the Ribbon
Step 3. Click **Decision Tree** in the **Tools** group
   Select **Node**, and click **Copy Node**
Step 4. Select cell F13
Step 5. Click the **ANALYTIC SOLVER PLATFORM** tab in the Ribbon
Step 6. Click **Decision Tree** in the **Tools** group
   Select **Node**, and click **Paste Node**

This copy-and-paste procedure places a chance node at the end of the Medium decision branch. Repeating the same copy-and-paste procedure for the Large decision branch completes the structure of the PDC decision tree, as shown in Figure 13.25.

FIGURE 13.25   PDC DECISION TREE CREATED WITH ANALYTIC SOLVER PLATFORM

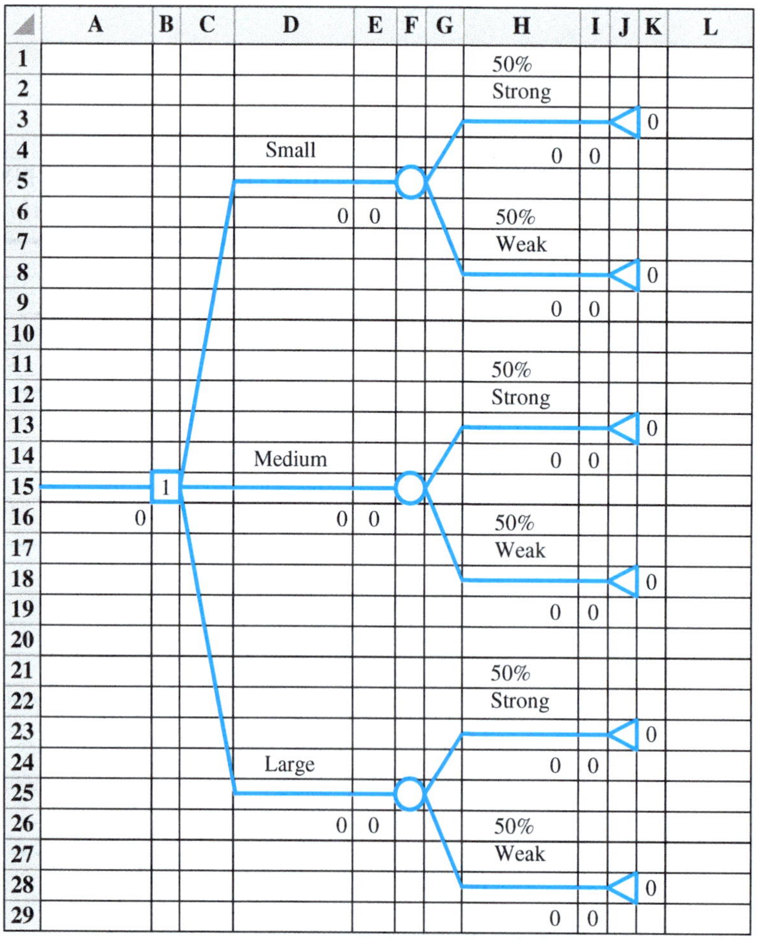

Inserting Probabilities and Payoffs

We now insert probabilities and payoffs into the decision tree. In Figure 13.25, we see that an equal probability of 0.5 is assigned automatically to each of the chance outcomes. For PDC, the probability of strong demand is 0.8 and the probability of weak demand is 1 minus the probability of strong demand, $= 1 - 0.8 = 0.2$. We can enter *0.8* into cell H1 and the formula $=1 - H1$ into cell H6. We enter the formula $=H1$ into cells H11 and H21, and we enter the formula $=H6$ into cells H16 and H26. In this way, all probabilities will be updated correctly if we change the value in cell H1.

To insert the payoffs, we enter *8* in H4, *7* in cell H9, *14* in cell H14, *5* in cell H19, *20* in cell H24, and *−9* in cell H29. Note in Figure 13.26 that the payoffs also appear in the right-hand margin of the decision tree. The payoffs in the right margin are computed by a formula that adds the payoffs on all of the branches leading to the associated terminal node. For the PDC problem, no payoffs are associated with the decision alternatives branches, so we leave the default values of zero in cells D6, D16, and D26. The PDC decision tree is now complete. After inserting the PDC probabilities and payoffs, the PDC decision tree appears as shown in Figure 13.26.

FIGURE 13.26   PDC DECISION TREE WITH BRANCH PROBABILITIES AND PAYOFFS CREATED WITH ANALYTIC SOLVER PLATFORM

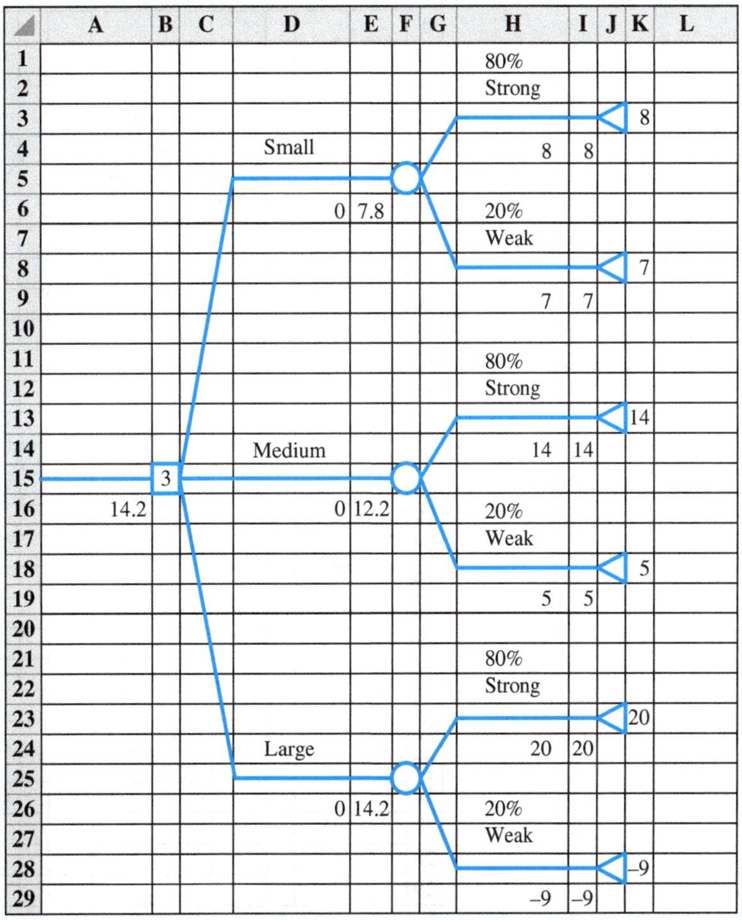

Interpreting the Result

When probabilities and payoffs are inserted, Analytic Solver Platform automatically makes the rollback computations necessary to determine the optimal solution. Optimal decisions are identified by the number in the corresponding decision node. In the PDC decision tree in Figure 13.26, cell B15 contains the decision node. Note that a "3" appears in this node, which tells us that decision alternative branch 3 provides the optimal decision. We can also easily identify the best decision using the Highlight function in Analytic Solver Platform. To highlight the best decision follow these steps:

Step 1. Click the **ANALYTIC SOLVER PLATFORM** tab in the Ribbon
Step 2. Click **Decision Tree** in the **Tools** group
Select **Highlight**, and click **Highlight Best**

Analytic Solver Platform highlights the best decision for the PDC problem. From Figure 13.27, we see that decision analysis recommends that PDC construct the Large

FIGURE 13.27   DECISION TREE FOR THE PDC PROBLEM WITH BEST DECISION HIGHLIGHTED CREATED WITH ANALYTIC SOLVER PLATFORM

	A	B	C	D	E	F	G	H	I	J	K
1								80%			
2								Strong			
3											8
4				Small				8	8		
5											
6				0	7.8			20%			
7								Weak			
8											7
9								7	7		
10											
11								80%			
12								Strong			
13											14
14				Medium				14	14		
15		3									
16	14.2			0	12.2			20%			
17								Weak			
18											5
19								5	5		
20											
21								80%			
22								Strong			
23											20
24				Large				20	20		
25											
26				0	14.2			20%			
27								Weak			
28											−9
29								−9	−9		

condominium complex. The expected value of this decision appears at the beginning of the tree in cell A16. Thus, we see that the optimal expected value is $14.2 million. The expected values of the other decision alternatives are displayed at the end of the corresponding decision branch. Thus, referring to cells E6 and E16, we see that the expected value of the Small complex is $7.8 million and the expected value of the Medium complex is $12.2 million.

Using software such as Analytic Solver Platform to develop decision trees allows for quick and easy sensitivity analysis. We can easily analyze the impact of changing branch probabilities and payoffs by simply changing these values in Excel and observing the impact on the optimal decision using Analytic Solver Platform. For instance, if we want to examine the impact of different values of Strong demand on our decision, we can change the value of cell H1 and see whether this changes the optimal decision.

A convenient way to summarize the sensitivity of a decision to a particular parameter is to combine the decision tree from XLMiner with a Data Table in Excel. Suppose we want to evaluate the impact of different probabilities of strong demand over a wide range of possibilities. The Excel worksheet shown in Figure 13.28 demonstrates the use of a Data

FIGURE 13.28 DECISION TREE AND DATA TABLE ILLUSTRATING SENSITIVITY ANALYSIS FOR THE PDC PROBLEM CREATED WITH ANALYTIC SOLVER PLATFORM

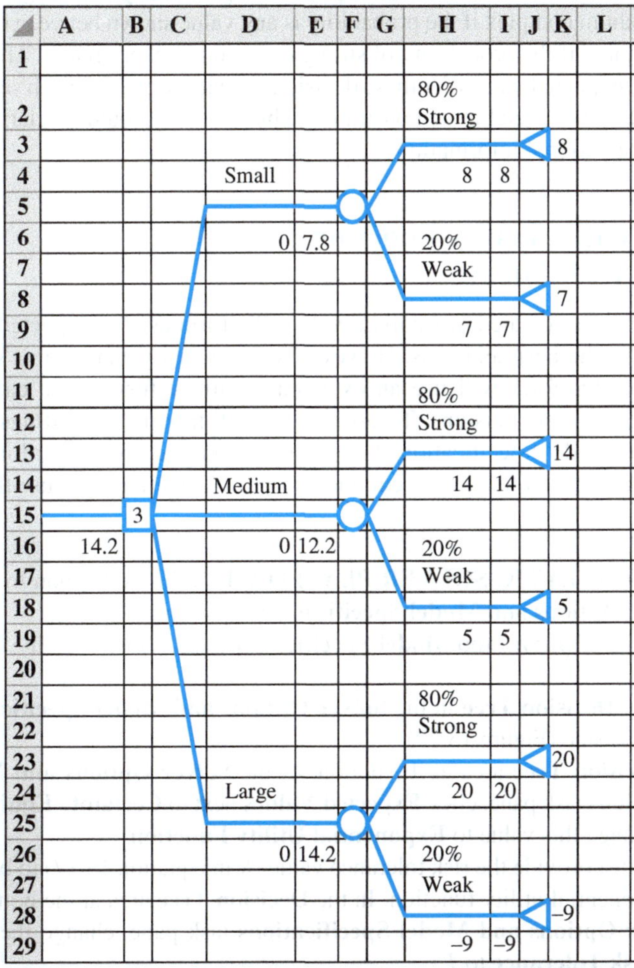

M	N	O
Data Table		
Probability Strong Demand	**Expected Value**	**Best Decision**
	14.2	Large
0.0	7	Small
0.1	7.1	Small
0.2	7.2	Small
0.3	7.7	Medium
0.4	8.6	Medium
0.5	9.5	Medium
0.6	10.4	Medium
0.7	11.3	Medium
0.8	14.2	Large
0.9	17.1	Large
1.0	20	Large

Table to perform this sensitivity analysis. To create this Data Table, we follow these steps once we have created the decision tree for this problem in XLMiner:

Step 1. Enter the values *0.0, 0.1, 0.2*, etc. into cells M4 to M14, as shown in Figure 13.27, to represent the different scenarios for the probability of Strong demand

Step 2. Enter =A16 into cell N3 to keep track of the optimal expected value in each scenario

Step 3. Enter the formula =CHOOSE(B15,"Small","Medium","Large") into cell O3. This will return the best decision in each scenario

Step 4. Select cells M3:O14

Step 5. Click the **DATA** tab in the Ribbon

Step 6. Click **What-If Analysis** from the **Data Tools** group
Select **Data Table...**

Step 7. When the **Data Table** dialog box opens, enter =H1 into the **Column input cell:** box
Click **OK**

The Excel function CHOOSE chooses a value from a list of possibilities based on the index in the referenced cell. Here, the CHOOSE function chooses "Small" in cell O3 if the value in cell B15 is 1; it enters "Medium" if the value in cell B15 is 2; it enters "Large" if the value in cell B15 is 3.

By entering =H1 in Step 7, we tell Excel to substitute the values of 0, 0.1, 0.2, and so on for the probability of Strong demand and then return the related outputs.

Figure 13.28 shows the completed decision tree and Data Table. From Figure 13.28, we see that the best decision is to construct the Small complex if the probability of strong demand is 0, 0.1, or 0.2, the Medium complex if the probability is any value shown between 0.3 and 0.7, and the Large complex if the probability of strong demand is 0.8 or greater. The Data Table also provides the expected values for these decisions in each scenario. Such sensitivity analysis can be greatly beneficial in demonstrating which values should be clarified, if possible, by procuring additional information.

Using the Exponential Utility Function in Analytic Solver Platform

By default, the decision trees created in Analytic Solver Platform use the expected value approach for calculating the best decisions. However, we can easily change this setting so that Analytic Solver Platform will use an exponential utility function to calculate utilities and determine the best decisions. To do this, we will modify the settings using the Solver Options and Model Specifications task pane of Analytic Solver Platform. To change the settings in a decision tree to use exponential utility functions, we use the following steps.

*If the **Solver Options and Model Specifications** task pane is not visible, it can be activated by clicking the **Model** button in the **Model** group under the **ANALYTIC SOLVER PLATFORM** tab in the Ribbon.*

Step 1. Click the **ANALYTIC SOLVER PLATFORM** tab in the Ribbon to reveal the **Solver Options and Model Specifications** task pane

Step 2. In the **Solver Options and Model Specifications** task pane, click the **Model** tab
Select **Decision Tree** in the **Solver Options and Model Specifications** task pane (Figure 13.29)

Step 3. In the **Decision Tree** area at the bottom of the **Solver Options and Model Specifications** task pane, click **Expected Values** next to **Certainty Equivalent**
Change this value to **Exponential Utility Function**

Step 4. We also must provide the risk tolerance value (R in equation 13.17) to be used in the exponential utility function. In the **Decision Tree** area at the bottom of the **Solver Options and Model Specifications** task pane, change the value next to **Risk Tolerance** to *1*

FIGURE 13.29   DECISION TREE IN ANALYTIC SOLVER PLATFORM USING AN EXPONENTIAL UTILITY FUNCTION WITH R = $1 MILLION

											Data Table		
											Probability Strong Demand	**Expected Value**	**Best Decision**
						80% Strong				8		7.7046	Small
		Small				8	8				0.0	7.0000	Small
							0.9997				0.1	7.0653	Small
		0	7.7046			20%					0.2	7.1352	Small
			0.9995			Weak					0.3	7.2103	Small
										7	0.4	7.2915	Small
						7	7				0.5	7.3799	Small
							0.9991				0.6	7.4769	Small
						80%					0.7	7.5843	Small
						Strong					0.8	7.7046	Small
										14	0.9	7.8414	Small
		Medium				14	14				1.0	20.0000	Large
	1						1.0000						
7.7046		0	6.6089			20%							
0.9995			0.9987			Weak							
										5			
						5	5						
							0.9933						
						80%							
						Strong							
										20			
		Large				20	20						
							1.0000						
		0	−7.3906			20%							
			−1619.6168			Weak							
										−9			
						−9	−9						
							−8102.0839						

Figure 13.29 shows the completed decision tree using the exponential utility function. Step 4 indicates that we are using a value of $1 million as the R value in equation (13.17). We know that the units here are in millions of dollars because those are the units used by the values in our decision tree. Recall that a small risk tolerance (R value), relative to the payoff values in the decision tree, indicates that the decision maker is very risk averse. Once we make this change in Analytic Solver Platform, the decision tree calculations are done using utilities based on the exponential function rather than using the expected value method.

In the Data Table in Figure 13.29, we see that the decision maker often prefers to build the Small complex to limit downside risk due to the decision maker being very risk averse. However, if we change the risk tolerance (R) to be $9 million, this means that the decision maker is less risk averse. Figure 13.30 shows the decision tree with an exponential utility function and R = $9 million; here we see that the decision maker is more likely to choose

FIGURE 13.30   DECISION TREE IN ANALYTIC SOLVER PLATFORM USING AN EXPONENTIAL UTILITY FUNCTION WITH R = \$9 MILLION

Data Table

	Probability Strong Demand	Expected Value	Best Decision
		11.3414	Medium
	0.0	7.0000	Small
	0.1	7.0951	Small
	0.2	7.1913	Small
	0.3	7.2885	Small
	0.4	7.6234	Medium
	0.5	8.4190	Medium
	0.6	9.2918	Medium
	0.7	10.2584	Medium
	0.8	11.3414	Medium
	0.9	12.5729	Medium
	1.0	20.0000	Large

Decision tree values:

- Small: 0   7.7909   0.5792
  - 80% Strong: 8, 8, 0.5889 → 8
  - 20% Weak: 7, 7, 0.5406 → 7
- Medium: 0   11.3414   0.7164
  - 80% Strong: 14, 14, 0.7889 → 14
  - 20% Weak: 5, 5, 0.4262 → 5
- Large: 0   4.1533   0.3696
  - 80% Strong: 20, 20, 0.8916 → 20
  - 20% Weak: −9, −9, −1.7183 → −9

Node value (A15): 2   (A16) 11.3414   (A17) 0.7164

Solver Options and Model Specifications

Model | Platform | Engine | Output

- Sensitivity
- Optimization
- Simulation
- Decision Tree
  - New Node
    - Small
      - New Node
        - Strong
          - Terminal
        - Weak
          - Terminal
    - Medium
      - New Node
        - Strong
          - Terminal
        - Weak
          - Terminal
    - Large
      - New Node

Decision Tree
Location	$A$1
Certainty Equivalents	Exponential Utility Function
Decision Node EV/CE	Maximize
Risk Tolerance	9
Scalar A	1
Scalar B	1

Risk Tolerance
The Risk Tolerance parameter of the exponential utility function

the Medium complex for many different probabilities of Strong demand as compared to the more risk averse decision maker shown in Figure 13.29. Figure 13.30 reflects a decision maker who is less risk averse and more willing to accept decisions that could have higher payoffs but that also have higher likelihoods of worse payoffs.

The complete decision tree and data table for the PDC problem is contained in the file *PDCModel*.

WEB file

PDCModel

Appendix 13.2   DECISION ANALYSIS WITH TREEPLAN

TreePlan[2] is an Excel add-in that can be used to develop decision trees for decision analysis problems. The software package is provided at the website that accompanies this text. Instructions for installation and a manual containing additional information are also available at the website. In this appendix we show how to use TreePlan to build a decision tree and solve the PDC problem presented in Section 13.3. The decision tree for the PDC problem is shown in Figure 13.31.

Getting Started: An Initial Decision Tree

We begin by assuming that TreePlan has been installed and an Excel workbook is open. To build a TreePlan version of the PDC decision tree, proceed as follows:

Step 1. Select cell A1
Step 2. Select the **Add-Ins tab** and choose **Decision Tree** from the **Menu Commands** group
Step 3. When the **TreePlan - New Tree** dialog box appears:
Click **New Tree**

A decision tree with one decision node and two branches (initially labeled as *Alternatives*) is provided in Figure 13.32.

FIGURE 13.31   PDC DECISION TREE

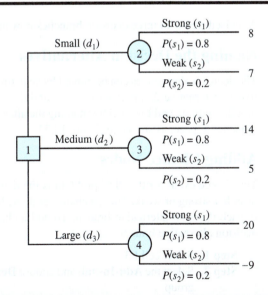

---

[2]TreePlan was developed by Professor Michael R. Middleton at the University of San Francisco and modified for use by Professor James E. Smith at Duke University. The TreePlan website is *http://www.treeplan.com*.

FIGURE 13.32   A DECISION TREE WITH ONE DECISION NODE AND TWO BRANCHES
DEVELOPED BY TREEPLAN

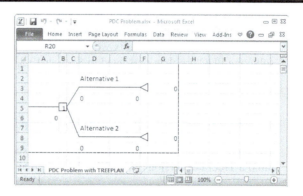

Adding a Branch

The PDC problem has three decision alternatives (small, medium, and large condominium complexes), so we must add another decision branch to the tree.

> **Step 1.** Select cell B5
> **Step 2.** Select the **Add-Ins tab** and choose **Decision Tree** from the **Menu Commands** group
> **Step 3.** When the **TreePlan - Decision Node** dialog box appears:
> Select **Add branch**
> Click **OK**

A revised tree with three decision branches now appears in the Excel worksheet.

Naming the Decision Alternatives

The decision alternatives can be named by selecting the cells containing the labels Alternative 1, Alternative 2, and Alternative 3, and then entering the corresponding PDC names Small, Medium, and Large. After naming the alternatives, the PDC tree with three decision branches appears as shown in Figure 13.33.

Adding Chance Nodes

The chance event for the PDC problem is the demand for the condominiums, which may be either strong or weak. Thus, a chance node with two branches must be added at the end of each decision alternative branch. To add a chance node with two branches to the top decision alternative branch:

> **Step 1.** Select cell F3
> **Step 2.** Select the **Add-Ins tab** and choose **Decision Tree** from the **Menu Commands** group
> **Step 3.** When the **TreePlan - Terminal Node** dialog box appears:
> Select **Change to event node**
> Select **Two** in the **Branches** section
> Click **OK**

FIGURE 13.33   TREEPLAN DECISION TREE WITH AN ADDITIONAL DECISION NODE AND LABELS ON THE BRANCHES

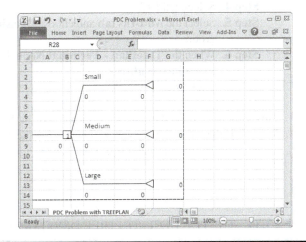

The tree now appears as shown in Figure 13.34.

   We next select the cells containing Outcome 4 and Outcome 5 and rename them Strong and Weak to provide the proper names for the PDC states of nature. After doing so we can copy the subtree for the chance node in cell F5 to the other two decision branches to complete the structure of the PDC decision tree as follows:

   Step 1.   Select cell F5
   Step 2.   Select the **Add-Ins tab** and choose **Decision Tree** from the **Menu Commands** group

FIGURE 13.34   TREEPLAN DECISION TREE WITH A CHANCE NODE ADDED TO THE END OF THE FIRST DECISION BRANCH

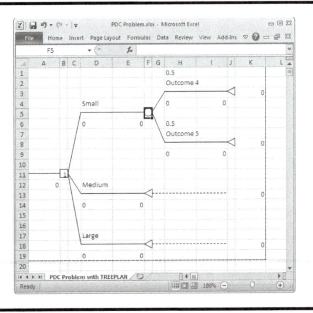

Step 3. When the **TreePlan Event** dialog box appears:
Select **Copy subtree**
Click **OK**

Step 4. Select cell F13

Step 5. Select the **Add-Ins tab** and choose **Decision Tree** from the **Menu Commands** group

Step 6. When the **TreePlan - Terminal Node** dialog box appears:
Select **Paste subtree**
Click **OK**

This copy/paste procedure places a chance node at the end of the Medium decision branch. Repeating the same copy/paste procedure for the Large decision branch completes the structure of the PDC decision tree as shown in Figure 13.35.

FIGURE 13.35   THE PDC DECISION TREE DEVELOPED BY TREEPLAN

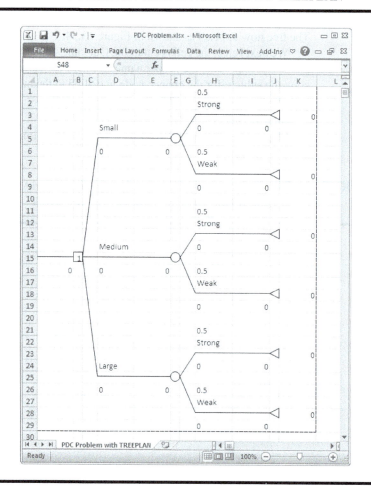

FIGURE 13.36   THE PDC DECISION TREE WITH BRANCH PROBABILITIES AND PAYOFFS

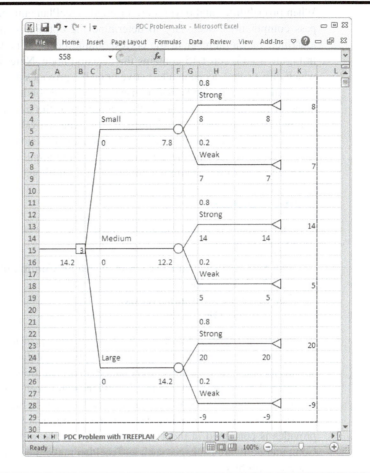

Inserting Probabilities and Payoffs

TreePlan provides the capability of inserting probabilities and payoffs into the decision tree. In Figure 13.32 we see that TreePlan automatically assigned an equal probability 0.5 to each of the chance outcomes. For PDC, the probability of strong demand is 0.8 and the probability of weak demand is 0.2. We can select cells H1, H6, H11, H16, H21, and H26 and insert the appropriate probabilities. The payoffs for the chance outcomes are inserted in cells H4, H9, H14, H19, H24, and H29. After inserting the PDC probabilities and payoffs, the PDC decision tree appears as shown in Figure 13.36.

Note that the payoffs also appear in the right-hand margin of the decision tree (column K in this problem). The payoffs in the right margin are computed by a formula that adds the payoffs on all of the branches leading to the associated terminal node. For the PDC problem, no payoffs are associated with the decision alternatives branches so we leave the default values of zero in cells D6, D16, and D26. The PDC decision tree is now complete.

Interpreting the Result

When probabilities and payoffs are inserted, TreePlan automatically makes the backward pass computations necessary to determine the optimal solution. Optimal decisions are identified by the number in the corresponding decision node. In the PDC decision tree in Figure 13.33, cell B15 contains the decision node. Note that a 3 appears in this node, which tells us that decision alternative branch 3 provides the optimal decision. Thus, decision analysis recommends PDC construct the Large condominium complex. The expected value of this decision appears at the beginning of the tree in cell A16. Thus, we see the optimal expected value is $14.2 million. The expected values of the other decision alternatives are displayed at the end of the corresponding decision branch. Thus, referring to cells E6 and E16, we see that the expected value of the Small complex is $7.8 million and the expected value of the Medium complex is $12.2 million.

Other Options

TreePlan defaults to a maximization objective. If you would like a minimization objective, follow these steps:

Step 1. Select **Decision Tree** from the **Menu Commands** group
Step 2. Select **Options**
Step 3. Choose **Minimize (costs)**
Click **OK**

In using a TreePlan decision tree, we can modify probabilities and payoffs and quickly observe the impact of the changes on the optimal solution. Using this "what if" type of sensitivity analysis, we can identify changes in probabilities and payoffs that would change the optimal decision. Also, because TreePlan is an Excel add-in, most of Excel's capabilities are available. For instance, we could use boldface to highlight the name of the optimal decision alternative on the final decision tree solution. A variety of other options TreePlan provides is contained in the TreePlan manual on the website that accompanies this text. Computer software packages such as TreePlan make it easier to do a thorough analysis of a decision problem.

CHAPTER 9

Time Series Analysis and Forecasting

CONTENTS

The purpose of this chapter is to provide an introduction to time series analysis and forecasting. Suppose we are asked to provide quarterly forecasts of sales for one of our company's products over the coming one-year period. Production schedules, raw materials purchasing, inventory policies, and sales quotas will all be affected by the quarterly forecasts we provide. Consequently, poor forecasts may result in poor planning and increased costs for the company. How should we go about providing the quarterly sales forecasts? Good judgment, intuition, and an awareness of the state of the economy may give us a rough idea or "feeling" of what is likely to happen in the future, but converting that feeling into a number that can be used as next year's sales forecast is challenging. The Management Science in Action, Forecasting Energy Needs in the Utility Industry, describes the role that forecasting plays in the utility industry.

A forecast is simply a prediction of what will happen in the future. Managers must accept that regardless of the technique used, they will not be able to develop perfect forecasts.

Forecasting methods can be classified as qualitative or quantitative. Qualitative methods generally involve the use of expert judgment to develop forecasts. Such methods are appropriate when historical data on the variable being forecast are either unavailable or not applicable. Quantitative forecasting methods can be used when (1) past information about the variable being forecast is available, (2) the information can be quantified, and (3) it is reasonable to assume that past is prologue (i.e. the pattern of the past will continue into the future). We will focus exclusively on quantitative forecasting methods in this chapter.

If the historical data are restricted to past values of the variable to be forecast, the forecasting procedure is called a *time series method* and the historical data are referred to as a

MANAGEMENT SCIENCE IN ACTION

FORECASTING ENERGY NEEDS IN THE UTILITY INDUSTRY*

Duke Energy is a diversified energy company with a portfolio of natural gas and electric businesses and an affiliated real estate company. In 2006, Duke Energy merged with Cinergy of Cincinnati, Ohio, to create one of North America's largest energy companies, with assets totaling more than $70 billion. As a result of this merger the Cincinnati Gas & Electric Company became part of Duke Energy. Today, Duke Energy services over 5.5 million retail electric and gas customers in North Carolina, South Carolina, Ohio, Kentucky, Indiana, and Ontario, Canada.

Forecasting in the utility industry offers some unique perspectives. Because energy is difficult to store, this product must be generated to meet the instantaneous requirements of the customers. Electrical shortages are not just lost sales, but "brownouts" or "blackouts." This situation places an unusual burden on the utility forecaster. On the positive side, the demand for energy and the sale of energy are more predictable than for many other products. Also, unlike the situation in a multiproduct firm, a great amount of forecasting effort and expertise can be concentrated on the two products: gas and electricity.

The largest observed electric demand for any given period, such as an hour, a day, a month, or a year, is defined as the peak load. The forecast of the annual electric peak load guides the timing decision for constructing future generating units, and the financial impact of this decision is great. Obviously, a timing decision that leads to having the unit available no sooner than necessary is crucial.

The energy forecasts are important in other ways also. For example, purchases of coal as fuel for the generating units are based on the forecast levels of energy needed. The revenue from the electric operations of the company is determined from forecasted sales, which in turn enters into the planning of rate changes and external financing. These planning and decision-making processes are among the most important managerial activities in the company. It is imperative that the decision makers have the best forecast information available to assist them in arriving at these decisions.

*Based on information provided by Dr. Richard Evans of Duke Energy.

time series. The objective of time series analysis is to uncover a pattern in the historical data or time series and then extrapolate the pattern into the future; the forecast is based solely on past values of the variable and/or on past forecast errors.

In Section 15.1 we discuss the various kinds of time series that a forecaster might be faced with in practice. These include a constant or horizontal pattern, a trend, a seasonal pattern, both a trend and a seasonal pattern, and a cyclical pattern. In order to build a quantitative forecasting model it is also necessary to have a measurement of forecast accuracy. Different measurements of forecast accuracy, and their respective advantages and disadvantages, are discussed in Section 15.2. In Section 15.3 we consider the simplest case, which is a horizontal or constant pattern. For this pattern, we develop the classical moving average, weighted moving average, and exponential smoothing models. Many time series have a trend, and taking this trend into account is important; in Section 15.4 we provide regression models for finding the best model parameters when a linear trend is present. Finally, in Section 15.5 we show how to incorporate both a trend and seasonality into a forecasting model.

15.1 TIME SERIES PATTERNS

A **time series** is a sequence of observations on a variable measured at successive points in time or over successive periods of time. The measurements may be taken every hour, day, week, month, or year, or at any other regular interval.[1] The pattern of the data is an important factor in understanding how the time series has behaved in the past. If such behavior can be expected to continue in the future, we can use it to guide us in selecting an appropriate forecasting method.

To identify the underlying pattern in the data, a useful first step is to construct a time series plot. A **time series plot** is a graphical presentation of the relationship between time and the time series variable; time is represented on the horizontal axis and values of the time series variable are shown on the vertical axis. Let us first review some of the common types of data patterns that can be identified when examining a time series plot.

Horizontal Pattern

A horizontal pattern exists when the data fluctuate randomly around a constant mean over time. To illustrate a time series with a horizontal pattern, consider the 12 weeks of data in Table 15.1. These data show the number of gallons of gasoline (in 1000s) sold by a gasoline distributor in Bennington, Vermont, over the past 12 weeks. The average value or mean for this time series is 19.25 or 19,250 gallons per week. Figure 15.1 shows a time series plot for these data. Note how the data fluctuate around the sample mean of 19,250 gallons. Although random variability is present, we would say that these data follow a horizontal pattern.

The term **stationary time series**[2] is used to denote a time series whose statistical properties are independent of time. In particular this means that

1. The process generating the data has a constant mean.
2. The variability of the time series is constant over time.

---

[1] We limit our discussion to time series for which the values of the series are recorded at equal intervals. Cases in which the observations are made at unequal intervals are beyond the scope of this text.

[2] For a formal definition of stationarity, see K. Ord and R. Fildes (2012), *Principles of Business Forecasting*. Mason, OH: Cengage Learning, p. 155.

TABLE 15.1   GASOLINE SALES TIME SERIES

Week	Sales (1000s of gallons)
1	17
2	21
3	19
4	23
5	18
6	16
7	20
8	18
9	22
10	20
11	15
12	22

WEB file

Gasoline

FIGURE 15.1   GASOLINE SALES TIME SERIES PLOT

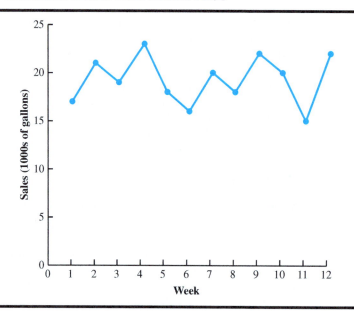

A time series plot for a stationary time series will always exhibit a horizontal pattern with random fluctuations. However, simply observing a horizontal pattern is not sufficient evidence to conclude that the time series is stationary. More advanced texts on forecasting discuss procedures for determining if a time series is stationary and provide methods for transforming a time series that is nonstationary into a stationary series.

Changes in business conditions often result in a time series with a horizontal pattern that shifts to a new level at some point in time. For instance, suppose the gasoline distributor signs a contract with the Vermont Sate Police to provide gasoline for state police cars located in southern Vermont beginning in Week 13. With this new contract,

TABLE 15.2   GASOLINE SALES TIME SERIES AFTER OBTAINING THE CONTRACT
WITH THE VERMONT STATE POLICE

Week	Sales (1000s of gallons)	Week	Sales (1000s of gallons)
1	17	12	22
2	21	13	31
3	19	14	34
4	23	15	31
5	18	16	33
6	16	17	28
7	20	18	32
8	18	19	30
9	22	20	29
10	20	21	34
11	15	22	33

WEB file

GasolineRevised

FIGURE 15.2   GASOLINE SALES TIME SERIES PLOT AFTER OBTAINING THE
CONTRACT WITH THE VERMONT STATE POLICE

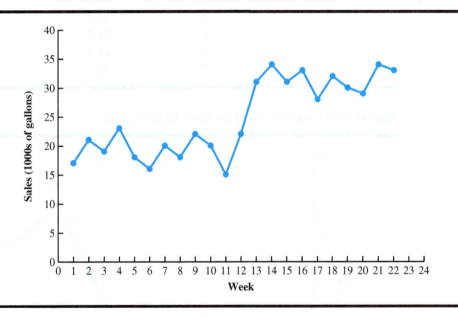

the distributor naturally expects to see a substantial increase in weekly sales starting
in Week 13. Table 15.2 shows the number of gallons of gasoline sold for the original
time series and the 10 weeks after signing the new contract. Figure 15.2 shows the corresponding time series plot. Note the increased level of the time series beginning in
Week 13. This change in the level of the time series makes it more difficult to choose
an appropriate forecasting method. Selecting a forecasting method that adapts well to
changes in the level of a time series is an important consideration in many practical
applications.

Trend Pattern

Although time series data generally exhibit random fluctuations, a time series may also show gradual shifts or movements to relatively higher or lower values over a longer period of time. If a time series plot exhibits this type of behavior, we say that a **trend pattern** exists. A trend is usually the result of long-term factors such as population increases or decreases, shifting demographic characteristics of the population, improving technology, and/or changes in consumer preferences.

To illustrate a time series with a linear trend pattern, consider the time series of bicycle sales for a particular manufacturer over the past 10 years, as shown in Table 15.3 and Figure 15.3. Note that 21,600 bicycles were sold in Year 1, 22,900

WEB file

Bicycle

TABLE 15.3   BICYCLE SALES TIME SERIES

Year	Sales (1000s)
1	21.6
2	22.9
3	25.5
4	21.9
5	23.9
6	27.5
7	31.5
8	29.7
9	28.6
10	31.4

FIGURE 15.3   BICYCLE SALES TIME SERIES PLOT

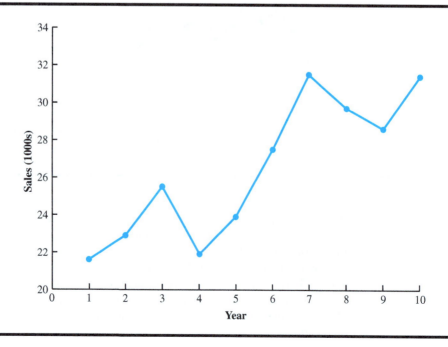

were sold in Year 2, and so on. In Year 10, the most recent year, 31,400 bicycles were sold. Visual inspection of the time series plot shows some up and down movement over the past 10 years, but the time series seems also to have a systematically increasing or upward trend.

The trend for the bicycle sales time series appears to be linear and increasing over time, but sometimes a trend can be described better by other types of patterns. For instance, the data in Table 15.4 and the corresponding time series plot in Figure 15.4 show the sales revenue for a cholesterol drug since the company won FDA approval for the drug 10 years ago. The time series increases in a nonlinear fashion; that is, the rate of change of revenue does not increase by a constant amount from one year to the next. In fact, the revenue appears to be growing in an exponential fashion. Exponential relationships such as this are appropriate when the percentage change from one period to the next is relatively constant.

TABLE 15.4   CHOLESTEROL DRUG REVENUE TIME SERIES ($ MILLIONS)

WEB file

Cholesterol

Year	Revenue
1	23.1
2	21.3
3	27.4
4	34.6
5	33.8
6	43.2
7	59.5
8	64.4
9	74.2
10	99.3

FIGURE 15.4   CHOLESTEROL DRUG REVENUE TIME SERIES PLOT ($ MILLIONS)

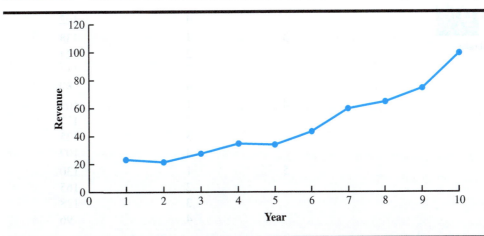

Seasonal Pattern

The trend of a time series can be identified by analyzing movements in historical data over multiple years. **Seasonal patterns** are recognized by observing recurring patterns over successive periods of time. For example, a manufacturer of swimming pools expects low sales activity in the fall and winter months, with peak sales in the spring and summer months to occur each year. Manufacturers of snow removal equipment and heavy clothing, however, expect the opposite yearly pattern. Not surprisingly, the pattern for a time series plot that exhibits a recurring pattern over a one-year period due to seasonal influences is called a seasonal pattern. While we generally think of seasonal movement in a time series as occurring within one year, time series data can also exhibit seasonal patterns of less than one year in duration. For example, daily traffic volume shows within-the-day "seasonal" behavior, with peak levels occurring during rush hours, moderate flow during the rest of the day and early evening, and light flow from midnight to early morning. Another example of an industry with sales that exhibit easily discernable seasonal patterns within a day is the restaurant industry.

As an example of a seasonal pattern, consider the number of umbrellas sold at a clothing store over the past five years. Table 15.5 shows the time series and Figure 15.5 shows the corresponding time series plot. The time series plot does not indicate a long-term trend in sales. In fact, unless you look carefully at the data, you might conclude that the data follow a horizontal pattern with random fluctuation.

TABLE 15.5   UMBRELLA SALES TIME SERIES

Umbrella

Year	Quarter	Sales
1	1	125
	2	153
	3	106
	4	88
2	1	118
	2	161
	3	133
	4	102
3	1	138
	2	144
	3	113
	4	80
4	1	109
	2	137
	3	125
	4	109
5	1	130
	2	165
	3	128
	4	96

FIGURE 15.5 UMBRELLA SALES TIME SERIES PLOT

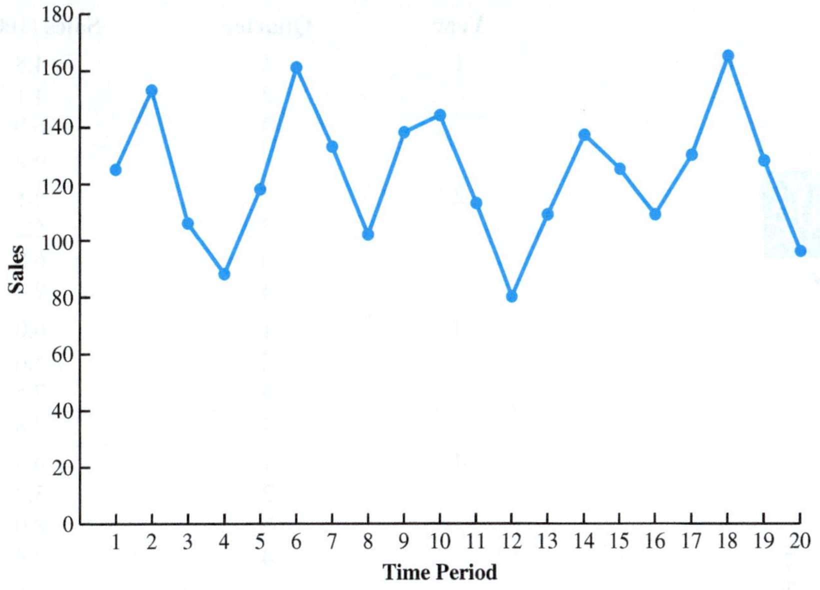

However, closer inspection of the fluctuations in the time series plot reveals a systematic pattern in the data that occurs within each year. That is, the first and third quarters have moderate sales, the second quarter has the highest sales, and the fourth quarter tends to have the lowest sales volume. Thus, we would conclude that a quarterly seasonal pattern is present.

Trend and Seasonal Pattern

Some time series include both a trend and a seasonal pattern. For instance, the data in Table 15.6 and the corresponding time series plot in Figure 15.6 show quarterly television set sales for a particular manufacturer over the past four years. Clearly an increasing trend is present. However, Figure 15.6 also indicates that sales are lowest in the second quarter of each year and highest in quarters 3 and 4. Thus, we conclude that a seasonal pattern also exists for television sales. In such cases we need to use a forecasting method that is capable of dealing with both trend and seasonality.

Cyclical Pattern

A **cyclical pattern** exists if the time series plot shows an alternating sequence of points below and above the trend line that lasts for more than one year. Many economic time series exhibit cyclical behavior with regular runs of observations below and above the trend line. Often the cyclical component of a time series is due to multiyear business cycles. For example, periods of moderate inflation followed by periods of rapid inflation can lead to a time series that alternates below and above a generally increasing trend line (e.g., a time series for housing costs). Business cycles are extremely difficult, if not impossible, to forecast. As a result, cyclical effects are often combined with long-term trend effects and referred to as trend-cycle effects. In this chapter we do not deal with cyclical effects that may be present in the time series.

TABLE 15.6   QUARTERLY TELEVISION SET SALES TIME SERIES

Year	Quarter	Sales (1000s)
1	1	4.8
	2	4.1
	3	6.0
	4	6.5
2	1	5.8
	2	5.2
	3	6.8
	4	7.4
3	1	6.0
	2	5.6
	3	7.5
	4	7.8
4	1	6.3
	2	5.9
	3	8.0
	4	8.4

WEB file

SalesTV

FIGURE 15.6   QUARTERLY TELEVISION SET SALES TIME SERIES PLOT

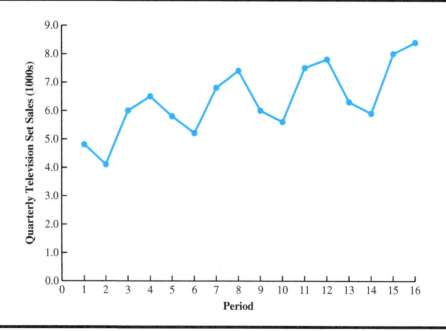

Selecting a Forecasting Method

The underlying pattern in the time series is an important factor in selecting a forecasting method. Thus, a time series plot should be one of the first analytic tools employed when trying to determine which forecasting method to use. If we see a horizontal pattern, then we need to select a method appropriate for this type of pattern. Similarly, if we observe a trend in the data, then we need to use a forecasting method that is capable of handling a trend effectively. In the next two sections we illustrate methods for assessing forecast accuracy and consider forecasting models that can be used in situations for which the underlying pattern is horizontal; in other words, no trend or seasonal effects are present. We then consider methods appropriate when trend and/or seasonality are present in the data. The Management Science in Action, Forecasting Demand for a Broad Product Line of Office Products, describes the considerations made by ACCO Brands when forecasting demand for its consumer and office products.

MANAGEMENT SCIENCE IN ACTION

FORECASTING DEMAND FOR A BROAD PRODUCT LINE OF OFFICE PRODUCTS*

ACCO Brands Corporation is one of the world's largest suppliers of branded office and consumer products and print finishing solutions. The company's widely recognized brands include AT-A-GLANCE*, Day-Timer*, Five Star*, GBC*, Hilroy*, Kensington*, Marbig*, Mead*, NOBO, Quartet*, Rexel, Swingline*, Tilibra*, Wilson Jones*, and many others.

Because it produces and markets a wide array of products with a myriad of demand characteristics, ACCO Brands relies heavily on sales forecasts in planning its manufacturing, distribution, and marketing activities. By viewing its relationship in terms of a supply chain, ACCO Brands and its customers (which are generally retail chains) establish close collaborative relationships and consider each other to be valued partners. As a result, ACCO Brands' customers share valuable information and data that serve as inputs into ACCO Brands' forecasting process.

In her role as a forecasting manager for ACCO Brands, Vanessa Baker appreciates the importance of this additional Information. "We do separate forecasts of demand for each major customer," said Baker, "and we generally use twenty-four to thirty-six months of history to generate monthly forecasts twelve to eighteen months into the future. While trends are important, several of our major product lines, including school, planning and organizing, and decorative calendars, are heavily seasonal, and seasonal sales make up the bulk of our annual volume."

Daniel Marks, one of several account-level strategic forecast managers for ACCO Brands, adds:

The supply chain process includes the total lead time from identifying opportunities to making or procuring the product to getting the product on the shelves to align with the forecasted demand; this can potentially take several months, so the accuracy of our forecasts is critical throughout each step of the supply chain. Adding to this challenge is the risk of obsolescence. We sell many dated items, such as planners and calendars, which have a natural, built-in obsolescence. In addition, many of our products feature designs that are fashion-conscious or contain pop culture images, and these products can also become obsolete very quickly as tastes and popularity change. An overly optimistic forecast for these products can be very costly, but an overly pessimistic forecast can result in lost sales potential and give our competitors an opportunity to take market share from us.

In addition to looking at trends, seasonal components, and cyclical patterns, Baker and Marks must contend with several other factors. Baker notes, "We have to adjust our forecasts for upcoming promotions by our customers." Marks agrees and adds:

We also have to go beyond just forecasting consumer demand; we must consider the retailer's specific needs in our order forecasts, such as what type of display will be used and how many units of a product must be on display to satisfy their presentation requirements. Current inventory is another factor—if a customer is carrying either too much or too little inventory, that will affect their future orders, and we need lo reflect that in our forecasts. Will the product have a short life because it is tied lo a cultural fad? What are the retailer's marketing and markdown strategics? Our knowledge of the environments in which our supply chain partners are competing helps us to forecast demand more accurately, and that reduces waste and makes our customers, as well as ACCO Brands, far more profitable.

*The authors are indebted to Vanessa Baker and Daniel Marks of ACCO Brands for providing input for this Management Science in Action.

15.2   FORECAST ACCURACY

In this section we begin by developing forecasts for the gasoline time series shown in Table 15.1 using the simplest of all the forecasting methods, an approach that uses the most recent week's sales volume as the forecast for the next week. For instance, the distributor sold 17,000 gallons of gasoline in Week 1; this value is used as the forecast for Week 2. Next, we use 21, the actual value of sales in Week 2, as the forecast for Week 3, and so on. The forecasts obtained for the historical data using this method are shown in Table 15.7 in the column labeled Forecast. Because of its simplicity, this method is often referred to as a naïve forecasting method.

How accurate are the forecasts obtained using this naïve forecasting method? To answer this question we will introduce several measures of forecast accuracy. These measures are used to determine how well a particular forecasting method is able to reproduce the time series data that are already available. By selecting the method that is most accurate for the data already known, we hope to increase the likelihood that we will obtain more accurate forecasts for future time periods.

The key concept associated with measuring forecast accuracy is **forecast error**. If we denote Y_t and F_t as the actual and forcasted values of the time series for period t, respectively, the forecasting error for period t is

$$e_t = Y_t - \hat{Y}_t \qquad (15.1)$$

That is, the forecast error for time period t is the difference between the actual and the forecasted values for period t.

TABLE 15.7   COMPUTING FORECASTS AND MEASURES OF FORECAST ACCURACY USING THE MOST RECENT VALUE AS THE FORECAST FOR THE NEXT PERIOD

Week	Time Series Value	Forecast	Forecast Error	Absolute Value of Forecast Error	Squared Forecast Error	Percentage Error	Absolute Value of Percentage Error
1	17						
2	21	17	4	4	16	19.05	19.05
3	19	21	−2	2	4	−10.53	10.53
4	23	19	4	4	16	17.39	17.39
5	18	23	−5	5	25	−27.78	27.78
6	16	18	−2	2	4	−12.50	12.50
7	20	16	4	4	16	20.00	20.00
8	18	20	−2	2	4	−11.11	11.11
9	22	18	4	4	16	18.18	18.18
10	20	22	−2	2	4	−10.00	10.00
11	15	20	−5	5	25	−33.33	33.33
12	22	15	7	7	49	31.82	31.82
		Total	5	41	179	1.19	211.69

For instance, because the distributor actually sold 21,000 gallons of gasoline in Week 2 and the forecast, using the sales volume in Week 1, was 17,000 gallons, the forecast error in Week 2 is

$$\text{Forecast Error in Week 2} = e_2 = Y_2 - \hat{Y}_2 = 21 - 17 = 4$$

The fact that the forecast error is positive indicates that in Week 2 the forecasting method underestimated the actual value of sales. Next we use 21, the actual value of sales in Week 2, as the forecast for Week 3. Since the actual value of sales in Week 3 is 19, the forecast error for Week 3 is $e_3 = 19 - 21 = -2$. In this case, the negative forecast error indicates the forecast overestimated the actual value for Week 3. Thus, the forecast error may be positive or negative, depending on whether the forecast is too low or too high. A complete summary of the forecast errors for this naïve forecasting method is shown in Table 15.7 in the column labeled Forecast Error. It is important to note that because we are using a past value of the time series to produce a forecast for period t, we do not have sufficient data to produce a naïve forecast for the first week of this time series.

A simple measure of forecast accuracy is the mean or average of the forecast errors. If we have n periods in our time series and k is the number of periods at the beginning of the time series for which we cannot produce a naïve forecast, the mean forecast error (MFE) is

$$\text{MFE} = \frac{\sum_{t=k+1}^{n} e_t}{n - k} \tag{15.2}$$

Table 15.7 shows that the sum of the forecast errors for the gasoline sales time series is 5; thus, the mean or average error is 5/11 = 0.45. Because we do not have sufficient data to produce a naïve forecast for the first week of this time series, we must adjust our calculations in both the numerator and denominator accordingly. This is common in forecasting; we often use k past periods from the time series to produce forecasts, and so we frequently cannot produce forecasts for the first k periods. In those instances the summation in the numerator starts at the first value of t for which we have produced a forecast (so we begin the summation at $t = k + 1$), and the denominator (which is the number of periods in our time series for which we are able to produce a forecast) will also reflect these circumstances. In the gasoline example, although the time series consists of 12 values, to compute the mean error we divided the sum of the forecast errors by 11 because there are only 11 forecast errors (we cannot generate forecast sales for the first week using this naïve forecasting method).

Also note that in the gasoline time series, the mean forecast error is positive, which implies that the method is generally underforecasting; in other words, the observed values tend to be greater than the forecasted values. Because positive and negative forecast errors tend to offset one another, the mean error is likely to be small; thus, the mean error is not a very useful measure of forecast accuracy.

The **mean absolute error**, denoted MAE, is a measure of forecast accuracy that avoids the problem of positive and negative forecast errors offsetting one another. As you might expect given its name, MAE is the average of the absolute values of the forecast errors:

$$\text{MAE} = \frac{\sum_{t=k+1}^{n} |e_t|}{n - k} \tag{15.3}$$

This is also referred to as the mean absolute deviation or MAD. Table 15.7 shows that the sum of the absolute values of the forecast errors is 41; thus

$$\text{MAE} = \text{average of the absolute value of forecast errors} = \frac{41}{11} = 3.73$$

Another measure that avoids the problem of positive and negative errors offsetting each other is obtained by computing the average of the squared forecast errors. This measure of forecast accuracy, referred to as the **mean squared error**, is denoted MSE:

$$\text{MSE} = \frac{\displaystyle\sum_{t=k+1}^{n} e_t^2}{n - k} \tag{15.4}$$

From Table 15.7, the sum of the squared errors is 179; hence,

$$\text{MSE} = \text{average of the sum of squared forecast errors} = \frac{179}{11} = 16.27$$

The size of MAE and MSE depends upon the scale of the data. As a result, it is difficult to make comparisons for different time intervals (such as comparing a method of forecasting monthly gasoline sales to a method of forecasting weekly sales) or to make comparisons across different time series (such as monthly sales of gasoline and monthly sales of oil filters). To make comparisons such as these we need to work with relative or percentage error measures. The **mean absolute percentage error**, denoted MAPE, is such a measure. To compute MAPE we must first compute the percentage error for each forecast:

$$\left(\frac{e_t}{Y_t}\right)100$$

For example, the percentage error corresponding to the forecast of 17 in Week 2 is computed by dividing the forecast error in Week 2 by the actual value in Week 2 and multiplying the result by 100. For Week 2 the percentage error is computed as follows:

$$\text{Percentage error for Week 2} = \left(\frac{e_2}{Y_2}\right)100 = \left(\frac{4}{21}\right)100 = 19.05\%$$

Thus, the forecast error for Week 2 is 19.05% of the observed value in Week 2. A complete summary of the percentage errors is shown in Table 15.7 in the column labeled Percentage Error. In the next column, we show the absolute value of the percentage error. Finally, we find the MAPE, which is calculated as

$$\text{MAPE} = \frac{\displaystyle\sum_{t=k+1}^{n} \left|\left(\frac{e_t}{Y_t}\right)100\right|}{n - k} \tag{15.5}$$

Table 15.7 shows that the sum of the absolute values of the percentage errors is 211.69; thus

$$\text{MAPE} = \text{average of the absolute value of percentage forecast errors}$$

$$= \frac{211.69}{11} = 19.24\%$$

In summary, using the naïve (most recent observation) forecasting method, we obtained the following measures of forecast accuracy:

$$\text{MAE} = 3.73$$
$$\text{MSE} = 16.27$$
$$\text{MAPE} = 19.24\%$$

Try Problem 1 for practice in computing measures of forecast accuracy.

These measures of forecast accuracy simply measure how well the forecasting method is able to forecast historical values of the time series. Now, suppose we want to forecast sales for a future time period, such as Week 13. In this case the forecast for Week 13 is 22, the actual value of the time series in Week 12. Is this an accurate estimate of sales for Week 13? Unfortunately there is no way to address the issue of accuracy associated with forecasts for future time periods. However, if we select a forecasting method that works well for the historical data, and we have reason to believe the historical pattern will continue into the future, we should obtain forecasts that will ultimately be shown to be accurate.

Before closing this section, let us consider another method for forecasting the gasoline sales time series in Table 15.1. Suppose we use the average of all the historical data available as the forecast for the next period. We begin by developing a forecast for Week 2. Since there is only one historical value available prior to Week 2, the forecast for Week 2 is just the time series value in Week 1; thus, the forecast for Week 2 is 17,000 gallons of gasoline. To compute the forecast for Week 3, we take the average of the sales values in Weeks 1 and 2. Thus,

$$\hat{Y}_3 = \frac{17 + 21}{2} = 19$$

Similarly, the forecast for Week 4 is

$$\hat{Y}_4 = \frac{17 + 21 + 19}{3} = 19$$

The forecasts obtained using this method for the gasoline time series are shown in Table 15.8 in the column labeled Forecast. Using the results shown in Table 15.8, we obtained the following values of MAE, MSE, and MAPE:

$$\text{MAE} = \frac{26.81}{11} = 2.44$$
$$\text{MSE} = \frac{89.07}{11} = 8.10$$
$$\text{MAPE} = \frac{141.34}{11} = 12.85\%$$

TABLE 15.8   COMPUTING FORECASTS AND MEASURES OF FORECAST ACCURACY
USING THE AVERAGE OF ALL THE HISTORICAL DATA AS THE
FORECAST FOR THE NEXT PERIOD

Week	Time Series Value	Forecast	Forecast Error	Absolute Value of Forecast Error	Squared Forecast Error	Percentage Error	Absolute Value of Percentage Error
1	17						
2	21	17.00	4.00	4.00	16.00	19.05	19.05
3	19	19.00	0.00	0.00	0.00	0.00	0.00
4	23	19.00	4.00	4.00	16.00	17.39	17.39
5	18	20.00	−2.00	2.00	4.00	−11.11	11.11
6	16	19.60	−3.60	3.60	12.96	−22.50	22.50
7	20	19.00	1.00	1.00	1.00	5.00	5.00
8	18	19.14	−1.14	1.14	1.31	−6.35	6.35
9	22	19.00	3.00	3.00	9.00	13.64	13.64
10	20	19.33	0.67	0.67	0.44	3.33	3.33
11	15	19.40	−4.40	4.40	19.36	−29.33	29.33
12	22	19.00	3.00	3.00	9.00	13.64	13.64
		Total	4.52	26.81	89.07	2.75	141.34

We can now compare the accuracy of the two forecasting methods we have considered in this section by comparing the values of MAE, MSE, and MAPE for each method.

	Naïve Method	Average of Past Values
MAE	3.73	2.44
MSE	16.27	8.10
MAPE	19.24%	12.85%

For each of these measures, the average of past values provides more accurate forecasts than using the most recent observation as the forecast for the next period. In general, if the underlying time series is stationary, the average of all the historical data will provide the most accurate forecasts.

Evaluating different forecasts based on historical accuracy is only helpful if historical patterns continue in to the future. As we note in Section 15.1, the 12 observations of Table 15.1 comprise a stationary time series. In Section 15.1 we mentioned that changes in business conditions often result in a time series that is not stationary. We discussed a situation in which the gasoline distributor signed a contract with the Vermont State Police to provide gasoline for state police cars located in southern Vermont. Table 15.2 shows the number of gallons of gasoline sold for the original time series and the 10 weeks after signing the new contract, and Figure 15.2 shows the corresponding time series plot. Note the change in level in Week 13 for the resulting time series. When a shift to a new level such as this occurs, it takes several periods for the forecasting method that uses the average of all the historical data to adjust to the new level of the time series. However, in this case the simple naïve method adjusts very rapidly to the change in level because it uses only the most recent observation available as the forecast.

Measures of forecast accuracy are important factors in comparing different forecasting methods, but we have to be careful to not rely too heavily upon them. Good judgment and knowledge about business conditions that might affect the value of the variable to be forecast also have to be considered carefully when selecting a method. Historical forecast accuracy is not the sole consideration, especially if the pattern exhibited by the time series is likely to change in the future.

In the next section we will introduce more sophisticated methods for developing forecasts for a time series that exhibits a horizontal pattern. Using the measures of forecast accuracy developed here, we will be able to assess whether such methods provide more accurate forecasts than we obtained using the simple approaches illustrated in this section. The methods that we will introduce also have the advantage that they adapt well to situations in which the time series changes to a new level. The ability of a forecasting method to adapt quickly to changes in level is an important consideration, especially in short-term forecasting situations.

15.3   MOVING AVERAGES AND EXPONENTIAL SMOOTHING

In this section we discuss three forecasting methods that are appropriate for a time series with a horizontal pattern: moving averages, weighted moving averages, and exponential smoothing. These methods are also capable of adapting well to changes in the level of a horizontal pattern such as what we saw with the extended gasoline sales time series (Table 15.2 and Figure 15.2). However, without modification they are not appropriate when considerable trend, cyclical, or seasonal effects are present. Because the objective of each of these methods is to "smooth out" random fluctuations in the time series, they are referred to as smoothing methods. These methods are easy to use and generally provide a high level of accuracy for short-range forecasts, such as a forecast for the next time period.

Moving Averages

The moving averages method uses the average of the most recent k data values in the time series as the forecast for the next period. Mathematically, a **moving average** forecast of order k is as follows:

$$\hat{Y}_{t+1} = \frac{\sum(\text{most recent } k \text{ data values})}{k} = \frac{\sum_{i=t-k+1}^{t} Y_i}{k}$$

$$= \frac{Y_{t-k+1} + \cdots + Y_{t-1} + Y_t}{k} \tag{15.6}$$

where

$\hat{Y}_{t+1} =$ forecast of the time series for period $t + 1$

$Y_i =$ actual value of the time series in period i

$k =$ number of periods of time series data used to generate the forecast

The term *moving* is used because every time a new observation becomes available for the time series, it replaces the oldest observation in the equation and a new average is computed. Thus, the periods over which the average is calculated change, or move, with each ensuing period.

To illustrate the moving averages method, let us return to the original 12 weeks of gasoline sales data in Table 15.1 and Figure 15.1. The time series plot in Figure 15.1 indicates that the gasoline sales time series has a horizontal pattern. Thus, the smoothing methods of this section are applicable.

To use moving averages to forecast a time series, we must first select the order k, or number of time series values to be included in the moving average. If only the most recent values of the time series are considered relevant, a small value of k is preferred. If a greater number of past values are considered relevant, then we generally opt for a larger value of k. As mentioned earlier, a time series with a horizontal pattern can shift to a new level over time. A moving average will adapt to the new level of the series and resume providing good forecasts in k periods. Thus a smaller value of k will track shifts in a time series more quickly (the naïve approach discussed earlier is actually a moving average for $k = 1$). On the other hand, larger values of k will be more effective in smoothing out random fluctuations. Thus, managerial judgment based on an understanding of the behavior of a time series is helpful in choosing an appropriate value of k.

To illustrate how moving averages can be used to forecast gasoline sales, we will use a three-week moving average ($k = 3$). We begin by computing the forecast of sales in Week 4 using the average of the time series values in Weeks 1 to 3.

$$\hat{Y}_4 = \text{average of Weeks 1 to 3} = \frac{17 + 21 + 19}{3} = 19$$

Thus, the moving average forecast of sales in Week 4 is 19 or 19,000 gallons of gasoline. Because the actual value observed in Week 4 is 23, the forecast error in Week 4 is $e_4 = 23 - 19 = 4$.

We next compute the forecast of sales in Week 5 by averaging the time series values in Weeks 2–4.

$$\hat{Y}_5 = \text{average of Weeks 2 to 4} = \frac{21 + 19 + 23}{3} = 21$$

Hence, the forecast of sales in Week 5 is 21 and the error associated with this forecast is $e_5 = 18 - 21 = -3$. A complete summary of the three-week moving average forecasts for the gasoline sales time series is provided in Table 15.9. Figure 15.7 shows the original time series plot and the three-week moving average forecasts. Note how the graph of the moving average forecasts has tended to smooth out the random fluctuations in the time series.

Can you now use moving averages to develop forecasts? Try Problem 7.

To forecast sales in Week 13, the next time period in the future, we simply compute the average of the time series values in Weeks 10, 11, and 12.

$$\hat{Y}_{13} = \text{average of Weeks 10 to 12} = \frac{20 + 15 + 22}{3} = 19$$

Thus, the forecast for Week 13 is 19 or 19,000 gallons of gasoline.

TABLE 15.9   SUMMARY OF THREE-WEEK MOVING AVERAGE CALCULATIONS

Week	Time Series Value	Forecast	Forecast Error	Absolute Value of Forecast Error	Squared Forecast Error	Percentage Error	Absolute Value of Percentage Error
1	17						
2	21						
3	19						
4	23	19	4	4	16	17.39	17.39
5	18	21	−3	3	9	−16.67	16.67
6	16	20	−4	4	16	−25.00	25.00
7	20	19	1	1	1	5.00	5.00
8	18	18	0	0	0	0.00	0.00
9	22	18	4	4	16	18.18	18.18
10	20	20	0	0	0	0.00	0.00
11	15	20	−5	5	25	−33.33	33.33
12	22	19	3	3	9	13.64	13.64
		Total	0	24	92	−20.79	129.21

FIGURE 15.7   GASOLINE SALES TIME SERIES PLOT AND THREE-WEEK MOVING AERAGE FORECASTS

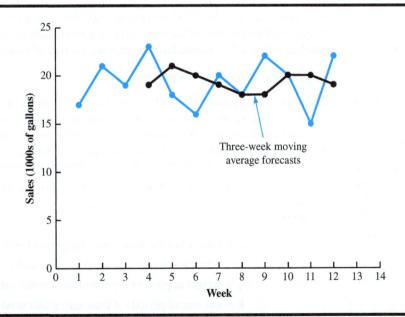

Forecast Accuracy   In Section 15.2 we discussed three measures of forecast accuracy: mean absolute error (MAE); mean squared error (MSE); and mean absolute percentage error (MAPE). Using the three-week moving average calculations in Table 15.9, the values for these three measures of forecast accuracy are

$$\text{MAE} = \frac{\sum_{t=4}^{12} |e_t|}{12 - 3} = \frac{24}{9} = 2.67$$

$$\text{MSE} = \frac{\sum_{t=4}^{12} e_t^2}{12 - 3} = \frac{92}{9} = 10.22$$

$$\text{MAPE} = \frac{\sum_{t=4}^{12} \left| \left(\frac{e_t}{Y_t} \right) 100 \right|}{12 - 3} = \frac{129.21}{9} = 14.36\%$$

In situations where you need to compare forecasting methods for different time periods, such as comparing a forecast of weekly sales to a forecast of monthly sales, relative measures such as MAPE are preferred.

In Section 15.2 we showed that using the most recent observation as the forecast for the next week (a moving average of order $k = 1$) resulted in values of MAE = 3.73, MSE = 16.27, and MAPE = 19.24%. Thus, in each case the three-week moving average approach has provided more accurate forecasts than simply using the most recent observation as the forecast. Also note how the formulas for the MAE, MSE, and MAPE reflect that our use of a three-week moving average leaves us with insufficient data to generate forecasts for the first three weeks of our time series.

To determine if a moving average with a different order k can provide more accurate forecasts, we recommend using trial and error to determine the value of k that minimizes the MSE. For the gasoline sales time series, it can be shown that the minimum value of MSE corresponds to a moving average of order $k = 6$ with MSE = 6.79. If we are willing to assume that the order of the moving average that is best for the historical data will also be best for future values of the time series, the most accurate moving average forecasts of gasoline sales can be obtained using a moving average of order $k = 6$.

Weighted Moving Averages

A moving average forecast of order k is just a special case of the weighted moving averages method in which each weight is equal to 1/k; for example, a moving average forecast of order k = 3 is just a special case of the weighted moving averages method in which each weight is equal to $\frac{1}{3}$.

In the moving averages method, each observation in the moving average calculation receives equal weight. One variation, known as **weighted moving averages**, involves selecting a different weight for each data value in the moving average and then computing a weighted average of the most recent k values as the forecast.

$$\hat{Y}_{t+1} = w_t Y_t + w_{t-1} Y_{t-1} + \cdots + w_{t-k+1} Y_{t-k+1} \tag{15.7}$$

where

$\hat{Y}_{t+1}$ = forecast of the time series for period $t + 1$

Y_t = actual value of the time series in period t

w_t = weight applied to the actual time series value for period t

k = number of periods of time series data used to generate the forecast

Generally the most recent observation receives the largest weight, and the weight decreases with the relative age of the data values. Let us use the gasoline sales time series in Table 15.1 to illustrate the computation of a weighted three-week moving average. We will assign a weight of $w_t = \frac{3}{6}$ to the most recent observation, a weight of $w_{t-1} = \frac{2}{6}$ to the second most recent observation, and a weight of $w_{t-2} = \frac{1}{6}$ to the third most recent observation. Using this weighted average, our forecast for Week 4 is computed as follows:

$$\text{Forecast for Week 4} = \frac{1}{6}(17) + \frac{2}{6}(21) = \frac{3}{6}(19) = 19.33$$

Use Problem 8 to practice using weighted moving averages to produce forecasts.

Note that the sum of the weights is equal to 1 for the weighted moving average method.

Forecast Accuracy   To use the weighted moving averages method, we must first select the number of data values to be included in the weighted moving average and then choose weights for each of these data values. In general, if we believe that the recent past is a better predictor of the future than the distant past, larger weights should be given to the more recent observations. However, when the time series is highly variable, selecting approximately equal weights for the data values may be preferable. The only requirements in selecting the weights are that they be nonnegative and that their sum must equal 1. To determine whether one particular combination of number of data values and weights provides a more accurate forecast than another combination, we recommend using MSE as the measure of forecast accuracy. That is, if we assume that the combination that is best for the past will also be best for the future, we would use the combination of number of data values and weights that minimized MSE for the historical time series to forecast the next value in the time series.

Exponential Smoothing

Exponential smoothing also uses a weighted average of past time series values as a forecast; it is a special case of the weighted moving averages method in which we select only one weight—the weight for the most recent observation. The weights for the other data values are computed automatically and become smaller as the observations move farther into the past. The exponential smoothing model follows.

$$\hat{Y}_{t+1} = \alpha Y_t + (1 - \alpha)\hat{Y}_t \qquad (15.8)$$

where

$$\hat{Y}_{t+1} = \text{forecast of the time series for period } t + 1$$
$$Y_t = \text{actual value of the time series in period } t$$
$$\hat{Y}_t = \text{forecast of the time series for period } t$$
$$\alpha = \text{smoothing constant } (0 \le \alpha \le 1)$$

There are several exponential smoothing procedures. Because it has a single smoothing constant α, the method presented here is often referred to as single exponential smoothing.

Equation (15.8) shows that the forecast for period $t + 1$ is a weighted average of the actual value in period t and the forecast for period t. The weight given to the actual value in period t is the **smoothing constant** α and the weight given to the forecast in period t is $1 - \alpha$. It turns out that the exponential smoothing forecast for any period is actually a weighted average of *all the previous actual values* of the time series. Let us illustrate by working with a time series involving only three periods of data: Y_1, Y_2, and Y_3.

To initiate the calculations, we let $\hat{Y}_1$ equal the actual value of the time series in period 1; that is, $\hat{Y}_1 = Y_1$. Hence, the forecast for period 2 is

$$
\begin{aligned}
\hat{Y}_2 &= \alpha Y_1 + (1 - \alpha)\hat{Y}_1 \\
&= \alpha Y_1 + (1 - \alpha)Y_1 \\
&= Y_1
\end{aligned}
$$

We see that the exponential smoothing forecast for period 2 is equal to the actual value of the time series in period 1.

The forecast for period 3 is

$$
\hat{Y}_3 = \alpha Y_2 + (1 - \alpha)\hat{Y}_2 = \alpha Y_2 + (1 - \alpha)Y_1
$$

Finally, substituting this expression for $\hat{Y}_3$ into the expression for $\hat{Y}_4$, we obtain

$$
\begin{aligned}
\hat{Y}_4 &= \alpha Y_3 + (1 - \alpha)\hat{Y}_3 \\
&= \alpha Y_3 + (1 - \alpha)[\alpha Y_2 + (1 - \alpha)Y_1] \\
&= \alpha Y_3 + \alpha(1 - \alpha)Y_2 + (1 - \alpha)^2 Y_1
\end{aligned}
$$

The term exponential smoothing comes from the exponential nature of the weighting scheme for the historical values.

We now see that $\hat{Y}_4$ is a weighted average of the first three time series values. The sum of the coefficients, or weights, for Y_1, Y_2, and Y_3 equals 1. A similar argument can be made to show that, in general, any forecast $\hat{Y}_{t+1}$ is a weighted average of all the t previous time series values.

Despite the fact that exponential smoothing provides a forecast that is a weighted average of all past observations, all past data do not need to be retained to compute the forecast for the next period. In fact, equation (15.8) shows that once the value for the smoothing constant α is selected, only two pieces of information are needed to compute the forecast for period $t + 1$: Y_t, the actual value of the time series in period t; and $\hat{Y}_t$, the forecast for period t.

To illustrate the exponential smoothing approach to forecasting, let us again consider the gasoline sales time series in Table 15.1 and Figure 15.1. As indicated previously, to initialize the calculations we set the exponential smoothing forecast for period 2 equal to the actual value of the time series in period 1. Thus, with $Y_1 = 17$, we set $\hat{Y}_2 = 17$ to initiate the computations. Referring to the time series data in Table 15.1, we find an actual time series value in period 2 of $Y_2 = 21$. Thus, in period 2 we have a forecast error of $e_2 = 21 - 17 = 4$.

Continuing with the exponential smoothing computations using a smoothing constant of $\alpha = 0.2$, we obtain the following forecast for period 3.

$$
\hat{Y}_3 = 0.2Y_2 + 0.8\hat{Y}_2 = 0.2(21) + 0.8(17) = 17.8
$$

Once the actual time series value in period 3, $Y_3 = 19$, is known, we can generate a forecast for period 4 as follows:

$$
\hat{Y}_4 = 0.2Y_3 + 0.8\hat{Y}_3 = 0.2(19) + 0.8(17.8) = 18.04
$$

Continuing the exponential smoothing calculations, we obtain the weekly forecast values shown in Table 15.10. Note that we have not shown an exponential smoothing forecast or a forecast error for Week 1 because no forecast was made (we used actual sales for Week 1 as the forecasted sales for Week 2 to initialize the exponential smoothing process). For Week 12, we have $Y_{12} = 22$ and $\hat{Y}_{12} = 18.48$. We can we use this information to generate a forecast for Week 13.

$$
\hat{Y}_{13} = 0.2Y_{12} + 0.8\hat{Y}_{12} = 0.2(22) + 0.8(18.48) = 19.18
$$

TABLE 15.10 SUMMARY OF THE EXPONENTIAL SMOOTHING FORECASTS AND FORECAST ERRORS FOR THE GASOLINE SALES TIME SERIES WITH SMOOTHING CONSTANT $\alpha = 0.2$

Week	Time Series Value	Forecast	Forecast Error	Squared Forecast Error
1	17			
2	21	17.00	4.00	16.00
3	19	17.80	1.20	1.44
4	23	18.04	4.96	24.60
5	18	19.03	−1.03	1.06
6	16	18.83	−2.83	8.01
7	20	18.26	1.74	3.03
8	18	18.61	−0.61	0.37
9	22	18.49	3.51	12.32
10	20	19.19	0.81	0.66
11	15	19.35	−4.35	18.92
12	22	18.48	3.52	12.39
		Total	10.92	98.80

FIGURE 15.8 ACTUAL AND FORECAST GASOLINE TIME SERIES WITH SMOOTHING CONSTANT $\alpha = 0.2$

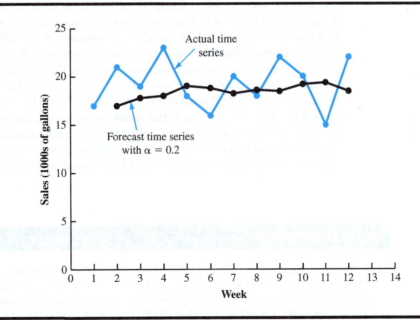

Try Problem 9 for practice using exponential smoothing to produce forecasts.

Thus, the exponential smoothing forecast of the amount sold in Week 13 is 19.18, or 19,180 gallons of gasoline. With this forecast, the firm can make plans and decisions accordingly.

Figure 15.8 shows the time series plot of the actual and forecast time series values. Note in particular how the forecasts "smooth out" the irregular or random fluctuations in the time series.

Forecast Accuracy   In the preceding exponential smoothing calculations, we used a smoothing constant of $\alpha = 0.2$. Although any value of α between 0 and 1 is acceptable, some values will yield more accurate forecasts than others. Insight into choosing a good value for α can be obtained by rewriting the basic exponential smoothing model as follows:

$$\hat{Y}_{t+1} = \alpha Y_t + (1 - \alpha)\hat{Y}_t$$
$$\hat{Y}_{t+1} = \alpha Y_t + \hat{Y}_t - \alpha\hat{Y}_t \qquad\qquad (15.9)$$
$$\hat{Y}_{t+1} = \hat{Y}_t + \alpha(Y_t - \hat{Y}_t) = \hat{Y}_t + \alpha e_t$$

Thus, the new forecast $\hat{Y}_{t+1}$ is equal to the previous forecast $\hat{Y}_t$ plus an adjustment, which is the smoothing constant α times the most recent forecast error, $e_t = Y_t - \hat{Y}_t$. That is, the forecast in period $t + 1$ is obtained by adjusting the forecast in period t by a fraction of the forecast error from period t. If the time series contains substantial random variability, a small value of the smoothing constant is preferred. The reason for this choice is that if much of the forecast error is due to random variability, we do not want to overreact and adjust the forecasts too quickly. For a time series with relatively little random variability, a forecast error is more likely to represent a real change in the level of the series. Thus, larger values of the smoothing constant provide the advantage of quickly adjusting the forecasts to changes in the time series; this allows the forecasts to react more quickly to changing conditions.

The criterion we will use to determine a desirable value for the smoothing constant α is the same as the criterion we proposed for determining the order or number of periods of data to include in the moving averages calculation. That is, we choose the value of α that minimizes the MSE. A summary of the MSE calculations for the exponential smoothing forecast of gasoline sales with $\alpha = 0.2$ is shown in Table 15.10. Note that there is one less squared error term than the number of time periods; this is because we had no past values with which to make a forecast for period 1. The value of the sum of squared forecast errors is 98.80; hence MSE = 98.80/11 = 8.98. Would a different value of α provide better results in terms of a lower MSE value? Trial and error is often used to determine if a different smoothing constant α can provide more accurate forecasts, but we can avoid trial and error and determine the value of α that minimizes MSE through the use of nonlinear optimization as discussed in Chapter 8 (see Problem 8.12).

NOTES AND COMMENTS

1. Spreadsheet packages are effective tools for implementing exponential smoothing. With the time series data and the forecasting formulas in a spreadsheet as shown in Table 15.10, you can use the MAE, MSE, and MAPE to evaluate different values of the smoothing constant α.

2. We presented the moving average, weighted moving average, and exponential smoothing methods in the context of a stationary time series. These methods can also be used to forecast a nonstationary time series that shifts in level but exhibits no trend or seasonality. Moving averages with small values of k adapt more quickly than moving averages with larger values of k. Weighted moving averages that place relatively large weights on the most recent values adapt more quickly than weighted moving averages that place relatively equal weights on the k time series values used in calculating the forecast. Exponential smoothing models with smoothing constants closer to 1 adapt more quickly than models with smaller values of the smoothing constant.

15.4 LINEAR TREND PROJECTION

In this section we present forecasting methods that are appropriate for time series exhibiting trend patterns. Here we show how **regression analysis** may be used to forecast a time series with a linear trend. In Section 15.1 we used the bicycle sales time series in Table 15.3 and Figure 15.3 to illustrate a time series with a trend pattern. Let us now use this time series to illustrate how regression analysis can be used to forecast a time series with a linear trend. The data for the bicycle time series are repeated in Table 15.11 and Figure 15.9.

Although the time series plot in Figure 15.9 shows some up and down movement over the past 10 years, we might agree that the linear trend line shown in Figure 15.10 provides a reasonable approximation of the long-run movement in the series. We can use regression analysis to develop such a linear trend line for the bicycle sales time series.

TABLE 15.11   BICYCLE SALES TIME SERIES

Year	Sales (1000s)
1	21.6
2	22.9
3	25.5
4	21.9
5	23.9
6	27.5
7	31.5
8	29.7
9	28.6
10	31.4

WEB file

Bicycle

FIGURE 15.9   BICYCLE SALES TIME SERIES PLOT

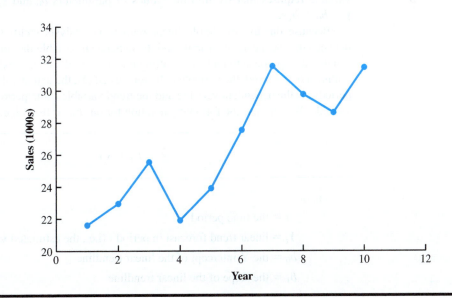

FIGURE 15.10   TREND REPRESENTED BY A LINEAR FUNCTION FOR THE BICYCLE
SALES TIME SERIES

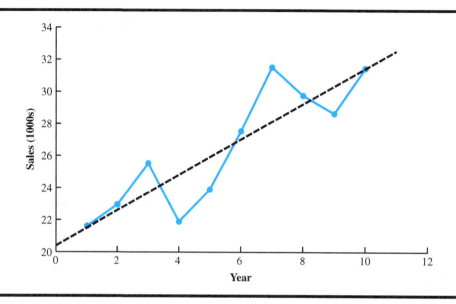

In regression analysis we use known values of variables to estimate the relationship between one variable (called the **dependent variable**) and one or more other related variables (called **independent variables**). This relationship is usually found in a manner that minimizes the sum of squared errors (and so also minimizes the MSE). With this relationship we can then use values of the independent variables to estimate the associated value of the dependent variable. When we estimate a linear relationship between the dependent variable (which is usually denoted as y) and a single independent variable (which is usually denoted as x), this is referred to as **simple linear regression**. Estimating the relationship between the dependent variable and a single independent variable requires that we find the values of parameters b_0 and b_1 for the straight line $y = b_0 + b_1x$.

Because our use of simple linear regression analysis yields the linear relationship between the independent variable and the dependent variable that minimizes the MSE, we can use this approach to find a best-fitting line to a set of data that exhibits a linear trend. In finding a linear trend, the variable to be forecasted (Y_t, the actual value of the time series in period t) is the dependent variable and the trend variable (time period t) is the independent variable. We will use the following notation for our linear trendline.

$$\hat{Y}_t = b_0 + b_1t \tag{15.10}$$

where

t = the time period

$\hat{Y}_t$ = linear trend forecast in period t (i.e., the estimated value of Y_t in period t)

b_0 = the Y-intercept of the linear trendline

b_1 = the slope of the linear trendline

In equation (15.10) the time variable begins at $t = 1$ corresponding to the first time series observation (Year 1 for the bicycle sales time series) and continues until $t = n$ corresponding to the most recent time series observation (Year 10 for the bicycle sales time series). Thus, for the bicycle sales time series $t = 1$ corresponds to the oldest time series value and $t = 10$ corresponds to the most recent year. Calculus may be used to show that the equations given below for b_0 and b_1 yield the line that minimizes the MSE. The equations for computing the values of b_0 and b_1 are

$$b_1 = \frac{\displaystyle\sum_{t=1}^{n} tY_t - \sum_{t=1}^{n} t \sum_{t=1}^{n} Y_t \Big/ n}{\displaystyle\sum_{t=1}^{n} t^2 - \left(\sum_{t=1}^{n} t\right)^2 \Big/ n} \tag{15.11}$$

$$b_0 = \bar{Y} - b_1 \bar{t} \tag{15.12}$$

where

$t = $ the time period

$Y_t = $ actual value of the time series in period t

$n = $ number of periods in the time series

$\bar{Y} = $ average value of the time series; that is, $\bar{Y} = \displaystyle\sum_{t=1}^{n} Y_t \Big/ n$

$\bar{t} = $ mean value of t; that is, $\bar{t} = \displaystyle\sum_{t=1}^{n} t \Big/ n$

Let us calculate b_0 and b_1 for the bicycle data in Table 15.11; the intermediate summary calculations necessary for computing the values of b_0 and b_1 are

t	Y_t	tY_t	t^2
1	21.6	21.6	1
2	22.9	45.8	4
3	25.5	76.5	9
4	21.9	87.6	16
5	23.9	119.5	25
6	27.5	165.0	36
7	31.5	220.5	49
8	29.7	237.6	64
9	28.6	257.4	81
10	31.4	314.0	100
Total 55	264.5	1545.5	385

And the final calculations of the values of b_0 and b_1 are

$$\bar{t} = \frac{55}{10} = 5.5$$

$$\bar{Y} = \frac{264.5}{10} = 26.45$$

$$b_1 = \frac{1545.5 - (55)(264.5)/10}{385 - 55^2/10} = 1.10$$

$$b_0 = 26.45 - 1.10(5.5) = 20.40$$

Problem 20 provides additional practice in using regression analysis to estimate the linear trend in a time series data set.

Therefore,

$$\hat{Y}_t = 20.4 + 1.1t \tag{15.13}$$

is the regression equation for the linear trend component for the bicycle sales time series.

The slope of 1.1 in this trend equation indicates that over the past 10 years, the firm has experienced an average growth in sales of about 1100 units per year. If we assume that the past 10-year trend in sales is a good indicator for the future, we can use equation (15.13) to project the trend component of the time series. For example, substituting $t = 11$ into equation (15.13) yields next year's trend projection, $\hat{Y}_{11}$:

$$\hat{Y}_{11} = 20.4 + 1.1(11) = 32.5$$

Thus, the linear trend model yields a sales forecast of 32,500 bicycles for the next year.

Table 15.12 shows the computation of the minimized sum of squared errors for the bicycle sales time series. As previously noted, minimizing sum of squared errors also minimizes the commonly used measure of accuracy, MSE. For the bicycle sales time series,

$$\text{MSE} = \frac{\sum_{t=1}^{n} e_t^2}{n} = \frac{30.7}{10} = 3.07$$

TABLE 15.12   SUMMARY OF THE LINEAR TREND FORECASTS AND FORECAST ERRORS FOR THE BICYCLE SALES TIME SERIES

Week	Sales (1000s) Y_t	Forecast $\hat{Y}_t$	Forecast Error	Squared Forecast Error
1	21.6	21.5	0.1	0.01
2	22.9	22.6	0.3	0.09
3	25.5	23.7	1.8	3.24
4	21.9	24.8	−2.9	8.41
5	23.9	25.9	−2.0	4.00
6	27.5	27.0	0.5	0.25
7	31.5	28.1	3.4	11.56
8	29.7	29.2	0.5	0.25
9	28.6	30.3	−1.7	2.89
10	31.4	31.4	0.0	0.00
			Total	30.70

Note that in this example we are not using past values of the time series to produce forecasts, and so $k = 0$; that is, we can produce a forecast for each period of the time series and so do not have to adjust our calculations of the MAE, MSE, or MAPE for k.

We can also use the trendline to forecast sales farther into the future. For instance, using equation (15.13), we develop annual forecasts for two and three years into the future as follows:

$$\hat{Y}_{12} = 20.4 + 1.1(12) = 33.6$$
$$\hat{Y}_{13} = 20.4 + 1.1(13) = 34.7$$

Note that the forecasted value increases by 1100 bicycles in each year.

NOTES AND COMMENTS

1. Statistical packages such as Minitab and SAS, as well as Excel, have routines to perform regression analysis. Regression analysis minimizes the sum of squared error and under certain assumptions it also allows the analyst to make statistical statements about the parameters and the forecasts.

2. While the use of a linear function to model the trend is common, some time series exhibit a curvilinear (nonlinear) trend. More advanced texts discuss how to develop nonlinear models such as quadratic models and exponential models for these more complex relationships.

In this section we used simple linear regression to estimate the relationship between the dependent variable (Y_t, the actual value of the time series in period t) and a single independent variable (the trend variable t). However, some regression models include several independent variables. When we estimate a linear relationship between the dependent variable and more than one independent variable, this is referred to as multiple linear regression. In the next section we will apply multiple linear regression to time series that include seasonal effects and to time series that include both seasonal effects and a linear trend.

15.5   SEASONALITY

In this section we show how to develop forecasts for a time series that has a seasonal pattern. To the extent that seasonality exists, we need to incorporate it into our forecasting models to ensure accurate forecasts. We begin the section by considering a seasonal time series with no trend and then discuss how to model seasonality with a linear trend.

Seasonality Without Trend

Let us consider again the data from Table 15.5, the number of umbrellas sold at a clothing store over the past five years. We repeat the data here in Table 15.13, and Figure 15.11 again shows the corresponding time series plot. The time series plot does not indicate any long-term trend in sales. In fact, unless you look carefully at the data, you might conclude that the data follow a horizontal pattern with random fluctuation and that single exponential smoothing could be used to forecast sales. However, closer inspection of the time series plot reveals a pattern in the fluctuations. That is, the first and third quarters have moderate sales, the second quarter the highest sales, and the fourth quarter tends to be the lowest quarter in terms of sales volume. Thus, we conclude that a quarterly seasonal pattern is present.

We can model a time series with a seasonal pattern by treating the season as a categorical variable. **Categorical variables** are data used to categorize observations of data. When

TABLE 15.13 UMBRELLA SALES TIME SERIES

Year	Quarter	Sales
1	1	125
	2	153
	3	106
	4	88
2	1	118
	2	161
	3	133
	4	102
3	1	138
	2	144
	3	113
	4	80
4	1	109
	2	137
	3	125
	4	109
5	1	130
	2	165
	3	128
	4	96

WEB file

Umbrella

FIGURE 15.11 UMBRELLA SALES TIME SERIES PLOT

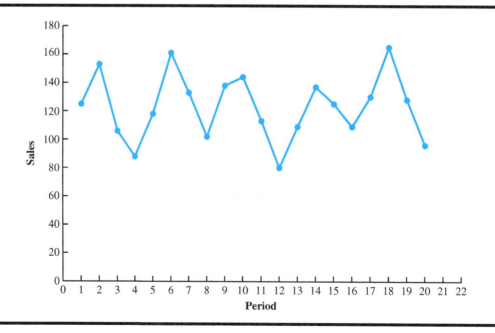

a categorical variable has k levels, $k - 1$ dummy variables (sometimes called 0-1 variables) are required. So if there are four seasons, we need three dummy variables. For instance, in the umbrella sales time series, the quarter to which each observation corresponds is treated as a season; it is a categorical variable with four levels: Quarter 1, Quarter 2, Quarter 3, and

Quarter 4. Thus, to model the seasonal effects in the umbrella time series we need $4 - 1 = 3$ dummy variables. The three dummy variables can be coded as follows:

$$\text{Qtr1}_t = \begin{cases} 1 & \text{if period } t \text{ is a Quarter 1} \\ 0 & \text{otherwise} \end{cases}$$

$$\text{Qtr2}_t = \begin{cases} 1 & \text{if period } t \text{ is a Quarter 2} \\ 0 & \text{otherwise} \end{cases}$$

$$\text{Qtr3}_t = \begin{cases} 1 & \text{if period } t \text{ is a Quarter 3} \\ 0 & \text{otherwise} \end{cases}$$

Using $\hat{Y}_t$ to denote the forecasted value of sales for period t, the general form of the equation relating the number of umbrellas sold to the quarter the sales take place follows.

$$\hat{Y}_t = b_0 + b_1 \text{ Qtr1}_t + b_2 \text{ Qtr2}_t + b_3 \text{ Qtr3}_t \qquad (15.14)$$

Note that we have numbered the observations in Table 15.14 as periods 1 to 20. For example, Year 3, quarter 3 is observation 11.

Note that the fourth quarter will be denoted by a setting of all three dummy variables to 0. Table 15.14 shows the umbrella sales time series with the coded values of the dummy variables shown. We can use a multiple linear regression model to find the values of b_0, b_1, b_2, and b_3 that minimize the sum of squared errors. For this regression model Y_t is the dependent variable and the quarterly dummy variables Qtr1$_t$, Qtr2$_t$, and Qtr3$_t$ are the independent variables.

TABLE 15.14   UMBRELLA SALES TIME SERIES WITH DUMMY VARIABLES

Period	Year	Quarter	Qtr1	Qtr2	Qtr3	Sales
1	1	1	1	0	0	125
2		2	0	1	0	153
3		3	0	0	1	106
4		4	0	0	0	88
5	2	1	1	0	0	118
6		2	0	1	0	161
7		3	0	0	1	133
8		4	0	0	0	102
9	3	1	1	0	0	138
10		2	0	1	0	144
11		3	0	0	1	113
12		4	0	0	0	80
13	4	1	1	0	0	109
14		2	0	1	0	137
15		3	0	0	1	125
16		4	0	0	0	109
17	5	1	1	0	0	130
18		2	0	1	0	165
19		3	0	0	1	128
20		4	0	0	0	96

Using the data in Table 15.14 and regression analysis, we obtain the following equation:

$$\hat{Y}_t = 95.0 + 29.0\ Qtr1_t + 57.0\ Qtr2_t + 26.0\ Qtr3_t \qquad (15.15)$$

we can use Equation (15.15) to forecast quarterly sales for next year.

For practice using categorical variables to estimate seasonal effects, try Problem 24.

Quarter 1: Sales = 95.0 + 29.0(1) + 57.0(0) + 26.0(0) = 124
Quarter 2: Sales = 95.0 + 29.0(0) + 57.0(1) + 26.0(0) = 152
Quarter 3: Sales = 95.0 + 29.0(0) + 57.0(0) + 26.0(1) = 121
Quarter 4: Sales = 95.0 + 29.0(0) + 57.0(0) + 26.0(0) = 95

It is interesting to note that we could have obtained the quarterly forecasts for next year by simply computing the average number of umbrellas sold in each quarter, as shown in the following table:

Year	Quarter 1	Quarter 2	Quarter 3	Quarter 4
1	125	153	106	88
2	118	161	133	102
3	138	144	113	80
4	109	137	125	109
5	130	165	128	96
Average	124	152	121	95

Nonetheless, for more complex problem situations, such as dealing with a time series that has both trend and seasonal effects, this simple averaging approach will not work.

Seasonality with Trend

We now consider situations for which the time series contains both a seasonal effect and a linear trend by showing how to forecast the quarterly television set sales time series introduced in Section 15.1. The data for the television set time series are shown in Table 15.15. The time series plot in Figure 15.12 indicates that sales are lowest in the second quarter of each year and increase in quarters 3 and 4. Thus, we conclude that a seasonal pattern exists for television set sales. However, the time series also has an upward linear trend that will need to be accounted for in order to develop accurate forecasts of quarterly sales. This is easily done by combining the dummy variable approach for handling seasonality with the approach we discussed in Section 15.4 for handling a linear trend.

The general form of the regression equation for modeling both the quarterly seasonal effects and the linear trend in the television set time series is:

$$\hat{Y}_t = b_0 + b_1 Qtr1_t + b_2 Qtr2_t + b_3 Qtr3_t + b_4 t \qquad (15.16)$$

where

$\hat{Y}_t$ = forecast of sales in period t

$Qtr1_t$ = 1 if time period t corresponds to the first quarter of the year; 0, otherwise

$Qtr2_t$ = 1 if time period t corresponds to the second quarter of the year; 0, otherwise

$Qtr3_t$ = 1 if time period t corresponds to the third quarter of the year; 0, otherwise

t = time period

TABLE 15.15   TELEVISION SET SALES TIME SERIES

Year	Quarter	Sales (1000s)
1	1	4.8
	2	4.1
	3	6.0
	4	6.5
2	1	5.8
	2	5.2
	3	6.8
	4	7.4
3	1	6.0
	2	5.6
	3	7.5
	4	7.8
4	1	6.3
	2	5.9
	3	8.0
	4	8.4

WEB file

SalesTV

FIGURE 15.12   TELEVISION SET SALES TIME SERIES PLOT

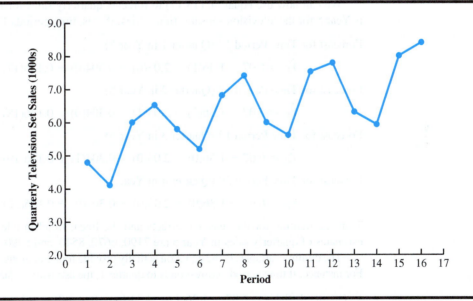

For this regression model Y_t is the dependent variable and the quarterly dummy variables $Qtr1_t$, $Qtr2_t$, and $Qtr3_t$ and the time period t are the independent variables.

Table 15.16 shows the revised television set sales time series that includes the coded values of the dummy variables and the time period t. Using the data in Table 15.16 with the regression model that includes both the seasonal and trend components, we obtain the following equation that minimizes our sum of squared errors:

$$\hat{Y}_t = 6.07 - 1.36\ Qtr1_t - 2.03\ Qtr2_t - 0.304\ Qtr3_t + 0.146t \qquad (15.17)$$

TABLE 15.16   TELEVISION SET SALES TIME SERIES WITH DUMMY VARIABLES AND
TIME PERIOD

Period	Year	Quarter	Qtr1	Qtr2	Qtr3	Sales (1000s)
1	1	1	1	0	0	4.8
2		2	0	1	0	4.1
3		3	0	0	1	6.0
4		4	0	0	0	6.5
5	2	1	1	0	0	5.8
6		2	0	1	0	5.2
7		3	0	0	1	6.8
8		4	0	0	0	7.4
9	3	1	1	0	0	6.0
10		2	0	1	0	5.6
11		3	0	0	1	7.5
12		4	0	0	0	7.8
13	4	1	1	0	0	6.3
14		2	0	1	0	5.9
15		3	0	0	1	8.0
16		4	0	0	0	8.4

We can now use equation (15.17) to forecast quarterly sales for next year. Next year is Year 5 for the television set sales time series; that is, time periods 17, 18, 19, and 20.

Forecast for Time Period 17 (Quarter 1 in Year 5)

$$\hat{Y}_{17} = 6.07 - 1.36(1) - 2.03(0) - 0.304(0) + 0.146(17) = 7.19$$

Forecast for Time Period 18 (Quarter 2 in Year 5)

$$\hat{Y}_{18} = 6.07 - 1.36(0) - 2.03(1) - 0.304(0) + 0.146(18) = 6.67$$

Forecast for Time Period 19 (Quarter 3 in Year 5)

$$\hat{Y}_{19} = 6.07 - 1.36(0) - 2.03(0) - 0.304(1) + 0.146(19) = 8.54$$

Forecast for Time Period 20 (Quarter 4 in Year 5)

$$\hat{Y}_{20} = 6.07 - 1.36(0) - 2.03(0) - 0.304(0) + 0.146(20) = 8.99$$

Thus, accounting for the seasonal effects and the linear trend in television set sales, the estimates of quarterly sales in Year 5 are 7190, 6670, 8540, and 8990.

The dummy variables in the equation actually provide four equations, one for each quarter. For instance, if time period t corresponds to quarter 1, the estimate of quarterly sales is

Quarter 1: Sales $= 6.07 - 1.36(1) - 2.03(0) - 0.304(0) + 0.146t = 4.71 + 0.146t$

Similarly, if time period t corresponds to quarters 2, 3, and 4, the estimates of quarterly sales are

Quarter 2: Sales $= 6.07 - 1.36(0) - 2.03(1) - 0.304(0) + 0.146t = 4.04 + 0.146t$

Quarter 3: Sales $= 6.07 - 1.36(0) - 2.03(0) - 0.304(1) + 0.146t = 5.77 + 0.146t$

Quarter 4: Sales $= 6.07 - 1.36(0) - 2.03(0) - 0.304(0) + 0.146t = 6.07 + 0.146t$

Problem 28 provides another example of using regression analysis to forecast time series data with both trend and seasonal effects.

The slope of the trend line for each quarterly forecast equation is 0.146, indicating a consistent growth in sales of about 146 sets per quarter. The only difference in the four equations is that they have different intercepts.

Models Based on Monthly Data

Whenever a categorical variable such as season has k levels, k − 1 dummy variables are required.

In the preceding television set sales example, we showed how dummy variables can be used to account for the quarterly seasonal effects in the time series. Because there were four levels for the categorical variable season, three dummy variables were required. However, many businesses use monthly rather than quarterly forecasts. For monthly data, season is a categorical variable with 12 levels, and thus $12 - 1 = 11$ dummy variables are required. For example, the 11 dummy variables could be coded as follows:

$$\text{Month1} = \begin{cases} 1 & \text{if January} \\ 0 & \text{otherwise} \end{cases}$$

$$\text{Month2} = \begin{cases} 1 & \text{if February} \\ 0 & \text{otherwise} \end{cases}$$

.
.
.

$$\text{Month11} = \begin{cases} 1 & \text{if November} \\ 0 & \text{otherwise} \end{cases}$$

Other than this change, the approach for handling seasonality remains the same.

SUMMARY

This chapter provided an introduction to basic methods of time series analysis and forecasting. We first showed that the underlying pattern in the time series can often be identified by constructing a time series plot. Several types of data patterns can be distinguished, including a horizontal pattern, a trend pattern, and a seasonal pattern. The forecasting methods we have discussed are based on which of these patterns are present in the time series.

We also discussed that the accuracy of the method is an important factor in determining which forecasting method to use. We considered three measures of forecast accuracy: mean absolute error (MAE), mean squared error (MSE), and mean absolute percentage error (MAPE). Each of these measures is designed to determine how well a particular forecasting method is able to reproduce the time series data that are already available. By selecting the method that is most accurate for the data already known, we hope to increase the likelihood that we will obtain more accurate forecasts for future time periods.

For a time series with a horizontal pattern, we showed how moving averages, weighted moving averages, and exponential smoothing can be used to develop a forecast. The moving averages method consists of computing an average of past data values and then using that average as the forecast for the next period. In the weighted moving average and exponential smoothing methods, weighted averages of past time series values are used to compute forecasts. These methods also adapt well to a horizontal pattern that shifts to a different level and then resumes a horizontal pattern.

For time series that have only a long-term linear trend, we showed how regression analysis can be used to make trend projections. For a time series with a seasonal pattern, we showed how dummy variables and regression analysis can be used to develop an equation with seasonal effects. We then extended the approach to include situations where the time series contains both a seasonal and a linear trend effect by showing how to combine the dummy variable approach for handling seasonality with the approach for handling a linear trend.

GLOSSARY

Categorical (dummy) variable A variable used to categorize observations of data. Used when modeling a time series with a seasonal pattern.

Cyclical pattern A cyclical pattern exists if the time series plot shows an alternating sequence of points below and above the trend line lasting more than one year.

Dependent variable The variable that is being predicted or explained in a regression analysis.

Exponential smoothing A forecasting method that uses a weighted average of past time series values as the forecast; it is a special case of the weighted moving averages method in which we select only one weight—the weight for the most recent observation.

Forecast error The difference between the actual time series value and the forecast.

Independent variable A variable used to predict or explain values of the dependent variable in regression analysis.

Mean absolute error (MAE) The average of the absolute values of the forecast errors.

Mean absolute percentage error (MAPE) The average of the absolute values of the percentage forecast errors.

Mean squared error (MSE) The average of the sum of squared forecast errors.

Moving averages A forecasting method that uses the average of the k most recent data values in the time series as the forecast for the next period.

Regression analysis A procedure for estimating values of a dependent variable given the values of one or more independent variables in a manner that minimizes the sum of the squared errors.

Seasonal pattern A seasonal pattern exists if the time series plot exhibits a repeating pattern over successive periods.

Smoothing constant A parameter of the exponential smoothing model that provides the weight given to the most recent time series value in the calculation of the forecast value.

Stationary time series A time series whose statistical properties are indepepndent of time. For a stationary time series, the process generating the data has a constant mean and the variability of the time series is constant over time.

Time series A sequence of observations on a variable measured at successive points in time or over successive periods of time.

Time series plot A graphical presentation of the relationship between time and the time series variable. Time is shown on the horizontal axis and the time series values are shown on the verical axis.

Trend pattern A trend pattern exists if the time series plot shows gradual shifts or movements to relatively higher or lower values over a longer period of time.

Weighted moving averages A forecasting method that involves selecting a different weight for the k most recent data values in the time series and then computing a weighted average of the of the values. The sum of the weights must equal one.

PROBLEMS

1. Consider the following time series data:

Week	1	2	3	4	5	6
Value	18	13	16	11	17	14

Using the naïve method (most recent value) as the forecast for the next week, compute the following measures of forecast accuracy.

   a. Mean absolute error
   b. Mean squared error
   c. Mean absolute percentage error
   d. What is the forecast for Week 7?

2. Refer to the time series data in Exercise 1. Using the average of all the historical data as a forecast for the next period, compute the following measures of forecast accuracy:

   a. Mean absolute error
   b. Mean squared error
   c. Mean absolute percentage error
   d. What is the forecast for Week 7?

3. Exercises 1 and 2 used different forecasting methods. Which method appears to provide the more accurate forecasts for the historical data? Explain.

4. Consider the following time series data:

Month	1	2	3	4	5	6	7
Value	24	13	20	12	19	23	15

   a. Compute MSE using the most recent value as the forecast for the next period. What is the forecast for Month 8?
   b. Compute MSE using the average of all the data available as the forecast for the next period. What is the forecast for Month 8?
   c. Which method appears to provide the better forecast?

5. Consider the following time series data:

Week	1	2	3	4	5	6
Value	18	13	16	11	17	14

   a. Construct a time series plot. What type of pattern exists in the data?
   b. Develop a three-week moving average for this time series. Compute MSE and a forecast for Week 7.
   c. Use $\alpha = 0.2$ to compute the exponential smoothing values for the time series. Compute MSE and a forecast for Week 7.
   d. Compare the three-week moving average forecast with the exponential smoothing forecast using $\alpha = 0.2$. Which appears to provide the better forecast based on MSE? Explain.
   e. Use trial and error to find a value of the exponential smoothing coefficient α that results in a smaller MSE than what you calculated for $\alpha = 0.2$.

6. Consider the following time series data:

Month	1	2	3	4	5	6	7
Value	24	13	20	12	19	23	15

   a. Construct a time series plot. What type of pattern exists in the data?
   b. Develop a three-week moving average for this time series. Compute MSE and a forecast for Month 8.
   c. Use $\alpha = 0.2$ to compute the exponential smoothing values for the time series. Compute MSE and a forecast for Month 8.
   d. Compare the three-week moving average forecast with the exponential smoothing forecast using $\alpha = 0.2$. Which appears to provide the better forecast based on MSE?

e. Use trial and error to find a value of the exponential smoothing coefficient α that results in a smaller MSE than what you calculated for $\alpha = 0.2$.

Gasoline

7. Refer to the gasoline sales time series data in Table 15.1.
    a. Compute four-week and five-week moving averages for the time series.
    b. Compute the MSE for the four-week and five-week moving average forecasts.
    c. What appears to be the best number of weeks of past data (three, four, or five) to use in the moving average computation? Recall that MSE for the three-week moving average is 10.22.

8. Refer again to the gasoline sales time series data in Table 15.1.
    a. Using a weight of 1/2 for the most recent observation, 1/3 for the second most recent, and 1/6 for third most recent, compute a three-week weighted moving average for the time series.
    b. Compute the MSE for the weighted moving average in part (a). Do you prefer this weighted moving average to the unweighted moving average? Remember that the MSE for the unweighted moving average is 10.22.
    c. Suppose you are allowed to choose any weights as long as they sum to 1. Could you always find a set of weights that would make the MSE smaller for a weighted moving average than for an unweighted moving average? Why or why not?

9. With the gasoline time series data from Table 15.1, show the exponential smoothing forecasts using $\alpha = 0.1$.
    a. Applying the MSE measure of forecast accuracy, would you prefer a smoothing constant of $\alpha = 0.1$ or $\alpha = 0.2$ for the gasoline sales time series?
    b. Are the results the same if you apply MAE as the measure of accuracy?
    c. What are the results if MAPE is used?

10. With a smoothing constant of $\alpha = 0.2$, equation (15.8) shows that the forecast for Week 13 of the gasoline sales data from Table 15.1 is given by $\hat{Y}_{13} = 0.2Y_{12} + 0.8\,\hat{Y}_{12}$. However, the forecast for Week 12 is given by $\hat{Y}_{12} = 0.2Y_{11} + 0.8\hat{Y}_{11}$. Thus, we could combine these two results to show that the forecast for Week 13 can be written

$$\hat{Y}_{13} = 0.2Y_{12} + 0.8(0.2Y_{11} + 0.8\hat{Y}_{11}) = 0.2Y_{12} + 0.16Y_{11} + 0.64\hat{Y}_{11}$$

    a. Making use of the fact that $\hat{Y}_{11} = 0.2Y_{10} + 0.8\hat{Y}_{10}$ (and similarly for $\hat{Y}_{10}$ and $\hat{Y}_9$), continue to expand the expression for $\hat{Y}_{13}$ until it is written in terms of the past data values $Y_{12}, Y_{11}, Y_{10}, Y_9, Y_8$, and the forecast for Week 8.
    b. Refer to the coefficients or weights for the past values $Y_{12}, Y_{11}, Y_{10}, Y_9$, and Y_8. What observation can you make about how exponential smoothing weights past data values in arriving at new forecasts? Compare this weighting pattern with the weighting pattern of the moving averages method.

11. For the Hawkins Company, the monthly percentages of all shipments received on time over the past 12 months are 80, 82, 84, 83, 83, 84, 85, 84, 82, 83, 84, and 83.
    a. Construct a time series plot. What type of pattern exists in the data?
    b. Compare a three-month moving average forecast with an exponential smoothing forecast for $\alpha = 0.2$. Which provides the better forecasts using MSE as the measure of model accuracy?
    c. What is the forecast for next month?

12. Corporate triple A bond interest rates for 12 consecutive months follow.

    9.5   9.3   9.4   9.6   9.8   9.7   9.8   10.5   9.9   9.7   9.6   9.6

    a. Construct a time series plot. What type of pattern exists in the data?

b. Develop three-month and four-month moving averages for this time series. Does the three-month or four-month moving average provide the better forecasts based on MSE? Explain.

c. What is the moving average forecast for the next month?

13.  The values of Alabama building contracts (in millions of dollars) for a 12-month period follow.

240 350 230 260 280 320 220 310 240 310 240 230

a. Construct a time series plot. What type of pattern exists in the data?

b. Compare a three-month moving average forecast with an exponential smoothing forecast. Use $\alpha = 0.2$. Which provides the better forecasts based on MSE?

c. What is the forecast for the next month?

14. The following time series shows the sales of a particular product over the past 12 months.

Month	Sales	Month	Sales
1	105	7	145
2	135	8	140
3	120	9	100
4	105	10	80
5	90	11	100
6	120	12	110

a. Construct a time series plot. What type of pattern exists in the data?

b. Use $\alpha = 0.3$ to compute the exponential smoothing values for the time series.

c. Use trial and error to find a value of the exponential smoothing coefficient α that results in a relatively small MSE.

15. Ten weeks of data on the Commodity Futures Index are 7.35, 7.40, 7.55, 7.56, 7.60, 7.52, 7.52, 7.70, 7.62, and 7.55.

a. Construct a time series plot. What type of pattern exists in the data?

b. Use trial and error to find a value of the exponential smoothing coefficient α that results in a relatively small MSE.

16. Since its inception in 1967, the Super Bowl is one of the most watched events on television in the United States every year. The number of U.S. households that tuned in for each Super Bowl, reported by Nielson.com, is provided in the data set SuperBowlRatings.

SuperBowlRatings

a. Construct a time series plot for the data. What type of pattern exists in the data? Discuss some of the patterns that may have resulted in the pattern exhibited in the time series plot of the data.

b. Given the pattern of the time series plot developed in part (a), do you think the forecasting methods discussed in this chapter are appropriate to develop forecasts for this time series? Explain.

c. Use simple linear regression analysis to find the parameters for the line that minimizes MSE for this time series.

17. Consider the following time series:

t	1	2	3	4	5
Y_t	6	11	9	14	15

a. Construct a time series plot. What type of pattern exists in the data?

b. Use simple linear regression analysis to find the parameters for the line that minimizes MSE for this time series.

c. What is the forecast for $t = 6$?

18. The following table reports the percentage of stocks in a portfolio for nine quarters from 2012 to 2014.

Quarter	Stock%
1st—2012	29.8
2nd—2012	31.0
3rd—2012	29.9
4th—2012	30.1
1st—2013	32.2
2nd—2013	31.5
3rd—2013	32.0
4th—2013	31.9
1st—2014	30.0

    a. Construct a time series plot. What type of pattern exists in the data?
    b. Use trial and error to find a value of the exponential smoothing coefficient α that results in a relatively small MSE.
    c. Using the exponential smoothing model you developed in part (b), what is the forecast of the percentage of stocks in a typical portfolio for the second quarter of 2014?

19. Consider the following time series:

t	1	2	3	4	5	6	7
Y_t	120	110	100	96	94	92	88

    a. Construct a time series plot. What type of pattern exists in the data?
    b. Use simple linear regression analysis to find the parameters for the line that minimizes MSE for this time series.
    c. What is the forecast for $t = 8$?

20. Because of high tuition costs at state and private universities, enrollments at community colleges have increased dramatically in recent years. The following data show the enrollment (in thousands) for Jefferson Community College for the nine most recent years.

Year	Enrollment (1000s)
1	6.5
2	8.1
3	8.4
4	10.2
5	12.5
6	13.3
7	13.7
8	17.2
9	18.1

    a. Construct a time series plot. What type of pattern exists in the data?
    b. Use simple linear regression analysis to find the parameters for the line that minimizes MSE for this time series.
    c. What is the forecast for Year 10?

AdultSmokers

21. The Centers for Disease Control and Prevention Office on Smoking and Health (OSH) is the lead federal agency responsible for comprehensive tobacco prevention and control. OSH was established in 1965 to reduce the death and disease caused by tobacco use and exposure to second-hand smoke. One of the many responsibilities of the OSH is

to collect data on tobacco use. The following data show the percentage of adults in the United States who were users of tobacco from 2001 through 2011 (http://www.cdc.gov /tobacco/data_statistics/tables/trends/cig_smoking/index.htm).

Year	Percentage of Adults Who Smoke
2001	22.8
2002	22.5
2003	21.6
2004	20.9
2005	20.9
2006	20.8
2007	19.8
2008	20.6
2009	20.6
2010	19.3
2011	18.9

a. Construct a time series plot. What type of pattern exists in the data?
b. Use simple linear regression to find the parameters for the line that minimizes MSE for this time series.
c. One of OSH's *Healthy People 2020 Goals* is to cut the percentage of adults in the United States who were users of tobacco to 12% or less by the year 2020. Does your regression model from part (b) suggest that the OSH is on target to meet this goal? If not, use your model from part (b) to estimate the year in which the OSH will achieve this goal.

22. The president of a small manufacturing firm is concerned about the continual increase in manufacturing costs over the past several years. The following figures provide a time series of the cost per unit for the firm's leading product over the past eight years.

Year	Cost/Unit ($)	Year	Cost/Unit ($)
1	20.00	5	26.60
2	24.50	6	30.00
3	28.20	7	31.00
4	27.50	8	36.00

a. Construct a time series plot. What type of pattern exists in the data?
b. Use simple linear regression analysis to find the parameters for the line that minimizes MSE for this time series.
c. What is the average cost increase that the firm has been realizing per year?
d. Compute an estimate of the cost/unit for next year.

WEB file

Exercise

23. The medical community unanimously agrees on the health benefits of regular exercise, but are adults listening? During each of the past 15 years, a polling organization has surveyed Americans about their exercise habits. In the most recent of these polls, slightly over half of all American adults reported that they exercise for 30 or more minutes at least three times per week. The following data show the percentages of adults who reported that they exercise for 30 or more minutes at least three times per week during each of the 15 years of this study.

Year	Percentage of Adults Who Reported That They Exercise for 30 or More Minutes at Least Three Times per Week
1	41.0
2	44.9
3	47.1
4	45.7
5	46.6
6	44.5
7	47.6
8	49.8
9	48.1
10	48.9
11	49.9
12	52.1
13	50.6
14	54.6
15	52.4

a. Construct a time series plot. Does a linear trend appear to be present?
b. Use simple linear regression to find the parameters for the line that minimizes MSE for this time series.
c. Use the trend equation from part (b) to forecast the percentage of adults next year (Year 16 of the study) who will report that they exercise for 30 or more minutes at least three times per week.
d. Would you feel comfortable using the trend equation from part (b) to forecast the percentage of adults three years from now (Year 18 of the study) who will report that they exercise for 30 or more minutes at least three times per week?

24. Consider the following time series:

Quarter	Year 1	Year 2	Year 3
1	71	68	62
2	49	41	51
3	58	60	53
4	78	81	72

a. Construct a time series plot. What type of pattern exists in the data?
b. Use a multiple linear regression model with dummy variables as follows to develop an equation to account for seasonal effects in the data. Qtr1 = 1 if Quarter 1, 0 otherwise; Qtr2 = 1 if Quarter 2, 0 otherwise; Qtr3 = 1 if Quarter 3, 0 otherwise.
c. Compute the quarterly forecasts for next year.

25. Consider the following time series data.

Quarter	Year 1	Year 2	Year 3
1	4	6	7
2	2	3	6
3	3	5	6
4	5	7	8

a. Construct a time series plot. What type of pattern exists in the data?
b. Use a multiple regression model with dummy variables as follows to develop an equation to account for seasonal effects in the data. Qtr1 = 1 if Quarter 1, 0 otherwise; Qtr2 = 1 if Quarter 2, 0 otherwise; Qtr3 = 1 if Quarter 3, 0 otherwise.
c. Compute the quarterly forecasts for next year.

26. The quarterly sales data (number of copies sold) for a college textbook over the past three years follow.

Quarter	Year 1	Year 2	Year 3
1	1690	1800	1850
2	940	900	1100
3	2625	2900	2930
4	2500	2360	2615

a. Construct a time series plot. What type of pattern exists in the data?
b. Use a regression model with dummy variables as follows to develop an equation to account for seasonal effects in the data. Qtr1 = 1 if Quarter 1, 0 otherwise; Qtr2 = 1 if Quarter 2, 0 otherwise; Qtr3 = 1 if Quarter 3, 0 otherwise.
c. Compute the quarterly forecasts for next year.
d. Let $t = 1$ to refer to the observation in Quarter 1 of Year 1; $t = 2$ to refer to the observation in Quarter 2 of Year 1; . . . ; and $t = 12$ to refer to the observation in Quarter 4 of Year 3. Using the dummy variables defined in part (b) and also using t, develop an equation to account for seasonal effects and any linear trend in the time series. Based upon the seasonal effects in the data and linear trend, compute the quarterly forecasts for next year.

Pollution

27. Air pollution control specialists in southern California monitor the amount of ozone, carbon dioxide, and nitrogen dioxide in the air on an hourly basis. The hourly time series data exhibit seasonality, with the levels of pollutants showing patterns that vary over the hours in the day. On July 15, 16, and 17, the following levels of nitrogen dioxide were observed for the 12 hours from 6:00 A.M. to 6:00 P.M.

July 15: 25 28 35 50 60 60 40 35 30 25 25 20
July 16: 28 30 35 48 60 65 50 40 35 25 20 20
July 17: 35 42 45 70 72 75 60 45 40 25 25 25

a. Construct a time series plot. What type of pattern exists in the data?
b. Use a multiple linear regression model with dummy variables as follows to develop an equation to account for seasonal effects in the data:

Hour1 = 1 if the reading was made between 6:00 A.M. and 7:00 A.M.; 0 otherwise

Hour2 = 1 if the reading was made between 7:00 A.M. and 8:00 A.M.; 0 otherwise

$$\vdots$$

Hour11 = 1 if the reading was made between 4:00 P.M. and 5:00 P.M.; 0 otherwise

Note that when the values of the 11 dummy variables are equal to 0, the observation corresponds to the 5:00 P.M. to 6:00 P.M. hour.

c. Using the equation developed in part (b), compute estimates of the levels of nitrogen dioxide for July 18.
d. Let $t = 1$ to refer to the observation in Hour 1 on July 15; $t = 2$ to refer to the observation in Hour 2 of July 15; . . . ; and $t = 36$ to refer to the observation in Hour 12 of July 17. Using the dummy variables defined in part (b) and t, develop an equation to

account for seasonal effects and any linear trend in the time series. Based upon the seasonal effects in the data and linear trend, compute estimates of the levels of nitrogen dioxide for July 18.

SouthShore

28. South Shore Construction builds permanent docks and seawalls along the southern shore of Long Island, New York. Although the firm has been in business for only five years, revenue has increased from $308,000 in the first year of operation to $1,084,000 in the most recent year. The following data show the quarterly sales revenue in thousands of dollars:

Quarter	Year 1	Year 2	Year 3	Year 4	Year 5
1	20	37	75	92	176
2	100	136	155	202	282
3	175	245	326	384	445
4	13	26	48	82	181

a. Construct a time series plot. What type of pattern exists in the data?
b. Use a multiple regression model with dummy variables as follows to develop an equation to account for seasonal effects in the data. Qtr1 = 1 if Quarter 1, 0 otherwise; Qtr2 = 1 if Quarter 2, 0 otherwise; Qtr3 = 1 if Quarter 3, 0 otherwise.
c. Let Period = 1 to refer to the observation in Quarter 1 of Year 1; Period = 2 to refer to the observation in Quarter 2 of Year 1; . . . and Period = 20 to refer to the observation in Quarter 4 of Year 5. Using the dummy variables defined in part (b) and Period, develop an equation to account for seasonal effects and any linear trend in the time series. Based upon the seasonal effects in the data and linear trend, compute estimates of quarterly sales for Year 6.

Case Problem 1   FORECASTING FOOD AND BEVERAGE SALES

The Vintage Restaurant, on Captiva Island near Fort Myers, Florida, is owned and operated by Karen Payne. The restaurant just completed its third year of operation. During that time, Karen sought to establish a reputation for the restaurant as a high-quality dining establishment that specializes in fresh seafood. Through the efforts of Karen and her staff, her restaurant has become one of the best and fastest-growing restaurants on the island.

To better plan for future growth of the restaurant, Karen needs to develop a system that will enable her to forecast food and beverage sales by month for up to one year in advance. Table 15.17 shows the value of food and beverage sales ($1000s) for the first three years of operation.

Managerial Report

Perform an analysis of the sales data for the Vintage Restaurant. Prepare a report for Karen that summarizes your findings, forecasts, and recommendations. Include the following:

1. A time series plot. Comment on the underlying pattern in the time series.
2. Using the dummy variable approach, forecast sales for January through December of the fourth year.

Assume that January sales for the fourth year turn out to be $295,000. What was your forecast error? If this error is large, Karen may be puzzled about the difference between your forecast and the actual sales value. What can you do to resolve her uncertainty in the forecasting procedure?

TABLE 15.17   FOOD AND BEVERAGE SALES FOR THE VINTAGE RESTAURANT ($1000s)

Vintage

Month	First Year	Second Year	Third Year
January	242	263	282
February	235	238	255
March	232	247	265
April	178	193	205
May	184	193	210
June	140	149	160
July	145	157	166
August	152	161	174
September	110	122	126
October	130	130	148
November	152	167	173
December	206	230	235

Case Problem 2   FORECASTING LOST SALES

The Carlson Department Store suffered heavy damage when a hurricane struck on August 31. The store was closed for four months (September through December), and Carlson is now involved in a dispute with its insurance company about the amount of lost sales during the time the store was closed. Two key issues must be resolved: (1) the amount of sales Carlson would have made if the hurricane had not struck and (2) whether Carlson is entitled to any compensation for excess sales due to increased business activity after the storm. More than $8 billion in federal disaster relief and insurance money came into the county, resulting in increased sales at department stores and numerous other businesses.

Table 15.18 gives Carlson's sales data for the 48 months preceding the storm. Table 15.19 reports total sales for the 48 months preceding the storm for all department stores in the county, as well as the total sales in the county for the four months the Carlson Department Store was closed. Carlson's managers asked you to analyze these data and develop estimates of the lost sales at the Carlson Department Store for the months of September

TABLE 15.18   SALES FOR CARLSON DEPARTMENT STORE ($ MILLIONS)

CarlsonSales

Month	Year 1	Year 2	Year 3	Year 4	Year 5
January		1.45	2.31	2.31	2.56
February		1.80	1.89	1.99	2.28
March		2.03	2.02	2.42	2.69
April		1.99	2.23	2.45	2.48
May		2.32	2.39	2.57	2.73
June		2.20	2.14	2.42	2.37
July		2.13	2.27	2.40	2.31
August		2.43	2.21	2.50	2.23
September	1.71	1.90	1.89	2.09	
October	1.90	2.13	2.29	2.54	
November	2.74	2.56	2.83	2.97	
December	4.20	4.16	4.04	4.35	

TABLE 15.19   DEPARTMENT STORE SALES FOR THE COUNTY ($ MILLIONS)

CountySales

Month	Year 1	Year 2	Year 3	Year 4	Year 5
January		46.80	46.80	43.80	48.00
February		48.00	48.60	45.60	51.60
March		60.00	59.40	57.60	57.60
April		57.60	58.20	53.40	58.20
May		61.80	60.60	56.40	60.00
June		58.20	55.20	52.80	57.00
July		56.40	51.00	54.00	57.60
August		63.00	58.80	60.60	61.80
September	55.80	57.60	49.80	47.40	69.00
October	56.40	53.40	54.60	54.60	75.00
November	71.40	71.40	65.40	67.80	85.20
December	117.60	114.00	102.00	100.20	121.80

through December. They also asked you to determine whether a case can be made for excess storm-related sales during the same period. If such a case can be made, Carlson is entitled to compensation for excess sales it would have earned in addition to ordinary sales.

Managerial Report

Prepare a report for the managers of the Carlson Department Store that summarizes your findings, forecasts, and recommendations. Include the following:

1. An estimate of sales for Carlson Department Store had there been no hurricane
2. An estimate of countywide department store sales had there been no hurricane
3. An estimate of lost sales for the Carlson Department Store for September through December

In addition, use the countywide actual department stores sales for September through December and the estimate in part (2) to make a case for or against excess storm-related sales.

Appendix 15.1   FORECASTING WITH EXCEL DATA ANALYSIS TOOLS

In this appendix we show how Excel can be used to develop forecasts using three forecasting methods: moving averages, exponential smoothing, and trend projection. We also show how to use Excel Solver for least-squares fitting of models to data.

Moving Averages

*If the **Data Analysis** option does not appear in the **Analysis** group, you will have to include the Add-In in Excel. To do so, click on the **File** tab, then click **Options**, and then **Add-Ins**. Click **Go** next to the **Excel Add-Ins** drop-down box. Click the box next to **Analysis ToolPak** and click **OK**.*

To show how Excel can be used to develop forecasts using the moving averages method, we develop a forecast for the gasoline sales time series in Table 15.1 and Figure 15.1. We assume that the user has entered the week in rows 2 through 13 of column A and the sales data for the 12 weeks into worksheet rows 2 through 13 of column B (as in Figure 15.13).

The following steps can be used to produce a three-week moving average:

Step 1. Select the **Data** tab
Step 2. From the **Analysis** group select the **Data Analysis** option
Step 3. When the **Data Analysis** dialog box appears, choose **Moving Average** and click **OK**

FIGURE 15.13   GASOLINE SALES DATA IN EXCEL ARRANGED TO USE THE MOVING AVERAGES FUNCTION TO DEVELOP FORECASTS

Week	Sales (1000s of gallons)
1	17
2	21
3	19
4	23
5	18
6	16
7	20
8	18
9	22
10	20
11	15
12	22

Step 4. When the **Moving Average** dialog box appears:
Enter B2:B13 in the **Input Range** box
Enter 3 in the **Interval** box
Enter C2 in the **Output Range** box
Click **OK**

Once you have completed this step (as shown in Figure 15.14), the three-week moving average forecasts will appear in column C of the worksheet as in Figure 15.15. Note that forecasts for periods of other lengths can be computed easily by entering a different value in the **Interval** box.

FIGURE 15.14   EXCEL MOVING AVERAGE DIALOGUE BOX FOR A 3-PERIOD MOVING AVERAGE

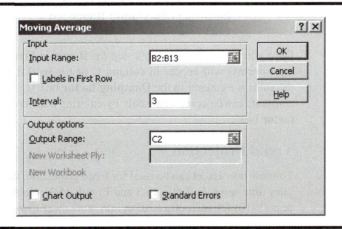

FIGURE 15.15 GASOLINE SALES DATA AND OUTPUT OF MOVING AVERAGES FUNCTION IN EXCEL

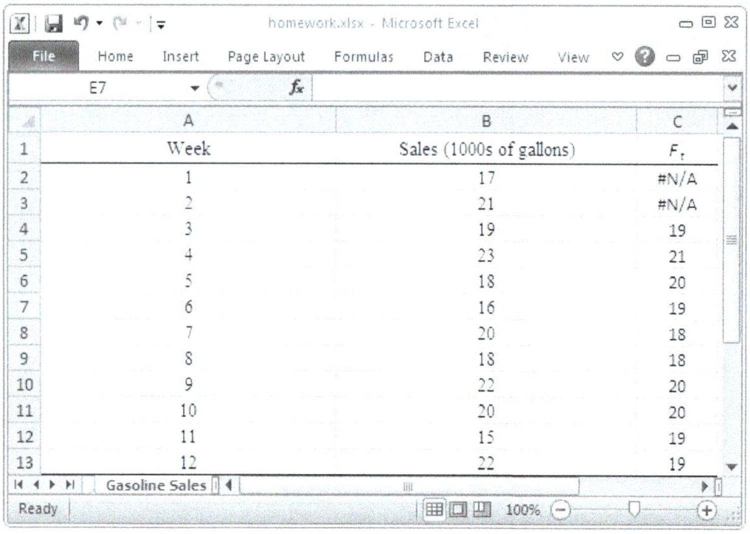

	A	B	C
1	Week	Sales (1000s of gallons)	F_t
2	1	17	#N/A
3	2	21	#N/A
4	3	19	19
5	4	23	21
6	5	18	20
7	6	16	19
8	7	20	18
9	8	18	18
10	9	22	20
11	10	20	20
12	11	15	19
13	12	22	19

Exponential Smoothing

To show how Excel can be used for exponential smoothing, we again develop a forecast for the gasoline sales time series in Table 15.1 and Figure 15.1. We assume that the user has entered the week in rows 2 through 13 of column A and the sales data for the 12 weeks into worksheet rows 2 through 13 of column B (as in Figure 15.13), and that the smoothing constant is $\alpha = 0.2$. The following steps can be used to produce a forecast:

Step 1. Select the **Data** tab
Step 2. From the **Analysis** group select the **Data Analysis** option
Step 3. When the **Data Analysis** dialog box appears, choose **Exponential Smoothing** and click **OK**
Step 4. When the **Exponential Smoothing** dialog box appears:
Enter B2:B13 in the **Input Range** box
Enter 0.8 in the **Damping factor** box
Enter C2 in the **Output Range** box
Click **OK**

Once you have completed this step (as shown in Figure 15.16), the exponential smoothing forecasts will appear in column C of the worksheet (as in Figure 15.17). Note that the value we entered in the **Damping factor** box is $1 - \alpha$; forecasts for other smoothing constants can be computed easily by entering a different value for $1 - \alpha$ in the **Damping factor** box.

Trend Projection

To show how Excel can be used for trend projection, we develop a forecast for the bicycle sales time series in Table 15.3 and Figure 15.3. We assume that the user has entered the year (1–10) for each observation into worksheet rows 2 through 11 of column A and the

FIGURE 15.16   EXCEL EXPONENTIAL SMOOTHING DIALOGUE BOX FOR $\alpha = 0.20$

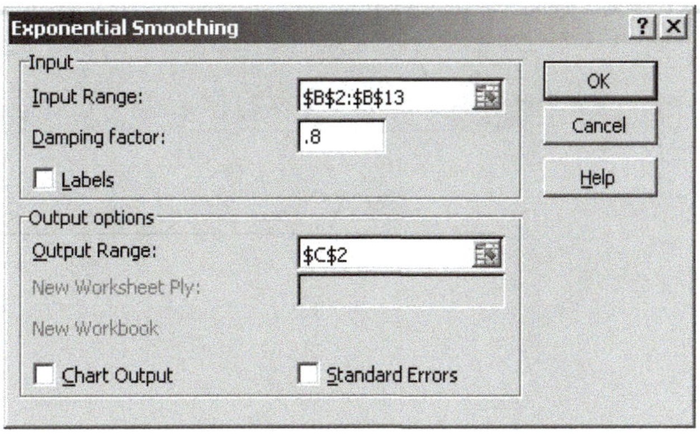

FIGURE 15.17   GASOLINE SALES DATA AND OUTPUT OF EXPONENTIAL SMOOTHING FUNCTION IN EXCEL

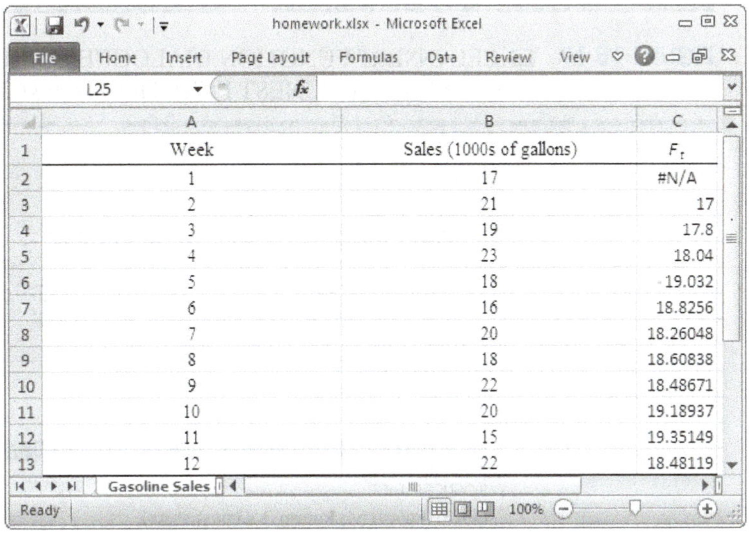

Week	Sales (1000s of gallons)	F_t
1	17	#N/A
2	21	17
3	19	17.8
4	23	18.04
5	18	19.032
6	16	18.8256
7	20	18.26048
8	18	18.60838
9	22	18.48671
10	20	19.18937
11	15	19.35149
12	22	18.48119

sales values into worksheet rows 2 through 11 of column B as shown in Figure 15.18. The following steps can be used to produce a forecast for Year 11 by trend projection:

Step 1. Select the **Formulas** tab

Step 2. Select two cells in the row where you want the regression coefficients b_1 and b_0 to appear (for this example, choose D1 and E1)

Step 3. Click on the **Insert Function** key

Step 4. When the **Insert Function** dialog box appears:
Choose **Statistical** in the **Or select a category** box
Choose **LINEST** in the **Select a function** box
Click **OK**

FIGURE 15.18   BICYCLE SALES DATA IN EXCEL ARRANGED TO USE THE LINEST
FUNCTION TO FIND THE LINEAR TREND

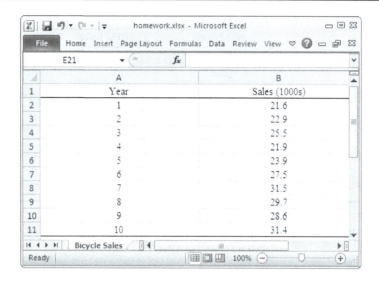

FIGURE 15.19   EXCEL INSERT FUNCTION DIALOGUE BOX FOR FINDING THE TREND
LINE USING THE LINEST FUNCTION IN EXCEL

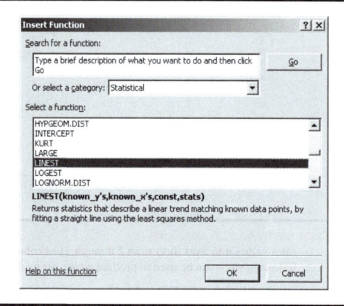

See Figure 15.19 for an example of this step.

Step 5. When the **Function Arguments** dialog box appears:
Enter B2:B11 in the **Known_y's** box
Enter A2:A11 in the **Known_x's** box
Click **OK**

FIGURE 15.20   EXCEL FUNCTION ARGUMENTS DIALOGUE BOX FOR FINDING THE
TREND LINE USING THE LINEST FUNCTION IN EXCEL

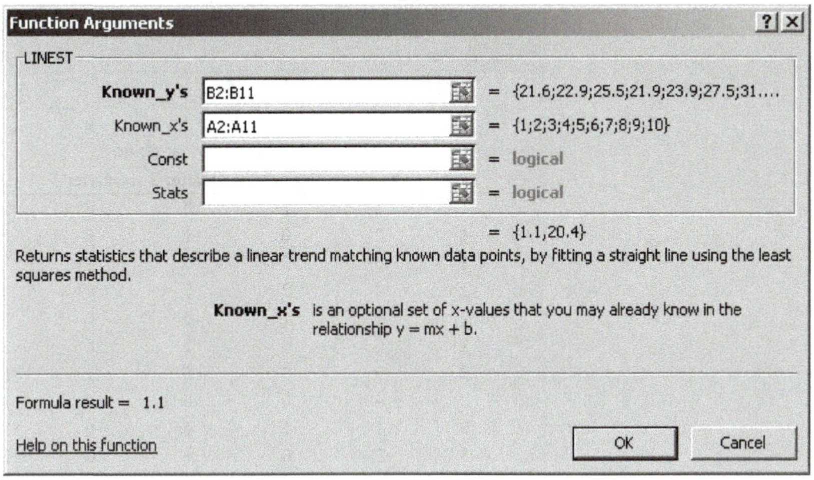

See Figure 15.20 for an example of this step.

Step 6. Hit the F2 key and then simultaneously hit the Shift, Control, and Enter keys
(Shift + Control + Enter) to create an array that contains the values of the
regression coefficients b_1 and b_0

At this point you have generated the regression coefficients b_1 and b_0 in the two cells
you originally selected in step 1. It is important to note that cell D1 contains b_1 and cell E1
contains b_0.

To generate a forecast, in a blank cell, multiply the value of the independent variable t
by b_1 and add the value of b_0 to this product. For example, if you wish to use this linear
trend model to generate a forecast for Year 11 and the value of b_1 is in cell D1 and the value
of b_0 is in cell E1, then enter =11*D1+E1 in a blank cell. The forecast for Year 11, in this
case 32.5, will appear in the blank cell in which you enter this formula.

Models with Seasonality and No Trend

To show how Excel can be used to fit models with seasonality, we develop a forecast for
the umbrella sales time series in Table 15.13 and Figure 15.11. We assume that the user has
entered the year (1–5) for each observation into worksheet rows 3 through 22 of column
A; the values for the quarter in worksheet rows 3 through 22 of column B; the values for
the quarterly dummy variables $Qtr1_t$, $Qtr2_t$, and $Qtr3_t$ in worksheet rows 3 through 22 of
columns C, D, and E, respectively; and the sales values into worksheet rows 3 through 22
of column F. The following steps can be used to produce a forecast for Year 11 by trend
projection as shown in Figure 15.21.

Step 1. Select the **Formulas** tab
Step 2. Select four cells in the row where you want the regression coefficients b_3, b_2,
b_1, and b_0 to appear (for this example, choose G1:J1)
Step 3. Click on the **Insert Function** key

FIGURE 15.21 UMBRELLA SALES DATA IN EXCEL ARRANGED TO USE THE LINEST FUNCTION TO FIND THE SEASONAL COMPONENTS

	A	B	C	D	E	F
1			Dummy Variables			
2	Year	Quarter	Quarter 1	Quarter 2	Quarter 3	Y_t
3	1	1	1	0	0	125
4	1	2	0	1	0	153
5	1	3	0	0	1	106
6	1	4	0	0	0	88
7	2	1	1	0	0	118
8	2	2	0	1	0	161
9	2	3	0	0	1	133
10	2	4	0	0	0	102
11	3	1	1	0	0	138
12	3	2	0	1	0	144
13	3	3	0	0	1	113
14	3	4	0	0	0	80
15	4	1	1	0	0	109
16	4	2	0	1	0	137
17	4	3	0	0	1	125
18	4	4	0	0	0	109
19	5	1	1	0	0	130
20	5	2	0	1	0	165
21	5	3	0	0	1	128
22	5	4	0	0	0	96
23						

Umbrella Sales (season only)

Step 4. When the **Insert Function** dialog box appears:
Choose **Statistical** in the **Or select a category** box
Choose **LINEST** in the **Select a function** box
Click **OK**

Step 5. When the **Function Arguments** dialog box appears:
Enter F3:F22 in the **Known_y's** box
Enter C3:E22 in the **Known_x's** box
Click **OK**

See Figure 15.22 for an example of this step.

Step 6. Hit the F2 key and then simultaneously hit the Shift, Control, and Enter keys (Shift + Control + Enter) to create an array that contains the values of the regression coefficients b_3, b_2, b_1, and b_0

At this point you have generated the regression coefficients b_3, b_2, b_1, and b_0 in cells G1:J1 selected in step 1. It is important to note that the first cell you selected contains b_3, the second cell you selected contains b_2, the third cell you selected contains b_1, and the fourth cell you selected contains b_0 (i.e., if you selected cells G1:J1 in step 1, the value of b_1 will be in cell G1, the value of b_2 will be in cell H1, the value of b_1 will be in I1, and the value of b_0 will be in cell J1).

FIGURE 15.22   EXCEL FUNCTION ARGUMENTS DIALOGUE BOX FOR FINDING THE
SEASONAL COMPONENTS USING THE LINEST FUNCTION IN EXCEL

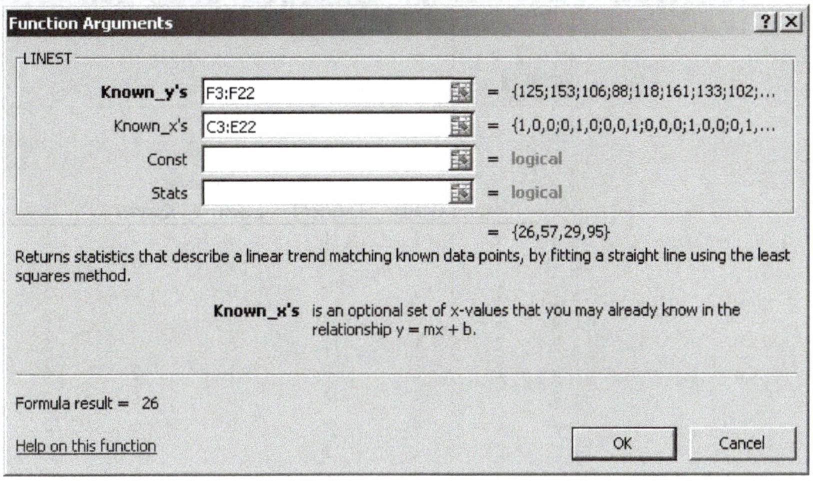

To generate a forecast, in a blank cell, add together b_0 and the product of b_1 and $Qtr1_t$, the product of b_2 and $Qtr2_t$, and the product of b_3 and $Qtr3_t$. For example, if you wish to use this linear trend model to generate a forecast for the first quarter of next year and the value of b_3 is in cell G1, the value of b_2 is in cell H1, the value of b_1 is in cell I1, and the value of b_0 is in cell J1, then enter =1*G1+0*H1+0*I1+J1 in a blank cell. The forecast for the first quarter of next year, in this case 124.0, will appear in the blank cell in which you enter this formula.

Models with Seasonality and Linear Trend

To show how Excel can be used to fit models with seasonality and a linear trend, we develop a forecast for the umbrella set time series in Table 15.13 and Figure 15.11. We assume that the user has entered the year (1–5) for each observation into worksheet rows 3 through 22 of column A; the values for the quarter in worksheet rows 3 through 22 of column B; the values for the quarterly dummy variables $Qtr1_t$, $Qtr2_t$, and $Qtr3_t$ into worksheet rows 3 through 22 of columns C, D, and E, respectively; the values of period t into worksheet rows 3 through 22 of column F; and the sales values into worksheet rows 3 through 22 of column G. The following steps can be used to produce a forecast for Year 11 by trend projection as shown in Figure 15.23.

Step 1. Select the **Formulas** tab
Step 2. Select five cells in the row where you want the regression coefficients b_4, b_3, b_2, b_1, and b_0 to appear for this example; choose H1:L1
Step 3. Click on the **Insert Function** key
Step 4. When the **Insert Function** dialog box appears:
Choose **Statistical** in the **Or select a category** box
Choose **LINEST** in the **Select a function** box
Click **OK**
Step 5. When the **Function Arguments** dialog box appears:
Enter G3:G22 in the **Known_y's** box
Enter C3:F22 in the **Known_x's** box
Click **OK**

FIGURE 15.23 UMBRELLA TIME SERIES DATA IN EXCEL ARRANGED TO USE THE LINEST FUNCTION TO FIND BOTH THE SEASONAL COMPONENTS AND TREND COMPONENT

homework.xlsx - Microsoft Excel

F8 f_x 6

	A	B	C	D	E	F	G
1				Dummy Variables			
2	Year	Quarter	Quarter 1	Quarter 2	Quarter 3	t	Y_t
3	1	1	1	0	0	1	125
4	1	2	0	1	0	2	153
5	1	3	0	0	1	3	106
6	1	4	0	0	0	4	88
7	2	1	1	0	0	5	118
8	2	2	0	1	0	6	161
9	2	3	0	0	1	7	133
10	2	4	0	0	0	8	102
11	3	1	1	0	0	9	138
12	3	2	0	1	0	10	144
13	3	3	0	0	1	11	113
14	3	4	0	0	0	12	80
15	4	1	1	0	0	13	109
16	4	2	0	1	0	14	137
17	4	3	0	0	1	15	125
18	4	4	0	0	0	16	109
19	5	1	1	0	0	17	130
20	5	2	0	1	0	18	165
21	5	3	0	0	1	19	128
22	5	4	0	0	0	20	96
23							

Umbrella Sales (season & trend)

Ready 100%

Step 6. Hit the F2 key and then simultaneously hit the Shift, Control, and Enter keys (Shift + Control + Enter) to create an array that contains the values of the regression coefficients b_4, b_3, b_2, b_1, and b_0

At this point you have generated the regression coefficients b_4, b_3, b_2, b_1, and b_0 in cells H1:L1 selected in step 1. It is important to note that the first cell you selected contains b_4, the second cell you selected contains b_3, the third cell you selected contains b_2, the fourth cell you selected contains b_1, and the fifth cell you selected contains b_0 (i.e., if you selected cells H1:L1 in step 1, the value of b_4 will be in cell H1, the value of b_1 will be in cell I1, the value of b_2 will be in J1, the value of b_1 will be in K1, and the value of b_0 will be in cell L1).

To generate a forecast, in a blank cell, add together b_0 and the product of b_1 and Qtr1_t, the product of b_2 and Qtr2_t, the product of b_3 and Qtr3_t, and the product of b_4 and t. For example, if you wish to use this linear trend model to generate a forecast for the first quarter of Year 5 and the value of b_4 is in cell H1, the value of b_3 is in cell I1, the value of b_2 is in cell J1, the value of b_1 is in cell K1, and the value of b_0 is in cell L1, then enter = 17*H1+1*I1+0*J1+0*K1+L1 in a blank cell. The forecast for the first quarter of next year, in this case 7.19, will appear in the blank cell in which you enter this formula.

CHAPTER 10

Statistical Methods for Quality Control

CONTENTS

STATISTICS *in* PRACTICE

DOW CHEMICAL COMPANY*
FREEPORT, TEXAS

In 1940 the Dow Chemical Company purchased 800 acres of Texas land on the Gulf Coast to build a magnesium production facility. That original site has expanded to cover more than 5000 acres and holds one of the largest petrochemical complexes in the world. Among the products from Dow Texas Operations are magnesium, styrene, plastics, adhesives, solvent, glycol, and chlorine. Some products are made solely for use in other processes, but many end up as essential ingredients in products such as pharmaceuticals, toothpastes, dog food, water hoses, ice chests, milk cartons, garbage bags, shampoos, and furniture.

Dow's Texas Operations produce more than 30% of the world's magnesium, an extremely lightweight metal used in products ranging from tennis racquets to suitcases to "mag" wheels. The Magnesium Department was the first group in Texas Operations to train its technical people and managers in the use of statistical quality control. Some of the earliest successful applications of statistical quality control were in chemical processing.

In one application involving the operation of a drier, samples of the output were taken at periodic intervals; the average value for each sample was computed and recorded on a chart called an $\bar{x}$ chart. Such a chart enabled Dow analysts to monitor trends in the output that might indicate the process was not operating correctly. In one instance, analysts began to observe values for the sample mean that were not indicative of a process operating within its

Statistical quality control has enabled Dow Chemical Company to improve its processing methods and output.

design limits. On further examination of the control chart and the operation itself, the analysts found that the variation could be traced to problems involving one operator. The $\bar{x}$ chart recorded after retraining the operator showed a significant improvement in the process quality.

Dow achieves quality improvements everywhere it applies statistical quality control. Documented savings of several hundred thousand dollars per year are realized, and new applications are continually being discovered.

In this chapter we will show how an $\bar{x}$ chart such as the one used by Dow can be developed. Such charts are a part of statistical quality control known as statistical process control. We will also discuss methods of quality control for situations in which a decision to accept or reject a group of items is based on a sample.

*The authors are indebted to Clifford B. Wilson, Magnesium Technical Manager, The Dow Chemical Company, for providing this Statistics in Practice.

ASQ's Vision: "By making quality a global priority, an organizational imperative, and a personal ethic, the American Society for Quality becomes the community for everyone who seeks quality concepts, technology, and tools to improve themselves and their world" (ASQ website).

The American Society for Quality (ASQ) defines quality as "the totality of features and characteristics of a product or service that bears on its ability to satisfy given needs." In other words, quality measures how well a product or service meets customer needs. Organizations recognize that to be competitive in today's global economy, they must strive for a high level of quality. As a result, they place increased emphasis on methods for monitoring and maintaining quality.

Today, the customer-driven focus that is fundamental to high-performing organizations has changed the scope that quality issues encompass, from simply eliminating defects on a production line to developing broad-based corporate quality strategies. Broadening the scope of quality naturally leads to the concept of **total quality (TQ)**.

Total Quality (TQ) is a people-focused management system that aims at continual increase in customer satisfaction at continually lower real cost. TQ is a total system approach (not a separate area or work program) and an integral part of high-level strategy; it works horizontally across function and departments, involves all employees, top to bottom, and extends backward and forward to include the supply chain and the customer chain. TQ stresses learning and adaptation to continual change as keys to organization success.[1]

Regardless of how it is implemented in different organizations, total quality is based on three fundamental principles: a focus on customers and stakeholders; participation and teamwork throughout the organization; and a focus on continuous improvement and learning. In the first section of the chapter we provide a brief introduction to three quality management frameworks: the Malcolm Baldrige Quality Award, ISO 9000 standards, and the Six Sigma philosophy. In the last two sections we introduce two statistical tools that can be used to monitor quality: statistical process control and acceptance sampling.

19.1 Philosophies and Frameworks

After World War II, Dr. W. Edwards Deming became a consultant to Japanese industry; he is credited with being the person who convinced top managers in Japan to use the methods of statistical quality control.

In the early twentieth century, quality control practices were limited to inspecting finished products and removing defective items. But this all changed as the result of the pioneering efforts of a young engineer named Walter A. Shewhart. After completing his doctorate in physics from the University of California in 1917, Dr. Shewhart joined the Western Electric Company, working in the inspection engineering department. In 1924 Dr. Shewhart prepared a memorandum that included a set of principles that are the basis for what is known today as process control. And his memo also contained a diagram that would be recognized as a statistical control chart. Continuing his work in quality at Bell Telephone Laboratories until his retirement in 1956, he brought together the disciplines of statistics, engineering, and economics and in doing so changed the course of industrial history. Dr. Shewhart is recognized as the father of statistical quality control and was the first honorary member of the ASQ.

Two other individuals who have had great influence on quality are Dr. W. Edwards Deming, a student of Dr. Shewhart, and Joseph Juran. These men helped educate the Japanese in quality management shortly after World War II. Although quality is everybody's job, Deming stressed that the focus on quality must be led by managers. He developed a list of 14 points that he believed represent the key responsibilities of managers. For instance, Deming stated that managers must cease dependence on mass inspection; must end the practice of awarding business solely on the basis of price; must seek continual improvement in all production processes and service; must foster a team-oriented environment; and must eliminate goals, slogans, and work standards that prescribe numerical quotas. Perhaps most important, managers must create a work environment in which a commitment to quality and productivity is maintained at all times.

Juran proposed a simple definition of quality: *fitness for use*. Juran's approach to quality focused on three quality processes: quality planning, quality control, and quality improvement. In contrast to Deming's philosophy, which required a major cultural change in the organization, Juran's programs were designed to improve quality by working within the current organizational system. Nonetheless, the two philosophies are similar in that they both focus on the need for top management to be involved and stress the need for continuous improvement, the importance of training, and the use of quality control techniques.

Many other individuals played significant roles in the quality movement, including Philip B. Crosby, A. V. Feigenbaum, Karou Ishikawa, and Genichi Taguchi. More specialized texts dealing exclusively with quality provide details of the contributions of each of

---

[1]J. R. Evans and W. M. Lindsay, *Managing for Quality and Performance Excellence*, 8th ed. (Cincinnati, OH: South-Western, 2011), p. 11.

these individuals. The contributions of all individuals involved in the quality movement helped define a set of best practices and led to numerous awards and certification programs. The two most significant programs are the U.S. Malcolm Baldrige National Quality Award and the international ISO 9000 certification process. In recent years, use of Six Sigma—a methodology for improving organizational performance based on rigorous data collection and statistical analysis—has also increased.

Malcolm Baldrige National Quality Award

The U.S. Commerce Department's National Institute of Standards and Technology (NIST) manages the Baldrige National Quality Program. More information can be obtained at the NIST website.

The Malcolm Baldrige National Quality Award is given by the president of the United States to organizations that apply and are judged to be outstanding in seven areas: leadership; strategic planning; customer and market focus; measurement, analysis, and knowledge management; human resource focus; process management; and business results. Congress established the award program in 1987 to recognize U.S. organizations for their achievements in quality and performance and to raise awareness about the importance of quality as a competitive edge. The award is named for Malcolm Baldrige, who served as secretary of commerce from 1981 until his death in 1987.

2004 was the final year for the Baldrige Stock Study because of the increase in the number of recipients that are either nonprofit or privately held businesses.

Since the presentation of the first awards in 1988, the Baldrige National Quality Program (BNQP) has grown in stature and impact. Approximately 2 million copies of the criteria have been distributed since 1988, and wide-scale reproduction by organizations and electronic access add to that number significantly. For eight years in a row, a hypothetical stock index, made up of publicly traded U.S. companies that had received the Baldrige Award, outperformed the Standard & Poor's 500. In one year, the "Baldrige Index" outperformed the S&P 500 by 4.4 to 1. Bob Barnett, executive vice president of Motorola, Inc., said, "We applied for the Award, not with the idea of winning, but with the goal of receiving the evaluation of the Baldrige Examiners. That evaluation was comprehensive, professional, and insightful... making it perhaps the most cost-effective, value-added business consultation available anywhere in the world today."

ISO 9000

ISO 9000 standards are revised periodically to improve the quality of the standard.

ISO 9000 is a series of five international standards published in 1987 by the International Organization for Standardization (ISO), Geneva, Switzerland. Companies can use the standards to help determine what is needed to maintain an efficient quality conformance system. For example, the standards describe the need for an effective quality system, for ensuring that measuring and testing equipment is calibrated regularly, and for maintaining an adequate record-keeping system. ISO 9000 registration determines whether a company complies with its own quality system. Overall, ISO 9000 registration covers less than 10% of the Baldrige Award criteria.

Six Sigma

In the late 1980s Motorola recognized the need to improve the quality of its products and services; their goal was to achieve a level of quality so good that for every million opportunities no more than 3.4 defects will occur. This level of quality is referred to as the six sigma level of quality, and the methodology created to reach this quality goal is referred to as **Six Sigma**.

An organization may undertake two kinds of Six Sigma projects:

- DMAIC (Define, Measure, Analyze, Improve, and Control) to help redesign existing processes
- DFSS (Design for Six Sigma) to design new products, processes, or services

In helping to redesign existing processes and design new processes, Six Sigma places a heavy emphasis on statistical analysis and careful measurement. Today, Six Sigma is a major tool in helping organizations achieve Baldrige levels of business performance and process quality. Many Baldrige examiners view Six Sigma as the ideal approach for implementing Baldrige improvement programs.

Six Sigma limits and defects per million opportunities   In Six Sigma terminology, a *defect* is any mistake or error that is passed on to the customer. The Six Sigma process defines quality performance as defects per million opportunities (dpmo). As we indicated previously, Six Sigma represents a quality level of at most 3.4 dpmo. To illustrate how this quality level is measured, let us consider the situation at KJW Packaging.

KJW operates a production line where boxes of cereal are filled. The filling process has a mean of $\mu = 16.05$ ounces and a standard deviation of $\sigma = .10$ ounces. It is reasonable to assume the filling weights are normally distributed. The distribution of filling weights is shown in Figure 19.1. Suppose management considers 15.45 to 16.65 ounces to be acceptable quality limits for the filling process. Thus, any box of cereal that contains less than 15.45 or more than 16.65 ounces is considered to be a defect. Using Excel, it can be shown that 99.9999998% of the boxes filled will have between $16.05 - 6(.10) = 15.45$ ounces and $16.05 + 6(.10) = 16.65$ ounces. In other words, only .0000002% of the boxes filled will contain less than 15.45 ounces or more than 16.65 ounces. Thus, the likelihood of obtaining a defective box of cereal from the filling process appears to be extremely unlikely, because on average only two boxes in 10 million will be defective.

Using Excel, NORM.S.DIST (6,TRUE)−NORM.S.DIST (−6,TRUE) = .999999998.

Motorola's early work on Six Sigma convinced them that a process mean can shift on average by as much as 1.5 standard deviations. For instance, suppose that the process mean for KJW increases by 1.5 standard deviations or $1.5(.10) = .15$ ounces. With such a shift, the normal distribution of filling weights would now be centered at $\mu = 16.05 + .15 = 16.20$ ounces. With a process mean of $\mu = 16.05$ ounces, the probability of obtaining a box

Using Excel, 1−NORM.S.DIST (4.5,TRUE) = .0000034.

FIGURE 19.1   NORMAL DISTRIBUTION OF CEREAL BOX FILLING WEIGHTS WITH A PROCESS MEAN $\mu = 16.05$

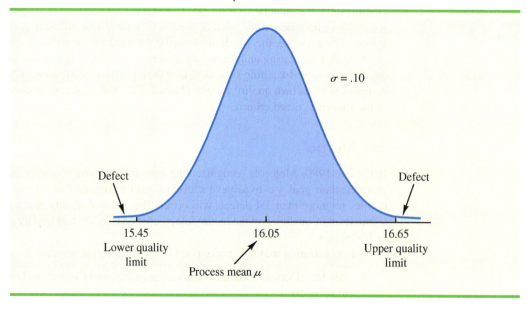

FIGURE 19.2 NORMAL DISTRIBUTION OF CEREAL BOX FILLING WEIGHTS WITH A PROCESS MEAN $\mu = 16.20$

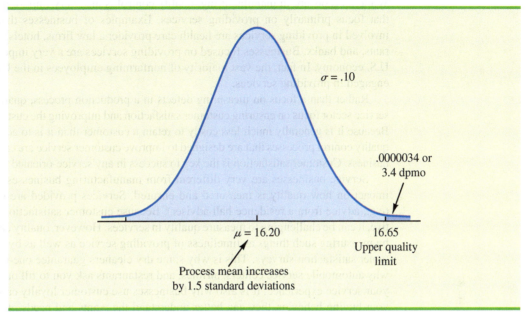

$\sigma = .10$

.0000034 or
3.4 dpmo

$\mu = 16.20$

16.65
Upper quality
limit

Process mean increases
by 1.5 standard deviations

of cereal with more than 16.65 ounces is extremely small. But how does this probability change if the mean of the process shifts up to $\mu = 16.20$ ounces? Figure 19.2 shows that for this case, the upper quality limit of 16.65 is 4.5 standard deviations to the right of the new mean $\mu = 16.20$ ounces. Using this mean and Excel, we find that the probability of obtaining a box with more than 16.65 ounces is .0000034. Thus, if the process mean shifts up by 1.5 standard deviations, approximately $1,000,000(.0000034) = 3.4$ boxes of cereal will exceed the upper limit of 16.65 ounces. In Six Sigma terminology, the quality level of the process is said to be 3.4 defects per million opportunities. If management of KJW considers 15.45 to 16.65 ounces to be acceptable quality limits for the filling process, the KJW filling process would be considered a Six Sigma process. Thus, if the process mean stays within 1.5 standard deviations of its target value $\mu = 16.05$ ounces, a maximum of only 3.4 defects per million boxes filled can be expected.

Organizations that want to achieve and maintain a Six Sigma level of quality must emphasize methods for monitoring and maintaining quality. *Quality assurance* refers to the entire system of policies, procedures, and guidelines established by an organization to achieve and maintain quality. Quality assurance consists of two principal functions: quality engineering and quality control. The object of *quality engineering* is to include quality in the design of products and processes and to identify quality problems prior to production. **Quality control** consists of a series of inspections and measurements used to determine whether quality standards are being met. If quality standards are not being met, corrective or preventive action can be taken to achieve and maintain conformance. In the next two sections we present two statistical methods used in quality control. The first method, *statistical process control,* uses graphical displays known as control charts to monitor a process; the goal is to determine whether the process can be continued or whether corrective action should be taken to achieve a desired quality level. The second method, *acceptance sampling,* is used in situations where a decision to accept or reject a group of items must be based on the quality found in a sample.

Quality in the Service Sector

While its roots are in manufacturing, quality control is also very important for businesses that focus primarily on providing services. Examples of businesses that are primarily involved in providing services are health care providers, law firms, hotels, airlines, restaurants, and banks. Businesses focused on providing services are a very important part of the U.S. economy. In fact, the vast majority of nonfarming employees in the United States are engaged in providing services.

Rather than a focus on measuring defects in a production process, quality efforts in the service sector focus on ensuring customer satisfaction and improving the customer experience. Because it is generally much less costly to retain a customer than it is to acquire a new one, quality control processes that are designed to improve customer service are critical to a service business. Customer satisfaction is the key to success in any service-oriented business.

Service businesses are very different from manufacturing businesses and this has an impact on how quality is measured and ensured. Services provided are often intangible (e.g., advice from a residence hall adviser). Because customer satisfaction is very subjective, it can be challenging to measure quality in services. However, quality can be monitored by measuring such things as timeliness of providing service as well as by conducting customer satisfaction surveys. This is why some dry cleaners guarantee one-hour service and why automobile service centers, airlines, and restaurants ask you to fill out a survey about your service experience. It is also why businesses use customer loyalty cards. By tracking your buying behavior, they can better understand the wants and needs of their customers and consequently provide better service.

19.2 Statistical Process Control

In this section we consider quality control procedures for a production process whereby goods are manufactured continuously. On the basis of sampling and inspection of production output, a decision will be made to either continue the production process or adjust it to bring the items or goods being produced up to acceptable quality standards.

Continuous improvement is one of the most important concepts of the total quality management movement. The most important use of a control chart is in improving the process.

Despite high standards of quality in manufacturing and production operations, machine tools will invariably wear out, vibrations will throw machine settings out of adjustment, purchased materials will be defective, and human operators will make mistakes. Any or all of these factors can result in poor quality output. Fortunately, procedures are available for monitoring production output so that poor quality can be detected early and the production process can be adjusted or corrected.

If the variation in the quality of the production output is due to **assignable causes** such as tools wearing out, incorrect machine settings, poor quality raw materials, or operator error, the process should be adjusted or corrected as soon as possible. Alternatively, if the variation is due to what are called **common causes**—that is, randomly occurring variations in materials, temperature, humidity, and so on, which the manufacturer cannot possibly control—the process does not need to be adjusted. The main objective of statistical process control is to determine whether variations in output are due to assignable causes or common causes.

Whenever assignable causes are detected, we conclude that the process is *out of control.* In that case, corrective action will be taken to bring the process back to an acceptable level of quality. However, if the variation in the output of a production process is due only to common causes, we conclude that the process is *in statistical control,* or simply *in control;* in such cases, no changes or adjustments are necessary.

Process control procedures are closely related to hypothesis testing procedures discussed earlier in this text. Control charts provide an ongoing test of the hypothesis that the process is in control.

The statistical procedures for process control are based on the hypothesis testing methodology presented in Chapter 9. The null hypothesis H_0 is formulated in terms of the production process being in control. The alternative hypothesis H_a is formulated in terms of the

TABLE 19.1   THE OUTCOMES OF STATISTICAL PROCESS CONTROL

		State of Production Process	
		H_0 **True** **Process in Control**	H_0 **False** **Process Out of Control**
	Continue Process	Correct decision	Type II error (allowing an out-of-control process to continue)
Decision			
	Adjust Process	Type I error (adjusting an in-control process)	Correct decision

production process being out of control. Table 19.1 shows that correct decisions to continue an in-control process and adjust an out-of-control process are possible. However, as with other hypothesis testing procedures, both a Type I error (adjusting an in-control process) and a Type II error (allowing an out-of-control process to continue) are also possible.

Control Charts

A **control chart** provides a basis for deciding whether the variation in the output is due to common causes (in control) or assignable causes (out of control). Whenever an out-of-control situation is detected, adjustments or other corrective action will be taken to bring the process back into control.

Control charts based on data that can be measured on a continuous scale are called variables control charts. The $\bar{x}$ chart is a variables control chart.

Control charts can be classified by the type of data they contain. An $\bar{x}$ **chart** is used if the quality of the output of the process is measured in terms of a variable such as length, weight, temperature, and so on. In that case, the decision to continue or to adjust the production process will be based on the mean value found in a sample of the output. To introduce some of the concepts common to all control charts, let us consider some specific features of an $\bar{x}$ chart.

Figure 19.3 shows the general structure of an $\bar{x}$ chart. The center line of the chart corresponds to the mean of the process when the process is *in control*. The vertical line identifies the scale of measurement for the variable of interest. Each time a sample is taken from the production process, a value of the sample mean $\bar{x}$ is computed and a data point showing the value of $\bar{x}$ is plotted on the control chart.

FIGURE 19.3 $\bar{x}$ CHART STRUCTURE

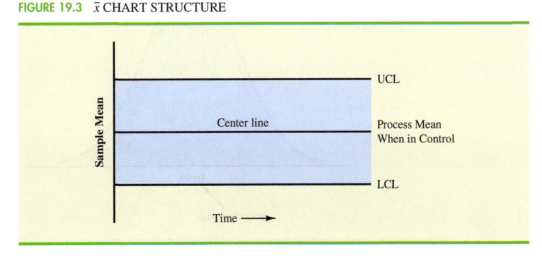

The two lines labeled UCL and LCL are important in determining whether the process is in control or out of control. The lines are called the *upper control limit* and the *lower control limit,* respectively. They are chosen so that when the process is in control, there will be a high probability that the value of $\bar{x}$ will be between the two control limits. Values outside the control limits provide strong statistical evidence that the process is out of control and corrective action should be taken.

Over time, more and more data points will be added to the control chart. The order of the data points will be from left to right as the process is sampled. In essence, every time a point is plotted on the control chart, we are carrying out a hypothesis test to determine whether the process is in control.

In addition to the $\bar{x}$ chart, other control charts can be used to monitor the range of the measurements in the sample (**R chart**), the proportion defective in the sample (**p chart**), and the number of defective items in the sample (**np chart**). In each case, the control chart has a LCL, a center line, and an UCL similar to the $\bar{x}$ chart in Figure 19.3. The major difference among the charts is what the vertical axis measures; for instance, in a p chart the measurement scale denotes the proportion of defective items in the sample instead of the sample mean. In the following discussion, we will illustrate the construction and use of the $\bar{x}$ chart, R chart, p chart, and np chart.

$\bar{x}$ Chart: Process Mean and Standard Deviation Known

To illustrate the construction of an $\bar{x}$ chart, let us reconsider the situation at KJW Packaging. Recall that KJW operates a production line where cartons of cereal are filled. When the process is operating correctly—and hence the system is in control—the mean filling weight is $\mu = 16.05$ ounces, and the process standard deviation is $\sigma = .10$ ounces. In addition, the filling weights are assumed to be normally distributed. This distribution is shown in Figure 19.4.

The sampling distribution of $\bar{x}$, as presented in Chapter 7, can be used to determine the variation that can be expected in $\bar{x}$ values for a process that is in control. Let us first briefly review the properties of the sampling distribution of $\bar{x}$. First, recall that the expected value or mean of $\bar{x}$ is equal to μ, the mean filling weight when the production line is in control.

FIGURE 19.4 NORMAL DISTRIBUTION OF CEREAL CARTON FILLING WEIGHTS

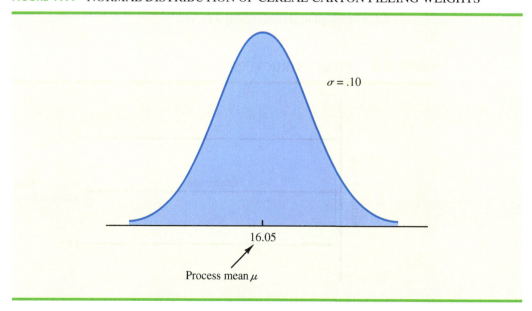

FIGURE 19.5   SAMPLING DISTRIBUTION OF $\bar{x}$ FOR A SAMPLE OF n FILLING WEIGHTS

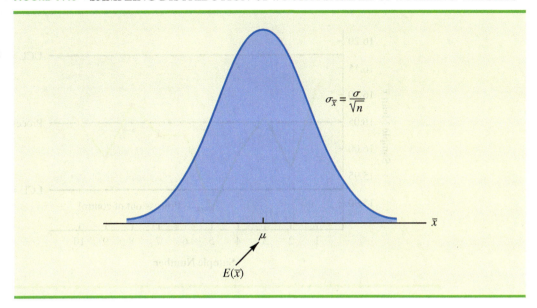

For samples of size n, the equation for the standard deviation of $\bar{x}$, called the standard error of the mean, is

$$\sigma_{\bar{x}} = \frac{\sigma}{\sqrt{n}} \qquad \textbf{(19.1)}$$

In addition, because the filling weights are normally distributed, the sampling distribution of $\bar{x}$ is normally distributed for any sample size. Thus, the sampling distribution of $\bar{x}$ is a normal distribution with mean μ and standard deviation $\sigma_{\bar{x}}$. This distribution is shown in Figure 19.5.

The sampling distribution of $\bar{x}$ is used to determine what values of $\bar{x}$ are reasonable if the process is in control. The general practice in quality control is to define as reasonable any value of $\bar{x}$ that is within 3 standard deviations, or standard errors, above or below the mean value. Recall from the study of the normal probability distribution that approximately 99.7% of the values of a normally distributed random variable are within ± 3 standard deviations of its mean value. Thus, if a value of $\bar{x}$ is within the interval $\mu - 3\sigma_{\bar{x}}$ to $\mu + 3\sigma_{\bar{x}}$, we will assume that the process is in control. In summary, then, the control limits for an $\bar{x}$ chart are as follows:

CONTROL LIMITS FOR AN $\bar{x}$ CHART: PROCESS MEAN AND STANDARD DEVIATION KNOWN

$$\text{UCL} = \mu + 3\sigma_{\bar{x}} \qquad \textbf{(19.2)}$$

$$\text{LCL} = \mu - 3\sigma_{\bar{x}} \qquad \textbf{(19.3)}$$

Reconsider the KJW Packaging example with the process distribution of filling weights shown in Figure 19.4 and the sampling distribution of $\bar{x}$ shown in Figure 19.5. Assume that a quality control inspector periodically samples six cartons and uses the sample mean filling weight to determine whether the process is in control or out of control. Using equation (19.1), we find that the standard error of the mean is $\sigma_{\bar{x}} = \sigma/\sqrt{n} = .10/\sqrt{6} = .04$. Thus, with the process mean at 16.05, the control limits are UCL $= 16.05 + 3(.04) = 16.17$

FIGURE 19.6   THE $\bar{x}$ CHART FOR THE CEREAL CARTON FILLING PROCESS

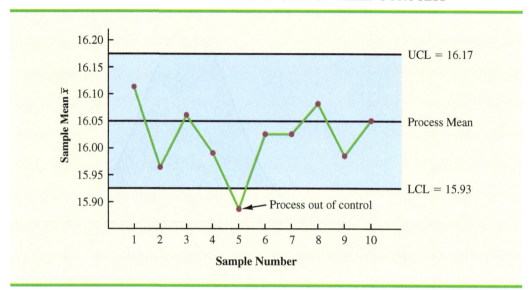

and LCL $= 16.05 - 3(.04) = 15.93$. Figure 19.6 is the control chart with the results of 10 samples taken over a 10-hour period. For ease of reading, the sample numbers 1 through 10 are listed below the chart.

Note that the mean for the fifth sample in Figure 19.6 shows there is strong evidence that the process is out of control. The fifth sample mean is below the LCL, indicating that assignable causes of output variation are present and that underfilling is occurring. As a result, corrective action was taken at this point to bring the process back into control. The fact that the remaining points on the $\bar{x}$ chart are within the upper and lower control limits indicates that the corrective action was successful.

$\bar{x}$ Chart: Process Mean and Standard Deviation Unknown

In the KJW Packaging example, we showed how an $\bar{x}$ chart can be developed when the mean and standard deviation of the process are known. In most situations, the process mean and standard deviation must be estimated by using samples that are selected from the process when it is in control. For instance, KJW might select a random sample of five boxes each morning and five boxes each afternoon for 10 days of in-control operation. For each subgroup, or sample, the mean and standard deviation of the sample are computed. The overall averages of both the sample means and the sample standard deviations are used to construct control charts for both the process mean and the process standard deviation.

It is important to maintain control over both the mean and the variability of a process.

In practice, it is more common to monitor the variability of the process by using the range instead of the standard deviation because the range is easier to compute. The range can be used to provide good estimates of the process standard deviation; thus it can be used to construct upper and lower control limits for the $\bar{x}$ chart with little computational effort. To illustrate, let us consider the problem facing Jensen Computer Supplies, Inc.

Jensen Computer Supplies (JCS) manufactures 3.5-inch-diameter solid-state drives; they just finished adjusting their production process so that it is operating in control. Suppose random samples of five drives were selected during the first hour of operation, five drives were selected during the second hour of operation, and so on, until 20 samples were obtained. Table 19.2 provides the diameter of each drive sampled as well as the mean $\bar{x}_j$ and range R_j for each of the samples.

TABLE 19.2   DATA FOR THE JENSEN COMPUTER SUPPLIES PROBLEM

Sample Number	Observations					Sample Mean $\bar{x}_j$	Sample Range R_j
1	3.5056	3.5086	3.5144	3.5009	3.5030	3.5065	.0135
2	3.4882	3.5085	3.4884	3.5250	3.5031	3.5026	.0368
3	3.4897	3.4898	3.4995	3.5130	3.4969	3.4978	.0233
4	3.5153	3.5120	3.4989	3.4900	3.4837	3.5000	.0316
5	3.5059	3.5113	3.5011	3.4773	3.4801	3.4951	.0340
6	3.4977	3.4961	3.5050	3.5014	3.5060	3.5012	.0099
7	3.4910	3.4913	3.4976	3.4831	3.5044	3.4935	.0213
8	3.4991	3.4853	3.4830	3.5083	3.5094	3.4970	.0264
9	3.5099	3.5162	3.5228	3.4958	3.5004	3.5090	.0270
10	3.4880	3.5015	3.5094	3.5102	3.5146	3.5047	.0266
11	3.4881	3.4887	3.5141	3.5175	3.4863	3.4989	.0312
12	3.5043	3.4867	3.4946	3.5018	3.4784	3.4932	.0259
13	3.5043	3.4769	3.4944	3.5014	3.4904	3.4935	.0274
14	3.5004	3.5030	3.5082	3.5045	3.5234	3.5079	.0230
15	3.4846	3.4938	3.5065	3.5089	3.5011	3.4990	.0243
16	3.5145	3.4832	3.5188	3.4935	3.4989	3.5018	.0356
17	3.5004	3.5042	3.4954	3.5020	3.4889	3.4982	.0153
18	3.4959	3.4823	3.4964	3.5082	3.4871	3.4940	.0259
19	3.4878	3.4864	3.4960	3.5070	3.4984	3.4951	.0206
20	3.4969	3.5144	3.5053	3.4985	3.4885	3.5007	.0259

DATA *file*

Jensen

The estimate of the process mean μ is given by the overall sample mean.

> **OVERALL SAMPLE MEAN**
>
> $$\bar{\bar{x}} = \frac{\bar{x}_1 + \bar{x}_2 + \cdots + \bar{x}_k}{k} \tag{19.4}$$
>
> where
>
> $\bar{x}_j$ = mean of the jth sample $j = 1, 2, \ldots, k$
> k = number of samples

For the JCS data in Table 19.2, the overall sample mean is $\bar{\bar{x}} = 3.4995$. This value will be the center line for the $\bar{x}$ chart. The range of each sample, denoted R_j, is simply the difference between the largest and smallest values in each sample. The average range for k samples is computed as follows:

> **AVERAGE RANGE**
>
> $$\bar{R} = \frac{R_1 + R_2 + \cdots + R_k}{k} \tag{19.5}$$
>
> where
>
> R_j = range of the jth sample, $j = 1, 2, \ldots, k$
> k = number of samples

For the JCS data in Table 19.2, the average range is $\overline{R} = .0253$.

In the preceding section we showed that the upper and lower control limits for the $\overline{x}$ chart are

$$\overline{x} \pm 3 \frac{\sigma}{\sqrt{n}} \qquad (19.6)$$

The overall sample mean $\overline{\overline{x}}$ is used to estimate μ and the sample ranges are used to develop an estimate of σ.

Hence, to construct the control limits for the $\overline{x}$ chart, we need to estimate μ and σ, the mean and standard deviation of the process. An estimate of μ is given by $\overline{\overline{x}}$. An estimate of σ can be developed by using the range data.

It can be shown that an estimator of the process standard deviation σ is the average range divided by d_2, a constant that depends on the sample size n. That is,

$$\text{Estimator of } \sigma = \frac{\overline{R}}{d_2} \qquad (19.7)$$

The *American Society for Testing and Materials Manual on Presentation of Data and Control Chart Analysis* provides values for d_2 as shown in Table 19.3. For instance, when $n = 5$, $d_2 = 2.326$, and the estimate of σ is the average range divided by 2.326.

TABLE 19.3 FACTORS FOR $\overline{x}$ AND R CONTROL CHARTS

Observations in Sample, n	d_2	A_2	d_3	D_3	D_4
2	1.128	1.880	0.853	0	3.267
3	1.693	1.023	0.888	0	2.574
4	2.059	0.729	0.880	0	2.282
5	2.326	0.577	0.864	0	2.114
6	2.534	0.483	0.848	0	2.004
7	2.704	0.419	0.833	0.076	1.924
8	2.847	0.373	0.820	0.136	1.864
9	2.970	0.337	0.808	0.184	1.816
10	3.078	0.308	0.797	0.223	1.777
11	3.173	0.285	0.787	0.256	1.744
12	3.258	0.266	0.778	0.283	1.717
13	3.336	0.249	0.770	0.307	1.693
14	3.407	0.235	0.763	0.328	1.672
15	3.472	0.223	0.756	0.347	1.653
16	3.532	0.212	0.750	0.363	1.637
17	3.588	0.203	0.744	0.378	1.622
18	3.640	0.194	0.739	0.391	1.608
19	3.689	0.187	0.734	0.403	1.597
20	3.735	0.180	0.729	0.415	1.585
21	3.778	0.173	0.724	0.425	1.575
22	3.819	0.167	0.720	0.434	1.566
23	3.858	0.162	0.716	0.443	1.557
24	3.895	0.157	0.712	0.451	1.548
25	3.931	0.153	0.708	0.459	1.541

Source: Reprinted with permission from Table 27 of ASTM STP 15D, *ASTM Manual on Presentation of Data and Control Chart Analysis,* Copyright ASTM International, 100 Barr Harbor Drive, West Conshohocken, PA 19428.

FIGURE 19.7 $\bar{x}$ CHART FOR THE JENSEN COMPUTER SUPPLIES PROBLEM

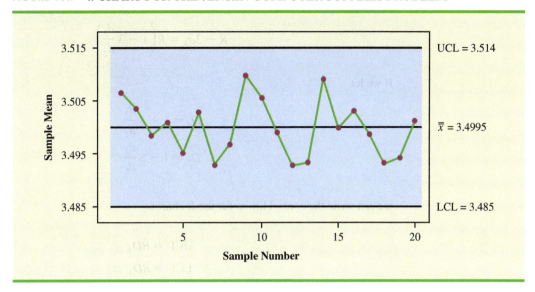

If we substitute $\bar{R}/d_2$ for σ in expression (19.6), we can write the control limits for the $\bar{x}$ chart as

$$\bar{\bar{x}} \pm 3\,\frac{\bar{R}/d_2}{\sqrt{n}} = \bar{\bar{x}} \pm \frac{3}{d_2\sqrt{n}}\,\bar{R} = \bar{\bar{x}} \pm A_2\bar{R} \tag{19.8}$$

Note that $A_2 = 3/(d_2\sqrt{n})$ is a constant that depends only on the sample size. Values for A_2 are provided in Table 19.3. For $n = 5$, $A_2 = .577$; thus, the control limits for the $\bar{x}$ chart are

$$3.4995 \pm (.577)(.0253) = 3.4995 \pm .0146$$

Hence, UCL = 3.514 and LCL = 3.485.

Figure 19.7 shows the $\bar{x}$ chart for the Jensen Computer Supplies problem. The center line is shown at the overall sample mean $\bar{\bar{x}} = 3.4995$. The upper control limit (UCL) is 3.514 and the lower control (LCL) is 3.485. The $\bar{x}$ chart shows the 20 sample means plotted over time. Because all 20 sample means are within the control limits, we confirm that the process mean was in control during the sampling period.

R **Chart**

Let us now consider a range chart (R chart) that can be used to control the variability of a process. To develop the R chart, we need to think of the range of a sample as a random variable with its own mean and standard deviation. The average range $\bar{R}$ provides an estimate of the mean of this random variable. Moreover, it can be shown that an estimate of the standard deviation of the range is

$$\hat{\sigma}_R = d_3\,\frac{\bar{R}}{d_2} \tag{19.9}$$

where d_2 and d_3 are constants that depend on the sample size; values of d_2 and d_3 are provided in Table 19.3. Thus, the UCL for the R chart is given by

$$\bar{R} + 3\hat{\sigma}_R = \bar{R}\!\left(1 + 3\,\frac{d_3}{d_2}\right) \tag{19.10}$$

and the LCL is

$$\overline{R} - 3\hat{\sigma}_R = \overline{R}\left(1 - 3\frac{d_3}{d_2}\right) \qquad (19.11)$$

If we let

$$D_4 = 1 + 3\frac{d_3}{d_2} \qquad (19.12)$$

$$D_3 = 1 - 3\frac{d_3}{d_2} \qquad (19.13)$$

we can write the control limits for the R chart as

$$UCL = \overline{R}D_4 \qquad (19.14)$$

$$LCL = \overline{R}D_3 \qquad (19.15)$$

Values for D_3 and D_4 are also provided in Table 19.3. Note that for $n = 5$, $D_3 = 0$ and $D_4 = 2.114$. Thus, with $\overline{R} = .0253$, the control limits are

$$UCL = .0253(2.114) = .053$$
$$LCL = .0253(0) = 0$$

If the R chart indicates that the process is out of control, the x̄ chart should not be interpreted until the R chart indicates the process variability is in control.

Figure 19.8 shows the R chart for the Jensen Computer Supplies problem. The center line is shown at the overall mean of the 20 sample ranges, $\overline{R} = .0253$. The UCL is .053 and the LCL is .000. The R chart shows the 20 sample ranges plotted over time. Because all 20 sample ranges are within the control limits, we confirm that the process variability was in control during the sampling period.

FIGURE 19.8 R CHART FOR THE JENSEN COMPUTER SUPPLIES PROBLEM

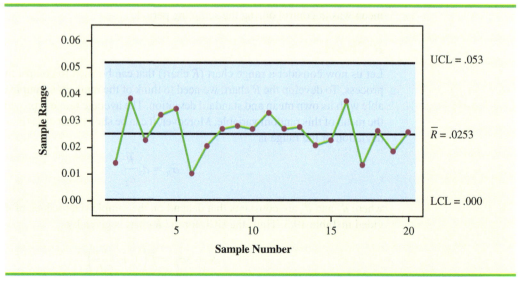

p **Chart**

Control charts that are based on data indicating the presence of a defect or a number of defects are called attributes control charts. A p chart is an attributes control chart.

Let us consider the case in which the output quality is measured by either nondefective or defective items. The decision to continue or to adjust the production process will be based on $\bar{p}$, the proportion of defective items found in a sample. The control chart used for proportion-defective data is called a p chart.

To illustrate the construction of a p chart, consider the use of automated mail-sorting machines in a post office. These automated machines scan the zip codes on letters and divert each letter to its proper carrier route. Even when a machine is operating properly, some letters are diverted to incorrect routes. Assume that when a machine is operating correctly, or in a state of control, 3% of the letters are incorrectly diverted. Thus p, the proportion of letters incorrectly diverted when the process is in control, is .03.

The sampling distribution of $\bar{p}$, as presented in Chapter 7, can be used to determine the variation that can be expected in $\bar{p}$ values for a process that is in control. Recall that the expected value or mean of $\bar{p}$ is p, the proportion defective when the process is in control. With samples of size n, the formula for the standard deviation of $\bar{p}$, called the standard error of the proportion, is

$$\sigma_{\bar{p}} = \sqrt{\frac{p(1-p)}{n}} \qquad\qquad \textbf{(19.16)}$$

We also learned in Chapter 7 that the sampling distribution of $\bar{p}$ can be approximated by a normal distribution whenever the sample size is large. With $\bar{p}$, the sample size can be considered large whenever the following two conditions are satisfied.

$$np \geq 5$$
$$n(1-p) \geq 5$$

In summary, whenever the sample size is large, the sampling distribution of $\bar{p}$ can be approximated by a normal distribution with mean p and standard deviation $\sigma_{\bar{p}}$. This distribution is shown in Figure 19.9.

FIGURE 19.9   SAMPLING DISTRIBUTION OF $\bar{p}$

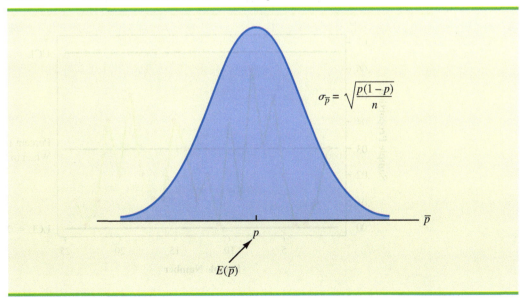

To establish control limits for a p chart, we follow the same procedure we used to establish control limits for an chart. That is, the limits for the control chart are set at 3 standard deviations, or standard errors, above and below the proportion defective when the process is in control. Thus, we have the following control limits.

CONTROL LIMITS FOR A p CHART

$$UCL = p + 3\sigma_{\bar{p}} \qquad\qquad \text{(19.17)}$$
$$LCL = p - 3\sigma_{\bar{p}} \qquad\qquad \text{(19.18)}$$

With $p = .03$ and samples of size $n = 200$, equation (19.16) shows that the standard error is

$$\sigma_{\bar{p}} = \sqrt{\frac{.03(1 - .03)}{200}} = .0121$$

Hence, the control limits are UCL $= .03 + 3(.0121) = .0663$ and LCL $= .03 - 3(.0121) = -.0063$. Whenever equation (19.18) provides a negative value for LCL, LCL is set equal to zero in the control chart.

Figure 19.10 is the p chart for the mail-sorting process. The points plotted show the sample proportion defective found in samples of letters taken from the process. All points are within the control limits, providing no evidence to conclude that the sorting process is out of control.

If the proportion of defective items for a process that is in control is not known, that value is first estimated by using sample data. Suppose, for example, that k different samples, each of size n, are selected from a process that is in control. The fraction or proportion of defective items in each sample is then determined. Treating all the data collected as one large sample, we can compute the proportion of defective items for all the data; that value can then be used to estimate p, the proportion of defective items observed when the process is in control. Note that this estimate of p also enables us to estimate the standard error of the proportion; upper and lower control limits can then be established.

FIGURE 19.10 p CHART FOR THE PROPORTION DEFECTIVE IN A MAIL-SORTING PROCESS

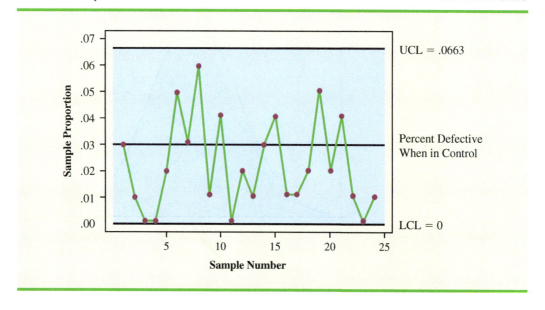

np **Chart**

An *np* chart is a control chart developed for the number of defective items in a sample. In this case, *n* is the sample size and *p* is the probability of observing a defective item when the process is in control. Whenever the sample size is large, that is, when $np \geq 5$ and $n(1 - p) \geq 5$, the distribution of the number of defective items observed in a sample of size *n* can be approximated by a normal distribution with mean *np* and standard deviation $\sqrt{np(1 - p)}$. Thus, for the mail-sorting example, with $n = 200$ and $p = .03$, the number of defective items observed in a sample of 200 letters can be approximated by a normal distribution with a mean of $200(.03) = 6$ and a standard deviation of $\sqrt{200(.03)(.97)} = 2.4125$.

The control limits for an *np* chart are set at 3 standard deviations above and below the expected number of defective items observed when the process is in control. Thus, we have the following control limits.

> **CONTROL LIMITS FOR AN *np* CHART**
>
> $$UCL = np + 3\sqrt{np(1 - p)} \qquad \textbf{(19.19)}$$
> $$LCL = np - 3\sqrt{np(1 - p)} \qquad \textbf{(19.20)}$$

For the mail-sorting process example, with $p = .03$ and $n = 200$, the control limits are $UCL = 6 + 3(2.4125) = 13.2375$ and $LCL = 6 - 3(2.4125) = -1.2375$. When LCL is negative, LCL is set equal to zero in the control chart. Hence, if the number of letters diverted to incorrect routes is greater than 13, the process is concluded to be out of control.

The information provided by an *np* chart is equivalent to the information provided by the *p* chart; the only difference is that the *np* chart is a plot of the number of defective items observed, whereas the *p* chart is a plot of the proportion of defective items observed. Thus, if we were to conclude that a particular process is out of control on the basis of a *p* chart, the process would also be concluded to be out of control on the basis of an *np* chart.

Interpretation of Control Charts

The location and pattern of points in a control chart enable us to determine, with a small probability of error, whether a process is in statistical control. A primary indication that a process may be out of control is a data point outside the control limits, such as point 5 in Figure 19.6. Finding such a point is statistical evidence that the process is out of control; in such cases, corrective action should be taken as soon as possible.

In addition to points outside the control limits, certain patterns of the points within the control limits can be warning signals of quality control problems. For example, assume that all the data points are within the control limits but that a large number of points are on one side of the center line. This pattern may indicate that an equipment problem, a change in materials, or some other assignable cause of a shift in quality has occurred. Careful investigation of the production process should be undertaken to determine whether quality has changed.

Even if all points are within the upper and lower control limits, a process may not be in control. Trends in the sample data points or unusually long runs above or below the center line may also indicate out-of-control conditions.

Another pattern to watch for in control charts is a gradual shift, or trend, over time. For example, as tools wear out, the dimensions of machined parts will gradually deviate from their designed levels. Gradual changes in temperature or humidity, general equipment deterioration, dirt buildup, or operator fatigue may also result in a trend pattern in control charts. Six or seven points in a row that indicate either an increasing or decreasing trend should be cause for concern, even if the data points are all within the control limits. When such a pattern occurs, the process should be reviewed for possible changes or shifts in quality. Corrective action to bring the process back into control may be necessary.

NOTES AND COMMENTS

1. Because the control limits for the $\bar{x}$ chart depend on the value of the average range, these limits will not have much meaning unless the process variability is in control. In practice, the R chart is usually constructed before the $\bar{x}$ chart; if the R chart indicates that the process variability is in control, then the $\bar{x}$ chart is constructed.

2. An np chart is used to monitor a process in terms of the number of defects. The Motorola Six Sigma Quality Level sets a goal of producing no more than 3.4 defects per million operations; this goal implies $p = .0000034$.

Exercises

Methods

1. A process that is in control has a mean of $\mu = 12.5$ and a standard deviation of $\sigma = .8$.
   a. Construct the $\bar{x}$ control chart for this process if samples of size 4 are to be used.
   b. Repeat part (a) for samples of size 8 and 16.
   c. What happens to the limits of the control chart as the sample size is increased? Discuss why this is reasonable.

2. Twenty-five samples, each of size 5, were selected from a process that was in control. The sum of all the data collected was 677.5 pounds.
   a. What is an estimate of the process mean (in terms of pounds per unit) when the process is in control?
   b. Develop the $\bar{x}$ control chart for this process if samples of size 5 will be used. Assume that the process standard deviation is .5 when the process is in control, and that the mean of the process is the estimate developed in part (a).

3. Twenty-five samples of 100 items each were inspected when a process was considered to be operating satisfactorily. In the 25 samples, a total of 135 items were found to be defective.
   a. What is an estimate of the proportion defective when the process is in control?
   b. What is the standard error of the proportion if samples of size 100 will be used for statistical process control?
   c. Compute the upper and lower control limits for the control chart.

SELF*test*

4. A process sampled 20 times with a sample of size 8 resulted in $\bar{\bar{x}} = 28.5$ and $\overline{R} = 1.6$. Compute the upper and lower control limits for the $\bar{x}$ and R charts for this process.

Applications

5. Temperature is used to measure the output of a production process. When the process is in control, the mean of the process is $\mu = 128.5$ and the standard deviation is $\sigma = .4$.
   a. Construct the $\bar{x}$ chart for this process if samples of size 6 are to be used.
   b. Is the process in control for a sample providing the following data?

128.8	128.2	129.1	128.7	128.4	129.2

   c. Is the process in control for a sample providing the following data?

129.3	128.7	128.6	129.2	129.5	129.0

6. A quality control process monitors the weight per carton of laundry detergent. Control limits are set at UCL = 20.12 ounces and LCL = 19.90 ounces. Samples of size 5 are

used for the sampling and inspection process. What are the process mean and process standard deviation for the manufacturing operation?

7. The Goodman Tire and Rubber Company periodically tests its tires for tread wear under simulated road conditions. To study and control the manufacturing process, 20 samples, each containing three radial tires, were chosen from different shifts over several days of operation, with the following results. Assuming that these data were collected when the manufacturing process was believed to be operating in control, develop the R and $\bar{x}$ charts.

Tires

Sample	Tread Wear*		
1	31	42	28
2	26	18	35
3	25	30	34
4	17	25	21
5	38	29	35
6	41	42	36
7	21	17	29
8	32	26	28
9	41	34	33
10	29	17	30
11	26	31	40
12	23	19	25
13	17	24	32
14	43	35	17
15	18	25	29
16	30	42	31
17	28	36	32
18	40	29	31
19	18	29	28
20	22	34	26

*Hundredths of an inch

8. Over several weeks of normal, or in-control, operation, 20 samples of 150 packages each of synthetic-gut tennis strings were tested for breaking strength. A total of 141 packages of the 3000 tested failed to conform to the manufacturer's specifications.
    a. What is an estimate of the process proportion defective when the system is in control?
    b. Compute the upper and lower control limits for a p chart.
    c. With the results of part (b), what conclusion should be made about the process if tests on a new sample of 150 packages find 12 defective? Do there appear to be assignable causes in this situation?
    d. Compute the upper and lower control limits for an np chart.
    e. Answer part (c) using the results of part (d).
    f. Which control chart would be preferred in this situation? Explain.

9. An airline operates a call center to handle customer questions and complaints. The airline monitors a sample of calls to help ensure that the service being provided is of high quality. Ten random samples of 100 calls each were monitored under normal conditions. The center can be thought of as being in control when these 10 samples were taken. The number of calls in each sample not resulting in a satisfactory resolution for the customer is as follows:

    4   5   3   2   3   3   4   6   4   7

    a. What is an estimate of the proportion of calls not resulting in a satisfactory outcome for the customer when the center is in control?

b. Construct the upper and lower limits for a *p* chart for the manufacturing process, assuming each sample has 100 calls.

c. With the results of part (b), what conclusion should be made if a sample of 100 has 12 calls not resulting in a satisfactory resolution for the customer?

d. Compute the upper and lower limits for the *np* chart.

e. With the results of part (d), what conclusion should be made if a sample of 100 calls has 12 not resulting in a satisfactory conclusion for the customer?

 # Acceptance Sampling

In acceptance sampling, the items of interest can be incoming shipments of raw materials or purchased parts as well as finished goods from final assembly. Suppose we want to decide whether to accept or reject a group of items on the basis of specified quality characteristics. In quality control terminology, the group of items is a **lot**, and **acceptance sampling** is a statistical method that enables us to base the accept-reject decision on the inspection of a sample of items from the lot.

The general steps of acceptance sampling are shown in Figure 19.11. After a lot is received, a sample of items is selected for inspection. The results of the inspection are compared to specified quality characteristics. If the quality characteristics are satisfied, the lot is accepted and sent to production or shipped to customers. If the lot is rejected, managers must decide on its disposition. In some cases, the decision may be to keep the lot and remove the unacceptable or nonconforming items. In other cases, the lot may be returned to the supplier at

FIGURE 19.11   ACCEPTANCE SAMPLING PROCEDURE

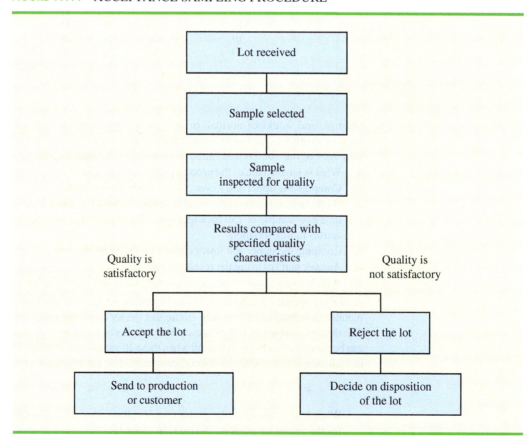

TABLE 19.4   THE OUTCOMES OF ACCEPTANCE SAMPLING

	State of the Lot	
	H_0 True Good-Quality Lot	H_0 False Poor-Quality Lot
Decision		
Accept the Lot	Correct decision	Type II error (accepting a poor-quality lot)
Reject the Lot	Type I error (rejecting a good-quality lot)	Correct decision

the supplier's expense; the extra work and cost placed on the supplier can motivate the supplier to provide high-quality lots. Finally, if the rejected lot consists of finished goods, the goods must be scrapped or reworked to meet acceptable quality standards.

The statistical procedure of acceptance sampling is based on the hypothesis testing methodology presented in Chapter 9. The null and alternative hypotheses are stated as follows:

$$H_0: \text{Good-quality lot}$$
$$H_a: \text{Poor-quality lot}$$

Acceptance sampling has the following advantages over 100% inspection:
1. Usually less expensive
2. Less product damage due to less handling and testing
3. Fewer inspectors required
4. The only approach possible if destructive testing must be used

Table 19.4 shows the results of the hypothesis testing procedure. Note that correct decisions correspond to accepting a good-quality lot and rejecting a poor-quality lot. However, as with other hypothesis testing procedures, we need to be aware of the possibilities of making a Type I error (rejecting a good-quality lot) or a Type II error (accepting a poor-quality lot).

The probability of a Type I error creates a risk for the producer of the lot and is known as the **producer's risk**. For example, a producer's risk of .05 indicates a 5% chance that a good-quality lot will be erroneously rejected. The probability of a Type II error, on the other hand, creates a risk for the consumer of the lot and is known as the **consumer's risk**. For example, a consumer's risk of .10 means a 10% chance that a poor-quality lot will be erroneously accepted and thus used in production or shipped to the customer. Specific values for the producer's risk and the consumer's risk can be controlled by the person designing the acceptance sampling procedure. To illustrate how to assign risk values, let us consider the problem faced by KALI, Inc.

KALI, Inc.: An Example of Acceptance Sampling

KALI, Inc., manufactures home appliances that are marketed under a variety of trade names. However, KALI does not manufacture every component used in its products. Several components are purchased directly from suppliers. For example, one of the components that KALI purchases for use in home air conditioners is an overload protector, a device that turns off the compressor if it overheats. The compressor can be seriously damaged if the overload protector does not function properly, and therefore KALI is concerned about the quality of the overload protectors. One way to ensure quality would be to test every component received through an approach known as 100% inspection. However, to determine proper functioning of an overload protector, the device must be subjected to time-consuming and expensive tests, and KALI cannot justify testing every overload protector it receives.

Instead, KALI uses an acceptance sampling plan to monitor the quality of the overload protectors. The acceptance sampling plan requires that KALI's quality control inspectors select and test a sample of overload protectors from each shipment. If very few defective units are found in the sample, the lot is probably of good quality and should be accepted.

However, if a large number of defective units are found in the sample, the lot is probably of poor quality and should be rejected.

An acceptance sampling plan consists of a sample size n and an acceptance criterion c. The **acceptance criterion** is the maximum number of defective items that can be found in the sample and still indicate an acceptable lot. For example, for the KALI problem let us assume that a sample of 15 items will be selected from each incoming shipment or lot. Furthermore, assume that the manager of quality control states that the lot can be accepted only if no defective items are found. In this case, the acceptance sampling plan established by the quality control manager is $n = 15$ and $c = 0$.

This acceptance sampling plan is easy for the quality control inspector to implement. The inspector simply selects a sample of 15 items, performs the tests, and reaches a conclusion based on the following decision rule.

- *Accept the lot* if zero defective items are found.
- *Reject the lot* if one or more defective items are found.

Before implementing this acceptance sampling plan, the quality control manager wants to evaluate the risks or errors possible under the plan. The plan will be implemented only if both the producer's risk (Type I error) and the consumer's risk (Type II error) are controlled at reasonable levels.

Computing the Probability of Accepting a Lot

The key to analyzing both the producer's risk and the consumer's risk is a "what-if" type of analysis. That is, we will assume that a lot has some known percentage of defective items and compute the probability of accepting the lot for a given sampling plan. By varying the assumed percentage of defective items, we can examine the effect of the sampling plan on both types of risks.

Let us begin by assuming that a large shipment of overload protectors has been received and that 5% of the overload protectors in the shipment are defective. For a shipment or lot with 5% of the items defective, what is the probability that the $n = 15$, $c = 0$ sampling plan will lead us to accept the lot? Because each overload protector tested will be either defective or nondefective and because the lot size is large, the number of defective items in a sample of 15 has a *binomial distribution*. The binomial probability function, which was presented in Chapter 5, follows.

BINOMIAL PROBABILITY FUNCTION FOR ACCEPTANCE SAMPLING

$$f(x) = \frac{n!}{x!(n-x)!} p^x (1-p)^{(n-x)} \tag{19.21}$$

where

$n =$ the sample size
$p =$ the proportion of defective items in the lot
$x =$ the number of defective items in the sample
$f(x) =$ the probability of x defective items in the sample

For the KALI acceptance sampling plan, $n = 15$; thus, for a lot with 5% defective ($p = .05$), we have

$$f(x) = \frac{15!}{x!(15-x)!} (.05)^x (1 - .05)^{(15-x)} \tag{19.22}$$

TABLE 19.5 PROBABILITY OF ACCEPTING THE LOT FOR THE KALI PROBLEM WITH $n = 15$ AND $c = 0$

Percent Defective in the Lot	Probability of Accepting the Lot
1	.8601
2	.7386
3	.6333
4	.5421
5	.4633
10	.2059
15	.0874
20	.0352
25	.0134

Using equation (19.22), $f(0)$ will provide the probability that zero overload protectors will be defective and the lot will be accepted. In using equation (19.22), recall that $0! = 1$. Thus, the probability computation for $f(0)$ is

$$f(0) = \frac{15!}{0!(15-0)!}(.05)^0(1 - .05)^{(15-0)}$$

$$= \frac{15!}{0!(15)!}(.05)^0(.95)^{15} = (.95)^{15} = .4633$$

We now know that the $n = 15$, $c = 0$ sampling plan has a .4633 probability of accepting a lot with 5% defective items. Hence, there must be a corresponding $1 - .4633 = .5367$ probability of rejecting a lot with 5% defective items.

Excel's BINOM.DIST function can be used to simplify making these binomial probability calculations. Using this function, we can determine that if the lot contains 10% defective items, there is a .2059 probability that the $n = 15$, $c = 0$ sampling plan will indicate an acceptable lot. The probability that the $n = 15$, $c = 0$ sampling plan will lead to the acceptance of lots with 1%, 2%, 3%, ... defective items is summarized in Table 19.5.

Using the probabilities in Table 19.5, a graph of the probability of accepting the lot versus the percent defective in the lot can be drawn as shown in Figure 19.12. This graph, or curve, is called the **operating characteristic (OC) curve** for the $n = 15$, $c = 0$ acceptance sampling plan.

Perhaps we should consider other sampling plans, ones with different sample sizes n or different acceptance criteria c. First consider the case in which the sample size remains $n = 15$ but the acceptance criterion increases from $c = 0$ to $c = 1$. That is, we will now accept the lot if zero or one defective component is found in the sample. For a lot with 5% defective items ($p = .05$), the binomial probability function in equation (19.21), or Excel's BINOM.DIST function, can be used to compute $f(0) = .4633$ and $f(1) = .3658$. Thus, there is a $.4633 + .3658 = .8291$ probability that the $n = 15$, $c = 1$ plan will lead to the acceptance of a lot with 5% defective items.

Continuing these calculations, we obtain Figure 19.13, which shows the operating characteristic curves for four alternative acceptance sampling plans for the KALI problem. Samples of size 15 and 20 are considered. Note that regardless of the proportion defective in the lot, the $n = 15$, $c = 1$ sampling plan provides the highest probabilities of accepting the lot. The $n = 20$, $c = 0$ sampling plan provides the lowest probabilities of accepting the lot; however, that plan also provides the highest probabilities of rejecting the lot.

FIGURE 19.12   OPERATING CHARACTERISTIC CURVE FOR THE $n = 15, c = 0$
ACCEPTANCE SAMPLING PLAN

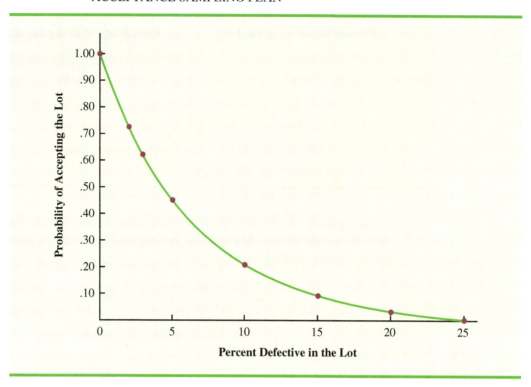

FIGURE 19.13   OPERATING CHARACTERISTIC CURVES FOR FOUR ACCEPTANCE
SAMPLING PLANS

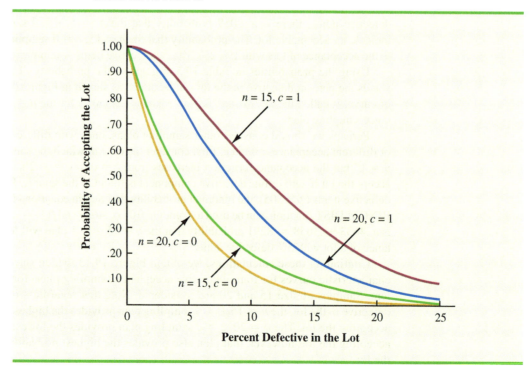

Selecting an Acceptance Sampling Plan

Now that we know how to use the binomial distribution to compute the probability of accepting a lot with a given proportion defective, we are ready to select the values of n and c that determine the desired acceptance sampling plan for the application being studied. To develop this plan, managers must specify two values for the fraction defective in the lot. One value, denoted p_0, will be used to control for the producer's risk, and the other value, denoted p_1, will be used to control for the consumer's risk.

We will use the following notation.

α = the producer's risk; the probability of rejecting a lot with p_0 defective items

β = the consumer's risk; the probability of accepting a lot with p_1 defective items

Suppose that for the KALI problem, the managers specify that $p_0 = .03$ and $p_1 = .15$. From the OC curve for $n = 15$, $c = 0$ in Figure 19.14, we see that $p_0 = .03$ provides a producer's risk of approximately $1 - .63 = .37$, and $p_1 = .15$ provides a consumer's risk of approximately .09. Thus, if the managers are willing to tolerate both a .37 probability of rejecting a lot with 3% defective items (producer's risk) and a .09 probability of accepting a lot with 15% defective items (consumer's risk), the $n = 15$, $c = 0$ acceptance sampling plan would be acceptable.

Suppose, however, that the managers request a producer's risk of $\alpha = .10$ and a consumer's risk of $\beta = .19$. We see that now the $n = 15$, $c = 0$ sampling plan has a better-than-desired consumer's risk but an unacceptably large producer's risk. The fact that $\alpha = .37$ indicates that 37% of the lots will be erroneously rejected when only 3% of the items in them are defective. The producer's risk is too high, and a different acceptance sampling plan should be considered.

FIGURE 19.14   OPERATING CHARACTERISTIC CURVE FOR $n = 15$, $c = 0$ WITH $p_0 = .03$ AND $p_1 = .15$

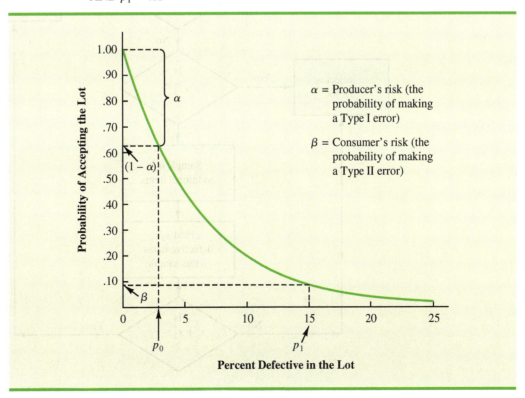

Exercise 13 at the end of this section will ask you to compute the producer's risk and the consumer's risk for the $n = 20$, $c = 1$ sampling plan.

Using $p_0 = .03$, $\alpha = .10$, $p_1 = .15$, and $\beta = .20$, Figure 19.13 shows that the acceptance sampling plan with $n = 20$ and $c = 1$ comes closest to meeting both the producer's and the consumer's risk requirements.

As shown in this section, several computations and several operating characteristic curves may need to be considered to determine the sampling plan with the desired producer's and consumer's risk. Fortunately, tables of sampling plans are published. For example, the American Military Standard Table, MIL-STD-105D, provides information helpful in designing acceptance sampling plans. More advanced texts on quality control, such as those listed in the bibliography, describe the use of such tables. The advanced texts also discuss the role of sampling costs in determining the optimal sampling plan.

FIGURE 19.15   A TWO-STAGE ACCEPTANCE SAMPLING PLAN

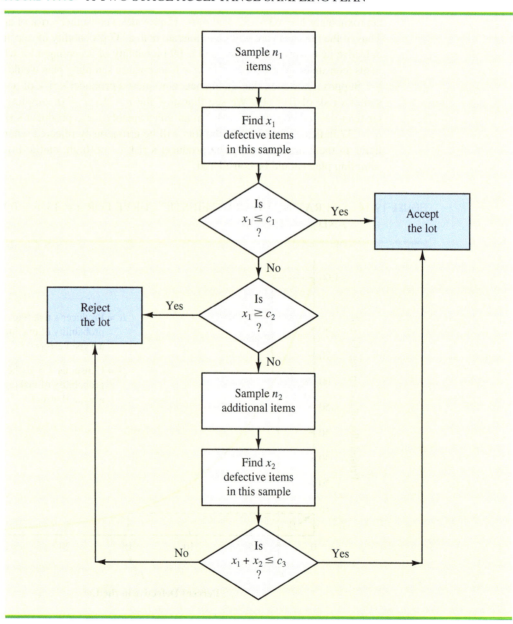

Multiple Sampling Plans

The acceptance sampling procedure we presented for the KALI problem is a *single-sample* plan. It is called a single-sample plan because only one sample or sampling stage is used. After the number of defective components in the sample is determined, a decision must be made to accept or reject the lot. An alternative to the single-sample plan is a **multiple sampling plan**, in which two or more stages of sampling are used. At each stage a decision is made among three possibilities: stop sampling and accept the lot, stop sampling and reject the lot, or continue sampling. Although more complex, multiple sampling plans often result in a smaller total sample size than single-sample plans with the same α and β probabilities.

The logic of a two-stage, or double-sample, plan is shown in Figure 19.15. Initially a sample of n_1 items is selected. If the number of defective components x_1 is less than or equal to c_1, accept the lot. If x_1 is greater than or equal to c_2, reject the lot. If x_1 is between c_1 and c_2 ($c_1 < x_1 < c_2$), select a second sample of n_2 items. Determine the combined, or total, number of defective components from the first sample (x_1) and the second sample (x_2). If $x_1 + x_2 \leq c_3$, accept the lot; otherwise reject the lot. The development of the double-sample plan is more difficult because the sample sizes n_1 and n_2 and the acceptance numbers c_1, c_2, and c_3 must meet both the producer's and consumer's risks desired.

NOTES AND COMMENTS

1. The use of the binomial distribution for acceptance sampling is based on the assumption of large lots. If the lot size is small, the hypergeometric distribution is appropriate.

2. In the MIL-STD-105D sampling tables, p_0 is called the acceptable quality level (AQL). In some sampling tables, p_1 is called the lot tolerance percent defective (LTPD) or the rejectable quality level (RQL). Many of the published sampling plans also use quality indexes such as the indifference quality level (IQL) and the average outgoing quality limit (AOQL). The more advanced texts listed in the bibliography provide a complete discussion of these other indexes.

3. In this section we provided an introduction to *attributes sampling plans.* In these plans each item sampled is classified as nondefective or defective. In *variables sampling plans,* a sample is taken and a measurement of the quality characteristic is taken. For example, for gold jewelry a measurement of quality may be the amount of gold it contains. A simple statistic such as the average amount of gold in the sample jewelry is computed and compared with an allowable value to determine whether to accept or reject the lot.

Exercises

Methods

10. For an acceptance sampling plan with $n = 25$ and $c = 0$, find the probability of accepting a lot that has a defect rate of 2%. What is the probability of accepting the lot if the defect rate is 6%?

11. Consider an acceptance sampling plan with $n = 20$ and $c = 0$. Compute the producer's risk for each of the following cases.
    a.   The lot has a defect rate of 2%.
    b.   The lot has a defect rate of 6%.

12. Repeat exercise 11 for the acceptance sampling plan with $n = 20$ and $c = 1$. What happens to the producer's risk as the acceptance number c is increased? Explain.

Applications

13. Refer to the KALI problem presented in this section. The quality control manager requested a producer's risk of .10 when p_0 was .03 and a consumer's risk of .20 when p_1 was .15. Consider the acceptance sampling plan based on a sample size of 20 and an acceptance number of 1. Answer the following questions.
    a. What is the producer's risk for the $n = 20$, $c = 1$ sampling plan?
    b. What is the consumer's risk for the $n = 20$, $c = 1$ sampling plan?
    c. Does the $n = 20$, $c = 1$ sampling plan satisfy the risks requested by the quality control manager? Discuss.

14. To inspect incoming shipments of raw materials, a manufacturer is considering samples of sizes 10, 15, and 19. Use the binomial probabilities from Table 5 of Appendix B to select a sampling plan that provides a producer's risk of $\alpha = .03$ when p_0 is .05 and a consumer's risk of $\beta = .12$ when p_1 is .30.

15. A domestic manufacturer of watches purchases quartz crystals from a Swiss firm. The crystals are shipped in lots of 1000. The acceptance sampling procedure uses 20 randomly selected crystals.
    a. Construct operating characteristic curves for acceptance numbers of 0, 1, and 2.
    b. If p_0 is .01 and $p_1 = .08$, what are the producer's and consumer's risks for each sampling plan in part (a)?

Summary

In this chapter we discussed how statistical methods can be used to assist in the control of quality. We first presented the $\bar{x}$, R, p, and np control charts as graphical aids in monitoring process quality. Control limits are established for each chart; samples are selected periodically, and the data points plotted on the control chart. Data points outside the control limits indicate that the process is out of control and that corrective action should be taken. Patterns of data points within the control limits can also indicate potential quality control problems and suggest that corrective action may be warranted.

We also considered the technique known as acceptance sampling. With this procedure, a sample is selected and inspected. The number of defective items in the sample provides the basis for accepting or rejecting the lot. The sample size and the acceptance criterion can be adjusted to control both the producer's risk (Type I error) and the consumer's risk (Type II error).

Glossary

Acceptance criterion The maximum number of defective items that can be found in the sample and still indicate an acceptable lot.

Acceptance sampling A statistical method in which the number of defective items found in a sample is used to determine whether a lot should be accepted or rejected.

Assignable causes Variations in process outputs that are due to factors such as machine tools wearing out, incorrect machine settings, poor-quality raw materials, operator error, and so on. Corrective action should be taken when assignable causes of output variation are detected.

Common causes Normal or natural variations in process outputs that are due purely to chance. No corrective action is necessary when output variations are due to common causes.

Consumer's risk The risk of accepting a poor-quality lot; a Type II error.

Control chart A graphical tool used to help determine whether a process is in control or out of control.

Lot A group of items such as incoming shipments of raw materials or purchased parts as well as finished goods from final assembly.

Multiple sampling plan A form of acceptance sampling in which more than one sample or stage is used. On the basis of the number of defective items found in a sample, a decision will be made to accept the lot, reject the lot, or continue sampling.

np **chart** A control chart used to monitor the quality of the output of a process in terms of the number of defective items.

Operating characteristic (OC) curve A graph showing the probability of accepting the lot as a function of the percentage defective in the lot. This curve can be used to help determine whether a particular acceptance sampling plan meets both the producer's and the consumer's risk requirements.

p **chart** A control chart used when the quality of the output of a process is measured in terms of the proportion defective.

Producer's risk The risk of rejecting a good-quality lot; a Type I error.

Quality control A series of inspections and measurements that determine whether quality standards are being met.

R **chart** A control chart used when the quality of the output of a process is measured in terms of the range of a variable.

Six Sigma A methodology that uses measurement and statistical analysis to achieve a level of quality so good that for every million opportunities no more than 3.4 defects will occur.

Total quality (TQ) A total system approach to improving customer satisfaction and lowering real cost through a strategy of continuous improvement and learning.

$\bar{x}$ **chart** A control chart used when the quality of the output of a process is measured in terms of the mean value of a variable such as a length, weight, temperature, and so on.

Key Formulas

Standard Error of the Mean

$$\sigma_{\bar{x}} = \frac{\sigma}{\sqrt{n}} \tag{19.1}$$

Control Limits for an $\bar{x}$ Chart: Process Mean and Standard Deviation Known

$$\text{UCL} = \mu + 3\sigma_{\bar{x}} \tag{19.2}$$
$$\text{LCL} = \mu - 3\sigma_{\bar{x}} \tag{19.3}$$

Overall Sample Mean

$$\bar{\bar{x}} = \frac{\bar{x}_1 + \bar{x}_2 + \cdots + \bar{x}_k}{k} \tag{19.4}$$

Average Range

$$\bar{R} = \frac{R_1 + R_2 + \cdots + R_k}{k} \tag{19.5}$$

Control Limits for an $\bar{x}$ Chart: Process Mean and Standard Deviation Unknown

$$\bar{\bar{x}} \pm A_2\bar{R} \tag{19.8}$$

Control Limits for an R Chart

$$\text{UCL} = \bar{R}D_4 \tag{19.14}$$

$$\text{LCL} = \bar{R}D_3 \tag{19.15}$$

Standard Error of the Proportion

$$\sigma_{\bar{p}} = \sqrt{\frac{p(1-p)}{n}} \tag{19.16}$$

Control Limits for a p Chart

$$\text{UCL} = p + 3\sigma_{\bar{p}} \tag{19.17}$$

$$\text{LCL} = p - 3\sigma_{\bar{p}} \tag{19.18}$$

Control Limits for an np Chart

$$\text{UCL} = np + 3\sqrt{np(1-p)} \tag{19.19}$$

$$\text{LCL} = np - 3\sqrt{np(1-p)} \tag{19.20}$$

Binomial Probability Function for Acceptance Sampling

$$f(x) = \frac{n!}{x!(n-x)!}p^x(1-p)^{(n-x)} \tag{19.21}$$

Supplementary Exercises

16. Samples of size 5 provided the following 20 sample means for a production process that is believed to be in control.

95.72	95.24	95.18
95.44	95.46	95.32
95.40	95.44	95.08
95.50	95.80	95.22
95.56	95.22	95.04
95.72	94.82	95.46
95.60	95.78	

a. Based on these data, what is an estimate of the mean when the process is in control?

b. Assume that the process standard deviation is $\sigma = .50$. Develop the $\bar{x}$ control chart for this production process. Assume that the mean of the process is the estimate developed in part (a).

c. Do any of the 20 sample means indicate that the process was out of control?

17. Product filling weights are normally distributed with a mean of 350 grams and a standard deviation of 15 grams.
    a. Develop the control limits for the $\bar{x}$ chart for samples of size 10, 20, and 30.
    b. What happens to the control limits as the sample size is increased?
    c. What happens when a Type I error is made?
    d. What happens when a Type II error is made?
    e. What is the probability of a Type I error for samples of size 10, 20, and 30?
    f. What is the advantage of increasing the sample size for control chart purposes? What error probability is reduced as the sample size is increased?

18. Twenty-five samples of size 5 resulted in $\bar{\bar{x}} = 5.42$ and $\bar{R} = 2.0$. Compute control limits for the $\bar{x}$ and R charts, and estimate the standard deviation of the process.

19. The following are quality control data for a manufacturing process at Kensport Chemical Company. The data show the temperature in degrees centigrade at five points in time during a manufacturing cycle. The company is interested in using control charts to monitor the temperature of its manufacturing process. Construct the $\bar{x}$ chart and R chart. What conclusions can be made about the quality of the process?

Sample	$\bar{x}$	R	Sample	$\bar{x}$	R
1	95.72	1.0	11	95.80	.6
2	95.24	.9	12	95.22	.2
3	95.18	.8	13	95.56	1.3
4	95.44	.4	14	95.22	.5
5	95.46	.5	15	95.04	.8
6	95.32	1.1	16	95.72	1.1
7	95.40	.9	17	94.82	.6
8	95.44	.3	18	95.46	.5
9	95.08	.2	19	95.60	.4
10	95.50	.6	20	95.74	.6

20. The following were collected for the Master Blend Coffee production process. The data show the filling weights based on samples of 3-pound cans of coffee. Use these data to construct the $\bar{x}$ and R charts. What conclusions can be made about the quality of the production process?

Coffee

	Observations				
Sample	1	2	3	4	5
1	3.05	3.08	3.07	3.11	3.11
2	3.13	3.07	3.05	3.10	3.10
3	3.06	3.04	3.12	3.11	3.10
4	3.09	3.08	3.09	3.09	3.07
5	3.10	3.06	3.06	3.07	3.08
6	3.08	3.10	3.13	3.03	3.06
7	3.06	3.06	3.08	3.10	3.08
8	3.11	3.08	3.07	3.07	3.07
9	3.09	3.09	3.08	3.07	3.09
10	3.06	3.11	3.07	3.09	3.07

21. An insurance company samples claim forms for errors created by its employees as well as the amount of time it takes to process a claim.
    a. When the process is in control, the proportion of claims with an error is .033. A p chart has LCL = 0 and UCL = .068. Plot the following seven sample results: .035, .062,

.055, .049, .058, .066, and .055. Comment on whether there might be concern about the quality of the process.

b.   An $\bar{x}$ chart for the mean processing time has LCL = 22.2 and UCL = 24.5. The mean is μ = 23.35 when the claim process is in control. Plot the following seven sample results: 22.4, 22.6, 22.65, 23.2, 23.4, 23.85, and 24.1. Comment on whether there might be concern about the quality of the process.

22.   Managers of 1200 different retail outlets make twice-a-month restocking orders from a central warehouse. Past experience shows that 4% of the orders result in one or more errors such as wrong item shipped, wrong quantity shipped, and item requested but not shipped. Random samples of 200 orders are selected monthly and checked for accuracy.

a.   Construct a control chart for this situation.

b.   Six months of data show the following numbers of orders with one or more errors: 10, 15, 6, 13, 8, and 17. Plot the data on the control chart. What does your plot indicate about the order process?

23.   An n = 10, c = 2 acceptance sampling plan is being considered; assume that p_0 = .05 and p_1 = .20.

a.   Compute both producer's and consumer's risk for this acceptance sampling plan.

b.   Would the producer, the consumer, or both be unhappy with the proposed sampling plan?

c.   What change in the sampling plan, if any, would you recommend?

24.   An acceptance sampling plan with n = 15 and c = 1 has been designed with a producer's risk of .075.

a.   Was the value of p_0 .01, .02, .03, .04, or .05? What does this value mean?

b.   What is the consumer's risk associated with this plan if p_1 is .25?

25.   A manufacturer produces lots of a canned food product. Let p denote the proportion of the lots that do not meet the product quality specifications. An n = 25, c = 0 acceptance sampling plan will be used.

a.   Compute points on the operating characteristic curve when p = .01, .03, .10, and .20.

b.   Plot the operating characteristic curve.

c.   What is the probability that the acceptance sampling plan will reject a lot containing .01 defective?

Appendix 19.1   Control Charts with Minitab

Jensen

In this appendix we describe the steps required to generate Minitab control charts using the Jensen Computer Supplies data shown in Table 19.2. The sample number appears in column C1. The first observation is in column C2, the second observation is in column C3, and so on. The following steps describe how to use Minitab to produce both the $\bar{x}$ chart and R chart simultaneously.

Step 1. Select the **Stat** menu
Step 2. Choose **Control Charts**
Step 3. Choose **Variables Charts for Subgroups**
Step 4. Choose **Xbar-R**
Step 5. When the Xbar-R Chart dialog box appears:
          Select **Observations for a subgroup are in one row of columns**
          In the box below, enter C2-C6
          Select **Xbar-R Options**

Step 6. When the Xbar-R-Options dialog box appears:
        Select the **Tests** tab
        Select **Perform selected tests for special causes**
        Choose **1 point > K standard deviations from center line***
        Enter 3 in the **K** box
        Click **OK**
Step 7. When the Xbar-R Chart dialog box appears:
        Click **OK**

The $\bar{x}$ chart and the R chart will be shown together on the Minitab output. The choices available under step 3 of the preceding Minitab procedure provide access to a variety of control chart options. For example, the $\bar{x}$ and the R chart can be selected separately. Additional options include the p chart, the np chart, and others.

---

*Minitab provides several additional tests for detecting special causes of variation and out-of-control conditions. The user may select several of these tests simultaneously.

APPENDIXES

Appendix A   Building Spreadsheet Models

The purpose of this appendix is twofold. First, we provide an overview of Excel and discuss the basic operations needed to work with Excel workbooks and worksheets. Second, we provide an introduction to building mathematical models using Excel, including a discussion of how to find and use particular Excel functions, how to design and build good spreadsheet models, and how to ensure that these models are free of errors.

OVERVIEW OF MICROSOFT EXCEL

A workbook is a file containing one or more worksheets.

When using Excel for modeling, the data and the model are displayed in workbooks, each of which contains a series of worksheets. Figure A.1 shows the layout of a blank workbook created each time Excel is opened. The workbook is named Book1 and contains a worksheet named **Sheet1**. Note that cell A1 is initially selected.

The wide bar located across the top of the workbook is referred to as the Ribbon. Tabs, located at the top of the Ribbon, provide quick access to groups of related commands. There are eight tabs: **HOME, INSERT, PAGE LAYOUT, FORMULAS, DATA, REVIEW, VIEW, and ADD-INS.** Each tab contains several groups of related commands. Note that the **HOME** tab is selected when Excel is opened. The seven groups associated with the **HOME** tab are displayed in Figure A.2. Under the **HOME** tab there are seven groups of related commands: **Clipboard, Font, Alignment, Number, Styles, Cells, and Editing**. Commands are arranged within each group. For example, to change selected text to boldface, click the HOME tab and click the Bold button **B** in the **Font** group.

Figure A.3 illustrates the location of the **FILE** tab, the **Quick Access Toolbar**, and the **Formula Bar**. When you click the **FILE** tab, Excel provides a list of workbook

FIGURE A.1   BLANK WORKBOOK CREATED WHEN EXCEL IS STARTED

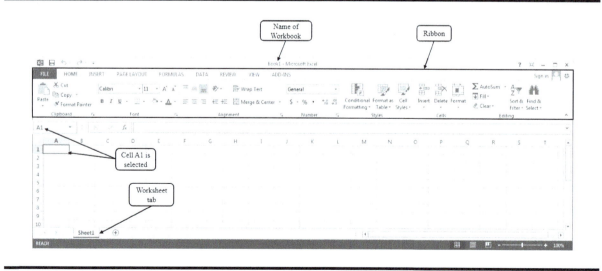

FIGURE A.2   PORTION OF THE HOME TAB

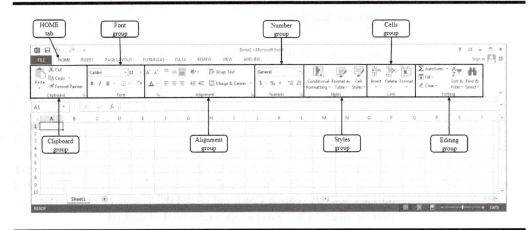

FIGURE A.3   EXCEL FILE TAB, QUICK ACCESS TOOLBAR, AND
FORMULA BAR

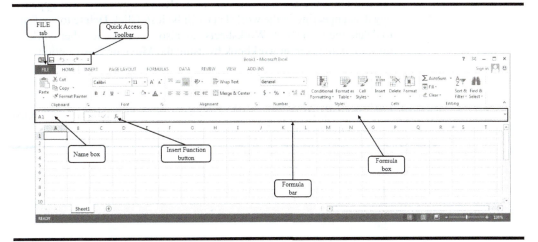

options such as opening, saving, and printing (worksheets). The **Quick Access Toolbar** allows you to quickly access these workbook options. For instance, the **Quick Access Toolbar** shown in Figure A.3 includes a **Save** button 🖫 that can be used to save files without having to first click the **FILE** tab. To add or remove features on the **Quick Access Toolbar** click the **Customize Quick Access Toolbar** button ▾ on the **Quick Access Toolbar**.

The Formula Bar contains a **Name** box, the **Insert Function** button *fx*, and a Formula box. In Figure A.3, "A1" appears in the **Name** box because cell A1 is selected. You can select any other cell in the worksheet by using the mouse to move the cursor to another cell and clicking or by typing the new cell location in the name box and pressing the Enter key. The Formula box is used to display the formula in the currently selected cell. For instance, if you had entered $=A1+A2$ into cell A3, whenever you select cell A3, the formula $=A1+A2$ will be shown in the Formula box. This feature makes it very easy to see and edit a formula in a particular cell. The **Insert Function** button allows you to quickly access all of the functions available in Excel. Later, we show how to find and use a particular function.

BASIC WORKBOOK OPERATIONS

Figure A.4 illustrates the worksheet options that can be performed after right clicking on a worksheet tab. For instance, to change the name of the current worksheet from "Sheet1" to "NowlinModel," right click the worksheet tab named "Sheet1" and select the **Rename** option. The current worksheet name (Sheet1) will be highlighted. Then, simply type the new name (NowlinModel) and press the Enter key to rename the worksheet.

Suppose that you wanted to create a copy of "Sheet 1." After right clicking the tab named "Sheet1," select the **Move or Copy** option. When the **Move or Copy** dialog box appears, select **Create a Copy** and click **OK**. The name of the copied worksheet will appear as "Sheet1 (2)." You can then rename it, if desired.

To add a worksheet to the workbook, right click any worksheet tab and select the Insert option; when the **Insert dialog box** appears, select Worksheet and click **OK**. An additional blank worksheet titled Sheet2 will appear in the workbook. You can also insert a new worksheet by clicking the Insert Worksheet tab button ⊕ that appears to the right of the last worksheet tab displayed. Worksheets can be deleted by right clicking the worksheet tab and choosing **Delete**. After clicking **Delete**, a window will appear warning you that any data appearing in the worksheet will be lost. Click **Delete** to confirm that you do want to delete the worksheet. Worksheets can also be moved to other workbooks or a different position in the current workbook by using the **Move or Copy** option.

FIGURE A.4   WORKSHEET OPTIONS OBTAINED AFTER RIGHT CLICKING ON A
                 WORKSHEET TAB

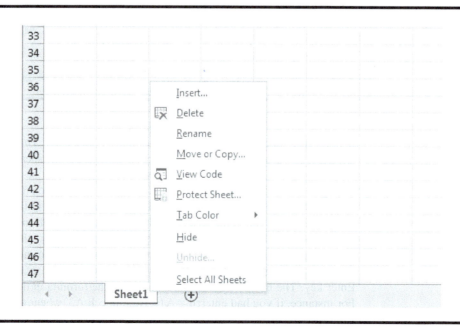

Creating, Saving, and Opening Files

As an illustration of manually entering, saving, and opening a file, we will use the Nowlin Plastics production example from Chapter 1. The objective is to compute the breakeven point for a product that has a fixed cost of $3000, a variable cost per unit of $2, and a selling price per unit of $5. We begin by creating a worksheet containing the problem data.

If you have just opened Excel, a blank workbook containing Sheet1 will be displayed. The Nowlin data can now be entered manually by simply typing the fixed cost of $3000, the variable cost of $2, and the selling price of $5 into one of the worksheets. If Excel is currently running and no blank workbook is displayed, you can create a new blank workbook using the following steps:

Step 1. Click the **File** tab
Step 2. Click **New** in the list of options
Step 3. Click **Blank Workbook**

A new workbook will appear.

We will place the data for the Nowlin example in the top portion of Sheet1 of the new workbook. First, we enter the label "Nowlin Plastics" into cell A1. To identify each of the three data values we enter the label "Fixed Cost" into cell A3, the label "Variable Cost Per Unit" into cell A5, and the label "Selling Price Per Unit" into cell A7. Next, we enter the actual cost and price data into the corresponding cells in column B: the value of $3000 in cell B3; the value of $2 in cell B5; and the value of $5 into cell B7. Finally, we will change the name of the worksheet from "Sheet1" to "NowlinModel" using the procedure described previously. Figure A.5 shows a portion of the worksheet we have just developed.

Before we begin the development of the model portion of the worksheet, we recommend that you first save the current file; this will prevent you from having to reenter the

FIGURE A.5 NOWLIN PLASTICS DATA

	A	B
1	**Nowlin Plastics**	
2		
3	**Fixed Cost**	$3,000
4		
5	**Variable Cost Per Unit**	$2
6		
7	**Selling Price Per Unit**	$5
8		
9		
10		
11		
12		
13		
14		
15		
16		
17		
18		

data in case something happens that causes Excel to close. To save the workbook using the filename "Nowlin," we perform the following steps:

Step 1. Click the **FILE** tab on the Ribbon
Step 2. Click **Save** in the list of options
Step 3. Select **Computer** under **Save As** and click **Browse**
Step 4. When the **Save As** dialog box appears
    Select the location where you want to save the file
    Enter the file name *Nowlin* in the **File name** box
    Click **Save**

Step 3 is only necessary for Excel 2013. In previous versions of Excel you may skip to Step 4.

Excel's **Save** command is designed to save the file as an Excel workbook. As you work with and build models in Excel, you should follow the practice of periodically saving the file so you will not lose any work. Simply follow the procedure described above, using the Save command.

*Keyboard shortcut: To save the file, press **CTRL S**.*

Sometimes you may want to create a copy of an existing file. For instance, suppose you change one or more of the data values and would like to save the modified file using the filename "NowlinMod." The following steps show how to save the modified workbook using filename "NowlinMod."

Step 1. Click the **FILE** tab in the Ribbon
Step 2. Click **Save As** in the list of options
Step 3. Select **Computer** under **Save As** and click **Browse**
Step 4. When the **Save As** dialog box appears
    Select the location where you want to save the file
    Type the file name *NowlinMod* in the **File name** box
    Click **Save**

Once the NowlinMod workbook has been saved, you can continue to work with the file to perform whatever type of analysis is appropriate. When you are finished working with the file, simply click the close window button ✖ located at the top right-hand corner of the Ribbon.

You can easily access a saved file at another point in time. For example, the following steps show how to open the previously saved Nowlin workbook.

*Step 3 is only necessary in Excel 2013. The filename Nowlin may also appear under the **Recent Workbooks** list in Excel to allow you to open it directly without navigating to where you saved the file.*

Step 1. Click the **FILE** tab in the Ribbon
Step 2. Click **Open** in the list of options
Step 3. Select **Computer** under **Open** and click **Browse**
Step 4. When the **Open** dialog box appears:
    Find the location where you previously saved the *Nowlin* file
    Click on the filename **Nowlin** so that it appears in the **File name** box
    Click **Open**

The procedures we showed for saving or opening a workbook begin by clicking on the **Office Button** to access the **Save** and **Open** commands. Once you have used Excel for a while, you will probably find it more convenient to add these commands to the **Quick Access Toolbar**.

CELLS, REFERENCES, AND FORMULAS IN EXCEL

Assume that the Nowlin workbook is open again and that we would like to develop a model that can be used to compute the profit or loss associated with a given production volume. We will use the bottom portion of the worksheet shown in Figure A.5 to develop the model. The model will contain formulas that *refer to the location of the data cells* in the upper section of the worksheet. By putting the location of the data cells in the formula, we will build a model that can be easily updated with new data. This will be discussed in more detail later in this appendix in the section Principles for Building Good Spreadsheet Models.

We enter the label "Model" into cell A10 to provide a visual reminder that the bottom portion of this worksheet will contain the model. Next, we enter the labels "Production Volume" into cell A12, "Total Cost" into cell A14, "Total Revenue" into cell A16, and "Total Profit (Loss)" into cell A18. Cell B12 is used to contain a value for the production volume. We will now enter formulas into cells B14, B16, and B18 that use the production volume in cell B12 to compute the values for total cost, total revenue, and total profit or loss.

Total cost is the sum of the fixed cost (cell B3) and the total variable cost. The total variable cost is the product of the variable cost per unit (cell B5) and production volume (cell B12). Thus, the formula for total variable cost is B5*B12 and to compute the value of total cost, we enter the formula =B3+B5*B12 into cell B14. Next, total revenue is the product of the selling price per unit (cell B7) and the number of units produced (cell B12), which we enter in cell B16 as the formula =B7*B12. Finally, the total profit or loss is the difference between the total revenue (cell B16) and the total cost (cell B14). Thus, in cell B18 we enter the formula =B16-B14. Figure A.6 shows a portion of the formula worksheet just described.

*To display all formulas in the cells of a worksheet, hold down the **CTRL** key and then press the ~ key.*

We can now compute the total profit or loss for a particular production volume by entering a value for the production volume into cell B12. Figure A.7 shows the results after entering a value of 800 into cell B12. We see that a production volume of 800 units results in a total cost of $4600, a total revenue of $4000, and a loss of $600.

USING EXCEL FUNCTIONS

Excel provides a wealth of built-in formulas or functions for developing mathematical models. If we know which function is needed and how to use it, we can simply enter the function into the appropriate worksheet cell. However, if we are not sure which functions are available to accomplish a task or are not sure how to use a particular function, Excel can provide assistance.

FIGURE A.6   NOWLIN PLASTICS DATA AND MODEL

	A	B
1	**Nowlin Plastics**	
2		
3	**Fixed Cost**	3000
4		
5	**Variable Cost Per Unit**	2
6		
7	**Selling Price Per Unit**	5
8		
9		
10	**Models**	
11		
12	**Production Volume**	
13		
14	**Total Cost**	=B3+B5*B12
15		
16	**Total Revenue**	=B7*B12
17		
18	**Total Profit (Loss)**	=B16-B14

FIGURE A.7   NOWLIN PLASTICS RESULTS

	A	B
1	**Nowlin Plastics**	
2		
3	**Fixed Cost**	$3,000
4		
5	**Variable Cost Per Unit**	$2
6		
7	**Selling Price Per Unit**	$5
8		
9		
10	**Models**	
11		
12	**Production Volume**	800
13		
14	**Total Cost**	$4,600
15		
16	**Total Revenue**	$4,000
17		
18	**Total Profit (Loss)**	−$600

Finding the Right Excel Function

To identify the functions available in Excel, click the **Formulas** tab on the Ribbon and then click the **Insert Function** button in the **Function Library** group. Alternatively, click the Insert Function button *fx* on the formula bar. Either approach provides the **Insert Function dialog box** shown in Figure A.8.

The Search for a function box at the top of the **Insert Function dialog box** enables us to type a brief description for what we want to do. After doing so and clicking Go, Excel will search for and display, in the **Select a function box**, the functions that may accomplish our task. In many situations, however, we may want to browse through an entire category of functions to see what is available. For this task, the **Or select a category box** is helpful.

It contains a dropdown list of several categories of functions provided by Excel. Figure A.8 shows that we selected the Math & Trig category. As a result, Excel's Math & Trig functions appear in alphabetical order in the Select a function box. We see the ABS function listed first, followed by the ACOS function, and so on.

Colon Notation

Although many functions, such as the ABS function, have a single argument, some Excel functions depend on arrays. Colon notation provides an efficient way to convey arrays and matrices of cells to functions. The colon notation may be described as follows: B3:B5 means cell B1 "through" cell B5, namely the array of values stored in the locations (B1,B2,B3,B4,B5). Consider for example the following function =SUM(B1:B5). The sum function adds up the elements contained in the function's argument. Hence, =SUM(B1:B5) evaluates the following formula:

$$=B1+B2+B3+B4+B5$$

FIGURE A.8   INSERT FUNCTION DIALOG BOX

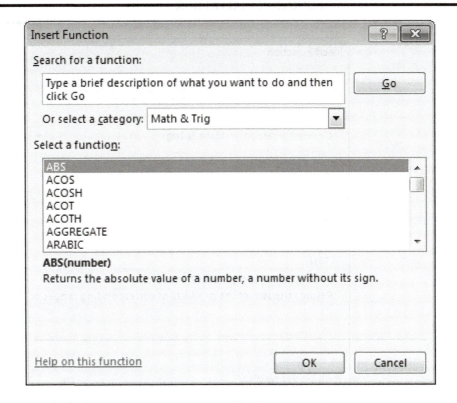

Inserting a Function into a Worksheet Cell

Through the use of an example, we will now show how to use the **Insert Function** and **Function Arguments** dialog boxes to select a function, develop its arguments, and insert the function into a worksheet cell. We also illustrate the use of a very useful function, the SUMPRODUCT function, and how to use colon notation in the argument of a function.

The SUMPRODUCT function, as shown in Figure A.9, is used in many of the Solver examples in the textbook. Note that SUMPRODUCT is now highlighted, and that immediately below the **Select a function** box we see SUMPRODUCT(array1,array2, array3, . . .), which indicates that the SUMPRODUCT function contains the array arguments array1, array2, array3, ... In addition, we see that the description of the SUMPRODUCT function is "Returns the sum of the products of corresponding ranges or arrays." For example, the function =SUMPRODUCT(A1:A3, B1:B3) evaluates the formula A1*B1 + A2*B2 + A3*B3. As shown in the following example, this function can be very useful in calculations of cost, profit, and other such functions involving multiple arrays of numbers.

Figure A.10 displays an Excel worksheet for the Foster Generators Problem that appears in Chapter 6. This problem involves the transportation of a product from three plants (Cleveland, Bedford, and York) to four distribution centers (Boston, Chicago, St. Louis, and Lexington). The costs for each unit shipped from each plant to each distribution center are shown in cells B5:E7, and the values in cells B17:E19 are the number of units shipped

FIGURE A.9   DESCRIPTION OF THE SUMPRODUCT FUNCTION IN THE INSERT
FUNCTION DIALOG BOX

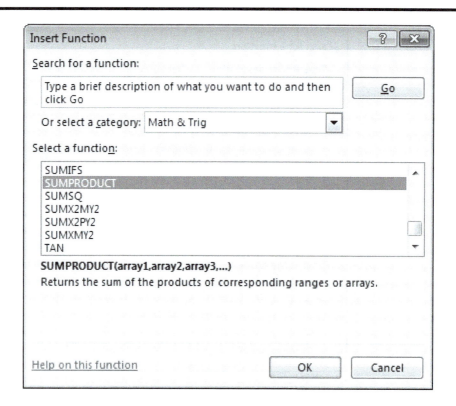

from each plant to each distribution center. Cell B13 will contain the total transportation
cost corresponding to the transportation cost values in cells B5:E7 and the values of the
number of units shipped in cells B17:E19.

The following steps show how to use the SUMPRODUCT function to compute the
total transportation cost for Foster Generators.

Step 1. Select **cell C13**
Step 2. Click *fx* on the formula bar
Step 3. When the **Insert Function** dialog box appears:
Select **Math & Trig** in the **Or select a category** box
Select **SUMPRODUCT** in the **Select a function** box (as shown in Figure A.9)
Click **OK**
Step 4. When the **Function Arguments** box appears (see Figure A.11):
Enter B5:E7 in the **Array1** box
Enter B17:E19 in the **Array2** box
Click **OK**

The worksheet then appears as shown in Figure A.12. The value of the total transportation
cost in cell C13 is 39500, or $39,500.

FIGURE A.10   EXCEL WORKSHEET USED TO CALCULATE TOTAL SHIPPING COSTS
FOR THE FOSTER GENERATORS TRANSPORTATION PROBLEM

	A	B	C	D	E	F	G	H
1	**Foster Generators**							
2								
3			**Destination**					
4	**Origin**	Boston	Chicago	St. Louis	Lexington	**Supply**		
5	Cleveland	3	2	7	6	5000		
6	Bedford	7	5	2	3	6000		
7	York	2	5	4	5	2500		
8	**Demand**	6000	4000	2000	1500			
9								
10								
11	**Model**							
12								
13		**Min Cost**						
14								
15			**Destination**					
16	**Origin**	Boston	Chicago	St. Louis	Lexington	**Total**		
17	Cleveland	3500	1500	0	0	5000	<=	5000
18	Bedford	0	2500	2000	1500	6000	<=	6000
19	York	2500	0	0	0	2500	<=	2500
20	**Total**	6000	4000	2000	1500			
21		=	=	=	=			
22		6000	4000	2000	1500			

WEB file

FosterGenerators

FIGURE A.11   COMPLETED FUNCTION ARGUMENTS DIALOG BOX FOR THE
SUMPRODUCT FUNCTION

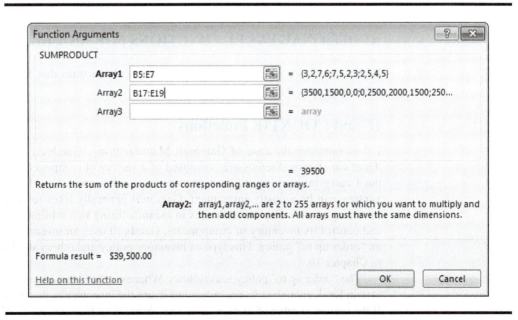

FIGURE A.12   EXCEL WORKSHEET SHOWING THE USE OF EXCEL'S SUMPRODUCT FUNCTION TO CALCULATE TOTAL SHIPPING COSTS

	A	B	C	D	E	F	G	H
1	**Foster Generators**							
2								
3				**Destination**				
4	**Origin**	Boston	Chicago	St. Louis	Lexington	**Supply**		
5	Cleveland	3	2	7	6	5000		
6	Bedford	7	5	2	3	6000		
7	York	2	5	4	5	2500		
8	**Demand**	6000	4000	2000	1500			
9								
10								
11	**Model**							
12								
13		**Min Cost**	39500					
14								
15				**Destination**				
16	**Origin**	Boston	Chicago	St. Louis	Lexington	**Total**		
17	Cleveland	3500	1500	0	0	5000	<=	5000
18	Bedford	0	2500	2000	1500	6000	<=	6000
19	York	2500	0	0	0	2500	<=	2500
20	**Total**	6000	4000	2000	1500			
21		=	=	=	=			
22		6000	4000	2000	1500			

We illustrated the use of Excel's capability to provide assistance in using the SUMPRODUCT function. The procedure is similar for all Excel functions. This capability is especially helpful if you do not know which function to use or forget the proper name and/or syntax for a function.

ADDITIONAL EXCEL FUNCTIONS FOR MODELING

In this section we introduce some additional Excel functions that have proven useful in modeling decision problems.

IF and COUNTIF Functions

Let us consider the case of Gambrell Manufacturing. Gambrell Manufacturing produces car stereos. Stereos are composed of a variety of components that the company must carry in inventory to keep production running smoothly. However, because inventory can be a costly investment, Gambrell generally likes to keep the amount of inventory of the components it uses in manufacturing to a minimum. To help monitor and control its inventory of components, Gambrell uses an inventory policy known as an "order up to" policy. This type of inventory policy and others are discussed in detail in Chapter 10.

The "order up to" policy is as follows. Whenever the inventory on hand drops below a certain level, enough units are ordered to return the inventory to that predetermined level. If the current number of units in inventory, denoted by H, drops below M units, we order enough to get the inventory level back up to M units. M is called the Order Up to Point. Stated mathematically, if Q is the amount we order, then

$$Q = M - H$$

An inventory model for Gambrell Manufacturing appears in Figure A.13. In this worksheet, labeled "OrderQuantity" in the upper half of the worksheet, the component ID number, inventory on hand (H), order up to point (M), and cost per unit are given for each of four components. Also given in this sheet is the fixed cost per order. The fixed cost is interpreted as follows: Each time a component is ordered, it costs Gambrell $120 to process the order. The fixed cost of $120 is incurred regardless of how many units are ordered.

The model portion of the worksheet calculates the order quantity for each component. For example, for component 570, $M = 100$ and $H = 5$, so $Q = M - H = 100 - 5 = 95$. For component 741, $M = 70$ and $H = 70$ and no units are ordered because the on-hand inventory of 70 units is equal to the order point of 70. The calculations are similar for the other two components.

Depending on the number of units ordered, Gambrell receives a discount on the cost per unit. If 50 or more units are ordered, there is a quantity discount of 10% on every unit purchased. For example, for component 741, the cost per unit is $4.50 and 95 units are ordered. Because 95 exceeds the 50-unit requirement, there is a 10% discount and the cost per unit is reduced to $4.50 - 0.1(\$4.50) = \$4.50 - \$0.45 = \$4.05$. Not including the fixed cost, the cost of goods purchased is then $4.05(95) = \$384.75$.

The Excel functions used to perform these calculations are shown in Figure A.14. The IF function is used to calculate the purchase cost of goods for each component in row 15. The general form of the IF function is

$$=\text{IF}(condition,\ result\ if\ condition\ is\ true,\ result\ if\ condition\ is\ false)$$

FIGURE A.13   THE GAMBRELL MANUFACTURING COMPONENT ORDERING MODEL

	A	B	C	D	E	F
4	Component ID	570	578	741	755	
5	Inventory On-Hand	5	30	70	17	
6	Up to Order Point	100	55	70	45	
7	Cost per unit	$4.50	$12.50	$3.26	$4.15	
8						
9	Fixed Cost per Order	$120				
10						
11	**Model**					
12						
13	Component ID	570	578	741	755	
14	Order Quantity	95	25	0	28	
15	Cost of Goods	$384.75	$312.50	$0.00	$116.20	
16						
17	Total Number of Orders	3				
18						
19	Total Fixed costs	$360.00				
20	Total Cost of Goods	$813.45				
21	Total Cost	$1,173.45				
22						

FIGURE A.14   FORMULAS AND FUNCTIONS FOR GAMBRELL MANUFACTURING

	A	B	C	D	E
1					
2	**Gambrell Manufacturing**				
3					
4	Component ID	570	578	741	755
5	Inventory On-Hand	5	30	70	17
6	Up to Order Point	100	55	70	45
7	Cost per unit	4.5	12.5	3.26	4.15
8					
9	Fixed Cost per Order	120			
10					
11	**Model**				
12					
13	Component ID	=B4	=C4	=D4	=E4
14	Order Quantity	=B6-B5	=C6-C5	=D6-D5	=E6-E5
15	Cost of Goods	=IF(B14>=50,0.9*B7,B7)*B14	=IF(C14>=50, 0.9*C7,C7)*C14	=IF(D14>=50, 0.9*D7,D7)*D14	=IF(E14>=50, 0.9*E7,E7)*E14
16					
17	Total Number of Orders	=COUNTIF(B14:E14,">0")			
18					
19	Total Fixed Costs	=B17*B9			
20	Total Cost of Goods	=SUM(B15:E15)			
21	Total Cost	=SUM(B19:B20)			
22					

For example, in cell B15 we have $=IF(B14>=50,0.9*B7,B7)*B14$. This statement says if the order quantity (cell B14) is greater than or equal to 50, then the cost per unit is 0.9*B7 (there is a 10% discount); otherwise, there is no discount and the cost per unit is the amount given in cell B7. The purchase cost of goods for the other components are computed in a like manner.

The total cost in cell B21 is the sum of the purchase cost of goods ordered in row 15 and the fixed ordering costs. Because we place three orders (one each for components 570, 578, and 755), the fixed cost of the orders is 3*120 = $360.

The COUNTIF function in cell B17 is used to count how many times we order. In particular, it counts the number of components having a positive order quantity. The general form of the COUNTIF function is

$$=COUNTIF(\textit{range, condition})$$

The *range* is the range to search for the *condition*. The condition is the test to be counted when satisfied. *Note that quotes are required for the condition with the COUNTIF function.* In the Gambrell model in Figure A.14, cell B17 counts the number of cells that are greater than zero in the range of cells B14:E14. In the model, because only cells B14, C14, and E14 are greater than zero, the COUNTIF function in cell B17 returns 3.

As we have seen, IF and COUNTIF are powerful functions that allow us to make calculations based on a condition holding (or not). There are other such conditional functions available in Excel. In the problems at the end of this appendix, we ask you to investigate one such function, the SUMIF function. Another conditional function that is extremely useful in modeling is the VLOOKUP function. We discuss the VLOOKUP function with an example in the next section.

VLOOKUP Function

Next, consider the workbook named *OM455* shown in Figure A.15. The worksheet named Grades is shown. This worksheet calculates the course grades for the course OM 455. There are 11 students in the course. Each student has a midterm exam score and a final exam score, and these are averaged in column D to get the course average. The scale given in the upper portion of the worksheet is used to determine the course grade for each student. Consider, for example, the performance of student Choi in row 16. This student earned an 82 on the midterm, an 80 on the final, and a course average of 81. From the grading scale, this equates to a course grade of B.

The course average is simply the average of the midterm and final scores, but how do we get Excel to look in the grading scale table and automatically assign the correct course letter grade to each student? The VLOOKUP function allows us to do just that. The formulas and functions used in *OM455* are shown in Figure A.16.

The VLOOKUP function allows the user to pull a subset of data from a larger table of data based on some criterion. The general form of the VLOOKUP function is

$$=\text{VLOOKUP}(arg1,arg2,arg3,arg4)$$

where arg1 is the value to search for in the first column of the table, arg2 is the table location, arg3 is the column location in the table to be returned, and arg4 is TRUE if looking for the first partial match of arg1 and FALSE for looking for an exact match of arg1. We will explain the difference between a partial and exact match in a moment. VLOOKUP assumes that the first column of the table is sorted in ascending order.

FIGURE A.15   OM455 GRADE SPREADSHEET

WEB file

OM455

	A	B	C	D	E	F
1	OM455					
2	Section 001					
3	Course Grading Scale Based on Course Average:					
4		Lower	Upper	Course		
5		Limit	Limit	Grade		
6		0	59	F		
7		60	69	D		
8		70	79	C		
9		80	89	B		
10		90	100	A		
11						
12		Midterm	Final	Course	Course	
13	Lastname	Score	Score	Average	Grade	
14	Benson	70	56	63.0	D	
15	Chin	95	91	93.0	A	
16	Choi	82	80	81.0	B	
17	Cruz	45	78	61.5	D	
18	Doe	68	45	56.5	F	
19	Honda	91	98	94.5	A	
20	Hume	87	74	80.5	B	
21	Jones	60	80	70.0	C	
22	Miranda	80	93	86.5	B	
23	Murigami	97	98	97.5	A	
24	Ruebush	90	91	90.5	A	
25						

FIGURE A.16   THE FORMULAS AND FUNCTIONS USED IN OM455

	A	B	C	D	E
1	OM 455				
2	Section 001				
3	Course Grading Scale Based on Course Average:				
4		Lower	Upper	Course	
5		Limit	Limit	Grade	
6		0	59	F	
7		60	69	D	
8		70	79	C	
9		80	89	B	
10		90	100	A	
11					
12		Midterm	Final	Course	Course
13	Lastname	Score	Score	Average	Grade
14	Benson	70	56	=AVERAGE(B14:C14)	=VLOOKUP(D14,B6:D10,3,TRUE)
15	Chin	95	91	=AVERAGE(B15:C15)	=VLOOKUP(D15,B6:D10,3,TRUE)
16	Choi	82	80	=AVERAGE(B16:C16)	=VLOOKUP(D16,B6:D10,3,TRUE)
17	Cruz	45	78	=AVERAGE(B17:C17)	=VLOOKUP(D17,B6:D10,3,TRUE)
18	Doe	68	45	=AVERAGE(B18:C18)	=VLOOKUP(D18,B6:D10,3,TRUE)
19	Honda	91	98	=AVERAGE(B19:C19)	=VLOOKUP(D19,B6:D10,3,TRUE)
20	Hume	87	74	=AVERAGE(B20:C20)	=VLOOKUP(D20,B6:D10,3,TRUE)
21	Jones	60	80	=AVERAGE(B21:C21)	=VLOOKUP(D21,B6:D10,3,TRUE)
22	Miranda	80	93	=AVERAGE(B22:C22)	=VLOOKUP(D22,B6:D10,3,TRUE)
23	Murigami	97	98	=AVERAGE(B23:C23)	=VLOOKUP(D23,B6:D10,3,TRUE)
24	Ruebush	90	91	=AVERAGE(B24:C24)	=VLOOKUP(D24,B6:D10,3,TRUE)
25					

The VLOOKUP function for student Choi in cell E16 is as follows:

$$=VLOOKUP(D16,B6:D10,3,TRUE)$$

This function uses the course average from cell D16 and searches the first column of the table defined by B6:D10. In the first column of the table (column B), Excel searches from the top until it finds a number strictly greater than the value of D16 (81). It then backs up one row (to row 9). That is, it finds the last value in the first column less than or equal to 81. Because there is a 3 in the third argument of the VLOOKUP function, it takes the element in row 9 in the third column of the table, which is the letter "B." In summary, the VLOOKUP takes the first argument and searches the first column of the table for the last row that is less than or equal to the first argument. It then selects from that row the element in the column number of the third argument.

Note: If the last element of the VLOOKUP function is "False," the only change is that Excel searches for an exact match of the first argument in the first column of the data. VLOOKUP is very useful when you seek subsets of a table based on a condition.

PRINCIPLES FOR BUILDING GOOD SPREADSHEET MODELS

We have covered some of the fundamentals of building spreadsheet models. There are some generally accepted guiding principles for how to build a spreadsheet so that it is more easily used by others and so that the risk of error is mitigated. In this section we discuss some of those principles.

Separate the Data from the Model

One of the first principles of good modeling is to separate the data from the model. This enables the user to update the model parameters without fear of mistakenly typing over a formula or function. For this reason, it is good practice to have a data section at the top of the spreadsheet. A separate model section should contain all calculations and in general should not be updated by a user. For a what-if model or an optimization model, there might also be a separate section for decision cells (values that are not data or calculations, but are the outputs we seek from the model).

The Nowlin model in Figure A.6 is a good example. The data section is in the upper part of the spreadsheet followed by the model section that contains the calculations. The Gambrell model in Figure A.13 does not totally employ the principle of data/model separation. A better model would have the 50-unit hurdle and the 90% cost (10% discount) as data in the upper section. Then the formulas in row 15 would simply refer to the cells in the upper section. This would allow the user to easily change the discount, for example, without having to change all four formulas in row 15.

Document the Model

A good spreadsheet model is well documented. Clear labels and proper formatting and alignment make the spreadsheet easier to navigate and understand. For example, if the values in a worksheet are cost, currency formatting should be used. No cells should be unlabeled. A new user should be able to easily understand the model and its calculations. Figure A.17 shows a better-documented version of the Foster Generators model previously

FIGURE A.17   A BETTER-DOCUMENTED FOSTER GENERATORS MODEL

WEB file

FosterRev

	A	B	C	D	E	F	G	H
1	**Foster Generators**							
2								
3	Origin to Destination—Cost per unit to ship							
4			**Destination**					
5	**Origin**	Boston	Chicago	St. Louis	Lexington	**Units Available**		
6	Cleveland	$3.00	$2.00	$7.00	$6.00	5000		
7	Bedford	$7.00	$5.00	$2.00	$3.00	6000		
8	York	$2.00	$5.00	$4.00	$5.00	2500		
9	**Units Demanded**	6000	4000	2000	1500			
10								
11								
12	**Model**							
13								
14		**Min Cost**	$39,500.00					
15								
16	Origin to Destination—Units Shipped							
17			**Destination**					
18	**Origin**	Boston	Chicago	St. Louis	Lexington	**Units Shipped**		
19	Cleveland	3500	1500	0	0	5000	<=	5000
20	Bedford	0	2500	2000	1500	6000	<=	6000
21	York	2500	0	0	0	2500	<=	2500
22	**Units Received**	6000	4000	2000	1500			
23		=	=	=	=			
24		6000	4000	2000	1500			

discussed (Figure A.10). The tables are more explicitly labeled, and shading focuses the user on the objective and the decision cells (amount to ship). The per-unit shipping cost data and total (Min) cost have been properly formatted as currency.

Use Simple Formulas and Cell Names

Clear formulas can eliminate unnecessary calculations, reduce errors, and make it easier to maintain your spreadsheet. Long and complex calculations should be divided into several cells. This makes the formula easier to understand and easier to edit. Avoid using numbers in a formula. Instead, put the number in a cell in the data section of your worksheet and refer to the cell location of the data in the formula. Building the formula in this manner avoids having to edit the formula for a simple data change.

Using cell names can make a formula much easier to understand. To assign a name to a cell, use the following steps:

Step 1. Select the cell or range of cells you would like to name
Step 2. Select the **Formulas** tab from the Ribbon
Step 3. Choose **Define Name** from the Define Names section
Step 4. The **New Name** dialog box will appear, as shown in Figure A.18
Enter the name you would like to use in the top portion of the dialog box and Click **OK**

Following this procedure and naming all cells in the *Nowlin Plastics* spreadsheet model leads to the model shown in Figure A.19. Compare this to Figure A.6 to easily understand the formulas in the model.

A name is also easily applied to range as follows. First, highlight the range of interest. Then click on the Name Box in the Formula Bar (refer back to Figure A.3) and type in the desired range name.

FIGURE A.18   THE DEFINE NAME DIALOG BOX

WEB file

NowlinPlastics

FIGURE A.19   THE NOWLIN PLASTICS MODEL FORMULAS WITH NAMED CELLS

	A	B
1	**Nowlin Plastics**	
2		
3	**Fixed Cost**	3000
4		
5	**Variable Cost Per Unit**	2
6		
7	**Selling Price Per Unit**	5
8		
9		
10	**Models**	
11		
12	**Production Volume**	800
13		
14	**Total Cost**	=Fixed_Cost+Variable_Cost*Production_Volume
15		
16	**Total Revenue**	=Selling_Price*Production_Volume
17		
18	**Total Profit (Loss)**	=Total_Revenue-Total_Cost

Use of Relative and Absolute Cell References

There are a number of ways to copy a formula from one cell to another in an Excel worksheet. One way to copy the a formula from one cell to another is presented here:

Step 1. Select the cell you would like to copy
Step 2. Right click on the mouse
Step 3. Click **Copy**
Step 4. Select the cell where you would like to put the copy
Step 5. Right click on the mouse
Step 6. Click **Paste**

When copying in Excel, one can use a relative or an absolute address. When copied, a relative address adjusts with the move of the copy, whereas an absolute address stays in its original form. Relative addresses are of the form C7. Absolute addresses have $ in front of the column and row, for example, $C$7. How you use relative and absolute addresses can have an impact on the amount of effort it takes to build a model and the opportunity for error in constructing the model.

Let us reconsider the OM455 grading spreadsheet previously discussed in this appendix and shown in Figure A.16. Recall that we used the VLOOKUP function to retrieve the appropriate letter grade for each student. The following formula is in cell E14:

$$=VLOOKUP(D14,B6:D10,3,TRUE)$$

Note that this formula contains only relative addresses. If we copy this to cell E15, we get the following result:

$$=VLOOKUP(D15,B7:D11,3,TRUE)$$

Although the first argument has correctly changed to D15 (we want to calculate the letter grade for the student in row 15), the table in the function has also shifted to B7:D11. What we desired was for this table location to remain the same. A better approach would have been to use the following formula in cell E14:

$$=VLOOKUP(D14,\$B\$6:\$D\$10,3,TRUE)$$

Copying this formula to cell E15 results in the following formula:

$$=VLOOKUP(D15,\$B\$6:\$D\$10,3,TRUE)$$

This correctly changes the first argument to D15 and keeps the data table intact. Using absolute referencing is extremely useful if you have a function that has a reference that should not change when applied to another cell and you are copying the formula to other locations. In the case of the OM455 workbook, instead of typing the VLOOKUP for each student, we can use absolute referencing on the table and then copy from row 14 to rows 15 through 24.

In this section we have discussed guidelines for good spreadsheet model building. In the next section we discuss EXCEL tools available for checking and debugging spreadsheet models.

AUDITING EXCEL MODELS

EXCEL contains a variety of tools to assist you in the development and debugging of spreadsheet models. These tools are found in the Formula Auditing group of the **FORMULAS** tab as shown in Figure A.20. Let us review each of the tools available in this group.

Trace Precedents and Dependents

The **Trace Precedents** button creates arrows pointing to the selected cell from cells that are part of the formula in that cell. The **Trace Dependents** button, on the other hand, shows arrows pointing from the selected cell, to cells that depend on the selected cell. Both of the tools are excellent for quickly ascertaining how parts of a model are linked.

An example of **Trace Precedents** is shown in Figure A.21. Here we have opened the *Foster Rev* worksheet, selected cell C14, and clicked the Trace Precedents button in the **Formula Auditing** group. Recall that the cost in cell C14 is calculated as the SUMPRODUCT of the per-unit shipping cost and units shipped. In Figure A.21, to show this relationship, arrows are drawn to these respective areas of the spreadsheet to cell C14. These arrows may be removed by clicking on the **Remove Arrows** button in the **Auditing Tools** group.

FIGURE A.20   THE FORMULA AUDITING GROUP OF THE FORMULAS TAB

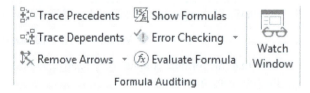

FIGURE A.21   TRACE PRECEDENTS FOR CELL C14 (COST) IN THE FOSTER GENERATORS REV MODEL

| C14 | | fx | =SUMPRODUCT(B6:E8,B19:E21) | | | | |

	A	B	C	D	E	F	G	H
1	**Foster Generators**							
2								
3	Origin to Destination—Cost per unit to ship							
4				**Destination**				
5	**Origin**	Boston	Chicago	St. Louis	Lexington	**Units Available**		
6	Cleveland	$3.00	$2.00	$7.00	$6.00	5000		
7	Bedford	$7.00	$5.00	$2.00	$3.00	6000		
8	York	$2.00	$5.00	$4.00	$5.00	2500		
9	**Units Demanded**	6000	4000	2000	1500			
10								
11								
12	**Model**							
13								
14			**Min Cost**	$39,500.00				
15								
16	Origin to Destination—Units Shipped							
17				**Destination**				
18	**Origin**	Boston	Chicago	St. Louis	Lexington	**Units Shipped**		
19	Cleveland	3500	1500	0	0	5000	<=	5000
20	Bedford	0	2500	2000	1500	6000	<=	6000
21	York	2500	0	0	0	2500	<=	2500
22	**Units Received**	6000	4000	2000	1500			
23		=	=	=	=			
24		6000	4000	2000	1500			

WEB file

FosterRev

An example of **Trace Dependents** is shown in Figure A.22. We have selected cell E20, the units shipped from Bedford to Lexington, and clicked on the **Trace Dependents** button in the **Formula Auditing** group. As shown in Figure A.22, units shipped from Bedford to Lexington impacts the cost function in cell C14, the total units shipped from Bedford given in cell F20, and the total units shipped to Lexington in cell E22. These arrows may be removed by clicking on the **Remove Arrows** button in the **Auditing Tools** group.

Trace Precedents and **Trace Dependents** can highlight errors in copying and formula construction by showing that incorrect sections of the worksheet are referenced.

Show Formulas

The **Show Formulas** button, [icon] Show Formulas , does exactly that. To see the formulas in a worksheet, simply click on any cell in the worksheet and then click on **Show Formulas**. You will see the formulas that exist in that worksheet. To go back to hiding the formulas, click again on the **Show Formulas** button. Figure A.6 gives an example of the show formulas view. This allows you to inspect each formula in detail in its cell location.

Evaluate Formulas

The **Evaluate Formula** button, [icon] Evaluate Formula , allows you to investigate the calculations of particular cell in great detail. To invoke this tool, we simply select a cell containing

FIGURE A.22   TRACE DEPENDENTS FOR CELL C14 (COST) IN THE FOSTER
GENERATORS REV MODEL

E20		▼	●	f_x	1500			
	A	**B**	**C**	**D**	**E**	**F**	**G**	**H**
12	Model							
13								
14		**Min Cost**	$39,500.00					
15								
16	Origin to Destination—Units Shipped							
17				Destination				
18	**Origin**	Boston	Chicago	St. Louis	Lexington	**Units Shipped**		
19	Cleveland	3500	1500	0	0	5000	<=	5000
20	Bedford	0	2500	2000	1500	6000	<=	6000
21	York	2500	0	0	0	2500	<=	2500
22	**Units Received**	6000	4000	2000	1500			
23		=	=	=	=			
24		6000	4000	2000	1500			

a formula and click on the **Evaluate Formula** button in the **Formula Auditing** group. As
an example, we select cell B15 of the Gambrell Manufacturing model (see Figures A.13
and A.14). Recall we are calculating cost of goods based upon whether or not there is a
quantity discount. Clicking on the Evaluate button allows you to evaluate this formula explicitly. The **Evaluate Formula** dialog box appears in Figure A.23. Figure A.24 shows the
result of one click of the Evaluate button. The B14 has changed to its value of 95. Further
clicks would evaluate in order, from left to right, the remaining components of the formula.
We ask the reader to further explore this tool in an exercise at the end of this appendix.

FIGURE A.23   THE EVALUATE FORMULA DIALOG BOX FOR CELL B15 OF THE
GAMBRELL MANUFACTURING MODEL

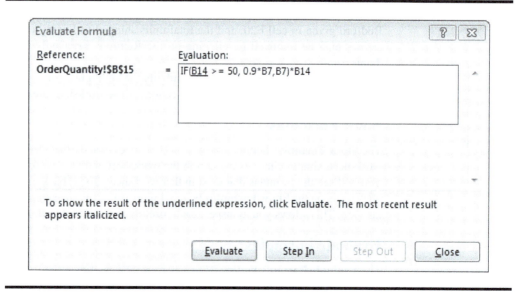

FIGURE A.24   THE EVALUATE FORMULA FOR CELL B15 OF THE GAMBRELL
MANUFACTURING MODEL AFTER ONE CLICK OF THE EVALUATE
BUTTON

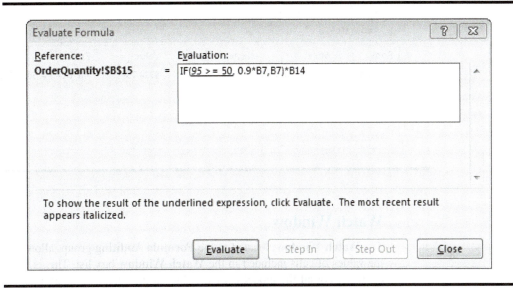

The **Evaluate Formula** tool provides an excellent means of identifying the exact location of an error in a formula.

Error Checking

The **Error Checking** button, 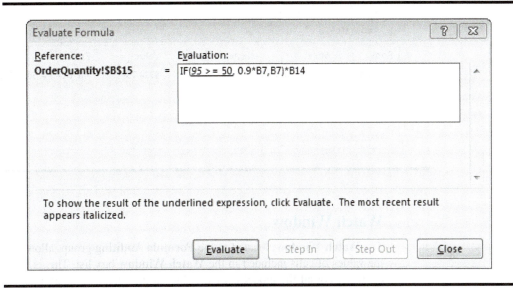 Error Checking ▾ , provides an automatic means of checking for mathematical errors within formulas of a worksheet. Clicking on the **Error Checking** button causes Excel to check every formula in the sheet for calculation errors. If an error is found, the **Error Checking** dialog box appears. An example for a hypothetical division by zero error is shown in Figure A.25. From this box, the formula can be edited or the calculation steps can be observed (as in the previous section on **Evaluate Formulas**).

FIGURE A.25   THE ERROR CHECKING DIALOG BOX FOR A DIVISION
BY ZERO ERROR

FIGURE A.26   THE WATCH WINDOW FOR THE GAMBRELL MANUFACTURING MODEL

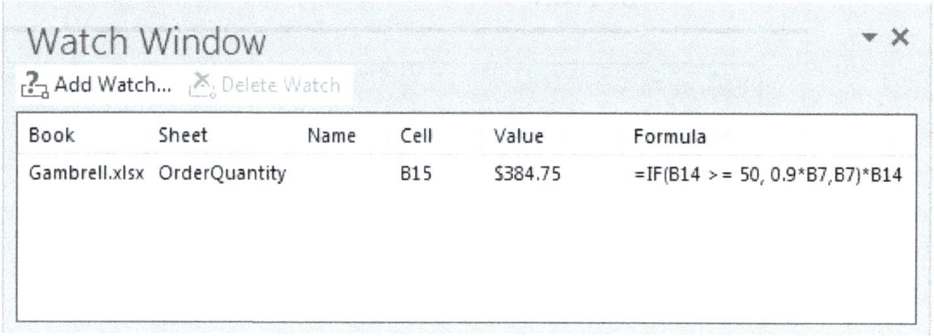

Watch Window

The **Watch Window**, located in the **Formula Auditing** group, allows the user to observe the values of cells included in the **Watch Window** box list. This is useful for large models when not all the model is observable on the screen or when multiple worksheets are used. The user can monitor how the listed cells change with a change in the model without searching through the worksheet or changing from one worksheet to another.

A **Watch Window** for the Gambrell Manufacturing model is shown in Figure A.26. The following steps were used from the OrderQuantity worksheet to add cell B15 of the OrderQuantity worksheet to the watch list:

Step 1. Select the **Formulas** tab
Step 2. Select **Watch Window** from the Formula Auditing group
The Watch Window will appear
Step 3. Select **Add Watch**
Step 4. Click on the cell you would like to add to the watch list (in this case B15)

As shown in Figure A.26, the list gives the workbook name, worksheet name, cell name (if used), cell location, cell value, and cell formula. To delete a cell from the watch list, select the entry from the list and then click on the **Delete Watch** button in the upper part of the **Watch Window**.

The Watch Window, as shown in Figure A.26, allows us to monitor the value of B15 as we make changes elsewhere in the worksheet. Furthermore, if we had other worksheets in this workbook, we could monitor changes to B15 of the OrderQuantity worksheet even from these other worksheets. The **Watch Window** is observable regardless of where we are in any worksheet of a workbook.

SUMMARY

In this appendix we have discussed how to build effective spreadsheet models using Excel. We provided an overview on workbooks and worksheets and details on useful Excel functions. We also discussed a set of principles for good modeling and tools for auditing spreadsheet models.

PROBLEMS

NowlinPlastics

1. Open the file *NowlinPlastics*. Recall that we have modeled total profit for the product CD-50 in this spreadsheet. Suppose we have a second product called a CD-100, with the following characteristics:

$$\text{Fixed Cost} = \$2500$$
$$\text{Variable Cost per Unit} = \$1.67$$
$$\text{Selling Price per Unit} = \$4.40$$

Extend the model so that the profit is calculated for each product and then totaled to give an overall profit generated for the two products. Use a CD-100 production volume of 1200. Save this file as *NowlinPlastics2*. *Hint:* Place the data for CD-100 in column C and copy the formulas in rows 14, 16, and 18 to column C.

2. Assume that in an empty Excel worksheet in cell A1 you enter the formula =B1*$F$3. You now copy this formula into cell E6. What is the modified formula that appears in E6?

FosterRev

3. Open the file *FosterRev*. Select cells B6:E8 and name these cells Shipping_Cost. Select cells B19:E21 and name these cells Units_Shipped. Use these names in the SUMPRODUCT function in cell C14 to compute cost and verify that you obtain the same cost ($39,500).

4. Open the file *NowlinPlastics*. Recall that we have modeled total profit for the product CD-50 in this spreadsheet. Modify the spreadsheet to take into account production capacity and forecasted demand. If forecasted demand is less than or equal to capacity, Nowlin will produce only the forecasted demand; otherwise, they will produce the full capacity. For this example, use forecasted demand of 1200 and capacity of 1500. *Hint:* Enter demand and capacity into the data section of the model. Then use an IF statement to calculate production volume.

CoxElectric

5. Cox Electric makes electronic components and has estimated the following for a new design of one of its products:

$$\text{Fixed Cost} = \$10,000$$
$$\text{Revenue per unit} = \$0.65$$
$$\text{Material cost per unit} = \$0.15$$
$$\text{Labor cost per unit} = \$0.10$$

These data are given in the spreadsheet *CoxElectric*. Also in the spreadsheet in row 14 is a profit model that gives the profit (or loss) for a specified volume (cell C14).

   a. Use the Show Formula button in the Formula Auditing Group of the Formulas tab to see the formulas and cell references used in row 14.

   b. Use the Trace Precedents tool to see how the formulas are dependent on the elements of the data section.

   c. Use trial and error, by trying various values of volume in cell C14, to arrive at a break-even volume.

6. Return to the CoxElectric spreadsheet. Build a table of profits based on different volume levels by doing the following: In cell C15, enter a volume of 20,000. Look at each formula in row 14 and decide which references should be absolute or relative for purposes of copying the formulas to row 15. Make the necessary changes to row 14 (change any references that should be absolute by putting in $). Copy cells D14:I14 to row 15. Continue this with new rows until a positive profit is found. Save your file as *CoxBreakeven*.

OM455

7. Open the workbook *OM455*. Save the file under a new name, *OM455COUNTIF*. Suppose we wish to automatically count the number of each letter grade.
    a. Begin by putting the letters A, B, C, D, and F in cells C29:C33. Use the COUNTIF function in cells D29:D33 to count the number of each letter grade. *Hint:* Create the necessary COUNTIF function in cell D29. Use absolute referencing on the range ($E14:$E$24) and then copy the function to cells D30:D33 to count the number of each of the other letter grades.
    b. We are considering a different grading scale as follows:

Lower	Upper	Grade
0	69	F
70	76	D
77	84	C
85	92	B
93	100	A

For the current list of students, use the COUNTIF function to determine the number of A, B, C, D, and F letter grades earned under this new system.

OM455

8. Open the workbook *OM455*. Save the file under a new name, *OM4555Revised*. Suppose we wish to use a more refined grading system, as shown below:

Lower	Upper	Grade
0	59	F
60	69	D
70	72	C−
73	76	C−
77	79	C+
80	82	B−
83	86	B
87	89	B+
90	92	A−
93	100	A

Update the file to use this more refined grading system. How many of each letter grade are awarded under the new system? *Hint:* Build a new grading table and use VLOOKUP and an absolute reference to the table. Then use COUNTIF to count the number of each letter grade.

9. Richardson Ski Racing (RSR) sells equipment needed for downhill ski racing. One of RSR's products is fencing used on downhill courses. The fence product comes in 150-foot rolls and sells for $215 per roll. However, RSR offers quantity discounts. The following table shows the price per roll depending on order size:

RSR

	Quantity Ordered	
From	**To**	**Price per Roll**
1	50	$215
51	100	$195
101	200	$175
201	and up	$155

The file RSR contains 172 orders that have arrived for the coming six weeks.

a. Use the VLOOKUP function with the preceding pricing table to determine the total revenue from these orders.

b. Use the COUNTIF function to determine the number of orders in each price bin.

NewtonData

10. Newton Manufacturing produces scientific calculators. The models are N350, N450, and the N900. Newton has planned its distribution of these products around eight customer zones: Brazil, China, France, Malaysia, U.S. Northeast, U.S. Southeast, U.S. Midwest, and U.S. West. Data for the current quarter (volume to be shipped in thousands of units) for each product and each customer zone are given in the file *NewtonData*.

Newton would like to know the total number of units going to each customer zone and also the total units of each product shipped. There are several ways to get this information from the data set. One way is to use the SUMIF function.

The SUMIF function extends the SUM function by allowing the user to add the values of cells meeting a logical condition. This general form of the function is

$$=\text{SUMIF}(\textit{test range, condition, range to be summed})$$

The *test range* is an area to search to test the *condition,* and the *range to be summed* is the position of the data to be summed. So, for example, using the *NewtonData* file, we would use the following function to get the total units sent to Malaysia:

$$=\text{SUMIF}(A3{:}A26,A3,C3{:}C26)$$

Here, A3 is Malaysia, A3:A26 is the range of customer zones, and C3:C26 are the volumes for each product for these customer zones. The SUMIF looks for matches of Malaysia in column A and, if a match is found, adds the volume to the total. Use the SUMIF function to get each total volume by zone and each total volume by product.

Williamson

11. Consider the transportation model given in the Excel file *Williamson*. It is a model that is very similar to the Foster Generators model. Williamson produces a single product and has plants in Atlanta, Lexington, Chicago, and Salt Lake City and warehouses in Portland, St. Paul, Las Vegas, Tuscon, and Cleveland. Each plant has a capacity and each warehouse has a demand. Williamson would like to find a low-cost shipping plan. Mr. Williamson has reviewed the results and notices right away that the total cost is way out of line. Use the Formula Auditing Tools under the Formulas tab in Excel to find any errors in this model. Correct the errors. *Hint:* There are two errors in this model. Be sure to check every formula.

Appendix B Areas for the Standard Normal Distribution

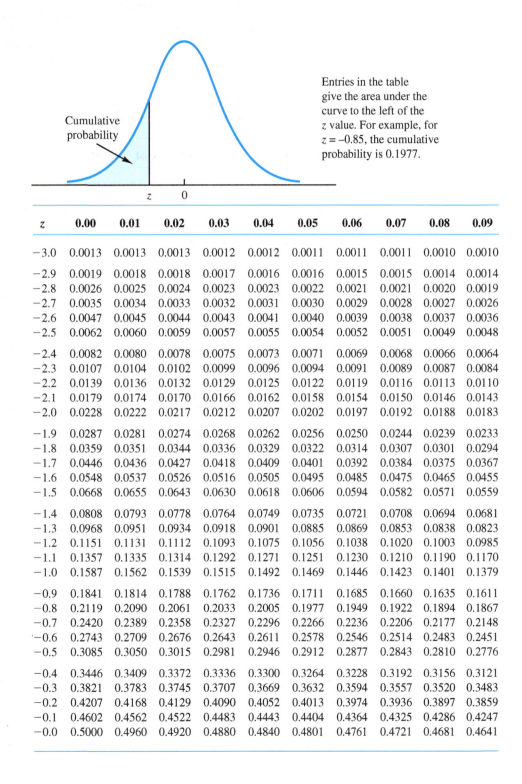

Cumulative probability

Entries in the table give the area under the curve to the left of the z value. For example, for $z = -0.85$, the cumulative probability is 0.1977.

z	0.00	0.01	0.02	0.03	0.04	0.05	0.06	0.07	0.08	0.09
−3.0	0.0013	0.0013	0.0013	0.0012	0.0012	0.0011	0.0011	0.0011	0.0010	0.0010
−2.9	0.0019	0.0018	0.0018	0.0017	0.0016	0.0016	0.0015	0.0015	0.0014	0.0014
−2.8	0.0026	0.0025	0.0024	0.0023	0.0023	0.0022	0.0021	0.0021	0.0020	0.0019
−2.7	0.0035	0.0034	0.0033	0.0032	0.0031	0.0030	0.0029	0.0028	0.0027	0.0026
−2.6	0.0047	0.0045	0.0044	0.0043	0.0041	0.0040	0.0039	0.0038	0.0037	0.0036
−2.5	0.0062	0.0060	0.0059	0.0057	0.0055	0.0054	0.0052	0.0051	0.0049	0.0048
−2.4	0.0082	0.0080	0.0078	0.0075	0.0073	0.0071	0.0069	0.0068	0.0066	0.0064
−2.3	0.0107	0.0104	0.0102	0.0099	0.0096	0.0094	0.0091	0.0089	0.0087	0.0084
−2.2	0.0139	0.0136	0.0132	0.0129	0.0125	0.0122	0.0119	0.0116	0.0113	0.0110
−2.1	0.0179	0.0174	0.0170	0.0166	0.0162	0.0158	0.0154	0.0150	0.0146	0.0143
−2.0	0.0228	0.0222	0.0217	0.0212	0.0207	0.0202	0.0197	0.0192	0.0188	0.0183
−1.9	0.0287	0.0281	0.0274	0.0268	0.0262	0.0256	0.0250	0.0244	0.0239	0.0233
−1.8	0.0359	0.0351	0.0344	0.0336	0.0329	0.0322	0.0314	0.0307	0.0301	0.0294
−1.7	0.0446	0.0436	0.0427	0.0418	0.0409	0.0401	0.0392	0.0384	0.0375	0.0367
−1.6	0.0548	0.0537	0.0526	0.0516	0.0505	0.0495	0.0485	0.0475	0.0465	0.0455
−1.5	0.0668	0.0655	0.0643	0.0630	0.0618	0.0606	0.0594	0.0582	0.0571	0.0559
−1.4	0.0808	0.0793	0.0778	0.0764	0.0749	0.0735	0.0721	0.0708	0.0694	0.0681
−1.3	0.0968	0.0951	0.0934	0.0918	0.0901	0.0885	0.0869	0.0853	0.0838	0.0823
−1.2	0.1151	0.1131	0.1112	0.1093	0.1075	0.1056	0.1038	0.1020	0.1003	0.0985
−1.1	0.1357	0.1335	0.1314	0.1292	0.1271	0.1251	0.1230	0.1210	0.1190	0.1170
−1.0	0.1587	0.1562	0.1539	0.1515	0.1492	0.1469	0.1446	0.1423	0.1401	0.1379
−0.9	0.1841	0.1814	0.1788	0.1762	0.1736	0.1711	0.1685	0.1660	0.1635	0.1611
−0.8	0.2119	0.2090	0.2061	0.2033	0.2005	0.1977	0.1949	0.1922	0.1894	0.1867
−0.7	0.2420	0.2389	0.2358	0.2327	0.2296	0.2266	0.2236	0.2206	0.2177	0.2148
−0.6	0.2743	0.2709	0.2676	0.2643	0.2611	0.2578	0.2546	0.2514	0.2483	0.2451
−0.5	0.3085	0.3050	0.3015	0.2981	0.2946	0.2912	0.2877	0.2843	0.2810	0.2776
−0.4	0.3446	0.3409	0.3372	0.3336	0.3300	0.3264	0.3228	0.3192	0.3156	0.3121
−0.3	0.3821	0.3783	0.3745	0.3707	0.3669	0.3632	0.3594	0.3557	0.3520	0.3483
−0.2	0.4207	0.4168	0.4129	0.4090	0.4052	0.4013	0.3974	0.3936	0.3897	0.3859
−0.1	0.4602	0.4562	0.4522	0.4483	0.4443	0.4404	0.4364	0.4325	0.4286	0.4247
−0.0	0.5000	0.4960	0.4920	0.4880	0.4840	0.4801	0.4761	0.4721	0.4681	0.4641

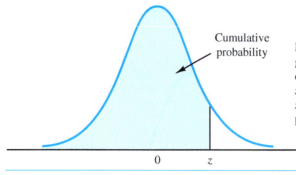

Cumulative probability

Entries in the table give the area under the curve to the left of the z value. For example, for $z = 1.25$, the cumulative probability is 0.8944.

z	0.00	0.01	0.02	0.03	0.04	0.05	0.06	0.07	0.08	0.09
0.0	0.5000	0.5040	0.5080	0.5120	0.5160	0.5199	0.5239	0.5279	0.5319	0.5359
0.1	0.5398	0.5438	0.5478	0.5517	0.5557	0.5596	0.5636	0.5675	0.5714	0.5753
0.2	0.5793	0.5832	0.5871	0.5910	0.5948	0.5987	0.6026	0.6064	0.6103	0.6141
0.3	0.6179	0.6217	0.6255	0.6293	0.6331	0.6368	0.6406	0.6443	0.6480	0.6517
0.4	0.6554	0.6591	0.6628	0.6664	0.6700	0.6736	0.6772	0.6808	0.6844	0.6879
0.5	0.6915	0.6950	0.6985	0.7019	0.7054	0.7088	0.7123	0.7157	0.7190	0.7224
0.6	0.7257	0.7291	0.7324	0.7357	0.7389	0.7422	0.7454	0.7486	0.7517	0.7549
0.7	0.7580	0.7611	0.7642	0.7673	0.7704	0.7734	0.7764	0.7794	0.7823	0.7852
0.8	0.7881	0.7910	0.7939	0.7967	0.7995	0.8023	0.8051	0.8078	0.8106	0.8133
0.9	0.8159	0.8186	0.8212	0.8238	0.8264	0.8289	0.8315	0.8340	0.8365	0.8389
1.0	0.8413	0.8438	0.8461	0.8485	0.8508	0.8531	0.8554	0.8577	0.8599	0.8621
1.1	0.8643	0.8665	0.8686	0.8708	0.8729	0.8749	0.8770	0.8790	0.8810	0.8830
1.2	0.8849	0.8869	0.8888	0.8907	0.8925	0.8944	0.8962	0.8980	0.8997	0.9015
1.3	0.9032	0.9049	0.9066	0.9082	0.9099	0.9115	0.9131	0.9147	0.9162	0.9177
1.4	0.9192	0.9207	0.9222	0.9236	0.9251	0.9265	0.9279	0.9292	0.9306	0.9319
1.5	0.9332	0.9345	0.9357	0.9370	0.9382	0.9394	0.9406	0.9418	0.9429	0.9441
1.6	0.9452	0.9463	0.9474	0.9484	0.9495	0.9505	0.9515	0.9525	0.9535	0.9545
1.7	0.9554	0.9564	0.9573	0.9582	0.9591	0.9599	0.9608	0.9616	0.9625	0.9633
1.8	0.9641	0.9649	0.9656	0.9664	0.9671	0.9678	0.9686	0.9693	0.9699	0.9706
1.9	0.9713	0.9719	0.9726	0.9732	0.9738	0.9744	0.9750	0.9756	0.9761	0.9767
2.0	0.9772	0.9778	0.9783	0.9788	0.9793	0.9798	0.9803	0.9808	0.9812	0.9817
2.1	0.9821	0.9826	0.9830	0.9834	0.9838	0.9842	0.9846	0.9850	0.9854	0.9857
2.2	0.9861	0.9864	0.9868	0.9871	0.9875	0.9878	0.9881	0.9884	0.9887	0.9890
2.3	0.9893	0.9896	0.9898	0.9901	0.9904	0.9906	0.9909	0.9911	0.9913	0.9913
2.4	0.9916	0.9920	0.9922	0.9925	0.9927	0.9929	0.9931	0.9932	0.9934	0.9936
2.5	0.9938	0.9940	0.9941	0.9943	0.9945	0.9946	0.9948	0.9949	0.9951	0.9952
2.6	0.9953	0.9955	0.9956	0.9957	0.9959	0.9960	0.9961	0.9962	0.9963	0.9964
2.7	0.9965	0.9966	0.9967	0.9968	0.9969	0.9970	0.9971	0.9972	0.9973	0.9974
2.8	0.9974	0.9975	0.9976	0.9977	0.9977	0.9978	0.9979	0.9979	0.9980	0.9981
2.9	0.9981	0.9982	0.9982	0.9983	0.9984	0.9984	0.9985	0.9985	0.9986	0.9986
3.0	0.9987	0.9987	0.9987	0.9988	0.9988	0.9989	0.9989	0.9989	0.9990	0.9990

Appendix C   Values of $e^{-\lambda}$

λ	$e^{-\lambda}$	λ	$e^{-\lambda}$	λ	$e^{-\lambda}$
0.05	0.9512	2.05	0.1287	4.05	0.0174
0.10	0.9048	2.10	0.1225	4.10	0.0166
0.15	0.8607	2.15	0.1165	4.15	0.0158
0.20	0.8187	2.20	0.1108	4.20	0.0150
0.25	0.7788	2.25	0.1054	4.25	0.0143
0.30	0.7408	2.30	0.1003	4.30	0.0136
0.35	0.7047	2.35	0.0954	4.35	0.0129
0.40	0.6703	2.40	0.0907	4.40	0.0123
0.45	0.6376	2.45	0.0863	4.45	0.0117
0.50	0.6065	2.50	0.0821	4.50	0.0111
0.55	0.5769	2.55	0.0781	4.55	0.0106
0.60	0.5488	2.60	0.0743	4.60	0.0101
0.65	0.5220	2.65	0.0707	4.65	0.0096
0.70	0.4966	2.70	0.0672	4.70	0.0091
0.75	0.4724	2.75	0.0639	4.75	0.0087
0.80	0.4493	2.80	0.0608	4.80	0.0082
0.85	0.4274	2.85	0.0578	4.85	0.0078
0.90	0.4066	2.90	0.0550	4.90	0.0074
0.95	0.3867	2.95	0.0523	4.95	0.0071
1.00	0.3679	3.00	0.0498	5.00	0.0067
1.05	0.3499	3.05	0.0474	5.05	0.0064
1.10	0.3329	3.10	0.0450	5.10	0.0061
1.15	0.3166	3.15	0.0429	5.15	0.0058
1.20	0.3012	3.20	0.0408	5.20	0.0055
1.25	0.2865	3.25	0.0388	5.25	0.0052
1.30	0.2725	3.30	0.0369	5.30	0.0050
1.35	0.2592	3.35	0.0351	5.35	0.0047
1.40	0.2466	3.40	0.0334	5.40	0.0045
1.45	0.2346	3.45	0.0317	5.45	0.0043
1.50	0.2231	3.50	0.0302	5.50	0.0041
1.55	0.2122	3.55	0.0287	5.55	0.0039
1.60	0.2019	3.60	0.0273	5.60	0.0037
1.65	0.1920	3.65	0.0260	5.65	0.0035
1.70	0.1827	3.70	0.0247	5.70	0.0033
1.75	0.1738	3.75	0.0235	5.75	0.0032
1.80	0.1653	3.80	0.0224	5.80	0.0030
1.85	0.1572	3.85	0.0213	5.85	0.0029
1.90	0.1496	3.90	0.0202	5.90	0.0027
1.95	0.1423	3.95	0.0193	5.95	0.0026
2.00	0.1353	4.00	0.0183	6.00	0.0025
				7.00	0.0009
				8.00	0.000335
				9.00	0.000123
				10.00	0.000045

Appendix D   References and Bibliography

Chapter 1   Introduction

Churchman, C. W., R. L. Ackoff, and E. L. Arnoff. *Introduction to Operations Research*. Wiley, 1957.

Horner, Peter. "The Sabre Story," *OR/MS Today* (June 2000).

Leon, Linda, Z. Przasnyski, and K. C. Seal. "Spreadsheets and OR/MS Models: An End-User Perspective," *Interfaces* (March/April 1996).

Powell, S. G. "Innovative Approaches to Management Science," *OR/MS Today* (October 1996).

Savage, S. "Weighing the Pros and Cons of Decision Technology and Spreadsheets," *OR/MS Today* (February 1997).

Winston, W. L. "The Teachers' Forum: Management Science with Spreadsheets for MBAs at Indiana University," *Interfaces* (March/April 1996).

Chapters 2 to 7   Linear, Integer Programming

Ahuja, R. K., T. L. Magnanti, and J. B. Orlin. *Network Flows, Theory, Algorithms, and Applications*. Prentice Hall, 1993.

Bazarra, M. S., J. J. Jarvis, and H. D. Sherali. *Linear Programming and Network Flows,* 2d ed. Wiley, 1990.

Carino, H. F., and C. H. Le Noir, Jr. "Optimizing Wood Procurement in Cabinet Manufacturing," *Interfaces* (March/April 1988): 10–19.

Dantzig, G. B. *Linear Programming and Extensions*. Princeton University Press, 1963.

Davis, Morton D. *Game Theory: A Nontechnical Introduction*. Dover, 1997.

Evans, J. R., and E. Minieka. *Optimization Algorithms for Networks and Graphs,* 2d ed. Marcel Dekker, 1992.

Ford, L. R., and D. R. Fulkerson. *Flows and Networks*. Princeton University Press, 1962.

Geoffrion, A., and G. Graves. "Better Distribution Planning with Computer Models," *Harvard Business Review* (July/August 1976).

Greenberg, H. J. "How to Analyze the Results of Linear Programs—Part 1: Preliminaries," *Interfaces* 23, no. 4 (July/August 1993): 56–67.

Greenberg, H. J. "How to Analyze the Results of Linear Programs—Part 2: Price Interpretation," *Interfaces* 23, no. 5 (September/October 1993): 97–114.

Greenberg, H. J. "How to Analyze the Results of Linear Programs—Part 3: Infeasibility Diagnosis," *Interfaces* 23, no. 6 (November/December 1993): 120–139.

Lillien, G., and A. Rangaswamy. *Marketing Engineering: Computer-Assisted Marketing Analysis and Planning*. Addison-Wesley, 1998.

Martin, R. K. *Large Scale Linear and Integer Optimization: A Unified Approach*. Kluwer Academic Publishers, 1999.

McMillian, John. *Games, Strategies, and Managers*. Oxford University Press, 1992.

Myerson, Roger B. *Game Theory: Analysis of Conflict*. Harvard University Press, 1997.

Nemhauser, G. L., and L. A. Wolsey. *Integer and Combinatorial Optimization*. Wiley, 1999.

Osborne, Martin J. *An Introduction to Game Theory*. Oxford University Press, 2004.

Schrage, Linus. *Optimization Modeling with LINDO,* 4th ed. LINDO Systems Inc., 2000.

Sherman, H. D. "Hospital Efficiency Measurement and Evaluation," *Medical Care* 22, no. 10 (October 1984): 922–938.

Winston, W. L., and S. C. Albright. *Practical Management Science,* 2d ed. Duxbury Press, 2001.

Chapter 8   Nonlinear Optimization Models

Bazarra, M. S., H. D. Sherali, and C. M. Shetty. *Nonlinear Programming Theory and Applications*. Wiley, 1993.

Benninga, Simon. *Financial Modeling*. MIT Press, 2000.

Luenberger, D. *Linear and Nonlinear Programming,* 2d ed. Addison-Wesley, 1984.

Rardin, R. L. *Optimization in Operations Research*. Prentice Hall, 1998.

Chapter 9   Project Scheduling: PERT/CPM

Moder, J. J., C. R. Phillips, and E. W. Davis. *Project Management with CPM, PERT and Precedence Diagramming,* 3d ed. Blitz, 1995.

Wasil, E. A., and A. A. Assad. "Project Management on the PC: Software, Applications, and Trends," *Interfaces* 18, no. 2 (March/April 1988): 75–84.

Wiest, J., and F. Levy. *Management Guide to PERT-CPM,* 2d ed. Prentice Hall, 1977.

Chapter 10   Inventory Models

Fogarty, D. W., J. H. Blackstone, and T. R. Hoffman. *Production and Inventory Management,* 2d ed. South-Western, 1990.

Hillier, F., and G. J. Lieberman. *Introduction to Operations Research,* 7th ed. McGraw-Hill, 2000.

Narasimhan, S. L., D. W. McLeavey, and P. B. Lington. *Production Planning and Inventory Control,* 2d ed. Prentice Hall, 1995.

Orlicky, J., and G. W. Plossi. *Orlicky's Material Requirements Planning.* McGraw-Hill, 1994.

Vollmann, T. E., W. L. Berry, and D. C. Whybark. *Manufacturing Planning and Control Systems,* 4th ed. McGraw-Hill, 1997.

Zipkin, P. H. *Foundations of Inventory Management.* McGraw-Hill/Irwin, 2000.

Chapter 11   Waiting Line Models

Bunday, B. D. *An Introduction to Queueing Theory.* Wiley, 1996.

Gross, D., and C. M. Harris. *Fundamentals of Queueing Theory,* 3d ed. Wiley, 1997.

Hall, R. W. *Queueing Methods: For Services and Manufacturing.* Prentice Hall, 1997.

Hillier, F., and G. J. Lieberman. *Introduction to Operations Research,* 7th ed. McGraw-Hill, 2000.

Kao, E. P. C. *An Introduction to Stochastic Processes.* Duxbury, 1996.

Chapter 12   Simulation

Banks, J., J. S. Carson, and B. L. Nelson. *Discrete-Event System Simulation,* 2d ed. Prentice Hall, 1995.

Fishwick, P. A. *Simulation Model Design and Execution: Building Digital Worlds.* Prentice Hall, 1995.

Harrell, C. R., and K. Tumau. *Simulation Made Easy: A Manager's Guide.* Institute of Industrial Engineers, 1996.

Kelton, W. D., R. P. Sadowski, and D. A. Sadowski. *Simulation with Arena,* 4th ed. McGraw-Hill, 2007.

Law, A. M., and W. D. Kelton. *Simulation Modeling and Analysis,* 3d ed. McGraw-Hill, 1999.

Pidd, M. *Computer Simulation in Management Science,* 4th ed. Wiley, 1998.

Thesen, A., and L. E. Travis. *Simulation for Decision Making.* Wadsworth, 1992.

Chapter 13   Decision Analysis

Berger, J. O. *Statistical Decision Theory and Bayesian Analysis,* 2d ed. Springer-Verlag, 1985.

Chernoff, H., and L. E. Moses. *Elementary Decision Theory.* Dover, 1987.

Clemen, R. T., and T. Reilly. *Making Hard Decisions with Decision Tools.* Duxbury, 2001.

Goodwin, P., and G. Wright. *Decision Analysis for Management Judgment,* 2d ed. Wiley, 1999.

Gregory, G. *Decision Analysis.* Plenum, 1988.

Pratt, J. W., H. Raiffa, and R. Schlaifer. *Introduction to Statistical Decision Theory.* MIT Press, 1995.

Raiffa, H. *Decision Analysis.* McGraw-Hill, 1997.

Schlaifer, R. *Analysis of Decisions Under Uncertainty.* Krieger, 1978.

Chapter 14   Multicriteria Decisions

Dyer, J. S. "A Clarification of Remarks on the Analytic Hierarchy Process," *Management Science* 36, no. 3 (March 1990): 274–275.

Dyer, J. S. "Remarks on the Analytic Hierarchy Process," *Management Science* 36, no. 3 (March 1990): 249–258.

Harker, P. T., and L. G. Vargas. "Reply to Remarks on the Analytic Hierarchy Process by J. S. Dyer," *Management Science* 36, no. 3 (March 1990): 269–273.

Harker, P. T., and L. G. Vargas. "The Theory of Ratio Scale Estimation: Saaty's Analytic Hierarchy Process," *Management Science* 33, no. 11 (November 1987): 1383–1403.

Ignizio, J. *Introduction to Linear Goal Programming.* Sage, 1986.

Keeney, R. L., and H. Raiffa. *Decisions with Multiple Objectives: Preferences and Value Tradeoffs.* Cambridge, 1993.

Saaty, T. *Decision Making for Leaders: The Analytic Hierarchy Process for Decisions in a Complex World,* 3d ed. RWS, 1999.

Saaty, T. *Multicriteria Decision Making,* 2d ed. RWS, 1996.

Saaty, T. L. "An Exposition of the AHP in Reply to the Paper Remarks on the Analytic Hierarchy Process," *Management Science* 36, no. 3 (March 1990): 259–268.

Saaty, T. L. "Rank Generation, Preservation, and Reversal in the Analytic Hierarchy Decision Process," *Decision Sciences* 18 (1987): 157–177.

Winkler, R. L. "Decision Modeling and Rational Choice: AHP and Utility Theory," *Management Science* 36, no. 3 (March 1990): 247–248.

Chapter 15   Forecasting

Bowerman, B. L., and R. T. O'Connell. *Forecasting and Time Series: An Applied Approach,* 3d ed. Duxbury, 2000.

Box, G. E. P., G. M. Jenkins, and G. C. Reinsel. *Time Series Analysis: Forecasting and Control,* 3d ed. Prentice Hall, 1994.

Hanke, J. E., and A. G. Reitsch. *Business Forecasting,* 6th ed. Prentice Hall, 1998.

Makridakis, S. G., S. C. Wheelwright, and R. J. Hyndman. *Forecasting: Methods and Applications,* 3d ed. Wiley, 1997.

Wilson, J. H., and B. Keating. *Business Forecasting,* 3d ed. Irwin, 1998.

Chapter 16   Markov Processes

Bharucha-Reid, A. T. *Elements of the Theory of Markov Processes and Their Applications.* Dover, 1997.

Bhat, U. N. *Elements of Applied Stochastic Processes,* 2d ed. Wiley, 1984.

Filar, J. A., and K. Vrieze. *Competitive Markov Decision Processes.* Springer-Verlag, 1996.

Norris, J. *Markov Chains.* Cambridge, 1997.

Appendix E   Self-Test Solutions and Answers to Even-Numbered Problems

Chapter 1

2. Define the problem; identify the alternatives; determine the criteria; evaluate the alternatives; choose an alternative.

4. A quantitative approach should be considered because the problem is large, complex, important, new, and repetitive.

6. Quicker to formulate, easier to solve, and/or more easily understood.

8. a. Max $10x + 5y$
   s.t.
   $$5x + 2y \leq 40$$
   $$x \geq 0, y \geq 0$$
   b. Controllable inputs: x and y
   Uncontrollable inputs: profit (10, 5), labor-hours (5, 2), and labor-hour availability (40)
   c. See Figure 1.8c.
   d. $x = 0, y = 20$; Profit = $100 (solution by trial and error)
   e. Deterministic

10. a. Total units received = $x + y$
   b. Total cost = $0.20x + 0.25y$
   c. $x + y = 5000$
   d. $x \leq 4000$ Kansas City
   $y \leq 3000$ Minneapolis
   e. Min $0.20x + 0.25y$
   s.t.
   $$\begin{aligned} x + \quad y &= 5000 \\ x \quad\quad &\leq 4000 \\ y &\leq 3000 \\ x, y &\geq 0 \end{aligned}$$

FIGURE 1.8C   SOLUTION

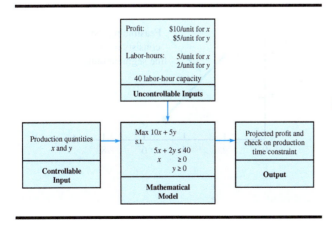

12. a. $TC = 2000 + 60x$
   b. $P = 80x - (2000 + 60x) = 20x - 2000$
   c. Break even when $P = 0$
   Thus, $20x - 2000 = 0$
   $$20x = 2000$$
   $$x = 100$$

14. a. 4000
   b. Loss of $8000
   c. $48.11
   d. $10,810 profit

16. a. Max $6x + 4y$
   b. $50x + 30y \leq 800,000$
   $50x \quad\quad \leq 500,000$
   $\quad\quad 30y \leq 450,000$

18. a. max $2.80x_1 + 2.90y_1 + 2.70x_2 + 2.80y_2 + 2.62x_3 + 2.72y_3$
   b. (1) $x_1 + y_1 \leq 12,000$
   (2) $x_2 + y_2 \leq 20,000$
   (3) $x_3 + y_3 \leq 24,000$
   c. $.65x_1 - .35x_2 - .35x_3 \geq 0$
   $-.50x_1 + .50x_2 - .50x_3 \leq 0$
   $-.15x_1 - .15x_2 + .85x_3 \geq 0$
   $.80y_1 - .20y_2 - .20y_3 \geq 0$
   $-.30y_1 + .70y_2 - .30y_3 \geq 0$
   $-.40y_1 - .40y_2 + .60y_3 \leq 0$
   $x_1 + x_2 + x_3 \geq 20,000$
   $y_1 + y_2 + y_3 \geq 20,000$

20. a. max $7000x + 4000y$
   b. $500x + 250y \leq 100,000$
   c. $x \leq 20$
   d. $y \geq 50$
   e. $2/3x - 1/3y \geq 0$
   f. If the number of television ads purchased (x) must be less than or equal to 20 and the number of Internet ads purchased (y) must be at least 50, the producers' desire that at least one-third of all ads will be placed on television cannot be satisfied.

Chapter 2

1. Parts (a), (b), and (e) are acceptable linear programming relationships.
   Part (c) is not acceptable because of $-2x_2^2$.
   Part (d) is not acceptable because of $3\sqrt{x_1}$.
   Part (f) is not acceptable because of $1x_1x_2$.
   Parts (c), (d), and (f) could not be found in a linear programming model because they contain nonlinear terms.

2. a.

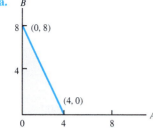

b.

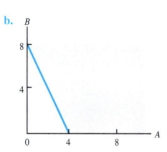

c.

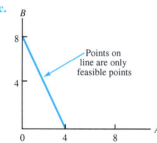

6. $7A + 10B = 420$
        $6A + 4B = 420$
        $-4A + 7B = 420$

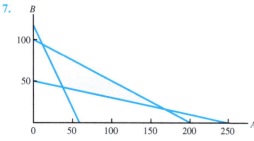

7.

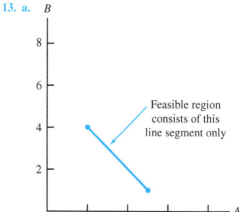

10.

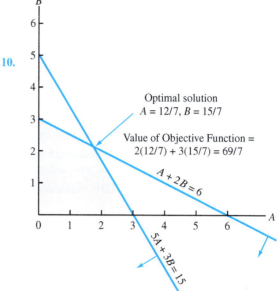

Optimal solution
$A = 12/7, B = 15/7$

Value of Objective Function =
$2(12/7) + 3(15/7) = 69/7$

$$A + 2B = 6 \quad (1)$$
$$5A + 3B = 15 \quad (2)$$

Equation (1) times 5: $5A + 10B = 30 \quad (3)$
Equation (2) minus equation (3): $-7B = -15$
                                    $B = 15/7$
From equation (1): $A = 6 - 2(15/7)$
                            $= 6 - 30/7 = 12/7$

12. a. $A = 3, B = 1.5$; value of optimal solution $= 13.5$
  b. $A = 0, B = 3$; value of optimal solution $= 18$
  c. Four: $(0, 0), (4, 0), (3, 1.5)$, and (0.3)

13. a.

Feasible region consists of this line segment only

b. The extreme points are (5, 1) and (2, 4).

c.

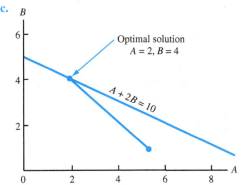

14. a. Let F = number of tons of fuel additive
S = number of tons of solvent base

Max $40F + 30S$

s.t.

$$\tfrac{2}{5}F + \tfrac{1}{2}S \leq 20 \quad \text{Material 1}$$
$$\tfrac{1}{5}S \leq 5 \quad \text{Material 2}$$
$$\tfrac{3}{5}F + \tfrac{3}{10}S \leq 21 \quad \text{Material 3}$$
$$F, S \geq 0$$

b. $F = 25, S = 20$

c. Material 2:4 tons are used; 1 ton is unused.

d. No redundant constraints

16. a. $3S + 9D$

b. (0, 540)

c. 90, 150, 348, 0

17. Max $5A + 2B + 0s_1 + 0s_2 + 0s_3$

s.t.

$$1A - 2B + 1s_1 \qquad\qquad = 420$$
$$2A + 3B - \qquad + 1s_2 \qquad = 610$$
$$6A - 1B + \qquad\qquad + 1s_3 = 125$$
$$A, B, s_1, s_2, s_3 \geq 0$$

18. b. $A = 18/7, B = 15/7$

c. 0, 0, 4/7

20. b. $A = 3.43, B = 3.43$

c. 2.86, 0, 1.43, 0

22. b.

Extreme Point	Coordinates	Profit ($)
1	(0, 0)	0
2	(1700, 0)	8500
3	(1400, 600)	9400
4	(800, 1200)	8800
5	(0, 1680)	6720

Extreme point 3 generates the highest profit.

c. $A = 1400, C = 600$

d. Cutting and dyeing constraint and the packaging constraint

e. $A = 800, C = 1200$; profit = \$9200

24. a. Let R = number of units of regular model
C = number of units of catcher's model

Max $5R + 8C$

$$1R + \tfrac{3}{2}C \leq 900 \quad \text{Cutting and sewing}$$
$$\tfrac{1}{2}R + \tfrac{1}{3}C \leq 300 \quad \text{Finishing}$$
$$\tfrac{1}{8}R + \tfrac{1}{4}C \leq 100 \quad \text{Packaging and shipping}$$
$$R, C \geq 0$$

b.

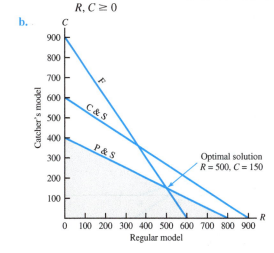

c. $5(500) + 8(150) = \$3700$

d. C & S $\qquad 1(500) + \tfrac{3}{2}(150) = 725$

F $\qquad\qquad \tfrac{1}{2}(500) + \tfrac{1}{3}(150) = 300$

P & S $\qquad \tfrac{1}{8}(500) + \tfrac{1}{4}(150) = 100$

e.

Department	Capacity	Usage	Slack
Cutting and sewing	900	725	175 hours
Finishing	300	300	0 hours
Packaging and shipping	100	100	0 hours

26. a. Max $50N + 80R$

s.t.

$$N + R = 1000$$
$$N \geq 250$$
$$R \geq 250$$
$$N - 2R \geq 0$$
$$N, R \geq 0$$

b. $N = 666.67, R = 333.33$; Audience exposure = 60,000

28. a. Max $1W + 1.25M$

s.t.

$$5W + 7M \leq 4480$$
$$3W + 1M \leq 2080$$
$$2W + 2M \leq 1600$$
$$W, M \geq 0$$

b. $W = 560, M = 240$; Profit = 860

30. a. Max $15E + 18C$
    s.t.
$$40E + 25C \le 50{,}000$$
$$40E \qquad\quad \ge 15{,}000$$
$$25C \ge 10{,}000$$
$$25C \le 25{,}000$$
$$E, C \ge 0$$

c. (375, 400); (1000, 400); (625, 1000); (375, 1000)

d. $E = 625, C = 1000$
    Total return = \$27,375

31.

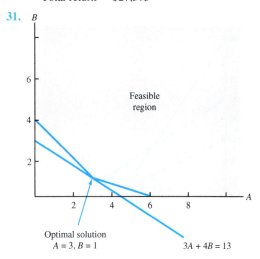

Optimal solution
$A = 3, B = 1$

$3A + 4B = 13$

Objective function value = 13

32.

Extreme Points	Objective Function Value	Surplus Demand	Surplus Total Production	Slack Processing Time
(250, 100)	800	125	—	—
(125, 225)	925	—	—	125
(125, 350)	1300	—	125	—

34. a.

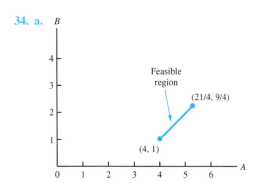

b. The two extreme points are
    $(A = 4, B = 1)$ and $(A = 21/4, B = 9/4)$

c. The optimal solution (see part (a)) is $A = 4, B = 1$.

35. a. Min $6A + 4B + 0s_1 + 0s_2 + 0s_3$
    s.t.
$$2A + 1B - s_1 \qquad\qquad = 12$$
$$1A + 1B \qquad - s_2 \qquad = 10$$
$$1B \qquad\qquad + s_3 = 4$$
$$A, B, s_1, s_2, s_3 \ge 0$$

b. The optimal solution is $A = 6, B = 4$.

c. $s_1 = 4, s_2 = 0, s_3 = 0$

36. a. Min $10{,}000T + 8{,}000P$
    s.t.
$$T \qquad\qquad \ge 8$$
$$P \ge 10$$
$$T + \qquad P \ge 25$$
$$3T + \qquad 2P \le 84$$

c. (15, 10); (21.33, 10); (8, 30); (8, 17)

d. $T = 8, P = 17$
    Total cost = \$216,000

38. a. Min $7.50S + 9.00P$
    s.t.
$$0.10S + 0.30P \le 6$$
$$0.06S + 0.12P \le 3$$
$$S + \qquad P = 30$$
$$S, P \le 0$$

c. Optional solution is $S = 15, P = 15$.

d. No

e. Yes

40. $P_1 = 30, P_2 = 25$; Cost = \$55

42.

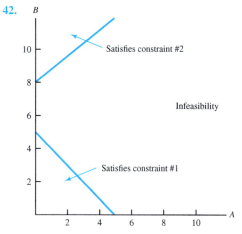

43.

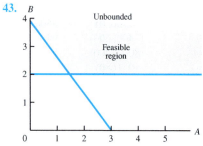

44. a. $A = {}^{30}\!/_{16}$, $B = {}^{30}\!/_{16}$; Value of optimal solution $= {}^{60}\!/_{16}$

b. $A = 0$, $B = 3$; Value of optimal solution $= 6$

46. a. 180, 20

b. Alternative optimal solutions

c. 120, 80

48. No feasible solution

50. $M = 65.45$, $R = 261.82$; Profit $= \$45,818$

52. $S = 384$, $O = 80$

54. a.   Max $160M_1 + 345M_2$

s.t.

$$
\begin{aligned}
M_1 \qquad\qquad &\leq\ 15 \\
M_2 &\leq\ 10 \\
M_1 \qquad\qquad &\geq\ 5 \\
M_2 &\geq\ 5 \\
40M_1 +\ 50M_2 &\leq 1000 \\
M_1, M_2 &\geq 0
\end{aligned}
$$

b. $M_1 = 12.5$, $M_2 = 10$

56. No, this could not make the problem infeasible. Changing an equality constraint to an inequality constraint can only make the feasible region larger, not smaller. No solutions have been eliminated and anything that was feasible before is still feasible.

58. The statement by the boss shows a fundamental misunderstanding of optimization models. If there were an optimal solution with 15 or less products, the model would find it, because it is trying to minimize. If there is no solution with 15 or less, adding this constraint will make the model infeasible.

Chapter 3

1. a.

b. The same extreme point, $A = 7$ and $B = 3$, remains optimal; value of the objective function becomes $5(7) + 2(3) = 41$.

c. A new extreme point, $A = 4$ and $B = 6$, becomes optimal; value of the objective function becomes $3(4) + 4(6) = 36$.

d. The objective coefficient range for variable A is 2 to 6; the optimal solution, $A = 7$ and $B = 3$, does not change. The objective coefficient range for variable B is 1 to 3; re-solve the problem to find the new optimal solution.

2. a. The feasible region becomes larger with the new optimal solution of $A = 6.5$ and $B = 4.5$.

b. Value of the optimal solution to the revised problem is $3(6.5) + 2(4.5) = 28.5$; the one-unit increase in the right-hand side of constraint 1 improves the value of the optimal solution by $28.5 - 27 = 1.5$; therefore, the dual value for constraint 1 is 1.5.

c. The right-hand-side range for constraint 1 is 8 to 11.2; as long as the right-hand side stays within this range, the dual value of 1.5 is applicable.

d. The improvement in the value of the optimal solution will be 0.5 for every unit increase in the right-hand side of constraint 2 as long as the right-hand side is between 18 and 30.

4. a. $X = 2.5$, $Y = 2.5$

b. -2

c. 5 to 11

d. -3 between 9 and 18

5. a. Regular glove $= 500$; Catcher's mitt $= 150$; Value $= 3700$

b. The finishing, packaging, and shipping constraints are binding; there is no slack.

c. Cutting and sewing $= 0$
Finishing $= 3$
Packaging and shipping $= 28$
Additional finishing time is worth \$3 per unit, and additional packaging and shipping time is worth \$28 per unit.

d. In the packaging and shipping department, each additional hour is worth \$28.

6. a. 4 to 12
3.33 to 10

b. As long as the profit contribution for the regular glove is between \$4.00 and \$12.00, the current solution is optimal; as long as the profit contribution for the catcher's mitt stays between \$3.33 and \$10.00, the current solution is optimal; the optimal solution is not sensitive to small changes in the profit contributions for the gloves.

c. The dual values for the resources are applicable over the following ranges:

Constraint	Right-Hand-Side Range
Cutting and sewing	725 to No upper limit
Finishing	133.33 to 400
Packaging and shipping	75 to 135

d. Amount of increase $= (28)(20) = \$560$

8. a. More than $7.00

  b. More than $3.50

  c. None

10. a. $S = 4000, M = 10,000$; Total risk $= 62,000$

  b.

Variable	Objective Coefficient Range
S	3.75 to No upper limit
M	No lower limit to 6.4

  c. $5(4000) + 4(10,000) = \$60,000$

  d. $60,000/1,200,000 = 0.05$ or 5%

  e. 0.057 risk units

  f. $0.057(100) = 5.7\%$

12. a. $E = 80, S = 120, D = 0$

     Profit $= \$16,440$

  b. Fan motors and cooling coils

  c. Labor hours; 320 hours available

  d. Objective function coefficient range of optimality

             No lower limit to 159

     Because $150 is in this range, the optimal solution would not change.

13. a. Range of optimality

     E 47.5 to 75

     S 87 to 126

     D No lower limit to 159

  b.

Model	Profit	Change	Allowable Increase/Decrease	%
E	\$ 63	Increase \$6(100)	$\$75 - \$63 = \$12$	$\%_{12}(100) = 50$
S	\$ 95	Decrease \$2	$\$95 - \$87 = \$8$	$\frac{3}{8}(100) = 25$
D	\$135	Increase \$4	$\$159 - \$135 = \$24$	$\frac{4}{24}(100) = 17$
				92

     Because changes are 92% of allowable changes, the optimal solution of $E = 80, S = 120, D = 0$ will not change. The change in total profit will be

       E 80 units @ $+\$6 = \$480$

       S 120 units @ $-\$2 = -240$

                         \$240

     $\therefore$ Profit $= \$16,440 + \$240 = \$16,680$

  c. Range of feasibility

     Constraint 1   160 to 280

     Constraint 2   200 to 400

     Constraint 3   2080 to No upper limit

  d. Yes, Fan motors $= 200 + 100 = 300$ is outside the range of feasibility; the dual value will change.

14. a. Manufacture 100 cases of A and 60 cases of B, and purchase 90 cases of B; Total cost $= \$2170$

  b. Demand for A, demand for B, assembly time

c. $-12.25, -9.0, 0, 0.375$

d. Assembly time constraint

16. a. 100 suits, 150 sport coats

     Profit $= \$40,900$

     40 hours of cutting overtime

  b. Optimal solution will not change.

  c. Consider ordering additional material $34.50 is the maximum price.

  d. Profit will improve by $875.

18. a. The linear programming model is as follows:

     Min $30AN + 50AO + 25BN + 40BO$

     s.t.

$$
\begin{aligned}
AN + AO &\geq 50,000 \\
BN + BO &\geq 70,000 \\
AN + BN &\leq 80,000 \\
AO + BO &\leq 60,000 \\
AN, AO, BN, BO &\geq 0
\end{aligned}
$$

  b. Optimal solution

	New Line	Old Line
Model A	50,000	0
Model B	30,000	40,000

     Total cost: $3,850,000

  c. The first three constraints are binding.

  d. Because the dual value is negative, increasing the right-hand side of constraint 3 will *decrease (improve)* the solution; thus, an increase in capacity for the new production line is desirable.

  e. Because constraint 4 is not a binding constraint, any increase in the production line capacity of the old production line will have no effect on the optimal solution; thus, increasing the capacity of the old production line results in no benefit.

  f. The reduced cost for model A made on the old production line is 5; thus, the cost would have to decrease by at least $5 before any units of model A would be produced on the old production line.

  g. The right-hand-side range for constraint 2 shows a lower limit of 30,000; thus, if the minimum production requirement is reduced 10,000 units to 60,000, the dual value of 40 is applicable; thus, total cost would decrease by $10,000(40) = \$400,000$.

20. a. Max $0.07H + 0.12P + 0.09A$

     s.t.

$$
\begin{aligned}
H + P + A &= 1,000,000 \\
0.6H - 0.4P - 0.4A &\geq 0 \\
P - 0.6A &\leq 0 \\
H, P, A &\geq 0
\end{aligned}
$$

  b. $H = \$400,000, P = \$225,000, A = \$375,000$

     Total annual return $= \$88,750$

     Annual percentage return $= 8.875\%$

c. No change

d. Increase of $890

e. Increase of $312.50, or 0.031%

22. a. Min $30L +$ $25D +$ $18S$
s.t.

$$L + \quad D + \quad S = 100$$
$$0.6L - \quad 0.4D \qquad \geq \quad 0$$
$$-0.15L - 0.15D + 0.85S \geq \quad 0$$
$$-0.25L - 0.25D + \quad S \leq \quad 0$$
$$L \qquad\qquad \leq \quad 50$$
$$L, D, S \geq 0$$

b. $L = 48, D = 72, S = 30$
Total cost = $3780

c. No change

d. No change

24. Let A = number of shares of stock A
B = number of shares of stock B
C = number of shares of stock C
D = number of shares of stock D

a. To get data on a per share basis multiply price by rate of return or risk measure value.

Min $10A + 3.5B + \quad 4C + 3.2D$
s.t.

$$100A + 50B + \quad 80C + \quad 40D = 200,000$$
$$12A + \quad 4B + 4.8C + \quad 4D \geq \quad 18,000 \text{ (9% of 200,00)}$$
$$100A \qquad\qquad\qquad \leq 100,000$$
$$50B \qquad\qquad \leq 100,000$$
$$80C \qquad \leq 100,000$$
$$40D \leq 100,000$$

$$A, B, C, D \geq 0$$

Solution: $A = 333.3, B = 0, C = 833.3, D = 2500$
Risk: 14,666.7
Return: 18,000 (9%) from constraint 2

b.

Variable	Objective Coefficient Range
A	9.5 to 11
B	3.33 to No Upper Limit
C	3.2 to 4.4
D	No Lower Limit to 3.33

Individual changes in the risk measure coefficients within these ranges will not cause a change in the optimal investment decisions.

c. The dual value associated with the rate of return constraint is 0.833. If the firm requires a 10% rate of return, this will increase the right-hand side of this constraint to 0.1*200,000 = 20,000 which is an increase of 2000 units. Because this increase is within the right-hand-side range, this means that we would expect the objective function to increase by 2000*0.833 = 1666 units.

In other words, the increased rate of return would result in an increase in risk of 1660 units.

26. a. Let M_1 = units of component 1 manufactured
M_2 = units of component 2 manufactured
M_3 = units of component 3 manufactured
P_1 = units of component 1 purchased
P_2 = units of component 2 purchased
P_3 = units of component 3 purchased

Min $4.50M_1 + 5.00M_2 + 2.75M_3 + 6.50P_1 + 8.80P_2 + 7.00P_3$
s.t.

$2M_1 + 3M_2 + 4M_3$	$\leq 21,600$	Production
$1M_1 + 1.5M_2 + 3M_3$	$\leq 15,000$	Assembly
$1.5M_1 + 2M_2 + 5M_3$	$\leq 18,000$	Testing & Packaging
$1M_1 \qquad\qquad + 1P_1$	$= 6,000$	Component 1
$1M_2 \qquad\qquad + 1P_2$	$= 4,000$	Component 2
$1M_3 \qquad\qquad + 1P_3 =$	$3,500$	Component 3

$$M_1, M_2, M_3, P_1, P_2, P_3 \geq 0$$

b.

Source	Component 1	Component 2	Component 3
Manufacture	2000	4000	1400
Purchase	4000		2100

Total cost = $73,550

c. Production: $54.36 per hour
Testing & Packaging: $7.50 per hour

d. Dual values = $7.969; so it will cost Benson $7.969 to add a unit of component 2.

28. b. $G = 120,000; S = 30,000; M = 150,000$

c. 0.15 to 0.60; No lower limit to 0.122; 0.02 to 0.20

d. 4668

e. $G = 48,000; S = 192,000; M = 60,000$

f. The client's risk index and the amount of funds available

30. a. $L = 3, N = 7, W = 5, S = 5$

b. Each additional minute of broadcast time increases cost by $100.

c. If local coverage is increased by 1 minute, total cost will increase by $100.

d. If the time devoted to local and national news is increased by 1 minute, total cost will increase by $100.

e. Increasing the sports by 1 minute will have no effect because the dual value is 0.

32. a. Let P_1 = number of PT-100 battery packs produced at the Philippines plant
P_2 = number of PT-200 battery packs produced at the Philippines plant
P_3 = number of PT-300 battery packs produced at the Philippines plant
M_1 = number of PT-100 battery packs produced at the Mexico plant

M_2 = number of PT-200 battery packs produced at the Mexico plant

M_3 = number of PT-300 battery packs produced at the Mexico plant

Min $1.13P_1 + 1.16P_2 + 1.52P_3 + 1.08M_1 + 1.16M_2 + 1.25M_3$
s.t.

$$
\begin{array}{llll}
P_1 + & & M_1 & = 200{,}000 \\
& P_2 + & M_2 & = 100{,}000 \\
& P_3 + & M_3 & = 150{,}000 \\
P_1 + & P_2 & & \leq 175{,}000 \\
& & M_1 + M_2 & \leq 160{,}000 \\
& P_3 & & \leq 75{,}000 \\
& & M_3 & \leq 100{,}000
\end{array}
$$

$P_1, P_2, P_3, M_1, M_2, M_3 \geq 0$

b. The optimal solution is as follows:

	Philippines	**Mexico**
PT-100	40,000	160,000
PT-200	100,000	0
PT-300	50,000	100,000

Total production and transportation cost is $535,000.

c. The range of optimality for the objective function coefficient for P_1 shows a lower limit of $1.08; thus, the production and/or shipping cost would have to decrease by at least 5 cents per unit.

d. The range of optimality for the objective function coefficient for M_1 shows a lower limit of $1.11; thus, the production and/or shipping cost would have to decrease by at least 5 cents per unit.

Chapter 4

1. a. Let T = number of television advertisements
R = number of radio advertisements
N = number of newspaper advertisements

Max $100{,}000T + 18{,}000R + 40{,}000N$
s.t.

$$
\begin{array}{llllll}
2000T + & 300R + & 600N & \leq 18{,}200 & \text{Budget} \\
T & & & \leq 10 & \text{Max TV} \\
& R & & \leq 20 & \text{Max radio} \\
& & N & \leq 10 & \text{Max news} \\
-0.5T + & 0.5R - & 0.5N & \leq 0 & \text{Max 50\% radio} \\
0.9T - & 0.1R - & 0.1N & \geq 0 & \text{Min 10\% TV}
\end{array}
$$

$T, R, N \geq 0$

Solution:		**Budget $**
$T = 4$		$ 8000
$R = 14$		4200
$N = 10$		6000
		$18,200

Audience = 1,052,000

b. The dual value for the budget constraint is 51.30, meaning a $100 increase in the budget should provide an increase in audience coverage of approximately 5130;

the right-hand-side range for the budget constraint will show that this interpretation is correct.

2. a. $x_1 = 77.89$, $x_2 = 63.16$, $3284.21
  b. Department A $15.79; Department B $47.37
  c. $x_1 = 87.21$, $x_2 = 65.12$, $3341.34
  Department A 10 hours; Department B 3.2 hours

4. a. $x_1 = 500$, $x_2 = 300$, $x_3 = 200$, $550
  b. $0.55
  c. Aroma, 75; Taste 84.4
  d. −$0.60

6. 50 units of product 1; 0 units of product 2; 300 hours department A; 600 hours department B

8. Schedule 19 officers as follows:
3 begin at 8:00 A.M.; 3 begin at noon; 7 begin at 4:00 P.M.; 4 begin at midnight, 2 begin at 4:00 A.M.

9. Let X_i = the number of call-center employees who start work on day i
($i = 1 = $ Monday, $i = 2 = $ Tuesday ...)

Min $X_1 + X_2 + X_3 + X_4 + X_5 + X_6 + X_7$
s.t.

$$
\begin{array}{l}
X_1 + \qquad\qquad X_4 + X_5 + X_6 + X_7 \geq 75 \\
X_1 + X_2 + \qquad\quad X_5 + X_6 + X_7 \geq 50 \\
X_1 + X_2 + X_3 + \qquad X_6 + X_7 \geq 45 \\
X_1 + X_2 + X_3 + X_4 \qquad\quad + X_7 \geq 60 \\
X_1 + X_2 + X_3 + X_4 + X_5 \qquad\quad \geq 90 \\
\qquad X_2 + X_3 + X_4 + X_5 + X_6 \qquad \geq 75 \\
\qquad\qquad X_3 + X_4 + X_5 + X_6 + X_7 \geq 45
\end{array}
$$

$X_1, X_2, X_3, X_4, X_5, X_6, X_7 \geq 0$

Solution: $X_1 = 20$, $X_2 = 20$, $X_3 = 0$, $X_4 = 45$, $X_5 = 5$, $X_6 = 5$, $X_7 = 0$
Total number of employees = 95
Excess employees: Thursday = 25, Sunday = 10, all others = 0.

10. a. 40.9%, 14.5%, 14.5%, 30.0%
  Annual return = 5.4%
  b. 0.0%, 36.0%, 36.0%, 28.0%
  Annual return = 2.52%
  c. 75.0%, 0.0%, 15.0%, 10.0%
  Annual return = 8.2%
  d. Yes

12.

Week	Buy	Sell	Store
1	80,000	0	100,000
2	0	0	100,000
3	0	100,000	0
4	25,000	0	25,000

14. b.

Quarter	Production	Ending Inventory
1	4000	2100
2	3000	1100
3	2000	100
4	1900	500

15. Let x_{11} = gallons of crude 1 used to produce regular
x_{12} = gallons of crude 1 used to produce high octane
x_{21} = gallons of crude 2 used to produce regular
x_{22} = gallons of crude 2 used to produce high octane

Min $0.10x_{11} + 0.10x_{12} + 0.15x_{21} + 0.15x_{22}$

s.t.

Each gallon of regular must have at least 40% A.

$x_{11} + x_{21}$ = amount of regular produced
$0.4(x_{11} + x_{21})$ = amount of A required for regular
$0.2x_{11} + 0.50x_{21}$ = amount of A in $(x_{11} + x_{21})$ gallons of regular gas
$\therefore 0.2x_{11} + 0.50x_{21} \geq 0.4x_{11} + 0.40x_{21}$
$\therefore -0.2x_{11} + 0.10x_{21} \geq 0$

Each gallon of high octane can have at most 50% B.

$x_{12} + x_{22}$ = amount high octane
$0.5(x_{12} + x_{22})$ = amount of B required for high octane
$0.60x_{12} + 0.30x_{22}$ = amount of B in $(x_{12} + x_{22})$ gallons of high octane
$\therefore 0.60x_{12} + 0.30x_{22} \leq 0.5x_{12} + 0.5x_{22}$
$\therefore 0.1x_{12} - 0.2x_{22} \leq 0$
$x_{11} + x_{21} \geq 800,000$
$x_{12} + x_{22} \geq 500,000$
$x_{11}, x_{12}, x_{21}, x_{22} \geq 0$

Optimal solution: $x_{11} = 266,667, x_{12} = 333,333, x_{21} = 533,333,$
$x_{22} = 166,667$
Cost = \$165,000

16. x_i = number of 10-inch rolls processed by cutting alternative i
a. $x_1 = 0, x_2 = 125, x_3 = 500, x_4 = 1500, x_5 = 0, x_6 = 0,$
$x_7 = 0$; 2125 rolls with waste of 750 inches
b. 2500 rolls with no waste; however, 1½-inch size is overproduced by 3000 units

18. a. 5 Super, 2 Regular, and 3 Econo-Tankers
Total cost \$583,000; monthly operating cost \$4650

19. a. Let x_{11} = amount of men's model in month 1
x_{21} = amount of women's model in month 1
x_{12} = amount of men's model in month 2
x_{22} = amount of women's model in month 2
s_{11} = inventory of men's model at end of month 1
s_{21} = inventory of women's model at end of month 1
s_{12} = inventory of men's model at end of month 2
s_{22} = inventory of women's model at end of month 2

Min $120x_{11} + 90x_{21} + 120x_{12} + 90x_{22} + 2.4s_{11} + 1.8s_{21} + 2.4s_{12} + 1.8s_{22}$

s.t.

$$\left.\begin{array}{l} x_{11} - \phantom{x_{12}} s_{11} \phantom{- s_{12}} = 130 \\ x_{21} - \phantom{x_{22}} s_{21} \phantom{- s_{22}} = 95 \\ s_{11} + x_{12} - s_{12} = 200 \\ s_{21} + x_{22} - s_{22} = 150 \end{array}\right\} \text{Satisfy demand}$$

$$\left.\begin{array}{l} s_{12} \geq 25 \\ s_{22} \geq 25 \end{array}\right\} \text{Ending inventory requirement}$$

Labor-hours: Men's 2.0 + 1.5 = 3.5
Women's 1.6 + 1.0 = 2.6

$$\left.\begin{array}{l} 3.5x_{11} + 2.6x_{21} \phantom{- 3.5x_{12} - 2.6x_{22}} \geq 900 \\ 3.5x_{11} + 2.6x_{21} \phantom{- 3.5x_{12} - 2.6x_{22}} \leq 1100 \\ 3.5x_{11} + 2.6x_{21} - 3.5x_{12} - 2.6x_{22} \leq 100 \\ -3.5x_{11} - 2.6x_{21} + 3.5x_{12} + 2.6x_{22} \leq 100 \end{array}\right\} \text{Labor smoothing}$$

$x_{11}, x_{12}, x_{21}, x_{22}, s_{11}, s_{12}, s_{21}, s_{22} \geq 0$

Solution: $x_{11} = 193; x_{21} = 95; x_{12} = 162; x_{22} = 175$
Total cost = \$67,156
Inventory levels: $s_{11} = 63; s_{12} = 25; s_{21} = 0; s_{22} = 25$
Labor levels: Previous   1000 hours
Month 1   922.25 hours
Month 2   1022.25 hours
b. To accommodate the new policy, the right-hand sides of the four labor-smoothing constraints must be changed to 950, 1050, 50, and 50, respectively; the new total cost is \$67,175.

20. Produce 10,250 units in March, 10,250 units in April, and 12,000 units in May.

22. b. 5, 515, 887 sq. in. of waste
Machine 3: 492 minutes

24. Investment strategy: 45.8% of A and 100% of B
Objective function = \$4340.40
Savings/Loan schedule

	Period			
	1	**2**	**3**	**4**
Savings	242.11	—	—	341.04
Funds from loan	—	200.00	127.58	—

Chapter 5

2. b. $E = 0.924$
$wa = 0.074$
$wc = 0.436$
$we = 0.489$
c. D is relatively inefficient.
Composite requires 92.4 of D's resources.
d. 34.37 patient days (65 or older)
41.99 patient days (under 65)
e. Hospitals A, C, and E

4. b. $E = 0.960$
$wb = 0.074$
$wc = 0.000$
$wj = 0.436$
$wn = 0.489$
$ws = 0.000$
c. Yes; $E = 0.960$

d. More: $220 profit per week
   Less: Hours of Operation 4.4 hours
          FTE Staff 2.6
          Supply Expense $185.61
d. Bardstown, Jeffersonville, and New Albany

6. a. 19, 18, 12, 18

b.
PCQ = 8	PMQ = 0	POQ = 27
PCY = 4	PMY = 1	POY = 2
NCQ = 6	NMQ = 23	NOQ = 2
NCY = 4	NMY = 2	NOY = 1
CMQ = 37	CMY = 2	
COQ = 11	COY = 3	

c.
PCQ = 8	PMQ = 1	POQ = 3
PCY = 4	PMY = 1	POY = 2
NCQ = 6	NMQ = 3	NOQ = 2
NCY = 4	NMY = 2	NOY = 1
CMQ = 3	CMY = 2	
COQ = 7	COY = 3	

8. b. 65.7% small-cap growth fund
   34.3% of the portfolio in a small-cap value
   Expected return = 18.5%
c. 10% foreign stock
   50.8% small-cap growth fund
   39.2% of the portfolio in a small-cap value
   Expected return = 17.178%

10.

Player B

Player A		b_1	b_2	b_3	Minimum
	a_1	8	5	7	⑤
	a_2	2	4	10	4
	Maximum	8	⑤	7	Maximum

Minimum

The game has a pure strategy: Player A strategy a_1; Player B strategy b_2; and value of game = 5.

12. a. The payoff table is

Blue Army

Red Army		Attack	Defend	Minimum
	Attack	30	50	30
	Defend	40	0	0
	Maximum	40	50	

The maximum of the row minimums is 30 and the minimum of the column maximums is 40. Because these values are not equal, a mixed strategy is optimal. Therefore, we must determine the best probability, p, for which the Red Army should choose the Attack strategy. Assume the Red Army chooses Attack with probability p and Defend with probability $1 - p$. If the Blue Army chooses Attack, the expected payoff is $30p + 40(1 - p)$. If the Blue Army chooses Defend, the expected payoff is $50p + 0*(1 - p)$.

Setting these equations equal to each other and solving for p, we get $p = 2/3$. Red Army should choose to Attack with probability 2/3 and Defend with probability 1/3.

b. Assume the Blue Army chooses Attack with probability q and Defend with probability $1 - q$. If the Red Army chooses Attack, the expected payoff for the Blue Army is $30q + 50*(1 - q)$. If the Red Army chooses Defend, the expected payoff for the Blue Army is $40q + 0*(1 - q)$. Setting theses equations equal to each other and solving for q we get $q = 0.833$. Therefore the Blue Army should choose to Attack with probability 0.833 and Defend with probability $1 - 0.833 = 0.167$.

14. Pure strategies a_4 and b_3
   Value = 10

16. Company A: 0.0, 0.0, 0.8, 0.2
   Company B: 0.4, 0.6, 0.0, 0.0
   Expected gain for A = 2.8

Chapter 6

1. The network model is shown:

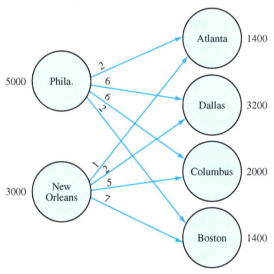

2. a. Let x_{11} = amount shipped from Jefferson City to Des Moines
   x_{12} = amount shipped from Jefferson City to Kansas City

$$\text{Min} \quad 14x_{11} + 9x_{12} + 7x_{13} + 8x_{21} + 10x_{22} + 5x_{23}$$
s.t.
$$
\begin{aligned}
x_{11} + x_{12} + x_{13} & & & \leq 30 \\
& x_{21} + x_{22} + x_{23} & & \leq 20 \\
x_{11} & + x_{21} & & = 25 \\
x_{12} & + x_{22} & & = 15 \\
x_{13} & + x_{23} & = 10 \\
\end{aligned}
$$
$$x_{11}, x_{12}, x_{13}, x_{21}, x_{22}, x_{23} \geq 0$$

b. Optimal Solution:

	Amount	Cost
Jefferson City–Des Moines	5	70
Jefferson City–Kansas City	15	135
Jefferson City–St. Louis	10	70
Omaha–Des Moines	20	160
	Total	435

4. The optimization model can be written as

x_{ij} = Red GloFish shipped from i to j i = M for Michigan, T for Texas; j = 1, 2, 3.

y_{ij} = Blue GloFish shipped from i to j, i = M for Michigan, T for Texas; j = 1, 2, 3.

Min $x_{M1} + 2.50x_{M2} + 0.50x_{M3} + y_{M1} + 2.50y_{M2} + 0.50y_{M3} + 2.00y_{T1} + 1.50y_{T2} + 2.80y_{T3}$

subject to

$$
\begin{array}{llllll}
x_{M1} + & x_{M2} + & x_{M3} & & & \leq 1{,}000{,}000 \\
& & y_{M1} + & y_{M2} + & y_{M3} & \leq 1{,}000{,}000 \\
& & & y_{T1} + & y_{T2} + y_{T3} \leq & 600{,}000 \\
x_{M1} & & & & & \geq 320{,}000 \\
& x_{M2} & & & & \geq 300{,}000 \\
& & x_{M3} & & & \geq 160{,}000 \\
& & y_{M1} + & & y_{T1} & \geq 380{,}000 \\
& & & y_{M2} + & y_{T2} & \geq 450{,}000 \\
& & & & y_{M3} + & y_{T3} \geq 290{,}000 \\
\end{array}
$$

$x_{ij} \geq 0$

Solving this linear program, we find that we should produce 780,000 red GloFish in Michigan, 670,000 blue GloFish in Michigan, and 450,000 blue GloFish in Texas.

Using the notation in the model, the number of GloFish shipped from each farm to each retailer can be expressed as follows:

x_{M1} = 320,000
x_{M2} = 300,000
x_{M3} = 160,000
y_{M1} = 380,000
y_{M2} = 0
y_{M3} = 290,000
y_{T1} = 0
y_{T2} = 450,000
y_{T3} = 0

a. The minimum transportation cost is $2.35 million.
b. We have to add variables x_{T1}, x_{T2}, and x_{T3} for Red GloFish shipped between Texas and Retailers 1, 2 and 3. The revised objective function is
Minimize $x_{M1} + 2.50x_{M2} + 0.50x_{M3} + y_{M1} + 2.50y_{M2} + 0.50y_{M3} + 2.00y_{T1} + 1.50y_{T2} + 2.80y_{T3} + x_{T1} + 2.50x_{T2} + 0.50x_{T3}$
We replace the third constraint above with
$x_{T1} + x_{T2} + x_{T3} + y_{T1} + y_{T2} + y_{T3} \leq 600{,}000$

And we change the constraints

$$
\begin{array}{ll}
x_{M1} & \geq 320{,}000 \\
x_{M2} & \geq 300{,}000 \\
x_{M3} & \geq 160{,}000 \\
\end{array}
$$

to

$$
\begin{array}{l}
x_{M1} + x_{T1} \geq 320{,}000 \\
x_{M2} + x_{T2} \geq 300{,}000 \\
x_{M3} + x_{T3} \geq 160{,}000 \\
\end{array}
$$

Using this new objective function and constraint the optimal solution is $2.2 million, so the savings are $150,000.

6. The network model, the linear programming formulation, and the optimal solution are shown. Note that the third constraint corresponds to the dummy origin. The variables x_{31}, x_{32}, x_{33}, and x_{34} are the amounts shipped out of the dummy origin; they do not appear in the objective function because they are given a coefficient of zero.

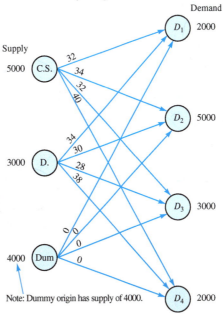

Note: Dummy origin has supply of 4000.

Max $32x_{11} + 34x_{12} + 32x_{13} + 40x_{14} + 34x_{21} + 30x_{22} + 28x_{23} + 38x_{24}$
s.t.

$$
\begin{array}{llll}
x_{11} + x_{12} + x_{13} + x_{14} & \leq 5000 \\
\quad x_{21} + x_{22} + x_{23} + x_{24} & \leq 3000 \\
\quad x_{31} + x_{32} + x_{33} + x_{34} & \leq 4000 & \text{Dummy} \\
x_{11} \quad\quad + x_{21} \quad\quad + x_{31} & = 2000 \\
\quad x_{12} \quad\quad + x_{22} \quad\quad + x_{32} & = 5000 \\
\quad\quad x_{13} \quad\quad + x_{23} \quad\quad + x_{33} & = 3000 \\
\quad\quad\quad x_{14} \quad\quad + x_{24} \quad\quad + x_{34} & = 2000 \\
\end{array}
$$

$x_{ij} \geq 0$ for all i, j

Optimal Solution	Units	Cost
Clifton Springs–D_2	4000	$136,000
Clifton Springs–D_4	1000	40,000
Danville–D_1	2000	68,000
Danville–D_4	1000	38,000
	Total Cost	$282,000

Customer 2 demand has a shortfall of 1000.

Customer 3 demand of 3000 is not satisfied.

8. a.

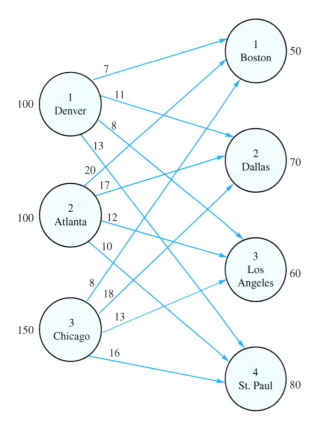

b. There are alternative optimal solutions.

Solution 1		Solution 2	
Denver to St. Paul:	10	Denver to St. Paul:	10
Atlanta to Boston:	50	Atlanta to Boston:	50
Atlanta to Dallas:	50	Atlanta to Los Angeles:	50
Chicago to Dallas:	20	Chicago to Dallas:	70
Chicago to Los Angeles:	60	Chicago to Los Angeles:	10
Chicago to St. Paul:	70	Chicago to St. Paul:	70
Total Profit: $4240			

If solution 1 is used, Forbelt should produce 10 motors at Denver, 100 motors at Atlanta, and 150 motors at Chicago. There will be idle capacity for 90 motors at Denver.

If solution 2 is used, Forbelt should adopt the same production schedule but a modified shipping schedule.

10. a. The total cost is the sum of the purchase cost and the transportation cost. We show the calculation for Division 1–Supplier 1 and present the result for the other Division-Supplier combinations.

Division 1–Supplier 1

Purchase cost (40,000 × $12.60)	$504,000
Transportation Cost (40,000 × $2.75)	110,000
Total Cost:	$614,000

Cost Matrix ($1000s)

			Supplier			
Division	1	2	3	4	5	6
1	614	660	534	680	590	630
2	603	639	702	693	693	630
3	865	830	775	850	900	930
4	532	553	511	581	595	553
5	720	648	684	693	657	747

b. Optimal Solution:

Supplier 1–Division 2	$ 603
Supplier 2–Division 5	648
Supplier 3–Division 3	775
Supplier 5–Division 1	590
Supplier 6–Division 4	553
Total	$3169

11. a. Network Model

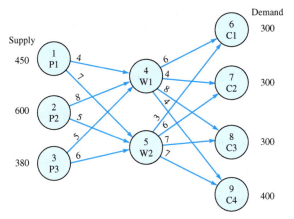

b. & c. The linear programming formulation and solution is shown below:

```
LINEAR PROGRAMMING PROBLEM

MIN 4X14 + 7X15 + 8X24 + 5X25 + 5X34 + 6X35
+ 6X46 + 4X47 + 8X48 + 4X49 + 3X56 + 6X57
+ 7X58 + 7X59

S.T.

(1) X14 + X15 < 450
(2) X24 + X25 < 600
(3) X34 + X35 < 380
(4) X46 + X47 + X48 + X49 − X14 − X24
    − X34 = 0
(5) X56 + X57 + X58 + X59 − X15 − X25
    − X35 = 0
(6) X46 + X56 = 300
(7) X47 + X57 = 300
(8) X48 + X58 = 300
(9) X49 + X59 = 400
```

```
OPTIMAL SOLUTION

Objective Function Value =     11850.000
```

Variable	Value	Reduced Costs
X14	450.000	0.000
X15	0.000	3.000
X24	0.000	3.000
X25	600.000	0.000
X34	250.000	0.000
X35	0.000	1.000
X46	0.000	3.000
X47	300.000	0.000
X48	0.000	1.000
X49	400.000	0.000
X56	300.000	0.000
X57	0.000	2.000
X58	300.000	0.000
X59	0.000	3.000

There is an excess capacity of 130 units at plant 3.

12. a. Three arcs must be added to the network model in Problem 11a. The new network is shown:

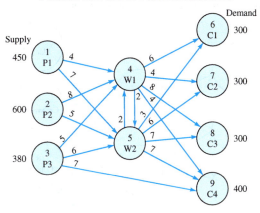

b. & c. The linear programming formulation and optimal solution is shown below:

```
LINEAR PROGRAMMING PROBLEM

MIN 4X14 + 7X15 + 8X24 + 5X25 + 5X34 +
6X35 + 6X46 + 4X47 + 8X48 + 4X49 + 3X56 +
6X57 + 7X58 + 7X59 + 7X39 + 2X45 + 2X54

S.T.

(1) X14 + X15 < 450
(2) X24 + X25 < 600
(3) X34 + X35 + X39 < 380
(4) X45 + X46 + X47 + X48 + X49 − X14 − X24
    − X34 − X54 = 0
(5) X54 + X56 + X57 + X58 + X59 − X15 − X25
    − X35 − X45 = 0
(6) X46 + X56 = 300
(7) X47 + X57 = 300
(8) X48 + X58 = 300
(9) X39 + X49 + X59 = 400
```

```
OPTIMAL SOLUTION

Objective Function Value = 11220.000
```

Variable	Value	Reduced Costs
X14	320.000	0.000
X15	0.000	2.000
X24	0.000	4.000
X25	600.000	0.000
X34	0.000	2.000
X35	0.000	2.000
X46	0.000	2.000
X47	300.000	0.000
X48	0.000	0.000
X49	20.000	0.000
X56	300.000	0.000
X57	0.000	3.000
X58	300.000	0.000
X59	0.000	4.000
X39	380.000	0.000
X45	0.000	1.000
X54	0.000	3.000

The value of the solution here is $630 less than the value of the solution for Problem 23. The new shipping route from plant 3 to customer 4 has helped ($x_{39} = 380$). There is now excess capacity of 130 units at plant 1.

14.

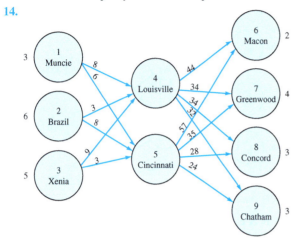

A linear programming model is

$$\text{Min } 8x_{14}+6x_{15}+3x_{24}+8x_{25}+9x_{34}+3x_{35}+44x_{46}+34x_{47}+34x_{48}+32x_{49}+57x_{56}+35x_{57}+28x_{58}+24x_{59}$$

s.t.

$$
\begin{aligned}
x_{14}+ x_{15} &\leq 3 \\
x_{24}+ x_{25} &\leq 6 \\
x_{34}+ x_{35} &\leq 5 \\
-x_{14} \quad - x_{24} \quad - x_{34} \quad + x_{46}+ x_{47}+ x_{48}+ x_{49} &= 0 \\
- x_{15} \quad - x_{25} \quad - x_{35} \quad + x_{56}+ x_{57}+ x_{58}+ x_{59} &= 0 \\
x_{46} \quad + x_{56} &= 2 \\
x_{47} \quad + x_{57} &= 4 \\
x_{48} \quad + x_{58} &= 3 \\
x_{49} \quad + x_{59} &= 3 \\
\end{aligned}
$$

$x_{ij} \geq 0 \quad \text{for all } i, j$

Optimal Solution	Units Shipped	Cost
Muncie–Cincinnati	1	6
Cincinnati–Concord	3	84
Brazil–Louisville	6	18
Louisville–Macon	2	88
Louisville–Greenwood	4	136
Xenia–Cincinnati	5	15
Cincinnati–Chatham	3	72
		419

Two rail cars must be held at Muncie until a buyer is found.

16. a.

$$\text{Min } 20x_{12} + 25x_{15} + 30x_{25} + 45x_{27} + 20x_{31} + 35x_{36}$$
$$+ 30x_{42} + 25x_{53} + 15x_{54} + 28x_{56} + 12x_{67} + 27x_{74}$$

s.t.

$$
\begin{aligned}
x_{31} - \quad x_{12} - \quad x_{15} &= 8 \\
x_{25} + \quad x_{27} - \quad x_{12} - \quad x_{42} &= 5 \\
x_{31} + \quad x_{36} \quad - x_{53} &= 3 \\
x_{54} \quad + x_{74} - \quad x_{42} &= 3 \\
x_{53} + \quad x_{54} + \quad x_{56} - \quad x_{15} - \quad x_{25} &= 2 \\
x_{36} + \quad x_{56} - \quad x_{67} &= 5 \\
x_{74} - \quad x_{27} - \quad x_{67} &= 6 \\
\end{aligned}
$$

$x_{ij} \geq 0 \text{ for all } i, j$

b.

$x_{12} = 0$	$x_{53} = 5$
$x_{15} = 0$	$x_{54} = 0$
$x_{25} = 8$	$x_{56} = 5$
$x_{27} = 0$	$x_{67} = 0$
$x_{31} = 8$	$x_{74} = 6$
$x_{36} = 0$	$x_{56} = 5$
$x_{42} = 3$	

Total cost of redistributing cars = $917

17. a.

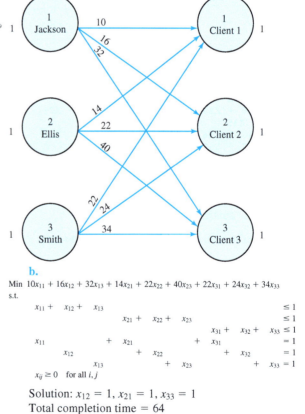

b.

$$\text{Min } 10x_{11} + 16x_{12} + 32x_{13} + 14x_{21} + 22x_{22} + 40x_{23} + 22x_{31} + 24x_{32} + 34x_{33}$$

s.t.

$$
\begin{aligned}
x_{11} + \quad x_{12} + \quad x_{13} &\leq 1 \\
x_{21} + \quad x_{22} + \quad x_{23} &\leq 1 \\
x_{31} + \quad x_{32} + \quad x_{33} &\leq 1 \\
x_{11} \quad + x_{21} \quad + x_{31} &= 1 \\
x_{12} \quad + x_{22} \quad + x_{32} &= 1 \\
x_{13} \quad + x_{23} \quad + x_{33} &= 1 \\
\end{aligned}
$$

$x_{ij} \geq 0 \quad \text{for all } i, j$

Solution: $x_{12} = 1$, $x_{21} = 1$, $x_{33} = 1$
Total completion time = 64

18. a.

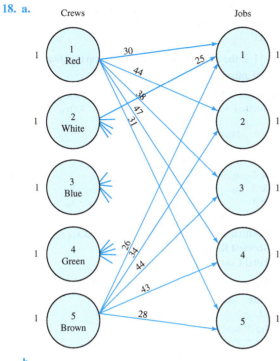

Crews   Jobs

b.

$$\text{Min } 30x_{11} + 44x_{12} + 38x_{13} + 47x_{14} + 31x_{15} + 25x_{21} + \cdots + 28x_{55}$$

s.t.

$$
\begin{array}{lr}
x_{11} + x_{12} + x_{13} + x_{14} + x_{15} & \leq 1 \\
x_{21} + x_{22} + x_{23} + x_{24} + x_{25} & \leq 1 \\
x_{31} + x_{32} + x_{33} + x_{34} + x_{35} & \leq 1 \\
x_{41} + x_{42} + x_{43} + x_{44} + x_{45} & \leq 1 \\
x_{51} + x_{52} + x_{53} + x_{54} + x_{55} & \leq 1 \\
x_{11} + x_{21} + x_{31} + x_{41} + x_{51} & = 1 \\
x_{12} + x_{22} + x_{32} + x_{42} + x_{52} & = 1 \\
x_{13} + x_{23} + x_{33} + x_{43} + x_{53} & = 1 \\
x_{14} + x_{24} + x_{34} + x_{44} + x_{54} & = 1 \\
x_{15} + x_{25} + x_{35} + x_{45} + x_{55} & = 1 \\
\end{array}
$$

$$x_{ij} \geq 0, \ i = 1, 2, \ldots, 5; \ j = 1, 2, \ldots, 5$$

Optimal Solution:

Green to Job 1	$ 26
Brown to Job 2	34
Red to Job 3	38
Blue to Job 4	39
White to Job 5	25
	$162

Because the data are in hundreds of dollars, the total installation cost for the five contracts is $16,200.

20. a. This is the variation of the assignment problem in which multiple assignments are possible. Each distribution center may be assigned up to three customer zones.

The linear programming model of this problem has 40 variables (one for each combination of distribution center and customer zone). It has 13 constraints. There are five supply (≤ 3) constraints and eight demand ($=1$) constraints.

The optimal solution is as follows:

	Assignments	Cost ($1000s)
Plano	Kansas City, Dallas	34
Flagstaff	Los Angeles	15
Springfield	Chicago, Columbus, Atlanta	70
Boulder	Newark, Denver	97
	Total Cost	$216

b. The Nashville distribution center is not used.

c. All the distribution centers are used. Columbus is switched from Springfield to Nashville. Total cost increases by $11,000 to $227,000.

22. A linear programming formulation of this problem can be developed as follows. Let the first letter of each variable name represent the professor and the second two the course. Note that a *DPH* variable is not created because the assignment is unacceptable.

$$\text{Max } 2.8AUG + 2.2AMB + 3.3AMS + 3.0APH + 3.2BUG + \cdots + 2.5DMS$$

s.t.

$$
\begin{array}{lr}
AUG + AMB + AMS + APH & \leq 1 \\
BUG + BMB + BMS + BPH & \leq 1 \\
CUG + CMB + CMS + CPH & \leq 1 \\
DUG + DMB + DMS & \leq 1 \\
AUG + BUG + CUG + DUG & = 1 \\
AMB + BMB + CMB + DMB & = 1 \\
AMS + BMS + CMS + DMS & = 1 \\
APH + BPH + CPH & = 1 \\
\end{array}
$$

All Variables ≥ 0

Optimal Solution	Rating
A to MS course	3.3
B to Ph.D. course	3.6
C to MBA course	3.2
D to Undergraduate course	3.2
Max Total Rating	13.3

23. Origin—Node 1

Transshipment—Nodes 2–5

Destination—Node 7

The linear program will have 14 variables for the arcs and 7 constraints for the nodes.

Let

$$x_{ij} = \begin{cases} 1 & \text{if the arc from node } i \text{ to node } j \text{ is on the shortest route} \\ 0 & \text{otherwise} \end{cases}$$

Min $7x_{12} + 9x_{13} + 18x_{14} + 3x_{23} + 5x_{25} + 3x_{32} + 4x_{35}$
    $+ 3x_{46} + 5x_{52} + 4x_{53} + 2x_{56} + 6x_{57} + 2x_{65} + 3x_{67}$
s.t.

	Flow Out	Flow In	
Node 1	$x_{12} + x_{13} + x_{14}$		$= 1$
Node 2	$x_{23} + x_{25}$	$-x_{12} - x_{32} - x_{52}$	$= 0$
Node 3	$x_{32} + x_{35}$	$-x_{13} - x_{23} - x_{53}$	$= 0$
Node 4	x_{46}	$-x_{14}$	$= 0$
Node 5	$x_{52} + x_{53} + x_{56} + x_{57}$	$-x_{25} - x_{35} - x_{65}$	$= 0$
Node 6	$x_{65} + x_{67}$	$-x_{46} - x_{56}$	$= 0$
Node 7		$+x_{57} + x_{67}$	$= 1$

$x_{ij} \geq 0$ for all i and j

Optimal Solution: $x_{12} = 1$, $x_{25} = 1$, $x_{56} = 1$, and $x_{67} = 1$
Shortest Route: 1–2–5–6–7
Length $= 17$

24. The linear program has 13 variables for the arcs and 6 constraints for the nodes. Use the same 6 constraints for the Gorman shortest route problem, as shown in the text. The objective function changes to travel time as follows:

Min $40x_{12} + 36x_{13} + 6x_{23} + 6x_{32} + 12x_{24} + 12x_{42} +$
    $25x_{26} + 15x_{35} + 15x_{53} + 8x_{45} + 8x_{54} + 11x_{46} +$
    $23x_{56}$

Optimal Solution: $x_{12} = 1$, $x_{24} = 1$, and $x_{46} = 1$
Shortest Route: 1–2–4–6
Total Time $= 63$ minutes

26. Origin—Node 1
Transshipment—Nodes 2–5 and node 7
Destination—Node 6

    The linear program will have 18 variables for the arcs and 7 constraints for the nodes.
Let

$x_{ij} = \begin{cases} 1 & \text{if the arc from node } i \text{ to node } j \text{ is on the shortest route} \\ 0 & \text{otherwise} \end{cases}$

Min $35x_{12} + 30x_{13} + 20x_{14} + 8x_{23} + 12x_{25} + 8x_{32} + 9x_{34} + 10x_{35}$
    $+ 20x_{36} + 9x_{43} + 15x_{47} + 12x_{52} + 10x_{53} + 5x_{56} + 20x_{57} + 15x_{74}$
    $+ 20x_{75} + 5x_{76}$
s.t.

	Flow Out	Flow In	
Node 1	$x_{12} + x_{13} + x_{14}$		$= 1$
Node 2	$x_{23} + x_{25}$	$-x_{12} - x_{32} - x_{52}$	$= 0$
Node 3	$x_{32} + x_{34} + x_{35} + x_{36}$	$-x_{13} - x_{23} - x_{43} - x_{53}$	$= 0$
Node 4	$x_{43} + x_{47}$	$-x_{14} - x_{34} - x_{74}$	$= 0$
Node 5	$x_{52} + x_{53} + x_{56} + x_{57}$	$-x_{25} - x_{35} - x_{75}$	$= 0$
Node 6		$+x_{36} + x_{56} + x_{76}$	$= 1$
Node 7	$x_{74} + x_{75} + x_{76}$	$-x_{47} - x_{57}$	$= 0$

$x_{ij} \geq 0$ for all i and j

Optimal Solution: $x_{14} = 1$, $x_{47} = 1$, and $x_{76} = 1$
Shortest Route: 1–4–7–6
Total Distance $= 40$ miles

28. Origin—Node 0
Transshipment—Nodes 1 to 3
Destination—Node 4

The linear program will have 10 variables for the arcs and 5 constraints for the nodes.
Let

$x_{ij} = \begin{cases} 1 & \text{if the arc from node } i \text{ to node } j \text{ is on the shortest route} \\ 0 & \text{otherwise} \end{cases}$

Min $600x_{01} + 1000x_{02} + 2000x_{03} + 2800x_{04} + 500x_{12} +$
    $1400x_{13} + 2100x_{14} + 800x_{23} + 1600x_{24} + 700x_{34}$
s.t.

	Flow Out	Flow In	
Node 0	$x_{01} + x_{02} + x_{03} + x_{04}$		$= 1$
Node 1	$x_{12} + x_{13} + x_{14}$	$-x_{01}$	$= 0$
Node 2	$x_{23} + x_{24}$	$-x_{02} - x_{12}$	$= 0$
Node 3	x_{34}	$-x_{03} - x_{13} - x_{23}$	$= 0$
Node 4		$-x_{04} - x_{14} - x_{24} - x_{34}$	$= 1$

$x_{ij} \geq 0$ for all i and j

Optimal Solution: $x_{02} = 1$, $x_{23} = 1$, and $x_{34} = 1$
Shortest Route: 0–2–3–4
Total Cost $= \$2500$

29. The capacitated transshipment problem to solve is given:

Max x_{61}
s.t.

$x_{12} + x_{13} + x_{14} - x_{61}$	$= 0$
$x_{24} + x_{25} - x_{12} - x_{42}$	$= 0$
$x_{34} + x_{36} - x_{13} - x_{43}$	$= 0$
$x_{42} + x_{43} + x_{45} + x_{46} - x_{14} - x_{24} - x_{34} - x_{54}$	$= 0$
$x_{54} + x_{56} - x_{25} - x_{45}$	$= 0$
$x_{61} - x_{36} + x_{46} - x_{56}$	$= 0$

$x_{12} \leq 2$	$x_{13} \leq 6$	$x_{14} \leq 3$
$x_{24} \leq 1$	$x_{25} \leq 4$	
$x_{34} \leq 3$	$x_{36} \leq 2$	
$x_{42} \leq 1$	$x_{43} \leq 3$	$x_{45} \leq 1$ $x_{46} \leq 3$
$x_{54} \leq 1$	$x_{56} \leq 6$	

$x_{ij} \geq 0$ for all i, j

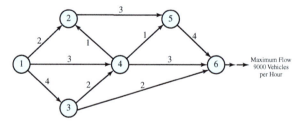

The system cannot accommodate a flow of 10,000 vehicles per hour.

30.

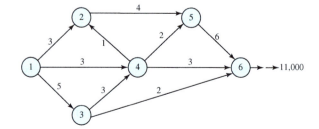

32. a. 10,000 gallons per hour or 10 hours

  b. Flow reduced to 9000 gallons per hour; 11.1 hours.

34. Maximal Flow = 23 gallons/minute. Five gallons will flow from node 3 to node 5.

36. a. Let R_1, R_2, R_3 represent regular time production in months 1, 2, 3

  O_1, O_2, O_3 represent overtime production in months 1, 2, 3

  D_1, D_2, D_3 represent demand in months 1, 2, 3

Using these nine nodes, a network model is shown:

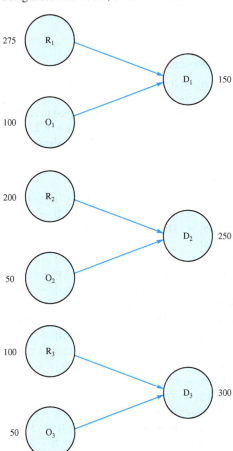

b. Use the following notation to define the variables: The first two characters designate the "from node" and the second two characters designate the "to node" of the arc. For instance, R_1D_1 is amount of regular time production available to satisfy demand in month 1; O_1D_1 is amount of overtime production in month 1 available to satisfy demand in month 1; D_1D_2 is the amount of inventory carried over from month 1 to month 2; and so on.

$$\text{Min } 50R_1D_1 + 80O_1D_1 + 20D_1D_2 + 50R_2D_2 + 80O_2D_2$$
$$+ 20D_2D_3 + 60R_3D_3 + 100O_3D_3$$

S.T.

(1) $R_1D_1 \leq 275$
(2) $O_1D_1 \leq 100$
(3) $R_2D_2 \leq 200$
(4) $O_2D_2 \leq 50$
(5) $R_3D_3 \leq 100$
(6) $O_3D_3 \leq 50$
(7) $R_1D_1 + O_1D_1 - D_1D_2 = 150$
(8) $R_2D_2 + O_2D_2 + D_1D_2 - D_2D_3 = 250$
(9) $R_3D_3 + O_3D_3 + D_2D_3 = 300$

  c. Optimal Solution:

Variable	Value
R_1D_1	275.000
O_1D_1	25.000
D_1D_2	150.000
R_2D_2	200.000
O_2D_2	50.000
D_2D_3	150.000
R_3D_3	100.000
O_3D_3	50.000

Value = \$46,750

Note: Slack variable for constraint 2 = 75

  d. The values of the slack variables for constraints 1 through 6 represent unused capacity. The only nonzero slack variable is for constraint 2; its value is 75. Thus, there are 75 units of unused overtime capacity in month 1.

Chapter 7

2. a.

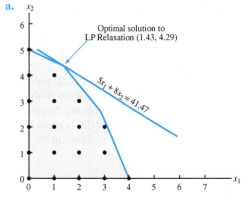

b. The optimal solution to the LP Relaxation is given by $x_1 = 1.43$, $x_2 = 4.29$, with an objective function value of 41.47. Rounding down gives the feasible integer solution $x_1 = 1$, $x_2 = 4$; its value is 37.

c.

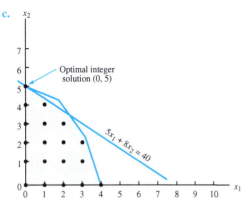

The optimal solution is given by $x_1 = 0$, $x_2 = 5$; its value is 40. It is not the same solution as found by rounding down; it provides a 3-unit increase in the value of the objective function.

4. a. $x_1 = 3.67$, $x_2 = 0$; Value = 36.7
     Rounded: $x_1 = 3$, $x_2 = 0$; Value = 30
     Lower bound = 30; Upper bound = 36.7
   b. $x_1 = 3$, $x_2 = 2$; Value = 36
   c. Alternative optimal solutions: $x_1 = 0$, $x_2 = 5$
                                         $x_1 = 2$, $x_2 = 4$

5. a. The feasible mixed-integer solutions are indicated by the boldface vertical lines in the graph.

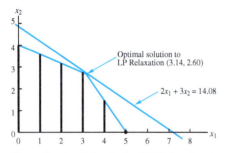

   b. The optimal solution to the LP Relaxation is given by $x_1 = 3.14$, $x_2 = 2.60$; its value is 14.08.
     Rounding down the value of x_1 to find a feasible mixed-integer solution yields $x_1 = 3$, $x_2 = 2.60$ with a value of 13.8; this solution is clearly not optimal; with $x_1 = 3$, x_2 can be made larger without violating the constraints.
   c. The optimal solution to the MILP is given by $x_1 = 3$, $x_2 = 2.67$; its value is 14, as shown in the following figure:

6. b. $x_1 = 1.96$, $x_2 = 5.48$; Value = 7.44
     Rounded: $x_1 = 1.96$, $x_2 = 5$; Value = 6.96
     Lower bound = 6.96; Upper bound = 7.44
   c. $x_1 = 1.29$, $x_2 = 6$; Value = 7.29

7. a. $x_1 + x_3 + x_5 + x_6 = 2$
   b. $x_3 - x_5 = 0$
   c. $x_1 + x_4 = 1$
   d. $x_4 \le x_1$
       $x_4 \le x_3$
   e. $x_4 \le x_1$
       $x_4 \le x_3$
       $x_4 \ge x_1 + x_3 - 1$

8. a. $x_3 = 1$, $x_4 = 1$, $x_6 = 1$; Value = 17,500
   b. Add $x_1 + x_2 \le 1$
   c. Add $x_3 - x_4 = 0$

10. b. Choose locations B and E.

12. a. Let $y[j] = 1$ if carrier j is selected, 0 if not
            $j = 1, 2, ..., 7$
         $x[i, j] = 1$ if city i is assigned to carrier j,
         0 if not $i = 1, 2, ..., 20$ $j = 1, 2, ..., 7$
   Minimize the cost of city-carrier assignments (note: for brevity, zeros are not shown).

Minimize

$65640x[1,5] + 49980x[1,6] + 53700x[1,7] + 14530x[2,2] +$
$26020x[2,5] + 17670x[2,6] + 30680x[3,2] + 45660x[3,5] +$
$37140x[3,6] + 37400x[3,7] + 67480x[4,2] + 104680x[4,5] +$
$69520x[4,6] + 15230x[5,2] + 22390x[5,5] + 17710x[5,6] +$
$18550x[5,7] + 15210x[6,2] + 15710x[6,5] + 15450x[6,7] +$
$25200x[7,2] + 23064x[7,4] + 23256x[7,5] + 24600x[7,7] +$
$45000x[8,2] + 35800x[8,4] + 35400x[8,5] + 43475x[8,7] +$
$28350x[9,2] + 30825x[9,4] + 29525x[9,5] + 28750x[9,7] +$
$22176x[10,2] + 20130x[10,4] + 22077x[10,5] + 22374x[10,7] +$
$7964x[11,1] + 7953x[11,3] + 6897x[11,4] + 7227x[11,5] +$
$7766x[11,7] + 22214x[12,1] + 22214x[12,3] + 20909x[12,4] +$
$19778x[12,5] + 21257x[12,7] + 8892x[13,1] + 8940x[13,3] +$
$8184x[13,5] + 8796x[13,7] + 19560x[14,1] + 19200x[14,2] +$
$19872x[14,3] + 17880x[14,5] + 19968x[14,7] + 9040x[15,1] +$
$8800x[15,3] + 8910x[15,5] + 9140x[15,7] + 9580x[16,1] +$
$9330x[16,3] + 8910x[16,5] + 9140x[16,7] + 21275x[17,1] +$
$21367x[17,3] + 21551x[17,5] + 22632x[17,7] + 22300x[18,1] +$
$21725x[18,3] + 20550x[18,4] + 20725x[18,5] + 21600x[18,7] +$
$11124x[19,1] + 11628x[19,3] + 11604x[19,5] + 12096x[19,7] +$
$9630x[20,1] + 9380x[20,3] + 9550x[20,5] + 9950x[20,7]$

subject to

$x[1,1] + x[1,2] + x[1,3] + x[1,4] + x[1,5] + x[1,6] + x[1,7] = 1$
$x[2,1] + x[2,2] + x[2,3] + x[2,4] + x[2,5] + x[2,6] + x[2,7] = 1$
$x[3,1] + x[3,2] + x[3,3] + x[3,4] + x[3,5] + x[3,6] + x[3,7] = 1$
$x[4,1] + x[4,2] + x[4,3] + x[4,4] + x[4,5] + x[4,6] + x[4,7] = 1$
$x[5,1] + x[5,2] + x[5,3] + x[5,4] + x[5,5] + x[5,6] + x[5,7] = 1$
$x[6,1] + x[6,2] + x[6,3] + x[6,4] + x[6,5] + x[6,6] + x[6,7] = 1$
$x[7,1] + x[7,2] + x[7,3] + x[7,4] + x[7,5] + x[7,6] + x[7,7] = 1$

$x[8,1] + x[8,2] + x[8,3] + x[8,4] + x[8,5] + x[8,6] + x[8,7] = 1$
$x[9,1] + x[9,2] + x[9,3] + x[9,4] + x[9,5] + x[9,6] + x[9,7] = 1$
$x[10,1] + x[10,2] + x[10,3] + x[10,4] + x[10,5] + x[10,6] + x[10,7] = 1$
$x[11,1] + x[11,2] + x[11,3] + x[11,4] + x[11,5] + x[11,6] + x[11,7] = 1$
$x[12,1] + x[12,2] + x[12,3] + x[12,4] + x[12,5] + x[12,6] + x[12,7] = 1$
$x[13,1] + x[13,2] + x[13,3] + x[13,4] + x[13,5] + x[13,6] + x[13,7] = 1$
$x[14,1] + x[14,2] + x[14,3] + x[14,4] + x[14,5] + x[14,6] + x[14,7] = 1$
$x[15,1] + x[15,2] + x[15,3] + x[15,4] + x[15,5] + x[15,6] + x[15,7] = 1$
$x[16,1] + x[16,2] + x[16,3] + x[16,4] + x[16,5] + x[16,6] + x[16,7] = 1$
$x[17,1] + x[17,2] + x[17,3] + x[17,4] + x[17,5] + x[17,6] + x[17,7] = 1$
$x[18,1] + x[18,2] + x[18,3] + x[18,4] + x[18,5] + x[18,6] + x[18,7] = 1$
$x[19,1] + x[19,2] + x[19,3] + x[19,4] + x[19,5] + x[19,6] + x[19,7] = 1$
$x[20,1] + x[20,2] + x[20,3] + x[20,4] + x[20,5] + x[20,6] + x[20,7] = 1$

$x[1,1] + x[2,1] + x[3,1] + x[4,1] + x[5,1] + x[6,1] + x[7,1] + x[8,1] +$
$x[9,1] + x[10,1] + x[11,1] + x[12,1] + x[13,1] + x[14,1] + x[15,1] +$
$x[16,1] + x[17,1] + x[18,1] + x[19,1] + x[20,1] <= 10y[1]$

$x[1,2] + x[2,2] + x[3,2] + x[4,2] + x[5,2] + x[6,2] + x[7,2] + x[8,2] +$
$x[9,2] + x[10,2] + x[11,2] + x[12,2] + x[13,2] + x[14,2] + x[15,2] +$
$x[16,2] + x[17,2] + x[18,2] + x[19,2] + x[20,2] <= 10y[2]$

$x[1,3] + x[2,3] + x[3,3] + x[4,3] + x[5,3] + x[6,3] + x[7,3] + x[8,3] +$
$x[9,3] + x[10,3] + x[11,3] + x[12,3] + x[13,3] + x[14,3] + x[15,3] +$
$x[16,3] + x[17,3] + x[18,3] + x[19,3] + x[20,3] <= 10y[3]$

$x[1,4] + x[2,4] + x[3,4] + x[4,4] + x[5,4] + x[6,4] + x[7,4] + x[8,4] +$
$x[9,4] + x[10,4] + x[11,4] + x[12,4] + x[13,4] + x[14,4] + x[15,4] +$
$x[16,4] + x[17,4] + x[18,4] + x[19,4] + x[20,4] <= 7y[4]$

$x[1,5] + x[2,5] + x[3,5] + x[4,5] + x[5,5] + x[6,5] + x[7,5] + x[8,5] +$
$x[9,5] + x[10,5] + x[11,5] + x[12,5] + x[13,5] + x[14,5] + x[15,5] +$
$x[16,5] + x[17,5] + x[18,5] + x[19,5] + x[20,5] <= 20y[5]$

$x[1,6] + x[2,6] + x[3,6] + x[4,6] + x[5,6] + x[6,6] + x[7,6] + x[8,6]$
$+ x[9,6] + x[10,6] + x[11,6] + x[12,6] + x[13,6] + x[14,6] + x[15,6]$
$+ x[16,6] + x[17,6] + x[18,6] + x[19,6] + x[20,6] <= 5y[6]$

$x[1,7] + x[2,7] + x[3,7] + x[4,7] + x[5,7] + x[6,7] + x[7,7] + x[8,7] +$
$x[9,7] + x[10,7] + x[11,7] + x[12,7] + x[13,7] + x[14,7] + x[15,7] +$
$x[16,7] + x[17,7] + x[18,7] + x[19,7] + x[20,7] <= 18y[7]$

$x[1,1] + x[2,1] + x[3,1] + x[4,1] + x[5,1] + x[6,1] + x[7,1] + x[8,1] +$
$x[9,1] + x[10,1] = 0$

$x[1,2] + x[11,2] + x[12,2] + x[13,2] + x[15,2] + x[16,2] + x[17,2] +$
$x[18,2] + x[19,2] + x[20,2] = 0$

$x[1,3] + x[2,3] + x[3,3] + x[4,3] + x[5,3] + x[6,3] + x[7,3] + x[8,3] +$
$x[9,3] + x[10,3] = 0$

$x[1,4] + x[2,4] + x[3,4] + x[4,4] + x[5,4] + x[6,4] + x[13,4] +$
$x[14,4] + x[15,4] + x[16,4] + x[17,4] + x[19,4] + x[20,4] = 0$

$x[6,6] + x[7,6] + x[8,6] + x[9,6] + x[10,6] + x[11,6] + x[12,6] +$
$x[13,6] + x[14,6] + x[15,6] + x[16,6] + x[17,6] + x[18,6] + x[19,6] +$
$x[20,6] = 0$

$x[2,7] + x[4,7] = 0$

$y[1] + y[2] + y[3] + y[4] + y[5] + y[6] + y[7] <= 3$

Solution: Total Cost = $436,512

Carrier 2: assigned cities 2, 3, 4, 5, 6, and 9

Carrier 5: assigned cities 7, 8, and 10–20

Carrier 6: assigned city 1

b.

# Carriers	Cost	Carriers Chosen
1	$524,677	5
2	$452,172	2,5
3	$436,512	2,5,6
4	$433,868	2,4,5,6
5	$433,112	1,2,4,5,6
6	$432,832	1,2,3,4,5,6
7	$432,832	1,2,3,4,5,6,7

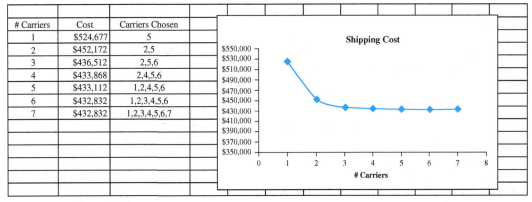

Given the incremental drop in cost, three seems like the correct number of carriers (the curve flattens considerably after three carriers).

13. a. Add the following multiple-choice constraint to the problem:

$y_1 + y_2 = 1$

New optimal solution: $y_1 = 1, y_3 = 1, x_{12} = 10, x_{31} = 30, x_{52} = 10, x_{53} = 20$

Value = 940

b. Because one plant is already located in St. Louis, it is only necessary to add the following constraint to the model:

$y_3 = y_4 \leq 1$

New optimal solution: $y_4 = 1, x_{42} = 20, x_{43} = 20, x_{51} = 30$

Value = 860

14. b. Modernize plants 1 and 3 or plants 4 and 5.
d. Modernize plants 1 and 3.

16. b. Use all part-time employees.
Bring on as follows: 9:00 A.M.–6, 11:00 A.M.–2, 12:00 noon–6, 1:00 P.M.–1, 3:00 P.M.–6
Cost = $672
c. Same as in part (b)
d. New solution is to bring on 1 full-time employee at 9:00 A.M., 4 more at 11:00 A.M., and part-time employees as follows:
9:00 A.M.–5, 12:00 noon–5, and 3:00 P.M.–2

18. a. 52, 49, 36, 83, 39, 70, 79, 59
b. Thick crust, cheese blend, chunky sauce, medium sausage: Six of eight consumers will prefer this pizza (75%).

20. a. New objective function: Min $25x_1 + 40x_2 + 40x_3 + 40x_4 + 25x_5$
b. $x_4 = x_5 = 1$; modernize the Ohio and California plants.
c. Add the constraint $x_2 + x_3 = 1$.
d. $x_1 = x_3 = 1$

22. $x_1 + x_2 + x_3 = 3y_1 + 5y_2 + 7y_3$
$y_1 + y_2 + y_3 = 1$

24. Let x_i = the amount (dollars) to invest in alternative i
$i = 1, 2, …, 10$
$y_i = 1$ if Dave invests in alternative i, 0 if not $i = 1, 2…, 10$
Max $.067x_1 + .0765x_2 + .0755x_3 + .0745x_4 + .075x_5 + .0645x_6 + .0705x_7 + .069x_8 + .052x_9 + .059x_{10}$
subject to
$x_1 + x_2 + x_3 + x_4 + x_5 + x_6 + x_7 + x_8 + x_9 + x_{10} = 100,000$

                                 Invest $100,000

$x_i \leq 25,000y_i \quad i = 1, 2,…, 10$

        Invest no more than $25,000 in any one fund

$x_i \geq 10,000y_i \quad i = 1, 2, …, 10$

        If invest in a fund, invest at least $10,000 in a fund

$y_1 + y_2 + y_3 + y_4 \leq 2$

        No more than 2 pure growth funds

$y_9 + y_{10} \geq 1$

        At least 1 must be a pure bond fund

$x_9 + x_{10} \geq x_1 + x_2 + x_3 + x_4$

Amount in pure bonds must be at least that invested in pure growth funds

$x_i \geq 0 \qquad i = 1, 2, …, 10$

The optimal solution follows: $x_2 = x_{10} = \$12,500, x_5 = x_7 = x_8 = \$25,000$; Total return = $7,056.25

Assumptions: (1) the expected annual returns are valid for the future. (2) All $100,000 will be invested. (3) These are the only alternatives for this $100,000.

Since these are annual returns, we would expect to run this no more often than once per year.

Chapter 8

2. a. $X = 4.32$ and $Y = 0.92$, for an optimal solution value of 4.84.
b. The dual value on the constraint $X + 4Y \leq 8$ is 0.88, which is the decrease in the optimal objective function value if we increase the right-hand-side from 8 to 9.
c. The new optimal objective function value is 4.0, so the actual decrease is only 0.84 rather than 0.88.

4. a. $q_1 = 2150$
$q_2 = 100$
Gross profit = $1,235,000
b. $G = -1.5p_1^2 - 0.5p_2^2 + p_1p_2 + 2000p_1 + 3450p_2 - 11,465,000$
c. $p_1 = \$2725$ and $p_2 = \$6175$; $q_1 = 1185$ and $q_2 = 230$; $G = \$1,911,875$
d. Max $p_1q_1 + p_2q_2 - c_1 - c_2$
s.t.
$c_1 = 10000 + 1500q_1$
$c_2 = 30000 + 4000q_2$
$q_1 = 950 - 1.5p_1 + 0.7p_2$
$q_2 = 2500 + 0.3p_1 - 0.5p_2$

5. a. If $1000 is spent on radio and $1000 is spent on direct mail, simply substitute those values into the sales function:

$$S = -2R^2 - 10M^2 - 8RM + 18R + 34M$$
$$= -2(2^2) - 10(1^2) - 8(2)(1) + 18(2) + 34(1)$$
$$= 18$$
Sales = $18,000
b. Max $-2R^2 - 10M^2 - 8RM + 18R + 34M$
s.t.
$$R + M \leq 3$$
c. The optimal solution is Radio = $2500 and Direct mail = $500
Total sales = $37,000

6. Substituting the given data into the model formulation gives us

$$\text{Min} \left[100 \times 2000 + \frac{150 \times 2000}{Q_1} + 0.20 \times 100 \times \frac{Q_1}{2} + \right.$$
$$50 \times 2000 + \frac{135 \times 2000}{Q_2} + 0.20 \times 50 \times \frac{Q_2}{2} + 80 \times$$
$$\left. 1000 + \frac{125 \times 1000}{Q_3} + 0.20 \times 80 \times \frac{Q_3}{2} \right]$$

s.t.

$$[100 \times Q_1 + 50 \times Q_2 + 80 \times Q_3] \le 20{,}000$$
$$Q_1, Q_2, Q_3 \ge 0$$

Using LINGO or Excel Solver, we find that the optimal solution is $Q_1 = 52.223$, $Q_2 = 70.065$, $Q_3 = 37.689$ with a total cost of $25,830.

8. b. $L = 2244.281$ and $C = 2618.328$; Optimal solution = $374,046.9$ (If Excel Solver is used for this problem, we recommend starting with an initial solution that has $L > 0$ and $C > 0$.)

10. a. Min $X^2 - X^2 + 5 + Y^2 + 2Y + 3$

s.t.

$$X + Y = 8$$
$$X, Y \ge 0$$

b. $X = 4.75$ and $Y = 3.25$; Optimal objective value = 42.875

11. The LINGO formulation:

Min = $(1/5)*((R1 - RBAR)^2 + (R2 - RBAR)^2 + (R3 - RBAR)^2 + (R4 - RBAR)^2 + (R5 - RBAR)^2$;

.1006*FS + .1764*IB + .3241*LG + .3236*LV + .3344*SG + .2456*SV = R1;
.1312*FS + .0325*IB + .1871*LG + .2061*LV + .1940*SG + .2532*SV = R2;
.1347*FS + .0751*IB + .3328*LG + .1293*LV + .0385*SG + .0670*SV = R3;
.4542*FS + .0133*IB + .4146*LG + .0706*LV + .5868*SG + .0543*SV = R4;
−.2193*FS + .0736*IB + .2326*LG + .0537*LV + .0902*SG + .1731*SV = R5;

FS +   IB +   LG +   LV +   SG +   SV = 50000;

(1/5)*(R1 + R2 + R3 + R4 + R5) = RBAR;
RBAR > RMIN;
RMIN = 5000;

@FREE(R1);
@FREE(R2);
@FREE(R3);
@FREE(R4);
@FREE(R5);

Optimal solution:

```
Local optimal solution found.
  Objective value:       6784038
  Total solver iterations:    19

  Model Title: MARKOWITZ
  Variable      Value      Reduced Cost
     R1      9478.492       0.000000
   RBAR      5000.000       0.000000
     R2      5756.023       0.000000
     R3      2821.951       0.000000
     R4      4864.037       0.000000
     R5      2079.496       0.000000
     FS      7920.372       0.000000
     IB      26273.98       0.000000
     LG      2103.251       0.000000
     LV      0.000000     208.2068
     SG      0.000000      78.04764
     SV      13702.40       0.000000
   RMIN      5000.000       0.000000
```

(Excel Solver will produce the same optimal solution.)

12. Optimal value of $\alpha = 0.1743882$
Sum of squared errors = 98.56

14. Optimal solution:

```
Local optimal solution found.
  Objective value:        0.1990478
  Total solver iterations:    12
  Model Title: MARKOWITZ

  Variable      Value      Reduced Cost
     R1      -0.1457056      0.000000
   RBAR      0.1518649       0.000000
     R2      0.7316081       0.000000
     R3      0.8905417       0.000000
     R4      -0.6823468E-02  0.000000
     R5      -0.3873745      0.000000
     R6      -0.5221017      0.000000
     R7      0.3499810       0.000000
     R8      0.2290317       0.000000
     R9      0.2276271       0.000000
   AAPL      0.1817734       0.000000
    AMD      0.1687534       0.000000
   ORCL      0.6494732       0.000000
```

15.

MODEL TITLE: MARKOWITZ;
! MINIMIZE VARIANCE OF THE PORTFOLIO;
MIN = (1/9) * ((R1 − RBAR)^2 + (R2 − RBAR)^2 + (R3 − RBAR)^2 + (R4 − RBAR)^2 + (R5 − RBAR)^2 + (R6 − RBAR)^2 + (R7 − RBAR)^2 + (R8 − RBAR)^2 + (R9 − RBAR)^2);
! SCENARIO 1 RETURN;
0.0962*AAPL − 0.5537*AMD − 0.1074*ORCL = R1;
! SCENARIO 2 RETURN;
0.8104*AAPL + 0.1272*AMD + 0.8666*ORCL = R2;
! SCENARIO 3 RETURN;
0.9236*AAPL + 0.4506*AMD + 0.9956*ORCL = R3;
! SCENARIO 4 RETURN;
−0.8753*AAPL + 0.3124*AMD + 0.1533*ORCL = R4;
! SCENARIO 5 RETURN;
0.1340*AAPL − 0.4270*AMD − 0.5230*ORCL = R5;
! SCENARIO 6 RETURN;
−0.5432*AAPL − 1.1194*AMD − 0.3610*ORCL = R6;
! SCENARIO 7 RETURN;
0.4517*AAPL + 1.0424*AMD + 0.1416*ORCL = R7;
! SCENARIO 8 RETURN;
1.2263*AAPL + 0.0613*AMD − 0.0065*ORCL = R8;
! SCENARIO 9 RETURN;
0.6749*AAPL + 0.9729*AMD − 0.0912*ORCL = R9;
! MUST BE FULLY INVESTED IN THE MUTUAL FUNDS;
AAPL + AMD + ORCL = 1;
! DEFINE THE MEAN RETURN;
(1/9) * (R1 + R2 + R3 + R4 + R5 + R6 + R7 + R8 + R9) = RBAR;
! THE MEAN RETURN MUST BE AT LEAST 10 PERCENT;
RBAR > 0.12;
! SCENARIO RETURNS MAY BE NEGATIVE;
@FREE(R1);
@FREE(R2);
@FREE(R3);
@FREE(R4);
@FREE(R5);
@FREE(R6);
@FREE(R7);
@FREE(R8);
@FREE(R9);
END

Optimal solution:

```
Local optimal solution found.
   Objective value:    0.4120213
   Total solver iterations:    8

Model Title: MATCHING S&P INFO TECH
RETURNS
      Variable     Value        Reduced Cost
        R1     -0.5266475E-01    0.000000
        R2      0.8458175        0.000000
        R3      0.9716207        0.000000
        R4     -0.1370104        0.000000
        R5     -0.3362695        0.000000
        R6     -0.4175977        0.000000
        R7      0.2353628        0.000000
        R8      0.3431437        0.000000
        R9      0.1328016        0.000000
       AAPL     0.2832558        0.000000
       AMD      0.6577707E-02    0.000000
       ORCL     0.7101665        0.000000
```

(Excel Solver produces the same return.)

16. Optimal solution:

```
Local optimal solution found.
   Objective value:    7.503540
   Total solver iterations:    18

Model Title: MARKOWITZ WITH SEMIVARIANCE
      Variable     Value        Reduced Cost
       D1N      0.000000         0.000000
       D2N      0.8595142        0.000000
       D3N      3.412762         0.000000
       D4N      2.343876         0.000000
       D5N      4.431505         0.000000
        FS      0.000000         6.491646
        IB      0.6908001        0.000000
        LG      0.6408726E-01    0.000000
        LV      0.000000         14.14185
        SG      0.8613837E-01    0.000000
        SV      0.1589743        0.000000
        R1      21.04766         0.000000
        R2      9.140486         0.000000
        R3      6.587238         0.000000
        R4      7.656124         0.000000
        R5      5.568495         0.000000
       RBAR     10.00000         0.000000
       RMIN     10.00000         0.000000
       D1P      11.04766         0.000000
       D2P      0.000000         0.3438057
       D3P      0.000000         1.365105
       D4P      0.000000         0.9375505
       D5P      0.000000         1.772602
```

The solution calls for investing 69.1% of the portfolio in the intermediate-term bond fund, 6.4% in the large-cap growth fund, 8.6% in the small-cap growth fund, and 15.9% in the small-cap value fund.

(Excel Solver may have trouble with this problem, depending upon the starting solution that is used; a starting solution of each fund at 0.167 will produce the optimal value.)

18.

Max Variance	Exp Return
20	Infeasible
25	9.645
30	10.449
35	11.172
40	11.835
45	12.450
50	13.022
55	13.526
60	13.976

20. Call option price for Friday, August 25, 2006, is approximately $C = \$1.524709$.

22. Optimal solution: Produce 10 chairs at Aynor, cost = $1350; 30 chairs at Spartanburg, cost = $3150; Total cost = $4500

Chapter 9

2.

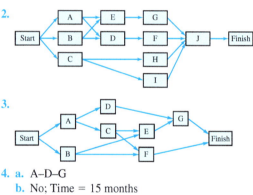

3.

4. a. A–D–G
   b. No; Time = 15 months

6. a. Critical path: A–D–F–H
   b. 22 weeks
   c. No, it is a critical activity.
   d. Yes, 2 weeks
   e. Schedule for activity E:

Earliest start	3
Latest start	4
Earliest finish	10
Latest finish	11

8. a.

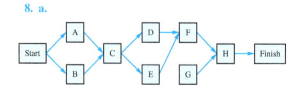

b. B–C–E–F–H

c.

Activity	Earliest Start	Latest Start	Earliest Finish	Latest Finish	Slack	Critical Activity
A	0	2	6	8	2	
B	0	0	8	8	0	Yes
C	8	8	20	20	0	Yes
D	20	22	24	26	2	
E	20	20	26	26	0	Yes
F	26	26	41	41	0	Yes
G	26	29	38	41	3	
H	41	41	49	49	0	Yes

d. Yes, time = 49 weeks

10. a.

Activity	Optimistic	Most Probable	Pessimistic	Expected Times	Variance
A	4	5.0	6	5.00	0.11
B	8	9.0	10	9.00	0.11
C	7	7.5	11	8.00	0.44
D	7	9.0	10	8.83	0.25
E	6	7.0	9	7.17	0.25
F	5	6.0	7	6.00	0.11

b. Critical activities: B–D–F
   Expected project completion time: 23.83
   Variance of projection completion time: 0.47

12. a. A–D–H–I

b. 25.66 days

c. 0.2578

13.

Activity	Expected Time	Variance
A	5	0.11
B	3	0.03
C	7	0.11
D	6	0.44
E	7	0.44
F	3	0.11
G	10	0.44
H	8	1.78

From Problem 6, A–D–F–H is the critical path, so
$E(T) = 5 + 6 + 3 + 8 = 22$.

$\sigma^2 = 0.11 + 0.44 + 0.11 + 1.78 = 2.44$

$$z = \frac{\text{Time} - E(T)}{\sigma} = \frac{\text{Time} - 22}{\sqrt{2.44}}$$

a. Time = 21: $z = -0.64$
   Cumulative Probability = 0.2611
   $P(21 \text{ weeks}) = 0.2611$

b. Time = 22: $z = 0$
   Cumulative Probability = 0.5000
   $P(22 \text{ weeks}) = 0.5000$

c. Time = 25: $z = +1.92$
   Cumulative Probability = 0.9726
   $P(25 \text{ weeks}) = 0.9726$

14. a. A–C–E–G–H

b. 52 weeks (1 year)

c. 0.0174

d. 0.0934

e. 10 month doubtful
   13 month very likely
   Estimate 12 months (1 year)

16. a.

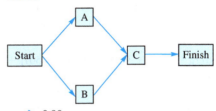

b. 0.90

c. 0.828

d. The probability estimate from (c) based on both paths is more accurate.

18. a.

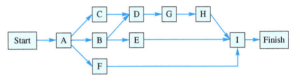

b.

Activity	Expected Time	Variance
A	1.17	0.03
B	6.00	0.44
C	4.00	0.44
D	2.00	0.11
E	3.00	0.11
F	2.00	0.11
G	2.00	0.11
H	2.00	0.11
I	1.00	0.00

Activity	Earliest Start	Latest Start	Earliest Finish	Latest Finish	Slack	Critical Activity
A	0.00	0.00	1.17	1.17	0.00	Yes
B	1.17	1.17	7.17	7.17	0.00	Yes
C	1.17	3.17	5.17	7.17	2.00	
D	7.17	7.17	9.17	9.17	0.00	Yes
E	7.17	10.17	10.17	13.17	3.00	
F	1.17	11.17	3.17	13.17	10.00	
G	9.17	9.17	11.17	11.17	0.00	Yes
H	11.17	11.17	13.17	13.17	0.00	Yes
I	13.17	13.17	14.17	14.17	0.00	Yes

c. A–B–D–G–H–I, 14.17 weeks

d. 0.0951, yes

20. a.

Activity	Maximum Crash	Crash Cost/Week
A	2	400
B	3	667
C	1	500
D	2	300
E	1	350
F	2	450
G	5	360
H	1	1000

Min $400Y_A + 667Y_B + 500Y_C + 300Y_D + 350Y_E + 450Y_F + 360Y_G + 1000Y_H$

s.t.

$x_A + y_A \geq 3$ $x_E + y_E - x_D \geq 4$ $x_H + y_H - x_G \geq 3$
$x_B + y_B \geq 6$ $x_F + y_F - x_E \geq 3$ $x_H \leq 16$
$x_C + y_C - x_A \geq 2$ $x_G + y_G - x_C \geq 9$
$x_D + y_D - x_C \geq 5$ $x_G + y_G - x_B \geq 9$
$x_D + y_D - x_B \geq 5$ $x_H + y_H - x_F \geq 3$

Maximum Crashing:

$$y_A \leq 2$$
$$y_B \leq 3$$
$$y_C \leq 1$$
$$y_D \leq 2$$
$$y_E \leq 1$$
$$y_F \leq 2$$
$$y_G \leq 5$$
$$y_H \leq 1$$
$$\text{All } x, y \geq 0$$

b. Crash B(1 week), D(2 weeks), E(1 week), F(1 week), G(1 week)
Total cost = $2427

c. All activities are critical

21. a.

Activity	Earliest Start	Latest Start	Earliest Finish	Latest Finish	Slack	Critical Activity
A	0	0	3	3	0	Yes
B	0	1	2	3	1	
C	3	3	8	8	0	Yes
D	2	3	7	8	1	
E	8	8	14	14	0	Yes
F	8	10	10	12	2	
G	10	12	12	14	2	

Critical path: A–C–E
Project completion time = 14 days

b. Total cost = $8400

22. a.

Activity	Max Crash Days	Crash Cost/Day
A	1	600
B	1	700
C	2	400
D	2	400
E	2	500
F	1	400
G	1	500

Min $600Y_A + 700Y_B + 400Y_C + 400Y_D + 500Y_E + 400Y_F + 400Y_G$

s.t.

$$X_A + Y_A \geq 3$$
$$X_B + Y_B \geq 2$$
$$-X_A + X_C + Y_C \geq 5$$
$$-X_B + X_D + Y_D \geq 5$$
$$-X_C + X_E + Y_E \geq 6$$
$$-X_D + X_E + Y_E \geq 6$$
$$-X_C + X_F + Y_F \geq 2$$
$$-X_D + X_F + Y_F \geq 2$$
$$-X_F + X_G + Y_G \geq 2$$
$$-X_E + X_{FIN} \geq 0$$
$$-X_G + X_{FIN} \geq 0$$
$$X_{FIN} \leq 12$$
$$Y_A \leq 1$$
$$Y_B \leq 1$$
$$Y_C \leq 2$$
$$Y_D \leq 2$$
$$Y_E \leq 2$$
$$Y_F \leq 1$$
$$Y_G \leq 1$$
$$\text{All } X, Y \geq 0$$

b. Solution of the linear programming model in part (a) shows

Activity	Crash	Crashing Cost
C	1 day	$400
E	1 day	500
		Total $900

c. Total cost = $9300

24. a.

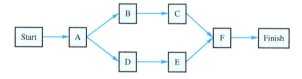

b.

Activity	Earliest Start	Latest Start	Earliest Finish	Latest Finish	Slack
A	0	0	10	10	0
B	10	10	18	18	0
C	18	18	28	28	0
D	10	11	17	18	1
E	17	18	27	28	1
F	28	28	31	31	0

c. A–B–C–F, 31 weeks

d. Crash A(2 weeks), B(2 weeks), C(1 week), D(1 week), E(1 week)

e. All activities are critical.

f. $112,500

Chapter 10

1. a. $Q^* = \sqrt{\dfrac{2DC_o}{C_h}} = \sqrt{\dfrac{2(3600)(20)}{0.25(3)}} = 438.18$

b. $r = dm = \dfrac{3600}{250}(5) = 72$

c. $T = \dfrac{250Q^*}{D} = \dfrac{250(438.18)}{3600} = 30.43$ days

d. $TC = \dfrac{1}{2}QC_h + \dfrac{D}{Q}C_o$

$\qquad = \dfrac{1}{2}(438.18)(0.25)(3) + \dfrac{3600}{438.18}(20) = \$328.63$

2. $164.32 for each; Total cost = $328.64

4. a. 1095.45

b. 240

c. 22.82 days

d. $273.86 for each; Total cost = $547.72

6. a. $Q^*_{pens} = 101$ days
$Q^*_{pencils} = 120$ days
$TC^*_{pens} = \$94.87$
$TC^*_{pencils} = \$80$
Total cost = $174.87

b. $22.88

8. $Q^* = 11.73$; use 12
5 classes per year
$225,200

10. $Q^* = 1414.21$
$T = 28.28$ days
Production runs of 7.07 days

12. a. 1500

b. 4 production runs; 3 month cycle time

c. Yes, savings = $12,510

13. a. $Q^* = \sqrt{\dfrac{2DC_o}{(1 - D/P)C_h}}$

$\qquad = \sqrt{\dfrac{2(7200)(150)}{(1 - 7200/25,000)(0.18)(14.50)}} = 1078.12$

b. Number of production runs $= \dfrac{D}{Q^*} = \dfrac{7200}{1078.12} = 6.68$

c. $T = \dfrac{250Q}{D} = \dfrac{250(1078.12)}{7200} = 37.43$ days

d. Production run length $= \dfrac{Q}{P/250}$

$\qquad = \dfrac{1078.12}{25,000/250} = 10.78$ days

e. Maximum inventory $= \left(1 - \dfrac{D}{P}\right)Q$

$\qquad = \left(1 - \dfrac{7200}{25,000}\right)(1078.12)$

$\qquad = 767.62$

f. Holiday cost $= \dfrac{1}{2}\left(a - \dfrac{D}{P}\right)QC_h$

$\qquad = \dfrac{1}{2}\left(1 - \dfrac{7200}{25,000}\right)(1078.12)(0.18)(14.50)$

$\qquad = \$1001.74$

Ordering cost $= \dfrac{D}{Q}C_o = \dfrac{7200}{1078.12}(150) = \$1001.74$

Total cost = $2003.48

g. $r = dm = \left(\dfrac{D}{250}\right)m = \dfrac{7200}{250}(15) = 432$

14. New $Q^* = 4509$

15. a. $Q^* = \sqrt{\dfrac{2DC_o}{C_h}\left(\dfrac{C_h + C_b}{C_b}\right)}$

$\qquad = \sqrt{\dfrac{2(12,000)(25)}{0.50}\left(\dfrac{0.50 + 5}{0.50}\right)} = 1148.91$

b. $S^* = Q^*\left(\dfrac{C_h}{C_h + C_b}\right) = 1148.91\left(\dfrac{0.50}{0.50 + 5}\right) = 104.45$

c. Max inventory $= Q^* - S^* = 1044.46$

d. $T = \dfrac{250Q^*}{D} = \dfrac{250(1148.91)}{12,000} = 23.94$ days

e. Holding $= \dfrac{(Q - S)^2}{2Q}C_h = \$237.38$

Ordering $= \dfrac{D}{Q}C_o = \$261.12$

Backorder $= \dfrac{S^2}{2Q}C_b = \$23.74$

Total cost = $522.24

The total cost for the EOQ model in Problem 4 was $547.72; allowing backorders reduces the total cost.

16. 135.55; $r = dm - S$; less than

18. 64, 24.44

20. $Q^* = 100$; Total cost = $3601.50

21. $Q = \sqrt{\dfrac{2DC_o}{C_h}}$

$Q_1 = \sqrt{\dfrac{2(500)(40)}{0.20(10)}} = 141.42$

$Q_2 = \sqrt{\dfrac{2(500)(40)}{0.20(9.7)}} = 143.59$

Because Q_1 is over its limit of 99 units, Q_1 cannot be optimal use $Q_2 = 143.59$ as the optimal order quantity.

Total cost $= \dfrac{1}{2}QC_h + \dfrac{D}{C}C_o + DC$

$= 139.28 + 139.28 + 4850.00 = 5128.56

22. $Q^* = 300$; Savings = $480

24. **a.** 8352 magazines
    b. 8828 magazines

25. **a.**
$$c_o = 80 - 50 = 30$$
$$c_u = 125 - 80 = 45$$

$$P(D \le Q^*) = \dfrac{c_u}{c_u + c_o} = \dfrac{45}{45 + 30} = 0.60$$

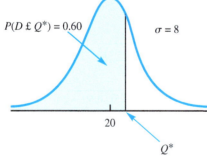

For the cumulative standard normal probability 0.60, $z = 0.25$.
$Q^* = 20 + 0.25(8) = 22$
    b. $P(\text{Sell all}) = P(D \ge Q^*) = 1 - 0.60 = 0.40$

26. **a.** $150
    b. $240 - $150 = $90
    c. 47
    d. 0.625

28. **a.** 440
    b. 0.60
    c. 710
    d. $c_u = $17

29. **a.** $r = dm = (200/250)15 = 12$
    b. $\dfrac{D}{Q} = \dfrac{200}{25} = 8$ orders/year

The limit of 1 stock-out per year means that $P(\text{Stock-out/cycle}) = 1/8 = 0.125$.

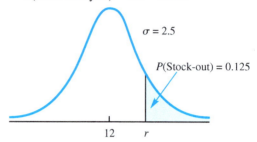

$P(\text{No Stock-out/cycle}) = 1 - 0.125 = 0.875$
For cumulative probability 0.875, $z = 1.15$

Thus, $z = \dfrac{r - 12}{2.5} = 1.15$

$r = 12 + 1.15(2.5) = 14.875$ Use 15.
    c. Safety stock = 3 units
    Added cost = 3($5) = $15/year

30. **a.** $Q^* = 56$ boxes
    b. $r = 475$ cups

32. **a.** 31.62
    b. 19.8; 0.2108
    c. 5, $15

33. **a.** $1/52 = 0.0192$
    b. $P(\text{No Stockout}) = 1 - 0.0192 = 0.9808$
    For cumulative probability 0.9808, $z = 2.07$

Thus, $z = \dfrac{M - 60}{12} = 2.07$

$M = \mu + z\sigma = 60 + 2.07(12) = 85$
    c. $M = 35 + (0.9808)(85 - 35) = 84$

34. **a.** 243
    b. 93, $54.87
    c. 613
    d. 163, $96.17
    e. Yes, added cost would only be $41.30 per year.
    f. Yes, added cost would be $4130 per year.

36. **a.** 40
    b. 62.25; 7.9
    c. 54
    d. 36

Chapter 11

2. **a.** 0.4512
    b. 0.6988
    c. 0.3012

4. 0.3333, 0.2222, 0.1481, 0.0988; 0.1976

5. a. $P_0 = 1 - \dfrac{\lambda}{\mu} = 1 - \dfrac{10}{12} = 0.1667$

  b. $L_q = \dfrac{\lambda^2}{\mu(\mu - \lambda)} = \dfrac{10^2}{12(12 - 10)} = 4.1667$

  c. $W_q = \dfrac{L_q}{\lambda} = 0.4167$ hour (25 minutes)

  d. $W = W_q + \dfrac{1}{\lambda} = 0.5$ hour (30 minutes)

  e. $P_w = \dfrac{\lambda}{\mu} = \dfrac{10}{12} = 0.8333$

6. a. 0.3750
  b. 1.0417
  c. 0.8333 minutes (50 seconds)
  d. 0.6250
  e. Yes

8. 0.20, 3.2, 4, 3.2, 4, 0.80
  Slightly poorer service

10. a. New: 0.3333, 1.3333, 2, 0.6667, 1, 0.6667
    Experienced: 0.50, 0.50, 1, 0.25, 0.50, 0.50
  b. New \$74; experienced \$50; hire experienced

11. a. $\lambda = 2.5; \ \mu = \dfrac{60}{10} = 6$ customers per hour

  $L_q = \dfrac{\lambda^2}{\mu(\mu - \lambda)} = \dfrac{(2.5)^2}{6(6 - 2.5)} = 0.2976$

  $L = L_q + \dfrac{\lambda}{\mu} = 0.7143$

  $W_q = \dfrac{L_q}{\lambda} = 0.1190$ hours (7.14 minutes)

  $W = W_q + \dfrac{1}{\mu} = 0.2857 \ hours$

  $P_w = \dfrac{\lambda}{\mu} = \dfrac{2.5}{6} = 0.4167$

  b. No; $W_q = 7.14$ minutes; firm should increase the service rate (μ) for the consultant or hire a second consultant.

  c. $\mu = \dfrac{60}{8} = 7.5$ customers per hour

  $L_q = \dfrac{\lambda^2}{\mu(\mu - \lambda)} = \dfrac{(2.5)^2}{7.5(7.5 - 2.5)} = 0.1667$

  $W_q = \dfrac{L_q}{\lambda} = 0.0667$ hours (4 minutes)

  The service goal is being met.

12. a. 0.25, 2.25, 3, 0.15 hours, 0.20 hours, 0.75
  b. The service needs improvement.

14. a. 8
  b. 0.3750
  c. 1.0417
  d. 12.5 minutes
  e. 0.6250
  f. Add a second consultant.

16. a. 0.50
  b. 0.50
  c. 0.10 hours (6 minutes)
  d. 0.20 hours (12 minutes)
  e. Yes, $W_q = 6$ minutes is most likely acceptable for a marina.

18. a. $k = 2; \lambda/\mu = 5.4/3 = 1.8; P_0 = 0.0526$

  $L_q = \dfrac{(\lambda/\mu)^2 \lambda \mu}{(k - 1)!(2\mu - \lambda)^2} P_0$

  $= \dfrac{(1.8)^2(5.4)(3)}{(2 - 1)!(6 - 5.4)^2}(0.0526) = 7.67$

  $L = L_q + \lambda/\mu = 7.67 + 1.8 = 9.47$

  $W_q = \dfrac{L_q}{\lambda} = \dfrac{7.67}{5.4} = 1.42$ minutes

  $W = W_q + 1/\mu = 1.42 + 0.33 = 1.75$ minutes

  $P_w = \dfrac{1}{k!}\left(\dfrac{\lambda}{\mu}\right)^k\left(\dfrac{k\mu}{k\mu - \lambda}\right)P_0$

  $= \dfrac{1}{2!}(1.8)^2\left(\dfrac{6}{6 - 5.4}\right)0.0526 = 0.8526$

  b. $L_q = 7.67$; Yes
  c. $W = 1.75$ minutes

20. a. Use $k = 2$
    $W = 3.7037$ minutes
    $L = 4.4444$
    $P_w = 0.7111$
  b. For $k = 3$
    $W = 7.1778$ minutes
    $L = 15.0735$ customers
    $P_N = 0.8767$
    Expand post office.

21. From Problem 11, a service time of 8 minutes has $\mu = 60/8 = 7.5$.

  $L_q = \dfrac{\lambda^2}{\mu(\mu - \lambda)} = \dfrac{(2.5)^2}{7.5(7.5 - 2.5)} = 0.1667$

  $L = L_q + \dfrac{\lambda}{\mu} = 0.50$

Total cost = $25 + $16
$$= 25(0.50) + 16 = \$28.50$$

Two channels: $\lambda = 2.5$; $\mu = 60/10 = 6$

With $P_0 = 0.6552$,

$$L_q = \frac{(\lambda/\mu)^2 \lambda \mu}{1!(2\mu - \lambda)^2} P_0 = 0.0189$$

$$L = L_q + \frac{\lambda}{\mu} = 0.4356$$

Total cost = $25(0.4356) + 2(16) = \$42.89$

Use one consultant with an 8-minute service time.

22.

Characteristic	A	B	C
a. P_0	0.2000	0.5000	0.4286
b. L_q	3.2000	0.5000	0.1524
c. L	4.0000	1.0000	0.9524
d. W_q	0.1333	0.0208	0.0063
e. W	0.1667	0.0417	0.0397
f. P_w	0.8000	0.5000	0.2286

The two-channel System C provides the best service.

24. $\lambda = 4$, $W = 10$ minutes
- **a.** $\mu = 0.5$
- **b.** $W_q = 8$ minutes
- **c.** $L = 40$

26.
- **a.** 0.2668, 10 minutes, 0.6667
- **b.** 0.0667, 7 minutes, 0.4669
- **c.** $25.33; $33.34; one-channel

27.
- **a.** ⅜ hours = 0.25 per hour
- **b.** 1/3.2 hours = 0.3125 per hour
- **c.** $L_q = \dfrac{\lambda^2 \sigma^2 + (\lambda/\mu)^2}{2(1 - \lambda/\mu)}$

$$= \frac{(0.25)^2(2)^2 + (2.5/0.3125)^2}{2(1 - 0.25/0.3125)} = 2.225$$

- **d.** $W_q = \dfrac{L_q}{\lambda} = \dfrac{2.225}{0.25} = 8.9$ hours

- **e.** $W = W_q + \dfrac{1}{\mu} = 8.9 + \dfrac{1}{0.3125} = 12.1$ hours

- **f.** Same as $P_w = \dfrac{\lambda}{\mu} = \dfrac{0.25}{0.3125} = 0.80$

The welder is busy 80% of the time.

28.
- **a.** 10, 9.6
- **b.** Design A with $\mu = 10$
- **c.** 0.05, 0.01
- **d.** A: 0.5, 0.3125, 0.8125, 0.0625, 0.1625, 0.5
  B: 0.4792, 0.2857, 0.8065, 0.0571, 0.1613, 0.5208
- **e.** Design B has slightly less waiting time.

30. a. $\lambda = 42$; $\lambda = 20$

i	$(\lambda/\mu)^i/i!$
0	1.0000
1	2.1000
2	2.2050
3	1.5435
	Total 6.8485

j	P_j	
0	1/6.8485	= 0.1460
1	2.1/6.8485	= 0.3066
2	2.2050/6.8485	= 0.3220
3	1.5435/6.8485	= 0.2254
		1.0000

- **b.** 0.2254
- **c.** $L = \lambda/\mu(1 - P_k) = 42/20(1 - 0.2254) = 1.6267$
- **d.** Four lines will be necessary; the probability of denied access is 0.1499

32. a. 31.03%
- **b.** 27.59%
- **c.** 0.2759, 0.1092, 0.0351
- **d.** 3, 10.92%

34. $N = 5$; $\lambda = 0.025$; $\mu = 0.20$; $\lambda/\mu = 0.125$
- **a.**

	$\dfrac{N!}{(N - n)!}\left(\dfrac{\lambda}{\mu}\right)^n$
0	1.0000
1	0.6250
2	0.3125
3	0.1172
4	0.0293
5	0.0037
	Total 2.0877

$$P_0 = 1/2.0877 = 0.4790$$

- **b.** $L_q = N - \left(\dfrac{\lambda + \mu}{\lambda}\right)(1 - P_0)$

$$= 5 - \left(\frac{0.225}{0.025}\right)(1 - 0.4790) = 0.3110$$

- **c.** $L = L_q + (1 - P_0) = 0.3110 + (1 - 0.4790)$
  $= 0.8321$

- **d.** $W_q = \dfrac{L_q}{(N - L)\lambda} = \dfrac{0.3110}{(5 - 0.8321)(0.025)}$
  $= 2.9854$ minutes

- **e.** $W = W_q + \dfrac{1}{\mu} = 2.9854 + \dfrac{1}{0.20} = 7.9854$ minutes

- **f.** Trips/day = (8 hours)(60 minutes/hour)(λ)
  $= (8)(60)(0.025) = 12$ trips

Time at copier: $12 \times 7.9854 = 95.8$ minutes/day
Wait time at copier: $12 \times 2.9854 = 35.8$ minutes/day

g. Yes, five assistants $\times$ 35.8 = 179 minutes (3 hours/day), so 3 hours per day are lost to waiting.
$(35.8/480)(100) = 7.5\%$ of each assistant's day is spent waiting for the copier.

Chapter 12

2. a. c = variable cost per unit
x = demand
Profit $= (50 - c)x - 30,000$

b. Base: Profit $= (50 - 20)1200 - 30,000 = 6,000$
Worst: Profit $= (50 - 24)300 - 30,000 = -22,200$
Best: Profit $= (50 - 16)2100 - 30,000 = 41,400$

c. Simulation will be helpful in estimating the probability of a loss.

4. a.

Number of New Accounts	Interval
0	0.00 but less than 0.01
1	0.01 but less than 0.05
2	0.05 but less than 0.15
3	0.15 but less than 0.40
4	0.40 but less than 0.80
5	0.80 but less than 0.95
6	0.95 but less than 1.00

b. 4, 3, 3, 5, 2, 6, 4, 4, 4, 2
37 new accounts

c. Commission from 10 seminars = $185,000
Cost of 10 seminars = $35,000
Yes

5. a.

Stock Price Change	Interval
-2	0.00 but less than 0.05
-1	0.05 but less than 0.15
0	0.15 but less than 0.40
$+1$	0.40 but less than 0.60
$+2$	0.60 but less than 0.80
$+3$	0.80 but less than 0.90
$+4$	0.90 but less than 1.00

b. Beginning price $39
0.1091 indicates -1 change; $38
0.9407 indicates $+4$ change; $42
0.1941 indicates 0 change; $42
0.8083 indicates $+3$ change; $45 (ending price)

6. a. 0.00–0.83, 0.83–0.89, 0.89–0.94, 0.94–0.96, 0.96–0.98, 0.98–0.99, 0.99–1.00

b. 4 claims paid; Total = $22,000

8. a. Atlanta wins each game if random number is in interval 0.00–0.60, 0.00–0.55, 0.00–0.48, 0.00–0.45, 0.00–0.48, 0.00–0.55, 0.00–0.50.

b. Atlanta wins games 1, 2, 4, and 6.
Atlanta wins series 4 to 2.

c. Repeat many times; record % of Atlanta wins.

9. a. Base-case based on most likely;
Time $= 6 + 5 + 14 + 8 = 33$ weeks

Worst: Time $= 8 + 7 + 18 + 10 = 43$ weeks
Best: Time $= 5 + 3 + 10 + 8 = 26$ weeks

b. 0.1778 for A: 5 weeks
0.9617 for B: 7 weeks
0.6849 for C: 14 weeks
0.4503 for D: 8 weeks; Total = 34 weeks

c. Simulation will provide an estimate of the probability of 35 weeks or less.

10. a.

Hand Value	Interval
17	0.0000 but less than 0.1654
18	0.1654 but less than 0.2717
19	0.2717 but less than 0.3780
20	0.3780 but less than 0.4797
21	0.4797 but less than 0.5769
Broke	0.5769 but less than 1.0000

b, c, & d. Dealer wins 13 hands, player wins 5, 2 pushes.

e. Player wins 7, dealer wins 13.

12. a. $7, $3, $12

b. Purchase: 0.00–0.25, 0.25–0.70, 0.70–1.00
Labor: 0.00–0.10, 0.10–0.35, 0.35–0.70, 0.70–1.00
Transportation: 0.00–0.75, 0.75–1.00

c. $5

d. $7

e. Provide probability profit less than $5/unit.

14. Selected cell formulas for the worksheet shown in Figure E12.14 are as follows:

Cell	Formula
B13	=$C$7+RAND()*($C$8−$C$7)
C13	=NORMINV(RAND(),$G$7,$G$8)
D13	=($C$3−B13)*C13−$C$4

a. The mean profit should be approximately $6000; simulation results will vary, with most simulations having a mean profit between $5500 and $6500.

b. 120 to 150 of the 500 simulation trials should show a loss; thus, the probability of a loss should be between 0.24 and 0.30.

c. This project appears too risky.

16. a. About 36% of simulation runs will show $130,000 as the winning bid.

b. $150,000; $10,000

c. Recommended $140,000

18. Selected cell formulas for the worksheet shown in Figure E12.18 are as follows:

Cell	Formula
B10	=$B$4 + RAND() * ($B$5-$B$4)
C10	=NORMINV(RAND(), $E$4, $E$5)
D10	=MAX(B10:C10)
C1013	=COUNTIF(D10:D1009, "<750000")
D1013	=C1013 / COUNT(D10:D1009)

FIGURE E12.14   WORSHEET FOR THE MADEIRA MANUFACTURING SIMULATION

	A	B	C	D	E	F	G	H
1	Madeira Manufacturing Company							
2								
3	Selling Price per Unit		$50					
4	Fixed Cost		$30,000					
5								
6	Variable Cost (Uniform Distribution)				Demand (Normal Distribution)			
7	Smallest Value		$16		Mean		1200	
8	Largest Value		$24		Standard Deviation		300	
9								
10	Simulation							
11								
12	Trial	Unit Variable Cost	Demand	Profit				
13	1	$17.81	788	($4,681)				
14	2	$18.86	1078	$3,580				
15								

FIGURE E12.18   WORKSHEET FOR THE CONTRACTOR BIDDING SIMULATION

	A	B	C	D	E
1	Contractor Bidding				
2					
3	Contractor A (Uniform Distribution)			Contractor A (Normal Distribution)	
4	Smallest Value	$600,000		Mean	$700,000
5	Largest Value	$800,000		Standard Deviation	$50,000
6					
7					
8	Simulation				
9	Trial	Contractor A's Bid	Contractor B's Bid	Highest Bid	
10	1	$785,020	$630,729	$785,020.16	
11	2	$698,925	$742,675	$742,675.28	
1008	999	$795,023	$822,027	$822,027.17	
1009	1000	$672,159	$708,791	$708,791.25	
1010					
1011		Results			
1012		Contractor's Bid	Number of Wins	Probability of Winning	
1013		$750,000	641	0.641	
1014		$775,000	826	0.826	
1015		$785,000	894	0.894	

a. The probability of winning the bid should be between 0.60 and 0.65.

b. Probability of $750,000 winning should be roughly 0.82; probability of $785,000 winning should be roughly 0.88.

20. a. Results vary with each simulation run.

Approximate results: 50,000 provided $230,000
60,000 provided $190,000
70,000 less than $100,000

b. Recommend 50,000 units.

c. Roughly 0.75

22. Very poor operation; some customers wait 30 minutes or more.

24. a. Mean interarrival time and mean service time are both approximately 4 minutes.

    b. Waiting time is approximately 0.8 minutes.

    c. 30% to 35% of customers have to wait.

Chapter 13

1. a.

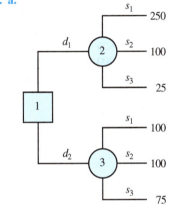

b.

Decision	Maximum Profit	Minimum Profit
d_1	250	25
d_2	100	75

Optimistic approach: Select d_1
Conservative approach: Select d_2
Regret or opportunity loss table:

Decision	s_1	s_2	s_3
d_1	0	0	50
d_2	150	0	0

Maximum regret: 50 for d_1 and 150 for d_2; select d_1

2. a. Optimistic: d_1
    Conservative: d_3
    Minimax regret: d_3
c. Optimistic: d_1
    Conservative: d_2 or d_3
    Minimax regret: d_2

3. a. Decision: Choose the best plant size from the two alternatives—a small plant and a large plant. Chance event: Market demand for the new product line with three possible outcomes (states of nature): low, medium, and high

    b. Influence Diagram:

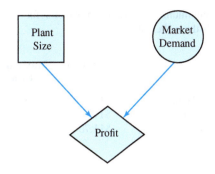

c.

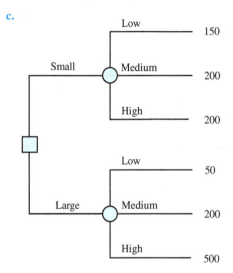

d.

Decision	Maximum Profit	Minimum Profit	Maximum Regret
Small	200	150	300
Large	500	50	100

Optimistic Approach: Large plant
Conservative Approach: Small plant
Minimax Regret: Large plant

4. a. The decision faced by Amy is to select the best lease option from three alternatives (Hepburn Honda, Midtown Motors, and Hopkins Automotive). The chance event is the number of miles Amy will drive.

Dealer	Actual Miles Driven Annually		
	12,000	15,000	18,000
Hepburn Honda	$10,764	$12,114	$13,464
Midtown Motors	$11,160	$11,160	$12,960
Hopkins Automotive	$11,700	$11,700	$11,700

c. The minimum and maximum payoffs for each of Amy's three alternatives are:

Dealer	Minimum Cost	Maximum Cost
Hepburn Honda	$10,764	$13,464
Midtown Motors	$11,160	$12,960
Hopkins Automotive	$11,700	$11,700

Thus:

The optimistic approach results in selection of the Hepburn Automotive lease option (which has the smallest minimum cost of the three alternatives—$10,764).

The conservative approach results in selection of the Hopkins Automotive lease option (which has the smallest maximum cost of the three alternatives—$11,700).

The minimax regret approach results in selection of the Hopkins Automotive lease option (which has the smallest regret of the three alternatives: $936).

d. The expected value approach results in selection of the Midtown Motors lease option (which has the minimum expected value of the three alternatives—$11,340).

e. The risk profile for the decision to lease from Midtown Motors is as follows:

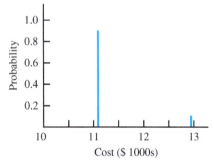

Note that although we have three chance outcomes (drive 12,000 miles annually, drive 15,000 miles annually, and drive 18,000 miles annually), we only have two unique costs on this graph. This is because for this decision alternative (lease from Midtown Motors) there are only two unique payoffs associated with the three chance outcomes—the payoff (cost) associated with the Midtown Motors lease is the same for two of the chance outcomes (whether Amy drives 12,000 miles or 15,000 miles annually, her payoff is $11,160).

The expected value approach results in selection of either the Midtown Motors lease option or the Hopkins Automotive lease option (both of which have the minimum expected value of the three alternatives—$11,700).

5. a. $EV(d_1) = 0.65(250) + 0.15(100) + 0.20(25) + 182.5$
$EV(d_2) = 0.65(100) + 0.15(100) + 0.20(75) + 95$
The optimal decision is d_1.

6. a. Pharmaceuticals; 3.4%
   b. Financial; 4.6%

7. a. $EV(\text{own staff}) = 0.2(650) + 0.5(650) + 0.3(600) = 635$
$EV(\text{outside vendor}) = 0.2(900) + 0.5(600) + 0.3(300) = 570$
$EV(\text{combination}) = 0.2(800) + 0.5(650) + 0.3(500) = 635$
Optimal decision: Hire an outside vendor with an expected cost of $570,000

b.

	Cost	Probability
Own staff	300	0.3
Outside vendor	600	0.5
Combination	900	0.2
		1.0

8. a. $EV(d_1) = p(10) + (1 - p)(1) = 9p + 1$
$EV(d_2) = p(4) + (1 - p)(3) = 1p + 3$

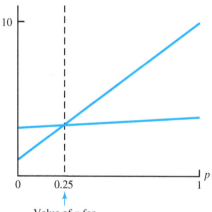

Value of p for which EVs are equal

$9p + 1 = 1p + 3$ and hence $p = 0.25$
d_2 is optimal for $p \geq 0.25$, d_1 is optimal for $p \geq 0.25$
b. d_2
c. As long as the payoff for $s_1 \geq 2$, then d_2 is optimal.

10. b. Space Pirates
EV = $724,000
$84,000 better than Battle Pacific
c. $200   0.18
$400   0.32
$800   0.30
$1600   0.20
d. $P(\text{Competition}) > 0.7273$

12. a. Decision: Whether to lengthen the runway
Chance event: The location decisions of Air Express and DRI
Consequence: Annual revenue

b. $255,000

c. $270,000

d. No

e. Lengthen the runway.

14. a. If s_1, then d_1; if s_2, then d_1 or d_2; if s_3, then d_2

b. EvwPI = 0.65(250) + 0.15(100) + 0.20(75) = 192.5

c. From the solution to Problem 5, we know that EV(d_1) = 182.5 and EV(d_2) = 95; thus, recommended decision is d_1; hence, EvwoPI = 182.5.

d. EVPI = EvwPI − EvwoPI = 192.5 − 182.5 = 10

16. a.

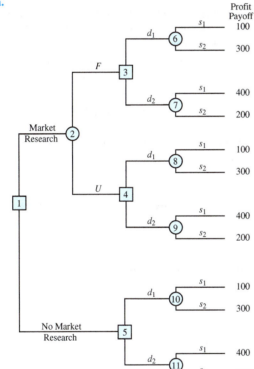

	Profit Payoff

EV (node 6) = 0.57(100) + 0.43(300) = 186
EV (node 7) = 0.57(400) + 0.43(200) = 314
EV (node 8) = 0.18(100) + 0.82(300) = 264
EV (node 9) = 0.18(400) + 0.82(200) = 236
EV (node 10) = 0.40(100) + 0.60(300) = 220
EV (node 11) = 0.40(400) + 0.60(200) = 280
EV (node 3) = Max(186,314) = 314d_2
EV (node 4) = Max(264,236) = 264d_1
EV (node 5) = Max(220,280) = 280d_2
EV (node 2) = 0.56(314) + 0.44(264) = 292
EV (node 1) = Max(292,280) = 292
    ∴ Market Research
    If favorable, decision d_2
    If unfavorable, decision d_1

18. a. 5000 − 200 − 2000 − 150 = 2650

3000 − 200 − 2000 − 150 = 650

b. Expected values at nodes:
8: 2350   5: 2350   9: 1100
6: 1150   10: 2000   7: 2000
4: 1870   3: 2000   2: 1560
1: 1560

c. Cost would have to decrease by at least $130,000.

d.

Payoff (in millions)	Probability
−$200	0.20
800	0.32
2800	0.48
	1.00

20. b. If Do Not Review, Accept
If Review and F, Accept
If Review and U, Accept
Always Accept

c. Do not review; EVSI = $0

d. $87,500; better method of predicting success

22. a. Order two lots; $60,000

b. If E, order two lots
If V, order one lot
EV = $60,500

c. EVPI = $14,000
EVSI = $500
Efficiency = 3.6%
Yes, use consultant.

23.

State of Nature	$P(s_j)$	$P(I\|s_j)$	$P(I \cap s_j)$	$P(s_j\|I)$
s_1	0.2	0.10	0.020	0.1905
s_2	0.5	0.05	0.025	0.2381
s_3	0.3	0.20	0.060	0.5714
	1.0		$P(I) = 0.105$	1.0000

24. a. 0.695, 0.215, 0.090
0.98, 0.02
0.79, 0.21
0.00, 1.00

c. If C, Expressway
If O, Expressway
If R, Queen City
26.6 minutes

26. a. EV(d_1) = 10,000
EV(d_2)=0.96(0)+0.03(100,000)+0.01(200,000)= 5,000
Using EV approach, we should choose No Insurance (d_2).

b. Lottery:

    p = probability of a \$0 Cost

    $1 - p$ = probability of a \$200,000 Cost

c.

		s_1 None	s_2 Minor	s_3 Major
Insurance	d_1	9.9	9.9	9.9
No Insurance	d_1	10.0	6.0	0.0

$EU(d_1) = 9.9$

$EU(d_2) = 0.96(10.0) + 0.03(6.0) + 0.01(0.0) = 9.78$

∴ Using EU approach → Insurance (d_1)

d. Use expected utility approach. The EV approach results in a decision that can be very risky since it means that the decision maker could lose up to \$200,000. Most decision makers (particularly those considering insurance) are risk averse.

28. a.

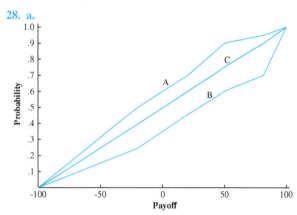

b. A - Risk avoider

    B - Risk taker

    C - Risk neutral

c. Risk avoider A, at \$20 payoff $p = 0.70$

    Thus, EV(Lottery) = $0.70(100) + 0.30(-100) = \$40$

    Therefore, will pay $40 - 20 = \$20$

    Risk taker B, at \$20 payoff $p = 0.45$

    Thus, EV(Lottery) = $0.45(100) + 0.55(-100) = -\$10$

    Therefore, will pay $20 - (-10) = \$30$

30.

Monetary Payoff, x	Utility, $U(x)$
-200	-1.226
-100	-0.492
0	0.000
100	0.330
200	0.551
300	0.699
400	0.798
500	0.865

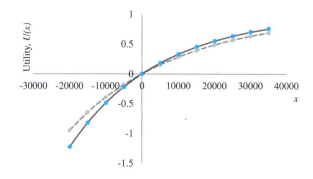

Chapter 14

2. a. Let x_1 = number of shares of AGA Products purchased

    x_2 = number of shares of Key Oil purchased

To obtain an annual return of exactly 9%:

$$0.06(50)x_1 + 0.10(100)x_2 = 0.09(50,000)$$
$$3x_1 + 10x_2 = 4500$$

To have exactly 60% of the total investment in Key Oil:

$$100x_2 = 0.60(50,000)$$
$$x_2 = 300$$

Therefore, we can write the goal programming model as follows:

Min $P_1(d_1^-) + P_2(d_2^+)$

s.t.

$50x_1 + 100x_2$	$\leq 50,000$	Funds available
$3x_1 + 10x_2 - d_1^+ + d_1^- =$	$4,500$	P_1 goal
$x_2 - d_2^+ + d_2^- =$	300	P_2 goal

$$x_1, x_2, d_1^+, d_1^-, d_2^+, d_2^- \geq 0$$

b. In the following graphical solution, $x_1 = 250$ and $x_2 = 375$.

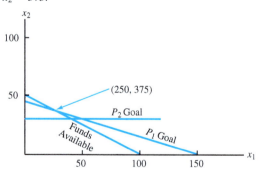

4. a. Min $P_1(d_1^-) + P_2(d_2^1) + P_2(d_3^-) + P_2(d_4^-) + P_3(d_5^-)$

    s.t.

$$20x_1 + 30x_2 - d_1^+ + d_1^- = 4800$$
$$20x_1 + 30x_2 - d_2^1 + d_2^- = 6000$$
$$x_1 - d_3^+ + d_3^- = 100$$
$$x_2 - d_4^+ + d_4^- = 120$$
$$x_1 + x_2 - d_3^1 + d_5^- = 300$$

$$x_1, x_2, \text{ all deviation variables} \geq 0$$

b. $x_1 = 120, x_2 = 120$

6. a. Let x_1 = number of letters mailed to group 1 customers
x_2 = number of letters mailed to group 2 customers

Min $P_1(d_1^-) + P_2(d_2^-) + P_2(d_3^+)$
s.t.

$$x_1 \qquad\quad - d_1^+ + d_1^- = 40{,}000$$
$$x_2 - d_2^+ + d_2^- = 50{,}000$$
$$x_1 + x_2 - d_3^+ + d_3^- = 70{,}000$$

$x_1, x_2,$ all deviation variables ≥ 0

b. $x_1 = 40{,}000, x_2 = 50{,}000$
c. Optimal solution does not change.

8. a. Min $d_1^- + d_1^+ + e_1^- + e_1^+ + d_2^- + d_2^+ + e_2^- +$
$e_2^+ + d_3^- + d_3^+ + e_3^- + e_3^+$

s.t.

$$x_1 \qquad + d_1^- - d_1^+ = 1$$
$$x_2 + e_1^- - e_1^+ = 7$$
$$x_1 \qquad + d_2^- - d_2^+ = 5$$
$$x_2 + e_2^- - e_2^+ = 9$$
$$x_1 \qquad + d_3^- - d_3^+ = 6$$
$$x_2 + e_3^- - e_3^+ = 2$$

all variables ≥ 0

b. $x_1 = 5, x_2 = 7$

9. Scoring calculations

Criterion	Analyst Chicago	Accountant Denver	Auditor Houston
Career advancement	35	20	20
Location	10	12	8
Management	30	25	35
Salary	28	32	16
Prestige	32	20	24
Job security	8	10	16
Enjoyment of the work	28	20	20
Total	171	139	139

The analyst position in Chicago is recommended.

10. 178, 184, 151
Marysville

12. 170, 168, 190, 183
Handover College

14. a. 220 Bowrider (194)
b. 240 Sundancer (144)

16. Step 1: Column totals are $^{17}/_4$, $^{31}/_{21}$, and 12.

Step 2:

Style	Accord	Saturn	Cavalier
Accord	$^4/_{17}$	$^7/_{31}$	$^4/_{12}$
Saturn	$^{12}/_{17}$	$^{21}/_{31}$	$^7/_{12}$
Cavalier	$^1/_{17}$	$^3/_{31}$	$^1/_{12}$

Step 3:

Style	Accord	Saturn	Cavalier	Row Average
Accord	0.235	0.226	0.333	0.265
Saturn	0.706	0.677	0.583	0.656
Cavalier	0.059	0.097	0.083	0.080

Consistency Ratio
Step 1:

$$0.265 \begin{bmatrix} 1 \\ 3 \\ 1/4 \end{bmatrix} + 0.656 \begin{bmatrix} 1/3 \\ 1 \\ 1/7 \end{bmatrix} + 0.080 \begin{bmatrix} 4 \\ 7 \\ 1 \end{bmatrix}$$

$$\begin{bmatrix} 0.265 \\ 0.795 \\ 0.066 \end{bmatrix} + \begin{bmatrix} 0.219 \\ 0.656 \\ 0.094 \end{bmatrix} + \begin{bmatrix} 0.320 \\ 0.560 \\ 0.080 \end{bmatrix} = \begin{bmatrix} 0.802 \\ 2.007 \\ 0.239 \end{bmatrix}$$

Step 2: $0.802/0.265 = 3.028$
$2.007/0.656 = 3.062$
$0.239/0.080 = 3.007$
Step 3: $\lambda_{max} = (3.028 + 3.062 + 3.007)/3 = 3.032$
Step 4: CI $= (3.032 - 3)/2 = 0.016$
Step 5: CR $= 0.016/0.58 = 0.028$
Because CR $= 0.028$ is less than 0.10, the degree of consistency exhibited in the pairwise comparison matrix for style is acceptable.

18. a. 0.724, 0.193, 0.083
b. CR $= 0.057$, yes

20. a.

Flavor	A	B	C
A	1	3	2
B	$^1/_3$	1	5
C	$^1/_2$	$^1/_5$	1

b. Step 1: Column totals are $^{11}/_6$, $^{21}/_5$, and 8.
Step 2:

Flavor	A	B	C
A	$^6/_{11}$	$^{15}/_{21}$	$^2/_8$
B	$^2/_{11}$	$^5/_{21}$	$^5/_8$
C	$^3/_{11}$	$^1/_{21}$	$^1/_8$

Step 3:

Flavor	A	B	C	Row Average
A	0.545	0.714	0.250	0.503
B	0.182	0.238	0.625	0.348
C	0.273	0.048	0.125	0.148

c. Step 1:

$$0.503 \begin{bmatrix} 1 \\ 1/3 \\ 1/2 \end{bmatrix} + 0.348 \begin{bmatrix} 3 \\ 1 \\ 1/5 \end{bmatrix} + 0.148 \begin{bmatrix} 2 \\ 5 \\ 1 \end{bmatrix}$$

$$\begin{bmatrix} 0.503 \\ 0.168 \\ 0.252 \end{bmatrix} + \begin{bmatrix} 1.044 \\ 0.348 \\ 0.070 \end{bmatrix} + \begin{bmatrix} 0.296 \\ 0.740 \\ 0.148 \end{bmatrix} = \begin{bmatrix} 1.845 \\ 1.258 \\ 0.470 \end{bmatrix}$$

Step 2: 1.845/0.503 = 3.668
1.258/0.348 = 3.615
0.470/0.148 = 3.123
Step 3: λ_{max} = (3.668 + 3.615 + 3.123)/3 = 3.469
Step 4: CI = (3.469 − 3)/2 = 0.235
Step 5: CR = 0.235/0.58 = 0.415
Because CR = 0.415 is greater than 0.10, the individual's judgments are not consistent.

22. a.

	D	S	N
D	1	1/4	1/7
S	4	1	1/3
N	7	3	1

b. 0.080, 0.265, 0.656
c. CR = 0.028, yes

24. Criteria: Yield and Risk
Step 1: Column totals are 1.5 and 3.
Step 2:

	Yield	Risk	Priority
Yield	0.667	0.667	0.667
Risk	0.333	0.333	0.333

With only two criteria, CR = 0; no need to compute CR; preceding calculations for Yield and Risk provide

Stocks	Yield Priority	Risk Priority
CCC	0.750	0.333
SRI	0.250	0.667

Overall Priorities:
CCC 0.667(0.750) + 0.333(0.333) = 0.611
SRI 0.667(0.250) + 0.333(0.667) = 0.389
CCC is preferred.

26. a. Criterion: 0.608, 0.272, 0.120
Price: 0.557, 0.123, 0.320
Sound: 0.137, 0.239, 0.623
Reception: 0.579, 0.187, 0.046
b. 0.446, 0.162, 0.392
System A is preferred.

Chapter 15

1. The following table shows the calculations for parts (a), (b), and (c).

Week	Time Series Value	Forecast	Forecast Error	Absolute Value of Forecast Error	Squared Forecast Error	Percentage Error	Absolute Value of Percentage Error
1	18						
2	13	18	−5	5	25	−38.46	38.46
3	16	13	3	3	9	18.75	18.75
4	11	16	−5	5	25	−45.45	45.45
5	17	11	6	6	36	35.29	35.29
6	14	17	−3	3	9	−21.43	21.43
			Total	22	104	−51.30	159.38

a. MAE = 22/5 = 4.4
b. MSE = 104/5 = 20.8

c. MAPE = 159.38/5 = 31.88
d. Forecast for week 7 is 14.

2. The following table shows the calculations for parts (a), (b), and (c).

Week	Time Series Value	Forecast	Forecast Error	Absolute Value of Forecast Error	Squared Forecast Error	Percentage Error	Absolute Value of Percentage Error
1	18						
2	13	18.00	−5.00	5.00	25.00	−38.46	38.46
3	16	15.50	0.50	0.50	0.25	3.13	3.13
4	11	15.67	−4.67	4.67	21.81	−42.45	42.45
5	17	14.50	2.50	2.50	6.25	14.71	14.71
6	14	15.00	−1.00	1.00	1.00	−7.14	7.14
			Total	13.67	54.31	−70.21	105.86

a. MAE = 13.67/5 = 2.73
b. MSE = 54.31/5 = 10.86
c. MAPE = 105.89/5 = 21.18
d. Forecast for week 7 is (18 + 13 + 16 + 11 + 17 + 14)/6 = 14.83.

3. By every measure, the approach used in Problem 2 appears to be the better method.

4. **a.** MSE = 363/6 = 60.5
   Forecast for month 8 is 15.
   b. MSE = 216.72/6 = 36.12
   Forecast for month 8 is 18.
   c. The average of all the previous values is better because MSE is smaller.

5. **a.** The data appear to follow a horizontal pattern.
   b.

Week	Time Series Value	Forecast	Forecast Error	Squared Forecast Error
1	18			
2	13			
3	16			
4	11	15.67	−4.67	21.78
5	17	13.33	3.67	13.44
6	14	14.67	−0.67	0.44
			Total	35.67

MSE = 35.67/3 = 11.89.
The forecast for week 7 = (11 + 17 + 14)/3 = 14.

c.

Week	Time Series Value	Forecast	Forecast Error	Squared Forecast Error
1	18			
2	13	18.00	−5.00	25.00
3	16	17.00	−1.00	1.00
4	11	16.80	−5.80	33.64
5	17	15.64	1.36	1.85
6	14	15.91	−1.91	3.66
			Total	65.15

MSE = 65.15/5 = 13.03
The forecast for week 7 is 0.2(14) + (1 − 0.2)15.91 = 15.53.

d. The three-week moving average provides a better forecast because it has a smaller MSE.

e.

Alpha   0.367694922

Week	Time Series Value	Forecast	Forecast Error	Squared Forecast Error
1	18			
2	13	18	−5.00	25.00
3	16	16.16	−0.16	0.03
4	11	16.10	−5.10	26.03
5	17	14.23	2.77	7.69
6	14	15.25	−1.25	1.55
			Total	60.30

MSE = 60.30/5 = 12.061

6. **a.** The data appear to follow a horizontal pattern.
   b. MSE = 110/4 = 27.5
   The forecast for week 8 is 19.
   c. MSE = 252.87/6 = 42.15
   The forecast for week 7 is 19.12.

d. The three-week moving average provides a better fore-cast because it has a smaller MSE.

e. $\alpha = 0.351404848$ MSE = 39.61428577

8. a.

Week	4	5	6	7	8	9	10	11	12
Forecast	19.3	21.3	19.8	17.8	18.3	18.3	20.3	20.3	17.8

b. MSE = 11.49

Prefer the unweighted moving average here; it has a smaller MSE.

c. You could always find a weighted moving average at least as good as the unweighted one. Actually, the unweighted moving average is a special case of the weighted ones where the weights are equal.

10. b. The more recent data receives the greater weight or importance in determining the forecast. The moving averages method weights the last n data values equally in determining the forecast.

12. a. The data appear to follow a horizontal pattern.

b. MSE(3-month) = 0.12
MSE(4-month) = 0.14
Use 3-month moving averages.

c. 9.63

13. a. The data appear to follow a horizontal pattern.

b.

Month	Time-Series Value	3-Month Moving Average Forecast	(Error)²	$\alpha = 0.2$ Forecast	(Error)²
1	240				
2	350			240.00	12100.00
3	230			262.00	1024.00

4	260	273.33	177.69	255.60	19.36
5	280	280.00	0.00	256.48	553.19
6	320	256.67	4010.69	261.18	3459.79
7	220	286.67	4444.89	272.95	2803.70
8	310	273.33	1344.69	262.36	2269.57
9	240	283.33	1877.49	271.89	1016.97
10	310	256.67	2844.09	265.51	1979.36
11	240	286.67	2178.09	274.41	1184.05
12	230	263.33	1110.89	267.53	1408.50
			17,988.52		27,818.49

MSE(3-Month) = 17,988.52/9 = 1998.72
MSE($\alpha = 0.2$) = 27,818.49/11 = 2528.95
Based on the above MSE values, the 3-month moving average appears better. However, exponential smoothing was penalized by including month 2, which was difficult for any method to forecast. Using only the errors for months 4–12, the MSE for exponential smoothing is
MSE($\alpha = 0.2$) = 14,694.49/9 = 1632.72
Thus, exponential smoothing was better considering months 4–12.

c. Using exponential smoothing,

$$F_{13} = \alpha Y_{12} + (1 - \alpha)F_{12} = 0.20(230) + 0.80(267.53)$$
$$= 260$$

14. a. The data appear to follow a horizontal pattern.

b. Values for months 2–12 are as follows:
105.00 114.00 115.80 112.56 105.79 110.05 120.54 126.38 118.46 106.92 104.85
MSE = 510.29

c. $\alpha = 0.032564518$ MSE = 459.69

16. a.

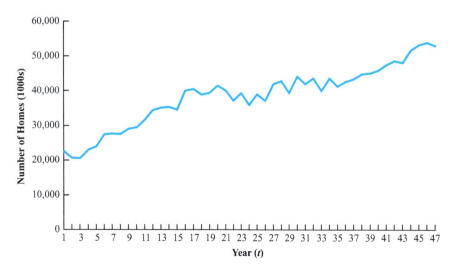

b. This time series plot indicates a possible linear trend in the data, so forecasting methods discussed in this chapter are appropriate to develop forecasts for this time series.

c. Equation for linear trend: $\hat{y}_t = 24170.506 + 596.366t$

17. a. The time series plot shows a linear trend.

b.

		b0	4.70		
		b1	2.10		
Year	Sales	Forecast	Forecast Error	Squared Forecast Error
1	6.00	6.80	−0.80	0.64
2	11.00	8.90	2.10	4.41
3	9.00	11.00	−2.00	4.00
4	14.00	13.10	0.90	0.81
5	15.00	15.20	−0.20	0.04
6		17.30	**Total**	9.9

MSE = 9.9/5 = 1.98

c. $T_6 = 4.7 + 2.1(6) = 17.3$

18. a.

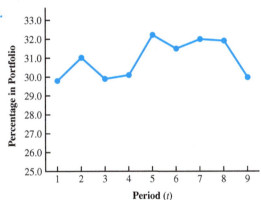

The time series plot indicates a horizontal pattern.

b. $\alpha = 0.467307293$; MSE = 1.222838367

c. Forecast for second quarter 2014 = 30.93

20. a. The time series plot shows a linear trend.

b.

		b0	4.72		
		b1	1.46		
Period	Year	Enrollment	Forecast	Forecast Error	Squared Forecast Error
1	2001	6.50	6.17	0.33	0.11
2	2002	8.10	7.63	0.47	0.22
3	2003	8.40	9.09	−0.69	0.47
4	2004	10.20	10.54	−0.34	0.12
5	2005	12.50	12.00	0.50	0.25
6	2006	13.30	13.46	−0.16	0.02
7	2007	13.70	14.91	−1.21	1.47
8	2008	17.20	16.37	0.83	0.69
9	2009	18.10	17.83	0.27	0.07
10	2010		19.28	**Total**	3.427333

$T_t = 4.72 + 1.46t$

c. $T_{10} = 4.72 + 1.46(10) = 19.28$

22. a. The time series plot shows a upward linear trend.

b. $T_t = 19.9928 + 1.7738t$

c. $1.77

d. $T_9 = 19.9928 + 1.7738(9) = 35.96$

24. a. The time series plot shows a horizontal pattern. But, there is a seasonal pattern in the data. For instance, in each year the lowest value occurs in quarter 2 and the highest value occurs in quarter 4.

b.

Year	Quarter	Period	Seasonality QTR1	QTR2	QTR3	Series	Forecast	Forecast Error	Squared Forecast Error
1	1	1	1	0	0	71	67.00	4.00	16.00
	2	2	0	1	0	49	47.00	2.00	4.00
	3	3	0	0	1	58	57.00	1.00	1.00
	4	4	0	0	0	78	77.00	1.00	1.00
2	1	5	1	0	0	68	67.00	1.00	1.00
	2	6	0	1	0	41	47.00	−6.00	36.00
	3	7	0	0	1	60	57.00	3.00	9.00
	4	8	0	0	0	81	77.00	4.00	16.00

(Continued)

Year	Quarter	Period	Seasonality QTR1	QTR2	QTR3	Series	Forecast	Forecast Error	Squared Forecast Error
3	1	9	1	0	0	62	67.00	−5.00	25.00
	2	10	0	1	0	51	47.00	4.00	16.00
	3	11	0	0	1	53	57.00	−4.00	16.00
	4	12	0	0	0	72	77.00	−5.00	25.00
								Total	166.00
		b0	b1	b2	b3				
		77.00	−10.00	−30.00	−20.00				

c. The quarterly forecasts for next year are as follows:
Quarter 1 forecast = 77.0 − 10.0(1) − 30.0(0) −
   20.0(0) = 67
Quarter 2 forecast = 77.0 − 10.0(0) − 30.0(1) −
   20.0(0) = 47
Quarter 3 forecast = 77.0 − 10.0(0) − 30.0(0) −
   20.0(1) = 57
Quarter 4 forecast = 77.0 − 10.0(0) − 30.0(0) −
   20.0(0) = 77

26. a. There appears to be a seasonal pattern in the data and perhaps a moderate upward linear trend.
b. $Sales_t = 2492 − 712 Qtr1_t − 1512 Qtr2_t + 327 Qtr3_t$
c. The quarterly forecasts for next year are as follows:
Quarter 1 forecast = 1780
Quarter 2 forecast = 980
Quarter 3 forecast = 2819
Quarter 4 forecast = 2492
d. $Sales_t = 2307 − 642 Qtr1_t − 1465 Qtr2_t + 350 Qtr3_t + 23.1 t$
The quarterly forecasts for next year are as follows:
Quarter 1 forecast = 2058
Quarter 2 forecast = 1258
Quarter 3 forecast = 3096
Quarter 4 forecast = 2769

28. a. The time series plot shows both a linear trend and seasonal effects.
b. $Revenue_t = 70.0 + 10.0 Qtr1_t + 105 Qtr2_t + 245 Qtr3_t$
Quarter 1 forecast = 80
Quarter 1 forecast = 175
Quarter 1 forecast = 315
Quarter 1 forecast = 70
c. The equation is
Revenue = −70.1 + 45.0 Qtr1 + 128 Qtr2
   + 257 Qtr3 + 11.7 Period
Quarter 1 forecast = 221
Quarter 1 forecast = 315
Quarter 1 forecast = 456
Quarter 1 forecast = 211

Appendix A

2. =F6*$F$3

4.

	A	B
1	Nowlin Plastics	
2		
3	Fixed Cost	$3,000.00
4		
5	Variable Cost Per Unit	$2.00
6		
7	Selling Price Per Unit	$5.00
8		
9	Capacity	1500
10		
11	Forecasted Demand	1200
12		
13	Model	
14		
15	Production Volume	1200
16		
17	Total Cost	$5,400.00
18		
19	Total Revenue	$6,000.00
20		
21	Total Profit (Loss)	$600.00
22		

	A	B
14		
15	Production Volume	=IF(B11<B9,B11,B9)
16		
17	Total Cost	=B3+B5*B15
18		
19	Total Revenue	=B7*B15
20		
21	Total Profit (Loss)	=B19-B17
22		

6.

Cell	Formula
D14	=C14*$B$3
E14	=C14*$B$7
F14	=C14*$B$9
G14	=$B$5
H14	=SUM(E14:G14)
I14	=D14-H14

	A	B	C	D	E	F	G	H	I
1	Cox Electric Breakeven Analysis								
2									
3	Revenue per Unit	$0.63							
4									
5	Fixed Costs	$10,000.00							
6									
7	Material Cost per Unit	$0.15							
8									
9	Labor Cost per Unit	$0.10							
10									
11									
12	Model								
13			Volume	Total Revenue	Material Cost	Labor Cost	Fixed Cost	Total Cost	Profit
14			10000	$6,300.00	$1,500.00	$1,000.00	$10,000.00	$12,500.00	-$6,200.00
15			20000	$12,600.00	$3,000.00	$2,000.00	$10,000.00	$15,000.00	-$2,400.00
16			30000	$18,900.00	$4,500.00	$3,000.00	$10,000.00	$17,500.00	$1,400.00
17									

8.

Grade	Count
F	1
D	2
C-	1
C-	1
C+	0
B-	2
B	1
B+	0
A-	1
A	3

	A	B	C	D	E	F	G	H	I	J	K	L	M
1	OM 455												
2	Section 001												
3	Course Grading Scale Based on Course Average:												
4		Lower	Upper	Course									
5		Limit	Limit	Garde									
6		0	59	F							New Scale		
7		60	69	D									
8		70	79	C						Lower	Upper	Grade	
9		80	89	B						0	59	F	
10		90	100	A						60	69	D	
11						Grade				70	72	C-	
12		Midterm	Final	Course	Course	Based on				73	76	C-	
13	Lastname	Score	Score	Average	Grade	New Scale				77	79	C-	
14	Benson	70	56	63.0	D	D				80	82	B-	
15	Chin	95	91	93.0	A	A				83	86	B	
16	Choi	82	80	81.0	B	B-				87	89	B-	
17	Cruz	45	78	61.5	D	D				90	92	A-	
18	Doe	68	45	56.5	F	F				93	100	A	
19	Honda	91	98	94.5	A	A							
20	Hume	87	74	80.5	B	B-							
21	Jones	60	80	70.0	C	C-							
22	Miranda	80	93	86.5	B	B							
23	Murigami	97	98	97.5	A	A							
24	Ruebush	90	91	90.5	A	A-							
25													
26													
27					Grade	Count							
28					F	1							
29					D	2							
30					C-	1							
31					C-	1							
32					C-	0							
33					B-	2							
34					B	1							
35					B-	0							
36					A-	1							
37					A	3							
38													

	D	E	F
12	Course	Course	Based on
13	Average	Grade	New Scale
14	=AVERAGE(B14:C14)	=VLOOKUP(D14,B6:D10,3,TRUE)	=VLOOKUP(D14,$J$9:$L$18,3,TRUE)
15	=AVERAGE(B15:C15)	=VLOOKUP(D15,B6:D10,3,TRUE)	=VLOOKUP(D15,$J$9:$L$18,3,TRUE)
16	=AVERAGE(B16:C16)	=VLOOKUP(D16,B6:D10,3,TRUE)	=VLOOKUP(D16,$J$9:$L$18,3,TRUE)
17	=AVERAGE(B17:C17)	=VLOOKUP(D17,B6:D10,3,TRUE)	=VLOOKUP(D17,$J$9:$L$18,3,TRUE)
18	=AVERAGE(B18:C18)	=VLOOKUP(D18,B6:D10,3,TRUE)	=VLOOKUP(D18,$J$9:$L$18,3,TRUE)
19	=AVERAGE(B19:C19)	=VLOOKUP(D19,B6:D10,3,TRUE)	=VLOOKUP(D19,$J$9:$L$18,3,TRUE)
20	=AVERAGE(B20:C20)	=VLOOKUP(D20,B6:D10,3,TRUE)	=VLOOKUP(D20,$J$9:$L$18,3,TRUE)
21	=AVERAGE(B21:C21)	=VLOOKUP(D21,B6:D10,3,TRUE)	=VLOOKUP(D21,$J$9:$L$18,3,TRUE)
22	=AVERAGE(B22:C22)	=VLOOKUP(D22,B6:D10,3,TRUE)	=VLOOKUP(D22,$J$9:$L$18,3,TRUE)
23	=AVERAGE(B23:C23)	=VLOOKUP(D23,B6:D10,3,TRUE)	=VLOOKUP(D23,$J$9:$L$18,3,TRUE)
24	=AVERAGE(B24:C24)	=VLOOKUP(D24,B6:D10,3,TRUE)	=VLOOKUP(D24,$J$9:$L$18,3,TRUE)
25			
26			
27		Grade	Count
28		F	=COUNTIF($F$14:$F$24,E28)
29		D	=COUNTIF($F$14:$F$24,E29)
30		C-	=COUNTIF($F$14:$F$24,E30)
31		C-	=COUNTIF($F$14:$F$24,E31)
32		C+	=COUNTIF($F$14:$F$24,E32)
33		B-	=COUNTIF($F$14:$F$24,E33)
34		B	=COUNTIF($F$14:$F$24,E34)
35		B+	=COUNTIF($F$14:$F$24,E35)
36		A-	=COUNTIF($F$14:$F$24,E36)
37		A	=COUNTIF($F$14:$F$24,E37)

10.

	A	B	C	D	E	F	G	H
1	Newton Scientific Calculators							Total Volume
2	Customer Zone	Model	Volume (000 units)					(000) Units
3	Malaysia	N350	399.0				Malaysia	1928.6
4	China	N350	3158.3				China	5328.5
5	France	N350	1406.0				France	3486.6
6	Brazil	N350	163.5				Brazil	1144.7
7	US Northeast	N350	68.7				US Northeast	430.2
8	US Southeast	N350	999.7				US Southeast	3203.3
9	US Midwest	N350	544.9				US Midwest	4482.7
10	US West	N350	1804.0				US West	5969.9
11	Malaysia	N450	228.0					
12	China	N450	540.9				Total	25974.5
13	France	N450	289.8					
14	Brazil	N450	240.5					
15	US Northeast	N450	313.2					Total Volume
16	US Southeast	N450	681.3					(000) Units
17	US Midwest	N450	1720.3				N350	8544.1
18	US West	N450	2922.3				N450	6936.3
19	Malaysia	N900	1301.6				N900	10494.1
20	China	N900	1629.3					
21	France	N900	1790.8				Total	25974.5
22	Brazil	N900	740.7					
23	US Northeast	N900	48.3					
24	US Southeast	N900	1522.3					
25	US Midwest	N900	2217.5					
26	US West	N900	1243.6					
27								
28		Total	25974.5					
29								

	G	H
1		Total Volume
2		(000) Units
3	Malaysia	=SUMIF($A$3:$A$26,G3,$C$3:$C$26)
4	China	=SUMIF($A$3:$A$26,G4,$C$3:$C$26)
5	France	=SUMIF($A$3:$A$26,G5,$C$3:$C$26)
6	Brazil	=SUMIF($A$3:$A$26,G6,$C$3:$C$26)
7	US Northeast	=SUMIF($A$3:$A$26,G7,$C$3:$C$26)
8	US Southeast	=SUMIF($A$3:$A$26,G8,$C$3:$C$26)
9	US Mideast	=SUMIF($A$3:$A$26,G9,$C$3:$C$26)
10	US West	=SUMIF($A$3:$A$26,G10,$C$3:$C$26)
11		
12	Total	=SUM(H3:H10)
13		
14		
15		Total Volume
16		(000) Units
17	N350	=SUMIF($B$3:$B$26,G17,$C$3:$C$26)
18	N450	=SUMIF($B$3:$B$26,G18,$C$3:$C$26)
19	N900	=SUMIF($B$3:$B$26,G19,$C$3:$C$26)
20		
21	Total	=SUM(H17:H19)
22		